AF513158

CONTENTS

Scheme of Examination

DSSSB will conduct **One Tier Exam** for PGT posts having two section:

Section-I

S.No.	Subject	Questions	Marks
1.	Mental Ability and Reasoning Ability	20	20
2.	General Awareness	20	20
3.	English Language & Comprehension	20	20
4.	Hindi Language & Comprehension	20	20
5.	Numerical Aptitude & Data Interpretation	20	20
	Total	**100**	**100**

Section-II

S.No.	Subject	Questions	Marks
1.	MCQs pertaining to Post-Graduation qualification and teaching methodology required for the post.	**200**	**200**

R. Gupta's®

POPULAR MASTER GUIDE

DSSSB–TEACHERS

PGT

BIOLOGY

Recruitment Exam

by

RPH Editorial Board

2026
EDITION

RAMESH PUBLISHING HOUSE, NEW DELHI

POPULAR MASTER GUIDE FOR THIS EXAM

DSSSB—TGT/PGT

COMMON SUBJECTS

• Mental Ability • General Awareness
• Arithmetic Ability • English • हिन्दी

Study Material with Previous Years' Papers (Solved)

Book Code : R-922 ❍ Price ₹ 495 ❍ ISBN : 978-93-89480-43-6

Email : order@rameshpublishinghouse.com

Published by
O.P. Gupta *for* Ramesh Publishing House
Admin. Office
12-H, New Daryaganj Road, Opp. Officers' Mess
New Delhi-110002 ✆ 23275224, 23245124
E-mail: info@rameshpublishinghouse.com
For Online Shopping: www.rameshpublishinghouse.com
Showroom
• Balaji Market, Nai Sarak, Delhi-110006 ✆ 23282525 📱 9354373464
• 4457, Nai Sarak, Delhi-110006

© *Reserved with the Publisher*

No Part of this book may be reproduced or transmitted in any form or by any means, electronic or mechanical including photocopying, recording or by any transformation storage and retrieval system without written permission from the Publisher.

Indemnification Clause: This book is being sold/distributed subject to the exclusive condition that neither the author nor the publishers, individually or collectively, shall be responsible to indemnify the buyer/user/possessor of this book beyond the selling price of this book for any reason under any circumstances. If you do not agree to it, please do not buy/accept/use/possess this book.

Book Code: R-1314

ISBN: 978-93-5012-013-2

Price: ₹ 390

Printed at: Deepak Offset, Delhi

Previous Years' Paper

Delhi Subordinate Services Selection Board (DSSSB)

PGT (Biology) Recruitment Exam, 2025

(Exam held on 23-07-2025)

Subject Knowledge – Biology & Teaching Methodology

1. The flower, which is formed during the reproductive phase of growth, may occur singly or as a part of an inflorescence is the characteristics features of _____.

1. Algae
2. Pteridophyte
3. Angiosperms
4. Bryophyta

2. What is the primary function of collenchyma cells in plant tissues?

1. Facilitate gas exchange and transpiration
2. Provide mechanical strength and elasticity
3. Regulate water and ion transport
4. Store starch and nutrients

3. During embryogenesis in higher plants with respect to embryonal axis, select the correct position of the radicle and the plumule.

1. The plumule is present at the upper end and the radicle is present at the lower end.
2. Both are present at the lower end of the embryonal axis.
3. Both are present at upper end of the embryonal axis.
4. The radicle is present at the upper end and the plumule is present at the lower end.

4. Which of the following is INCORRECT regarding phylum Annelida?

1. Examples are Nereis, Pheretima and Hirudinaria.
2. Open circulatory system is present.
3. Body surface is distinctly marked out into metameres.
4. Nephridia help in osmoregulation and excretion.

5. In case of algae, for sexual reproduction, which of the following shows fusion of two gametes dissimilar in size?

1. Ulothrix
2. Eudorina
3. Spirogyra
4. Hydrodictyon

6. Which of the following is a place of ex-situ conservation of endangered plant species as well as conservation of germplasm?

1. Plant museum
2. National park
3. Botanical garden
4. Biosphere reserve

7. What is the primary function of the stratum compactum layer in the skin of frogs?

1. To provide mechanical strength and protection
2. To produce mucus for skin lubrication
3. To regulate water and ion balance
4. To facilitate gas exchange

8. Which of the following types of vascular bundles occur in dicotyledonous stems?

1. Conjoint, close with exarch protoxylem
2. Conjoint, open with endarch protoxylem
3. Conjoint, close with endarch protoxylem
4. Conjoint, open with exarch protoxylem

9. Which of the following animal exhibits polymorphism and alternation of generation in which a solitary, sexual gonozooid alternates with the colonial, asexual oozoid?

1. Amphioxus 2. Balanoglossus
3. Star fish 4. Doliolum

10. The reserve food material in red algae is:

1. Floridean starch 2. Cellulose
3. Starch 4. Glycogen

11. Which of the following medicinal plants belongs to the family Solanaceae?

1. Cassia 2. Gulmohar
3. Belladonna 4. Mustard

12. Which of the following plant groups is characterised by the presence of a leptoid, a specialised cell type that is thought to be analogous to the sieve elements of seed plants?

1. Bryophyta 2. Angiospermae
3. Gymnospermae 4. Pteridophyta

13. In an old tree, the ascent of sap takes place through the:

1. Central light coloured duramen
2. Peripheral Light coloured alburnum
3. Peripheral dark coloured heartwood
4. Central dark coloured sap wood

14. Which of the following statements correctly describes the tissue composition of the human heart?

1. It is made up of all four types of tissue - epithelial, connective, muscular and neural.
2. It is made up of only connective tissue.
3. It is made up of only one type of tissue i.e., neural tissue.
4. It is composed of only two types of tissue.

15. Which of the following is NOT a class of mollusks?

1. Bivalvia 2. Cephalopoda
3. Crustacea 4. Gastropoda

16. In the binomial nomenclature system, which of the following is true about the names of species?

1. Both the genus and species names are written in uppercase.
2. Both names are written in uppercase.
3. The genus name is capitalised, and the species name is written in lowercase.
4. The genus name is written in lowercase, and the species name is capitalised.

17. Which of the following statements about leaves is correct?

1. Veins in leaves serve only a mechanical function and do not participate in transport.
2. Leaves are the most important organs for photosynthesis.
3. The leaf is a lateral, generally flattened structure borne on the root.
4. Leaves originate from shoot apical meristems and are arranged in basipetal order.

18. What is the primary characteristic that distinguishes gymnosperms from angiosperms in terms of seed development?

1. Structure of ovule
2. Type of pollination
3. Presence of endosperm
4. Absence of ovary wall

19. In angiosperms, male and female gametophyte develop in a specialised structure called the:

1. embryo sac 2. microsporangia
3. flower 4. megasporangia

20. Brown fat which is found in newborn babies and hibernating mammals has cytochrome pigments which contains which of the following elements?

1. Magnesium
2. Copper
3. Silver
4. Iron

21. The movement of ions across a membrane is called as _____.

1. Flex
2. Flux
3. Evaporation
4. Transpiration

22. In lactic acid and alcoholic fermentation, the percentage of energy released from glucose is:

1. About 38%
2. Less than 7%
3. More than 10% but less than 20%
4. More than 50%

23. Which of the following is the correct representation of an enzyme catalysed reaction?

1. E + S — ES ¾¾® EP ¾¾® E + P
2. E + S — EP ¾¾® ES ¾¾® E + P
3. E + S — ES ¾¾® E + P ¾¾® EP
4. E + P — EP ¾¾® ES ¾¾® E + S

24. Consider the following statements with regard to the effect of temperature on the activity of enzymes and select the most appropriate answer.

Statement A: High temperature destroys enzymatic activity because proteins are denatured by heat.

Statement B: Low temperature preserves the enzyme in a temporarily inactive state.

1. Statement B is correct, and statement A is incorrect.
2. Both statements A and B are incorrect.
3. Statement A is correct, and statement B is incorrect.
4. Both statements A and B are correct.

25. An inhibitor that inhibits the activity of the enzyme and shows close resemblance with the substrate in its molecular structure is called a/an _____.

1. uncompetitive inhibitor
2. mixed inhibitor
3. non-competitive inhibitor
4. competitive inhibitor

26. Which of the following organelles are involved in photorespiration?

1. Nucleus, chloroplast, and mitochondrion
2. Peroxisome, ER, and Golgi apparatus
3. Chloroplast, ribosome, and vacuole
4. Chloroplast, peroxisome, and mitochondrion

27. Which of the following statements is true about non-competitive inhibition?

1. The Km value decreases.
2. The inhibitor changes the shape of the enzyme, reducing its activity.
3. The inhibitor binds to the active site of the enzyme.
4. The inhibition can be overcome by increasing the substrate concentration.

28. What is the meaning of the EC number 1.1.1.1 assigned to an enzyme?

1. The enzyme is a lyase that catalyses the cleavage of C-C bonds.
2. The enzyme is a hydrolase that acts on ester bonds.
3. The enzyme is a transferase that catalyses the transfer of a methyl group.
4. The enzyme is an oxidoreductase that acts on CH-OH group of donors with NAD^+ as acceptor.

29. What is correct sequence of C3 cycle?

1. Carboxylation-regeneration-reduction
2. Carboxylation-reduction-regeneration
3. Carboxylation-reduction-regeneration-reduction
4. Regeneration-reduction-regeneration

30. RuBP is joined with carbon dioxide by the activity of enzyme RUBISCO. Select from the given options the metallic cofactor of RUBISCO.

1. Calcium 2. Manganese
3. Magnesium 4. Zinc

31. Which of these statements are true for cyclic photophosphorylation?

1. It occurs during low light intensity.
2. It leads to photolysis of water.
3. It leads to phosphorylation of ADP.
4. One of the products of the process is $NADPH^+H^+$.

1. 2 and 3 2. 3 and 4
3. 1 and 3 4. 2 and 4

32. Which of the following cell organelles are involved in photorespiration?

1. Chloroplast, mitochondria and lysosome
2. Chloroplast, mitochondria and vacuole
3. Chloroplast, mitochondria and Golgi complex
4. Chloroplast, mitochondria and peroxisome

33. Removal of shoot tips or decapitation results in enhanced growth of lateral buds because:

1. The auxin production reduces
2. The auxin production increases
3. The cytokinin increases in lateral buds
4. The gibberellin production increases

34. How many major classes are enzymes classified into based on their function?

1. 5 2. 7
3. 6 4. 4

35. Which of the following components of the chloroplast electron transport chain donates electrons directly to plastocyanin (PC)?

1. Ferredoxin
2. Cytochrome b6f complex
3. Photosystem I
4. $NADP^+$ reductase

36. Which class of enzyme catalyses oxidoreduction between two substrates of reaction?

1. Oxidoreductases 2. Transferases
3. Lyases 4. Isomerases

37. The graphic representation of the amount of absorption of different wavelengths of light by a substance is called as absorption spectrum of that substance. Chlorophyll pigments absorb maximum light in the:

1. Blue and Yellow region of the visible spectrum
2. Red and Green region of the visible spectrum
3. Blue and Red region of the visible spectrum
4. Yellow and Green region of the visible spectrum

38. What is the effect of increasing temperature on enzyme activity?

1. Enzyme activity increases up to an optimal temperature.
2. Enzyme activity remains unchanged.
3. Enzyme activity increases indefinitely.
4. Enzyme activity decreases indefinitely.

39. Which of the following can alter the activity of an enzyme?

1. Only temperature and pH
2. Only pH
3. Changes in pH, temperature, substrate concentration
4. Constant substrate concentration

40. During partial oxidation of glucose in cytoplasm, the first oxidation step is catalysed by which of the following enzymes?

1. Kinase 2. Mutase
3. Dehydrogenase 4. Phosphorylase

41. What is the most common cause of female infertility?

1. Uterine infections
2. Polycystic Ovary Syndrome (PCOS)
3. Tubal blockage
4. Endometriosis

42. Which of the following is the most common indication for kidney transplantation in adults?

1. Renal Colic
2. Renal Calculi
3. Hypotension
4. End-stage renal disease

43. During a baby's suckling, the oxytocin causes which cells to contract, thereby expressing the milk from the alveoli into the ducts?

1. Cartilage cells
2. Myoepithelial cells
3. Pancreatic cells
4. Hepatic cells

44. Which of the following correctly describes the composition and function of lymph in the human body?

1. Lymph is composed mostly of digestive enzymes and hormones, and it functions primarily in digestion and metabolic regulation.
2. Lymph is composed mainly of white blood cells, chyle and proteins, and it protects the body from foreign organisms and other materials by removing them from the interstitial fluid.
3. Lymph is composed primarily of carbon dioxide and urea, and it functions mainly in excreting metabolic waste.
4. Lymph is composed primarily of red blood cells and platelets, and it functions mainly in transporting oxygen to tissues.

45. Which of the following is NOT a common effect of alcohol consumption?

1. Impaired motor coordination
2. Decreased inhibitions
3. Increased risk of liver cirrhosis
4. Enhanced cognitive abilities

46. Which of the following is a common disorder of the excretory system characterised by the presence of kidney stones?

1. Pyelonephritis
2. Glomerulonephritis
3. Renal Calculi
4. Cystitis

47. In the context of human anatomy, which type of movement is characterised by a limb moving away from the body's midline?

1. Extension
2. Adduction
3. Flexion
4. Abduction

48. Which of the following structures is primarily responsible for integrating the neural and endocrine systems to regulate physiological processes?

1. Pituitary gland
2. Pineal gland
3. Adrenal cortex
4. Hypothalamus

49. The primary endosperm cell in flowering plants is formed _____.

1. without fusion
2. after triple fusion
3. after double fusion
4. after quadruple fusion

50. Which of the following factors is NOT commonly associated with influencing sexual behaviour in adolescents?

1. Parental guidance
2. Exposure to tobacco
3. Socioeconomic status
4. Peer pressure

51. During low light intensities, only cyclic photophosphorylation takes place. Cyclic photophosphorylation occurs mostly in the:

1. Grana lamellae
2. Mitochondria
3. Stroma lamellae
4. Thylakoid lumen

52. Which specialised procedure is used to form an embryo in the laboratory in which a sperm is directly injected into the ovum?

1. Artificial insemination
2. Intra-uterine insemination
3. Intra-cytoplasmic sperm injection
4. In-vivo fertilization

53. In humans, failure of a testis to descend from the abdomen into the scrotum at or near the time of birth of a foetus is called:

1. Endometriosis
2. Prostatitis
3. Cryptorchidism
4. Hematuria

54. Which of the following animals use tracheal tubes for respiration?

1. Amphibians 2. Insects
3. Reptiles 4. Fish

55. What is the role of the pancreas in digestion?

1. Breaks down food mechanically
2. Secretes enzymes that support the digestion of food in the intestines
3. Produces bile
4. Absorbs nutrients

56. Haematuria is a condition that indicates the presence of ____ in the urine.

1. glucose 2. blood
3. proteins 4. bacteria

57. With respect to the transport of organic solutes through phloem, the source-sink relationship is:

1. Not dependent on the season
2. Fixed and essentially unidirectional
3. Independent of the plant's need
4. Variable and bidirectional

58. Aldosterone increases which of the following in the cortical collecting tubules by reabsorption?

1. Sodium 2. Iron
3. Copper 4. Potassium

59. Which of the following hormones is primarily responsible for regulating the body's metabolism and energy levels?

1. Thyroxine 2. Estrogen
3. Cortisol 4. Insulin

60. In the process of urine formation, the maximum reabsorption of glucose occurs in ____.

1. collecting duct
2. distal convoluted tubule
3. loop of Henle
4. proximal convoluted tubule

61. Which scientist in 1924, has proposed that conditions on the primeval earth billions of years ago were definitely different from present conditions and the first form of life or self-duplicating particles did arise spontaneously from chemical inanimate or abiotic substances?

1. Van Leeuwenhoek
2. Louis Pasteur
3. Francesco Redi
4. Alexander I Oparin

62. The sequence of events that lead to the expression of a response of an organism towards a stimulus is called:

1. Anabolic pathways
2. Metabolic pathways
3. Amphibolic pathways
4. Signal transduction pathways

63. In a test cross involving a dihybrid plant (AaBb), what phenotypic ratio is expected if the genes assort independently?

1. 3 : 1
2. 9 : 3 : 3 : 1
3. 1 : 2 : 1
4. 1 : 1 : 1 : 1

64. What is the primary difference between a transition and a transversion mutation?

1. Type of base substitution
2. Location of mutation
3. Frequency of occurrence
4. Effect on protein function

65. A change in allele frequencies within a population indicates that:

1. mating is completely random
2. the population is genetically stable
3. evolution occurs in the population
4. the population is in Hardy-Weinberg equilibrium

66. Which of the following was NOT used by Nirenberg for deciphering the genetic code?

1. Enzyme Nucleoside phosphorylase
2. Cell free system of protein synthesis
3. Radioactive amino acids
4. Enzyme DNA Polymerase III

67. Kernel colour of wheat is an example of _____.

1. Supplementary Inheritance
2. Epistasis Inheritance
3. Complementary Inheritance
4. Polygenic Inheritance

68. How many true-breeding pea plant varieties did Mendel select?

1. 14
2. 2
3. 8
4. 24

69. In a hybridisation experiment it was found that genetic recombinants between gene A and C were 3%, gene B and C were 12%, gene A and B were 15% and between gene A and D were 19%. What will be the order of genes on the chromosome?

1. A, B, D, C
2. A, D, B, C
3. A, C, B, D
4. A, B, C, D

70. Which of the following statements about fetal and embryonic gonads is correct?

1. In the absence of Y chromosome influence, the indifferent gonads develop into testes.
2. The development of male gonads begins with the formation of the Müllerian ducts, which eventually become the epididymis.
3. Female gonads develop from the mesonephric duct, which is also involved in the formation of the male reproductive system.
4. The gonads in both males and females initially develop from the same embryonic tissue.

71. In a pedigree chart, horizontal lines connecting male and female and vertical lines extending downward from a couple, respectively, represent:

1. affected individual and siblings
2. siblings and children
3. children and mating
4. mating and children

72. Which of the following is an example of sex-linked inheritance?

1. Muscular dystrophy
2. Phenylketonuria
3. Red and green colour blindness
4. Sickle cell anaemia

73. The first fossil (a fragile upper jaw) of Ramapithecus was recovered by G Edward Lewis in 1932 from which of the following areas?

1. Taung Village, South Africa
2. Shivalik Hills, India
3. Hadar, Ethiopia
4. Swartkrans, South Africa

74. In DNA profiling, unique RFLP patterns are obtained due to which of the following?

1. Differences in the probe used for autoradiography
2. Difference in size of the VNTR segment
3. Difference in locus of the given VNTR
4. Difference in restriction endonucleases used

75. In breeding populations, random fluctuation in allele frequencies is called:

1. Genetic drift
2. Founder effect
3. Meiotic drive
4. Migration pressure

76. Which of the following experiments provided evidence supporting the idea that organic compounds necessary for life could be synthesised from abiogenic materials/inorganic molecules under Earth's prebiotic conditions?

1. Miller-Urey experiment
2. Pasteur's experiment
3. Griffith's experiment
4. Hershey-Chase experiment

77. Gregor Mendel selected seven pairs of contrasting characters for his experiments on pea plants. Which of the following trait selected by Mendel, turned out to be a dominant trait in his experiments?

1. Yellow pod colour
2. Axial flower position
3. Green seed colour
4. Terminal flower position

78. Which scientist in 1970 proposed the endosymbiotic hypothesis about mitochondria?

1. E. Zuckerkandl 2. Margoliash
3. Thompson 4. Lynn Margulis

79. Who proposed that the first form of life could have originated from pre-existing non-living organic molecules?

1. Charles Darwin
2. Oparin and Haldane
3. Ernst Heckel
4. Karl Ernst von Baer

80. At what stage of the blastomeres is the zygote transferred into the fallopian tube by Zygote Intra Fallopian Transfer (ZIFT)?

1. At 16 blastomeres
2. Upto 8 blastomeres
3. At 24 blastomeres
4. More than 8 blastomeres

81. Which of the following pairs associated with the Krebs cycle generates energy in the electron transport chain?

1. $FADH_2$ and ATP
2. NADH and $FADH_2$
3. ATP and NAD^+
4. $NADH_2$ and GTP

82. The central part of the proximal region of the centriole is proteinaceous, which is called?

1. The hub 2. Spindle fibres
3. Radial spokes 4. Basal body

83. Mitosis type of cell division is also called ____________.

1. reductional division
2. mixed division
3. equational division
4. free nuclear division

84. What type of transport is mediated by importins and exportins across the nuclear pore complex?

1. Facilitated diffusion
2. Active transport
3. Endocytosis
4. Passive diffusion

85. Which of the following scientists worked on the role of NO as a signaling molecule?

1. Walter Gering
2. Pribnow, Hogness and Goldberg
3. Robert Hooke, Louis Pasteur
4. Robert F. Furchgott, Louis J. Ignarro and Ferid Murad

86. Which of the following enzymes is responsible for the conversion of ADP into ATP by means of oxidative phosphorylation?

1. ADP carboxylase
2. ATP synthase
3. ATP carboxylase
4. ADP synthase

87. Which of the following is essential for the activity of coenzyme Nicotinamide Adenine Dinucleotide (NAD)?

1. Calciferol 2. Niacin
3. Retinol 4. Ascorbic acid

88. What is the primary role of enzymes in reducing the activation energy of a reaction?

1. To stabilise the transition state
2. To increase the temperature of the reaction
3. To increase the energy of the reactants
4. To decrease the energy of the products

89. What is the characteristic feature of polytene chromosomes that allows for their visualisation under a light microscope?

1. Presence of centromeres
2. Multiple rounds of replication without division
3. Association with nuclear lamina
4. High degree of condensation

90. Which fungus is commonly used as a biocontrol agent to control plant pathogens?

1. Trichoderma 2. Fusarium
3. Rhizopus 4. Aspergillus

91. Molecules move passively without any expenditure of energy across the membrane, EXCEPT by which of the given options?

1. By diffusion and osmosis
2. Only by diffusion
3. Only by Na^+-K^+ pump
4. Only by osmosis

92. Which of the following hormones has the ability to increase the length of the axis and is used to increase the length of the grape stalks?

1. Gibberellins
2. Abscisic acid
3. Auxins
4. Cytokinins

93. Which of the following microscopes are used to study the dynamic motility of mitochondria, mitotic chromosomes, and vacuoles?

1. Bright-field microscope
2. Confocal microscope
3. Compound light microscope
4. Phase-contrast microscope

94. Which of the following is the correct full form of RAPD in molecular biology?

1. Repetitive Amplification of DNA Polymorphism
2. Random Amplified Polymorphic DNA
3. Reverse Amplification of Primer-Derived DNA
4. Rapid Amplified Polymorphic DNA

95. Which of the following is the substrate for the enzyme β-galactosidase and regulates the switching on and off of the operon?

1. Fructose
2. Maltose
3. Sucrose
4. Lactose

96. How do B chromosomes typically behave during meiosis?

1. They do not pair with A chromosomes and segregate irregularly.
2. They are always lost during meiosis.
3. They always segregate to the same pole.
4. They pair with A chromosomes and segregate normally.

97. Which vitamin is the precursor to the coenzyme NAD^+?

1. Vitamin B_3
2. Vitamin B_{12}
3. Vitamin B_6
4. Vitamin C

98. What is the primary function of the centromere during mitosis?

1. To repair DNA damage
2. To synthesise new DNA strands
3. To facilitate the separation of sister chromatids
4. To regulate the attachment of microtubules to the chromosome

99. Which of the following is correct regarding the genetic code?

1. The genetic code is singlet, degenerate, comma-less and non-ambiguous.
2. The genetic code is triplet, degenerate, comma-less and ambiguous.
3. The genetic code is triplet, generate, comma-less and non-ambiguous.
4. The genetic code is triplet, degenerate, comma-less and non-ambiguous.

100. Which of the following enzymes is crucial in the rate-limiting step of steroid hormone biosynthesis?

1. Cholesterol desmolase
2. 5α-reductase
3. 17β-Hydroxysteroid dehydrogenase
4. Aromatase

101. Which of the following is NOT likely to be cultivated as a sustainable source of Single Cell Protein (SCP) due to limitations in biomass productivity and scalability?

1. *Mushrooms*
2. *Spirulina*
3. *Candida utilis*
4. *Methylophilus methylotrophus*

102. Plants, bacteria, fungi and animals whose genes have been altered by manipulation are called ______.

1. clonal populations
2. genetically mutated organisms
3. genetically modified organisms
4. selectively bred hybrids

103. Which breeding method involves the use of tissue culture techniques to produce large numbers of genetically identical plants?

1. Conventional breeding
2. Micropropagation
3. Mutation breeding
4. Hybrid breeding

104. Which of the given options is based on the principle of antigen-antibody interaction?

1. Polymerase Chain Reaction
2. Southern Blotting
3. Enzyme Linked Immunosorbent Assay
4. Northern Blotting

105. Semi-dwarf rice varieties were derived from ______.

1. IR-8   2. HR-20
3. LR-50   4. LM-6

106. Select the correct option with respect to the following statements.

Statement I: Antibiotic means 'pro-life' in context to disease-causing organisms.

Statement II: *Saccharomyces cerevisiae* is used in the production of immunosuppressive agent in organ transplant patients.

1. Both Statements I and II are incorrect
2. Both Statements I and II are correct
3. Statement I is incorrect, but Statement II is correct
4. Statement I is correct, but Statement II is incorrect

107. Which category of compounds are most expressed in genetically modified organisms (GMOs) engineered for pest resistance?

1. Toxins that kill specific pests
2. Antibiotics
3. Pest hormones
4. Growth factors for pests

108. In biological treatment, masses of bacteria associated with fungal filaments form mesh-like structures, which is known as?

1. Biochemical oxygen demand activators
2. Anaerobic microbes flocs
3. Aerobic microbes flocs
4. Anaerobic sludge digesters

109. Which of the given phenomena involves silencing of genes either through degradation of their corresponding mRNA or through blocking translation of its mRNA?

1. RNA interference
2. Non-coding RNA
3. RNA-mRNA interactions
4. Riboswitches

110. What is one potential application of RNAi technology?

1. Enhancing photosynthesis in plants
2. Increasing cell division
3. Stimulating cancer growth
4. Silencing disease-causing genes

111. What is a key advantage of cosmid vectors?

1. They can clone small DNA fragments.
2. They have multiple ori sites.
3. They can be used for gene expression.
4. They can clone large DNA fragments.

112. Which of the following is being developed for safety testing of vaccines before they are used on humans?

1. Transgenic cats
2. Transgenic dogs
3. Transgenic horses
4. Transgenic mice

113. What was the first transgenic animal ever created?

1. A transgenic mouse
2. A transgenic chicken
3. A transgenic cow
4. A transgenic goat

114. A distinct ecological community of plants and animals living together in a particular climate and has characteristic appearance along with distribution over a wide geographical area is called:

1. Biota
2. Biological community
3. Fens
4. Biome

115. In order to improve the plant varieties for various purposes, the most conventional method, still very useful with enormous unexplored possibilities is:

1. Genetic Engineering
2. Plant Introduction
3. Mutation Breeding
4. Hybridization

116. What is cryopreservation commonly used for storing?

1. Biological materials like cells, tissues, and gametes
2. Food items
3. Chemicals
4. Medicines

117. In which stage of sewage treatment does the breakdown of organic matter by microbes occur?

1. Sludge processing
2. Primary treatment
3. Tertiary treatment
4. Secondary treatment

118. What is the key component of an ELISA assay?

1. RNA
2. A lipid membrane
3. DNA polymerase
4. An enzyme-linked antibody

119. Which of the following is a collection of methods that allows the correction of a gene defect that has been diagnosed in a child/ embryo, where genes are inserted into a person's cells and tissues to treat a disease?

1. Recombinant DNA technology
2. Micro-propagation
3. Gene therapy
4. Somatic hybridization

120. During plant succession in a habitat, which of the following changes take place in the successive seral stages?

1. Total biomass remains constant, but species diversity increases.
2. Total biomass increases, but species diversity remains constant.
3. Both species diversity & total biomass increase.
4. The number of species increases, but total biomass decreases.

121. The succession of plants in water and dry areas is called _____.

1. Hydrarch succession and xerarch succession respectively
2. Xerarch succession and hydrarch succession respectively
3. Lithrarch succession and hydrarch succession respectively
4. Xerarch succession and halrarch succession respectively

122. Which earthworm species is commonly used in vermiculture?

1. *Dendrobaena octaedra*
2. *Allolobophora chlorotica*
3. *Lumbricus terrestris*
4. *Eisenia fetida*

123. Which of the following techniques relies on antigen-antibody interactions and is commonly used for detecting specific proteins in a sample?

1. Polymerase Chain Reaction (PCR)
2. Gel Electrophoresis
3. Enzyme-Linked Immunosorbent Assay (ELISA)
4. Mass Spectrometry

124. Which of the following organisms is considered a detritivore that breaks down detritus into smaller particles, aiding nutrient cycling?

1. *Volvox*
2. *Eisenia fetida* (Earthworm)
3. *Nostoc*
4. *Plasmodium vivax*

125. Which of the following is NOT used as catalytic converters that are fitted into automobiles for reducing emission of poisonous gases?

1. Platinum 2. Rhodium
3. Strontium 4. Palladium

126. Which organism index is utilised as a parameter for assessing water pollution in a unit volume of water?

1. *Bacillus thuringiensis*
2. *Bacillus subtilis*
3. *Streptomyces griseus*
4. *Escherichia coli*

127. Identify the rule which states that individuals of species in cooler climates tend to be larger than those in warmer climates.

1. Bergmann's Law
2. Allen's Rule
3. Shelford's Law
4. Lindmann's Rule

128. Immunologically active regions on a complex antigen are called ____.

1. MHC-I 2. MHC-II
3. Adjuvant 4. Epitopes

129. Nuclear wastes should be pre-treated and then stored in shielded containers buried within rocks ____ below the earth's surface.

1. about 300 metres
2. about 500 metres
3. about 200 metres
4. about 100 metres

130. Which of the following types of hypersensitivity is primarily mediated by IgE antibodies and is associated with allergic reactions such as asthma and anaphylaxis?

1. Type I 2. Type III
3. Type II 4. Type IV

131. Ecosystem are divided into how many basic categories?

1. Three 2. Two
3. Four 4. One

132. During the eighteenth and nineteenth centuries, tuberculosis spread with the growth of cities and created havoc throughout the industrialised world. It became known as:

1. Plague of Justinian
2. Great white plague
3. Great Influenza epidemic
4. Bubonic plague

133. These parts of an antigen that combine with the antigen-binding site on an antibody molecule or on a lymphocyte receptor are called:

1. Minigene
2. Antigenic determinants
3. Tail region
4. Hinge regions

134. Air pollution can be controlled effectively by adopting many preventative measures, EXCEPT which of the following?

1. A broad belt of trees and shrubs should be planted around the industrial areas.
2. Industries should use fuel with low sulphur content.
3. The chimneys and smoke stacks should be medium and placed at a lower level.
4. Industrial processes and equipments should be modified to reduce emissions.

135. What does afforestation refer to?

1. Conversion of forest land to agriculture
2. Planting trees in areas that have never been forested
3. Planting trees in areas that were previously forests
4. Cutting down trees for timber

136. What is the main purpose of using monoclonal antibodies in diagnostic tests?

1. To stimulate the production of multiple antibodies
2. To provide general protection against infections
3. To enhance natural immune responses
4. To specifically target and identify a single antigen

137. What method is commonly used to treat hazardous solid waste?

1. Open dumping
2. Ocean dumping
3. Incineration
4. Landfilling

138. Which of the following is an example of ex-situ conservation?

1. National parks 2. Biosphere reserve
3. Wildlife safari 4. Sacred groves

139. In a terrestrial ecosystem, which of the following will be the highest?

1. Net Community Productivity
2. Secondary Productivity
3. Gross Primary Productivity
4. Net Primary Productivity

140. Which of the following best explains the synergistic effect in air pollution?

1. When only one pollutant is active, and the other is inert
2. When two pollutants together have a lesser impact than each alone
3. When two pollutants neutralise each other
4. When combined pollutants produce a greater toxic effect than expected

141. Which of the following is the correct sequence in the life cycle of *Bombyx mori*?

1. Egg → Cocoon → Larva → Pupa → Adult
2. Larva → Pupa → Egg → Cocoon → Pupa
3. Egg → Larva → Cocoon → Pupa → Adult
4. Larva → Egg → Pupa → Cocoon → Adult

142. Which of the following is a protein primarily synthesised by silkworms?

1. Protease 2. Sericin
3. Lipase 4. Hematin

143. Chemicals that cause birth defects by disrupting the normal development of a foetus are called _____.

1. Mutagens 2. Carcinogens
3. Mitogens 4. Teratogens

144. Select from the given choices one of the characteristic spore of the fungus causing black stem rust disease of wheat.

1. Uninucleated Teleutospores
2. Binucleated Pycniospores
3. Binucleated Aeciospores
4. Binucleated Uredospores

145. Which of the following statements about gametogenesis is true?

1. Spermatogenesis occurs in the ovaries.
2. Both oogenesis and spermatogenesis are identical processes.
3. Oogenesis produces four functional ova from one primary oocyte.
4. Spermatogenesis results in four functional sperm cells from one primary spermatocyte.

146. Which of the following insects causes damage to citrus plants in India?

1. *Galerucella birmanica*
2. *Cosmopolites sordidus*
3. *Earias vetella*
4. *Papilio demoleus*

147. Which of the following is one of the significant therapeutic uses of stem cells in medicine?

1. Gene therapy
2. Cosmetic enhancement
3. Treatment of infections
4. Regeneration of damaged tissues

148. Which insect is known for having one of the highest protein contents per serving?

1. Mealworms
2. Silkworms
3. Grasshoppers
4. Crickets

149. Which of the following accurately describes the reproductive process of earthworms in vermiculture?

1. Earthworms reproduce asexually through binary fission.
2. Earthworms reproduce by budding, similar to hydra.
3. Earthworms are hermaphrodites and reproduce sexually through the exchange of sperm.
4. Earthworms lay eggs that develop into larvae without the need for fertilization.

150. What is the primary advantage of induced pluripotent stem cells (iPSCs)?

1. They are only found in adult tissues.
2. They are limited to differentiating into a specific cell type.
3. They can be generated from embryos.
4. They bypass the ethical concerns associated with embryonic stem cells.

151. Which of the extraembryonic membranes is first to make its appearance during chick embryo development?

1. Yolk sac 2. Amnion
3. Chorion 4. Allantoic

152. Which of the following is NOT a parasite of *lac* insect?

1. *Tricholyga sorbillans*
2. *Parenchthrodryinus clavicornis*
3. *Erenchyrtus dewitzii*
4. *Tachardiaephagus tacchardiae*

153. In plants, complete resistance for diseases is usually controlled by R genes, which codes for a particular type of protein which mediates with the process of induction of resistance. Identify the protein coded by the R genes.

1. Cyclin dependent mutases
2. Cyclin dependent kinases
3. Receptor like cyclases
4. Receptor like kinases

154. Xenopsylla cheopis, a chief transmitter of the bubonic plague, has which type of metamorphosis?

1. Gradual metamorphosis
2. No-metamorphosis
3. Incomplete metamorphosis
4. Complete metamorphosis

155. Which of the following is the correct chronological order in the process of In Vitro Fertilisation (IVF)?

1. Fertilisation → Superovulation → Oocyte retrieval → Embryo transfer
2. Superovulation → Oocyte retrieval → Embryo transfer → Fertilisation
3. Oocyte retrieval → Embryo transfer → Fertilisation → Superovulation
4. Superovulation → Oocyte retrieval → Fertilisation → Embryo transfer

156. Paedogenesis refers to the development of gonads and the production of young ones by an otherwise immature larval or preadult animal. Which of the following DO NOT show paedogenesis?

1. Spiders 2. Gall fly
3. Liver fluke 4. Salamanders

157. Which of the following diseases is NOT caused by a virus?

1. Turnip mosaic 2. Brown rust of wheat
3. Tobacco mosaic 4. Yellow mosaic

158. Which of the following toxins produced by phytopathogenic microbe induces accumulation of toxic concentrations of ammonia and destruction of thylakoid membrane of chloroplast leading to chlorosis?

1. Tabtoxin 2. Phaseolotoxin
3. Cercosporin 4. Victorin

159. The very famous Ladybird beetle is useful for getting rid of which of the following pests?

1. *Aphids*
2. *Mosquitoes*
3. *Trichoderma*
4. *Bacillus thuringiensis*

160. Which type of parasitism is shown by the Cuscuta plant?

1. Both Endo and Brood parasitism
2. Endo parasitism only
3. Brood parasitism only
4. Ecto parasitism

161. Which enzyme plays a crucial role in the PCR process?

1. Reverse transcriptase
2. RNA polymerase
3. DNA polymerase
4. Ligase

162. Which blood group is recognised as the universal donor?

1. A^+ 2. B^+
3. AB^+ 4. O

163. Who proposed the student's t-distribution?

1. Francis Galton
2. Karl Pearson
3. Ronald A Fisher
4. William Sealy Gosset

164. Which of the following fluids is utilised for counting red blood cells (RBCs) in a sample?

1. Carnoy's fluid 2. Normal saline
3. Hayem's fluid 4. Wright's stain

165. Which of the following statement is INCORRECT regarding blood?

1. WBC are enucleated cells and help in the production of antigens to fight infections.
2. Red blood cells carry oxygen from the lungs to the body's tissues, and also transport carbon dioxide from the tissues back to the lungs.
3. Plasma is mostly water, but also contains proteins, sugars, and fat particles.
4. Blood is a specialised body fluid that's made up of four main components- plasma, red blood cells, white blood cells, platelets.

166. By using which biotechniques can we check the different DNA fragments present in a sample and determine their absolute size with the help of a DNA ladder made up of DNA fragments of known sizes?

1. Ion-exchange Chromatography
2. Gel Filtration Chromatography
3. Fluorescent Microscopy
4. Agarose Gel Electrophoresis

167. Which of the following statements is INCORRECT regarding the spectroscopy technique?

1. It is used for the study of intramolecular bonding.
2. It is used for the identification of substances through the spectrum emitted from or absorbed by them.
3. It is used for the estimation of concentration of coloured compounds.
4. It used for the study of interaction of electromagnetic radiation with matter.

168. Which of the following platforms for testing pathogens is INCORRECT?

1. Enzyme technology on Sim Plate
2. Size exclusion chromatographic method
3. Immunoassay on Lateral Flow Sheets
4. Conventional method with culture media

169. What is the main difference between ANOVA and a t-test?

1. ANOVA is used for comparing two groups, while a t-test is used for comparing three or more groups.
2. ANOVA is used for comparing means of three or more groups, while a t-test is used for comparing means of two groups.
3. ANOVA is used for comparing means, while a t-test is used for comparing variances.
4. ANOVA is used for comparing variances, while a t-test is used for comparing means.

170. In RNA-Seq, what is the primary reason for converting RNA into cDNA before sequencing?

1. RNA has high fidelity for replication.
2. RNA cannot be fragmented.
3. Sequencing technologies are DNA-specific.
4. RNA is more stable than DNA.

171. What is SWISS-PROT known for?

1. Annotating protein sequences with high accuracy
2. Storing gene expression data
3. Archiving phylogenetic trees
4. Providing comprehensive nucleotide sequences

172. Which of the following components is most suitable for a patient with thrombocytopenia due to chemotherapy?

1. Whole blood
2. Fresh frozen plasma
3. Platelet concentrate
4. Packed red blood cells

173. What type of sample is commonly utilised in a DNA microarray experiment?

1. Protein
2. RNA
3. Lipids
4. Metabolites

174. Which algorithm is most widely used for global sequence alignment?

1. Needleman-Wunsch
2. FASTA
3. Smith-Waterman
4. BLAST

175. BLAST is an alignment tool. Here, BLAST stands for:

1. Basic Local And Search Tool
2. Basic Large Alignment Search Tool
3. Basic Local Alignment Search Tool
4. Basic Large Alignment Search Tutorial

176. Which of the following radioactive isotopes is commonly used in Radioimmunoassay (RIA)?

1. Iodine-125 (^{125}I)
2. Phosphorus-32 (^{32}P)
3. Carbon-14 (^{14}C)
4. Tritium (^{3}H)

177. Which of the following platforms is based on reversible dye terminator chemistry used in sequencing-by-synthesis?

1. Oxford Nanopore MinION
2. SOLiD by Applied Biosystems
3. Pacific Biosciences SMRT
4. Illumina HiSeq

178. Which statement is INCORRECT regarding the neighbor-joining method?

1. The neighbor-joining method is applicable to evolutionary distance data to obtain the correct tree topology and branch lengths of the final tree.
2. The neighbor-joining method produces unrooted trees and assumes a different rate of evolution among lineages under consideration.
3. The method of neighbor-joining was proposed by MO Dayhoff in 1978 for reconstructing the phylogenetic tree.
4. The method of neighbor-joining starts with a starlike topology assuming that there is no clustering of operational taxonomic units (OTU or neighbors).

179. What percentage of total blood volume is comprised of plasma?

1. 55% 2. 20%
3. 35% 4. 75%

180. In ANOVA, what is the F-test statistic defined as?

1. Between-group variance/Within-group variance
2. Within-group variance/Between-group variance
3. Total variance/Residual variance
4. Mean variance/Median variance

181. Which of the following statements best reflects the nature of gender roles?
1. Permanent and natural
2. Determined only by educational qualifications
3. Biological and identical across cultures
4. Socially constructed and vary across cultures

182. Which is NOT a type of art?
1. Logical reasoning
2. Creative writing
3. Dance
4. Music

183. What is a school subject?
1. A method of teaching
2. A discipline at the university level
3. A teaching-learning strategy
4. An area of learning within the school curriculum

184. Which approach to learning describes learning as a connection between stimulus and response?
1. Behaviorist
2. Humanistic perspective
3. Constructivist
4. Cognitive

185. A teacher develops three versions of a worksheet: basic recall, application-based, and critical thinking. This approach is an example of:
1. time-bound teaching
2. uniform instruction
3. differentiated instruction
4. standardised testing

186. Which principle of curriculum construction suggests that subject matter should be logically and psychologically arranged?
1. Principle of integration and correlation
2. Principle of time allocation
3. Principle of conservation
4. Principle of social utility

187. Which of the following is NOT one of Michael Halliday's dimensions of register variation?
1. Mode 2. Tenor
3. Region 4. Field

188. Which of the following qualities is socially expected of women in many cultures?
1. Nurturing, caring, and warmth
2. Authoritativeness and control
3. Aggressiveness and ambition
4. Physical strength and decisiveness

189. What is considered equivalent to accuracy in the context of assessments?
1. Generality 2. Reliability
3. Relevance 4. Validity

190. Scaffolding in learning refers to:
1. a permanent support structure
2. removing all difficulty from the task
3. teaching all students the same way
4. providing guided support that gradually fades as students gain mastery

191. Which of the following programmes aimed to achieve 'universalisation of elementary education'?
1. Project for Integrated Education for the Disabled
2. District Primary Education Programme
3. Integrated Education for Disabled Children
4. Sarva Shiksha Abhiyan

192. Which approach considers environment more important than heredity in the determination of behaviour?
1. Humanistic 2. Behaviourist
3. Cognitive 4. Constructivist

193. In which approach are the perceptions of a learner processed through differentiation, generalisation and restructuration?
1. Behaviourist 2. Cognitive
3. Constructivist 4. Humanistic

194. What does reliability refer to?
1. Time taken to complete
2. Repeatability and consistency
3. Teacher feedback
4. Level of difficulty

195. How many disabilities are recognised in Rights of Persons with Disabilities Act, 2016?
1. 25
2. 22
3. 26
4. 21

196. What does the principle of civic and social needs in curriculum construction emphasise?
1. Development of both the individual and society
2. Preparing students for foreign employment
3. Teaching only national history
4. Promoting competition among peers

197. According to _____ theorists, teaching is a process of developing understanding or insight in the learner.
1. cognitive 2. constructivist
3. humanistic 4. behaviourist

198. The word discipline is derived from the _____ word 'dicipulus'.
1. Latin 2. Spanish
3. Hebrew 4. Greek

199. What is measured in terms of height and weight?
1. Development 2. Growth
3. Nutritional level 4. Intelligence

200. Which of the following is NOT part of factors that influence growth and development?
1. Culture 2. Genetics
3. Nutrition 4. Caste

ANSWERS

1	2	3	4	5	6	7	8	9	10
3	2	1	2	2	3	1	2	4	1
11	**12**	**13**	**14**	**15**	**16**	**17**	**18**	**19**	**20**
3	1	2	1	3	3	2	4	3	4
21	**22**	**23**	**24**	**25**	**26**	**27**	**28**	**29**	**30**
2	2	1	4	4	4	2	4	2	3
31	**32**	**33**	**34**	**35**	**36**	**37**	**38**	**39**	**40**
3	4	1	3	2	1	3	1	3	3
41	**42**	**43**	**44**	**45**	**46**	**47**	**48**	**49**	**50**
2	4	2	2	4	3	4	4	2	2
51	**52**	**53**	**54**	**55**	**56**	**57**	**58**	**59**	**60**
3	3	3	2	2	2	4	1	1	4
61	**62**	**63**	**64**	**65**	**66**	**67**	**68**	**69**	**70**
4	4	4	1	3	4	4	1	3	4
71	**72**	**73**	**74**	**75**	**76**	**77**	**78**	**79**	**80**
4	3	2	2	1	1	2	4	2	2
81	**82**	**83**	**84**	**85**	**86**	**87**	**88**	**89**	**90**
2	1	3	2	4	2	2	1	2	1

91	**92**	**93**	**94**	**95**	**96**	**97**	**98**	**99**	**100**
3	1	4	2	4	1	1	4	4	1
101	**102**	**103**	**104**	**105**	**106**	**107**	**108**	**109**	**110**
1	3	2	3	1	1	1	3	1	4
111	**112**	**113**	**114**	**115**	**116**	**117**	**118**	**119**	**120**
4	4	1	4	4	1	4	4	3	3
121	**122**	**123**	**124**	**125**	**126**	**127**	**128**	**129**	**130**
1	4	3	2	3	4	1	4	2	1
131	**132**	**133**	**134**	**135**	**136**	**137**	**138**	**139**	**140**
2	2	2	3	2	4	3	3	3	4
141	**142**	**143**	**144**	**145**	**146**	**147**	**148**	**149**	**150**
3	2	4	4	4	4	4	4	3	4
151	**152**	**153**	**154**	**155**	**156**	**157**	**158**	**159**	**160**
1	1	4	4	4	1	2	1	1	4
161	**162**	**163**	**164**	**165**	**166**	**167**	**168**	**169**	**170**
3	4	4	3	1	4	1	2	2	3
171	**172**	**173**	**174**	**175**	**176**	**177**	**178**	**179**	**180**
1	3	2	1	3	1	4	3	1	1
181	**182**	**183**	**184**	**185**	**186**	**187**	**188**	**189**	**190**
4	1	4	1	3	1	3	1	4	4
191	**192**	**193**	**194**	**195**	**196**	**197**	**198**	**199**	**200**
4	2	2	2	4	1	2	1	2	4

EXPLANATORY ANSWERS

1. The flower is a reproductive structure that develops during the reproductive phase of growth in plants. It may occur singly or as part of an inflorescence. Flowers are a distinct feature of angiosperms, which are also known as flowering plants. Other groups like algae, bryophytes, and pteridophytes reproduce through spores and do not form flowers.

2. Collenchyma cells are a type of simple permanent plant tissue primarily responsible for providing mechanical support and elasticity to growing parts of the plant such as young stems and leaves. They have unevenly thickened cell walls made of cellulose and pectin, which allow them to stretch and provide flexibility without breaking.

3. During embryogenesis in higher plants, the embryonal axis gives rise to two poles: the plumule (which develops into the shoot system) and the radicle (which develops into the root system). The plumule is located at the upper end, while the radicle is located at the lower end of the embryonal axis.

4. Phylum Annelida includes organisms such as Nereis, Pheretima (Earthworm), and Hirudinaria (Leech). They have a closed circulatory system, not an open one. Their body is divided into ring-like segments called metameres, and nephridia are excretory organs that also play a role in osmoregulation. Therefore, the statement "open circulatory system is present" is incorrect.

5. In algae, sexual reproduction involves the fusion of gametes, which may be similar or dissimilar in size. The fusion of two gametes dissimilar in size is called anisogamy. Among the options, Eudorina shows anisogamous reproduction, where one gamete is larger and less motile, and the other is smaller and more motile.

6. Ex-situ conservation refers to the preservation of plants and animals outside their natural habitats. This includes gene banks, seed banks, zoos, and botanical gardens. Botanical gardens are specifically designed for the conservation of endangered plant species and the maintenance of germplasm for research, education, and reintroduction into the wild.

7. The stratum compactum is a dense connective tissue layer found beneath the epidermis in the skin of frogs. Its primary role is to provide mechanical strength and protection to the body by supporting the epidermal layers and resisting wear and tear. It does not secrete mucus, regulate ions, or aid in gas exchange.

8. In dicotyledonous stems, the vascular bundles are conjoint, collateral, and open, meaning xylem and phloem are arranged together in the same radius, and a cambium is present between them allowing secondary growth. The protoxylem is endarch, meaning it develops towards the center.

9. Doliolum, a urochordate (tunicate), exhibits both polymorphism and alternation of generations. In its life cycle, a solitary, sexual gonozooid alternates with a colonial, asexual oozoid. This alternation represents a shift between sexual and asexual reproductive forms.

10. The reserve food material in red algae (Rhodophyceae) is floridean starch, which is chemically different from plant starch and is stored in the cytoplasm rather than in plastids.

11. The medicinal plant Belladonna (*Atropa belladonna*), commonly known as deadly nightshade, belongs to the family Solanaceae. This family also includes plants like tobacco, tomato, potato, and Datura. Cassia belongs to Fabaceae, Gulmohar to Fabaceae, and Mustard to Brassicaceae.

12. Leptoids are specialized conducting cells found in Bryophytes, particularly in mosses (e.g., Polytrichum). They are functionally similar to the sieve elements of higher plants (Angiosperms and Gymnosperms), responsible for transporting food materials. Thus, their presence is a characteristic feature of Bryophyta.

13. In an old tree, the ascent of sap occurs through the peripheral, light-colored alburnum, also known as sapwood. Sapwood consists of active xylem vessels responsible for conducting water and minerals. The central, dark-colored part, known as heartwood (duramen), is non-functional in conduction and mainly provides mechanical strength.

14. The human heart is a complex organ composed of all four types of tissues:
    - Epithelial tissue (lines the chambers and valves)
    - Connective tissue (forms fibrous skeleton and valves)
    - Muscular tissue (cardiac muscle for pumping)
    - Neural tissue (controls heart rate via the nervous system)

    Hence, it is made up of all four types of tissues.

15. The phylum Mollusca includes classes such as Bivalvia (e.g., mussels), Cephalopoda (e.g., octopus), and Gastropoda (e.g., snail). Crustacea, however, belongs to a different phylum — Arthropoda, not Mollusca.

16. In the binomial nomenclature system (developed by Carolus Linnaeus), the scientific name of a species consists of two parts — the genus name and the species epithet. The genus name is always capitalized, while the species name is written in lowercase. Both are italicized (or underlined when handwritten). Example: Homo sapiens.

17. Leaves are the most important organs for photosynthesis in most plants. They contain chlorophyll and are designed to capture sunlight and exchange gases efficiently. Although veins help in transport and mechanical support, photosynthesis is their primary function.

18. The key difference between gymnosperms and angiosperms is that gymnosperms have naked seeds, i.e., their ovules are not enclosed within an ovary. In angiosperms, the ovules are enclosed within an ovary that later forms the fruit wall. Thus, gymnosperms are distinguished by the absence of an ovary wall around their seeds.

19. In angiosperms, the male gametophyte develops within the microsporangia (pollen sacs of the anther), and the female gametophyte develops within the megasporangia, which is part of the ovule. However, the structure that contains both male and female reproductive organs (anther and ovary) is the flower, where both gametophytes develop in a specialized arrangement for reproduction.

20. Brown fat (brown adipose tissue) is specialized for heat production (thermogenesis) and is rich in mitochondria containing cytochrome pigments. Cytochromes are iron-containing proteins involved in the electron transport chain, which is essential for energy metabolism.

21. The term flux refers to the movement of ions or molecules across a membrane. It represents the rate of flow of ions from one side of the membrane to the other and is influenced by concentration gradients, membrane permeability, and electrical potential.

22. In lactic acid and alcoholic fermentation, energy is released anaerobically (without oxygen). Only about 2 ATP molecules are produced per glucose molecule, which represents less than 7% of the total energy available from glucose oxidation (compared to ~38% in aerobic respiration).

23. The correct sequence for an enzyme-catalyzed reaction is as follows:

1. The enzyme (E) combines with the substrate (S) to form an enzyme-substrate complex (ES).
2. The ES complex then transitions to an enzyme-product complex (EP).
3. Finally, the enzyme (E) and product (P) separate, releasing the product and regenerating the enzyme.

Hence, the correct representation is: E + S — ES → EP → E + P.

24. **Statement A:** High temperature destroys enzymatic activity because enzymes are proteins, and excessive heat causes denaturation of their structure, rendering them inactive.

Statement B: Low temperature does not destroy enzymes but reduces their activity, placing them in a temporarily inactive state that can be restored upon warming.

Both statements are correct.

25. A competitive inhibitor closely resembles the substrate in molecular structure and competes for the active site of the enzyme. This type of inhibition can be overcome by increasing the substrate concentration.

26. Photorespiration is a light-dependent process that occurs in C3 plants when Rubisco binds oxygen instead of carbon dioxide. It involves the participation of three organelles — the chloroplast, peroxisome, and mitochondrion. These organelles work together to recycle 2-phosphoglycolate produced by oxygenation, resulting in energy loss.

27. In non-competitive inhibition, the inhibitor binds to a site other than the active site of the enzyme, leading to a change in the enzyme's shape. This alters the active site configuration and reduces enzyme activity. The inhibition cannot be overcome by increasing substrate concentration since the active site itself is affected.

28. The EC number (Enzyme Commission number) classifies enzymes based on the type of reaction they catalyze. The number 1.1.1.1 refers to alcohol dehydrogenase, which belongs to the oxidoreductase class.

- The first "1" indicates it's an oxidoreductase (catalyzes oxidation-reduction reactions).
- The second "1" shows it acts on the CH–OH group of donors.
- The third "1" means NAD^+ or $NADP^+$ is the electron acceptor.

29. The C3 cycle (Calvin cycle) consists of three main steps:

1. Carboxylation - CO_2 fixation by RUBISCO to form 3-phosphoglycerate (PGA).
2. Reduction - Conversion of PGA to glyceraldehyde-3-phosphate (G3P) using ATP and NADPH.
3. Regeneration - Regeneration of RuBP (ribulose-1,5-bisphosphate) to continue the cycle.

Thus, the correct sequence is Carboxylation → Reduction → Regeneration.

30. The enzyme RUBISCO (Ribulose-1,5-bisphosphate carboxylase/oxygenase) catalyzes the fixation of CO_2 to RuBP in the Calvin cycle. It requires magnesium (Mg^{2+}) as a metallic cofactor, which stabilizes the negative charges on the substrate and activates the enzyme.

31. In cyclic photophosphorylation, electrons excited from Photosystem I (PS I) return to the same photosystem after passing through an electron transport chain. This process:

- Occurs under low light intensity or when $NADP^+$ is not available.
- Produces ATP only (no NADPH or oxygen is formed).
- Does not involve photolysis of water.

Hence, statements 1 and 3 are correct.

32. Photorespiration occurs in C3 plants and involves three organelles working together — the chloroplast, mitochondrion, and peroxisome. These organelles collaborate in the metabolism of glycolate formed when Rubisco fixes oxygen instead of carbon dioxide.

33. Removal of shoot tips (decapitation) eliminates the source of auxin, which normally inhibits the growth of lateral buds (a phenomenon known as apical dominance). With reduced auxin concentration, lateral buds become active and grow more vigorously.

34. Enzymes are classified into six major classes by the Enzyme Commission (EC) based on the type of reaction they catalyze:

1. Oxidoreductases 2. Transferases
3. Hydrolases 4. Lyases
5. Isomerases 6. Ligases

35. In the chloroplast electron transport chain, the cytochrome b6f complex receives electrons from plastoquinone (PQ) and transfers them to plastocyanin (PC). Plastocyanin then delivers electrons to Photosystem I.

36. The class of enzymes that catalyze oxidation-reduction (redox) reactions between two substrates (one acting as an electron donor and the other as an acceptor) is known as oxidoreductases. These enzymes include dehydrogenases, oxidases, and reductases.

37. In the absorption spectrum of chlorophyll pigments, chlorophyll a and chlorophyll b absorb maximum light in the blue (around 430–450 nm) and red (around 640–680 nm) regions of the visible spectrum. They reflect green light, which is why leaves appear green.

38. As temperature increases, enzyme activity also increases up to a certain optimal temperature (usually around 35–40°C for most enzymes). Beyond this, the enzyme's protein structure denatures, leading to a rapid decline in activity.

39. The activity of enzymes can be influenced by several factors such as pH, temperature, and substrate concentration. Each enzyme has an optimal pH and temperature range within which it functions best. Deviations can reduce or destroy enzyme activity.

40. During the partial oxidation of glucose in the cytoplasm (glycolysis), the first oxidation step occurs when glyceraldehyde-3-phosphate is oxidized to 1,3-bisphosphoglycerate. This step is catalyzed by the enzyme glyceraldehyde-3-phosphate dehydrogenase, which is a dehydrogenase enzyme.

41. The most common cause of female infertility is Polycystic Ovary Syndrome (PCOS). It is a hormonal disorder characterized by irregular menstrual cycles, anovulation (lack of ovulation), and cyst formation in ovaries, leading to difficulty in conception. Other causes like uterine infections, tubal blockage, and endometriosis also contribute but are less frequent overall.

42. The most common indication for kidney transplantation in adults is End-Stage Renal Disease (ESRD). This condition occurs when the kidneys permanently lose their filtering capacity, leading to accumulation of toxins and waste in the body. Dialysis or kidney transplantation becomes essential for survival.

43. During suckling, the hormone oxytocin stimulates myoepithelial cells surrounding the alveoli in the mammary glands to contract. This contraction pushes milk from the alveoli into the ducts, allowing milk ejection or "let-down reflex."

44. Lymph is a clear, colorless fluid composed mainly of white blood cells (especially lymphocytes), proteins, and chyle (lipid-containing fluid). It plays a crucial role in immune defense by removing pathogens and foreign materials from interstitial fluid and returning excess tissue fluid to the bloodstream.

45. Alcohol consumption commonly causes impaired motor coordination, decreased inhibitions, and increased risk of liver cirrhosis with prolonged use. However, it does not enhance cognitive abilities—in fact, it impairs judgment, attention, and reaction time.

46. The disorder of the excretory system characterized by the formation of kidney stones is called renal calculi. These are solid deposits made up of minerals such as calcium oxalate or uric acid, which form in the kidneys and can obstruct urine flow, causing pain and discomfort.

47. The movement of a limb away from the body's midline is known as abduction. For example, lifting your arm sideways away from your body or spreading your fingers apart are examples of abduction. The opposite movement, toward the midline, is adduction.

48. The hypothalamus is the brain structure that integrates the neural and endocrine systems. It regulates various physiological processes such as temperature, hunger, thirst, circadian rhythms, and emotional responses. It also controls the pituitary gland, linking the nervous and endocrine systems.

49. In flowering plants, the primary endosperm cell is formed after triple fusion — that is, when one male gamete fuses with two polar nuclei in the central cell of the embryo sac. This process results in a triploid (3n) cell, which develops into the endosperm, providing nourishment to the developing embryo.

50. Factors such as parental guidance, socioeconomic status, and peer pressure are known to influence sexual behaviour in adolescents. However, exposure to tobacco is not directly associated with influencing sexual behaviour; it primarily affects health and addiction tendencies.

51. Cyclic photophosphorylation occurs mainly in the stroma lamellae (also called intergranal thylakoids) of chloroplasts. These regions contain Photosystem I (PS I) but lack Photosystem II (PS II), which makes them ideal for cyclic electron flow. This process produces ATP only, without the formation of NADPH or oxygen.

52. The specialised assisted reproductive technique in which a single sperm is directly injected into the cytoplasm of an ovum is called Intra-Cytoplasmic Sperm Injection (ICSI). This method is particularly useful in cases of male infertility where sperm count or motility is very low.

53. The condition in males where one or both testes fail to descend from the abdomen into the scrotum around the time of birth is known as cryptorchidism. If untreated, it can lead to infertility and increased risk of testicular cancer due to higher internal body temperatures.

54. Insects use a system of tracheal tubes for respiration. These tubes branch throughout the body, delivering oxygen directly to tissues through small openings called spiracles. This tracheal system bypasses the need for a circulatory system to transport oxygen.

55. The pancreas plays a vital role in digestion by secreting digestive enzymes (like amylase, lipase, and trypsin) into the small intestine via the pancreatic duct. These enzymes help in breaking down carbohydrates, fats, and proteins, supporting the chemical digestion of food.

56. Haematuria is a medical condition characterized by the presence of blood in the urine. It may result from urinary tract infections (UTIs), kidney stones, trauma, or other disorders affecting the kidneys or urinary tract.

57. The source-sink relationship in plants refers to the movement of organic solutes (mainly sucrose) through the phloem from a source (site of production, like leaves) to a sink (site of utilization or storage, like roots or fruits). This relationship is variable and bidirectional, depending on the plant's developmental stage and metabolic needs.

58. The hormone aldosterone, secreted by the adrenal cortex, acts on the cortical collecting tubules and distal convoluted tubule of the kidney to increase sodium reabsorption and potassium excretion. This helps regulate blood volume and pressure.

59. The hormone thyroxine (T_4), produced by the thyroid gland, is primarily responsible for regulating the body's metabolism and energy levels. It controls the rate of cellular respiration and influences protein synthesis, growth, and development.

60. During urine formation, the proximal convoluted tubule (PCT) is the site where maximum reabsorption of water, glucose, amino acids, and ions occurs. Nearly all glucose is reabsorbed here through active transport mechanisms.

61. In 1924, the Russian scientist Alexander I Oparin proposed that the early Earth had a reducing atmosphere, and that the first forms of life arose spontaneously from inorganic molecules through gradual chemical evolution. This idea is known as the Oparin–Haldane hypothesis, forming the foundation of modern abiogenesis theories.

62. The sequence of events that occurs when a cell or organism detects and responds to a stimulus is called a signal transduction pathway. It involves receptor activation, signal amplification, and the triggering of a specific cellular response such as enzyme activation or gene expression.

63. In a test cross involving a dihybrid plant (AaBb) crossed with a double recessive plant (aabb), and assuming independent assortment, the expected phenotypic ratio of the offspring is 1 : 1 : 1 : 1 — representing four different combinations of traits.

64. The primary difference between a transition and a transversion mutation lies in the type of base substitution:

- **Transition:** substitution between purines (A ↔ G) or pyrimidines (C ↔ T).
- **Transversion:** substitution between a purine and a pyrimidine (A ↔ T, A ↔ C, G ↔ T, G ↔ C).

65. A change in allele frequencies within a population over time indicates that evolution is occurring. Evolution is defined as any shift in the genetic composition of a population across generations, caused by factors such as mutation, natural selection, migration, or genetic drift.

66. In his famous experiment to decipher the genetic code, Marshall Nirenberg used:

- A cell-free system for protein synthesis,
- Enzyme nucleoside phosphorylase to synthesize artificial mRNA, and
- Radioactive amino acids to trace the incorporation into proteins.

However, he did not use DNA Polymerase III, as it is involved in DNA replication, not RNA synthesis or translation.

67. The kernel colour of wheat is determined by the cumulative effect of multiple genes, each contributing to the final phenotype in an additive manner. This is a classic example of polygenic inheritance, where multiple genes influence a single trait.

68. In his genetic experiments, Gregor Mendel selected 14 true-breeding pea plant varieties — two for each of the seven contrasting traits (like tall vs. dwarf, round vs. wrinkled seeds, etc.) to ensure consistent and predictable inheritance patterns.

69. The recombination frequency between genes helps determine their order on the chromosome — smaller percentages indicate closer linkage.

Given:

- A–C = 3%
- B–C = 12%
- A–B = 15%
- A–D = 19%

From these values:

- A and C are closest (3%)
- C and B are further apart (12%)
- A–B distance (15%) fits as A–C–B
- D is farthest from A (19%), placing it beyond B

Thus, the correct gene order is A – C – B – D.

70. During early embryonic development, the gonads of both sexes originate from the same indifferent (bipotential) gonadal tissue. Later differentiation depends on the presence or absence of the Y chromosome and its SRY gene. Therefore, both male and female gonads initially develop from the same embryonic tissue.

71. In a pedigree chart, a horizontal line connecting a male and a female represents mating (or marriage), while the vertical line extending downward from that couple represents their children (offspring). These conventions help in tracking inheritance patterns across generations.

72. Sex-linked inheritance refers to traits determined by genes located on the sex chromosomes, usually the X chromosome. Red and green colour blindness and muscular dystrophy are classic examples of X-linked disorders, but red-green colour blindness is the most common and clear example.

73. The first fossil of Ramapithecus, consisting of a fragile upper jaw, was discovered by G. Edward Lewis in 1932 from the Shivalik Hills in India. This fossil is considered an important link in primate evolution, representing an early ancestor of humans.

74. In DNA profiling, the unique RFLP (Restriction Fragment Length Polymorphism) patterns arise due to differences in the size of VNTR (Variable Number of Tandem Repeat) segments among individuals. These variations in the number of repeats make each person's DNA profile unique (except in identical twins).

75. In a breeding population, genetic drift refers to random fluctuations in allele frequencies over generations due to chance events. It is more pronounced in small populations and can lead to the loss or fixation of alleles independent of natural selection.

76. The Miller–Urey experiment (1953) provided strong evidence that organic compounds could form abiotically under conditions similar to those of early Earth. Stanley Miller and Harold Urey simulated a primitive atmosphere (methane, ammonia, hydrogen, and water vapor) and, after applying electric sparks, found amino acids — the building blocks of life.

77. In Mendel's pea plant experiments, he studied seven pairs of contrasting traits. Among them, axial flower position (flowers borne along the stem) was dominant, while terminal flower position was recessive. Mendel's work demonstrated the dominance of certain traits over others.

78. The endosymbiotic hypothesis, proposed by Lynn Margulis in 1970, suggested that mitochondria and chloroplasts originated from free-living prokaryotes that were engulfed by ancestral eukaryotic cells and formed a symbiotic relationship. This theory explains the presence of DNA and double membranes in these organelles.

79. The idea that the first form of life originated from pre-existing non-living organic molecules (chemical evolution) was proposed independently by A.I. Oparin and J.B.S. Haldane. They theorized that early Earth's conditions favored the formation of simple organic molecules, which gradually became more complex.

80. In the Zygote Intra Fallopian Transfer (ZIFT) technique, a zygote with up to 8 blastomeres (early cleavage stage) is transferred into the fallopian tube to facilitate implantation and further development inside the uterus. This technique is used in assisted reproductive technologies (ART).

81. In the Krebs cycle (citric acid cycle), energy-rich electron carriers NADH and $FADH_2$ are produced. These molecules transfer their high-energy electrons to the electron transport chain (ETC) in mitochondria, where they drive ATP synthesis through oxidative phosphorylation.

82. The central part of the proximal region of the centriole is a dense, proteinaceous structure known as the hub. It connects to the surrounding microtubule triplets through structures called radial spokes, helping in centriole organization and microtubule anchoring.

83. Mitosis is also known as equational division because the chromosome number in the daughter cells remains the same as in the parent cell. It ensures genetic stability and is essential for growth and repair in multicellular organisms.

84. The transport of molecules across the nuclear pore complex mediated by importins and exportins requires energy (in the form of GTP) and involves movement against concentration gradients. Therefore, this process is a form of active transport, not diffusion.

85. The discovery of nitric oxide (NO) as a signaling molecule (particularly as an endothelium-derived relaxing factor that regulates blood vessel dilation) was made by Robert F. Furchgott, Louis J. Ignarro, and Ferid Murad, for which they received the 1998 Nobel Prize in Physiology or Medicine.

86. The enzyme responsible for the conversion of ADP to ATP during oxidative phosphorylation is ATP synthase. It utilizes the proton motive force generated by the electron transport chain across the mitochondrial membrane to catalyze ATP formation from ADP and inorganic phosphate (Pi).

87. The coenzyme Nicotinamide Adenine Dinucleotide (NAD^+) is derived from niacin (vitamin B_3). Niacin is essential for the proper functioning of NAD^+, which acts as an electron carrier in oxidation-reduction (redox) reactions within cellular respiration and metabolism.

88. Enzymes reduce the activation energy of reactions by stabilizing the transition state, thereby lowering the energy barrier for the reaction to proceed. They do this without altering the reactants or products, increasing the reaction rate efficiently.

89. Polytene chromosomes, found in certain insect tissues (e.g., Drosophila salivary glands), are formed by multiple rounds of DNA replication without cell division (endomitosis). This results in large, thick chromosomes with distinct banding patterns, making them easily visible under a light microscope.

90. Trichoderma is a genus of fungi commonly used as a biocontrol agent against plant pathogens. It works by competing for nutrients, producing antifungal metabolites, and parasitizing harmful fungi in the soil, thereby promoting healthy plant growth.

91. Molecules can move passively across the membrane by diffusion and osmosis, both of which do not require energy. However, the Na^+–K^+ pump actively transports sodium and potassium ions against their concentration gradients, consuming ATP in the process. Therefore, this is not a passive transport mechanism.

92. Gibberellins are plant hormones known to promote stem elongation, seed germination, and fruit growth. They are used commercially to increase the length of the grape stalks and improve fruit size by stimulating cell elongation and division in the pedicels.

93. A phase-contrast microscope enhances contrast in transparent specimens, making it ideal for studying living cells and their internal structures such as mitochondria, mitotic chromosomes, and vacuoles — all without staining or killing the specimen.

94. In molecular biology, RAPD stands for Random Amplified Polymorphic DNA. It is a type of PCR-based DNA fingerprinting technique that uses short, random primers to amplify regions of genomic DNA, revealing polymorphisms among individuals.

95. In the lac operon model of *E. coli*, the enzyme β-galactosidase acts on lactose, which serves as the substrate and inducer. Lactose binds to the repressor, inactivating it and allowing transcription of the operon genes involved in lactose metabolism.

96. B chromosomes are supernumerary (extra) chromosomes that do not belong to the normal (A) chromosome set. During meiosis, they typically do not pair with A chromosomes and show irregular segregation. Their inheritance is non-Mendelian, often varying in number among individuals.

97. The vitamin that serves as a precursor to the coenzyme NAD^+ (Nicotinamide Adenine Dinucleotide) is Vitamin B_3 (Niacin). It is converted into nicotinamide, which forms the amide component of NAD^+, essential in redox reactions and energy metabolism.

98. The centromere is the region of a chromosome where spindle microtubules attach via the kinetochore complex during mitosis. This ensures that sister chromatids are accurately separated and distributed to opposite poles of the cell during anaphase.

99. The genetic code is:

- Triplet (each codon has 3 bases),
- Degenerate (more than one codon codes for the same amino acid),
- Comma-less (no punctuation between codons), and
- Non-ambiguous (each codon specifies only one amino acid).

100. The rate-limiting step in steroid hormone biosynthesis is catalyzed by cholesterol desmolase (also known as P450scc or CYP11A1). This enzyme converts cholesterol to pregnenolone, the first step in the synthesis of all steroid hormones (like cortisol, aldosterone, and sex steroids).

101. Single Cell Protein (SCP) refers to protein-rich biomass produced from microorganisms like algae, fungi, and bacteria. Mushrooms, being multicellular fungi with slower growth and lower yield, are not suitable for large-scale SCP production due to limited biomass productivity and scalability compared to unicellular organisms like *Spirulina, Candida utilis, or Methylophilus methylotrophus*.

102. Organisms such as plants, bacteria, fungi, and animals whose genetic material has been deliberately altered using molecular biology techniques are known as Genetically Modified Organisms (GMOs). These modifications enhance desirable traits like disease resistance, productivity, or nutrient content.

103. Micropropagation is a tissue culture-based breeding technique used to produce a large number of genetically identical (clonal) plants from a single explant under sterile conditions. It's widely applied in horticulture and forestry for rapid propagation of elite varieties.

104. The Enzyme-Linked Immunosorbent Assay (ELISA) is based on the antigen-antibody interaction principle. It is used for detecting and quantifying specific proteins, hormones, or pathogens (e.g., HIV testing) by linking antibodies to enzymes that produce a detectable color change.

105. Semi-dwarf rice varieties were developed from IR-8, a high-yielding variety produced during the Green Revolution. IR-8 was derived using dwarfing genes from the Dee-geo-woo-gen variety of rice and became the genetic base for many modern semi-dwarf rice cultivars.

106. **Statement I:** Incorrect — Antibiotic actually means "against life," not "pro-life." It refers to substances that kill or inhibit the growth of disease-causing organisms such as bacteria.

Statement II: Incorrect — *Saccharomyces cerevisiae* (yeast) is used in alcoholic fermentation, not for producing immunosuppressive agents. The immunosuppressant Cyclosporin A is produced by the fungus *Trichoderma polysporum*.

107. In genetically modified organisms (GMOs) developed for pest resistance, the most commonly expressed compounds are toxins that kill specific pests. For example, Bt cotton expresses the Cry toxin from *Bacillus thuringiensis*, which is lethal to insect larvae but safe for other organisms.

108. In biological wastewater treatment, masses of bacteria and fungal filaments form flocs — mesh-like structures that help in the aerobic degradation of organic matter. These are part of the activated sludge process under aerobic conditions.

109. RNA interference (RNAi) is a process of gene silencing where small RNA molecules (like siRNA or miRNA) inhibit gene expression by either degrading mRNA or blocking its translation. This is a natural defense mechanism in many eukaryotes against viruses and transposons.

110. A key application of RNAi technology is in silencing disease-causing genes, either to suppress viral infections, control harmful gene expression, or create pest-resistant crops by targeting essential genes in the pest's biology.

111. Cosmid vectors are hybrid plasmid–phage DNA molecules that combine features of plasmids and bacteriophage λ. Their key advantage is that they can clone large DNA fragments (up to about 45 kb), which is much larger than what standard plasmid vectors can accommodate.

112. Transgenic mice are widely used in vaccine safety testing before human trials. These animals are genetically modified to express specific human genes or immune system components, allowing scientists to study immune responses and detect potential adverse effects safely.

113. The first transgenic animal ever created was a mouse. In 1981, scientists introduced foreign DNA into mouse embryos, producing offspring that carried and expressed the inserted genes — marking a breakthrough in genetic engineering research.

114. A biome is a large, distinct ecological community composed of plants and animals adapted to a specific climate and geographical region. Examples include tundra, desert, grassland, and tropical rainforest. Biomes are defined by dominant vegetation and climatic conditions.

115. Among the traditional methods of crop improvement, hybridization remains the most conventional and widely used approach. It involves crossing two genetically different plants to combine desirable traits such as disease resistance, yield, or stress tolerance, offering immense potential for future breeding advancements.

116. Cryopreservation is a method of preserving biological materials such as cells, tissues, embryos, gametes, and microorganisms at very low temperatures (typically $-196°C$ in liquid nitrogen). This technique halts all metabolic and enzymatic activity, ensuring long-term storage without damage or degradation.

117. The breakdown of organic matter by microbes occurs during the secondary treatment (or biological treatment) stage of sewage processing. In this phase, aerobic microorganisms digest organic pollutants, forming biological flocs that help reduce the Biological Oxygen Demand (BOD) of the wastewater.

118. The key component of an ELISA (Enzyme-Linked Immunosorbent Assay) is an enzyme-linked antibody. This antibody binds specifically to the antigen being tested, and the enzyme catalyzes a color-producing reaction, allowing for detection and quantification of the target substance.

119. Gene therapy involves the introduction of functional genes into a person's cells or tissues to correct genetic defects or treat genetic diseases. It uses vectors (often viruses) to deliver therapeutic genes, offering potential cures for disorders such as cystic fibrosis and hemophilia.

120. During ecological succession, both species diversity and total biomass typically increase as the community progresses through successive seral stages toward a stable climax community. Early stages are dominated by pioneer species, followed by more complex and diverse communities.

121. The succession of plants in aquatic (water) habitats is called hydrarch succession, while succession in dry habitats is called xerarch succession. Hydrarch succession begins with submerged plants and ends in terrestrial vegetation, whereas xerarch succession starts in dry conditions and leads to a mesic (moderately moist) environment.

122. The species *Eisenia fetida*, commonly known as the red wiggler or red earthworm, is widely used in vermiculture and vermicomposting due to its high rate of organic matter degradation and tolerance to a wide range of environmental conditions.

123. The Enzyme-Linked Immunosorbent Assay (ELISA) is a biochemical technique based on antigen–antibody interactions. It is used for detecting and quantifying specific proteins or antigens in biological samples, commonly applied in diagnostics such as HIV and COVID-19 testing.

124. *Eisenia fetida* (earthworm) is a detritivore, meaning it feeds on dead and decaying organic matter (detritus). By breaking down this material into smaller particles, earthworms improve soil aeration and enhance nutrient cycling, making nutrients more available to plants.

125. Catalytic converters used in automobiles contain platinum, palladium, and rhodium as catalysts to reduce harmful emissions such as carbon monoxide, hydrocarbons, and nitrogen oxides. Strontium is not used in catalytic converters; it is mainly used in pyrotechnics and glass manufacturing.

126. The presence of *Escherichia coli* (*E. coli*) in water serves as a standard indicator of water pollution, particularly fecal contamination. Since *E. coli* originates from the intestines of warm-blooded animals, its detection in a unit volume of water indicates possible contamination with sewage or harmful pathogens.

127. Bergmann's Law states that individuals of a species (or closely related species) in colder climates tend to have larger body sizes than those in warmer climates. Larger bodies conserve heat more effectively due to a smaller surface area-to-volume ratio, aiding thermoregulation.

128. The immunologically active regions on a complex antigen that are specifically recognized and bound by antibodies or T-cell receptors are called epitopes (or antigenic determinants). These regions trigger immune responses by interacting with immune receptors.

129. Nuclear wastes are extremely hazardous and must be safely disposed of to prevent radiation leaks. They are pre-treated and stored in shielded containers, which are then buried about 500 metres below the Earth's surface in stable rock formations to isolate them from the biosphere.

130. Type I hypersensitivity is primarily mediated by IgE antibodies and is responsible for immediate allergic reactions such as asthma, hay fever, and anaphylaxis. Upon exposure to an allergen, IgE triggers mast cell degranulation and histamine release, leading to inflammation and allergic symptoms.

131. Ecosystems are broadly divided into two basic categories — natural ecosystems (such as forests, oceans, grasslands) and artificial ecosystems (man-made, such as crop fields, aquariums). This classification is based on the origin and maintenance of the ecosystem.

132. During the 18th and 19th centuries, tuberculosis (TB) spread rapidly with urbanization and industrialization, causing massive mortality across Europe. It was referred to as the "Great White Plague" because of the pale appearance of infected patients and its devastating impact.

133. The specific regions on an antigen that interact with the antigen-binding sites of antibodies or lymphocyte receptors are called antigenic determinants or epitopes. These regions are responsible for the specificity of immune recognition and response.

134. Air pollution can be effectively controlled by measures like planting trees, using low-sulphur fuels, and modifying industrial processes to reduce emissions. However, keeping chimneys and smoke stacks at a medium or lower level worsens pollution by keeping contaminants near the ground, thus this option is incorrect.

135. Afforestation refers to the planting of trees in areas that have never been forested before. It is a key environmental strategy to combat desertification, enhance biodiversity, and increase carbon sequestration.

136. The main purpose of using monoclonal antibodies in diagnostic tests is to specifically target and identify a single antigen. Because monoclonal antibodies are derived from a single clone of B cells, they bind with high specificity to one epitope, making them ideal for use in diagnostic assays like ELISA and rapid antigen tests.

137. Incineration is a common and effective method for treating hazardous solid waste. It involves burning waste materials at very high temperatures, converting them into ash, flue gases, and heat, thus reducing the volume of waste and destroying toxic organic compounds.

138. Ex-situ conservation involves protecting endangered species outside their natural habitats, such as in botanical gardens, zoological parks, seed banks, and gene banks. This approach ensures the survival and propagation of species under controlled conditions.

139. In a terrestrial ecosystem, Gross Primary Productivity (GPP) is the highest, as it represents the total amount of energy captured by autotrophs (plants) through photosynthesis before any losses due to respiration. It forms the energy base for all subsequent trophic levels.

140. The synergistic effect in air pollution occurs when two or more pollutants interact to produce a combined toxic effect greater than the sum of their individual effects. For example, the combination of Sulfur dioxide (SO_2) and particulates causes more severe respiratory issues than either pollutant alone.

141. The life cycle of the silkworm (*Bombyx mori*) follows a complete metamorphosis consisting of egg → larva → cocoon → pupa → adult. The larva (caterpillar) stage is the feeding and silk-producing phase, and the pupa develops inside the cocoon before emerging as an adult moth.

142. Sericin is a protein produced by silkworms, which, along with fibroin, forms the silk thread. Sericin acts as a gum-like substance that cements fibroin filaments together, while fibroin provides the strength and structure of silk.

143. Teratogens are chemicals or agents that cause birth defects by interfering with the normal development of the embryo or fetus. Examples include certain drugs (like thalidomide), alcohol, and radiation, which can result in congenital malformations.

144. The fungus *Puccinia graminis tritici*, which causes black stem rust of wheat, produces several types of spores during its life cycle. The binucleated uredospores are the repeating spores, responsible for spreading the infection during the growing season.

145. During spermatogenesis, each primary spermatocyte undergoes meiosis to produce four functional sperm cells (spermatids), which later mature into spermatozoa. In contrast, oogenesis produces only one functional ovum from one primary oocyte.

146. The lime butterfly (*Papilio demoleus*) is a major pest of citrus plants in India. Its larvae feed voraciously on the leaves of citrus trees, causing significant defoliation and reducing fruit yield. It is one of the most destructive pests in citrus orchards.

147. One of the most important therapeutic applications of stem cells in modern medicine is their use in regenerating damaged tissues. Stem cells can differentiate into various specialized cell types, allowing for treatments of conditions such as spinal cord injuries, heart disease, and burns.

148. Crickets are widely recognized as one of the most protein-rich edible insects, containing up to 60–70% protein by dry weight. They are sustainable and nutritious, making them a promising alternative protein source for humans and animals.

149. Earthworms are hermaphrodites (each individual has both male and female reproductive organs) but they reproduce sexually through cross-fertilization — two worms exchange sperm during copulation, and fertilized eggs are later enclosed in a cocoon.

150. The primary advantage of induced pluripotent stem cells (iPSCs) is that they bypass the ethical concerns associated with embryonic stem cells. iPSCs are created by reprogramming adult somatic cells to a pluripotent state, allowing them to differentiate into various cell types without using embryos.

151. In the development of a chick embryo, the yolk sac is the first extraembryonic membrane to appear. It forms around the yolk and functions in the absorption of nutrients during early development, before the formation of other membranes like the amnion, chorion, and allantois.

152. The species that is NOT a parasite of the lac insect is *Tricholygas orbillans*.

Tricholygas orbillans is not recorded in entomological literature as a parasite of the lac insect (*Kerria lacca*). The true parasites include *Parenchthrodryinus clavicornis*, *Erencyrtus dewitzii*, and *Tachardiaephagus tachardiae*, all belonging to the family Encyrtidae of chalcid wasps.

153. In plants, R genes (resistance genes) code for receptor-like kinases (RLKs) or similar proteins. These proteins recognize pathogen-associated molecular patterns and trigger defense signaling pathways that lead to the induction of disease resistance mechanisms.

154. The rat flea (*Xenopsylla cheopis*), the chief vector of bubonic plague, undergoes complete metamorphosis, passing through the stages of egg → larva → pupa → adult. Each stage is morphologically distinct and serves a different function in the insect's lifecycle.

155. The correct chronological sequence in In Vitro Fertilization (IVF) is:

1. Superovulation – Hormonal stimulation of ovaries to produce multiple eggs.
2. Oocyte retrieval – Collection of mature eggs from the ovaries.
3. Fertilisation – Fusion of sperm and egg outside the body in a laboratory dish.
4. Embryo transfer – Placement of the resulting embryo into the uterus.

156. Paedogenesis is the reproduction by immature or larval stages in some animals. It is seen in organisms such as gall flies, liver flukes, and salamanders. Spiders do not exhibit paedogenesis as they reproduce only after attaining full maturity.

157. Brown rust of wheat is caused by a fungus (*Puccinia triticina*), while turnip mosaic, tobacco mosaic, and yellow mosaic are caused by viruses. Hence, brown rust of wheat is not a viral disease.

158. Tabtoxin, produced by *Pseudomonas tabaci*, causes chlorosis by inducing the accumulation of toxic levels of ammonia and damaging the thylakoid membranes of chloroplasts.

159. The Ladybird beetle is a beneficial insect widely known for preying on aphids, which are common plant pests that suck sap from crops.

160. The plant Cuscuta (dodder) is a stem parasite that lives externally on the host and absorbs nutrients through haustorial connections, thus showing ectoparasitism.

161. The Polymerase Chain Reaction (PCR) relies on a heat-stable enzyme known as DNA polymerase, specifically Taq polymerase, which synthesises new DNA strands by extending primers during the amplification process.

162. Blood group O is known as the universal donor because it lacks A and B antigens on the surface of red blood cells, preventing immune reactions when transfused into individuals of other blood types.

163. The Student's t-distribution was proposed by William Sealy Gosset, who published it under the pseudonym "Student" while working at the Guinness Brewery. It is used for analysing small sample data.

164. Hayem's fluid is used for counting red blood cells (RBCs). It prevents coagulation and maintains the shape of RBCs, allowing for accurate counting under the microscope.

165. The statement "WBC are enucleated cells and help in the production of antigens to fight infections" is incorrect because WBCs are nucleated cells, and they produce antibodies, not antigens.

166. The technique used to separate and analyse DNA fragments based on size is Agarose Gel Electrophoresis. It allows the visualisation of DNA bands under UV light, and the DNA ladder helps estimate fragment sizes accurately.

167. The incorrect statement is "It is used for the study of intramolecular bonding." Spectroscopy primarily studies the interaction of electromagnetic radiation with matter, not specifically intramolecular bonding.

168. The size exclusion chromatographic method is not typically used for testing pathogens. It is mainly applied for separating molecules based on size, not for pathogen detection.

169. ANOVA (Analysis of Variance) is used for comparing the means of three or more groups, whereas a t-test compares the means of two groups.

170. In RNA-Seq, RNA is converted into cDNA because most sequencing platforms are DNA-specific and cannot directly read RNA molecules.

171. SWISS-PROT is a curated protein sequence database that provides highly accurate and manually annotated protein sequences with information on structure, function, and post-translational modifications.

172. For patients with thrombocytopenia (low platelet count), particularly due to chemotherapy, the most appropriate blood component is platelet concentrate, which helps restore normal clotting ability.

173. In a DNA microarray experiment, RNA samples are commonly used to measure gene expression levels, as cDNA is synthesized from RNA to detect which genes are active.

174. The Needleman-Wunsch algorithm is the most widely used method for global sequence alignment, as it aligns entire sequences from end to end.

175. BLAST stands for Basic Local Alignment Search Tool, and it is used to compare a query sequence against a database to identify regions of local similarity.

176. In Radioimmunoassay (RIA), the commonly used radioactive isotope is Iodine-125 (^{125}I), which labels antigens or antibodies to detect minute quantities of biological substances like hormones.

177. The Illumina HiSeq platform uses reversible dye terminator chemistry in sequencing-by-synthesis, allowing detection of nucleotide incorporation in real-time.

178. The incorrect statement is that the neighbor-joining method was proposed by M.O. Dayhoff in 1978. In reality, it was proposed by Saitou and Nei in 1987 for reconstructing phylogenetic trees.

179. Plasma makes up about 55% of total blood volume. It contains water, electrolytes, proteins, and other solutes necessary for physiological balance.

180. In ANOVA (Analysis of Variance), the F-test statistic is defined as the ratio of between-group variance to within-group variance, helping to determine if group means differ significantly.

181. Gender roles are socially constructed and differ across cultures, time, and social contexts. They are not biologically fixed but shaped by societal expectations and norms.

182. Logical reasoning is not a type of art; it belongs to the domain of analytical and cognitive skills. Arts include creative and expressive activities such as dance, music, and creative writing.

183. A school subject refers to an area of learning within the school curriculum, designed to help students gain knowledge, skills, and values in specific disciplines.

184. The behaviorist approach to learning describes it as a connection between stimulus and response, emphasizing observable behaviors shaped through conditioning.

185. Designing worksheets of varying levels—recall, application, and critical thinking—is an example of differentiated instruction, where teaching is tailored to meet diverse learner needs.

186. The principle of integration and correlation emphasizes that subject matter should be logically and psychologically arranged, ensuring content is meaningful, connected, and developmentally appropriate for learners.

187. Region is not one of Michael Halliday's three dimensions of register variation. The correct dimensions are Field (what is happening), Tenor (who is involved), and Mode (how communication occurs).

188. In many cultures, women are socially expected to display nurturing, caring, and warmth, reflecting traditional gender role expectations.

189. In the context of assessments, validity is considered equivalent to accuracy, as it measures how well an assessment truly evaluates what it is intended to assess.

190. Scaffolding refers to providing guided support to learners, which is gradually reduced as they become more independent and gain mastery over the task.

191. The Sarva Shiksha Abhiyan (SSA) is a flagship programme launched by the Government of India to achieve the goal of universalisation of elementary education and ensure that every child receives free and compulsory education.

192. The Behaviourist approach emphasizes the role of environment over heredity in shaping behaviour, asserting that learning results from interactions with the external environment through conditioning.

193. The Cognitive approach explains that learners process perceptions through differentiation, generalisation, and restructuration, focusing on how mental processes influence understanding and learning.

194. Reliability refers to the repeatability and consistency of an assessment — if the same test produces similar results under consistent conditions, it is said to be reliable.

195. The Rights of Persons with Disabilities Act, 2016 recognises 21 disabilities, expanding the scope from the previous 7 categories listed in the 1995 Act.

196. The principle of civic and social needs in curriculum construction emphasises the development of both the individual and society, ensuring learners become responsible citizens who contribute to social progress.

197. According to constructivist theorists, teaching is a process of developing understanding or insight in the learner. This approach emphasises that learners actively construct their own knowledge through experience, reflection, and interaction rather than passively receiving information.

198. The word discipline is derived from the Latin word 'discipulus', which means learner or pupil, highlighting its roots in learning and instruction.

199. Growth is measured in quantitative terms, such as height and weight, representing physical changes in an individual over time.

200. Caste is not considered a biological or environmental factor influencing growth and development; rather, it is a social classification.

Previous Paper (Solved)

Delhi Subordinate Services Selection Board

DSSSB-PGT—BIOLOGY

Recruitment Exam, 2021*

Subject Knowledge – Biology & Teaching Methodology

1. With which of the following is the book "Systema Naturae" associated with?

A. Natural selection

B. Classification of flora

C. Classification of plants and animals

D. Human body mechanism

2. ICBN makes the rules for nomenclature. Here ICBN stands for:

A. International Code for Botanical Nomenclature

B. International Committee of Botanical Nomenclature

C. International Committee of Biological Nomenclature

D. International Code for Biological Nomenclature

3. Consider the following:

1. This part of the plant bears both the nodes and internodes
2. It is generally green when young, but changes colour later.

Which of the following parts has been described?

A. Bud B. Root

C. Flower D. Stem

4. Solanum tuberosum is the scientific name of ______.

A. Potato B. Brinjal

C. Cabbage D. Tomato

5. Which of the following flowers is zygomorphic?

A. Chilli B. Mustard

C. Datura D. Gulmohur

6. We can eat the roots of many plants. Which of the following is an example of a plant with edible roots?

A. Potato B. Sweet potato

C. Wheat D. Mango

7. The alternation of generation in Obelia is termed as ______.

A. Metagenesis B. Metamerism

C. Metamorphosis D. Dimorphism

8. Families are characterised on the basis of:

1. Vegetative features of plant species
2. Reproductive feature of plant species

A. Neither 1 nor 2 B. 2 only

C. 1 only D. Both 1 and 2

9. Reproduction is a method by which one organism can produce their offspring, it can occur within members of:

A. Family B. Order

C. Species D. Genus

10. Pith is the anatomical part of plant, which is well developed in ______.

A. Monocot root and Dicot root

B. Monocot root and monocot stem

C. Dicot root and monocot stem

D. Monocot root and Dicot stem

* Online exam held on 16/07/2021

11. The organism that does not reproduce is:
A. Cockroach B. Mule
C. Spirogyra D. Fungi

12. Which of the following is known as the 'potato-family'?
A. Fabaceae B. Brassicaceae
C. Solanaceae D. Liliaceae

13. _____ has formalised Binomial Nomenclature.
A. Mendel B. Robert Hooke
C. Charles Darwin D. Carolus Linnaeus

14. Which plant is seen growing in swampy areas with many roots coming out of the ground and growing vertically upwards?
A. Monstera B. Banyan tree
C. Mirabilis D. Rhizophora

15. In which of the following plants, the primary root is short lived and is replaced by a large number of roots. These roots originate from the base of the stem and constitute the fibrous root system.
A. Monocotyledons B. Bryophyta
C. Gymnosperm D. Dicotyledons

16. Who has authored the book "Anatomy of Seed Plants"?
A. Susan E. Eichhorn
B. Katherine Esau
C. Vernon Cheadle
D. Ray F. Evert

17. Which of the following is incorrectly matched?
A. Gynoecium – Composed of stamens
B. Calyx – outermost whorl of the flower
C. Corolla – brightly coloured to attract insects
D. Placentation – Arrangement of ovules within the ovary

18. There are different branches of science. Which of the following branches of science deals with identification, nomenclature, and classification of organisms?
A. Environmental science
B. Ecology
C. Taxonomy
D. Genetics

19. The region of the stem from where leaves are born is called:
A. Bud B. Gemmule
C. Internodes D. Nodes

20. Consider the following:
1. When the incisions of the lamina reach up to the midrib breaking it into a number of leaflets, the leaf is called compound.
2. Phyllotaxy is the pattern of arrangement of leaves on the stem or branch.

Which of the above is incorrect?
A. Both 1 and 2 B. Only 1
C. Only 2 D. Neither 1 nor 2

21. A gravid proglottid has:
A. A fully developed male reproductive unit
B. An under-developed female reproductive unit
C. Branched uterus filled with fertilised eggs
D. Only female organs are well developed

22. Which of the following parasites show alternation of generation and alternation of host in its life cycle?
1. Fasciola 2. Taenia
A. Both 1 and 2 B. Only 2
C. Only 1 D. Neither 1 nor 2

23. ______ is the process where the microspores are formed from a pollen mother cell (PMC).
A. Exine B. Microspore tetrad
C. Pollen grains D. Microsporogenesis

24. Human haemoglobin is a quaternary protein, the structure of which is described as:
A. Tetramer of four different subunits
B. Tetramer of two different subunits
C. Tetramer of identical peptide subunits
D. Dimer of two myoglobin dimers

25. Which of the following can create electric-fields?
A. Dolphins B. Torpedoes
C. Porpoises D. Turtles

26. Synthesis of mRNA on DNA template is:
A. Bidirectional
B. Unidirectional
C. Bi-directional with the help of primer
D. Uni-directional with the help of primer

27. Which of the following works helped to establish the relationship of a gene to control synthesis of one enzyme?
A. The work of George Beadle and Edward Tatum during 1930s on the mould Neurospora crassa
B. The work of Johansen and Edward Tatum during 1930s on the mould Neurospora crassa
C. The work of Bateson and Edward Tatum during 1930s on the mould Neurospora crassa
D. The work of Morgan and Edward Tatum during 1930s on the mould Neurospora crassa

28. Lactose is the substrate for which of the following enzyme?
A. Beta-galactosidase
B. Glucosidases
C. Galactose
D. Beta-glucuronidase

29. With the help of ______ diagram, production of gametes by the parents, the formation of the zygotes, the F1 and F2 plants can be understood.
A. Heterozygous B. Punnett Square
C. Monohybrid Cross D. Test Cross

30. Which of the following removes the RNA primers from the lagging strand?
A. DNA polymerase I
B. 3′→5′ exonuclease
C. DNA polymerase III
D. DNA ligase

31. Consider the following statements:
1. This type of Immunoglobulin is a type of antibody representing approximately 75% of serum antibodies in humans.
2. It is present in most abundant quantity in the blood circulation.

Which type of immunoglobulin is being talked about?
A. IgG B. IgM
C. IgE D. IgD

32. What term is used for nephridia which discharge their excretory products into the lumen of gut?
A. Holocrine B. Exonephric
C. Enteronephric D. Exocrine

33. The breathing of blue whales occurs through:
A. Skin B. Gill
C. Blowhole D. Nose

34. Which of the following shows the characteristics of torsion?
A. Gastropoda B. Cephalopoda
C. Aplacophora D. Monaplacophora

35. Consider the following animals:
1. Cartilaginous fishes
2. Frogs
3. Crocodiles

Which of the above animals' heart auricle consist of single chamber?
A. Only 1
B. Only 3
C. Only 1 and 2
D. Only 2 and 3

36. How many occipital condyle(s) should be there in the skull of a snake?
A. Two B. Nil
C. Three D. One

37. The jawless vertebrates are known as:
A. Osteichthyes B. Dipnoi
C. Chondrichthynes D. Agnatha

38. The factors or gene on chromosome regulating the physical expression of the characters is called ______.
A. Co-dominance B. Genotype
C. Phenotype D. Allele

39. Which of the following is the phenomena where different genes interact with each other in a way that influences the phenotype?

A. Pleiotropy
B. Incomplete dominance
C. Epistasis
D. Codominance

40. Action of topoisomerase leads to change in ______.

A. Linking number of closed circular double stranded DNA
B. Linking number of closed circular single stranded DNA
C. Linking number of double stranded linear DNA
D. Linking number of linear single stranded DNA

41. The testosterone producing cells of the testes are called:

A. Spermatogonia B. Granulosa cells
C. Sertoli cells D. Leydig cells

42. Pollen grains are generally spherical measuring about ______ in diameter.

A. 25-50 Micrometers
B. 50-75 Micrometers
C. 75-100 Micrometers
D. More than 100 Micrometers

43. Cells found in the choroid plexus that secrete cerebrospinal fluid are:

A. Astrocytes
B. Oligodendrocytes
C. Microglia
D. Ependymal cells

44. ______ is the release of secondary oocyte from the ovary.

A. Fertilization B. Oogenesis
C. Ovulation D. Spermatogenesis

45. Nerve impulses are carried from the eye to the brain by the:

A. Optic nerve
B. Rod and cone cell
C. Bipolar cell
D. Cornea

46. Gene is the unit of inheritance that controls a specific trait or character and may also be expressed in alternative forms known as ______.

A. Alleles B. Central Dogma
C. Phenotypes D. Codominance

47. Mendel proposed two general rules to consolidate his understanding of inheritance in monohybrid crosses. The law consists of which of the following?

I. Law of Dominance
II. Law of Segregation
III. Law of Hereditary

A. Both I and II
B. Both II and III
C. Only I
D. I, II and III

48. Which part of pollen grains contain sporopollenin?

A. Intine
B. Exine
C. Pollen cytoplasm
D. Tapetum

49. Oxytocin is secreted by the ______.

A. Adenohypophysis
B. Zona glomerulosa
C. Neurohypophysis
D. Pars intermedia

50. Cells of the tapetum possess dense cytoplasm and generally have ______.

A. More than One Nucleus
B. More than Three Nucleus
C. More than Two Nucleus
D. More than Four Nucleus

51. Which of the following describes the process of Apomixis?

A. Production of seeds as result of sexual reproduction
B. Production of seeds without fertilisation
C. Production of seeds after fertilisation
D. No production of seeds even after sexual reproduction

52. An antrum is characteristic of ______ follicle.
A. Bone marrow B. Primary
C. Graafian D. Secondary

53. A neuron with many short dendrites and a single long axon is a:
A. Unipolar neuron
B. Bipolar neuron
C. Multipolar neuron
D. Varies from region to region

54. The process of formation of megaspores from the megaspore mother cell is called:
A. Megasporangium
B. Megasporexis
C. Megasporonium
D. Megasporogenesis

55. Without associating transiently with initiation-factor (σ) and termination-factor (ρ), the RNA polymerase is only capable of catalysing which of the following process?
1. Initiation
2. Elongation
3. Termination
A. Only 2 B. Only 1
C. 1, 2 and 3 D. Only 3

56. Human chorionic gonadotropin:
A. Begins to be produced four months after fertilization
B. Is produced by Corpus luteum
C. Is present only if a successful fertilization has occurred
D. Is produced by the prostate gland

57. Sutton united the knowledge of chromosomal segregation with Mendelian principles and called it the ______.
A. Chromosomal theory of Inheritance
B. Chromosomal theory of Behaviour
C. Chromosomal theory of Segregation
D. Chromosomal theory of Hereditary

58. The Generative Cell of the pollen grain divides to form:
A. Five Male Gametes
B. Three Male Gametes
C. Four Male Gametes
D. Two Male Gametes

59. Polyembryony Means:
I. Occurrence of Single Embryo in the seed
II. No occurrence of embryo in the seed
III. Occurrence of more than one embryo in the seed
A. I and III only
B. Only III
C. Only I
D. Only II

60. The total DNA content in one complete set of chromosomes (including all the genes and other parts of DNA) is called a ______.
A. Cytoplasm
B. Genome
C. Prokaryote Genome
D. Eukaryotic Genome

61. Which of the following methods of conservation of biodiversity is used only for threatened animals and plants?
A. Biosphere Reserves
B. In Situ conservation
C. Ex Situ conservation
D. National parks

62. The term living fossil refers to a:
A. Life like fossil well preserved in amber
B. Living animal which is about to be fossilized
C. Fossil formed from a living animal
D. Living organisms showing some very primitive characters

63. Consider the following gases:
(*a*) Carbon dioxide
(*b*) Methane
(*c*) CFCs
(*d*) Nitrous Oxide

Arrange these gases according to the decending order of their relative contribution to total global warming.
A. (*d*), (*c*), (*b*), (*a*) B. (*a*), (*b*), (*c*), (*d*)
C. (*a*), (*d*), (*c*), (*b*) D. (*a*), (*c*), (*b*), (*d*)

64. Which of the following best describes the Alpha Diversity?
1. The diversity of organisms sharing the same habitat or community.
2. The diversity of organisms which do not share the same habitat or community.
3. The diversity of organisms which has no preference for sharing the same habitat or community.

A. Only 3
B. Only 1
C. Neither 1, nor 2, nor 3
D. Only 2

65. From which of the following structures is the secondary oocyte ovulated?
A. Primary follicle
B. Germinal epithelium
C. Graafian follicle
D. Corpus luteum

66. Which of the following parts of the human body is effected the most due to the fluoride pollution?
A. Eyes
B. Liver
C. Pancreas
D. Teeth

67. Syphilis is caused by which of the following bacterium?
A. Treponema pallidum
B. Spirochaetales
C. Spirochaetes
D. Leptospira interrogans

68. Which one among the following is the most important factor in speciation?
A. Ethological isolation
B. Ecological isolation
C. Reproductive isolation
D. Geographical isolation

69. Which of the following best represents the approximate temperature of Cryopreservation?
A. –140°C B. 0°C
C. –130°C D. –196°C

70. The process that sperm undergoes in female genital tract of mammals before fertilization is called:
A. Activation B. Deactivation
C. Decapacitation D. Capacitation

71. Which of the following phrase is used for Eichhornia Crassipes?
A. Terror of South B. Terror of Bombay
C. Terror of North D. Terror of Bengal

72. Nilgiri was the first biosphere reserve of India. It was established in which year?
A. 1998 B. 1986
C. 1999 D. 1988

73. Which of the following can be a reason for biodiversity losses?
1. Alien species invasion
2. Co-extinctions

A. Neither 1 nor 2
B. Both 1 and 2
C. Only 1
D. Only 2

74. ______ is produced mainly by the Corpus luteum in the ovary following ovulation.
A. FSH B. Progesterone
C. hCG D. LH

75. Fertilization of human egg most of ten takes place in the ______.
A. Uterus B. Cervix
C. Ampulla D. Ovary

76. Which of the following diseases was caused due to the fish contamination with mercury?
A. Minamata Disease
B. Yokkaichi asthma
C. Itai-Itai Disease
D. Argyria

77. Which of the following term is used to categorise the species which is at the highest risk of extinction in near future?
A. Link species
B. Vulnerable
C. Critically endangered
D. Rare

78. The process in which the three germ layers form is called:
A. Cleavage B. Organogenesis
C. Gastrulation D. Fertilization

79. Coelom is formed from:
A. Endoderm B. Mesoderm
C. Cnidoblast D. Ectoderm

80. Which hormone from the hypothalamus stimulates the release of FSH from the anterior pituitary?
A. Oxytocin
B. Progesterone
C. Luteinizing hormone
D. GnRH

81. Cells that release histamine and other vaso-active substances in response to allergens are:
A. Mast cells B. NK cell
C. Macrophages D. Neutrophils

82. What is the principal health concern of Ozone depletion in the Stratosphere?
A. Hadley cell
B. Ilankovitch cycle
C. Cancer and other damage to the skin
D. Temperature inversions

83. Who was the founder of the 'Madras school' of conformational analysis of biopolymers?
A. S.S. Bhatnagar B. H.G. Khorana
C. Anna Mani D. G.N. Ramachandran

84. Who discovered Restriction endonuclease enzymes?
A. Smith and Nathans
B. Fleming
C. Baiger
D. Waxman

85. Consider the options and determine which of the following is not component of yeast artificial chromosome?
A. Centromere
B. Telomere
C. Origin of replication
D. COS site

86. Secretion of adrenaline hormone causes nervousness and irritability as an effect of which of the following?
A. Land Pollution
B. Noise Pollution
C. Air Pollution
D. Water Pollution

87. Which part connects foetus to placenta?
A. Chorion B. Amnion
C. Umbilical cord D. Yolk sac

88. Ecological Pyramids can determine ______.
A. The energy which the different organism show in the different atmosphere
B. The level at which different organisms stand in the food chain
C. The energy and biomass relationship between the organisms at different tropic levels
D. The life cycle of an organism

89. Which cells are most affected by AIDS?
A. Neutrophils B. T-cells
C. Monocytes D. B-cells

90. Which of the following are organisms that completely lack a cell wall and are the smallest living cells known and can survive without oxygen?
A. Cyanobacteria B. Mycoplasma
C. Eubacteria D. Heterocysts

91. Allergy and anaphylaxis are due to:
A. IgM B. IgA
C. IgE D. IgG

92. In 1838 ______ and ______ formulated the "cell theory."
A. Robert Hooke, Anton Van Leeuwenhoek
B. M.J. Schleiden, Theodore Schwann
C. Theodore Schwann, Robert Hooke
D. Anton Van Leeuwenhoek, M.J. Schleiden

93. Mendel would have explained the Law of independent assortment, if ______ was known at his time.
A. Linkage B. Heterogamete
C. Autosomes D. Recombination

94. An endemic species is ______.
A. One found only on island
B. One found in many different geographic areas
C. One found naturally in just one geographic area
D. One that has been introduced to a new geographic area

95. When was the concept of Joint Forest Movement (JFM) launched in India?
A. 1980s B. 1970s
C. 1960s D. 1990s

96. Asterias and Ophiura are examples of ______.
A. Phylum - Chordata
B. Phylum - Echinodermata
C. Phylum - Hemichordata
D. Phylum - Arthropoda

97. Which of the following statements is incorrect regarding Bt Cotton?
I. Bt stands for Bacillus thuringiensis.
II. The strains contain crystals which contain a toxic insecticidal protein.
A. Neither I nor II
B. Only I
C. Only II
D. Both I and II

98. In a choromosome there is a specific DNA sequence which is responsible for initiating replication. What is it called?
A. Promotor
B. Plasmid
C. Operator
D. Origin of replication

99. In which temperature range enzymes are most functional?
A. 35° - 40°C B. 50° - 60°C
C. (–15°) - (–25°C) D. 10° - 80°C

100. Which of the following secondary metabolite is a toxin?
A. Cartenoids B. Curcumin
C. Morphine D. Ricin

101. Which is the first visceral arch?
A. Mandibular arch
B. Hyoid arch
C. Branchial arch
D. Aortic arch

102. Which one of the following will represent low stability and high resilience?
A. An ecosystem which can be easily damaged and cannot recover even after damaging effect stops
B. An ecosystem which cannot be damaged at all
C. An ecosystem which cannot be easily damaged but can recover whatever damaged is caused after sometime if damaging effect stops
D. An ecosystem which can be easily damaged but can recover after sometime if damaging effect stops

103. A protozoan reproduces by binary fission. What will be the number of protozoans in its population after eight generations?
A. 256 B. 64
C. 128 D. 32

104. How many chambers are present in Crocodile's heart?
A. 5 B. 4
C. 3 D. 2

105. The individual monosaccharides are linked by a ______ to form a polysaccharide.
A. Glycosidic bond
B. Peptide bond
C. Phosphodiester bond
D. Ester bond

106. Retrogressive met amorphosis is commonly seen in ______.
A. Ascidia B. E.coli
C. Frog D. Snake

107. In a society, pattern of age of population is directly responsible for the kind of population growth, because:
A. Different age group have different reproductive capabilities

B. Younger females have more offspring than do older females
C. The habits of the newer society leads to less reproductive ability
D. The more the people are educated, the less do they want to reproduce

108. Which process is used to remove urea from the blood?
A. Sweating B. Digestion
C. Excretion D. Hemodialysis

109. Nephron is the structural and functional unit of ______.
A. Lungs B. Brain
C. Pancreas D. Kidney

110. Which of the following is the excretory organ of cockroach?
A. Nephridia
B. Malpighian tubules
C. Flame cell
D. Kidney

111. A group of vertebrates are without any amnion; they are called anamniota. Which of the following belongs to this group?
A. Amphibians and Reptiles
B. Reptiles
C. Fishes and amphibians
D. Fish

112. Western ghats are known as ______.
A. Best reserved national park in India
B. Best wildlife protection India
C. Hot-spot of biodiversity in India
D. Hot-spot of reserved sanctuary in India

113. Which of the following organs is affected in jaundice?
A. Lungs B. Liver
C. Kidney D. Heart

114. Which valve is present in the junction of right artery and ventricle in a human heart?
A. Seminular valve
B. Tricuspid valve
C. Bicuspid valve
D. Mitral valve

115. Frontal part of skull is made up of ______ bones.
A. 32 B. 23
C. 24 D. 14

116. The joint between humerus and pectoral girdle is ______.
A. Ball and socket joint
B. Pivot joint
C. Saddle joint
D. Hinge joint

117. Henle's loop is present in the ______ of human.
A. Lungs
B. Kidney
C. Blood
D. Nephridia

118. Rare and Endangered Species are given under which of the following?
A. Blue Data Book
B. Red Data Book
C. Green Data Book
D. Black Data Book

119. Which of the following describes the littoral zone?
1. The zone at the edge of a lake or ocean which is alternatively exposed to air and immersed in water.
2. The zone at the middle of a lake or ocean which is alternatively exposed to air and immersed in water.
3. The zone at the both the ends of a lake which is alternatively exposed to air and immersed in water.

A. Neither 1 nor 2 nor 3
B. Only 3
C. Only 1
D. Only 2

120. Jim Corbett was developed as:
A. First National Park of India
B. First Protected Forest for Endangered Species
C. First Protected Bird Reserve
D. First Wildlife Sanctuary of India

121. Kranz anatomy is found in ______ plant.
A. C_2 B. CAM
C. C_4 D. C_3

122. ______ is known as golden era of reptile.
A. Mesozoic era
B. Cenozoic era
C. Paleozoic era
D. Phanerozoic era

123. Which type of jaw attachment is found in mammals?
A. Hyostylic condition
B. Autostylic condition
C. Holostylic condition
D. Craniostylic condition

124. The lateral ventricles remain in communication with the third ventricle by a small opening called ______.
A. Foramen of Monro
B. Basal ganglia
C. Foramen of panizza
D. Fossa ovalis

125. Bipolar neurons are found in ______.
A. Heart B. Cerebral cortex
C. Retina of eye D. Embryonic stage

126. Coelom originates from which germinal layer?
A. Endoderm B. Mesoderm
C. Vacuoles D. Ectoderm

127. Jacobson's organ is useful in the process of communicating chemical messages in which organism?
A. Cat B. Snake
C. Monkey D. Rat

128. Which is not a part of lymphatic system?
A. Tonsil B. Adenoids
C. Stomach D. Spleen

129. Which type of Chlorophyll is present in Rhodophyceae?
A. Chlorophyll a, c
B. Chlorophyll a, b
C. Chlorophyll c, d
D. Chlorophyll a, d

130. If S = Species richness, A = Area, Z = slope of the line (regression coefficient), C = Y-intercept, then on a logarithmic scale, the species-area relationship is a straight line described by the equation:
A. log S = log C/Z log A
B. log S = log C – Z log A
C. log C = log S – Z log A
D. log S = log C + Z log A

131. In case of Ambystoma, the phenomenon of attainment of sexual maturity in larval phase is called ______.
A. Neoteny
B. Juvenile phase
C. Reproductive phase
D. Maturity

132. Which of the following is considered a living fossil?
A. Turtle B. Tuatara
C. Rhinocerous D. Tiger

133. All single celled eukaryotes are placed under ______.
A. Monera B. Protista
C. Bacteria D. Animalia

134. Outer subdermal fat layer of aquatic mammal is known as:
A. Blubber B. Epidermis
C. Skin D. Fat bodies

135. Which type of kidney is found in Frog?
A. Pronephric type B. Mesonephric type
C. Primitive type D. Metanephric type

136. The covering of brain is known as ______.
A. Suture B. Meninges
C. CSF D. Pleura

137. Which organism doesn't have Coelom?
A. Hirudinaria B. Platyhelminthes
C. Pheretima D. Nereis

138. Which of the following is responsible for causing "Red Tides"?
A. Gonyaulax B. Chrysophytes
C. Euglena D. Slime moulds

139. Which Fungi is commonly known as Imperfect Fungi?
A. Ascomycetes
B. Basidiomycetes
C. Phycomycetes
D. Deuteromycetes

140. The thyroid glands produces a hormone called ______.
A. T4 B. TSH
C. ADH D. FSH

141. The tail part of Chlorophyll molecule is made up of ______.
A. Phytol B. Hydrogen
C. Porphyria D. 10 carbon bond

142. Human heart consists of which tissue?
A. Epithelial
B. Connective, Epithelial
C. Neural, Muscular, Connective, Epithelial
D. Muscular, Connective

143. ______ is known as birth hormone.
A. Oxytocin B. LH
C. FSH D. Prolactin

144. Which of the following is known as traffic police of the cell?
A. Golgi body
B. Nucleus
C. Lysosome
D. Endoplasmic Reticulum

145. Which of the following cells function as nurse cells for the sperm?
A. Scrotum B. Acrosome
C. Sertoli cell D. Leydig cell

146. Blood is a fluid ______ tissue.
A. Nervous B. Connective
C. Muscle D. Epithelial

147. Testosterone is a ______.
A. Thyroid hormone
B. Steroid hormone
C. Pregnancy hormone
D. Peptide hormone

148. Which type of placenta is found in cats and dogs?
A. Discoidal placenta
B. Zonary placenta
C. Meta Discoidal placenta
D. Diffuse placenta

149. ___________ is the first body segment of earthworm.
A. Peristomium B. Epithelium
C. Prostomium D. Peritoneum

150. Earthworm bears a dark band of glandular tissue called Clitellum, it is present in ______.
A. 13-14 segment
B. 13-15 segment
C. 14-16 segment
D. 12-13 segment

151. The ______ are the compound lipids and they form the pigments of the animal and plant cells.
A. Anthocyanine B. Xanthophylls
C. Chlorophyll D. Carotenoids

152. The respiratory organ/organs of adult Frog is/are ______.
A. Lungs and skin B. Gill
C. Book gill D. Trachea

153. Which organ is known as graveyard of RBC?
A. Spleen B. Tonsil
C. Blood D. Stomach

154. Which of the following characters is a dominant character?
A. Rolling tongue
B. Folding tongue
C. Attached ear lobes
D. Fingers with no hair

155. Exoskeleton of arthropods is made up of ______.
A. Muscle B. Protein
C. Chitin D. Skeleton

156. Which hormone is used in pregnancy test?
A. ADH B. FSH
C. PRL D. HCG

157. Which of the following is the phenotypic ratio of incomplete dominance?
A. 1/5 : 1/8 : 1/5
B. 1 : 2 : 1
C. 4 : 2 : 1
D. 8 : 2 : 2 : 1

158. Chemical name of Vitamin E is ______.
A. Riboflavin B. Calciferol
C. Thiamine D. Tocopherol

159. Which is the most common and abundant biological product on earth?
A. Pepsin B. Cellulose
C. Glycerol D. Amino acid

160. Which plant pigment is present in tomatoes?
A. Phycobilins
B. Lycopene
C. Xanthophylls
D. Carotene

161. Which of the following scientists has proposed the Mutation Theory?
A. De Vries B. Darwin
C. Mendel D. Lamark

162. Sexual reproduction takes place through fusion of two gametes. These gametes can be flagellated and similar in size (as in Ulothrix) or non-flagellated (non-motile) but similar in size (as in Spirogyra). Such reproduction is called:
A. Anisogamous
B. Isogamous
C. Oogamous
D. Gametophyte

163. The Ganga Action Plan was launched in ______.
A. 1984 B. 1986
C. 1985 D. 1987

164. A genetic disease due to the XXY karyotype is called:
A. Klinefelter's syndrome
B. Equus caballlus
C. Cry du chat syndrome
D. Marasmus

165. The position or place on a chromosome occupied by particular gene or one of its alleles is:
A. Location B. Centromere
C. Position D. Locus

166. Which one is the vestigial organ of the human?
A. Eye B. Coccyx
C. Skin D. Stomach

167. Which antibody can pass from mother to foetus via the placenta?
A. IgG B. IgD
C. IgA D. IgM

168. Which of the following helps in the swimming of spermatozoa, maintenance of water current in the canal system of sponges and in locomotion of Protozoans like Euglena?
A. Flagellar movement
B. Visceral muscles
C. Skeletal muscles
D. Striated muscles

169. Frequency is denoted as ______.
A. Nanometer B. Hertz
C. Sone D. Decibel

170. Who is the founder or father of modern Palaeontology?
A. Cuvier
B. Watson
C. John Playfair
D. Leonardo da Vinci

171. Archaeopteryx was the connecting link between:
A. Fish and Amphibia
B. Reptile and Mammal
C. Amphibia and Reptile
D. Reptile and Bird

172. Which of the following is not a X linked disorder?
A. Fragile X syndrome
B. Colour blindness
C. Hemophilia
D. Thalassemia

173. Which pollutant is released from the refrigerator industry?

A. CO_2 B. Fe
C. NO_2 D. CFC

174. Zygotes do not undergo reduction division immediately. They produce a multicellular body called a:

A. Antheridium B. Archegonium
C. Gametophyte D. Sporophyte

175. Number of rectrices present in a pigeon is:

A. 12 B. 24 pair
C. 12 pair D. 24

176. The Nutrient enrichment of water causes the natural aging of the lake. This is called:

A. Accelerated Eutrophication
B. Eutrophication
C. Algae Bloom
D. Biomagnification

177. Which represents the modern horse?

A. Merychippus B. Equus
C. Eohippus D. Pliohippus

178. Which of the following is the phenomenon, where the living differentiated cells, that by now have lost the capacity to divide can regain the capacity of division under certain conditions?

A. Differentiation B. Redifferentiated
C. Divisioniated D. Dedifferentiation

179. Myotome muscle is present in ______.

A. Fish B. Bird
C. Reptilia D. Amphibia

180. Mycobiont part of Lichen is ______.

A. Rhizobium B. Bacteria
C. Fungi D. Algae

181. In a class, all the students are given a problem. All the students work on the problem individually in order to solve it. They bring their solutions in written form. They present their views in the class one by one and the other students listen to these attentively to criticize them later on. Which of the following methods of teaching has been described?

A. Seminar
B. This is not a teaching method
C. Brain Storming
D. Drill method

182. A biology-teacher can give which of the following types of home-works?

1. Informational
2. Problematic

A. Only 2
B. Both 1 and 2
C. Neither 1 nor 2
D. Only 1

183. Who is considered as the Father of Microbiology?

A. Robert Brown
B. Robert Hooke
C. Theodor Schwann
D. Antonie van Leeuwenhoek

184. Which of the following methods establishes a student's mastery level?

A. Bloom's mastery learning strategy
B. Gloom's mastery learning strategy
C. Albert's mastery learning strategy
D. Garrett's mastery learning strategy

185. What should be done to remove gender-disparity in science education?

1. The curriculum should strive to make the contribution of women to the field of science and technology 'visible'.
2. Studies should be undertaken to understand how gender bias operates in schools both within and outside the classrooms.

A. Only 1
B. Neither 1 nor 2
C. Both 1 and 2
D. Only 2

186. Which of the following statements is incorrect?

1. Studies have shown that girls in the same class get science education different from boys.

2. Science textbooks and science teachers, like others, are not free from gender bias.
   A. Only 2
   B. Neither 1 nor 2
   C. Only 1
   D. Both 1 and 2

187. Education can be:
   1. Formal
   2. Informal

   A. Neither 1 nor 2 B. Only 1
   C. Only 2 D. Both 1 and 2

188. Which of the following statements is incorrect?
   A. Training is only a specialized part of teaching
   B. Skill is developed through teaching while knowledge is imparted through training
   C. The word training refers to moulding of habits
   D. An idealist society gives importance to teaching while a pragmatic society gives importance to training

189. A biology-teacher wants to give home-work to her students. Which of the following thoughts should she not entertain while giving the homework?
   A. Home-work should be such that it increases the rate of learning further
   B. Home-works given to students should be based on their class work
   C. Home-work should be somewhat challenging to the students also
   D. Home-work should be time-consuming, so that the students don't get any freetime at home

190. Many Indian students perform very well in formal/scholastic tests, but relatively few make it to the grade of truly outstanding researchers or original thinkers. What can be the reason for this?
   A. Science education in India does not develop competence or inventiveness or creativity
   B. Science education in India at its best develops competence, but does not encourage inventiveness and creativity
   C. Science education in India at its best develops inventiveness, but does not encourage inventiveness and competence
   D. Science education in India at its best develops creativity, but does not encourage competence and inventiveness

191. In which year was EDUSAT launched?
   A. 2003 B. 2002
   C. 2005 D. 2004

192. In which stage, science should be introduced as separate disciplines with emphasis on experiments/technology and problem solving?
   A. Primary stage
   B. Secondary stage
   C. Upper primary stage
   D. Higher secondary stage

193. The primary stage extends from Class I to Class:
   A. V B. VII
   C. VI D. IV

194. Which of the following is not a function of a teacher related to class and classroom teaching?
   A. Maintaining records of pupils' attendance
   B. Evaluating the achievement of pupils
   C. Always scold the students to maintain strict discipline
   D. Planning for curricular and co-curricular activities

195. Which of the following should not be a personality trait of a teacher?
   A. A teacher should not take risk of experimenting with his teaching strategy
   B. A teacher has to be very active in and outside the class in the school which requires sound physical health
   C. A teacher should be amiable and friendly in his behaviour
   D. A teacher should not be hasty in his habits

196. Computer Literacy and Studies in Schools (CLASS) project was introduced in the:
A. early 60s B. early 80s
C. early 90s D. early 70s

197. Using non-formal channels in our education system and specially in science will increase:
A. Creative learning
B. Concentration among students
C. Indiscipline
D. Unattentiveness among students

198. Kilpatric is the investigator of which teaching-strategy?
A. Heuristic method
B. Project method
C. Discovery method
D. Role playing method

199. Who is known as the exponent of the Question-answer method of teaching?
A. Dewey
B. Newton
C. Socrates
D. Galileo

200. In which method is the whole class divided into different homogeneous small sections on the basis of abilities so that teacher can remove their difficulties by giving them individual guidance?
1. Demonstration method
2. Tutorial method
A. Both 1 and 2
B. Neither 1 nor 2
C. Only 1
D. Only 2

ANSWERS

1	2	3	4	5	6	7	8	9	10
C	A	D	A	D	B	A	D	C	D
11	**12**	**13**	**14**	**15**	**16**	**17**	**18**	**19**	**20**
B	C	D	D	A	B	A	C	D	D
21	**22**	**23**	**24**	**25**	**26**	**27**	**28**	**29**	**30**
C	C	D	B	B	B	A	A	B	A
31	**32**	**33**	**34**	**35**	**36**	**37**	**38**	**39**	**40**
A	C	C	A	A	D	D	C	C	A
41	**42**	**43**	**44**	**45**	**46**	**47**	**48**	**49**	**50**
D	A	D	C	A	A	A	B	C	A
51	**52**	**53**	**54**	**55**	**56**	**57**	**58**	**59**	**60**
B	C	C	D	A	C	A	D	B	B
61	**62**	**63**	**64**	**65**	**66**	**67**	**68**	**69**	**70**
C	D	B	B	C	D	A	C	D	D
71	**72**	**73**	**74**	**75**	**76**	**77**	**78**	**79**	**80**
D	B	B	B	C	A	C	C	B	D
81	**82**	**83**	**84**	**85**	**86**	**87**	**88**	**89**	**90**
A	C	D	A	D	B	C	C	B	B
91	**92**	**93**	**94**	**95**	**96**	**97**	**98**	**99**	**100**
C	B	A	C	A	B	A	D	A	D

101	**102**	**103**	**104**	**105**	**106**	**107**	**108**	**109**	**110**
A	D	A	B	A	A	A	D	D	B
111	**112**	**113**	**114**	**115**	**116**	**117**	**118**	**119**	**120**
C	C	B	B	D	A	B	B	C	A
121	**122**	**123**	**124**	**125**	**126**	**127**	**128**	**129**	**130**
C	A	D	A	C	B	B	C	D	D
131	**132**	**133**	**134**	**135**	**136**	**137**	**138**	**139**	**140**
A	B	B	A	B	B	B	A	D	A
141	**142**	**143**	**144**	**145**	**146**	**147**	**148**	**149**	**150**
A	C	A	A	C	B	B	B	A	C
151	**152**	**153**	**154**	**155**	**156**	**157**	**158**	**159**	**160**
D	A	A	A	C	D	B	D	B	B
161	**162**	**163**	**164**	**165**	**166**	**167**	**168**	**169**	**170**
A	B	B	A	D	B	A	A	B	A
171	**172**	**173**	**174**	**175**	**176**	**177**	**178**	**179**	**180**
D	D	D	D	A	B	B	D	A	C
181	**182**	**183**	**184**	**185**	**186**	**187**	**188**	**189**	**190**
A	B	D	A	C	B	D	B	D	B
191	**192**	**193**	**194**	**195**	**196**	**197**	**198**	**199**	**200**
D	D	A	C	A	B	A	B	C	D

Previous Paper (Solved)

Delhi Subordinate Services Selection Board

DSSSB–PGT (Biology) Recruitment Exam, 2018*

Subject Knowledge – Biology & Teaching Methodology

1. Which of the following is a condition where myosin heads are unable to detach from action due to complete lack of ATP?
A. Rigor mortis
B. Muscle fatigue
C. Muscle tone
D. Wave summation

2. What is a herbarium?
A. A centre for the preservation of dried specimen of plants
B. A collection of dried herbs
C. A garden with a collection of medicinal herbs
D. A garden with varied collection of herbs

3. What is a genetic clone?
A. A heterosexual plant produced by sexual means
B. A homozygous plant produced by sexual means
C. A hybrid produced by sexual means
D. A genetic composition

4. Which of the following would not result in increase in RBC production?
A. Polycythemia
B. Hemorrhage
C. Donating blood to blood bank
D. High altitude

5. What is "meatus" in skeletal system?
A. A shallow depression
B. A tube-like opening
C. A sharp, slender projection
D. A smooth, flat articular surface

6. Which of the following properties can be used for predicting function of a protein?
A. Overall charge of a molecule
B. Molecular weight
C. Spatial conformation
D. Number of amino acids

7. Which of the following is the most common degenerative joint disease in the elderly, often caused by wear and tear?
A. Rheumatism
B. Osteoarthritis
C. Rheumatoid arthritis
D. Gouty arthritis

8. What is the source of glucose for glycolysis in non-photosynthetic parts of plants?
A. Sucrose
B. Fructose
C. Glycogen
D. Photosynthesis end product is glucose

9. Which of the following is a secretion of Brunner's glands?
A. Mucus with HCl
B. Secretin
C. Chyme with pH 7
D. Urogastrone

10. Which of the following is not a cause of infertility in a couple?
A. Sexual dysfunction
B. Mental or psychological factors
C. Environmental pollutants
D. Infrared radiation

11. DNase is a type of:
A. Hydrolase B. Lyase
C. Ligase D. Isomerase

* Online exam held on 06/07/2018

12. Which of the following is NOT required for blood clotting?
A. Thrombin
B. Prostacyclin
C. Calcium
D. Vitamin K

13. During which of the following process contraceptives are not able to block conception?
A. Fertilisation
B. Implantation
C. Ovulation
D. Transport of egg by oviduct

14. What happens during the physiological condition called "heartburn"?
A. Inflammation of heart wall
B. Damage to the serous layer of heart wall
C. Irritation in the oesophagus mucosa due to HCl
D. Irritation in heart wall due to highly acidic blood

15. Which condition results in the "birth of fraternal twins"?
A. When two sperms fertilise two ovums simultaneously
B. When two sperms fertilise one ovum
C. When one sperm fertilises two ovums
D. When one sperm fertilises the ovum and zygote divides into two separate cells developing independently

16. When there is a decrease in the oxygen concentration in blood, the rate of breathing:
A. Increases or decreases depending on the density of blood
B. Increases
C. Decreases
D. Does not change

17. Which of the following contraceptives also protects against STDs?
A. Condom
B. Spermicide
C. Progesterone pills
D. Tubal ligation

18. Which of the following does not determine Glomerular Filtration Rate (GFR)?
A. Osmotic force by plasma urea in glomerular capillaries
B. Osmotic force by plasma proteins in glomerular capillaries
C. Hydrostatic pressure in the Bowman's space
D. Hydrostatic pressure in glomerular capillaries

19. Which of the following mammals undergo menopause?
A. Elephant
B. Chimpanzee
C. Short finned pilot whale
D. Monkey

20. What is "haemoglobin bound to carbon dioxide" termed as?
A. Carbaminohaemoglobin
B. Deoxyhaemoglobin
C. Carboxyhaemoglobin
D. Carboxylatedhaemoglobin

21. If the plasma glucose concentration is 90 mg/100 ml and GFR is 120 ml/min, how much glucose will be filtered and excreted out, respectively, per minute?
A. 108 mg/min, almost zero mg
B. 98 mg/min, 49 mg/min
C. 120 mg/min, almost zero mg
D. 90 mg/min, 25 mg/min

22. What are Nissl bodies?
A. Site of protein synthesis in neurons
B. Macrophages of CNS
C. Cells surrounding CSF-filled ventricles in brain
D. Most abundant cell types in CNS

23. Our body can acclimatise to high altitude by virtue of which of the following changes?
A. Increasing BPG concentration
B. Decreasing BPG concentration
C. Increasing the blood volume
D. Decreasing hematocrit

24. Which of the following takes place under the influence of estradiol during embryonic development?

A. Development of external genitalia
B. Development of seminal vesicle
C. Development of wolffian duct
D. Masculinisation of brain

25. The large intestine is characterised by which of the following features?
A. Presence of taeniae coli
B. Numerous villi
C. Less number of goblet cells
D. Well-developed plicae circulares

26. Which of the following is not a criteria of five kingdom classification as proposed by Whittaker?
A. Cell structure
B. Mode of locomotion
C. Body organisation
D. Mode of nutrition

27. In humans, the presence of more than one pair of mammary glands is called:
A. Gynecomastia
B. Polythelia
C. Polycythemia
D. Thelarche

28. The mouth parts in insects are the examples of:
A. Analogous organs
B. Homologous organs
C. Atavism
D. Vestigial organs

29. "Taxonomic keys" do not facilitate which one of the following activities?
A. Animal identification
B. Fossil identification
C. Plant identification
D. Evaluation phylogenetic history

30. Which of the following features make Ctenophores different from Cnidarians?
A. Absence of polymorphism
B. Presence of nematocyst
C. Presence of mesoglea
D. Absence of larval forms

31. What is the term given to signal the build-up due to simultaneous release of neurotransmitter by several presynaptic end bulbs nervous tissue?
A. Spatial summation
B. Temporal summation
C. Graded hyperpolarising potential
D. Graded depolarising potential

32. In skeletal muscle, the time period when a second action potential can be initiated with stronger stimulus is called:
A. Relative refractory period
B. Incomplete refractory period
C. Hyperpolarising phase
D. Hyperdepolarising phase

33. Which of the following contributes to high biodiversity in tropics?
A. Higher rate of inbreeding among plants
B. More stable climate
C. Less competition for available resources
D. Less pressure from pest, parasites and diseases

34. Which of the following chemical reactions is not responsible for the generation of smog?
A. Chlorofluorocarbons
B. Sunlight
C. Carbon monoxide
D. Nitrogen oxides

35. The sustained but wavering contraction with partial relaxation between stimuli in a skeletal muscle is called:
A. Muscle fatigue
B. Wave summation
C. Muscle tone
D. Unfused tetanus

36. Which of the following plant fatty acids is used to synthesise "Omega 6" fats in animals?
A. Palmitoleic acid
B. Oleic acid
C. Alpha-linolenic acid
D. Linoleic acid

37. What is the full form of IUCN?
A. Indian Union for Conservation of Nature
B. International Unit for Conservation of Nature

C. International Union for Conservation of Natural Resources

D. International Union for Conservation of Nature and Natural Resources

38. Which of the following features is found in males with extra Y chromosome?

A. Oligospermia

B. Normal testosterone levels

C. Elevated testosterone levels

D. Delayed puberty

39. What is Galactopoiesis?

A. Release of milk independent of infant suckling

B. Release of colostrum

C. Establishment of mature milk supply

D. Gathering of substrates for milk production in mammary glands

40. Which of the following physiological changes is not associated with pregnancy in human females?

A. Kidney enlargement

B. Increase in cardiac output

C. Increase in respiratory rate

D. Decrease in blood volume

41. Which of the following pollutants has direct effect on reproductive health?

A. Lead

B. Chlorofluorocarbons

C. Nitrogen oxide

D. Chlorine

42. The rate of enzyme catalyzed reaction is not dependent on which of the following?

A. Temperature

B. Substrate concentration

C. Enzyme concentration

D. Product concentration

43. Which of the following is not a diagnostic criterion for Polycystic ovary syndrome (PCOS)?

A. Oligomenorrhea

B. Hyperandrogenemia

C. Presence of polycystic ovary

D. Chronic anovulation

44. Which of the following is not present in the cell wall of algae?

A. Mannitol B. Algin

C. Cellulose D. Pectin

45. Which of the following is true for Lotka-Volterra equation?

A. It is the Logistic equation expressing intraspecific competition

B. It is altogether different from Logistic equation

C. It is same as Logistic equation

D. It is the Logistic equation expressing interspecific competition

46. Which of the following genus does not show metamerism?

A. Penaeus B. Labeo

C. Asterias D. Nereis

47. Aminotransferases and chymotrypsin enzymes are examples of which type of reaction?

A. Random bi-substrate reaction

B. Oxidation reduction reaction

C. Ping-pong reaction

D. Sequential bi-substrate reaction

48. Which of the following features are characteristics of Kingdom Monera?

A. Unicellular, with cell wall

B. Prokaryote, unicellular, without a cell wall

C. Prokaryote, unicellular, with a cell wall

D. Prokaryotes, unicellular, with or without a cell wall

49. Which of the following is/are not considered as a part of "five kingdom classification" defined by Whittaker?

A. Cyanobacteria

B. Mycoplasma

C. Lichens

D. Amphibious plants

50. "Zona pellucida" is dissolved just before which one of the following events?

A. Implantation

B. Beginning of cleavage

C. Morula formation

D. Fertilisation

51. Chaparral biome is located in which of the following climates?
A. Tundra B. Mediterranean
C. Temperate D. Tropical

52. What is "pneumothorax"?
A. Viral infection in lungs
B. Collapsed lungs
C. Thoracic inflammation
D. Bacterial infection of lungs

53. What happens to the enzyme activity with a gradual rise in temperature?
A. Increases
B. First decreases then increases
C. First increases then decreases
D. Decreases

54. Acetyl CoA is formed during catabolism of all EXCEPT which one of the following?
A. Nucleic acid B. Proteins
C. Carbohydrates D. Fats

55. The group of species that make their living by exploiting the same class of resources in a similar way is called:
A. Resprout species
B. Shredders
C. Sibling species
D. Guild

56. Which of the following is an asexual but not vegetative mode of reproduction in fungi?
A. Budding B. Spores
C. Fission D. Fragmentation

57. Who coined the term Biodiversity hotspot?
A. Ronald Good
B. Norman Myers
C. Ernest Meyer
D. W.G. Rosen

58. Which of the following reactions is catalysed by enzymes Oxygenases?
A. Transfer of hydrogen from one substrate to another
B. Removal of oxygen from substrate
C. Transport of electrons from substrate to oxygen
D Hydroxylation of drugs and steroids

59. Which of the following plants have haplo-diplontic life cycle?
A. Fucus B. Pinus
C. Laminaria D. Volvox

60. Bilateral true coelomates, with worm-like body divided into proboscis, collar and trunk are characteristic features of which of the following phylums?
A. Annelida
B. Hemichordata
C. Aschelhelminthes
D. Chordata

61. What will be the type of mutation if "U" is replaced with "G" at 9th position in the sequence AUGAAGUUUGGC?
A. Inversion
B. Transversion mutation
C. Frameshift mutation
D. Transition mutation

62. Which of the following is a process where either of the parental chromosome is modified by methylation to affect in phenotypic expression?
A. Autosomal inheritance
B. Sex linked inheritance
C. Genomic imprinting
D. Uniparental disomy

63. An individual can have how many different alleles for a gene?
A. Only one
B. More than 4
C. Many
D. Only 2

64. The DNA damage checkpoint works at which of the following stages of a cell cycle?
A. S and G2
B. G1 and S
C. G1, S and G2
D. Only S

65. What is the term given to a chromosomal aberration where a segment of chromosome turned around 180° within a chromosome inducting centromere?
A. Paracentric inversion

B. Diacentric inversion
C. Pericentric inversion
D. Acentric inversion

66. What is the most apparent change traced during evolutionary history of *Homo sapiens*?
A. Walking upright
B. Shortening of jaws
C. Loss of body hair
D. Remarkable increase in the brain size

67. "Agar" is obtained from which of the following?
A. Saraggasum B. Laminaria
C. Gelidium D. Fucus

68. Which of the following is a multiple fruit?
A. Pineapple B. Tomato
C. Apple D. Mango

69. The rate of transpiration will be maximum in which of the following conditions?
A. Both soil and atmosphere are dry
B. Soil is wet and atmosphere is humid
C. Soil is dry and atmosphere is humid
D. Soil is wet and atmosphere is dry

70. Which of the following is the first carboxylation product of C_3 plants?
A. Oxaloacetic acid
B. Phosphoglyceraldehyde
C. 3-phosphoglyceric acid
D. Maleic acid

71. Which of the following is a sex influenced trait?
A. Hemophilia
B. Achondroplasia
C. Baldness
D. Albinism

72. Which of the following enzymes are activated in cell death by apoptosis?
A. Protein kinases
B. Caspases
C. Phosphatases
D. Phosphodiesterases

73. In a Hardy Weinberg population, what will be frequency of individual with genotype "AA" frequency of allele "a" is 0.3?
A. 0.20 B. 0.49
C. 0.81 D. 0.32

74. Which of the following is primarily an embryonic connective tissue?
A. Adipose
B. Reticular
C. Areolar
D. Mesenchyme

75. In which part of a leguminous plant, leghemoglobin is present?
A. Stem B. Leaves
C. Root hairs D. Root nodules

76. Which of the following statement is true for temperature dependent sex determination in all species of reptiles?
A. There is narrow temperature range resulting in both male and female
B. Both low and high yield males
C. High temperature yield females
D. High temperature results in males

77. Which of the following epithelial tissue lines the Bowmen's capsule of kidney?
A. Simple squamous
B. Stratified columnar
C. Ciliated simple columnar
D. Simple cuboidal

78. Which of the following is not an X-linked disorder?
A. G6PD deficiency
B. Red-green colour blindness
C. Hemophilia
D. Achondroplasia

79. Who gave natural classification system of plants based on plant anatomy, ultrastructure & embryology?
A. Carl von Linnaeus
B. Carl Wilhelm Scheele
C. Whittakar
D. G. Bentham and J.D. Hooker

80. Which of the following is not a reason for change in enzyme activity of biological enzymes with moderate (pH 5-9) change in the pH value?

A. Change in substrate binding
B. Change in charged state of weakly acidic/ basic groups
C. Loss of secondary structure
D. Change in conformation of catalytic site

81. Which of the following statement is incorrect related to nervous system of earthworm?
A. Ganglia are located at the interface of two body segments
B. Nerve cord bifurcates at the anterior region
C. Nerve cord is paired and present ventrally
D. Anterior nerve ring includes cerebral ganglion

82. How many types of sperms (2n = 46) can be produced by a human male?
A. 2^{22} B. 2^{46}
C. 2^{23} D. 2^{8}

83. What is the reason of development of root pressure in plants?
A. Passive absorption
B. Active absorption
C. Both active and passive absorption
D. Increased rate of transpiration

84. Which of the following events inhibits Cdkl activity?
A. Association with cyclin
B. Phosphorylation at Tyr14 and Tyr 15
C. Dephosphorylation at Tyr14 and Tyr15
D. Phosphorylation at Thr-161

85. Coir is extracted from which part of the coconut plant?
A. Phloem B. Epicarp
C. Roots D. Mesocarp

86. Excess of which of the following hormones results in leave abscission in plants?
A. Auxin
B. Abscissic acid
C. Cytokinin
D. Gibberelic acid

87. Which of the following cell junction are present at intercalated discs?
A. Desmosomes, Adhering and Gap junctions
B. Desmosomes
C. Adhering and Gap junctions
D. Tight and Gap junctions

88. What is the phenotypic ratio for the progeny of dihybrid cross with recessive epistasis?
A. 9 : 3 : 3 : 1
B. 9 : 3 : 4
C. 9 : 6 : 1
D. 12 : 3 : 1

89. Decrease in which of the following factors is the result of Deforestation?
A. Soil erosion B. Land slide
C. Soil fertility D. Rainfall

90. Which of the following generically modified vectors was used for transfer of adenosine deaminase gene to SCID patients initially?
A. Herpes virus
B. Retrovirus
C. Adenovirus
D. Aeno-associated virus

91. What is the function of phenol in genomic DNA isolation technique?
A. to extract hydrophobic proteins
B. to dissolve RNA
C. to make a visible gradient
D. to dissolve DNA

92. Which of the following was first Bt crop in India?
A. Corn B. Potato
C. Tomato D. Cotton

93. "Apospory" can be observed in which of the following plants?
A. Algae B. Angiosperms
C. Pteridophytes D. Gymnosperms

94. Which of the following plants show Kranz anatomy?
A. C_3 plants
B. C_4 plants
C. Saprophytic plants
D. Algae

95. Which of the following scientist proved that oxygen is released in photosynthesis during light reaction?
A. Black Man

B. Robert Emerson
C. Daniel I. Arnon
D. Robert Hill

96. How many genetically different gametes are possible by an individual of genotype CcWwRr?
A. 8 B. 64
C. 16 D. 36

97. What is the probability that a plant with genotype PpWw will be produced by parental plants of genotypes PpWw and Ppww?
A. 1/3 B. 1/2
C. 1/4 D. 3/4

98. What is the end product of glycolysis in RBC?
A. Lactic acid
B. 3-phosphoglycerate
C. Acetyl CoA
D. Pyruvic acid

99. Which experimental model were used by Boveri and Sutton to give chromosome theory of inheritance?
A. Grasshopper and sea urchin respectively
B. Grasshopper
C. Sea urchin and grasshopper respectively
D. Sea urchin

100. At which of the following cell cycle stage cohesion-complex is established in the nucleus?
A. S phase
B. G1 phase
C. M and G1 phase
D. M phase

101. Which of the following honey bee products is known to increase the performance of athletes?
A. Bee venom
B. Bee pollen
C. Honey
D. Royal jelly

102. Which of the following antibodies is primarily synthesized during allergy?
A. IgD B. IgE
C. IgG D. IgM

103. What is a cross between a recessive parent and offspring called?
A. Back cross
B. Reciprocal cross
C. Monohybrid cross
D. Test cross

104. In which of the following species crossing over is observed in mitosis also?
A. Fucus B. Agaricus
C. Drosophila D. Zebra fish

105. In a Hardy Weinberg population, frequency of a gene is NOT influenced by which of the following factors?
A. Genetic recombination
B. Mutation
C. Natural selection
D. Natural death

106. Which of the following enzymes DOES NOT have a proof reading ability during DNA replication?
A. DNA polymerase II
B. Polymerase alpha
C. Polymerase epsilon
D. DNA polymerase I

107. Who wrote "The Families of Flowering Plants"?
A. Braun
B. Black Man
C. Bentham
D. John Hutchinson

108. Which of the following is surrounded by Accessory cells?
A. Guard cells B. Stomata
C. Xylem D. Phloem

109. What will be the potential phenotypes in the offspring of parents of blood group A and A?
A. $\frac{1}{4}$ A, $\frac{1}{2}$ B and $\frac{1}{4}$ O
B. $\frac{3}{4}$ B and $\frac{1}{4}$ O

C. $\frac{3}{4}$ A and $\frac{1}{4}$ O

D. $\frac{1}{2}$ A and $\frac{1}{2}$ O

110. During cytokinesis in plants, cell plate is formed by which of the following organelle?
A. RER
B. Golgi complex
C. Vacuoles
D. SER

111. Which of the following plasmid vector is used mostly in genetic engineering?
A. ColE1 B. pBR322
C. plasmid D. pSC101

112. Most of the transgenic studies have been performed on which of the following animal models?
A. Rodents B. Mice
C. Pig D. Sheep

113. Which of the following techniques can be used to visualize dosage compensation in Drosophila?
A. Autoradiography
B. Chromosome banding
C. Gel electrophoresis
D. 3H labelled DNA

114. Which of the following growth patterns indicates resource limitation?
A. Exponential
B. Logarithmic
C. Logistic
D. Geometric

115. Where does the Hardy Weinberg Equilibrium exist in nature?
A. Nowhere
B. Tropical zone
C. Temperate zone
D. Polar regions

116. What is the transfer of pollen grains from the anther to the stigma of another flower of the same plant called?
A. Geitonogamy
B. Autogamy
C. Xenogamy
D. Cleistogamy

117. What is the sedimentation coefficient of rRNA present in 30 S ribosomal subunit?
A. 18 S B. 5 S
C. 16 S D. 5.8 S

118. Which of the following is an exception to the Central Dogma of molecular biology?
A. Retrovirus
B. Bacteria
C. Virus
D. Archaebacteria

119. How many linkage groups are present in *Drosophila melanogaster*?
A. 4 B. 6
C. 3 D. 8

120. A protein containing 400 amino acids will required a gene for at least how many base pair long for its synthesis?
A. 1500 B. 1200
C. 1300 D. 1000

121. Which of the following results in appearance of brown spots surrounded by chlorotic veins in plants?
A. Manganese excess
B. Molybdenum excess
C. Deficiency of Zinc
D. Deficiency of Manganese

122. "Widal test" is a serological test based on which of the following techniques?
A. Cell culture
B. PCR
C. Biochemical
D. Antigen-antibody interaction

123. Discrete, un-encapsulated aggregate of lymphatic nodules are present in mucosal layer of which of the following organs?
A. Appendix B. Kidney
C. Stomach D. Ovary

124. Which of the following drugs is a modification of fungal product?
A. Crack
B. Charas

C. Lysergic acid diethyl amide (LSD)
D. Smack

125. Which of the following is not a radioactive isotope extensively used in molecular techniques'?
A. 15_N B. 14_C
C. 3_H D. 32_P

126. Which of the following plants has been extensively used for production of edible vaccine?
A. Potato B. Banana
C. Lettuce D. Tomato

127. At least how many epitopes an antigen must have in a Sandwich ELISA?
A. Two
B. Not required
C. One
D. More than five

128. In which of the following the enzyme reverse transcriptase is used?
A. Northern blotting
B. PCR
C. For identifying a gene from cDNA library
D. For creating cDNA library

129. Which of the following experimental model is best suited to study natural selection though mutation?
A. Mice B. Microbes
C. Algae D. Humans

130. What is the term given to the effect of high atmospheric CO_2 which results in increased rate of photosynthesis?
A. Green-house effect
B. CO_2 compensation effect
C. Climate change
D. CO_2 fertilization effect

131. Which of the following dairy cattle cross-breed is widely used in hilly regions of India?
A. Sahiwal
B. Holstein-Friesian (HF)
C. Red Dane
D. Jersey

132. What is the optimum temperature for *Taq polymerase* activity?
A. 55 °C B. 72 °C
C. 45 °C D. 92 °C

133. Which of the following is NOT an example of Adaptive radiation?
A. Human evolution
B. Darwin's finches
C. Cichlid fish in the river of East African Rift
D. Australian marsupials

134. Which day is designated as international day of Biological Diversity?
A. May 22 B. May 01
C. March 21 D. June 05

135. Which of the following micronutrient in plants showing symptoms of necrosis, chlorosis and inhabitation of cell division?
A. K B. Mo
C. S D. N

136. What is the term given to a small molecule which can bind to a preformed antibody but fails to stimulate B cells?
A. Hapten B. Antigen
C. Bacterial toxin D. Capsid

137. Skin colour in humans is an example of which of the following inheritance?
A. Polygenic
B. co-dominance
C. Epistasis
D. Incomplete dominance

138. Which of the following transgenic animal is used for producing a variant of human tissue plasminogen activator?
A. Goat B. Pig
C. Sheep D. Rodent

139. Which of the following mineral is required by plants in greatest amount?
A. Magnesium
B. Molybdenum
C. Nitrogen
D. Iron

140. Which of the following radiation is not used in cancer treatment?
A. UV radiation
B. X-ray
C. Gamma radiation
D. Charged particles

141. HIV cannot spread through which of the following ways from an infected mother to her child?
A. Delivery
B. Sharing meal
C. Pregnancy
D. Breast feeding

142. "Cyclosporin A" is an immunosuppressive agent, used in organ transplant patients produced by which of the following organisms?
A. Fungus
B. Transgenic animals
C. Bacteria
D. Algae

143. Which of the following is an inducer of *lac* operon?
A. Allolactose B. Glucose
C. Galactose D. Lactose

144. Which of the following is national aquatic animal of India?
A. Turtle
B. River Dolphin
C. Tortoise
D. A type of Fish

145. What would be the Respiratory Quotient if pure proteins are used as respiratory substrates?
A. 0.7 B. 0.9
C. 1 D. 0.6

146. Avian flu virus CANNOT spread through which of the following medium?
A. Air
B. Saliva
C. Nasal secretion
D. Feces

147. Which of the following pair is incorrect modification of plant parts?
A. Thorne-Axillary buds
B. Flower-shoot modification
C. Prop-root modification
D. *Colocasia*-modified root

148. The cellular respiratory pathway is categorized as which type of following metabolic pathways?
A. Catabolic
B. Anabolic
C. Amphibolic
D. Black Man pathway

149. What is the function of stilt roots?
A. Storage of food
B. Storage of food and water
C. Provide support to plant
D. Get oxygen for plant

150. Along with *Lactobacillus* which of the following micro-organism is used to make yogurt?
A. *S. cerevisiae*
B. *S. thermophilus*
C. *S. acidophilus*
D. *P. sharmanii*

151. "Cyathium inflorescence" is characteristic of which of the following genus?
A. *Euphorbia* B. *Brassica*
C. *Citrus* D. *Hibiscus*

152. "The Neel Kranti mission" is related to which of the following?
A. Water purification
B. Fish and fisheries
C. Ozone replenishment
D. Plants and plant products

153. Which of the following antibiotics inhibit cell wall synthesis?
A. Penicillins
B. Aminoglycosides
C. Nitrofurans
D. Chloramphenicols

154. Which of the following is a pentameric antibody?

A. IgE B. IgM
C. IgG D. IgA

155. Which of the following molecular technique is used extensively for preparing a karyotype?
A. FISH B. GISH
C. PCR D. ELISA

156. In which of the following parts of xylem lignin is absent from the cell wall?
A. Xylem fibers
B. Tracheids
C. Vessels
D. Xylem parenchyma

157. Who is the Father of Ecology in India?
A. Ramdeo Misra
B. G.N. Ramachandran
C. Alexander V. Humboldt
D. Panchanan Maheshwari

158. Hyper-accumulator plant species can be used for which of the following process?
A. Bio-fertilizers
B. Phytoremediation
C. Biofortification
D. Bioremediation

159. What is the term given to the arrangement of leaves in a plant stem?
A. Inflorescence
B. Phylloclade
C. Origami
D. Phyllotaxy

160. In animal breeding, what is the outcome of continuous and closed inbreeding of animals?
A. Increased heterozygosity
B. Reduced fertility
C. Increased productivity
D. Increased fertility

161. What is the process of inducing a woman to release more than one egg in a month called?
A. *Invivo* fertilization
B. Ovarian stimulation
C. Ovulation induction
D. Superovulation

162. What is GEAC?
A. Gene Expressing Authorizing Company
B. Genomic Expression Approval Committee
C. Gene Engineering Approval Committee
D. Genetic Engineering Approval Committee

163. How many layers are present in a Tropical Rainforest?
A. More than 5 B. 4
C. 5 D. 3

164. "An orchid growing on a mango branch" is an example of which type of population interaction?
A. Parasitism
B. Mutualism
C. Amensalism
D. Commensalism

165. Which of the following traits of Pea plant is NOT considered by Mendel?
A. Seed shape
B. Seed colour
C. Pod size
D. Flower colour

166. In humans, which of the following is the site of maximum fertilization?
A. Uterus B. Ovary
C. Cervix D. Oviduct

167. What is pollination by bees or bumblebees is termed as?
A. Myrmecophily
B. Entomophily
C. Melittophily
D. Anemophily

168. "Darwinian fitness" is related to which of the following aspects?
A. Psychological fitness
B. Stable population
C. Reproductive fitness
D. Physical fitness

169. "Desert Lizard keep their body temperature fairly constant" this is an example of which type of following adaptations?
A. Structural
B. Behavioural
C. Physiological
D. Reproductive

170. Which of the following is NOT used as fusogen in somatic cell hybridization?
A. $NaNO_3$
B. PEG
C. Agar
D. High pH/Ca^2

171. At which stage of menstrual cycle the concentration of Luteinizing hormone (LH) is maximum?
A. Just before ovulation
B. Throughout the ovulatory phase
C. Just after ovulation
D. At ovulation

172. Which of the following molecule pose hindrance in utilizing Single Cell Protein (SCP) as major food in humans?
A. Fat
B. Lipids
C. Protein
D. Nucleic acid

173. Which of the following is not force of interaction in antigen-antibody complex formation?
A. Covalent bond
B. Hydrophobic
C. Hydrogen bond
D. Van-der Walls

174. The saprophytes are placed at which tropic level in an ecological pyramid of biomass?
A. Primary consumer
B. Primary producer
C. Secondary consumer
D. Nowhere

175. Which of the following is a plant cytokinin receptor?
A. CRK 1
B. ABP 1
C. CRHR 1
D. CRE 1

176. What is the term given to the expansion of a species niche due to lack of a competitor species?
A. Niche overlap
B. Competitive exclusion
C. Competitive release
D. Realized niche

177. The genetically modified "Golden rice" is rich in which of the following vitamins?
A. Vitamin D
B. Vitamin B
C. Vitamin B4
D. Vitamin A

178. Which of the following elements are responsible for algal bloom?
A. Calcium
B. Carbon
C. Sulfates
D. Nitrates and phosphates

179. Which of the following organisms were first to evolve on the earth?
A. Chemoheterotrophs
B. Chemoautotrophs
C. Eukatyotes
D. Autotrophs

180. "Red Data Book" gives information related to which one of the following?
A. All existing species
B. Endangered species
C. Threatened species
D. Vulnerable species

181. The two much desirable benefits of integrating Music into school subjects are:
A. Language development and concept clarity
B. Developing language and reasoning, and improving memory and retention
C. Better understanding of concepts and improved learning pace
D. Improved peer relation and recognition for the school

182. Select the correct option to complete the following sentence.

Scope for non-verbal communication is more in:
A. Life Sciences
B. Algebra
C. English Literature
D. Environmental Science

183. Select the correct option to complete the following sentence.

One of the objectives of summative evaluation is:

A. giving feedback to the student
B. testing the student's learning in the middle of a session
C. giving response to the student
D. testing the student's achievement at the end of a session

184. Select the correct option to complete the following sentence.

BCC in e-mails differs from CC in that:

A. BCC hides the sender's e-mail address
B. BCC hides all the recipient e-mail addresses
C. BCC is sent over a secured connection
D. BCC supports attachments

185. Select the correct option to complete the following sentence.

Teacher can support Sneha, a dyslexic child, by:

A. allotting a buddy
B. giving printed notes
C. giving more writing practice
D. giving remediation

186. The teacher asks the children to tweeze cotton and paste it on the picture of a duck. Development of which of the following domains is taking place through this activity?

A. Social
B. Creative
C. Emotional
D. Fine motor

187. Select the correct option to complete the following sentence.

Ozone depletion is an adverse effect of:

A. natural calamities
B. urbanisation
C. deforestation
D. unseasonal rains

188. Select the correct option to complete the following sentence.

Bloom's cognitive domain include:

A. Knowledge, Comprehension, Application, Analysis and Evaluation
B. Interest, Values, Knowledge and Analysis
C. Receiving, Responding, Attitude, Evaluation and Comprehension
D. Knowledge, Application, Values and Interest

189. One of the critical aspects of Reflection is:

A. remembering events and incidents
B. making notes immediately
C. writing clearly
D. being critical about self and situations

190. Select the correct option to complete the following sentence.

FLAW — Functional Literacy for Adult Women — was initiated by ICDS in the year:

A. 1988-89 B. 1975-76
C. 1970-71 D. 1990-91

191. Select the correct option to complete the following sentence.

The impact of effective inclusive practices can be evidenced in:

A. good teachers
B. excellent infrastructural provisions
C. academic and social progress of students of the marginalised group
D. lesson plans

192. Select the correct option to complete the following sentence.

The first Indian university for women (SNDT) was founded on:

A. 2 July 1916
B. 2 July 1926
C. 2 July 1920
D. 2 July 1912

193. Select the correct option to complete the following sentence.

In the process of mastering independent reading skills, an individual goes through the different stages in the following sequence:

A. Recognition stage – Structuring stage – Interpretation stage

B. Model reading – Structuring stage – Understanding stage
C. Imitation stage – Recognition stage – Demonstration stage
D. Recognition stage – Interpretation stage – Structuring stage

194. Select the correct option to complete the following sentence.

An inter-connection of two or more computers created for exchanging information among themselves is known as:

A. Webpage B. Internet
C. LAN D. WAN

195. Select the correct option to complete the following sentence.

The important attributes that mark a divergent thinker from a convergent thinker are:

A. Fluency and Flexibility
B. Flexibility and Elaboration
C. Originality and Complexity
D. Imagination and Originality

196. Identify the most appropriate reason.

Checklist does not suit assessing all domains because:

A. it does not allow recording progress in development
B. it is not easy to use
C. it is not reliable
D. it is very simple

197. Select the correct option to complete the following sentence.

The most appropriate way to study science is by:

A. Discussing
B. Doing
C. Experimenting
D. Asking How and Why questions

198. Children in a primary class are sitting in groups and pairs. They would like to remain in these groups. We can relate this observation to the Motivation Theory by:

A. Hull B. Murray
C. Tolman D. Maslow

199. Select the correct option to complete the following sentence.

An activity to create a folk song and compose music for it is best suited for children with:

A. musical and naturalistic intelligence
B. naturalistic, linguistic and musical intelligence
C. logical and musical intelligence
D. linguistic and musical intelligence

200. Audio-visual aids are best suited for concepts:

A. that are difficult
B. that are interesting
C. that are better understood when visual representations are supported by animations
D. when there is excessive time

ANSWERS

1	2	3	4	5	6	7	8	9	10
A	A	D	C	B	C	B	A	D	D
11	**12**	**13**	**14**	**15**	**16**	**17**	**18**	**19**	**20**
A	B	B	C	A	B	A	A	D	A
21	**22**	**23**	**24**	**25**	**26**	**27**	**28**	**29**	**30**
A	A	A	D	A	B	B	B	D	A
31	**32**	**33**	**34**	**35**	**36**	**37**	**38**	**39**	**40**
A	A	B	A	D	D	D	B	C	D
41	**42**	**43**	**44**	**45**	**46**	**47**	**48**	**49**	**50**
A	D	A	A	D	C	C	D	C	A

51	52	53	54	55	56	57	58	59	60
B	B	C	A	D	B	B	D	C	B
61	**62**	**63**	**64**	**65**	**66**	**67**	**68**	**69**	**70**
B	C	D	C	C	D	C	A	D	C
71	**72**	**73**	**74**	**75**	**76**	**77**	**78**	**79**	**80**
C	B	B	D	D	A	A	D	D	C
81	**82**	**83**	**84**	**85**	**86**	**87**	**88**	**89**	**90**
A	C	B	B	D	B	A	B	D	B
91	**92**	**93**	**94**	**95**	**96**	**97**	**98**	**99**	**100**
A	D	C	B	D	A	C	A	C	A
101	**102**	**103**	**104**	**105**	**106**	**107**	**108**	**109**	**110**
B	B	D	C	D	B	D	A	C	B
111	**112**	**113**	**114**	**115**	**116**	**117**	**118**	**119**	**120**
B	B	A	C	A	A	C	A	A	B
121	**122**	**123**	**124**	**125**	**126**	**127**	**128**	**129**	**130**
A	D	A	C	A	A	A	D	B	D
131	**132**	**133**	**134**	**135**	**136**	**137**	**138**	**139**	**140**
B	B	A	A	A	A	A	A	C	A
141	**142**	**143**	**144**	**145**	**146**	**147**	**148**	**149**	**150**
B	A	A	B	B	A	D	C	C	B
151	**152**	**153**	**154**	**155**	**156**	**157**	**158**	**159**	**160**
A	B	A	B	A	D	A	B	D	B
161	**162**	**163**	**164**	**165**	**166**	**167**	**168**	**169**	**170**
D	D	B	D	C	D	C	C	B	C
171	**172**	**173**	**174**	**175**	**176**	**177**	**178**	**179**	**180**
A	D	A	D	D	C	D	D	B	B
181	**182**	**183**	**184**	**185**	**186**	**187**	**188**	**189**	**190**
B	A	D	B	B	D	B	A	D	B
191	**192**	**193**	**194**	**195**	**196**	**197**	**198**	**199**	**200**
C	A	A	C	D	A	D	D	B	C

Previous Paper (Solved)

Delhi Subordinate Services Selection Board
DSSSB–PGT (Biology) Recruitment Exam, 2015*

POST SPECIFIC SUBJECT RELATED QUESTIONS

1. Which of the following is the correct descending sequence of taxonomic categories?
A. Class – order – division – family – species – tribe
B. Family – order – genus – species – division – class
C. Division – class – order – family – tribe – genus
D. Family – order – division – genus – species – tribe

2. "Die naturlichen pflanzenfamilien" is written by:
A. Bentham Hooker
B. Engler and Prantle
C. Linnaeus
D. Hutchinson

3. Differential staining of bacteria on Gram staining is due to:
A. Difference in the cell wall layer components of Gram positive and Gram negative bacteria
B. Difference in the cell structure of Gram positive and Gram negative bacteria
C. Difference in the mode of the nutrition of Gram positive and Gram negative bacteria
D. None of the above

4. Ruminate Endosperm is present in which family?
A. Orchidaceae B. Rubiaceae
C. Annonaceae D. Asclepiadaceae

5. Which one is known as filamentous bacteria?
A. Mycoplasmas B. Spirochaetes
C. Actinomycetes D. Vibrios

6. Cork-screw shaped forms of bacteria are:
A. Bacilli B. Stalked bacteria
C. Spirochaetes D. Actinomycetes

7. Outside of living cell, the virus particle is called:
A. Virion B. Capsid
C. Obligate parasite D. None of these

8. "Eleterium" a dangerous drug is obtained from:
A. Ecballium B. Sechium
C. Trichosanthes D. Echinocystis

9. Scientific name of "Indian Telegraph" plant is:
A. Canavalia ensiformis
B. Indigofera tinetoria
C. Desmodium gyrans
D. Butea frondosa

10. AIDS virus contains:
A. DNA only B. RNA only
C. DNA + Protein D. RNA + Protein

11. *Ginkgo biloba* is not now an endangered species because of its:
A. *Exsitu* conservation
B. Offsite conservation
C. *Insitu* conservation
D. Cryopreservation

12. Cryopreservation is useful for:
A. Preservation of semen
B. Living cells
C. Very young foetuses
D. All the above

13. Who is known as the father of Phycology?
A. De Bary B. Fritach
C. Aristotle D. Hodgkin

14. "Ipecac" which is an excellent drug for Amoebic – dysentery is obtained from:
A. Roots of Morinda
B. Wood of Morinda
C. Roots of Celphalis
D. Wood of Celphalis

* Tite-I Exam.

15. On the top of the Ovary a nectar disc "stylopodium" is present in the family:
A. Euphorbiaceae B. Apiaceae
C. Orchidaceae D. Lamiaceae

16. Flavouring agent "Vanilla" belongs to the family:
A. Lamiaceae B. Apiaceae
C. Orchidaceae D. Asclepiadaceae

17. Feathery stigmas are seen in:
A. Orchidaceae B. Palmae
C. Oleaceae D. Gramineae

18. "Stamens are the male organs" of the flower was first stated by:
A. Camerarius B. Kolreuter
C. Grew D. Amici

19. In which type of ovule the cellular tissue remains single layered?
A. Unitegmic ovules
B. Bitegmic ovules
C. Tenuinucellate ovules
D. Crassinucellate ovules

20. Which of the following are the features that differentiates cilia from flagella?
A. Cilia are short compared to flagella
B. Flagella are less in number compared to cilia
C. Cilia are distributed throughout the cell surface
D. All of the above

21. Eukaryotic flagella is driven by:
A. ATP B. Proton
C. Both (A) and (B) D. None of these

22. Bioluminescence is a phenomenon associated with:
A. Chrysophyta B. Phaeophyta
C. Pyrrophyta D. Chlorophyta

23. Which of the following algal divisions is characterized by possession of chlorophylls A and B, starch as the energy storage material, cellulosic cell walls and live in fresh water and marine habitats?
A. Chlorophyta B. Chrysophyta
C. Phaeophyta D. Pyrrophyta

24. Which algal division is divided up into three main groups consisting of the golden-brown algae, the yellow-green algae and the diatoms?
A. Chlorophyta B. Chrysophyta
C. Phaeophyta D. Pyrrophyta

25. Origin and evolution of sex in algae is best seen in:
A. Blue-green algae
B. Green algae
C. Red algae
D. Brown algae

26. Zygotic meiosis is a characteristic feature of:
A. Algae B. Bryophytes
C. Pteridophytes D. Gymnosperms

27. Sargasso sea is named after an algae Sargassum which is a:
A. Green algae B. Brown algae
C. Red algae D. Blue-green algae

28. How many Antipodal cells are there in Oenothera type of Embryo sac?
A. 4 B. 8
C. 3 D. Zero

29. Central Drug Research Institute is situated at:
A. Delhi B. Bombay
C. Chennai D. Lucknow

30. In some parasitic fungi a globular or hook like structure is formed at the point of contact with the host. This is known as:
A. Haustoria B. Appressorium
C. Hold fast D. Hook

31. "Perfect stage" of fungus means:
A. When the fungus is perfectly healthy
B. When it produces asexually
C. When it forms perfectly sexual spores
D. None of these

32. Enzyme code of Glucose-6-Phosphotransferase is:
A. 2-7-1-2 B. 2-1-7-2
C. 2-7-2-2 D. 2-7-2-1

33. Assume that four molecules of an enzyme and 60000 molecules of substrate are taken into a test tube, containing water. All the substrate molecules are converted into products in five minutes. Considering this data, calculate the TON of that enzyme.

A. 2500 B. 3000
C. 3500 D. 4000

34. Plant hormone used as anti-transpirant is:

A. IAA B. GA
C. Ethylene D. ABA

35. Organisation of stem apex into corpus and tunica is determined mainly by:

A. Planes of cell division
B. Regions of meristematic activity
C. Rate of cell growth
D. Rate of shoot tip growth

36. Exanthema in citrus is due to:

A. Deficiency of Manganese
B. Deficiency of Copper
C. Deficiency of iron
D. Deficiency of Aluminium

37. The pahala blight of sugarcane is due to the deficiency of:

A. Copper
B. Manganese
C. Iron
D. None of the above

38. White rust of crucifers caused *Alugo candida* belongs to class:

A. Oomycetes
B. Plasmophora
C. Phytophothora
D. All of the above

39. Cleavage polyembryony is found in:

A. Pinus
B. Cycas
C. Cycas and Pinus both
D. None of these

40. Tunica Carpus theory was proposed by:

A. Hanstein B. Schmidt
C. Haberlandt D. Robert Hook

41. Mucilaginous canals in Cycas are found in:

A. Pith only
B. Cortex and pith
C. Vascular bundle
D. All of these

42. The fruits are not formed in gymnosperms because:

A. They are seedless plants
B. They are not pollinated
C. They have no ovary
D. The process of fertilization does not take place in them

43. Stomata are absent in:

A. Submerged plants
B. Xerophytes
C. Free-floating plants
D. All of the above

44. Enrichment of water bodies through human activity is:

A. Denudation B. Eutrophication
C. Naturosis D. Leaching

45. Plants growing on snow are known as:

A. Cryptophytes B. Cryophytes
C. Therophytes D. Oxylophytes

46. Carpogonial filament of polysiphonia consists of following number of cells:

A. 3 – 4 B. 4 – 5
C. 5 – 6 D. 6 – 7

47. Which of the following is **not** concerned with cyanophyceae?

A. Absence of sex organs and motile reproductive bodies
B. Simple protoplasts with plastids
C. The low state of the thallus organisation and extremely simple cell structure
D. Absence or well-organized nuclei

48. Phytochrome is involved in:

A. Phototropism
B. Photoperiodism
C. Photorespiration
D. Photophosphorylation

49. The branch of ecology that deals with the biological relationship between an individual organism or an individual species and its environment:

A. Autecological
B. Synecology
C. Phytogeography
D. None of the above

50. Cancer's are apart of every culture and have been around as long as people. The study of cancers is known as:
A. Physiology B. Pathology
C. Oncology D. Neurology

51. Which of the following was the cause of the "baby boom" in the last century?
A. Immigration
B. Ending of the war
C. Development of birth control
D. Mortality

52. Which one of the following molecules is **not** a component of the 30s initiation complex?
A. GTP B. mRNA
C. Initiation factor 2 D. ATP

53. Animals get nitrogen directly through:
A. Nitrogen fixation
B. Plants
C. Bacteria
D. Habitat

54. The king of Indian spices:
A. Foeniculum vulgare
B. Piper nigram
C. Curcuma longa
D. Zingiber officinale

55. Selaginella differs from Funaria in having:
A. Motile sperms
B. Well-developed vascular system
C. An independent gametophyte
D. Antheridia

56. Protonema occurs in the life cycle of:
A. Riccia B. Funaria
C. Dryopteris D. Spirogyra

57. Formation of gametophyte directly from sporophytic tissue without spores is:
A. Apogamy B. Apospory
C. Apocarpy D. Parthenogenesis

58. Fern gametophyte is:
A. Multicellular cordate prothallus
B. Liver shaped thallus
C. Unicellular colourless
D. Filamentous, multicellular and green

59. The enzyme responsible for continuing DNA replication in prokaryotes, once it is initiated is:
A. DNA polymerase I
B. DNA polymerase III
C. Polymerase beta
D. Polymerase delta

60. In Pyrimidine Synthesis, Eukaryotes can use uracil to feedback inhibit which of the following enzymes?
A. Carbamoyl phosphate synthase
B. Asparatate Transcarbamoylase
C. Dihydroorotase
D. Thymidylate synthase

61. Cytogenetic mapping
A. Requires that the gene have been cloned if *insitu* hybridization is to be used
B. Is a high resolution method of gene localization
C. Can be used to determine relative order of genes located very close to each other
D. All of the above

62. Which of the following questions could be easily answered by FISH?
A. How often does recombination occur between the *ebony* and *sepia* loci in Drosophila?
B. In a particular farmily affected with Becker muscular dystrophy, is the mutation due to a deletion of the entire gene.
C. How large a piece of DNA would you need to clone in order to clone the group of human globin genes from chromosome 11?
D. None of the above

Directions (Qs. 63 and 64): You have set up the following experiment to linkage map two RFLPs in pigs. For RFLP A, you can detect either a 5,000 bp band or a 3,350 bp band; for RFLP B, you can detect either a 4,300 bp band or a pair of bands of 2,300 and 2,000 bp. Beginning with strains homozygous for different forms of each RFLP, you generate compound heterozygotes, which you then cross to pigs that are homozygous for the smaller forms of each RFLP. By analysis of several litters you get the following results: 52 individuals with 5,000 bp and 4,300 bp; 48 individuals with 5,000 bp, 4,300 bp, 3,350 bp, 2,300 bp and 2,000 bp bands; 11 individuals with 5,000 bp, 4,300 bp, 2,300 bp and 2,000 bp bands; and 9 individuals with 5,000 bp, 4,300 bp and 3,350 bp bands.

63. What was the arrangement of the markers in the original parental strains?
A. A : 5,000 bp, B : 4,300 bp and A : 3,350 bp, B : 2,300/2,000 bp
B. A : 5,000 bp, B : 2,300/2,000 bp and A : 3,350 bp, B : 4,300 bp
C. A : 3,350 bp, B : 4,300 bp and A : 5,000 bp, B : 4,300 bp
D. A : 3,350 bp, B : 2,300/2,000 bp and A : 3,350 bp, B : 2,300/2,000 bp

64. Which of these genetic markers is most likely to be highly polymorphic (have many different alleles)?
A. An RFLP
B. A microsatellite
C. An SNP
D. All of these are equally polymorphic

65. Mendel's hybridization stratergy was use of two plants:
A. Differing in a pair of contrasting character
B. Differing in two pairs of contrasting character
C. Differing in many pairs of contrasting character
D. Differing in three pairs of contrasting character

66. Gene transfer in bacteria by transformation has the following characteristics:
A. A majority of the donor genes are transferred
B. It involves a plasmid
C. It depends on phage infection of the recipient cell
D. It can be carried out using free DNA extracted from the donor

67. Any process that results in the integration of new combinations of genes together in a single cell is:
A. Genetic recombination
B. Fusion
C. Genetic fission
D. Allelotyping

68. Common lymphomas in pediatric age:
A. Anaplastic large cell lymphoma
B. Burkitt's lymphoma
C. Follicular lymphoma
D. Diffuse large β-cell lymphoma

69. Myoepithelial carcinoma is immune reactive for:
A. S-100, CD1a and p53
B. EMA, desmin and fibrin
C. Cytokeratin, S-100 and calponin
D. CD20, CD3 and vimentin

70. Which of the following is associated with Burkitt's lymphoma?
A. EBV B. Arbovirus
C. Picornavirus D. Pox virus

71. Link the following cancers with their corresponding viruses:

(*a*) Cervical cancer	1. Epstein Barr virus
(*b*) Burkitt's lymphoma	2. Human papilloma virus
(*c*) Nasopharyngeal cancer	3. Hepatitis B
(*d*) Hepatocellular carcinoma	4. RNA retro virus
(*e*) T-cell leukaemia	

	(*a*)	(*b*)	(*c*)	(*d*)	(*e*)
A.	1	1	2	3	4
B.	4	1	1	3	4
C.	2	1	1	3	4
D.	3	1	2	1	4

72. The transfer of oncogenes from one cell to another is called:
A. Infection B. Transduction
C. Transfection D. Inductance

73. Organisms, which damage man's property, including plants and agricultural produce causing damage of significant economic importance are called:
A. Pests B. Pathogens
C. Parasites D. Aliens

74. What do the following insects have in common? sod webworm, bagworm, black cutworm and monarch:

A. They all belong to the order Lepidoptera
B. They all feed on trees
C. They all migrate
D. They are all butterflies

75. What is the major alfalfa insect pest insect in this region?

A. Alfalfa weevil
B. Alfalfa looper
C. Blister beetle
D. Alfalfa butterfly

76. Carpenter ants belong to which of the following orders?

A. Neuropteran
B. Lepidoptera
C. Plecoptera
D. Hymenoptera

77. What do the following insects have in common? mayfly, caddisfly, mosquito, dobsonfly:

A. They all belong to the order Lepidoptera
B. They all feed on trees
C. They all live in the water
D. They are all in the order dipteral

78. Which of the following is a function of air bladder?

A. Respiration
B. Sound production
C. Buoyant float
D. All of the above

79. Which of the following structure of a fish is homologous with lung of frog?

A. Gill pouch
B. Swim bladder
C. Stomach
D. Book lung

80. What is the scientific name of pinworm of man?

A. Enteroblus vernicularis
B. Trichinella spirals
C. Trichuris trichiura
D. Dracunculus medinensis

81. Which structure is called tongue of cockroach?

A. Labium B. Labrum
C. Hypopharynx D. Mandible

82. The skull of frog and rabbit are:

A. Dicondylic B. Monocondylic
C. Tricondylic D. Tetracondylic

83. Which of the following is used as emulsifier?

A. Algin B. Agar
C. Carrageenan D. Funoran

84. Recurrence of floods in the plains of North India is due to excessive:

A. Siltation of dams
B. Rainfall
C. Agriculture
D. Deforestation in catchment area

85. Genome comparisons have suggested that mouse DNA has mutated about twice as fast as human DNA. What is a possible explanation for this discrepancy?

A. Mice are much smaller than humans
B. Mice live in much less sanitary conditions than humans and are therefore exposed to a wider range of mutation-causing substances
C. Mice have a smaller genome size
D. Mice have a much shorter generation time.

[wp_campaign_1]

86. Why was the genome of the protist *P. falciparum* difficult to sequence?

A. This protist has a large genome
B. This organism hides inside red blood cells, making it difficult to obtain enough DNA for the sequencing project
C. The apicoplast structures in this protist inhibit sequencing reactions
D. The genome contains a high proportion of adenine and thymine

87. Which of the following best describes pseudogenes?

A. Two functional genes within an organism that arose from the duplication of one gene
B. Genes that share the same ancestral sequence, but are found in different organisms

C. Sequences of DNA that are very similar to functional genes, but do not produce a functional product

D. Sequences of DNA that are very similar to inactive genes, but do produce a functional product

88. The *Tbx5* gene is known to play a role in which process?

A. Notochord development

B. Limb formation

C. Eye formation

D. Sexual reproduction

89. How many pairs of chromosomes do chimpanzees carry?

A. 23 B. 46

C. 24 D. 48

90. Which of the following is the study of a collection of genetic material (genomes) from a mixed community of organisms. It is usually refers to the study of microbial communities?

A. Metagenomics

B. Genomics

C. Epigenetic

D. None of the above

91. In females, one of the X-chromosomes is inactive by:

A. The number of dominant genes on each X-chromosomes

B. Epigenetic markers

C. Environmental factors

D. Enzymes coded for by mitochondrial DNA

92. The only methylated base in mammals is:

A. 7-methyl guanine

B. Thymine

C. Methyl adenine

D. 5-methyl cytosine

93. Which of these is **not** secreted from anterior Hypophysis?

A. Thyroid Stimulating Hormone

B. Adrenocorticotropic Hormone

C. Oxytocin

D. Follicle Stimulating Hormone

94. Long-term management of hypercalcaemia does not include:

A. Bisphosphates B. Hydration

C. Calcitonin D. Loop diuretics

95. The "Master gland" of the endocrine system, located at the base of the brain, is the:

A. Apical gland

B. Bartholin gland

C. Pituitary gland

D. Thyroid gland

96. Which type of gland secretes hormones directly into the bloodstream rather than into ducts leading to the exterior of the body?

A. Endocrine gland

B. Exocrine gland

C. Serous gland

D. Target gland

97. In *Drosophila,* the pattern is established:

A. During production of the oocyte

B. As a result of environmental interactions with the oocyte

C. During gastrulation

D. After embryogenesis has completed

98. Morphogen:

A. Conveys positional information to cells within the embryo

B. Is typically present in similar amounts in all cells

C. Functions only at very low concentration

D. All of these

99. In Drosophila development, an embryonic segment:

A. Is the same thing as a parasegment

B. Will contribute to two different segments in the adult fly

C. Is a region of spatial control of gene expression

D. None of the above

100. Which of these would be an example of a homeotic phenotype?

A. The wings are shrunken and useless

B. The eyes of the fly are brown instead of normal red

C. The first abdominal segment has legs

D. None of the above

ANSWERS

1	2	3	4	5	6	7	8	9	10
C	B	A	C	C	C	A	A	C	D
11	**12**	**13**	**14**	**15**	**16**	**17**	**18**	**19**	**20**
A	B	B	C	B	C	D	C	C	D
21	**22**	**23**	**24**	**25**	**26**	**27**	**28**	**29**	**30**
A	C	A	B	B	A	B	C	D	B
31	**32**	**33**	**34**	**35**	**36**	**37**	**38**	**39**	**40**
C	A	B	D	A	B	B	A	A	B
41	**42**	**43**	**44**	**45**	**46**	**47**	**48**	**49**	**50**
B	C	A	B	B	A	B	B	A	C
51	**52**	**53**	**54**	**55**	**56**	**57**	**58**	**59**	**60**
B	D	B	B	B	B	B	A	B	A
61	**62**	**63**	**64**	**65**	**66**	**67**	**68**	**69**	**70**
A	B	A	B	A	B	A	C	C	A
71	**72**	**73**	**74**	**75**	**76**	**77**	**78**	**79**	**80**
C	B	A	A	A	D	C	D	B	A
81	**82**	**83**	**84**	**85**	**86**	**87**	**88**	**89**	**90**
C	A	C	B	D	D	C	B	C	A
91	**92**	**93**	**94**	**95**	**96**	**97**	**98**	**99**	**100**
B	D	C	C	C	A	A	A	D	C

BIOLOGY

Botany/Zoology/Life Sciences/Bio Sciences/Genetics/ Micro-Biology/Bio-Technology/Molecular Bio/Plant Physiology

1. DIVERSITY OF LIVING WORLD

PRINCIPLES AND METHODS OF TAXONOMY

INTRODUCTION

Diversity of Life

Diversity is the occurrence of different varieties/forms, develops due to organic evolution and their adaptation to overcome competition. About 1.5 million species of animals have been identified, classified and assigned their respective phyletic status.

- **Systematics (GK. systema–order or sequence) :** It is the scientific study of types and diversity of organisms and their comparative and evolutionary relationships based on comparative anatomy, physiology, ecology, biochemistry and other fields. It is based on following fundamentals.
- **Taxonomy (Caroleus Linnaeus-Father of Taxonomy) (GK. Taxis–arrangement, nomos-law) :** The term Taxonomy coinod by De Candolle. It is the srudy of identification, nomenclature and classification of an organism.
- **Identification :** It is to determine the exact place or position of an organism in the set plan of classification.
- **Classification :** It is the arrangement of organisms in hierarchical series of groups and subgroups on the basis of similarities and differences in their traits so as to bring out their relationships.
- **Nomenclature :** It is the process of providing scientific names to the organism.
- **Key :** It provides a convenient way for easy identification of an organism by using diagnostic or distinguishing characters.

The taxonomic groups are arranged in definite order from higher to lower categories. Total seven obligate categories are :

Kingdom – Division/Phylum – Class – Order – Family – Genus – Species →

Highest Taxonomic Category → Lowest and basic Taxonomic category

In the organisms placed in the lowest category, the number of common characters is maximum and they decreases with the rise in category. Such common character are called *correlated characters.* The highly acceptable five kingdom classification was proposed by R.H. Whittaker (1969) on the basis of

- Complexity of cell structure – prokaryote or eukaryote
- Complexity of body structure – unicellular or multicellular
- Mode of nutrition – autotroph or heterotroph
- Ecological lite style – producer or consumer or decomposer
- Phylogenetic relationships *i.e.,* how one category originate from the other.

This classification includes :

1. Kingdom monera - Prokaryotes
2. Kingdom Protista - Unicellular eukaryotes
3. Kingdom Fungi - Multicellular decomposers
4. Kingdom plantae — Multicellular producers
5. Kingdom Animalia/iMetazoa — Multicellular consumers.

Kingdom – Animalia or Metazoa

(Multiecllular consumers)

(Latin, **anima** = air or breath or soul)

Animals are metazoans like plants but differ in a number of characters like absence of plastids, cell wall and central vacuole. There are about 1.2 million animal species which shows a great diversity in their shapes, sizes, colours, habits, habitats, structures, and various processes.

CHARACTERISTIC FEATURES

1. They are *multicellular* consumers of the ecosystem.
2. They are made of eukaryotic cells and have no cell wall, plastids, central vacuole and photosynthetic pigments.
3. Lower animals exhibit cellular or tissue level of organization and higher animals have organ system level of organisation.
4. Mostly free living and some (sponges and several coelenterates) are fixed.
5. They take food by ingestion *i.e.,* holozoic in nutrition and digestion takes place in an internal cavity. Some forms have absorptive nutrition and digestive cavity is absent. The undigested food is removed by egestion.
6. They have muscle cells (contraction and relaxation of body parts) and nerve cells (transmit nerve impulses). Porifers lack nerve cells.
7. Lower animals have asexual and sexual reproduction. Higher animals have generally sexual reproduction.
8. They exhibit meiosis and form gametes (only haploid stage) before fertilization.
9. In adult stage of life cycle, they have typical diploid or triploid body. The zygote form a multicellular embryo.

LEVEL OF STRUCTURAL ORGANIZATION OF ANIMALS

SOME GENERAL FEATURES OF ANIMALS

(A) Habitat

Two habitats, (I) aquatic and (II) terrestrial

(I) Aquatic Animals

May be fresh or marine :

1. **Fresh Water Animals :** Found in ponds, rivers, streams etc. *e.g.,* Snails, Amoeba. Paramecium, Prawn etc.
2. **Marine Animals :** Found in sea water, where salt concentration is high *e.g.,* all echinoderms and cartilage fishes and most of sponges and coelenterates.
3. **Pelagic** animals live in sea or open water *e.g.,* jelly fishes.
   (*a*) **Zooplankton :** Drift with water currents *e.g.,* invertebrates and their larvae.
   (*b*) **Nektons :** Swim actively even against water flow *e.g.,* most of fishes.
4. **Benthic :** Animals live at the bottom of sea *e.g.,* star fish.
5. **Neuston :** Animals float or swim in the surface water.
6. **Seston :** Living or non-living things that float or swim in water.
7. **Tripton :** Non-living sestons float or swim in water.
8. **Neritic :** Animals are present in coastal waters.
9. **Sedentary (Sessile) :** Animals are attached to the substratum.
   (*a*) **Epizoons :** Animals fixed over other animals
   (*b*) **Periphylons or Epiphytic :** Fixed or attached over rooted plants
   (*c*) **Epilithic :** Fixed on rocks or stones.

(II) Terrestrial Animals

These animals lives on land

1. **Fossorial :** Live inside burrows *e.g.,* snake, earthworm, rabbit, duck billed platypus etc.
2. **Arboreal :** Live on the trees *e.g.,* bats, apes, monkeys, most of birds etc.
3. **Cursorial :** Fast runners *e.g.,* tiger, lion, horse, kangaroo, dog etc.
4. **Scansorial :** Climb the walls or rocks etc. *e.g.,* wall lizards, flying squirrels etc.
5. **Aerial/Volant/Flying :** Flying animals *e.g.,* birds, bats, most of insects etc.
6. **Cave dwellers :** Reside in caves *e.g.,* bats etc.
7. **Diurnal :** Active during day hours *e.g.,* non, housefly etc.

8. **Nocturnal :** Active during night hours *e.g.*, moth, bats, owl etc.
9. **Vespertine :** Active during evening hours *e.g.*, birds etc.
10. **Auroral :** Active during day *e.g.*, earthworm etc.
11. **Parasites :** Live on or in the body of others *e.g.*, fluke, tapeworm, ticks, mites etc.

(III) Aggregations

Animals may be **solitary** (living alone *e.g.*, tapeworm, grasshopper) or *gregarious* (living in aggregations *e.g.*, locust) or colonial (obligatory interdependence *e.g.*, termites, honeybees etc.)

Animals aggregate during migration or mating. The groups of these gregarious animals are known differently.

e.g.,		
Flock	–	Sheep, parrot
Swarm	–	Locust, bees
Shoal	–	Fishes
Herd	–	Cattle, zebra
Troop	–	Monkey, lions
Litters	–	Young ones of pig, dogs, cats
Pack	–	Horse
Shoan	–	Deer
School	–	Whale, porpoises
Muster	–	Peacock
Rookery	–	Seals
Broad	–	Chickens

Family may be –

Monogamous : One female and one male *e.g.*, Sparrow, white Band Gibbon etc.

Polygamous : One male with several females *e.g.*, Deer.

Matriarchy : Female is head of family *e.g.*, African elephant.

Patriarchy : Male is head of family *e.g.*, Deer, Zebra etc.

(B) Levels or Grades of Organization

Five types

1. **Acellular or Protoplasmic Level:** All the activities are functioned by one cell body *e.g.*, Protozoa or acellular protists.
2. **Cellular Level:** The animal is made up of many cells. But cells do not form definite tissues and no coordination among them. *e.g.*, mesozoans and sponges.
3. **Cell-Tissue Level :** The animal is made up of many cells which coordinate to perform a specific function. They form tour types of tissues *e.g.*, epithelial, connective, muscular and nervous tissues. *e.g.*, *Cnidaria* or *Coelenterata.* The body is made up of only two germ layers *e.g.*, ectoderm and endoderm *i.e.*, *Diploblastic* animals.
4. **Tissue-Organ Level :** The tissues are aggregated to form organs which have a more specialised function than tissues *e.g.*, Platyhelminthes. They have a third cellular germ layer in between the ectoderm and. endoderm *i.e.*, mesoderm. They are Triploblastic animals.
5. **Organ-System Level :** This is the highest level of organization. The animal is multicellular and several organs are associated to form a distinct system to perform a distinct function. *e.g.*, from roundworm to mammals.

(C) Body Plan

Three basic plans –

1. **Cell aggregate body plan :** The body is an aggregation of cells with meagre differentiation and no coordination. *e.g.*, sponges.
2. **Blind sac body plan :** The body is like a sac or cavity with one opening which acts as both mouth and anus (incomplete alimentary canal) *e.g.* flatworms, coelenterates.
3. **Tube within a tube plan :** The body wall forms an outer tube and alimentary canal forms an inner or second tube. Alimentary canal is complete with two openings – anterior *mouth* (for ingestion) and posterior *anus* (for egestion). Two types –
   (*a*) **Protostomous (Protostomy) plan :** Mouth is formed from blastopore of archenteron of gastrula larva and is formed earlier than anus *e.g.*, flatworms, roundworms, annelids, molluscs and arthropods.

(*b*) **Deuterostomous (Deterostomy) plan :** Anus is formed first from blastopore of gastrula *e.g.*, hemichordates, chordates and echinoderms.

(D) Symmetry

Arrangement of body parts on two sides of main axis of body. Two types

1. **Asymmetrical :** Body is so highly irregular that cannot be divided in two similar parts by any plane e.g., snails, certain sponges, Amoeba.
2. **Symmetrical :** The body is divided into two similar parts by one or more planes. Three types-

(*a*) **Spherical or Universal Symmetry :** The body is like a ball and can be divided into two equal parts by any plane passing through the centre of body *e.g., Volvox,* some corals.

(*b*) **Radial Symmetry :** The body is in the form of a flat or cylinder (tall). It can be divided into equal halves by any plane passing through the centre from top to bottom *e.g.,* some sponges, coelenterates, echinoderms. Three types:

(*i*) **Tetramerous Radial Symmetry :** Body parts arranged in 4 or multiple of 4. e.g., Jellyfish.

(*ii*) **Pentamerous Radial Symmetry :** Body parts arranged in S or multiple of *5.e.g.,* Echinoderms.

(*iii*) **Hexamerous Radial Symmetry :** Body parts arranged in 6 or multiple of 6. *e:g.,* Sea anemone. (In sea anemone body has biradial symmetry both radially and bilaterally symmetrical.

(*c*) **Bilateral symmetry :** Body is divided into two equal halves by one plane only mid-sagittal *e.g.,* all the vertebrates. The body has a *antetior* (head) end, *posterior* (tails) end, *proximal* (near site of body) end *distal* (head/mouth region or away from the site of origin) end, *dorsal* (upper or vertebral) side, *ventral* (lower or towards the substratum during locomotion) side and two *lateral* (right and left) sides.

(E) Cephalization

It is the differentiation of anterior or oral end of the animal due to concentration of brain and sense organs into a definite head. It is developed in flatworms and found in all phyla from platyhelminthes to chordata.

(F) Appendages

These are the out growth structures from the body which are used in feeding, locomotion and some other functions. *e.g., lentacles* (coelenterates) *parapodia* (many annelids), foot (molluscs *), fins* (fishes), *antennae* and legs (arthropods), *tubefeet* or *podia (*echilloderms), *limbs* and *wings* (tetrapods). These may be *paired* (one or either side) or *unpaired* (*e.g.,* dorsal fin and caudal fin in fishes).

(G) Metamerism (segmentation)

The repetition of internal body parts is called metamerism. Each segment is called a *metmnere* or *somite e.g.,* annelids, arthropods, mollusus and chordate. In *annelids,* the body is externally divided by *annuli* and internally by *septa.* The external division corresponds to internal division and is called *metameric segmentation. In adult chordates,* internal segmentation is exhibited by repetition of ribs, vertebral nerve, muscles and blood vessels. In arthropods, only external metamerism is present. In *tapeworm, pseudometamerism or false segmentation* is present because segmentation is not of embryonic origin.

(H) Germ Layers

All the tissues and organs develop from germ layers (layers of gastrula). Three types :

1. Ectoderm – Outer layer
2. Mesoderm – Middle layer
3. Endoderm – Inner layer

The animals may be –

1. **Diploblastic :** Two layers, outer ectoderm and inner endoderm or gastroderm. *e.g.,* Porifers and coelenterates.
2. **Triploblastic :** All the three layers are present *e.g.,* from platyhelminthes to mammals.

(I) Coelom (Body Cavity)

It is the space between body wall and alimentary canal which is filled with a fluid and lined by peritoneum derived trom mesoderm.

1. **Acoelomate :** No coelom. *e.g.*, porifers, coelenterates, ctenophores, flatworms and preboscis worms.
2. **Pseudocoelomate :** Developed from blastocoel. Coelom is present but not lined by peritoneal layer. The coelom is called as pseudocoel or false-coelom. *e.g.*, roundworms (*Ascaris*).
3. **Eucoelomates :** The body cavity is lined by peritoneal layers (outer side parietal epithelium and inner side visceral peritoneum. The coelom is called *true-coelom e.g.*, from annelids to mammals.
4. **Haemocoelomates :** In *arthropods,* coelom is reduced, filled with blood and called as haemocoel. Coelom is of two types on the basis of their origin.
    1. **Schizocoel :** Formed by splitting of mesodermal sheet *e.g.*, annelids, arthropods and molluscs.
    2. **Enterocoel :** Formed from the enteron of gastrula *e.g.*, echinoderms and chordates.

(J) Body Temperature:

1. **Homeothermal/Warm-blooded Endothermal :** Body temperature is constant and does not vary with surrounding temperature *e.g.*, birds and mammals.
2. **Poikiothermal/Cold-blood/Ectothermal :** Body temperature is not constant, it varies with change in surrounding temperature *e.g.*, invertebrates, fish, amphibians reptiles. They defend two ways.
    (*a*) **Hibernation** (winter sleep) : Remains inactive during winter months *e.g.*, amphibians and lizards.
    (*b*) **Aestivation** (summer sleep) : Remains inactive during hot summer months *e.g.*, amphibians.

(K) Skeleton

It is the hard structure of body which provides the shape, support and protection to the body. It is of two types:

1. **Exoskeleton :** Secreted by skin or ectoderm and made up of non-living material *e.g.*. *chitinous plates* or sclerites (arthropods) *epidermal scales* (reptiles,), *calcareous shell* (molluscs), *plates below skin* (echinoderms), horny scales, feathers, claws, hair, nails, hoofs and horns (vertebrates) It is absent in frog.
2. **Endoskeleton :** Internal skeleton, produced by mesoderm or sometimes endoderm, may be living (cartilages and bones in vertebrates) or non-living (*e.g., calcareous plates* in echinoderms and *calcareous or silicious spicules* in porifers). Bones and cartilages forms endoskdeton.

(L) Digestive system

Includes ingestion, digestion and egestion of food. The alimentary canal is of two types –

1. **Incomplete :** Mouth present, anus absent *e.g.*, coelenterates and flatworms.
2. **Complete :** Mouth for ingestion and anus for egestion *e.g.*, roundworms to mammals.

(M) Nutrition

Animals are heterotrophs (exception in some protozoan are autotroph) three types of feeding habits :

1. **Ingestive** (Holozoic) : *Herbivorous* (plant feeder), *carnivorous* (animal feeder), *omnivorous* (animal and plant feeder), *detrivorous* (detritus feeder), *scavanging* (scavengers feeds on *carrions*),.*frugivorous* (fruit eater), *insectivorous* (insect eater), *cannibalism* (eating other members of same species or own species), *sanguivorous* (blood feeder), *coprophagous* (eating faeces), *coprozoic* (feeding on dung) etc.
2. **Saprozoic**
3. **Parasites** *e.g.*, – roundworms, flukes etc.

(N) Respiratory System

Exchange of gases takes place by *general body surface* (sponges, coelentrates), *gills i.e.*, branchial respiration (crustaceans, mollusca, pisces), *lungs i.e.*, pulmonary respiration (tetrapods), *book lungs* (archnids), *book-gills (limulus),* trachea (insects, centipedes, millipedes) and *skin i.e.*, cutaneous respiration amphibians).

(O) Circulatory System

It includes transport of material in the body. Two types :

1. **Open Circulatory System :** Blood flows in spaces or *sinuses e.g.*, arthropods, molluscs and leeches.
2. **Closed Circulatory System :** Blood flows in closed vessels and heart. *e.g.*, annelids and all vertebrates.

Blood may be **colourless** (insects), bluish due to copper containing haemocyanin in plasma (molluscs), red due to haemoglobin in RBCs (vertebrates), red due to haemoglobin in plasma (annelids). Circulatory system is absent in *Taenia.*

(P) Excretory System

It includes removal of nitrogenous wastes out of the body to maintain homeostasis. Many aquatic animals have no excretory organs *e.g.*, porifers, coelenterates and echinoderms. There are various types of excretory organs. These are *protonephridia or flame cells* in platyhelminthes, *renett cell* or *excretory canals* in roundworms, *nephridia* annelids, *antennaly* or *green glands* in crustaceans, *coxal glands* and *malpighian tubules* in arachnids, *malpighian tubules* and *urate cells* in insects, centipedes and millipedes, *renal organ* or *kidneys* in molluscs and *kidneys* in vertebrates.

The animals may be of four types on the basis of nature of main nitrogenous waste.

1. **Ammonotelic Animals :** Excrete ammonia *e.g.*, mostly aquatic invertebrates (sponges, coelenterates) and some aquatic vertebrates (bony fishes, tailed amphibians).
2. **Ureotelic Animals :** Nitrogenous waste is urea *e.g.*, tailless amphibians, mammals and cartilage fishes (shark, rays).
3. **Uricotelic Animals :** Excretory waste is uric acid *e.g.*, insects, land snail, land reptiles and birds.
4. **Aminotelic Animals :** Excrete amino acids *e.g.*, some mollusc and some echinoderms.

(Q) Nervous System

It controls and coordinates body functions. It is *absent* in porifers, *diffuse type* in coelenterates, *ladder type* in flatworms and roundworms, *central nervous system* (circum-pharyngeal nerve ring and ventral solid and ganglionated nerve cord) in annelids, *central nervous system* (circum-oesophageal nerve ring and a double, ventral, solid and ganglionated nerve cord) in arthropods, *ganglia interconnected by commissures and connectives* in molluscs, *oral and aboral nerve rings and radial nerves* in echinoderms and *central nervous system* (anterior broader brain, posterior longer and narrow spinal cord. CNS is dorsal, hollow and non-ganglionated) in vertebrates.

The three classes of neurons in vertebrates and complex invertebrates are : Sensory neurons which receive information from sensory receptors and transmit it to the central nervous system, motor neurons, which transmit messages to the effectors, and inner neurons, which transmit messages between the two types of neuvous

(R) Reproduction

Animals may be

1. **Bisexual** or *monoecious* or *hermaphrodite i.e.*, male and female sex organs in one individual *e.g.*, tapeworms, earthworm, leech, liverfluke.
2. **Unisexual** or **dioecious :** When an individual have either male or female sex organ *e.g.*, frog, lizard, rabbit, man etc.

Sexual dimorphism : When male and female individual can be distinguished externally *e.g.*, peacock and peahen, lion and lioness,

Asexual methods : No formation and fusion of gametes *e.g.*, **binary fission** (Amoeba), **multiple fission** Amoeba **budding (Hydra)** and **fragmentation.**

Fertilization may be **external** (enchinoderms, bony fishes and amphibious) or **internal** (land vertebrates and cartilage fishes). It may be cross fertilization (different animal) or **self-fertilization** (same animal).

Cross fertilization takes place due to two conditions:

1. **Protandrous:** Testes mature earlier than avaries *e.g.*. leech. earthworm.
2. **Prtogynous :** Ovaries mature earlier than testes *e.g.*, Scypha, Herdmania, human beings.

Development may be **direct** *i.e.*, youngones resembles the adult (earthworm, cockroach, human beings) or **indirect** *i.e.*, young does not resembele the adult (honey bee-**larva**, dragon fly-raised, frog-tadpole etc.). Young ones or larva undergoes morphological, physiological and behavioural changes to become changes are called **metamorposis.**

OUTLINE CLASSIFICATION OF ANIMALS

It is divided into 35 phyla out of which 11 are **major phyla.** The **major phyla** are

1. Protozoa (acellular) – now excluded to protista
2. Porifera - porebearer
3. Coelenterata cnidaria – radiate animals
4. Ctenophora – combjellies
5. Platyhelminthes – flatworms
6. Aschelminthes/nemathelminthes – round worms
7. Annelida – metameric segmented animals
8. Arthropoda – animals with jointed appendages
9. Mollusca – soft bodied shelled animals
10. Echinodermata – first enterocoelous coelomates
11. Chordata – notochord is present.

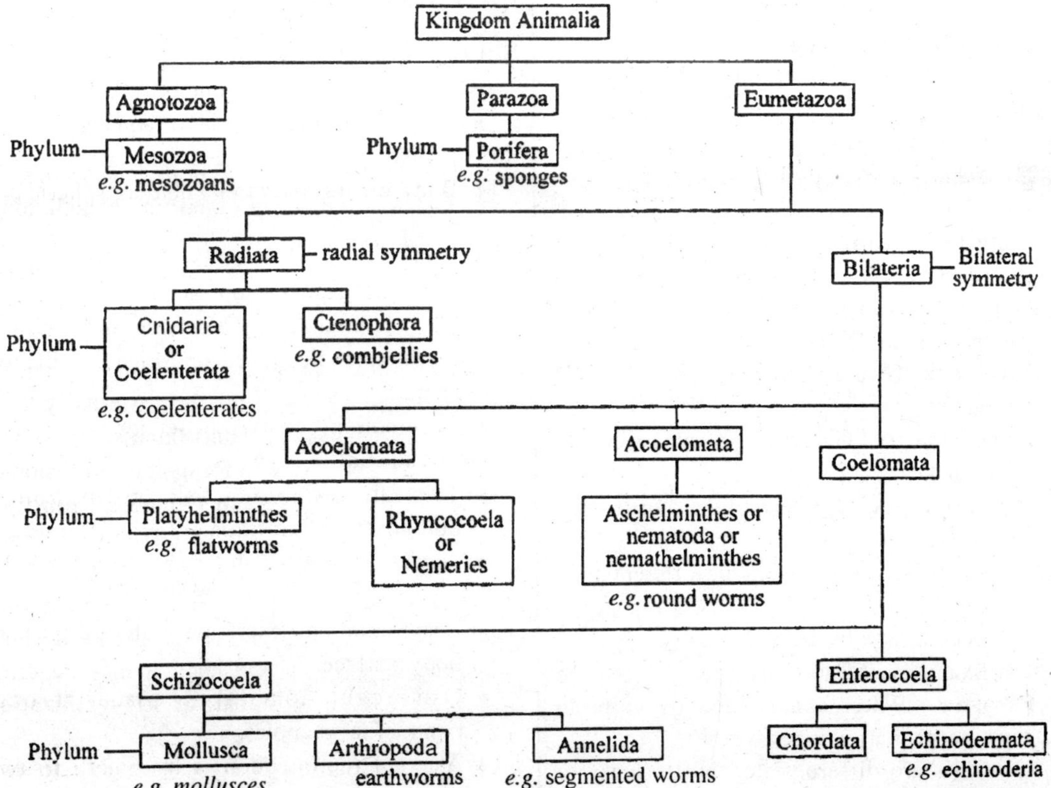

SOME IMPORTANT FACTS

- **Agamospecies :** Species depend on the basis of asexual traits due to the absence of sexual reproduction.
- **Gamespecies/Biospecies :** Species based on reproductive isolation.
- **Cleavage :** (*a*) Holoblastic – total cleavage of egg *e.g.,* many invertebrates, amphibians, mammals (*b*) **Meroblastic –** cleavage in some part of egg *e.g.,* reptiles, birds, many fishes.
- **Cuvier (1829) :** Coined the term **phylum.**
- **Linnaeus (1735) :** coined the term class.
- **Linnaeus (1693) :** first used the term **family. Genus** and **species.**
- Water circulation sponges and coelenterates.
  - Parenchymal circulation – flatworms
  - Pseudocoelomic circulation – Nematodes
- **Metamorphosis :** (*a*) **Progressive** – larvae is less advanced than adult *e.g.,* frog (*b*) **Retrogressive** – more advanced larva is changed into a degenerate adult *e.g.,* **Herdmania, sacculina.**
- **Planes :** Two body axis establish an anatomial plane.
- **Transverse plane :** Left-right and dorsoventral axis. Cut in frontal or horizontal section.
- **Saggital plane :** Longitudinal and dorsoventral axis. Cut in saggittal section.
- **Oviparity :** Female legs eggs *e.g.,* all birds, amphibians, most of fishes and insects.
- **Viviparity :** Give birth to youngsters *e.g.,* most of mammals.
- **Ovo-viviparity :** Give birth to youngones *e.g.,* rattle snake.
- **Agnotozoa :** surface cells. Take nutrition by absorption and ingestion.
  - Digestive system and tissue differentiation absent.
  - Locomotion by cilia.
  - Example – Mesozoans
- **Parazoa :** Water canal lined by cells so nutrition primarily ingestive.
  - Cells are differentiated but tissues are absent.
  - Animals are non-motile but cells have same motility.
  - Example – sponges.
- Eumetazoa: Advanced with tissue differentiation, multicellular
  - Digestive tract present (Enterozoa)
  - Example – Coelentrata to chordata
- **Invertebrates :** About 99% of animals backbone less.
- Vertebrates - with backbone. Most of the animals are present in sea.
- Arthropods and molluscs are most abundant and diverse groups.
- **Lower metazoa :** Porifera, coelenterata, platyhelminthes, Aschelminthes, *Entoprocta* and Acanthocephala.
- **Higher metazoa :** Mollusca, Annelida, Arthropoda, Echinodermata and chordata.

KINGDOM ANIMALIA : PHYLUM-PROTOZOA

Study-Protozoology

These are microscopic, colourless organisms.

- Occurs in both terrestrial or aquatic, living or parasitic.
- Body exhibit radial or bilateral, spherical or irregular symmetry.
- Body is naked consisting of uni or multinucleated protoplasm.
- Body is bounded by a delicate membrane or a firm pellicle, theca or lorica or siliceous shell.
- Locomotion occurs by pseudopodia or cilia or flagella.
- They are mainly holozoic or saprozoic or holophytic in nutrition.
- Digestion is intracellular and reserve food is glycogen.
- Respiration and excretion is through general body surface.
- Osmoregulation takes place through contractile vacuoles.
- Asexual reproduction is by binary fission. multiple fission or budding or cyst formation.

- Sexual reproduction is by syngamy or conjugation.
- They are immortal or no natural death occurs because their body is not differentiated into somatoplasm and germplasm.

CLASSIFICATION

Protozoa have been classified into four subphylum on the basis of locomotory organs.

Subphylum
- Zooflagellate
- Sarcodina
- Sporozoa
- Ciliophora

Zooflagellate	Sarcodina
– Endoparasitic or commensal or symbiotic	– Free floating or endoparasite
– Uninucleate (except Giardia) Opalina	– Uninucleate
– *Locomotion* by flagella	– By pseudopodia
– *Asexual reproduction* by binary fission and cyst formation	– Binary fission, multiple fusion, budding or spore formation
– *Sexual reproduction* absent	– By syngamy
– Inhabts female genital tract and male urinogenital tract.	
– It causes leucorrhoea in women.	
Trichonympha	

Zooflagellate

Inhabits the gut of termites, cockroaches and wood roaches. It is a symbiont and convert cellulose to glucose.

Giardia-Grand old man of Intestine. Inhabits the intestine of all kinds of the vertebrates. It causes diarrhoea or giardiasis or back packer's disease.

Trypanosoma gambienses

Its primary host is man and intermediate is tse-tse fly ***(Glossina palpalis).*** It causes fatal disease sleeping sickness.

Trypanosome cruzi is transmitted by kissing bug.
Panstronglyus magistus causes chagas disease.
Trypanosoma brucei causes Nagana disease.

Leishmania donovani

Its primary host is reticuloendothelial system man and sec-ondary host is sandfly ***(Phlebotomus argentipes).*** It causes Kala-azar, dum-dum fever and black fever and visceral leisamaniatis oriental sores **(L. tropica)** enlargement of spleen ***(L. intentum)*** **Opalina**

It inhabits the rectum of frogs. Tadpole get infection by ingesting cysts. Multinucleate protozoan undergo plasmotomy.

Proterospongia

Its a donial, free floating choanoflagellate, often regarded as connective link between protozoan and poriferans.

Mastigamoeba

Link between zoo flagellate and sarcodines. They possess flagella like flagellates and pseudopodia like sarcodiness.

Sarcodina

Class

- **Actinopodea**
  – Pseudopodia as filopodia or axopodia
  - *Sub class*
    - Heliozoa
      – Axopodia radiating
      e.g. Actinophecys
      – The sun animalcule
    - Radiolaria
      – Axopodia without axial filaments
      e.g. Actinomma
      Aulocantha – Highest number of chromosome
    - Proteomyxidia
      – Pseudopodia is filopodia type
      e.g. Pseudospora
- **Rhizopodea**
  – Pseudopodia as lobopodia or filopodia or reticulopodia
    - Lobosia
      – Pseudopodia as lobopodia
      e.g. Amoeba
      – The proteus animalcule
      Entamoeba histolitica
      – Intestinal amoeba
      It causes amoebic dysentary. It may invade liver, lungs and brain.
      Entamoeba gingivalis
      – Mouth amoeba
      – It causes pyrrhoea
    - Filosia
      – Pseudopodia is filotrodia
      e.g. Allorgromia
      Penardia
    - Granuloreticulosa
      – Pseudopodia is reticulopodia
      e.g. Babesia

Sporzoa	Ciliophora
– Endoparasite – Uninucleate – Absent – Multiple fission – Gamony *e.g.*, Telosporea - Spores are naked as lobopodia Toxoplasmea – No spores **e.g. Toxoplasma** Haplosporea – Spore case present **e.g. Ichthyosporidium** **Subclass** (of Telosporea) Gregarinea – Mature trophozoite are large and extracellular – Parasite of invertebrates **e.g. Monocystis** – It is found in the seminal vesicles of Indian earthworm **Gregarina** – It is a parasite of annelid and arthropods Coccidea – Small and intracellular – Parasite of vertebrates **e.g. Eimera** – Inhabits the epithetial cells of intestine of centipede **Plasmodium** Its primary host is femal Anopheles and secondary host is man It causes malaria.	– Free living or parasitic – Binucleate – By cilia – Binary fission – Conjugation *e.g.*, **Subclass** Holotricha – Body cilia simple and uniform **e. g. Balantidum** – It lives in the colon of human and causes ulcer by secreting cytolysin which results diarrhoea **Paramecium** – Slipper animalcule – Kappa particles produce paramecium. Peritricha – Body cilia absent and optical end bears cilia **e.g. Vorticella** – The bell organism – It is gregarous, having many contractile vacuoles and myonemes Suctoria – Young with cilia and adult with tentacles **e.g. Acineta, Ephelota** Spirotricha – Body cilia are reduced and buccal cilia are well marked **e.g. Bursaria** **Euplotes**

SOME IMPORTANT FACTS

- **Spleen index :** It is the enlargement of spleen which secrete lysolecithin and further destroy RBC and cause jaundice.
- **Black water fever :** It is the infection of *P.falciparum.* Haemoglobin is excreted in urine.
- Quinine from cinchona bark was the first malarial drug.
- Malaria Day - 20 August.
- Mosquito day - 29 August.
- GBP - General blood picture is to test malaria.
- **Larvaceous fishes :** *Gambusa* (Mosquito fish) *Poecilia* (Guppy fish)
- **P. praecox** causes malaria in birds and *P.gallinaecium* causes malaria in chicken and phesants.
- Malaria Research Centre (MRC) is located in New Delhi (since 1977).
- Prepatent period : Interval between inoculation and initiation of erythrocytic cycle.
- **Zoonosis :** A disease of man which also infect animals.
- **Paramecium bursaria** (green) exhibit symbiosis with green algae *zoochlorella.*
- **Hydramoeba :** It is the ectoparasite feeding on epidem1al cells of Hydra.

LIFE CYCLE OF AMOEBA

Amoeba always reproduce asexually. There are different methods of its multiplication (Fig. 1).

(I) Binary fission

- **Amoeba** reproduces by binary fission. In this process, the parent divides into two daughter amoebae in tavourable conditions when food is plentiful.
- The different phases of mitosis are accompanied with changes in the shape of body.
- In prophase : body becomes spherical with numerous pseudopodia and nucleus show intranuclear spindle. Chromatidia appears as duplicated chromosomes in the nucleus.
- In metaphase, chromosomes arrange at the equator.
- In anaphase, daughter chromosomes move towards opposite poles.
- In telophase, pseudopodia assume normal shape, constriction appears in the middle, one of the daughter retain contractile vacuole and the other acquires new vacuole.
- Now the parent after binary fission starts living as two individual which later on grow in size.

(II) Sporulation

- Some species of **Amoeba** reproduce by sporulation. Sporulation begins with breakdown of nuclear membrane and release of chromatin blocks in groups of 2 or 3 into the cytoplasm (*see* Fig. 2).
- Now cytoplasm of parent body segregate around daughter nucleus and this cytoplasmic layer changes into tough, resistant spore membrane.
- Later on residual cytoplasm disintegrates and releases spores (about 200) in water. These spores sink down at bottom of the pond.
- On return of favourable season, these spore membrane rupture and releases amoeba.

(III) Encystment and Multiple Fission (*see* Fig. 3)

- Under unfavourable conditions like draught, extreme temperature, **Amoeba** withdraw its pseudopodia and becomes spherical and secretes three layered cyst around itself.
- Now its nucleus undergo repeated mitosis and daughter nuclei (about 600) becomes surrounded by mass of cytoplasm called **amoebulae/pseudopodiospores.**
- This encysted amoeba lives under suspended animation with extremely slow metabolism. Encystment is also the means of dispersal.
- On return of favourable season, amoeba hatches out from its cyst and resume active life.

(IV) Regeneration

Amoeba has a great power of regeneration. If it is cut into small pieces. containing a part of the nucleus, it rapidly regenerate to complete amoeba.

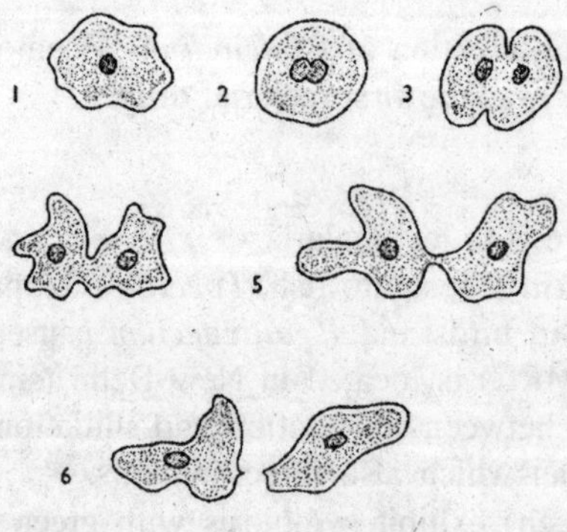

Fig. 1: *Stages of binary fission in amoeba*

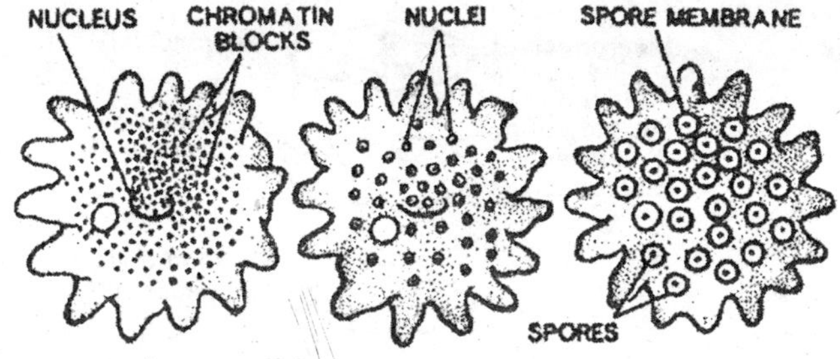

Fig. 2: *Sporulation in amoeba*

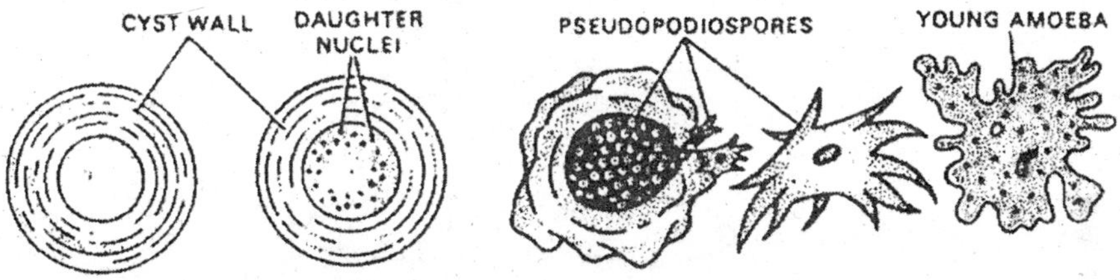

Fig. 3: *Encystment and multiple fission in amoeba*

REPRODUCTION IN PARAMECIUM

Paramecium although reproduce mainly by binary fission but several nuclear reorganising processes occurs at intervals as

- Asexual process – Endomixis, Hemixis
- Sexual process – Conjugation, autogamy, cytogamy.

Binary Fission

- In favourable environment when food is plenty, **paramecium** multiplies by transverse binary fission. Before fission, animals stops feeding and becomes spindle shaped.
- Micronucleus elongates and forms intranuclear spindle and chromosomes show mitotic division. Simultaneously the macronucleus divides amitotically by elongation and constriction.
- Nuclear division is followed by cytokinesis. Oral groove start disappearing, two new pellicular pores of contractile vacuoles appear, ingestatory apparatus starts forming a new one by budding.
- Finally a duplicated organelles move apart and constriction appears in equatorial plane.
- Anterior daughter is called proter with original contractile vacuole and posterior **opisthe** with one produced by buddmg.

ASEXUAL NUCLEAR REORGANISING PROCESSES

In these processes there is no formation of gametic nuclei.

Endomixis

- The macronucleus divide amitotically and the micronucleus divide mitotically (twice) to form 8 daughter nuclei. Out of these about 6 nuclei disintegrates.
- Now paramecium divide and each daughter receive single nucleus. This nucleus divides twice into 4 daughter nuclei of which two form micro and two macronuclei. Now each daughter individual itself divides into 2, each getting one macronucleus and 2 micronucleus by division (*see* Fig. 4).

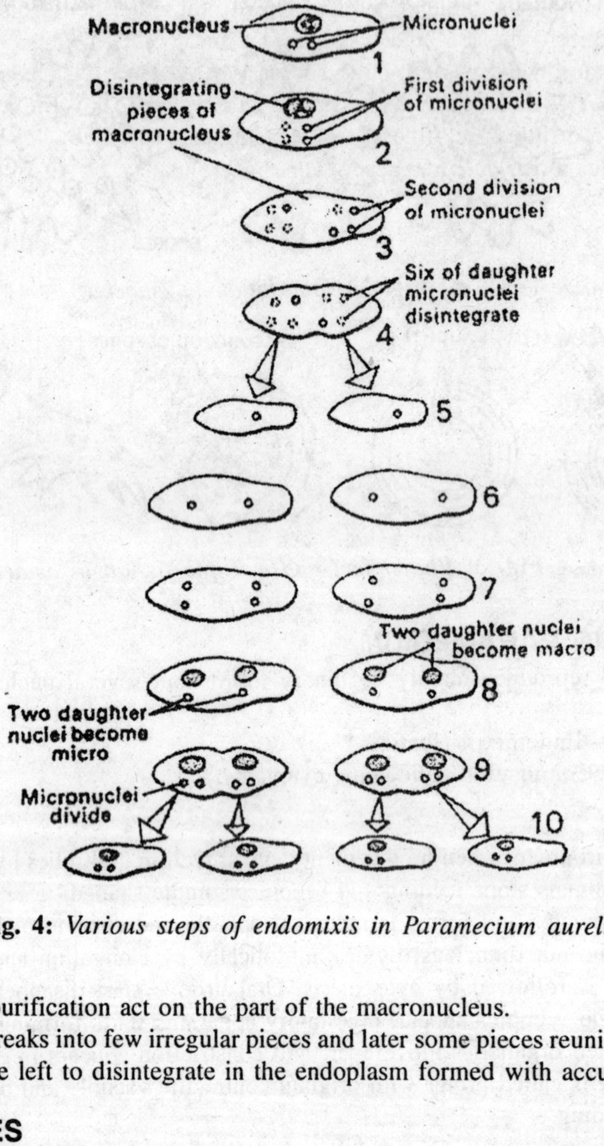

Fig. 4: *Various steps of endomixis in Paramecium aurelia*

Hemixis

- This process is the purification act on the part of the macronucleus.
- Macronucleus first breaks into few irregular pieces and later some pieces reunite to form the nucleus.
- Remaining pieces are left to disintegrate in the endoplasm formed with accumulated impurities.

SEXUAL PROCESSES

Conjugation

- It is the vigor – restoring method which involves a temporary union of two individuals for exhanging their micronuclear material *i.e.,* it is a "modified form of cross-fertilization".
- Feeding stops in conjugants and ingestatory apparatus, pellicle, cilia, trichocyst, kinetics of oral region disappear gradually and endoplasmic bridge is formed between two conjugants in this region.
- Macronucleus breaks and dissolve in endoplasm. The micronucleus undergo meiosis and form 4 haploid nuclei.
- Three of the haploid daughter nuclei disintegrate and one left divides again into two pronuclei/ gametic nuclei – smaller active male and larger stationary/passive female one.

- Male pronuclei of one conjugant crosses over to the other conjugant and fuses with its stationary pronuclei forming **zygotic nucleus/synkaryon** and then conjugants separate.
- Now its synkaryon divides by three successive mitotic divisions into 8 daughter nuclei called **amphinuclei.** Four of these nuclei enlarge to becomes macronuclei and four as micronuclei (later on three disintegrates) these exconjugants also divide by 2 successive division and form 4 daughter nuclei. Each daughter receive one macronucleus by distribution and one micronuclei by division (Fig. 5).

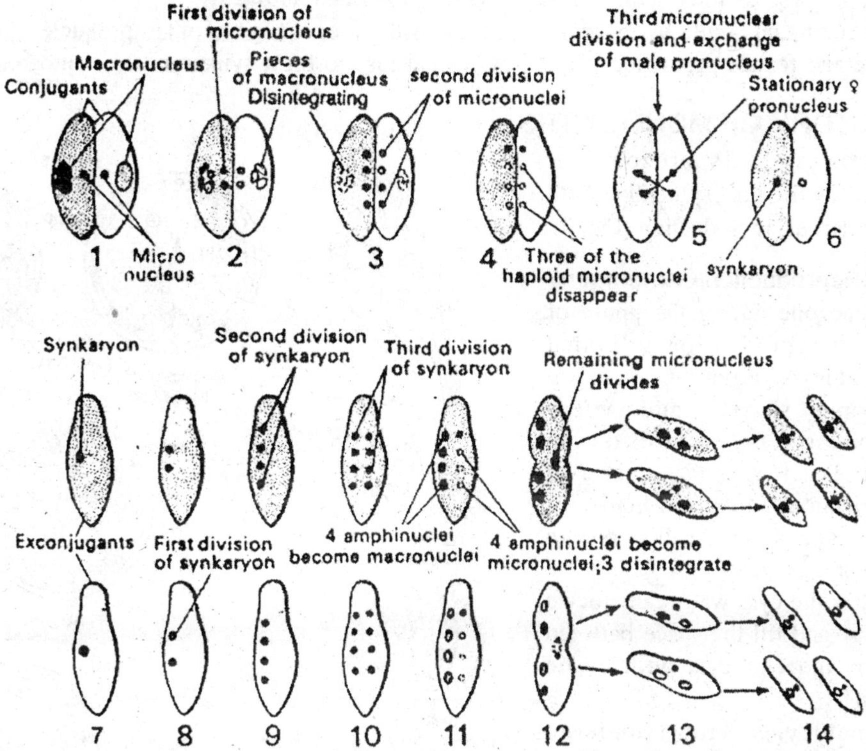

Fig. 5: *Various stages of conjugation in Paramecium caudatum*

Autogamy

- It is a modified form of self-fertilization. The purpose of this process is to replace the old, worn out macronucleus. The macronucleus breaks and disintegrates. The micronuclei divide once by meiosis and than by mitosis to form 8 haploid daughter nuclei (Fig. 6).

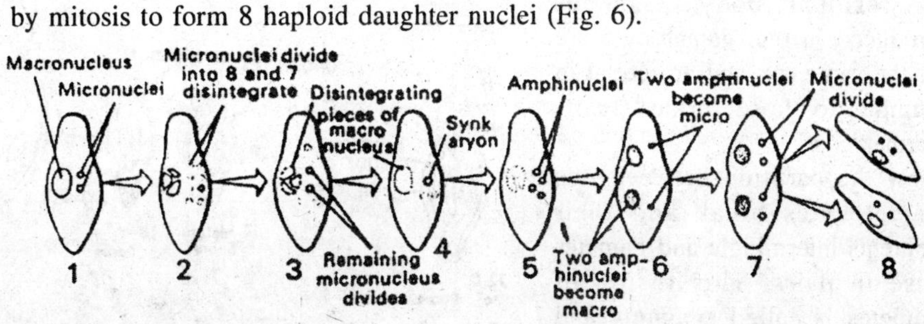

Fig. 6: *Various stages of autogamy in Paramecium aurelia*

- Now 7 daughter nuclei disintegrates and remaining one divide into male and female pronuclei. Both pronuclei fuse to form diploid **synkaryon.**
- This nuclei divide twice mitotically to form 4 **amphinuclei.** Two of them becomes micro and 2 macro nuclei.
- Animal also divides into two daughters recelvmg one macronuclei and another micronuclei.

Cytogamy

- It is the process intermediate between conjugation and autogamy.
- The conjugants unite as in conjugation but without exchange of male pronuclei.
- Male and female pronuclei of same individual fuse to form synkaryon like autogamy.

LIFE HISTORY OF MONOCYSTIS

Monocystis is a sporozoan of earthworm. Its life history involve both sexual and asexual reproduction (Fig. 7).

(I) Sexual Reproduction/Gametogony

- Trophozoite during the phase of sexual reproduction is called **gametocyte/gamont.** Gametocyte become shorter and wider assuming rounded form during monsexual association of two companions of its own kind.
- This association is called **syzygy** (Iso or anisogamy).
- Within the cyst wall, gametocyte shrink and fill the space between them and endocyst with cystic **fluid.**
- Gametocytes now undergo multiple fission/gamogony and produce gametes (about 64) which migrate to the periphery and giving it the appearance of mulberry. Some cytoplasm is left as residual body. Gametes produced in one gametocyte are of the same sex and are equal in number to those formed in its partner.
- Now the partition between two gametocytes break and their contents intermingle and gametes fuse in pairs. This fusion of gametes is called syngamy and they form zygote or sporont.

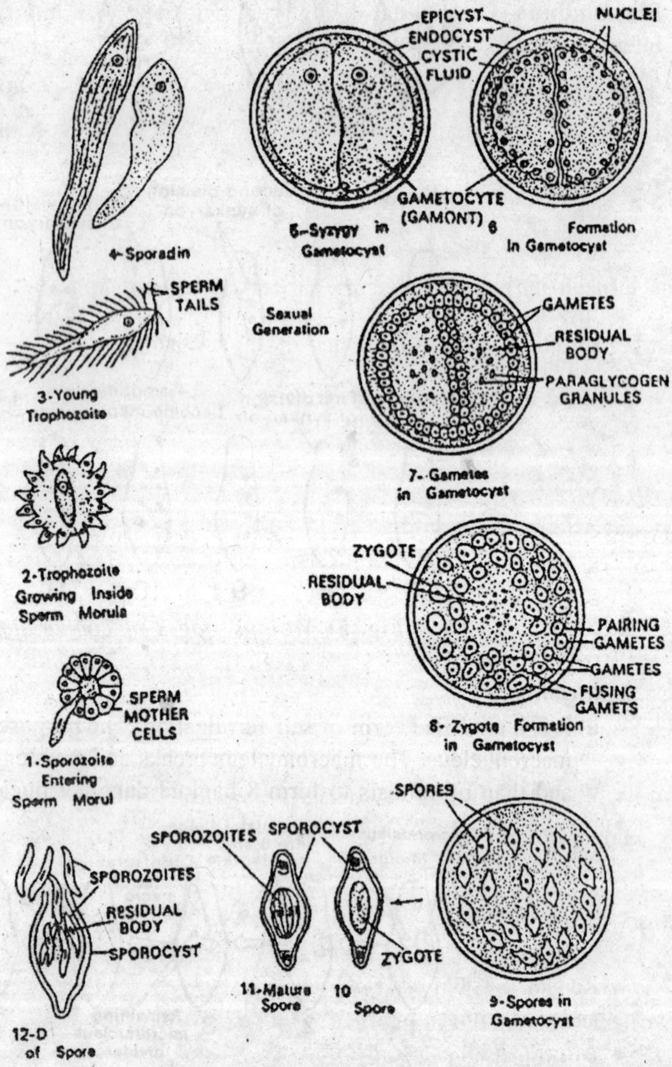

Fig. 7: *Life History of Monocystis*

- Zygote secretes around it a secondary covering, **spore case/sporocyst** and the structure formed is called **spore/oocyst**. Sometimes it is named as pseudonavicella of boat shaped structure.

(II) Asexual Reproduction

After some resting period, zygote undergo multiple fission, sporogony and form 8 uninucleated **sporozoite/ faliciform young** arranged like the loculi of an orange around a core of residual cytoplasm.

Further development does not occur in the same host. So the gametocytes may pass from one earthworm to another during copulation or by disintegration of host.

In *Monocystis,* sexual generation gives rise to asexual by gametic fusion and the asexual generation produces the sexual generation by means of sporozoites *i.e.,* they show alternation of generation.

LIFE HISTORY OF PLASMODIUM

Plasmodium is a digenetic, malarial parasite. Its primary host is female anopheles mosquito and intermediate host is man.

Asexual cycle and schizogony in man

Life cycle of **plasmodium** in man is divisible into **(I) Exerythrocytic cycle (II) Erythrocytic cycle**

(I) Exerythrocytic cycle

- The infective stage of **plasmodium** inoculated into human blood by female anopheles is sporozoite.
- Within half an hour after inoculation, all a sporozoites reach into the liver with blood circulation. They penetrate into liver cells by the lytic action of the secretions of their secretory organelles.
- In the liver cell, a sporozoite actively feeds upon its cytoplasm and grows into cryptozoite which further divides by repeated multiple fission (shizogony) and form **cryptomerozoite.**
- Due to the pressure of the shizont the host liver cell rupture and release cryptomerozoites into liver sinusoid. Some of these cryptomerozoites invade fresh liver cell while others remain in blood stream and invade RBCs.

(II) Erythrocytic Cycle

- After entering into an erythrocyte, a merozoite soon becomes a rounded disc like trophozoite. As it grows a large non-contractile vacuole appears in its centre, pushing nucleus towards one side giving it signet ring appearance.
- Soon the vacuole disappears and the trophozoite becomes **amoeboid.** It starts feeding upon cytoplasm of the host RBC. During its growth, the trophozoite acquires brownish-black haemozoin granules (Proteolytic breakdown of haemoglobin). Globin part of haemoglobin is digested and hematin part accumulates in trophozoites cytoplasm.
- In 2-3 days the trophozoite grows into adult, oocupying almost entire RBC. A number of granules of unknown nature appears in its cytoplasm (Schuffner's dot in ***P. vivax***).
- Now adult trophozoites undergo repeated mitotic divisions to form uninucleated **merozoites.** A small amount of residual cytoplasm with hemozoin granules is left in the centre of schizont. Both schizont and host RBCs burst due to pressure of merozoites and are referred as 'Ghost Cells', destroyed in spleen. This accumulation of hemozoin granules causes the characteristic attack of malarial fever.
- Repeated erythrocytic cycles results in intermittent attack of fever, large scale destruction of RBCs and weakening of patient to a considerable extent.
- After a number of erythrocytic cycles, merozoites invade fresh RBCs grow into different kind of round forms called gametocytes or **gamonts.** Fully formed gametocytes are dimorphic – smaller

male/microgametocyte and larger *female/macrogametocyte* with more reserve food and hemozoin granules. The formation of gametocytes is so regulated that they start appearing in blood at the onset of night and start disappearing completely by the morning.

LIFE CYCLE OF PLASMODIUM IN MOSQUITO (SEXUAL CYCLE)

- When a female **Anopheles** sucks the blood of infected human host, it receives RBC containing different stages of erythrocytic cycle. In its gut all the stages except gametocytes are digested. They hatch out from RBCs of host stomach and become active (at low temperature) to start sexual cycle.
- The microgametocyte undergoes spermatogensis and forms 6-8 haploid nuclei surrounded with cytoplasm. Soon they form whip like **sperm** or **microgamete** by exflagellation and they wriggle about in the lumen of the stomach of the host. The female, macrogametocyte undergo **oogenesis** to form **ovum** or **macrogamete** (*see* Fig. 8).
- Now fertilization cone is formed on one side of ovum and wriggling sperm when comes in contact with cone it enters into ovum and zygote is formed in the stomach of mosquito (syngamy; anisogamy).
- After remaining inactive for some time, it undergo certain changes in 9-10 hours. It becomes warm like organism called **ookinets/vermicule.** The ookinete when comes in contact with the gastric wall start penetrating into the wall by the action of lytic secretion.

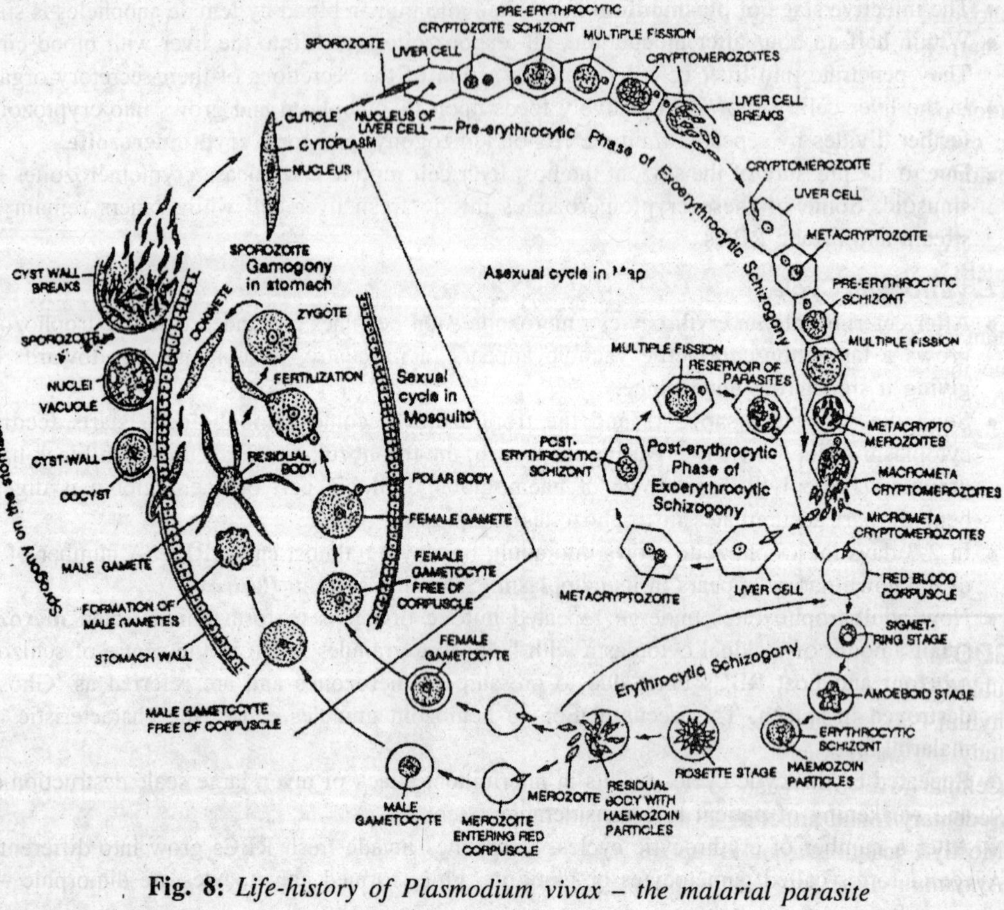

Fig. 8: *Life-history of Plasmodium vivax – the malarial parasite*

- On reaching beneath the peritoneum covering of stomach wall it becomes immobile, spherical and soon becomes enclosed in a thin, semipermeable elastic cyst (formed by zygote and stomach wall). It is called oocyst.
- Oocyst soon grows 5-6 times by initially activel) absorbing nourishment and later due to the formation of large non-contractile vacuoles now it is called **sporont.** Which undergo asexual multiplication by sporogony and from sporozoites. By the pressure of sporozoites oocyst rupture and release them in the haemocoel of the host.
- Floating freely in haemocoelonic fluid they reach the salivary glands of the host and ready to be inoculated into human blood.

Both asexual and sexual generation follow each other in the life cycle of **plasmodium.** This phenomenon is called **alternation** of **generating.** Their sexual generation begins in the human host and is completed in the mosquito while asexual generation starts in mosquito and is continued in man *i. e.,* change in generation cells for a change of host *i.e.,* they also show **alternation of hosts.**

A Comparison of Human Species of Plasmodium

	P. vivax	*P. malariae*	*P. falciparum*	*P. ovale*
No. of parasites per-cubic mm of blood	20-40000	5-10000	50-100000	Unknown
Trophozoite and sharply	Ring large, oval round, rarely amoeboid	Ring small, slit like, less amoeboid	Ring small, round rarely amoeboid	Ring small, amoeboid
Duration of erythro-cylic cycle	48 hours	72 hours	36-48 hours	48 hours
Haematin	Large brown in fine granules	Dark brown in coarse granules	Dark in one or two solid masses	Light brown scattered
Host RBC	Enlarged	Not enlarged	Not enlarged	Slightly enlarged
Pigment granules visible in it	Red Schuffner's dots	Zeimann's dots	Greenish maurer's dots	Schuffner's dots
Incubation period	10-14 days	28-35 days	7-12 days	14 days
Types of malariae	Benign tertian, recur every third day, seldom fatal	Quartan, recurs every fourth day, often fatal	Quotidian that occurs daily or malignant terti-an that recur every third day, often fatal	Benign tertian recurs every third day, not fatal

KINGDOM – ANIMALIA

Subkingdom – Parazoa

Phylum Porifera/Sponges/Pore bearers

Study – Parazoology

1. Cellular level of organisation
2. Sedentary/found attached to the rocks
3. Mostly aquactic-marine except *spongilla* (fresh watch)
4. Aysymmtrical except *leucosolinia*

5. Diploblastic (Mesogloea = mesohyle)
6. Skeleton – Calcareous $CaCO_3$ or silicious (silica) spicule or spongin fibres or absent.
7. Canal system – body is perforated by numerous pores, ostia for inflow of water and a single large opening *osculum* through which water comes out of the body.

There are three types of canal systems

- **Ascon (simplest)**

  Ostia → Spongocoel → Osculum (1) Leucosolenia

  (Ostia: Analogue to mouth; Osculum: Analogue to anus)

- **Sycon** Ostia (Myocytes) → Incurrent canal (Polygonal flat cells pinacoderm) —Prosophyle→ Radial (canal) (Choanocytes flagellated cells) —Apopyle→ Excurrent canal → Incurrent ostia → Spongocoel paragastric cavity (Common to all sponges) → Osculum (Myocytes)

- **Leucon** Most complicated and efficient system e.g., spongilla

  Ostia → Incurrent canal —Prosophyl→ Flagellated chamber (Modified radial canal) —Apopyle→ Excurrent canal → Incurrent ostia → Spongocoel → Osculum

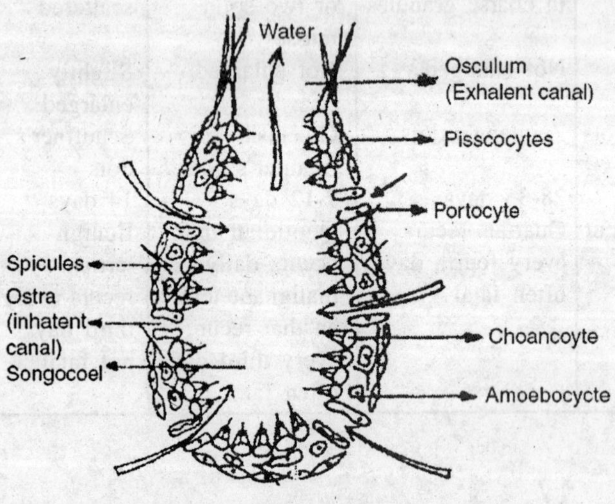

Fig. *Internal structure of* a *sponge.*

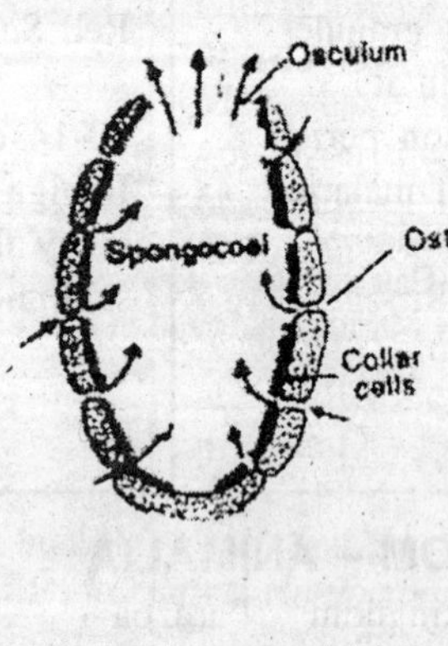

Fig. *Structure of sponogocoel.*

Rhagan canal system – It demospongeae, leuconoid condition is derived from a larval stages, rhagan characterised by pyramid like from with broad base the hypophore and spacious spongocoel. *e.g.*, **spongilla.**

Digestion : Filter feeder, amoebocytes, food-bacteria, protestans Intracellular (inside food vacuole) in thesocytes.

Respiration : Through surface

Circulation : With the help of amoebocytes called **trophocytes** exist in ditferent varieties.

Nervous system : Absent.

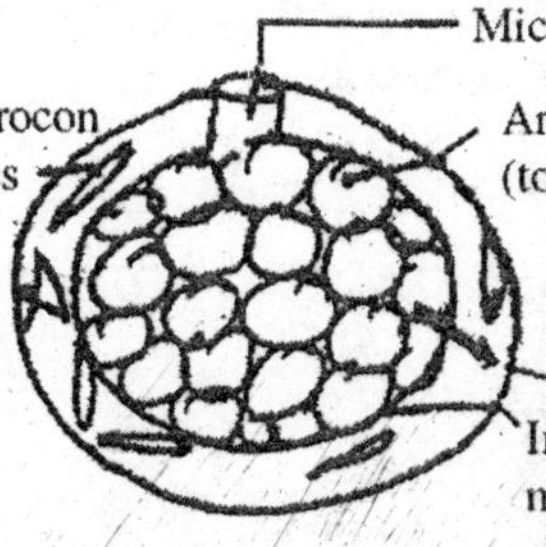

Fig. 9: *Gemmule earlier than* ♂

REPRODUCTIVE SYSTEM

Asexual: By internal budding/gemmule formation in adverse/unfavourable conditions. Also have a great power of regeneration (*see* Fig. 9).

Sexual: Hermaphrodite/monoecious/bisexual both ♂ and ♀ in same.

- Archeocytes produce gonads
- show internal cross fertilization **of protogyne** *i.e.,* ♀ mature.

Development is indirect, cleavage is holoblastic.

Larva – **Amphiblastula** *e.g.,* scypha, free swimming, anterior half flagellated and posterior half non-flagellated Hol1ow

Parenchymula/stomogastula/stereogastula – free swimming

Solid larva, external layer of flagellated cells inner mass of amoeboid cells. *e.g.* **leucosolenia.**

Class (on the basis of nature of skelton)

Calcarea
(Calcispongiae-lime sponge)
- Marine and found in shallow water
- Calcareous spicules
- Chaenocytes are large and body vase-like and measures 10 cm in height

e.g. Sycon (scypha)
- Grantia
- Leucosolenia

Hexactinellida
(Hyalospongiae)
- Marine and found in deep water
- Six rayed silcerous spicules.
- Choanocytes are relatively small
- Body coloured, cylindrical and may measure 90 cms in height

e.g. Euplectella
- (Venus flower basket)
- Hyalonema (Glass rope sponge)

Demospongiae
- Marine fresh water and found in shallow water
- 1–4 rayed siliceous spicules.
- Choanocytes small
- Body asymmetrical and brightly coloured.

e.g. Cliona (Suplhur sponge)
- Spongilla(fresh water sponge)
- Euspongia (Bath sponge)

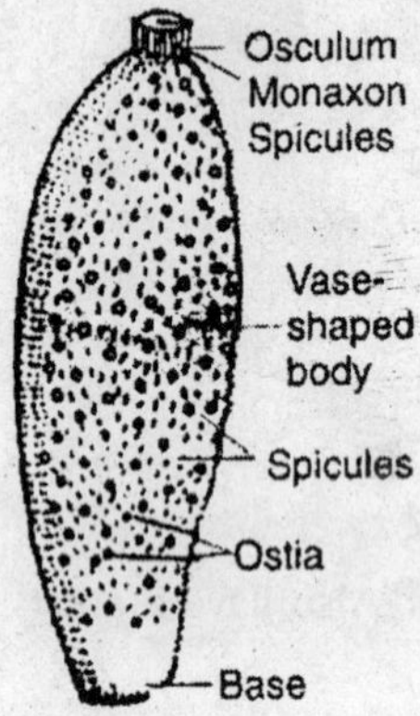

Fig. 10(a) Sycon (A)

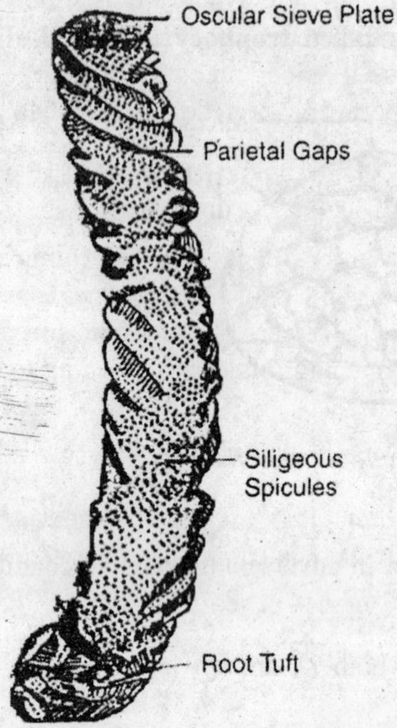

Fig. 10(b) Euplectella (B)

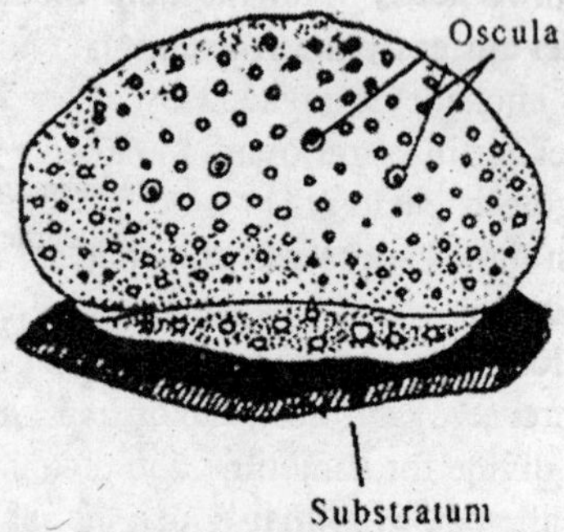

Fig. 10(c) Euspongia

Fig. 10(d) Spongilla (D)

SOME IMPORTANT FACTS

- Sponges are best found in mediterannian sea.
- **Chalina**/Dead man's finger/mermaid gloves.
- **Proterion**/ Neptune's cup/Tallest sponges.
- Connective link between protozoan and sponges is **proterospongia** because of having both amoeboid and collar cells.
- Costliest bath sponge – ***Spongia officinalis*** (natureTurkish/sponge)
- Spheclospongia is the largest sponge.

LIFE HISTORY OF SYCON

Sycon (Scypha) is a monoecious sponge and shows gamete formation. The sperm and the ova do not mature simultaneously as to ensure cross fertilization especially due to **protogyne.** Their gamete formation is initiated by changes in water temperature and photoperiod Gametes are formed from totipotent cells, archaeocytes and sometimes by choanocytes or amoebocytes (*see* Fig. 10 (a, b, c, d)).

Ova

Oogonia/ova mother cell (archaeocyte or meobocyte or choanocyte) migrate to radial canal and undergo double mitosis, producing 4 **oocytes.** These oocytes move to mesenchyme where they increase in size by engulfing nutrients. Once they attain considerable size they undergo meiosis and form **ovum.**

Sperm

Spermatogonium/sperm mother cell (amoebocyte or choanocyte) get surrounded by cover cell. These spermatogonium divide 2-3 times and form **spermatocyte** which later on undergo meiosis and produce sperms.

The different steps involve in the formation of complete sycon are as follows (*see* Fig. 11):

1. Fertilization is internal. Sperm of another organism reach upto radial canal of the **sycon** along with water current. Sperm enters the choancyte make it amoeboid and than migrate into mesohyle. Here this choanocyte invaded by sperm is called sperm transit cell, serves to carry sperm to the ovum. After fertilization ovum is called **zygote.**
2. Zygote is enclosed in a brood capsule formed by amoebocytes. It undergo cleavage.
3. First three successive divisions are vertical and holoblastic followed by unequal horizontal division producing two types of blastomeres named as **micromeres** and **macromeres.** These blastomeres enclose a small cavity, **blastocoel** and the embryonic stage is named as **Blastula**.
4. Micromeres multiply rapidly and develop flagella directed towards blastocoel. The macromere do not divide for sometime and develops a small opening, **blastopore** leading to blastocoel. This stage is called **stomoblastula.** It is a parasite on its parents.
5. Stomoblastula soon undergo **inversion** *i.e.,* turns inside out through mouth. Inverted embryo has flagella directed outward.
6. Now macromeres also divide and closes the mouth and embryo becomes elongated, ready for free life. It is termed as **Amphiblastula.** It is partly flagellated and partly non-flagellated.
7. Amphiblastula rupture the brood capsule and finally leaves the parent body through osculum.
8. After swimming for sometime, flagellated half of the larva invaginates and is overgrown by the large non-flagellated cells. It becomes two layered called **Gastrula** with blastopore.

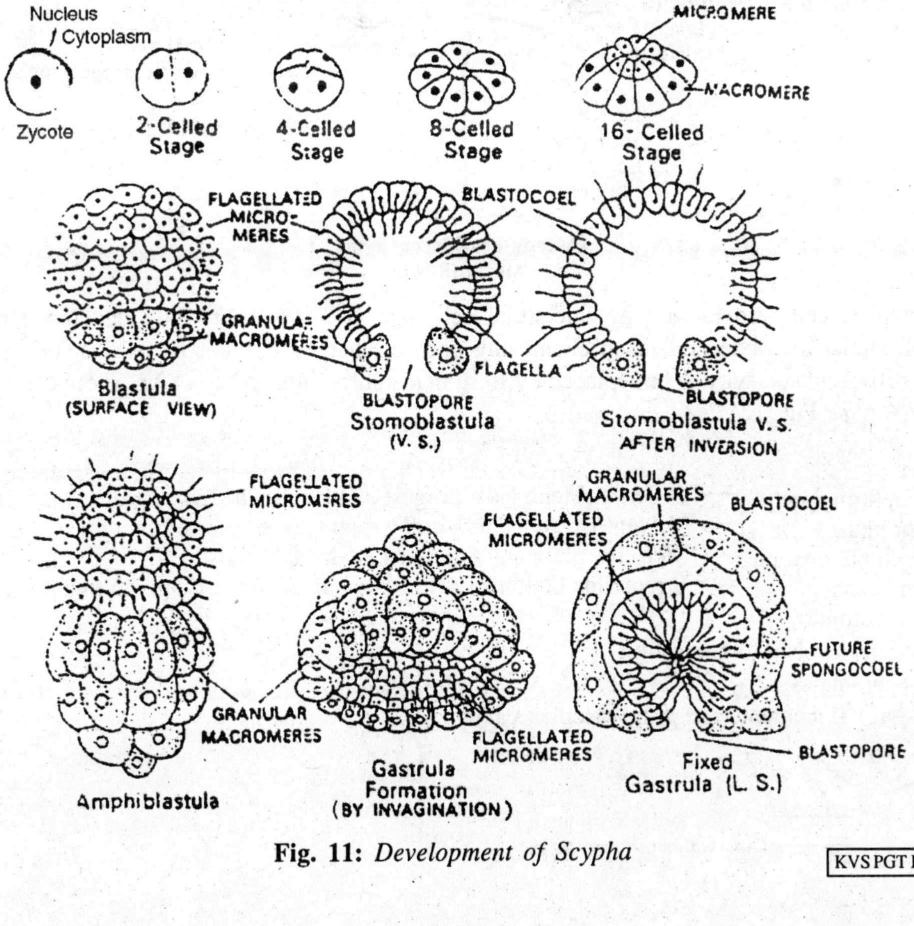

Fig. 11: *Development of Scypha*

9. Gastrula fixes itself to some substratum by blastopore side and form cylindrical structure. The outer non-flagellated cells form dermal layer and flagellated cells covers the spongocoel. At this stage **sycon** resembles **asconoid sponge**. All the pores appear on body surface form dermal ostia. This stage is called olynthus stage.
10. The walls of cylinder gradually thickened due to the formation of mesohyle between two cell layers. Evagination of spongocoel produce radial canal and invagination of dermal layer form incurrent canals. In the mean time archaeocytes produce other types of cells and spicules.

KINGDOM – ANIMALIA

Subkingdom – Eumetazoa

Study – Cnidology

- No. of species known – About 10,000
- Mostly marine except Hydra – Mostly colonical and spine are solitary *e.g.*, **Hydra.**
- Diploblastic

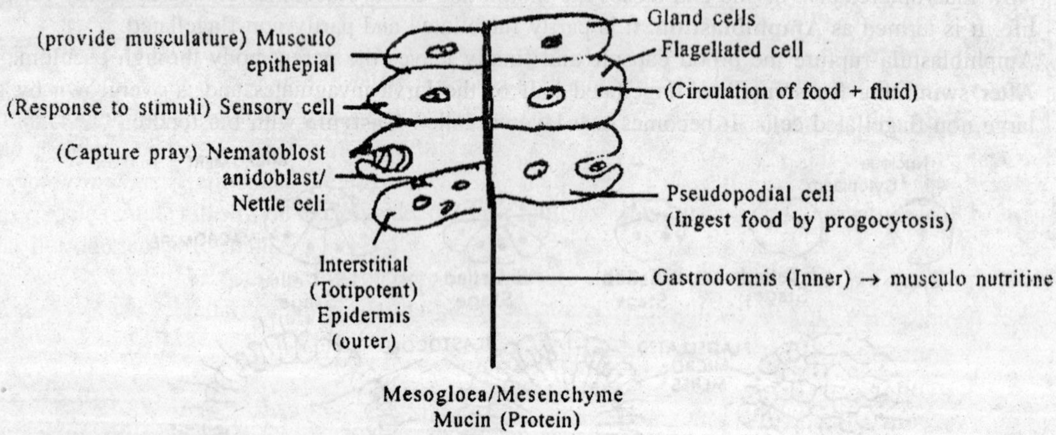

Nematoblast cells are formed by interstitial cells and later on when fully developed migrate to tentacles. Stimulated mechanically and chemically once discharged can not be used again and migrate back to gastrovascular. Cavity to be replaced by fresh nematoblast after every 48 hr. These cells are absent on basal disc (*see* Fig. 12).

Types

Capturing prety for glutination both glutimation and cozling
- Penetrant/stenotele – Largest – Hypnotoxin
- Volvent/Desmoneme – coil a round projections of the prey.
- Steroline glutinant/Atrichous Isorhizas-smalls
- Streptoline Glutinant / Holotrichous Isorhizas (large glutinant)

- Protostome
- Tissue level of organisation
- Acoelomates
- Cavity is coelenteron/gastrovascular cavity.

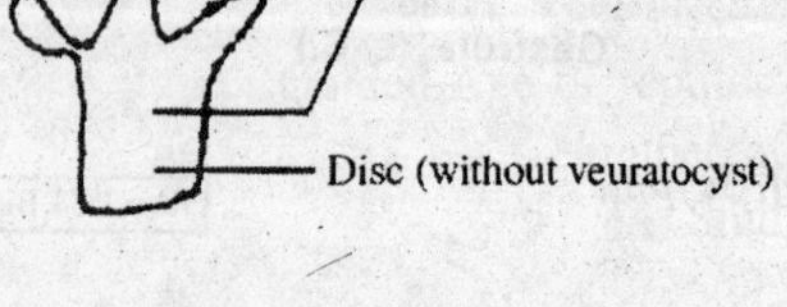

- Radially symmetrical
- Radially symmetrical – 2 Basic body forms (zooids)

Polyp/Hydranth/feeding zooids	Medusal/Gonozooids/Blastostyle
Fixed, sessile, found near low water attached to rocks/weeds	Swim in water
Cylindrical	Ball shaped
Tntacles face upward, surround the mouth and help incatching food	Tentacles face downwards and present all over the margin of the ball
Asexual stage	Sexual stage
Gives rise to redusal by budding	Give rise to polyp by sexual reproduction
	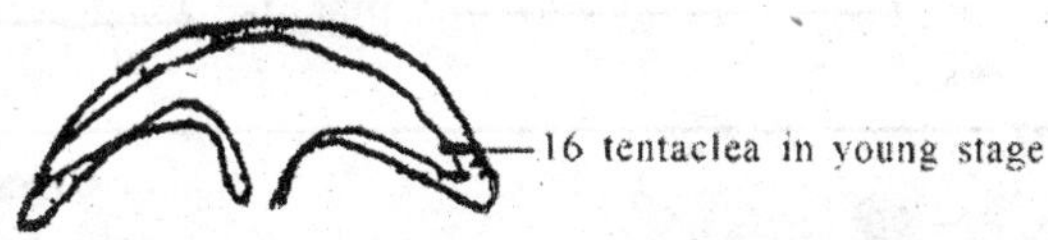
e.g., Gastrozoid – feeding polyp Dactylozooid – protective polyp Gonozooid - reproductive polyp	*e.g.,* Pneumatophore – floating medusant Gonophore – having gonads, incomplete digestive tract.

- **Digestion :** Carnivores, Holozoic,
  Intra cellular – In Gastrodermal cells
  Extra cellular – Coelenteron
  cannot digest starch in the absence of amylase
- **Respiration** – body surface
- **Circulation** – Water enters through mouth
- **Nervous** – Collection of cells forming an irregular network or **plexus** (either side of mesogloea)

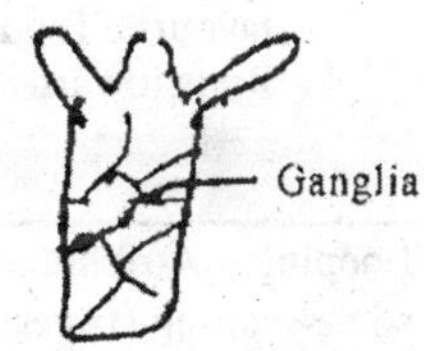

- **Sense organs** – Nematoblast / Cnidoblast

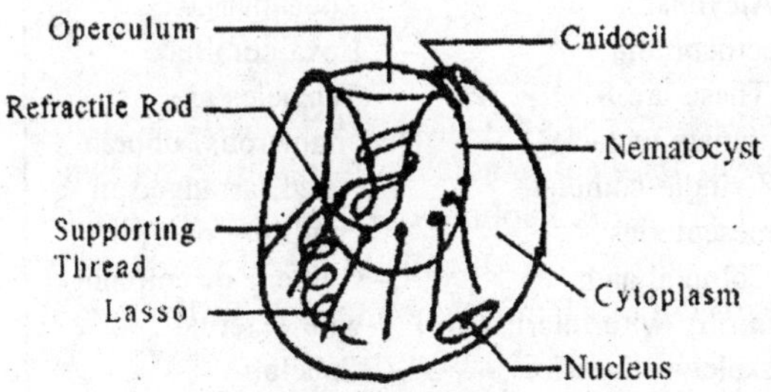

Undischarged

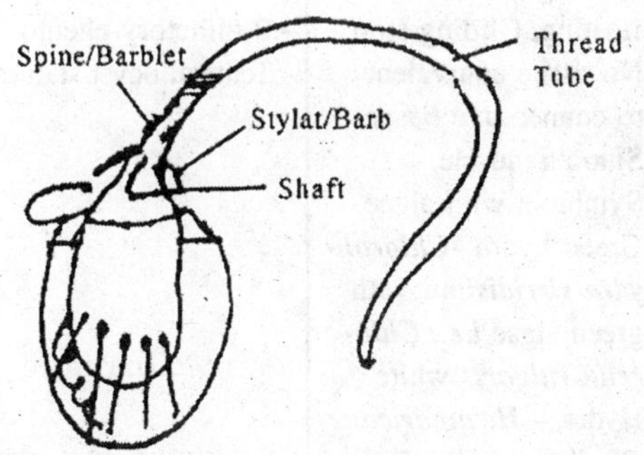

Cnidoblast

Medusae also have ocelli and statocyst.

- **Excretion** – General body surface, ammonotelic.
- **Reproduction**
  Asexual – By budding

Sexual – Hermaphrodite/Monoecious/Bisexual/Both of present show internal or external. Cross fertilization of **protandry** (♂ mature earlier than ♀).

- **Larva** – Planula (uniformly ciliated) tree swimming.

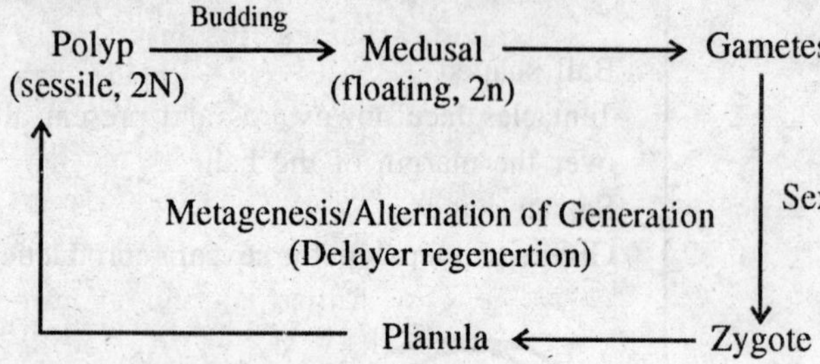

Classes

Hydrozoa
- Polyp stage is dominant
- Medusae simple
- Gonads ectodermal
  e.g., **Hydra** – 6 – 10 tentacles
- Only fresh water coelenterate of
- favourite food – Daphia cyclops
- Buds towards abaxial region

- Looping – Atrichous some-saulting (fastest walking-leasure hr. floating, Gliding stop
- No tissue equivalent to connec tive tissue
- Smooth muscle.
- Symbiont with algae Green hydra -***Chlorohydra virridisima*** with green algae *i.e.*, ***Chlorella vulgaris*** white Hydra – ***H. amaricane***
  Obelia – sea fun/zoophyte (it looks like a plant)
  Sertularia
  Bougainvillea (Like plants)

Scyphozoa
- Polyp reduced
- Medusae dominant
- Endodermal
  e.g., **Aurelia**/Moon Jelly Jelly fish
- Bioluminescent
- Planula – Hydratuba
- Seyphostoma
- Ephyra larval forms

Sense organs
- 8 Rhopalia
- 2 ocelli – Photoreceptor
- 2 olfactory-chemo
- Tentaculocyst/statocyst

Anthozoa
- Exclusively polyp
- No medusal
- Endodermal
  e.g., All corals

Sub classes

- Alcyonaria/octocorallia
  - These are 8 pinnate tentacles 8 single complete mesenteries
  - Colonial and mostly with internal skeleton lives in sea and attached to snails shell cupsied solitary, fixed by hermit crab.
  e.g. **Pennatula** (sea pen/sea feather)
  - **Gorgonia** – sea fan/

- Zooantharia/Hexa corallia
  - Tentacles are numerous, unbranched, arranged in multiple of 5 or 6
  - Solitary or coloning with external skeleton
  (Sea anaemone) solitary, fixed to various objects and can slowly creep when required.
  - *e.g.*, **Adamsia Metridium/Actinidia**

Valella (Sail by wind) **Physalia** (Portugess man of war) – 90% Nitrogen + 1.5% Argon – Neurotoxin like venom of cobra – Suddenly appears and disappears like active navy ship of portugees		Hormy coral – **Tubipora** – organ pipe coral – **Alcyonium** – Dead man's finger – **Corallium** – rubrum-Moonga most precious corel (red coral)	(Sea anaemone) see flower) – Separate sex without skeleton – **Astraea** – stage coral – **Madrepora** – star horn coral – **Meandrine** – Brain coral appears like sulcus and gyri of brain – **Fungia** – mushroom coral – **Heliopora** – Blue coral – Oculina – eye coral

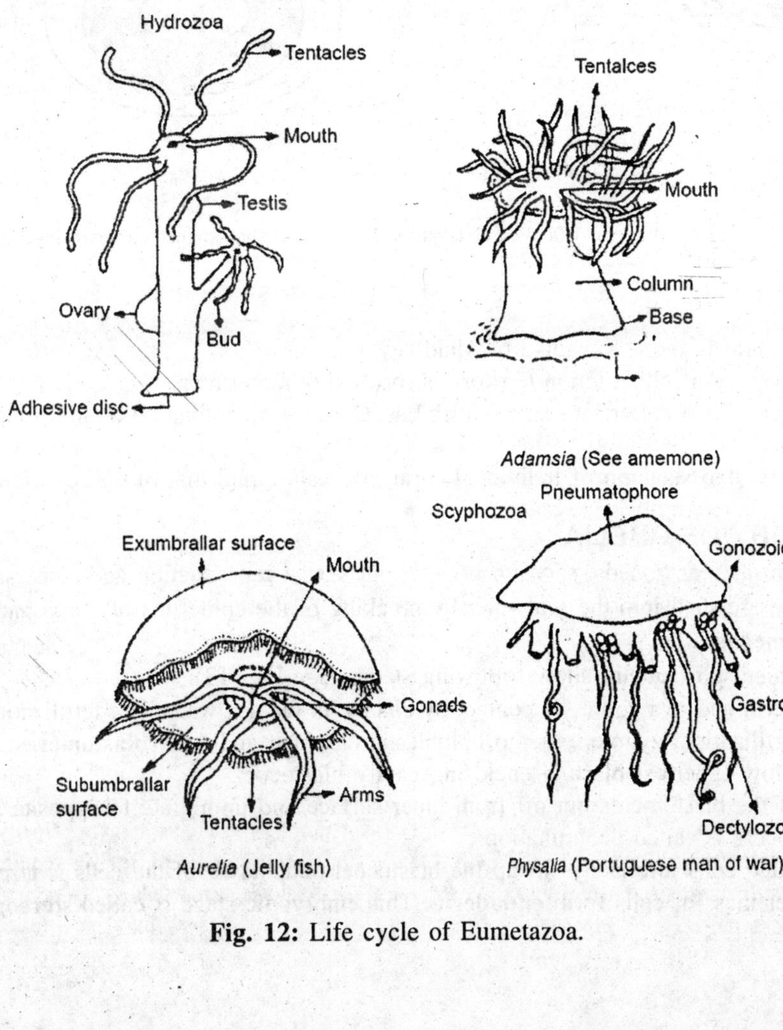

Fig. 12: Life cycle of Eumetazoa.

SOME IMPORTANT FACTS

- **Charybdea** (sea wasp) is the most poisonous coelenterate, can paralyse people swimming in sea.
- In Hydra - Blastocoel is surrounded by blastomere in blastula, some of the cells migrate in the centre tangentially, others divide by outer and inner division to make solid gastula. This repeated process of divison is called **Delanunation.**
- Corals – Marine, mostly colonial some solitary polypoid coelenterates living in a skeleton secreted by them.
- **Coral reef** – Island growing by budding of polypoids and form masses as coral reef. It needs shallw water like Indipecific, central western pacific. It is formed where temperature of water never falls 20°C.

Types of Coral reef

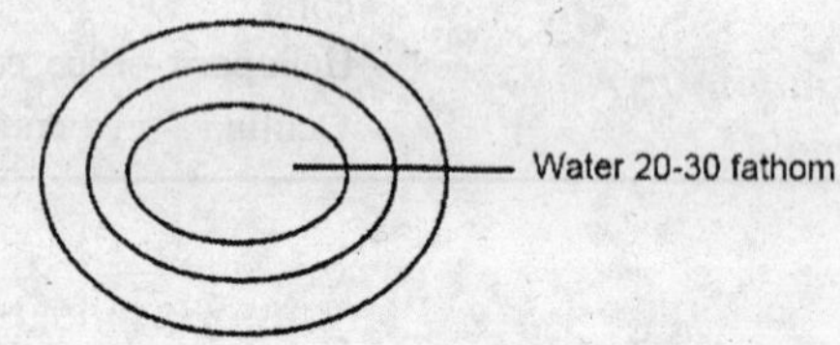

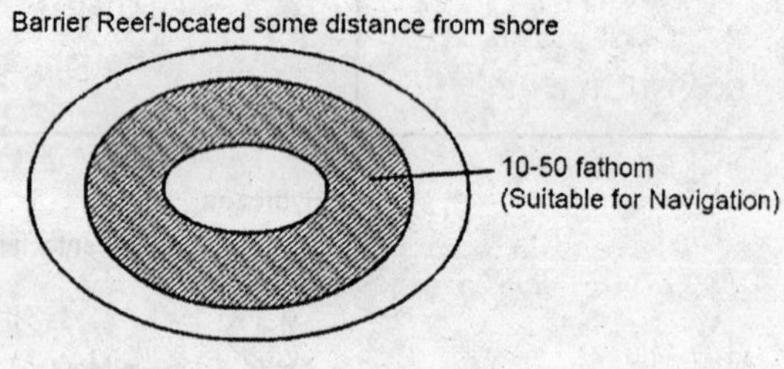

A toll/Lagoon Island/coral Island – Horse shoe shaped reef circles a lagoon. not an island 40-45 m across.

- Largest coral island – Suvadiva of Maldives
- Lakshdeep – An Indian union territory is fortified by coral reef.
- Largest coral reef is Barrier reef in North East Coast of Australia (1200 miles long) also called **coral sea.**
- Calcareous exo skeleton of individual coral in corallite and that of entire colony is corallium.

LIFE HISTORY OF OBELIA

In **obelia** medusal bear gonads, serve to bring about sexual reproduction and dispersal of species. Both sperm and egg are shed into the sea water by breaking of the epidermis of the gonads which results in the death of medusal.

The life history of **obelia** show following stages (*see* Fig. 13):

1. Both sperm and ova comes in contact by chance in the sea water *i.e.*, fertilization in external.
2. After fertilization, zygote undergo holoblastic cleavage and form **blastomeres.** It converts zygote into hollow spherical blastula enclosing cavity blastocoel.
3. Some of the blastomeres out off from inner surface and immigrate to opposite pole in blastocoel. This process is called delamination.
4. Immigrated cells ultimately fill up the blastocoel outer layer of the cells is termed as **ecotoderm** and inner mass of cells form **endoderm.** This embryonic stage is called **stereogastrule** *i.e.*, solid gastrula.

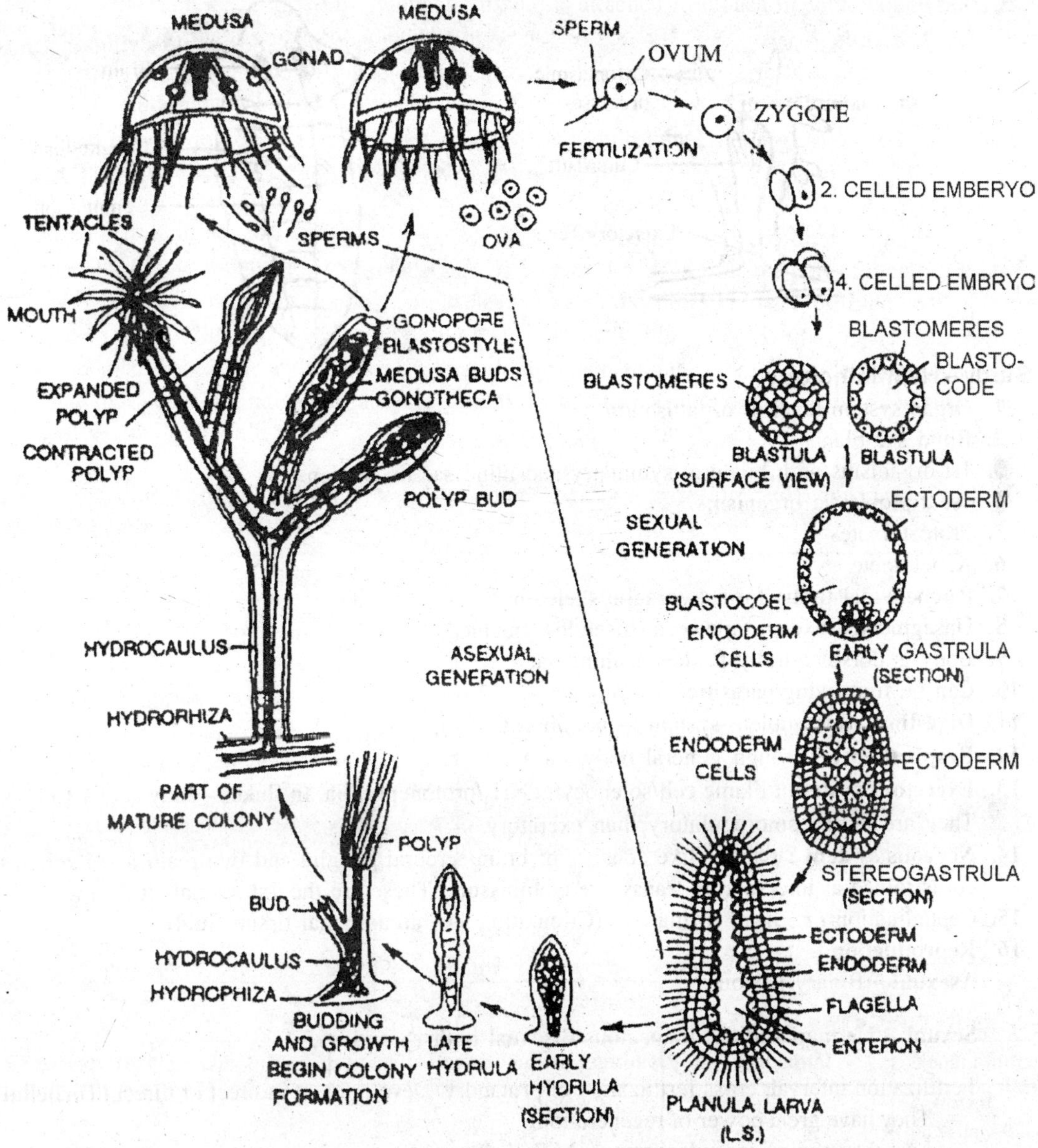

Fig. 13: *Life history of Obelia*

5. Gastrula elongates and its ectodermal cells acquire flagella. This stage is called planula. It has broad anterior end and narrow posterior end. It swims in water from few hours to several days.
6. During free swimming endoderm develops a cavity **enteron** and both the layers show cellular differentiation. Planula now settles on some object and its flagella disappears.
7. Planula's attached end flattens into a disc and free and develops tentacles with manubrium enclosing mouth. This stage resembles Hydra so is termed as **hydrula.**
8. Hydrula now start feeding and initiates a new colony made up of polyps and medusae.

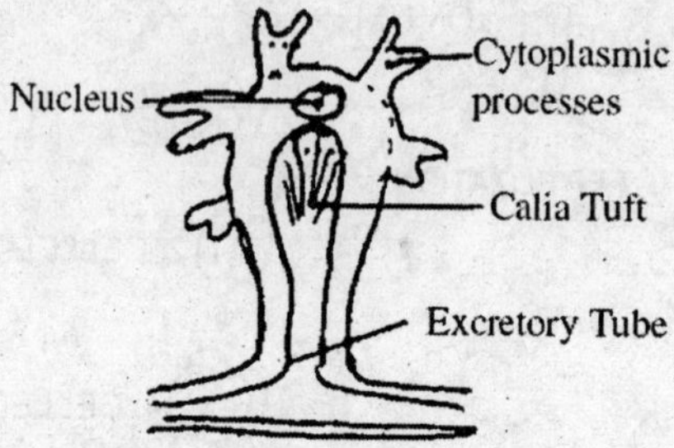

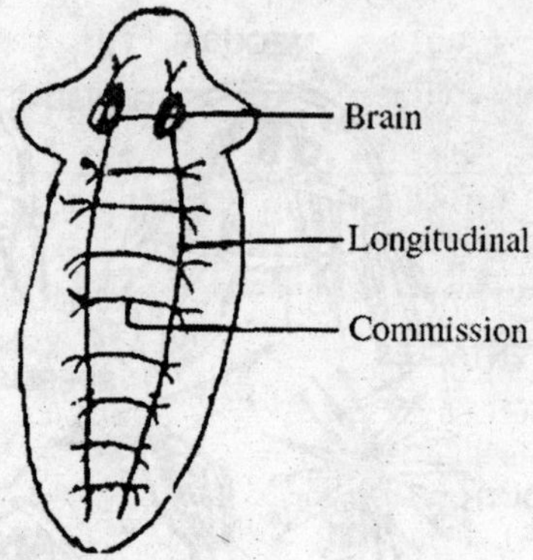

Study – Helminthology

1. Organ system level of organisation.
2. Blind sac plan
3. 1st organisms with bilateral symmetry and blind sac body plan.
4. 1st triploblastic organisms.
5. Protostomates
6. Acoelomete.
7. Parenchymal tissue form hydraulic skeleton
8. Unsegmented except tapeworm (pseudosegmented)
9. Body is dorsoventrally flattened, thin, flat.
10. Can be free living/parasitic
11. **Digestion :** Incomplete system; Anus absent
12. **Respiration :** Through general body surface
13. **Excretory system :** Flame cell/solenocyte; NH_3/protonephridia. In flukes – fatty acid + CO_2, + NH_3. They are more osmoregulatory than excretory.
14. **Nervous system :** Ladder like consists of brain/cerebral ganglia and two main longitudinal nerve cords joined at intervals by transverse commissure. These are the 1st animals to show.
15. Cephaligation *i.e.,* head formation. (Circulation → Parenchymal tissue fluid)
16. **Reproduction**

    Asexual – Binary fission.

    Sexual – Hermaphrodite/Monoecious/Bisexual both ♂ and ♀.

    Fertilization interval, cross fertilization of protandry. Development indirect or direct **(Turbellaria)**

    – They have great power of regeneration.

    – Larval stages – Some planarions – Miller's larva.

    Flukes → Miracidium (in faces) → Sporocyst → Radia Cercaria → Metacercaria

    (Attached to the trapa fruit)

    Tape worm → Hexaconth → onchosphere → cystacercus

(Bladder worm Inuaginate) Alive for 5-6 yr. than caicified by the host

Classes

Turbellaria	**Trematoda/flukes**	**Cestoda**
Sterring type e.g. swiming, Aquatic Ciliated epidermis without cuticle Suckers are rare Mouth is ventral Circular – Diagonal – Longitudnal Testis and ovary 2 Simple history	Hole Endoparasite leaf like body Thick cuticle pr. – Mesenchymal cells Bear 1 or more sucker Mouth is anterior vitelling gland → yolk Circular –Longitudinal oblique Complex history with alteration of host. Polyembryonic	Gurdle from endoparasite tape like body Thick cuticle of tapeworm are living (mitochondira, (ER) called **Tagumen** Head has hooks and sucker wall-ower they absorb food from body surface Ecolecithal eggs (yolk cells outside the egg) Polyembronic

The class trematoda is divided into 3 subclasses

Monogenea/Meterocotylea	**Digenea/Malacotylea**	**Aspidobothria** **Aspidocotylea** **Aspidogastra**
– ectorparasites of aquatic vertebrates – Have special adhesive apparatus, haptor – Life history simple and is without intermediate host. – One egg produces only one worm *i.e.*,one generation e,g., **Polystomum** (present in urinary bladder of frog or turtles)	– endoparasites – Life history includes many larval forms and more than one intermediate host. – There are atleast two infective stages accounts for the, name two generation e.g., **Liver fluke** digenetic host – ***Fasciola hepatica*** – Sheep – ***F. gigantica*** **– cattle** – ***F. buski*** – Intestine of ♂ pig. – **Schistosona** (Blood fluke)/ **Bilharzia** 10 host – human **blood vessels** 20 host – pont snail Sanguivorous, resp. Aerobic Radia absent, ♂ lives in canal pr. in ♂ Gynaecophoric canal Antimony bring used – ***S. raematobium*** – bladder and urinary tract – ***S. manosonic*** – Mesenteric and portal veins – ***S. japanica*** – small veins mesenteric portal schistosomiosis diarrhoea, anaemia enlargements of spleen, liver, pain, fever. – **Paragonium** – Lungfluke – **Clinorchis/Opisthorchis**	– endparasites in the gut of fish or in molluscs. – Adhesive structure is Suckers – Life cycle involves one or two hosts e.g. **Asipdogaster, cotylaspis**

The class cestoda is divided into two subclasses

Cestodaria/Monozoa

- Body is small, undivided
- Scolex is absent
- Single set of reproductive organs
- Embryo bears 10 hooks

e.g., Gyrocotyle

Eucestoda/Merozoa

- Body is long, divided into proglottid
- Scolex bear adhesive organs
- More than one set of reproductive organs
- Embryo bear 6 hooks

e.g., ***Taenia solium.*** (Pork T. worm)

Formation – Strobilation

Shadding – Apolysis people a niose beef eaters is called measly posk

T. saginata (Beef *T. worm*)

10 host – Man

20" – cow. (onchosphere)

Echinococcust – Dog *T. worm*

Hymenolepsis – Dwarf *T. worm* 10 cm (200 proglottids)

Diphyllobothrium – (largest. *T. worm*; 18m; fish *T. worm*)

Classes

Turbellaria

e.g. **Dugesla** (Planaria) Pharnx be can everted

Bipalium – only terrestrial planaria and cnivorous.

Gregosechs

Heteromorphoris the part develops complete dugestia causes – **Hyperplasia.**

Inflamation of liver bilducto block *i.e.,* Gallstone → Haemorrhage → **Fasciolitasis**

- Diarrhoea, anaemia enlargement of spleen liver. pain, fever

Polystomum – urinary bladder of frog/Turtle

Trematoda/flukes

e.g., Liver fluke

10 host

20 host – Pond snail

Cestoda

Appx. 30,000 eggs oviduct and vagina fuse to form ootype.

Single bilobed ovary vasdeference modify to form genital atrium. Protandrous

Formation - Strobilation

Shedding - Apolysis people and more

Hooks absent, 1500 proglottid disease

Taeniasis – Abdominal pain, false appetite, restlessness indigestion.

Due to immunity; large size; only sing tape worm exist in the intestine.

SOME IMPORTANT FACTS

Parasitic adaptations

1. Absence of epidermis and presence of tough horny cuticle.
2. Sense organs like **eye spots** are reduced/absent.
3. Have some **adhesive structures like suckers/hooks** for attachement to the host.
4. Presence of 1 or **more in intermediate hosts** in the life history reduce their period of exposure absence of **organs of locomotion.**
5. **Alimentary canal** is absent in tapeworms.

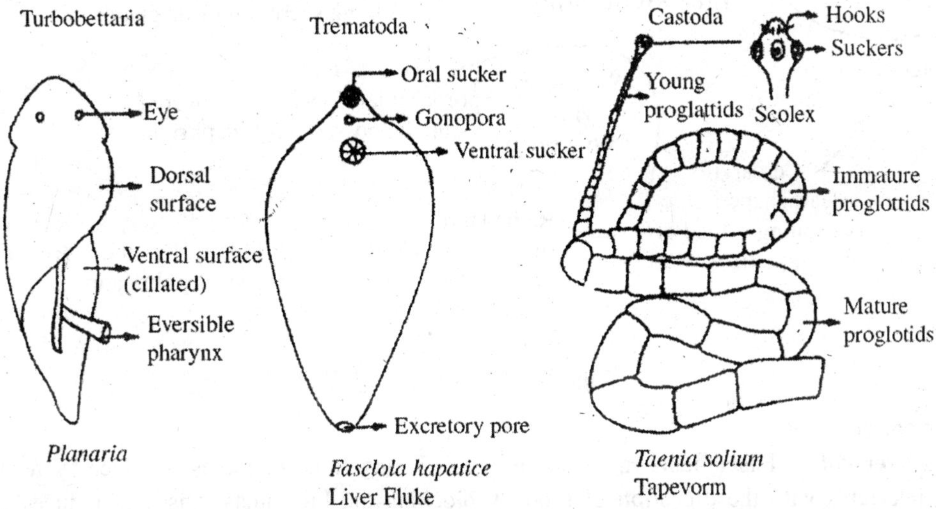

- Anterior sucker of fluke is prohaptor while posterior sucker of fluke is ophisthaptor.
- Man sometimes act as accidental final host of **echinococcus.**
- In **Dugesia** sometimes 10 zygotes and 1000 of yolk cells get enclosed in a prolectine proteinaceous shell called cocoon/egg capsule.
- In Diplozoon (trematode) two larva fuse morphologically and physiologically and remains as such throughout life. They are called **Diporpa larva.**

LIFE HISTORY OF FASCIOLA

It is a digenetic platyhelminthes

- Primary host: Sheep and Goat (Liver and Bile ducts)
- Intermediate/Secondary host : Fresh water snail **Limnaea Planorbis, Bulinus.**

Larval stages

Miracidium, sporocyst, radia, aria, metacercaria life cycle Fasciola includes a period of asexual reproduction during immature stages (sporocyst, radio) followed by a period of sexual reproduction in the adult stages *i.e.*, they show metagenesis (*see* Fig. 14).

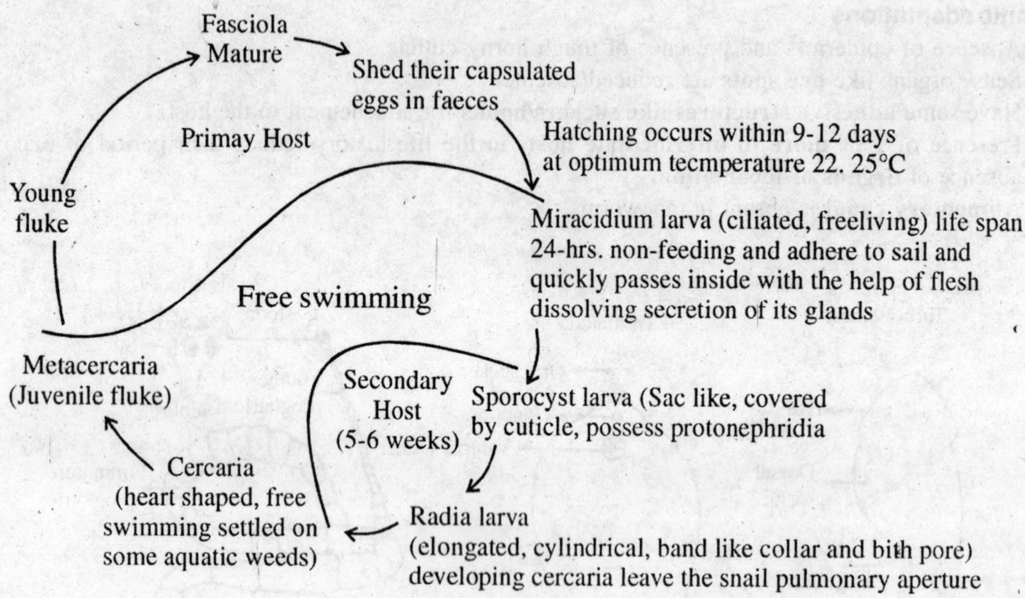

Fig. 14: *Life history of Fasciola*

Disease caused

It causes **liver rot** or **Fascioliasis** in sheep and goat. Young fluke damages the liver by feeding on its cells. It interferes with the digestion of food by blocking the bile ducts. Diseases reduces the vitality of the host and may prove fatal (*see* Fig. 15).

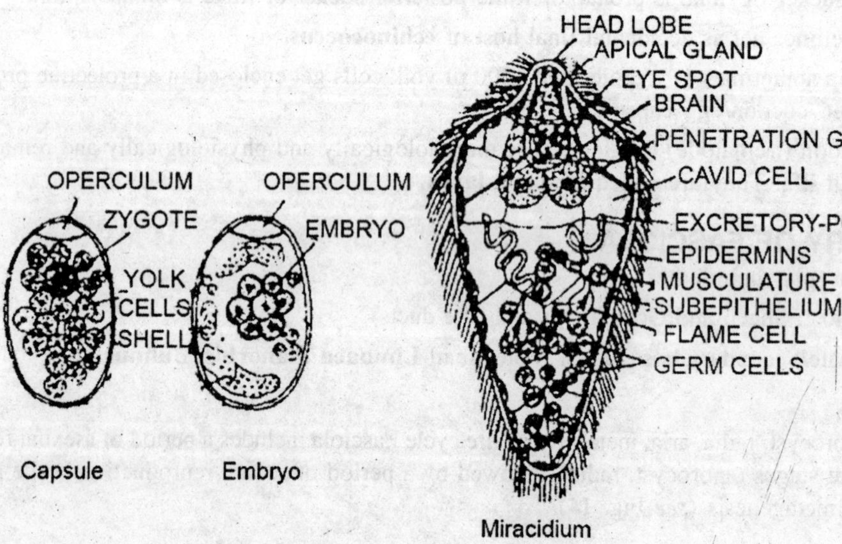

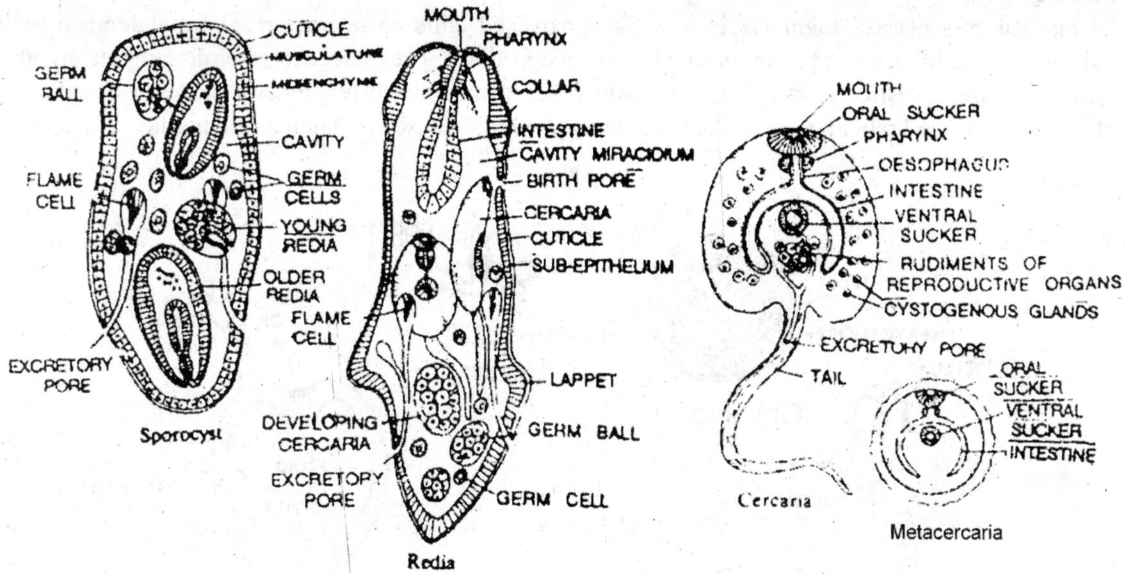

Fig. 15: *Life history of liver fluke. (Fasciola hepatica)*

LIFE HISTORY OF TAENIA

It is digenetic **cestode** Primary host – Man (small intestine). Intermediate/secondary host – pig sometimes dog and sheep.

Due to large size, only one worm normally occurs in one host (*see* Fig. 16).

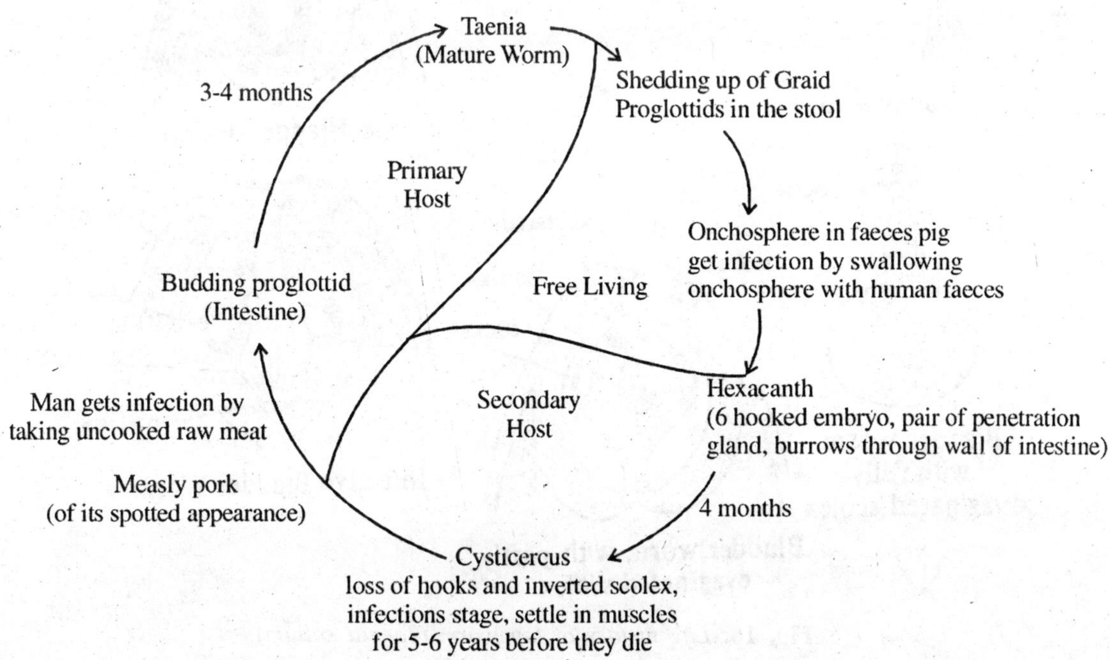

Pathogenicity

Taenia causes a disease **taeniasis** in a weak person and children characterised by abdominal pain, indigestion, vomiting, constipation, insomnia, loss of appetite, low resistance to other diseases etc. Another serious disease is **cysticercosis** caused by bladder worm infection. It may encyst in the eyes and cause blindness or in the brain and prove fatal. Large hydated cyst causes inflammation, diarrhoea, abdominal pain, vomiting etc.

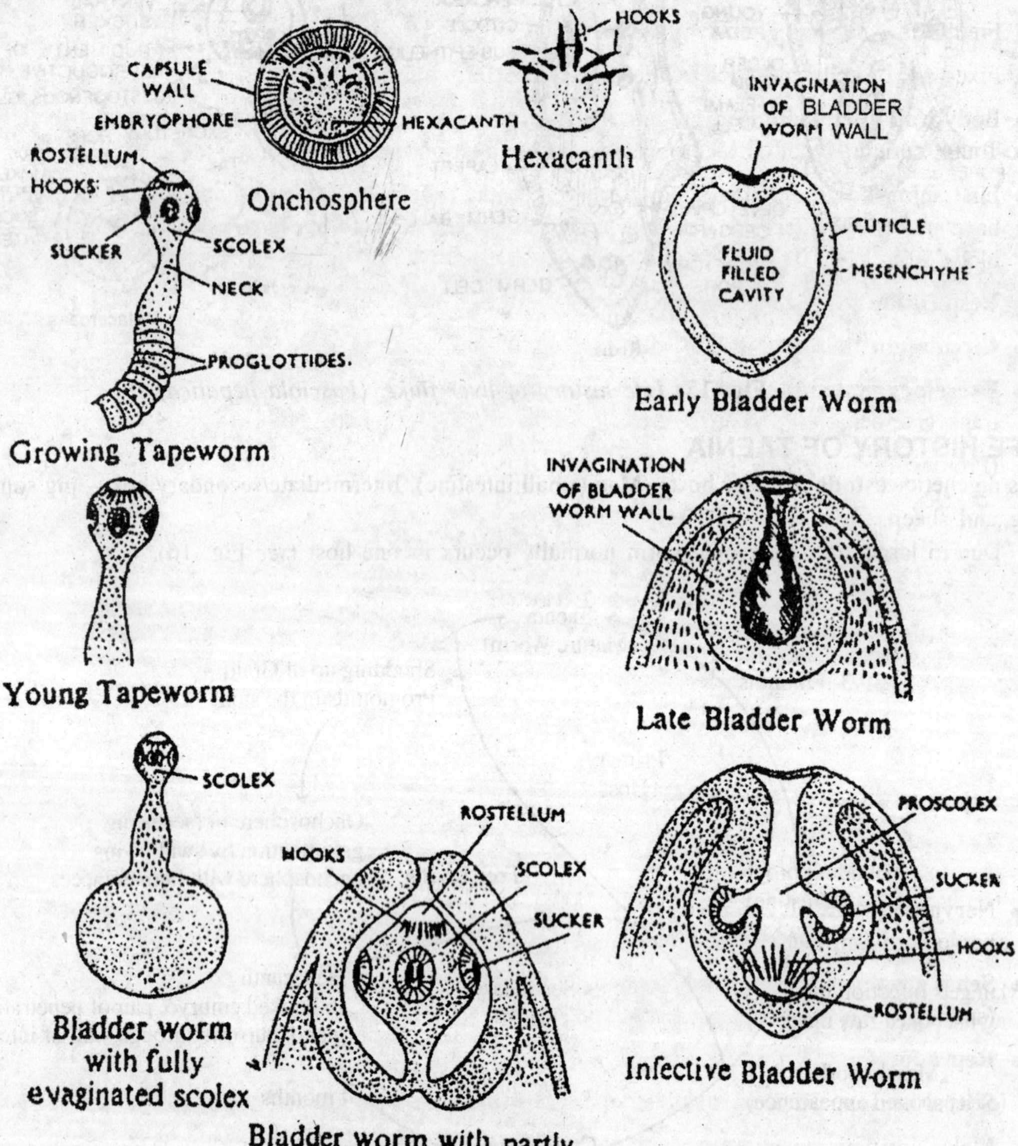

Fig. 16: *Life history of tapeworm (Taenia solium)*

Study – Nematology

- Largest phylum among pseudocoelomates – About 15000 species known organ system level of organisation Triploblastic.
- Unsegmented, round, tube like/ worm like pseudocoelomates act as Hydroskeleton.
- Bilateral symmetry
- Protostome
- Free living/parasitic forms/aquatic forms
- Fixed no. of cells and nuclei called **Eutely** (After maturity)
- **Body wall :** Only **longitudinal** muscle fibres; circular muscles absent so have only restricted length; Tough cuticle, syncitial **locomotion** is by contraction and relaxation of muscles.
- First animals with complete alimentary canal *i.e.*, tube with in tube organisation. Freeliving forms have mouth with teeth to cut and pierce plants. Parasitic forms have muscular pharymx to suck blood from host. Intestine is non muscular.
- **Respiration :** No specific system; through general body surface
- **Circulation :** No specific; by pseudocoel.
- **Excretory system :** In the form of H-shaped canals *i.e.*, 2 longitudinal excretory canals joined by transverse canal emptying through pore just behind the mouth; NH_3 urea.

  (Protonephridia) ; Renett cells (Fig. 17)

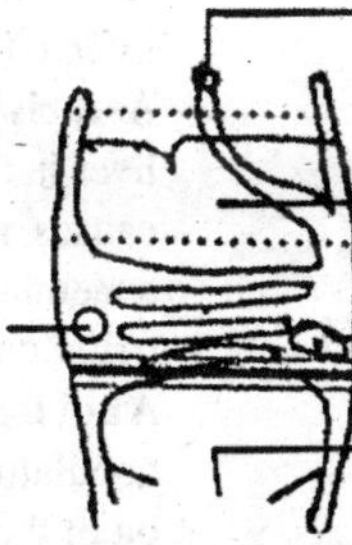

Fig. 17: *Ecretory system in Ascaris*

- **Nervous system :** It comprises of circum pharyngeal nerve ring around pharynx and dorsal, venteral nerve cord *i.e.*, ladder type, interconnected by connectives.
- **Sense organs :** Simple, poorly developed sensory cells as papillae (raised structure, tactile), amphids (small pits, olfactory, chemoreceptive), phasmid (glandulosecretory) and gustatory (taste) organs.
- **Reproduction :** Asexual – Absent

  Sexual unisexual/Dioecious/either male or female showing sexual dimorphism.
- Males are with pineal spicules, cloaca and are smaller than female.
- Fertilization is internal, development in direct.

Class

Aphasmida/Adenophorea

- Phasmids, a unicellular glandulosensory structure is absent
- Amphids are of various types
- Excretory organs are reduced or absent.
- Caudal adhesive glands present

e.g., **Trichinella** (Trichina worm) - present in the intestine of man, pigs. Causes disease **trichinosis** characterised by nausea and muscular pain.

Trichuris trichura (whip worm) : It inhabits the human caecum and appendix. Heavy infection of this worm causes diarrhoea, anaemia, abdominal pain and blood in the stool

Phasmida/Secermentea

- Phasmid present
- Amphids are pore like
- Excretory organs are developed
- Absent

e.g., **Phasmida**

Rhabditis : Freeliving, semiparasitic resides in soil or human vagina.

Meloidogyne (hook knot nematode) : It infect root nodules of all vegetables and a variety of agricultural and horticultural crops.

Strongyloidea: Parasitic female live buried in the mucous membrane of the intestine. Moderate infection leads to diarrohoea with blood and epigastric pain.

Entrerobius/Oxyuris (common pin worm or seat wonn) : It is characterised by cephalic alae :

Most common parasite live in caecum and appendix. Its infection leads to loss of appetite, insomnia, restlessness, inflamation of mucous membrane of infected region.

Ascaris/Giant intestinal round worm: This worm lives in the small intestine of man. Its heavy infection causes ascariasis characterised by weakness and anaemia. Toxin produced by the parasite causes irritation of intestinal mucosa and impair digestion.

Ancylostoma (Hook worm) : Male is having copulatory bursae. They live by firmly anchoring bit of the intestinal lining into its mouth. Its infection causes severe anaemia. bloody stool. decrease in immunity.

Dracunculus (Guinea worm/Fiery serpent) digenetic, inhabits the subcutaneous tissue in man and its intermediate host is cyclops (water flea). If form blisters in man. Its heavy infection causes itchiness, nausea, diarrhoea, vomiting, asthma and eosinophilia.

Wuchereria/Filarial worm

Viviparous, Digenetic, primary host is man and secondary host is culex or Aedes, diurnal and show day night periodicity *i.e.,* during day time it lives in deep seated blood vessels but at night they come to peripheral blood vessels so that it is sucked by mosquitoes. It causes disease elephantiasis or filariasis characterised by blocking of lymph vessel and swelling of the part affected.

Loa loa (eye worm)

It lives in the subdermal connective tissue of man. Man gets infection by bites of infected dearfly chrysops. Sometimes this worm pass across the eyeball and may produce conjunctivitis in the eye.

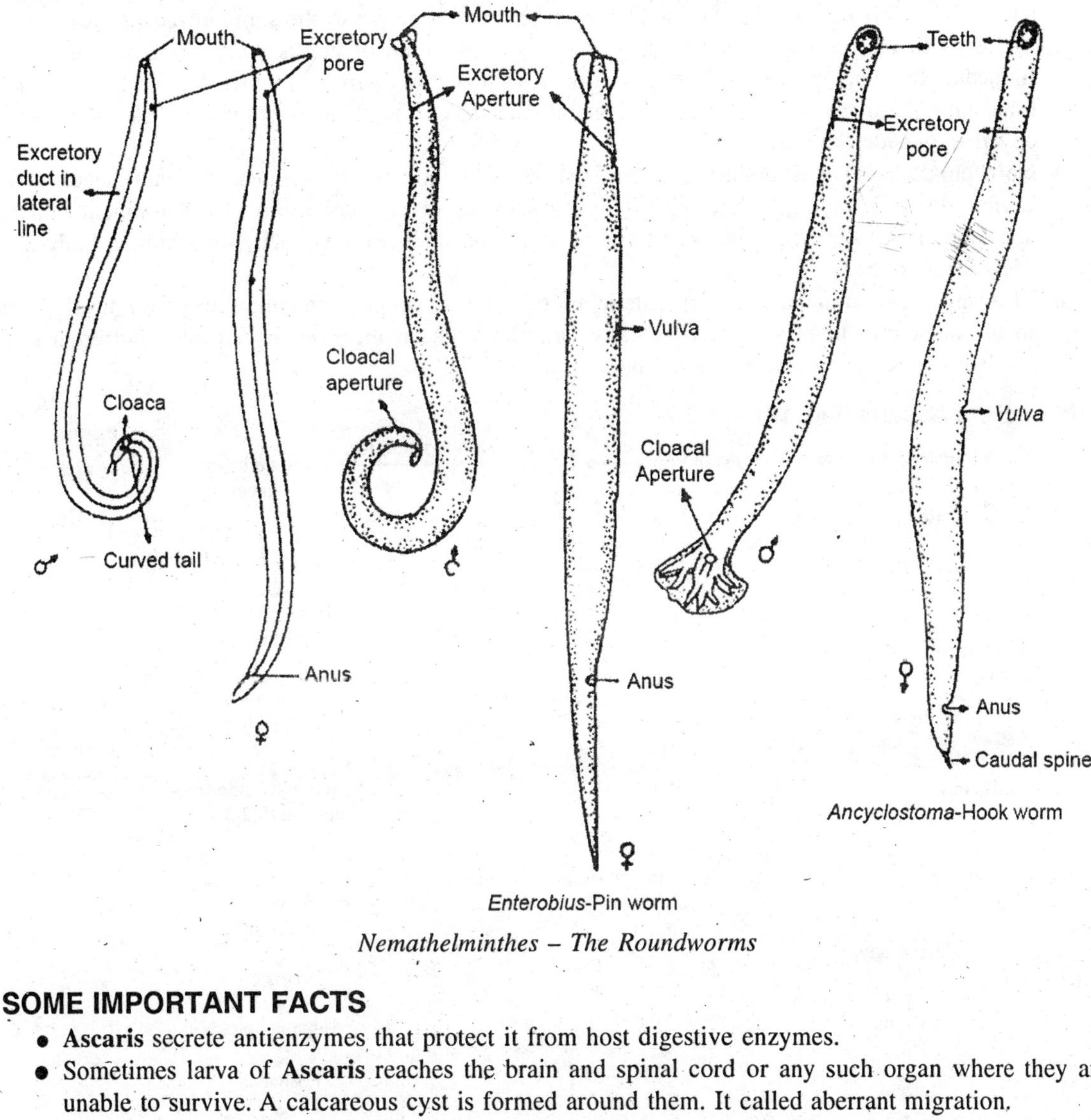

Ancyclostoma-Hook worm

Enterobius-Pin worm

Nemathelminthes – The Roundworms

SOME IMPORTANT FACTS

- **Ascaris** secrete antienzymes that protect it from host digestive enzymes.
- Sometimes larva of **Ascaris** reaches the brain and spinal cord or any such organ where they are unable to survive. A calcareous cyst is formed around them. It called aberrant migration.
- **Toxocara canis** (dog ascarid) : Larva hatching from eggs ingested by a pregnant female dog, migrate through placenta to enter the developing embryos of foeti. Larva is known as **larva migrans.**
- In **Ascaris, 4** moults takes place in life cycle first in the open, second and third in lung alveoli and fourth in human intestine.

LIFE HISTORY OF ASCARIS/INTESTINAL WORM

- Sexes are separate in **Ascaris** with distinct sexual dimorphism. Male are shorter in size, curved downward have cloacal opening with two pineal spicules.

- Male reproductive organs are monorchic *i.e.,* they occur in single set and female reproductive organs are didelphic *i.e.,* occur in double set.
- Both male and female worm copulate in the host intestine in such a way that males cloacal aperture apposes the vulva of female. Sperms by amoeboid action move to the seminal receptacles.
- The eggs in the secondary oocyte stage reach proximal end of uterus where fertilization occurs. Immediately after fertilization of egg fertilization membrane is formed which harden to form shell. Later on eggs cytoplasm produce lipid membrane inside the shell. Uterine wall also add protein covering outside the shell.
- Now female lay eggs through vulva into host intestine and are passed out along with faeces (about 27 million eggs/ laying). Eggs are highly resistant to adverse condition of environment. Further development of egg needs low oxygen, moisture and temperature (85°F) than human body so it starts in the open.
- Cleavage is determinate, spiral. In eutelic animals mitosis stops following embryonic development so the most growth in size of a nematode results from an increase in cell size. Different steps involved during life cycle are given below.

Life Cycle of Ascaris (Fig. 18)

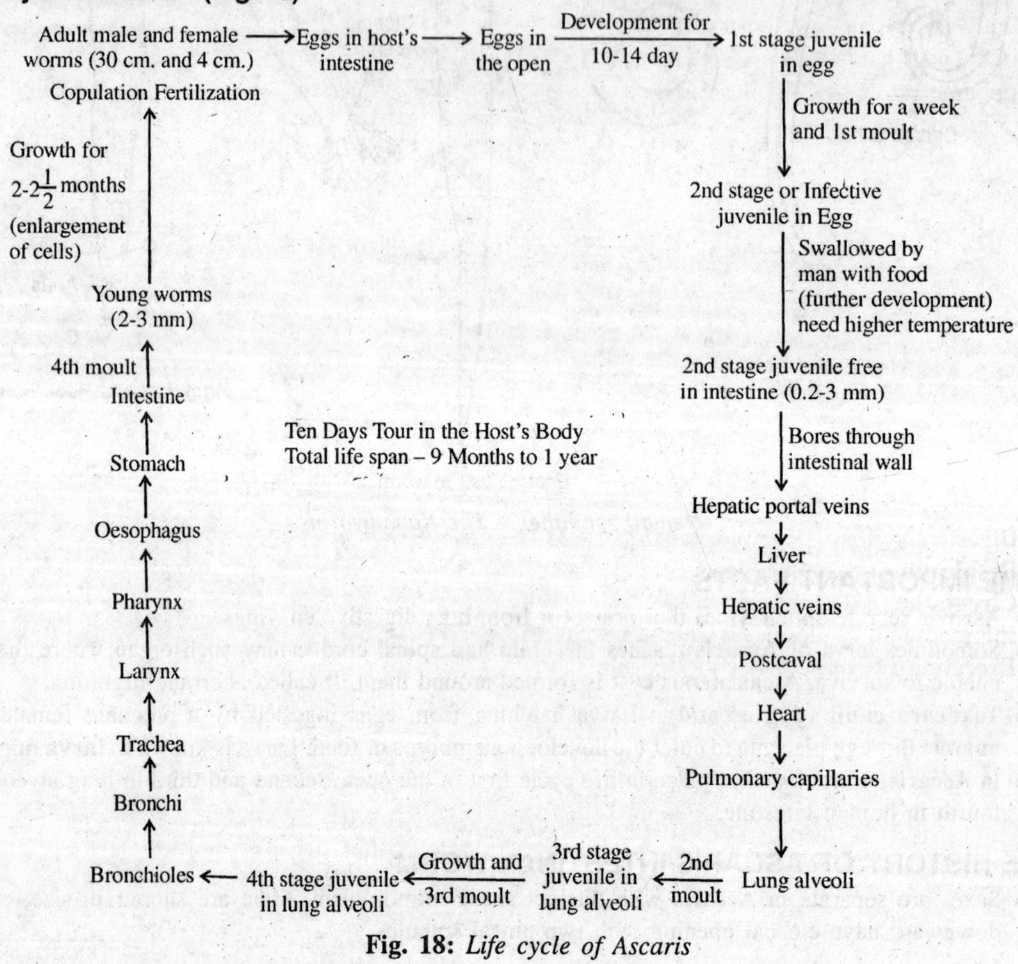

Fig. 18: *Life cycle of Ascaris*

Heavy infection of **Ascaris** proves serious. It causes weakness and anaemia as worm share host's food. Toxins produced by parasite causes irritation of intestinal mucosa and impair digestion. Blockage of intestine may cause death (at least 100 worms) can plug intestine sometimes worm migrate the vermiform appendix or bile ducts into the liver. The course of juvenile through the body may cause internal bleeding. **Ascaris** infection increases level of immunoglobulin G and E (IgG and IgE).

Kingdom — Anamalia
Sub-kingdom — Eumetazoa
Phylum — Annelida (Segmented Worms)
Annulus — Ring Worms

Includes over 9000 known species.

1. Organ system level of organisation.
2. Triploblastic
3. Bilateral symmetry, tube within tube body plan
4. Protostome
5. **Metameric** segmentation – segments called metameres or somites except clitellum region.
6. True coelomates/schizocoel : Act as hydroskeleton so can make body stiff.
7. Body is covered by transparent, moist nonchitinous cuticle secreted by ectoderm.
8. Body wall has outer **circular** inner longitudinal and **oblique** which helps in locomotion.
9. **Locomotion** is by chitinous **setae** or by appendages called **parapodia** (locomotion and respiration) or by suckers.

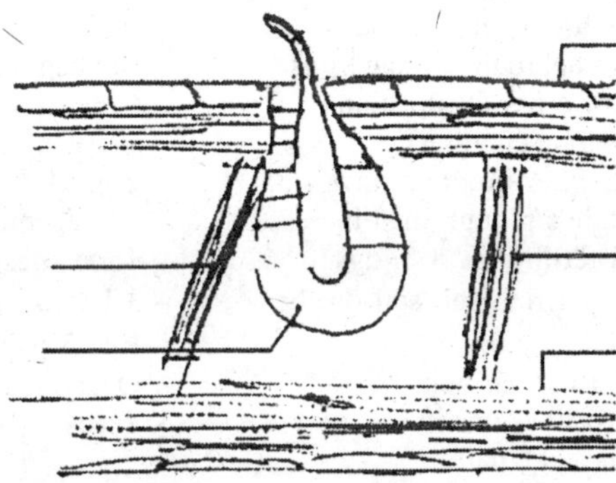

10. **Digestive** system is complete and digestion is extra-cellular.
11. **Respiration :** Skin or gills
12. **Circulation :** 1st animals with closed circulatory system **Haemoglobin** or **erythrocruorin** or chlorocrounin in plasma or called Haemocoelomic system.
13. **Excretion :** Nephridia, excretory material may be NH_3, Urea.

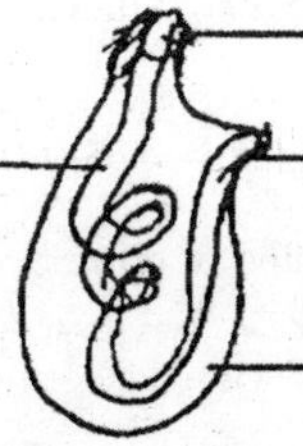

14. **Nervous system:** Dorsal cerebral ganglia/brain **nerve ring** and double ventral nerve cord with nerves ganglia in each segment or circumpharyngeal nerve ring.
15. **Reproduction**
    Asexual: Number of segments. There regeneration power is more at the posterior end.
    Sexual: Sexual dimorphism. Fertilization external or internal indirect development or direct development.
16. **Larva:** Trochophore.

Classes

Polychaetae Many Hair	**Oligochaetae** Few Hair	**Hirudinariae**
– Marine	– Terestrial and fresh water	– Ectoparasite with anterior and posterior suck and fresh water
– Clitellum cingullum absent so no cocoon formation	– **Clitellum** present so eggs are laid in cocoon (summers)	– Clitellum not distinct (appears during breeding season seg. 6, 7, 8, 9, 10, 11) (April, May, June)
– Body has setae/parapodia for locomotion *e.g.,* crawfing – parapodia swimning muscles	– Few setae; no parapodia (Ist and segment and last clitellum without setae)	– No setae; no parapodia
– Dioecious	– Hermaphrodite protandrous	– Hermaphrodite
– Fertilization external with larvae	– Show cross fertilization development direct	– Cross fertilization direct development
e.g., **Nereis** (Rag worm/sand worm/clam worm) closed circulation without heart	*e.g.,* **Pheretima** (earthworm)	*e.g.,* **Hirudinaria** (cattle fish)
	– Nature's plough man increase soil fertility as it brings mineral rich sub soil on the surface by digging	– 33 segements Ist 2 and last form sucker
– Nuchal organ-olfactory and chaemosen- sory behind detect pray. Ova and testis are not permanent	– Used as fish bait	– 3 Jaws so prode Y shaped worm
	– 100-120 segments	– Eye 5 pairs ♂ 10th ♀ 11th
	– Testis – 11 pair	– Ovary – 1 pair
		– Testis – 11 pairs
Meteronereis – with both sexual and asexual part.	– Mouth – Ist segment **peristomium**	– Anus – 26th segment
	– ♀ gonopore – 14 th	– Crop to store blood
Epitoke – Posterior parts with gonads and leafy outgrowth. Atoke – Anterior asexual part Heteronereis can swim actively on the surface of sea to	– ♂ gonopore – 18th Dorsal pores – 12, 13 seg. Coelom- comes out of it to moist skin. Copulatory papillae 17, 19th seg. 2 pairs	– **Nephridiopore** 17 pairs (6 to 22 segment)
		– Beneath muscle layer of conn- ective is primary cells
		– Botryoidal tissue meant for excreation.
shed ova and sperm (swarming)	blood gland– 4, 5, 6 in pair.	– **Protandrous**
compressed and functionless	Spermathecal pore ↓	– Salivary gland secrete very costly anticoagulant
Epitoky – Non sexual form to sexual form		– Hirudin used as anticoagulant of blood and used during bleeding

- ♀ produces **fertilium** attract ♂ is.

Anus – pygiduim
e.g., **Arenicola** – lug worm
Aphrodite – sea mouse
Chaetopterus – paddle bioluminescent worm

Tubifex – Blood worm Hb has high affinity for oxygen its presence indicates sewage contamination of aerated water *i.e.,* helps in purification of polluted fresh water.

5/6, 6/7, 7/8, 8/9.

Anus – Last seg. Lymph gland 10 Chloragogen cells/yellow cells = liver of vertebrates. 4re pair of heart 7,9 (Lateral) 12,13 (Lateroesoph – ageal)

Dorsal B. Vessel true heart Gizard- circular muscle highly developed **Nephridia** Pharyngeal – 4, 5, 6 Septal – behind 15 opens into intestine chromophil cells opens salivary chamber (pharynx to lubricate food) Calciferous gland in the stomach remove $CaCO_3$ from the blood and excrete it through anus. The pigment porphyrin protects it from sunlight.

- Typhlosole - large sized fold in intestine starts from 26th and till before 25 last segments. 50% urea 40% NH_3

- Open circulation
- Phlebotomy is method of blood-letting to suck the impure blood by applying a lean hungry leech to the skin.

e. g., **Hirudo** (Medicinalleech)

Pontobdella (Fish leech/shate sucker)
Acanthobdella - connective link between oligochaete and hirudinea.

ORGANISMS OF HEALTH AND AGRICULTURAL IMPORTANCE

OUTLINE OF CLASSIFICATION OF PHYLUM CHORDATA

Introduction

Kingdom-Animalia

Sub-kingdom – Eumetazoa (Multicellular)

Phylum-Chordata (Notochord, dorsal hollow nerve cord, paired gill slits)

Group

Protochordata/Acrania
(Head absent)
(Lower chordate)
Sub-phylum

Urochordata/tunicata
– Notochord & nerve cord only in tadpole like larva

Cephalochordata
– Notochord and nerve cord present throughout life along length of body

Euchordata/Craniata
(Higher chordate)

Distinct vertebral column & brain protected by skull
Sub – phylum
Vertebrata
– Notochord form vertebral column

Division

Agnatha
– Without jaws
– Paired appendages absent
– Inner ear with 2 semi-circular canals

Gnathostoma
– With jaws
– Paired appendages
– Inner ear with 3 semi-circular canals

Class

Ostracodermi
- World's first vertebrate include extinct armous fishes

Cyclostomata
- Circular mouth
- Parasite + Scavengers

Super Class

Pisces
- Fish like aquatic form
- Paired fins
- Respiration through gills
- Anamniotes

Tetrapoda
- Aquatic or terrestrial form
- Paired limbs
- Respiration through lungs

Class

Placodermi
- Extinct jawed fishes with bony head shield

Chondrichthyes
- Cartilagenous fishes
- Skin with placoid scales

Osteichthyes
- Bony fishes
- Skin with cycloid, ctenoid scales

Class

Amphibia
- Dual life *i.e.*, terrestorial & aquatic
- Skin thin, moist glandular, vascular and without exoskeleton
- Anamniote

Reptilia
- Terrestrial, creeping
- Skin dry, non glandular covered by ectodermal horny scales
- Amniote

Aves
- Flying vertebrates
- Forelimbs modified to form wings
- Warm blooded
- Amniote

Mammals
- Body covered by hair
- Female with mammary glands
- Warm blooded
- Amniote

KINGDOM – ANIMALIA

Sub-kingdom – Eumetazoa
Phylum – Chordata
Sub-phylum – Urochordata/Tunicata tail

General characters

- Number of species — About 2000
- They are marine & sedentary (fixed).
- Their body is enclosed in a *test/tunica* (cellulose like polysaccharide called Tunicine $(C_6H_{10}O_5)_n$).
- Their coelom is unrecognised.
- Notochord is present in tail region in larva.
- Alimentary canal is complete and are ciliary feeders.
- Respiration is through numerous gill slits (stigmata).
- They show open circulation. Their heart is neurogenic and their blood flow shows periodic reversal. They have special corpuscles, vanadocytes (except in *herdmania)* to extract vanadium from sea water and store it in blood vessels.
- Dorsal tubular nerve cord only in larval stage which is replaced by a single dorsal ganglia in adult.
- Sense organs in the form of receptors.
- Excretion is by nephrocytes, Pyloric gland or neural gland (Homologous to pituitary gland of vertebrates).
- Asexual reproduction is by buddings.
- Mostly hermaphrodite and development is indirect. Free swimming Ascidian larva show retrogressive metamorphosis.

- They possess the ability of dedifferentiation *i.e.*, grow smaller during starvation and develop again on normalization of conditions.

SUB-PHYLUM UROCHORDATA IS DIVIDED IN TO THREE CLASSES

Class

Ascidiacea	**Thaliaceae solitary orcolonial**	**Larvacea (Appendicularia)**
– Solitary & colonial bottom dweller	– Free swimming, pelagic	– Solitary, free swimming, pelagic or neotenic
– Test permanent, well develo-ped & thick	– Test permanent, thin and transparent	– Test forming a temporary" house, renewed periodically
– Atrium opens dorsally by atriopore	– Atriopore is located posteriorly	– Atrium & atrium aperture is absent.
– Pharynx large with many persistent gill slits	– Pharynx with 2 large or many	– Gill slits 2, opening directly to gill slits outside
– Larva show retrogressive metamorphosis	– Show remarkable alternation of generation by gonozooid (solitary, sexual form) and oozoid (asexual, gregareous form)	– No metamorphosis

Order

Enterogona	**Pleurogona**
– Gonads are unpaired and projecting behind the intestinal loop	– Gonads are paired and lies in the atrial wall
– Neural gland is neutral to nerve ganglia.	– Neural gland is dorsal or lateral to nerve ganglia
– Larva has cerebral eye & statocyst.	– Larva has statocyst but no separate eye
e.g., Ascidia – The British sea squort	*e.g., Herdmania* – Sea potato/sea squirt as it ejects two gets of water when disturbed
Ciona– The tube sea squirt.	*Molgula, Botlyllus*

Order

Doliolida/Cyclomyaria	**Pyrosomida/Meromyaria**	**Salpida/hemimyaria**
– Body is barrel shaped	– Compact cylindrical colonies	– Cylindrical/prism like
– Muscle bands are complete	– Muscle bands are feeble	– Muscle bands are incomplete ventrally
– Tailed larval stage is present	– Tailed larval stage is absent	– Tailed lorval stag~ is absent
e.g.. *Dolium*	e.g., *Pyrosoma*	e.g., *Salpa*

Order

Endostylophora
- House is bilaterally symmetrical with separate inhalent & exhalent aperture.
- Pharynx is with endostyle
e.g.. Oikopeurat, show neotony & liver is a temporary) gelationous house, *appendicularia*

Polystylophora
- House is biradially with single symmetrical aperture
- Pharynx is without endostyle
e.g., kowalevskia

KINGDOM – ANIMALIA

Sub-kingdom – Eumetazoa
Phylum – Chordata
Sub-phylum – Cephalochordata

General characters

- They are marine and mostly sedentary.
- Body is cylindrical, fish like having head and tail.
- Coelom is enterocoelous.
- Notochord is rod-like extending from rostrum to tail.
- Muscles dorso-lateral, segmented into V-shaped myotomes.
- Alimentary canal is complete. Buccal cavity has wheel organ called muller's organ/rotatory organ.
- Circulation is closed type. They lack heart so their contraction is by ventral aorta. They show typical vertebral pattern of blood flow.
- Dorsal, tubular nerve cord without nerve ganglia and brain.
- They have sensory cells over oral hood called cells of Joseph and have chemo or olfactory receptors in kolliker's pit.
- Excretion is by protonephridia. Single large nephridia above oral hood is called Hatschek's nephridia. They also have brown funnels & renal papillae.
- Asexual reproduction is absent.
- Sexes are separate and development is indirect including free swimming larva showing progressive metamorhosis. They shed their sperm and ova into atrium by bursting of inner wall of gonads at certain points called *cicatrices.* Their sperms are smallest among chordates.
e.g, *Amphioxus/Branchiostoma* – Lancelet.

KINGDOM – ANIMALIA

Sub-kingdom – Eumetazoa
Phylum – Chordata
Sub-phylum – Vertebrata
Super class – Agnatha (Jawless)
Class – Ostracodermi (Extinct) Armoured Fishes

General characters

- They were jawless fossil vertebrates.
- They were poikilothermus, sluggish bottom dwellar.

- Their body form was fish like, dorsoventrally flattened with huge head & muscular trunk.
- The head was covered by broad bony dermal plates and rest of the body is surrounded by small dermal scales. So are named as armoured fishes or bony skin fishes.
- They had no endoskeleton.
- Mouth was anteroventrally small and without jaws and teeth. They were filter feeders.
- Their internal ear was with two semicircular canals.
- Pair of lateral eyes & median pineal eye on top of head. They resemble the present day cyclostomes in many respects and are divided into two sub classes.

Sub-classes

Monorhina
- A single large, slit-like median nostril on top a head between eyes.

Diplorhina
- Two separate nasal openings

Order

Euphanerida
- Fusiform, blunt head
- Two lateral and a median dorsal finfilds.
- Gillslits absent

e.g., Jamoyticus kerwoodi Regarded as ancestor of ostracoderms

Anaspida
- Head covered by small plates
- Eyes laterally placed and nostril single median
- They were active subimmers

e.g., Birkenia, lasanius, pteroleps, rhyncholepis, pharyngolepis

Osteostraci/cephalaspida
- A single piece head shield or carapace wthout sutures.
- Several pairs of gill slits
- Tail heterocercal
- Lampreys were derived form osteostriaci

e.g. Cephalaspis, Hemicyclaspis, Tremataspis, Didymaspis, ,Benneviaspis etc.

Order

Heterostraci
- Body large, tail laterally compressed.
- Mouth is slit like aperture
- A single large gill slits
- A backwardly directed dorsal spine protected upwards from posterior part of cephalic sheld

e.g., Pteraspis, Drepanaspis etc.

Coelolepida
- Body small, fusifom1, torpedo like.
- Body surface is covered by placoid scales
- Lateral eyes widely apart.

e.g., *Phlebolepis, Coelolepis, Lanarkia*

KINGDOM—ANIMALIA

Sub-kingdom—Eumetazoa
Phylum—Chordata
Sub-phylum- Vertebrata
Superclass—Agnatha (jawless)
Class—Cyclostomata/Maripobranchii/circular mouth (living fossils)
No. of species = 50

General Features

- These are jawless vertebrates.
- They are pokilotherms
- Their living members are ectoparasites on fishes.
- They have cylindrical body with two single fins at the back which helps in swimming.
- Their endoskeleton is cartilagenous.
- A true coelom is present.
- Skin is soft, slimy due to unicellular mucus glands and scales are absent.
- Digestive system is without stomach. They have funnel like suctorial mouth with sharp teeth, rasping tongue. Intestine is with fold called typhlosole.
- Respiration is through 5 - 16 pairs of gills enclosed in a gill pouch (marsipobranchii).
- Heart is 2-chambered with conus arterious. RBC's are nucleated and circular. Hepatic portal system is present and renal portal system is absent.
- Excretion is through mesonephric kidneys.
- Dorsal nerve cord with differentiated brain.
- 8-10 pairs of cranial nerves.
- Sense organs as single, median, pineal functional eye, internal ear, single external nostrial and lateral line sense organ for balancing.
- Sexes separate or united. Single sex organ, discharge gametes in the coelom. Fertilization is external. Development include ammocoetus larva resembling *Amphioxus* larva in structure and function. It is a connective link between cephalochordate and cyclostone.

The class cyclostomata is divided into two orders

Petromyzontiformes	Myxinoidea
– Both marine as well as fresh water forms	– All marine forms.
– Mouth ventral, suctorial buccal funnel with horny teeth.	– Mouth terminal lack buccal funnel and have 4 pairs of tentacles.
– Nostril dorsal & nasohypophyseal sac closed behind & not connected to pharynx.	– Nostril terminal & nosohypohyseal duct open, behind the pharynx.
– Eyes are functional.	– Eyes are vestigial.
– 7 pairs of gill pouches & branchial basket is complete.	– 6 to 14 pairs of gill pouches and branchial basket is poorly developed.
– Ears with 2 semicircular canals.	– Ears with only semicircular canal.
– Development indirect. *e.g., Petromyzon-* The sea lamprey, they are anadromous *i.e.,* it is marine but migrate to freshwater for breeding. *Lampetra-the* freshwater lamprey.	– Development direct. *eg., Mvxine-the* hagfish. It bores the body of fish and eat its soft tissues. They also distroy pearl oysters & harm the pearl industry.

KINGDOM—ANIMALIA

Sub-kingdom-Eumetazoa
Phylum—Chordata
Sub-phylum—Vertebrata
Division—Gnathostomata
Super class—Pisces
Devonian period is the 'Golden age of fishes'
Study—Ichthology; cültivation—Pisciculture

General Features

- Poikilotherms, ectothermal or cold blooded. They are marine or fresh water fishes.
- Monocondylic and vertebrae amphicoelous type. Endoskeleton bony or cartilagenous, skull. Exoskeleton in the form of scales.
- Fins are supported by fin rays. Paired fins are pelvic fin (act as brakes) & pectoral fin (act as balancer). Unpaired fins are dorsal fin, ventral fin & caudal fin (all act as stearing organ). Caudal fin may be homocercal or heterocercal.
- Digestive system consists of complete alimentary canal. Their tongue is non-muscular & non-protrusible. Teeth are homodont and polyphyodont. Digestion is extracellular and food is stored in the liver in the form of glycogen & oil.
- Branchial respiration.
- Circulation is closed type. Heart is myogenic with one auricle, one ventricle and accessory chambers as sinus venosus or conus arteriosus. Both hepatic portal and renal portal circulation is present. Their RBC's are nucleated.
- Poikilotherm
- Kidney opisthonephric or mesonephric. Urinary bladder is absent. Excretion is ureotelic or ammonotelic.
- Brain with large olfactory lobes and cerebellum and optic lobes. Cranial nerves are 10 pairs.
- Lateral line system senses the changes in the surrounding water. Eyes are without eyelids. Only internal ear is present with 3 semicircular canals.
- Sexes separate, gonads paired, fertilization may be external or internal. They may be oviparous or ovoviviparous or viviparous. Development direct with no metamorphosis and their young ones are as hatchlings, fingerlings and fries. They are anammiotes *i.e.,* without embryonic membrane).

Super class Pisces is divided into three classes as :

- Placodermic • Chondrichthyes • Osteichthyes

Class Placodermic

These were extinct fishes with powerful immovable jaws, heavy external bony armourplate skinned and efficient fins. Placoderms survived for a short period (appeared in silurion, fluorished in devonion and carboniferous and became extinct in permian) and are often considered as 'unsuccessful ancient experiment' in the evolution of gnathostomes.

They were divided into two orders as Arthrodiriformes	Antiarchiformes
– Resemble ostracoderms – Heavy bony armour shields of head & trunk – Powerful gasping jaw with sharp shearing blades *e.g., Coccostens, Dunkleosteus, Dinichthyes*	– Bottom dweller – Resemble Agnathans – Head & forepart of trunk are covered by a depressed bony shield. – Long pectoral fins *e.g., Bothriolepis, pterichthyodes*

OTHER CLASSES

Chondrichthyes/Elasmobranchs	**Osteichthyes/teleosts**
Cartilagenous fishplate gills	
– About 600 species known.	– About 20,000 living species
– Cartilagenous fishes	– Bony fishes
– Always marine	– Marine or fresh water
– Laterally compressed body	– Spindle shaped body
– Skin covered by placoid scales/dermal dentine	– Skin covered by ganoid, cycloid or ctenoid scales.
– Mouth is on the ventral side	– Mouth is on the anterior side.
– Pelvic fin is posterior & bear clasper in males	– Pelvic fin is anterior & bear no clasper.
– Caudal fin is heterocercal	– Caudal fin is homocercal.
– Dorsal fins are 2	– Dorsal fin is 1.
– Ceratotrichia *i.e.,* fins with elastin fin rays.	– Lepidotrichia *i.e.,* fins with bony fin rays.
– 5-7 pairs of lamellar, uncovered gills.	– 4 pairs of filamentous gills covered by an operculum.
– Heavy body due to the absence of swim/air bladder	– Jaw suspension is autostylic.
– Alimentary canal ends into cloaca.	– Light weight body due to the presence of air fulled swim bladder which helps in respiration sound production and locomotion.
– Intestine has a spiral valve.	– Alimentary canal ends into anus.
– Liver is bilobed.	– Spiral valve absent.
– Heart has conus arteriosus	– Liver is trilobed.
– 5-7 pairs of aortic arches	– Heart has bulbus arteriosus.
– Ureotelic organisms with opisthonephric kidneys.	– 4 pairs of aortic arches
– Ampulla of lorenzini are present, act as thermoreceptor and sensitive to change in hydrostatic pressure.	– Ammonotelic or ureotelic with mesonephric kidney. – Absent.
– Restiform bodies are present brain	– Absent
– Retina lack cones	– Cones are present in the retina.
– Internal nares are absent.	– Internal nares are present in only lungfishes.
– Show sexual dimorphosm	– Male & female are not distinguishable externally.
– Oviducts (mullerian ducts) are not continious with ovaries.	– Ovidents are continuous with the ovaries.
– Fertilization is internal.	– Fertilization in external.

Class Chondrichthyes is divided into two sub classes sub-class Selachii	**Holocephalii**
– Skin is covered by placoid scales	– Skin is scaleless
– Upper jaw is not fused with cranium.	– Upper jaw is fused with cranium
– Teeth are numerous & occur in several rows	– Teeth are fused to form plates meant for crushing.
– Vertebrae are well developed	– Vertebrae are poorly developed
– Cloaca is present	– Separate opening for alimentary canal and urinogenital ducts.

Order

Pleurotremata
- Include sharks and dog fishes
- Spindle shaped body
- Gill slits are 5-7 pairs & lateral in position.
- Teeth are sharp & conical
- Anterior margin of pectoral fin is free

e.g. Scoliodon — Indian shark/ dog skin is used as abrasive (shagreen)
Sphyrna/zygaena–Hammer headed shark

Rhineodon–Largest living shark; whale shark

Hypotremata/Ragiformes
- Include saw fishes, rays & skates
- Dorsoventrally flattened body
- Gill slits are 4 pairs & ventral in position
- Teeth are blunt
- Anterior margin of pectoral fish is fused with sides of the body or head

e.g., Trygon-Stingray/whiptailed ray sting is a modified dorsal fin.

Torpedo–Electric ray; electric organ is a modified muscle and it gives electric shock of 50-60 volts.
Raja–The thornback skate.
Phinobatus Guitar fish

Order

Chimaeriformes
- They are carnivorous
- Oviparous, lay eggs in horney case

e.g., Chimaera – Rat fish/ rabbit fish/king of herrings they have characters of sharks (cartilagenous skeleton, pelvic clasper, placoid scales) and bony fishes (fleshy lips, operculum and distinct anus)

Class Osteichthyes is divided into two subclasses sub-class

Sacropterygii/choanichthyes	Actinoptergii
Fleshy fin nares fishes – Paired fins are leg like with fleshy bony central axis. – Olfactory sacs open into mouth cavity by internal – There are generally two dorsal fin. – Tail is disphycercal.	rayfin – Paired fins have broad bases & from like form & they lack fleshy basal lobes. – Olfactory sacs do not open into mouth cavity but have double external nares. – There is single dorsal fins. – Tail is homocereal.

Order

Crossopterygii

A fringe fin
- Fins are lobed
- Premaxillae and maxillae are present
- Internal nares are absent
- Spiracles are present

e.g. Latimeria – The coelacanth, feeding on other fishes and is the oldest living fish
Neoceratodu – Australain lung fish

Dipnoi

Double breathing
- They have gills as well as lungs.
- Premaxillae & maxillae absent
- Internal nares present
- Spiracles are absent
- Show discontinous distribution.

e.g.,
Protopterus – African lung fish-mud fish.
Lepidosiren – South American lung fish/
Neoceratodus – Australian lung fish/the brunett salmon.

Superorder

Chondrostei	Holostei	Teleostei
Cartilage Bone	Entire Bone	Complete Bone
–Scales Ganoid	–Scales ganoid or cycloid	–Scales cycloid or ctenoid
–Tail fin heterocercal	–Tail fin heterocercal	–Tail fin homocercal
–Skeleton is largely cartilagenous with dermal bony plates on the head	–Skeleton is moderately ossified	–Skeleton is fully bony

Order (Chondrostei) / Order (Holostei)

Polypteriformes	Acipenseriformes	Lepisosteiformes	Amiiformes
– Ganoid scales	– Scales absent	–Body is covered with rhomobiod scale having coat of ganoid scales	– Head has ganoid scales and trunk bears overlapping cycloid scales
– Notochord is constricted & is replaced by verterbrae	– Notochord is unconstricted	–Procoelusvertebrae	– Amphicoelous verdebrae
e.g., *Polyptertus* The bichir	*e.g., Acipenser* – The sturgeon Polydon – Spoon billed sturgeon	*e.g., Lepisosteus* The long nosed grapike; scales are used in jwellery.	*e.g.,* Ania–The mud fish/fresh water dog fish/ Bow fish.

Important orders

Anguilliformes	Siluriformes	Cypriniformes	Atheriniformes /beloniformes	Gasterosteriformes /syngnathiformes
– Body long, snake like	– Head bears sensory barbels	–Head is scaleless & Body bears cycloid scales	–Cycloid scales	–Trunk is covered with armour of bony plates
– Pectoral fins are reduced	– They bear adipose fin (fin without fin rays)	–Jaws lack teeth	–Dorsal fin is opposite	–Males have brood pouch on the underside of the abdomen to carry eggs till hatching. So males are said to be pregnant
– Pelvic fin absent			–Dorsal fin is opposite the anal fin	
e.g. Anguilla– Fresh water eel; catadromous	*e.g., Mystus arius clarias* The car fish The cat fish	*e.g.* Labeo–Rohu; used to control insects catla-Largest India CRAP	*e.g., Exocoetus* – the flying fish; it glides in air with modified pectoral fin.	*e.g., Hippocampus*– The sea horse; dried skin is used as ornament
Muraena–Moray		*Electrophorus*-Electric eel *Wallago*-Lachi	*Belone*-Garfish	*Syngnathus*-Pipe fish

Perciformes	Tetradoniformes
– Fin rays are hard and spiny – Weberian apparatus absent *e.g., Anabas* – the climbing perch *Remora/Echeneis* – The sucker fish; sucker is it modified dorsal fin	– Body is covered with spines – Belly is inflatable *e.g., Diodon*–The porcupine fish *Tetradon*–the globe/puffer fish *Ostracion* – the box/coffer fish/Trunk fish/Cow fish

Lophiformes	Pleuronectiformes	Cluperiformesl	Channiformes
– Huge head with very wide mouth	– Body is highly compressed	– Head & operculum are without scales	–Air bladder is long & extends upto the tail
– Spiny dorsal fin is tipped with a fleshy flap to attract the prey	– Both the eyes are on the same side	– Weberian ossicles absent	–Air
	– Spineless fins and are often very long	– Pelvic fins abdominal	–fins are without spines & are very long
e.g., Lophius – The angler /fishing frog	*e.g., Solea* – The flat fish/ sole; edible bottom dweller.	*e.g., Notopterus*–Chital fish *Clupea* – Herring *Salmo* – Atlantic salmon	*e.g., Ophioecphalus* Channa/The mullet headed fish

Advancement of Bony Fish Over Cartilagenous Fish

- Presence of homocercal tail
- Autostylic jaw suspension
- Better developed brain

SOME IMPORTANT FACTS

- Edible fishes
- **Freshwater fishes** – Rohu, Rita, catla, mrigall, carp, malhi, chital, chamla, sanghara, eel.
- **Marine fishes** – Pomfret, bombay duck, *exocoetus,* salmon, *solea, hilsa,* Indian eel.
- Lavaevorous fish – *Gambusia, Telapia, Oryzia*
- Most primitive fish – *Climatius*
- Most advanced fish – Lung fish
- Viviparous fish – *Zygaena, Rhinobatus, Pristis*
- Sound producing fish – *Mola, Balistis*
- Largest fish – Whale shark (18 m, 40 tonnes)
- Smallest fish – Pygmygoly (11 mm, 4–5 gm)
- Fastest fish – Sail fish (109 km/hr.)
- Most beautiful fish – Zebrafish
- Most poisonous fish – Stone fish
- Bioluminescent fish – *Porichthyes, Anamalops*

Migratory mode

- Catadromous fishes – Move from freshwater to sea for breeding *e.g., Anguilla*
- Anadromous tishes – Move from seawater to fresh water *e.g., Salmon, hi/sa* (move from Bay of Bengal to Ganga)
- Potamodramous fishes – Migrate from marine to marine water.

Range of tolerance

- Stenohaline fishes – Live within narrow range of salinity
- Euryhalimefishes – Live & loteratewide range of salinity.
- Oils are extracted from liver and body of several fishes. Liver oil is rich in vitamin A and D and the body oil are of two types.
- Drying oil – Having higher iodine value
- Semidrying oil – Having lower iodine value
- Ice fish is without haemoglobin
- **Anablelps** can see in above and below water simulataneously as it has two pupils in each eye.
- **Isinglass:** It is a gelatinous material obtained from the air bladder of some fishes *e.g.*, cods, catfishes. perches, salmons, sturgeons etc. used for making coments, jellies & for classification of wines & beers.
- Fish meal is the unpalatable, unmarkesable fishes, ground, dried & is used to feed poultry, pigs, cattles & pet animals.
- Fish manure is a sharks mixed with unpalatable fishes, crushed & ground bones & refuse of no use make good fertilizer for tea, coffee & rubber plants.
  It is rich in calcium, phosphate & nitrogen.

KINGDOM—ANIMALIA

Sub-kingdom — Eumetazoa
Phylum — Chordata
Sub-phylum— Vertebrata
Division — Gnathostomata
Super class — Tetrapoda
Class — Amphibia (Dual Life)
Carboniferous period was the 'Age of Amphibians'
Number of species — About 3000

General Features

- Poikilotherms, ectothermal or cold blooded.
- They are found in freshwater and moist land. They are the first terrestrial organism.
- Body is divisible into head and trunk. Trunk may be extended to tail region.
- They have smooth moist skin with large number of glands.
- Exoskeleton is absent.
- Endoskeleton is cartilagenous in larval form and bony in adults. Skull is dicondylic. Vertebrae are procoelous type and axis vertebra is absent. Sacral vertebrae is one in number. Jaws are autostylic.
- They have two pairs of pentadactyl limb. Forelims are smaller than hind limbs and hind limbs have webbed feet.
- Digestive system is complete. Opens out by cloacal aperture. Mouth is large with muscular and protrusible tongue. Lower jaw is without teeth. Teeth are homodont, acrodont and polyphyodont type.
- Respiration takes place through moist skin (cutaneous) gills (Branchial), buccopharyngeal cavity (buccopharyngeal) or lungs (pulmonary).
- Circulation is closed type, heart is three chambered (2 auricle & ventricle) with accessory chambers as sinus venosus and conus arteriosus. Both hepatic & renal portal circulationis well developed, RBCs are oval,biconvex and nucleated.

- Pronephros kidneys in larval form and mesonephros kidneys in adult. Larval are ammonotelic and adults are ureotelic.
- Nervous system consists of brain and spinal cord and are covered by two meningeal membrane (piamater and dura arachnoid). Cerebellum is reduced. Brain has 10 pairs of cranial nerves.
- Sense organs include Jacobson organ for olfactory function, middle ear & internal ear are present and tympanum lies on the surface to receive vibrations. Middle ear also contain collumella auris to transmit sound from tympanum to internal ear. Eyes are with movable nictitating membrane, lacrymal gland (moist eyes) and herdian gland (lubricate eye ball). Lateral line system is present only during development for balance.
- They show hibernation (winter sleep) and aestivation (summer sleep).
- Unisexual, exhibit sexual dimorphism, oviparous, mesolecithal eggs. Fertilization may be external or internal. Development may be direct (terrestrial form tree frogs) or indirect. Larval form is tadpole in frogs and axolotyl in salamanders. The axolotyl larva exhibit neotony and paedogenesis.

Class Amphibia is divided into three orders.

ORDERS

Urodela/Ecaudata	**Anura/Salientia**	**Apoda/Gymnophiona/Caecilian**
– Aquatic	– Amphibious	– Burrows in soil
– Body is divisible into head, neck, trunk & tail.	– Body is divisible into head & trunk.	– Worm like & apparently, segmented with head, trunk and tail
– Scales are absent	– Scales are absent	– Dermal scales are embedded in the skin & is transversely wrinkled.
– Two pairs of equal sized limbs.	– Forelimbs are shorter than hind limbs are adapted for leaping & swimming.	– Limb are absent
– Middle ear is absent	– Middle ear is present	– Middle ear absent
– Larva is axolotyl *e.g., Amphibiuma* – The congo eel; having gill slits without gills; largest sized RBC *Salamandra* (The salamander;) retains gills upto adult stage *Salamandra atra* – (Alpine salamander; ovoviviparous & give birth to 1 to 2 young ones. *Proteus*–The blind salamander/ The olm; Larva is with eyes; secondary fresh water amphibian; gills persist in adults – *Necturus*–Mud puppy/water dog; neotonous *Ambystoma*–The tiger salamender neotonous *Triton*–Crested newt *Siren*–The mud eel; only one pair of limbs; swim like eel & burrows in soft mud	– Larva is tadpole *e.g., Rana* – Frog; skin is used for glue and book binding *Phyllobates limbatus*–Smallest & poisonous frog (12.5 mm) *Hyla*–Indian tree frog; Insect feeder; absorb dew drops to moisten the skin **Phyllomedusae** – American tree frog; makes leaf nest *Rhacophora*–The flying frog; finger & toes are webbed *pipa*–Surinam toad; tongueless; carries eggs on its back *Bombirator/Discolossus*–Fire bellied Toad; red patches are enemies by directing his belly towards the enemy shaking water gives a flame like appearance to red patches	– No larval form *e.g., Icthyophis* – Blind worm; Tongue is absent; vertebrae amphicoelous; about 20 vertabrae; show parental care *Uroaeotyphlus*

(contd.)...

Urodela/Ecaudata	Anura/Salientia	Apoda/Gymnophiona/Caecilian
Triturus–The Himalayan salamander *Tylotriton*–Only Indian urodela found in Eastern Himalayan region *Megalobatrachus*–Giant salamander; largest amphibian (175 cm long)	*Alytes*–Midwife toad; fingers are free and toes are webbed; Female lay eggs in double string which male winds around his things. *Ascaphus*–American ball toad; cloacal appendae serve as copulatory organ of female eggs. *Xenopus*–Tongueless clawed toad of south African; used as a test in diagnosis of human pregnanacy. Has horny claws on that first three toes. *Rhinoderma*–South American Darwin frog; carries eggs and tadpole in its vocal sacs. *Rheobatrachus*–Australian frog; keeps eggs in her stomach and expelled it through mouth.	

OTHER IMPORTANT FACTS

- Largest amphibian is *Megalobatrachus japonica* (Japanese giant salamander, 1.6 m).
- Smallest amphibian is South American arrow poison frog (1.3 m).
- Most poisonous frog is Golden dart poison frog.
- *Cryptobranchus* (Hellbender; largeAmerican Salamander) is fully aquatic because of the presence of spiracle (single gill slit) on the left side, used for outlet of water during buccal respiration;poisonous but not dangerous to man.
- Poisonous secretions (Bufotoxins) of *Bufo marinus* are fatal to dogs & cats.
- *Neotony* is the retention of certain larval characteristics beyond the normal period or during adult life.

Type of Neotony

- *Partial neotony* means when metamorphosis is delayed due to temporary ecological or physiological changes in the environment *e.g.,* tadpole.
- *Intermediate neotony* is exhibited by axolotyls which also reproduce sexually but undergo metamorphosis in suitable conditions.
- *Total/Extreme neotony* is exhibited by several salamanders *e.g., protens, siren. necturus.* They remain larva throughout, even the treatment with thyroxine fails to induce metamorphosis.
- Paedogenesis is the development of sexual maturity and reproductive capacity of larval or other pre-adult states.
- Seymouria (fossil amphibian) is a connective link between amphibians and reptiles.

KINGDOM – ANIMALIA

Sub-kingdom—Eumetazoa

Phylum—Chordata

Division—Gnathostomata

Supper class—Tetrapoda

Class—Reptillia (to Creep)

'Golden Age of reptiles' is Jurassic period of mesozoic era.

Number of species—About 7000

Study—Herpetology

General Features

- Poikilotherm exothermal or cold blooded.
- They are the first true terrestrial vertebrates.
- Their body is divisible into head, neck trunk & tail.
- Their skin is dry, cornified and non-glandular.
- Exoskeleton is in the form of epidermal scales (scutes) which helps in water conservation.
- Endoskeleton is bony. Skull is monocondylic. Vertebrae are procoelous type and both atlas & axis vertebrae are present. Sacral vertebral are two in number. Interclavicle is T-shaped. These are the first vertebrates with monoheaded ribs.
- They have two pairs of pentadactyl limbs that end claws (corneoscutes.) Limbs are secondarily lost is snakes and few lizards.
- Alimentary canal terminates into cloaca. Jaws bear simple homodont, acrodont & polyphyodont teeth. In turtles at the place of teeth, horny beaks are present.
- Respiration is pulmonary type. Ribs and intercostal muscles increase the respiratory efficiency. Turtles also show cloacal respiration.
- Heart consists of two auricles and partially divided ventricle (except crocodile). Sinus venosis is present and conus arteriosus split into three arches. Hepatic portal system is well developed and renal portal is reduced. RBCs are oval biconvex and nucleated.
- They have metanephric kidneys & excretion is uric acid (uricotelic).
- Brain is with well developed cerebrum. 12 pairs of cranial nerves and 16 pairs of spinal nerves are present.
- Sense organs include Jacobson organ in the roof of buccal cavity meant for smelling, internal nares open into buccal cavity. Ear consists of external, males generally have muscular copulatory organ *e.g.*, hemipenis in lizards, 4 pairs in crocodile & turtles. Fertilization internal, polylecithal, cledoic eggs.
- Extra embryonic membranes appear during development. There is no metamorphosis.
- Extinct Reptiles are called dianosaurs.

CLASS REPTILLIA IS DIVIDED INTO TWO SUB-CLASSES

Anapsida

- Skull has soild bony roof with no temporal fossae.
- Order *Chelonia/Testudinaa Turtle.*
- Body is covered by dorsal carapace and ventral plastron.
- Body is covered by dorsal carapace and ventral plastron.
- Jaws are with horny sheaths & teeth are absent.
- Cloacal aperture is longitudinal slit.
- Copulatory organ is simple.
- Longest like span among animal (200-400 years)

  e.g., Chelone–the green turtle; green due to the presence of green faterrrapin; head cannot be with drawn completely under the shell.

  Testudo–The land tortoise/Starred torroise, Head & limbs are completely withdrawn inside the shell.

  Trionyx—The soft shelled turtle/soft shelled freshwater; terrapin, head & limbs are completely with drawn under the shell.

  Dermochelys–the leather back turtle; largest of all turtles, weight about 600 kg.

  Chrysemys.

Diapsida

Skull has two temporal fossal.

Orders

Rhynchocephalia	Squamata	Crocodilia
Snout Head	Scaly	
– Limbs pentadactyle & clawed	– Limbs clawed are absent	– Limbs short, powerful & webbed.
– Acrodont teeth.	– Pleurodont teeth	– thecodont teeth
– Ouadrate is fixed.	– Quadrate is movable	– Quadrate is immovable
– Vertebrae amphicoelous	– Vertebrae procoelous	– Vertebrae procoelous
– Heart incompletely 4 chambered	– Heart is incompletely 4 chambered	– Heart is 4 chambered
– Cloacal aperture is transverse	– Cloacal aperture is transverse	– Cloacal aperture is longitudinal slit
– Numerous abdominal ribs are present	– Ribs are simple headed	– Bicephalous abdominal ribs are present & diaphalous is incomplete
– Males are without copulatory organ	– Males are with copulatory organ, hemipenis	– Males are with copulatory organ, penis.
e.g. Sphenodon-tuataras, hatteria; living fossil and is a connective link between Amphibian & reptiles; possess/pineal or median/3rd eye. It belongs to New Zealand and was considered extinct.	*e.g.* Lizards (Study-Saurology) & snakes (study-ophiology) *Hemidactylus-the* wall lizard/ Gickio; produce sound by striking tongue against palate; digests bear adhesive pads or lamellae. *Varanus monitor*-Goya/monit-or lizard. *Varanus kemodensis-Feroci-ous* dragon *Draco–Flying* lizard/flying dragon; skin fold & pategia is supported by ribs helps in flying *Chamaeleon*-Chammaeleon; Arboral metachrosis; ability to rotate eye ball in all directions. *Calotes*–Garden lizard; blood sucker; show mimicry. *Phrynosoma*–Horned lizard/ Horned toad; on irritation it emits ajet of blood from eyes by contracting blood sinuses at the base of nictitating mem brane *Heloderma*–The Gila monster; only poisonous lizard. *Uromastix*–the spiny tailed lizard; fat bodies yield oil to cure potency; femoral glands secretion hardens to form temporary spines used as copulatory organ.	*e.g., Crocodilus porosus*–Maggar largest reptile (8 m, 495 kg) un-equal teeth not used for mastication; skin in used for making bags & shoes; Triangluar head & is very aggressive *Alligator mississipeienis*–Alligator; unequal teeth & carnivorous *Gavialis gangeticus*– Gavial/ Gharial; resides in Ganges & Brahmputra river; teeth nearly similar; pot like enlargment in males during breedy season.

Rhynchocephalia	Squamata	Crocodilia
	Ophisausus–The Indian Glass snake lizard limbless lizard; fixed jaws. *Iguano*–Arboreal lizard; favourite article in the native diet. *Amblyrhynchus*–Only existing marine lizard. *Mabouia*–Skink *Typhlops*–The blind snake; Insectivo rous non poisionous. *Naja Cobra*, hood formed by spreading of ribs of neck region which may bear spectacle marks dorsally diurnal, highly poisonous. *Bungarus*–Krait highly poisonous, nocturnal *Python*–Ajgar; Largest snake, bulkisest In adults claws/spur on either side of cloaca represent vestigial hind limbs. *Dendrophis*–Tree snake; non-poisonous. *Eryx*–the sand boa/Double mouthed snake Ptyas-the rat snake/dhaman; *Vipera*–The viper/Russel's viper; pitless *Crotalus*–The rattle snake Threadsnake–Smallest *Dryophis-Green* whip snake	

SOME IMPORTANT FACTS

- Neurotoxic snakes (paralyse nerves & muscles)–cobra krait, coral snake, sea snake.
- Haemotoxic snakes–(Tissue destruction & haemorrhage) Viper.
- Snakes venom is acidic in reaction.
- Indians largest non-poisonous snake is Boa.
- Indians largest poisonous snake is king cobra (*Naja hummah*)
- Haffkin Research Institute, Bombay prepares antivenom injections.
- Párapsida (aquatic reptiles) & synapsida (mammal like reptile) sub-classes include exctinct reptiles.
- Lizards show autocomy *i.e.,* easily broken off their tail when threatened.
- Tail of lizards is without bones.
- Order squamata includes two suborders as lacertilia (lizards) and ophidia (snakes).
- *Seymoria* is a missing link between amphibians & reptiles.
- Smallest snake of India is *Typhlina brahmina.*
- Most poisonous snake is *Hydrophis beicheri* (sea snake).

- The smallest reptile is *Sphaerodactylus partinopion.*
- The most famous serpentarium of India is at Chennai.
- *Brontosaurus* is a herbivore and is a largest dinosaur.
- *Tyranosaurus* is a carnivore & is known as king of dinosaurs.
- Terrible lizards or reptilian dinosaurs belongs to order Saurischia while plated lizard belongs to order Ornthischia.

KINGDOM—ANIMALIA

Sub-kingdom—Eumetazoa
Phylum—Chordata
Division—Gnathostomata
Super class—Tetrapoda
Class—Aves (Birds)
Age of Birds is Jurassic period of mesozoic era
Number of species—About 9000
Study—Ornithology

General Features

- Homeothermal, endothermal or warm blooded. Their body temperature is generally 42°C & may reach up to 45°C in some cases.
- Their body is streamlined with head, neck (long sized), trunk and tail (reduced & stumpy).
- Skin is dry, devoid or glands except oil of preen gland at type root of the short tail (uropygium. It used for dressing feathers of birds).
- Exoskeleton is in the form of feathers, scales, claws and toothless beak (rhamphotheca). All are epidermal in orgin.
- Endoskeleton is bony. Skull is monocondylic. Skull bones and vertebrae of trunk and tail are fused. Vertebrae are heterocoelous and tail vertebrae fused to form pygostyle. Bones are pneumatic (with air cavities). Presence of furcula or merry thought bone or wish bone (fused clavicle & interclavicle). They have bicephalous ribs. Lower jaw or mandible articulates with quadrate. The sternum is largely expanded & bears a large mid ventral ridge or keel for the attachement of major light muscles as pectoralis major and pectoralis minor.
- They have two pairs of pentadactyl limbs. Forelimbs are modified to form wings/feathers. Hindlimbs are modified for perching or walking or food capturing or swimming or wading or running and end into 4 clawed toes (Hallux is directed backwards).
- Alimentary canal is complete and have additional chamber crop (modified oesophagus), muscular gizards, a pair of rectal caeca (junction of small intestine & rectum) and three chambered cloaca (to conserve water). Tongue is pointed in front & bifid behind. It lacks the muscle for the movement which is done by the altering movement of hyoid apparatus. Gall blader is absent.
- Respiration is pulmonary. Lungs are spongy and elastic with air sacs. Trachea is with comlete bony rings and bronchi is covered with cartilagenous rings and is slightly expand to form sound producing organ, syrinx. Air sacs (cervical, anterior thoracic, posterior thoracic and abdominal) are the expansion of mucous membrane of secondary bronchi. These air sacs act as internal cooling agents. Larynx is without vocal cords.
- Heart is four chambered (2 auricle, 2 ventricle). Hepatic portal system is well developed and renal portal system is vestigial. RBC's are oval, biconvex and nucleated. Hepatic portal system has special coccygeomes senteric vein.

- Bursa fabricii/cloacal thymus (lymphatic tissue) is attached to cloaca in some young birds & takes part in the formation of lymphocytes.
- They have metanephric, trilobed kidney. Excretion is uricotelic (uric acid) sea birds deposit it as Guano (phosphate rich). Urinary bladder is absent except in ostrich, American rhea.
- Brain is well developed cerebrum, cerebellum and optic lobes are large sized. Olfactory lobes are poorly developed. They have 12 pairs of cranial nerves.
- Sense organs include eyes with comb like structure or pecten (except kiwi) and double accomodation power. (ciliary muscle–crompton + Bruke muscle are well developed), internal ear with single ear ossicle (stapes), cochlea is Columella auris is present. Lagaena is also a part of membrane labyrinth. associates with hearing Grandy's corpuscles are touch receptors in the skin of the beak of birds and Herb's corpuscles are heat & vibration receptor in the dermis of the birds.
- Sexes separate with well marked sexual dimorphism female is with single functional left ovary and oviduct. Copulatory organs are absent except in ostrich, ducks, geese & setites. Eggs are polylecithal, Cledoic and are amniotes. External incubation of eggs, meroblastic cleavage, direct development.
- Show courtship, nest building (nidicolous), parental care(altricial), migration and territory behaviour.

Class Aves have two sub-classes	Sub-Class
Archaeornithes Ancient birds – Extinct, toothed birds – Long tail with more than 30 amphico-elous vertebra. – Sternum was without keel – Carpals & metacarpals free – Abdominal ribs were present *e.g. Archaeopteryx lithographica*–It is a missing link between reptiles & birds.	**Neornithes** Modern birds – Modern birds without teeth (except some fossil birds) – Short tail with less than 13, procoelous vertebrae. – Sternum is with keel. – Carpals & metacarpals fused to form carpometacarpals – Abdominal ribs are present

Superorder

Odontognathae	Ratitae/palaeo gnathae	Impennal	Neognathae
– Extinct, cretaceous birds **Hesperornithiformes** – Flightless, swimming *e.g., Hesperornis* **Ichthyornithiformes** – Fligtless, toothed bird *e.g., Icthyornis*	old new' – Flightless – Running birds – Without teeth	– Flightless with paddle like wings/flippers & webbed Feet *e.g., Aptenodytes*–Penguin of antarctica; gregareous. Blubber beneath the skin; bird with double trachea	*carinatal* New jaw kai – wings weel developed – Feathers with inter-locking mechanism

Super order Ratitae is divided into different orders

Struthiniformes	Rheiformes	Casuariformes	Apterygiformes	Tinamiformes
Ostrich form	Mother of zeus	Genus of cassowary form	No wing form	Genus of tinamous form
– Head, neck & legs sparsely feathhered. Feathers lack aftershaft.	– Head and neck partly feathered. lack aftershaft	– Neck & body denesly feathered. Feathers with aftershaft	– Flightless birds with hair like feathers without aftershaft	–Flightless bird, cursorial
– Pygostyle absent sternum lack keel.	– Sternum lack keel	–Head bears comb	– Legs with 4 toes	– Sternum is keeled – Eggsell with high gloss
– Legs with two toes Stunted nails which are unequal	– Legs with three toes	– Sternum keeless – Legs with three toes with claws		
e.g. *Struthio*-Ostrich of Africa & Arabia; largest sized herds; used as food fastest runner; Bird with penis; largest living	e.g., *Rhea americana*–American ostrich; only ratitae bird with syrinx	e.g., *Casuarius*–cassowarine of Australia third largest flightless bird *Dromaius*–Emus of of New Zealand. 2nd largest flight lessbird	e.g.,*Apteryx*–Kiwis of New Zealand; smallest flightless bird; acute sense of smell for food on the ground.	e.g., *Tinamus*–Tinamous

Super order Neognathae is divided into different orders as

Order

Passeriformes	Piciformes	Columbiformes
Sparrow form – Largest order – Arboreal bird – Feet are adapted for perching – Beak is adapted for cutting e.g. *Passer domesticus*–House sparrow; most abundant bird *Corvus splendens*–Common House crow; scavenger; nest is crude & Untidy *Orthotomous*–Tailor bird; restless bird, nest consists of soft fibres, cotton or wool & is placed in funnel formed of green leaves stitched together with plant fibres hence its name.	wood pecker form – Arboreal bird – Their 1st & 4th toe facing backward (Zygodactylus) e.g., *Brachyptermus benghalensis*- – The golden backed wood pecker; Beak is strong & insectivoros chisal shaped; Toes with strong claws *Pickus*–The wood peacker.	dove form – Arboreal bird – Beak is short & bear cere at its base – Crop secrete pigeon milk – Mostly frugivorous e.g., *Columba livia*–Blue rock pigeon maximum diversitry among birds; possess homing instinct *Raphus*–Doda *Streptopelia*–The dove; sexes alike Enblem of the sign of peace.
Psittaciformes	**Galliformes**	**Cuculiformes**
Parrot form – Arboreal bird	Cock form – Terrestrial game birds	Cuckoo form – Terrestrial bird

Psittaciformes	Galliformes	Cuculiformes
– Orgagreous & have loud voice – Feet are adapted for grasping e.g., *Psittacula*- The parakeet/parrot; pet bird/cage bird; carries germs of disease psittacosis; exhibit both syndactyly & zygodactyly.	– Graminivorous – Their flight is powerful but short – Bony spur for fighting *e.g., Gallus domesticus*–The domestic fowl; provides eggs & meat *Phasianus*–Pheasants *Pavo cristatus*–Peafowl; national bird in India; feathers are decorative.	–Zygodactylous feet & are not used for grasping *e.g., Eudynamis*–The koel, Feeds on fruits caterpillars & insects; characteristic kucoo-kuoo call by males is a sex call & territory marker; brood parasite; Indian nightingale.
Anseriformes Goose form – Swimming & diving bird & strong fliers – Herbivorous, fish eaters or filter feeder *e.g., Anas*–The duck; polygamous; nest is formed on the ground near water; eggs & flesh is eatable. *Cygnus*–The swan	**Falconiformes** Falcon – Birds of prey – Diurnal, hooked beak – Curved claws – Keen eyesight. *e.g., Milvus*–Pariah kite, scavenger *Falco*–The falcon; It was employed for hunting birds in the past *Gypsa*–Vulture; highest flight, heaviest bird of prey	**Strigiformes** owl form –Birds of prey –Nocturanal. Reenest eyesight –Powerful grasping feet. *e.g.,Tyto alba*– The barn owl; Their Pupil size increases tremendously during night; eyes are fixed so they rotate their head at 270° angle; distroy rats & mice. *Bubo bubo*– The great horned owl; keeps checks on the rodent population fully feathered legs.

Coraciiformes
Crow form
- Swimming & diving bird
- Feet are fused at the base (syndactylous)
- Beak is very strong

e.g. Halcyon smyrnensis- The white brested kingfisher
Upupa epops– The hoope; their call is soft & musical hoopo., crest is folded & directed back like needle. Opposite the beak.
Dichoceros bicornis–Great hornbill; Emblem of Bombay very small size.
Natural History Society (BNHS)

Ciconiiformes
- Long necked & long legged form
- Fish eaters in marshes & mudflats
- Good fliers

e.g., Ardes–Greatblue heron; S-shaped neck
Bulblcus–The cattle egret *i.e.,* relieves cattle of parasites.

Apodiformes
Without feet *form*
- Small birds
- Legs and feet are very small
- Beak is small and weak.

e.g., Micropodu swift–Fastest flying birds (171 km/hr.); use its saliva to make nest.
Mellisuga humming birds–Can fly forward and backward; built smallest nest (57mm) smallest eggs; Beat their wings 60 times/ second cold blodded during nights due to their

GENERAL INFORMATION REGARDING BIRDS

Migration (Study–Phenology)

It means a regular, periodic, to and fro movement of a population of some birds for breeding, nesting, feeding, resting etc. Migration depends on stimulus and guidance whereas impulse for migration is due to instinct and gradual changes.

Migratory birds–Migrate from one place to another.

Resident birds–Do not migrate *e.g.,* Bobwhite and the ruffled sand grouse.

Kind of Migration

1. **Latitudinal or vertical**–Migration trom plains to hills or from tropical parts to north temperate and subarctic region *e.g.,* common wood cock, American golden plover.
2. **Longitudinal** – Migration from east to west or *vice-versa. e.g.,* Patagonian polver.
3. **Seasonal Migration**:
   - **Summer Visitors**–South to spring for breeding and leave for south in autumn *e.g.,* swifts, swallows, cuckoos.
   - **Winter Vistors**–Form north to autumn and again northwards in spring. *e.g.,* field fare, redwing, snow bunting.
   - **Birds of Passage**–Seen for a short time twice a year on their way to colder or warmer countries in spring and autumn. *e.g.,* snipes and sand pipers.
   - Migration may be daily, seasonal and cyclic (snow owl).
   - Bird migration is studied by *ringing* or *banding.*
   - Arctic tern (*Sterna parasisaea*) travelled longest distance from arctic to antarctic and back (17600 km migration 40,000 km/yr.)
   - Golden plover travels nonstop for 3600 km and utilise only two ounces of high octane fuel.
   - Ducks, shore birds, gulls etc. may migrate at night or in the day.

Feathers

- **Pterylosis** is arrangement of feathers in the body.
- Feathers are arranged in definite feather tracts (*Pterylae*), separate by featherless areas (*apteria*) which have only a few.
  1. **Quills** (flight feather)–Large, found in wings (remiges) and tail, (retrices) shaft (centre axis), *calamus* (small, hollow, translucent and cylindrical, proximal part of shaft), *rachis* (long distal solid and opaque part of stem), inferior *umbicus* small hole on the proximal end of calamus, *superior cumblicus* (hole on the distal end of calamus), *barbs* (parallel filaments with *barbules).*
  2. **Coverts** – Small feathers, similar to quills, meant for filling gaps between the quill feathers on wings and tail, short calamus
  3. **Contours**–form general covering of the body. Barbs can be easily separated.
  4. **Filoplumes or hair feathers** – Present beneath contours, very small in size, short calamus, long rachis and few barbs and barbules of the free end.
  5. **Down feather or plumules**–Cover body of a newly hatched bird *i.e.,first feathery covering* of the young bird. Small calamus and long flexible barbs containing barbules without interlocking hooklets.
  6. **Bristles**–Short calamus, slender rachis with a few barbs in rudimentary form at its base. Found in *flycatchers.*
- First digit of the hand (*thumb or pollex*) bear a tuft of small feathers known as *bastard wing* or *alaspuria* or *false wing.*

Beaks

Modified according to different functions.

1. **Cutting beak**–in crows, beaks with cutting edge.
2. **Fruit eating beak**–is parrots, deeply hooked and extremely strong
3. **Seed eating beak**–in sparrows, finches and cardinals, peg-like and conical beaks.
4. **Mud probing beak**–in snipe, stilt, sand piper etc., extremely long and slender.
5. **Fish catching beak**–Long, sharply pointed, powerful, spearing beaks, *e.g.*, snake-birds or darters, *cormorants.*
6. **Spatulate beak**–in spoon-bill, flattened and terminates into a spatulate or spoon like expansion.
7. **Insectivorous beak** in swallows and swifts, small wide and delicate to scoop up their living insect prey.
8. **Wood chiselling beak**–is wood peakers, elongated, straight and stout chisel-like beaks.
9. **Tearing and piercing beak**–in carrion feeding and flesh eating birds *e.g.*, vultures, owls, kites, hawks etc., pointed, sharp edged and powerful, hooked beaks.
10. **Water and mus straining beak**–in ducks, geese and teal, broad and flat.
11. **Flower probing beak**–Is tropical humming bird, long, pointed and rapier like.
12. **Pouched beak**–is *pelicans,* beak with a capacious gular pouch of extensile skin.

Feet of Claws

1. Cursorial or *running–Ostrich* (2 toes), *Emu* (3 toes).
2. Climbing–Parrots, wood peckers.
3. Clinging–Swift, humming bird.
4. Swimming–diving birds (coots, grebes), paddling birds (ducks, teals.)
5. Wading–Wading or marshy birds (herons, jacana, lapuing).
6. Raptorial–Predatory or carnivorous birds (eagles, vultures, owls).
7. Perching–Perching birds or passers (sparrows, crows, bulbuls, mynah).
8. Scraching–Fowls, quails, pheasants.
9. Snow shoe like–ruffled grouse.

Perching

Birds are able to sleep on a branch of tree. The specialised muscles are *Ambiens muscles. Gastrocnemius* (calf muscles), *peroneus long us* (anterior side of crus) and *extenser muscles* as

- Pectoralis major which bring the wing downward, forward & backward keeping the bird up & carrying it onward.
- Pectoralis minor raises the wing for the next stroke.

SOME IMPORTANT FACTS

- **Royal Allbatross** *(Diomedea)* is largest flying sea bird (wingspan 80-125 inches).
- Famous ornithologist of India is Professor Salim Ali–Bird man of India.
- Smallest bird of India is sun bird/tickel flower pocker; suck nectar from flowers.
- Smallest bird of the world is Bee humming bird of Cuba.
- Study of nests is nidology.
- Pygostyle is homologous to coccyx of man.
- Monal is the state bird of Himachal Pradesh.
- Aviary–Enclosure for keeping birds.
- Largest/Tallest crane is *Grus antigone* (Garus crone).
- Hawk possess both functional ovaries.

- Highes bird flier is *Cygnus lygnus* (whooper swan; 27000 ft.).
- Deepest diver bird is *Aptenodytes fosteri* (emperor penguin).
- Fastest swimming bird is *Pygoscelis pupua* (gentoo Penguin)
- Slowest flying bird is *scolopax minos* (American woockock, 8 km;hr.).
- Poisonous bird is *Pitohui dichrous* (Hooded pitonui) of papua, New Guinea have toxins in its skin & feathers.
- Irds & bony fishes are the two most successful classes of vertebrates.
- *Caprimulgus europens* (poor will/Good sucker/Night Jar), a short billed, wide mouthed, nocturnal, insectivorous bird undergoes hibernation.
- Ostrich has the largest eyes of any land animal.
- Study of birds eggs in Oology.
- Feathered young ones of birds are called precoicial.
- World champion bird is *sterna.*

KINGDOM—ANIMALIA

Sub-kingdom—Eumetazoa
Phylum—Chordata
Division—Gnathostomata
Super Class-Tetrapoda
Class—Mammalia
Age of mammals is coenozoic era
Number of species—About 4000
Study—Mammology

General Characteristics

- Homeothermal, endothennal or warm blooded.
- Their body is divisible into head, neck, trunk and tail.
- Skin is glandular with sweat gland or sudoriferous gland, oil gland or sebaceous gland, ceruminous (ear wax) and mammary gland.
- Exoskeleton as horns, epidermal hairs, claws, spines, nails, hoofs, bony dermal plates etc.
- Endoskeleton is ossified, skull is dicondylic, cranium is large, single zygomatic arch, acoelous vertebrae, 7 cervical vertebrae (except 2 toed loth (6), three toed sloth (9) ribs bicephalous.
- Presence of muscular diphragm which separate anterior thoracic cavity from the posterior abdominal cavity.
- They have two pairs of pentadactyl limbs, each with 5 or fewer digits. Digits have nails or hoofs or claws. Hind limbs are absent in ceteans and sirenians.
- Alimentary canal ends by anus. They show development of secondary palate (premaxillae, maxillae & palatine) which separates buccal cavity & nasal passage. Teeth are heterodont, diphyodont and the codont.
- Respiration is pulmonary. Glottis is protected by a fleshy, cartilagenous epiglottis which is present over the opening of trachea or larynx. Larynx enclose vocal cords.
- Heart is four chambered showing double circulation. Renal portal systems absent & only hepatic portal system is present. RBC's are small circular & non-nucleated (oval & flat in llama & camel).
- They have metanephric kidneys and excretion is ureotelic (urea).
- Brain is highly developed with large, convoluted cerebrum and cerebellum. A band like connection as corpus callosum is present between two cerebral hemispheres. They have 12 pairs of cranial nerves.

- Sense organs include external ear with fleshy pinna, middle ear with 3 ear ossicles (malels, incus, stapes) & cochlea of internal ear is highly coiled. Eyes are protected with eye lids.
- Sexes separate well marked sexual dimorphism. Males are with copulatory organ (erectile penis). Fertilization is internal & are viviparous. Development occurs in uterus through placenta. The extra embryonic membranes are present.
- After birth young ones are nourished by milk secreted from mammary gland of mother. Parental care is well developed.
- Mammals exhibit greatest intelligence among all animals.

Class mammalia is divided into two sub-classes

Sub-class

Prototheria	**Theria**	
First beast – Primitive reptile like, oviparous	Animal – Modern mammal viviparous **Infraclass**	
	Metatheria/between/after Marsupials/pouched mammals	**Eutheria/placental mammal**
– External ear is absent. – Marsupial pouch is absent. – Teats absent. – Placenta is absent – Testis is abdominal – Confined to Australia	– External ear is present. – Marsupial pouch is present – Teats are abdominal with or without placenta. – Placenta is less developecd – Tests is infront of penis in scrotal – Confined to Australia & neighbouring islands	– External ear is present. – Marsupila pouch is absent – Teats are thoracic or abdominal – Placenta is well developed – Testis is behind the penis in Scrotal sac. – They constitute vast majority of mammals
Order **Monotremata**	**Order** **Marsupialia**	**Order** **Echidna/Tachyglossus**
Single opening – Cloaca opening is present – Thecodont teeth – Ramer called them unfinished mammals *e.g. Ornithorhyncus*–Platypus/duck bill male has spur on hind limb connected to poison gland, lay eggs in the nest made up of grass leaves.	– Born in immature state and complete their development attached to teats – Vagina double – 3 premolar & 4 molars in each jaw. *e.g., Macropus*–Kangaroo; National animal of Australia Didelphis–Opossum; arboreal & possess prehensile tail, shorter gastation period (12-13 days) Phascolarctos-Koala; orboreal	– Spiny ant eater; hair modified to form spines, male develop mammary gland; Toilet claw (IInd claw of hind limb) is larger & curved used to clean spine & fur.
Insectivora	**Chiroptera**	**Dermoptera**
Insect to eat – Most primitive with pointed snout	Hand wing – Flying mammals, forelimbs are modified to form wings/ are	Skin wing – Gliding mammals – Four equal sized limbs

Insectivora	**Chiroptera**	**Dermoptera**
– Live in burrows *e.g., Sorex*–Shrew*;* smallest mammal; saliva contain poisonous substance to kill the prey. *Hemiechinus–Hedgehog;* largest insectivore; can eat snakes; If disturbed it rolls into ball; nocturnal.	– Eyes poorly developed so they locate object by echo – Pneumatic bones – Milk teeth are shed & permanent teeth appear before birth *e.g.,Pterous*–Flying fox; frugivorus *Scotophilus*–Small bat; carnivorous *Desmodus*–Vampirebats, sanguivours	– Tail included in lateral furry fold skin, petagia *e.g., Cynocephalus*
Pholiodata	**Edentata**	**Tubulidenta**
Horny scale – Body covered by overlapping horny scales – Tongue used to capture insects *e.g., Main*–Scaly ant eater	Toothless – Toothless – Toes with curved claws *e.g., Bradypus*–3 toed sloth	Tube like tooth – Tube like tooth – Each jaw with 4-5 teeth, enamel absent & perforated by numerous tubules of pulp *e.g., Orycteropus*–Cape anteater
Rodentia	**Lagomorpha**	**Cetacea**
Gnaw – Canines absent (Diastema) – Gnawing mammals – Cut hair lip – 2 pair of incisors *e.g., Rattus*–Rat; fussorial; nocturnal; grayish *Mus*–Mouse; dark brown; smaller than rat *Cavia*-Guinea pig; herbivore; prolific breeder; pinna small sized; milk teeth are shed & permanant teeth appear before birth *Funambulus*–squirrel	Hair form – Canines absent – 4 pairs of incisors *e.g., Oryctologus*–Rabbit herbivorous crepuslar; cursorial; coprophagic *Lepas*–Hare	Whale – Aquatic mammals – Forelimbs form flappers – Sweat glands absent – True salivary glands absent. – Hair only on the lips – Skin has thick layer of fats called blubber – Pelvic girdle is absent – Abdominal testis *e.g.,Platanista gangetica*–Ganga dolphin; jaws bear teeth well adapted for feeding on bottom living crustaceans. *Delphinus delphis*–common dolphin; toothed whale. *Balaenoptera masculus*–Blue whale/whalebond whale; gregareous; carnivorous; fastest growing mammal; largest heart

Sirenia	**Carnivora**
Sea nymph – Aquatic mammals with paddle like forelimbs – Flattened tail with horizontal fleshy fluke with or without a notch – Inhabit esturies & coastal sea e.g., *Dugong*–Dugong *Rhytina*–Steller's sea cow; recently extinct; 6 cervical vertebrae	Flesh to eat – Flesh eating mammals – Sharp, pointed teeth with strong jaws – Well developed claws *e.g., Canis familaris*–Dog, claws retractile *Canis lupus*–Wolf; cloaws non-retractifile *Acinonyx*–cheetah; fastest mammal; (120km/hr.) exctinct from India but present in Africa

Sirenia	**Carnivora**
	Pantheraleo–Lion; restricted to Gir forest Gujarat; cannon bones occur in its limbs *Panthera tigris*–Tiger; National animal of India declared in 1973. *Ailuropoda*–Panda

Proboscidea **Lophiiformes** **Infront to eat**	**Perissodactyla/** **Pleuronectiformes** **odd toes**	**Artiodactyla/** **Cluperiformes** **even toes**	**Primates/** **Channiformes/** **of the first rank**
– Long trunk without bones – Long tusks (made up of ivory) as modified incisors – Herbivorous – Largest land animal – Padded feet & hoobs absent *e.g., Elphas maximus* -Elephant beast of burden longest gestation period (609 days); Indian female elephants in without tusks. *Elephas cyclotis*–Pigmy African elephant *Loscodonta africana*–African elephant; largest land animal	– Odd toed hoofed mammal – Herbivorous – Both upper & lower incisors are present – Horns are absent – Simple stomach *e;g; Rhinoceros-Rhino;* second largest mammal; skin form sheild urine has antiseptic properties Two horned rhino has become extinct from India *Equus cabalus*–Horse; largest eyes *Equus zebra*–Zebra; vertical stripes; very strong sense of hearing. No two zebra are alike. *Equus vulgaris*–Ass; small body with narrow hoofs; erect mane; mone; only lower part of tail is hairy.	– Even toad hoofed mammal – herbivorous – Upper incisors are absent – Horns or antlers are present – Compound stomach *e.g., Hippopotomus amphibius* Horse of river; bulkiest mammal; red sweat; amphibious *Bos indicus*–Cow; two digits functional *Sus scrofa*–Pig *Cervus*–Deer; solid antlers *Moschus moschiferus*–Musk deer; without antlers; male musk deep has mush-bag or gland from which musk is squeezed. *Camelus dromedarius*–Arabian Camel; one humped; ship of desert; state animal Rajasthan. *Camelus bacterianus*–Turkish camel; two humped. *Giraffa cameloparadolis*–Giraffe, tallest mammal; has highest blood pressure. *Llama*–lama.	– Firsh digit opposable – Plantigrades – Arbogeal terrestrial *e.g., Lemur*–lemurs; confined to Medagascar island *Loris*–Loris; large forwardly directed eyes *Tarsius*–Tarsier; common in phillipines New world monkeys Cheek pouch absent nose flat, Prehensile tail; premolar 3 *e.g., Ateles*–Spider monkey old world monkeys–Cheek pouch present, nose is raised; tail is not prehensile; premolar 2 *e.g., Macaca*–Rhesus monkey; *Presbytis*–Langur *Hylobates*–gibbon, most intelligent ape; only race found in India *Pango/Simia*–Orangeutan; make nest for living *Pan*–Chimpanzee; Intelligent ape near to man *Gorilla*–Largest ape; dangerous; travel in group lead by male *Homo sapiens*–Man/Naked ape, most intelligent; social cultured; bipedal & erect posture; ability to communicate; jaw suspension is craniostylic.

GENERAL INFORMATION REGARDING MAMMALS

- **Digitigrade**–Digits touching the ground during walking or running *e.g.,* elephant, rabbit.
- **Unguligrade**–Tip of digits during running or walking. Heels raised above the ground *e.g.,* Cow, Horse, Ass, Deer.
- **Plantigrade**–(Palmigrade) whole sole of feet touching the ground during walking or running e.g., Human, Bear.
- Human beings are plantigrade while walking but become digitigrade while running.

LOCOMOTION	EXAMPLE
Digging	Anteater
Walking	Elephant
Arboseal climbing	Squirrel
Arboreal gliding	Flying squirrel
Arboreal hanging	Sloth
Brachiating	Gibbous urangutan
Scansosial (cave dwelling)	Bata
Scansorial (climbing)	Monkey, loris
Volant	Bats
Aquatic (naatorial)	Sirenians, cetaceans, seals
Cursorial (rinning)	Deer, horse, Carnivorous
Fossorial (burrowing)	Mole, rodents
Saltatorial (jumping)	Kangaroo, rabbit, here
TEETH	**EXAMPLES**
Monophyodont	Platypus, marsupials, moles, sirenian,whale
Acrodont	Shark, frog
Thecodont	Crocodile, mammals, fossil toothed birds
Bunodont	Human being, monkey
Lophodont	Elephant
Pleurodont	Urodele, Lizards
Toothless mammals	Spiny outteater, scaly anteata, platypus

SOME IMPORTANT FACTS

- Hyaena is a mammial, with a similar voice to crackling human laughter.
- Nidifugous or precocial youngs *e.g.,* cattle.
- Niculous or altricial youngs *e.g.,* cats, rats.
- Smallest mammal is hog nose at (earlier it was pigmy water shrew).
- Carnassial teeth are cutting teeth in carnivores to crack bones. It is the fourth premolar of upper jaw and first molar of lower jaw.
- Slowest aquatic mammal–Sea other (*Erhydra lutric*)–10 km/hr.
- Slowest terrestrial mammal–3 toed sloth (*Brady pus tridactylus*)–10 m/hr.
- Echo location is useful in flight is bats.
- Whaling–Hunting of whales for its blubber.
- **Armadillo**–Only mammal with bony plates in skin, exhibit polyembyony *i.e.,* one zygote produec 4–8 youngones.

- **Dolphin** (*Platanista gongetica*) is second most intelligent mammal and has high learning powers.
- In *Prototherians,* eggs are polylecithal, shelled and cledoic like reptiles.
- *Thyroid cartilage* in the larynx is present only is the mammals.
- **Cervical vertebral–**
  3-toed sloth (*Bradypus*) – 9
  2-toed sloth (*Cholerpus*) – 6
  Manatee (*Trichechus*) – 6
  Ant bear *(Tamandua)* – 8
- Jaw suspension is *craniostylic i.e.,* dentary bone (lower jaw) suspended from squamosal bone (upper jaw).
- Indian female elephant do not have tusks.
- **Polyestrous mammals**–Many sexual season is a year *e.g.,* sheep, rat, goat etc.
- No particular mating season in man, baboon, giraffe and elephants.
- Proboscis (trunk) in elephants is prehensile and formed by the prolongation of Nose and upperlip jointly, present in both sexes.
- Tusks are enlarged upper incisors which are rudimentary is females and long is males,
- Camel has three chambered stomach.

CHORDATES

	Pisces	Amphibia	Reptilia	Aves	Mammalia
1. Skull	Dicondylic	Dicondylic	Monocondylic	Monocondylic	Dicondylic
2. Body temperature	Cold blooded	Cold blooded	Cold blooded	Warm blooded	Warm blooded
3. Kidney	Mesonephric	Mesonephric	Metanephric	Metanephric	Metanephric
4. Renal portal system	Well developed	Well developed	Less developed	Very much reduced	Absent
5 Ear	Internal only	Internal & middle ear tympanum covers middle ear	External, middle & internal Snakes have have only internal	External, middle & internal	External middle Internal Pinna-part of external ear
6. Cranial nerves	Ten pairs	Ten pairs	Twelve pairs	Twelve pairs	Twelve pairs
7. Heart	Two chambered, in ling fish three chambered	Three chambered–two auricles, one ventricle	Two auricles, one partly divided ventricle. Crocodile has 4-chambered	Four chambered	Four-chambered
8. Amnion	-	-	Present	Present	Present
9. Respiratory system	Gills, except in lung Fishes	Gills, lungs. skin. buccophyrangal cavity	Lungs	Lungs	Lungs
10. Lateral lines system	Well developed	Found during development	Absent	Absent	Absent
11. Fertilization Development	Internal in chondichthyes & external in osteichthyes Oviparous/ Ovoviviparous usually direct	Mostly external Mostly oviparous Indirect	Internal, Oviparous/Ovoviviparous Direct	Internal; Oviparous Direct	Internal Except-egg laying mammals all viviparous

	Pisces	Amphibia	Reptilia	Aves	Mammalia
12. Excretory product	Chondrichthyes -urea, Osteichthyes-ammonia	Larvae & amphibians ammonia, Frogs toads urea	Crocodile-ammonia Turtle & alligator--urea, Lizard & snakes uric acid	Uric acid	Urea
13. Special features	Except in lung fishes, internal nares absent; operculum; paired and unpaired fins; swim bladder; dermal scales	Upaired fins may be present, scales if present, hidden beneath the skin	Epidermal scales: typical cloaca	Wings are fore limbs, beak formed by upper & lower jaws; lacks teeth in alimentary canal-crop & gizzard; for voice-syrinx; air sacs; pneumatic bones; urinary bladder absent except in American Ostrich; keel on sternum; Right ovary & oviduct absent or vestigeal	Nourish young ones with milk, well developed placenta present, except in egg laying mammals
14. Cloaca	Chondrichthyes–Present Osteichthyes –absent	Present	Present	Present	Absent except in monotremes (egg-laying mammals)

GYMNOSPERMS

Introduction

- Gymnosperm (*gymnos* = naked; *sperma* = seed).
- Term **"Gymnospermae"** was coined by Theophrastus.
- Commonly known as **naked seed plant** because their ovules (later becomes seed) are **not covered** and lie naked on the **megasporophylls** or **ovuliferous scales** or **carpels** which are arranged into cones.
- Perrenial, dominant flora in colder areas, xerophytic, evergreen trees or shrubs. Annual and herbacious forms are absent.
- Sporophytic plant body and differentiated into roots, stems and leaves.
- Root system (tap root) well developed.
- Leaves **dimorphic** (2 types) (*a*) green **foliage** leaves (needle shaped or pinnately compound) (*b*) brown **scaly** leaves (minute, deciduous). Leaves with sunken stomata and covered with thick cuticle.
- **Lateral veins** are absent in the leaves of most gymnosperms. Instead **transfusion tissue (hydrostereom)** present for lateral translocation of nutrient.
- Vascular bundles in stem are **conjoint, collateral** and **open** arranged in a ring.
- Xylem with **tracheids and parenchyma only.** Vessels absent (present only in members of **Gnetales).** Phloem lacks companion cells.
- **Monoxylic** (*e.g., Cycas*) or **pycnoxylic** (*e.g., Pinus*) wood.
- **Heterosporous** (2 types of spores)—microspores and megaspores which are produced in microsporangia (microsporophylls) and megasporangia (megasporophylls), respectively. These sporophylls produce compact **cones** or **strobili.** Flowers are absent.
- Generally **monosporangiate** (unisexual) cones and development of microsporangia is **eusporangiate.**

- Ovules are **orthrotropous** and **unitegmic** (**bitegmic** in *Gnetum*) and lies naked on megasporophyll. Each ovule has a mass of tissue **(nucellus).** Megasporophylls aggregate to form female cones which persist for several years.
- Female gametophyte develops **archegonia** with a single egg and a venter canal cell. **Neck canal cells are absent.** Male gametes are **ciliated** and **motile** (*e.g.*, Cycas, Ginkgo) or non-ciliated and non-motile (*e.g., Pinus, Gnetum*).
- Pollination by wind **(anemophily)** which bring pollen grains over the micropylar end of ovules *i.e.*, direct pollination. **Siphonogamic** (through pollen tube) fertilization. **Meroblastic** embryo development. Sometimes exhibit **polyembryony.**
- Endosperm is **gametophytic** and develops before fertilization and is haploid.
- The number of cotyledons in seed is **one** (*e.g., Cycas*) or **two** (*e.g., Pinus*).
- In some gymnosperms, secondary growth present.

CLASSIFICATION OF GYMNOSPERMS

(1) **Cycads** *e.g., Cycas, Zamia*
(2) **Conifers** *e.g., Pinus*
(3) **Ginkophytes** *e.g.,* Ginkgo or Maiden Hair tree
(4) **Gnetophytes** *e.g., Gnetum, Ephedra*

Cycas

- Commonly called **sago palm,** found in tropical regions of the world.
- Sporophyte plant body and differentiated into root, stem and leaf.
- Tap root system present. Additional **contractile** and adventitious roots may present.
- Root branches are of 2 types **(normal** and **coralloid).** Corralloid roots lies near the soil surface which are irregular and dichotomously branched. Coralloid roots have symbiotic association with N_2-fixing blue-green algae either *Anabaena cycadacearum* or *Nostoc punctiforme.*
- Anomalous (abnormal) secondary growth occurs in *Cycas* stem. Wood is **manoxylic.**
- The cells of both cortex and pith of stem contains **starch grains** or **sago grains.**
- Vegetative reproduction by **bulbils** (on the stem).
- **Dioecious** *i.e.,* male and female plants are distinct. Male plant produces single terminal, oval, large (40-50 cm) **male cone** utilizes the growing apex. Male plant shows **"sympodial branching".** Male cone possess numerous micro-sporophylls on abaxial side arranged spirally on a **central axis** in **acropetal** succession. Each micro-sporophyll is horizontly flattened and wedge-shaped and it has basal sterile region, middle fertile region and terminal upcurved sterile apophysis. The microsporangia produce a large number of boat-shaped microspores or pollen grains arranged **tetrahedrally.** At **3-celled stage** (prothallial, generative and tube cells), pollen grains are dispersed.
- The female plant produces many megasporophylls near its tip, once in an year.
- The megasporophylls are loosely arranged in close spirals around the apex of columnar trunk. Each megasporophyll (15-30 cm long) is a flat leaf like and bears many (2-12) ovules arranged in two rows in the middle fertile region.
- Ovules of *Cycas* are **large,** naked, **orthrotropous, unitegmic,** reddish in colour. Integument is differentiated into outer **sarcotesta,** middle **sclerotesta** and inner **sarcotesta. Micropyle** is opening at the top of ovule. Integument is followed by **nucellus** and female gametophyte (or endosperm) with 2-8 archegonia. Each archegonium with 4-celled neck and a large egg.

- Pollination by **wind** (anemophilous). During pollination, the mature ovule ooze out a mucilagenous liquid drop through their micropyle. The pollen grains get entangled to the adhesive drop and sucked into the pollen chamber inside the ovule. They germinate by giving out pollen tube which pierces through the **nucellus** and absorbs nutrients from it. In *Cycas* pollen tube also acts as a **haustorium.**
- The generative cell divide to form a **stalk cell** and a large **body cell.** The body cell divides to form two **spermatozoids** (or **antherozoids).** Each antherozoid or sperm is oval, **top-shaped,** multiciliate with 4-5 spiral bands of cilia on the pointed end.
- Fertilization in **siphonogamous** which results in the formation of diploid zygote ($2n = 22$) which develops into **meroblastic** embryo. There are number of archegonia in each ovule, a number of embryos develop but finally only one attains maturity.
- The ovule is finally converted into seed containing single dicotyledinous embryo. Embryo consists of radicle, plumule, haustorium, suspensor, two cotyledons.
- Mature seed represents 3 generations–
  (1) Testa and nucellus—sporophytic parent generation
  (2) Endosperm—gametophytic generation
  (3) Diploid embryo—next sporophytic generation
- The post-fertilization changes are—
  (1) Nucellus → Perisperm
  (2) Female gametophyte → Endosperm
  (3) Zygote → Embryo
  (4) Integuement → Seed coat
  (5) Ovule → Seed
- Life cycle is **diplohaplontic** and exhibit **heteromorphic** or **heterologous** type of alternation of generation.

Pinus

- Tall (3-50 m) coniferous tree, perrenial, evergreen, xerophytes and appear conical or excurrent or pyramidal like a 'Christmas tree' due to radial branching.
- Common species are *P. roxburghii* and *P. wallichiana.*
- The main stem *i.e.,* shaft and the dominant branches are covered by **bark.** The branching is **monopodial** and **excurrent.**
- Branches are **dimorphic** (*a*) branches of unlimited growth (long shoots) and (b) branches of limited growth (or dwarf shoots) called as **spur shoots** or **brachyplasts.**
- Each dwarf shoot bear 8-10 spirally arranged scale leaves *i.e.,* cataphylls and terminates into 1-5 needle like foliage leaves at its apex.
- Roots of many conifers harbour **ectotrophic mycorrhizae** which help in the absorption of water and minerals.
- Secondary growth producing **non porous** (vessels absent) and **pycnoxylic** (compact with less parenchyma and narrow medullary rays) wood.
- Resin ducts are filled with an aromatic sticky material (resin) found in wood and bark.
- Foliage leaves are needle-shaped and with thick cuticle, sclerenchymatous hypodermis and sunken stomata to reduce the loss of water by transpiration.
- **Heterosporous, monoecious** *i.e.,* male and female cones on **separate branches** of **same tree.**
- Male cone (1.5-2.5 cm long and 0.5 cm in diameter) are rounded and arise in clusters (15-140 in each cluster) behind the apical buds at the bases of new shoots.

- Female cone (**ovulate strobili** or **seed cones**) arise singly or in groups of 2-4 in the axils of scale leaves at the tips of new strong shoots at some distance from the male cones. These are green when young but become reddish brown in the 2nd year. They take about 3 years to complete their growth.
- Both male and female cones are made up of spirally arranged, closely packed **microsporophylls** and **megasporophylls,** respectively.
- Each microsporophylls bears two elongated or pouch like **microsporangia** or **pollen sacs** on its **abaxial** (lower) surface. The pollen mother cell divide by meiosis inside the pollen sac and produces haploid **microspores** or pollen grains. Each pollen grain has two large air sacs to facilitate dispersal by wind. Large quantities of pollen grains are produced so that cones becomes yellow and **clouds of pollen** or **"shower of sulphur dust"** are released.
- Each megasporophyll consists of lower **scaly bract** scale and a large **ovuliferous** scale or megasporophyll. Each **ovuliferous** scale is shortly stalked and bears two naked, sessile and anatropous ovules towards the basal region on the upper side.
- Each ovule with a three layered integument which encloses a parenchymatous nucellus. The integument leaves a gap called **micropyle.** Within the nucellus a central megaspore mother cell divides by meiosis to produce 4 linearly arranged haploid **megaspores.** The lowest megaspore is functional while rest of three degenerate. The functional megaspore develops a female gametophyte with 1-8 (generally 3) **archegonia.**
- Each **archegonium** with **8 neck cells** (4 tiers of 2 cells each), whereas neck canal cells are absent. The large venter is made up of a small venter canal cell and a large egg.
- **Anemophilous** pollination. Pollen grains are **4 celled** (two prothallial cells, one generative cell and one tube cell) at the time of pollination. The time gap between pollination and fertilization is about fifteen months.
- The pollen grains enter into the opened micropyle of ovule and deposited over the top of nucellus where they germinate to form a **germ** or **pollen tubes.** Tube reaches to the **archegonium** pushing through the nucellus.
- The generative cell divides into a **sterile stalk cell** and a **fertile body cell.**
- The body cell migrates into pollen tube and divides a weak before fertilization into **two unequal non-flagellated male gametes.** The pollen tube enters into the **archegonium** where it bursts and liberating both the male gametes.
- Only one of these fuses with the egg nucleus to form a diploid **zygote** or oospore. The zygote develops into an embryo and the ovule matures into a seed.
- The embryo development shows **cleavage polyembryony** but only one embryo attains maturity.
- The upper surface layer of ovuliferous scale, close to the ovule becomes membranous and develops a **wing** of the seed which helps in the dispersal of **seed by wind.**
- Small portion of nucellus present in the form of **papery perisperm,** outer layer of integument **degenerates,** the middle layer forms the **hard seed coat** and the inner layer forms a thin membranous **tegmen.**

ECONOMIC IMPORTANCE OF GYMNOSPERMS

- Seeds of *Pinus gerardiana*, commonly called **chilgoza** (dry fruit).
- Stem and seeds of **cycads** yields **sago starch** which is used is as food.
- An alkaloid **ephedrine** obtained from *Ephedra* is for the preparation of medicines in the treatment of asthma, cough and bronchitis.

- The seeds of *Gnetum gnemon* and *G. latifolium* are edible.
- **Resins** secreted from **coniferous** trees which are complex oxidation products of various essential oils containing terpenes, resin acids and esters. They are used in the manufacture of waterproof paints, varnishes, sealing wax etc. Some common resins from various sources are–

  Copal — *Agathis australis*
  Manila copal—*Agathis alba*
  Rosin—As residue after the distillation of pine terpentine
  Canada balsam—*Abies balsamea*
  Amber—Fossil resin from extinct species of *Pinus*.
- Many gymnospermous trees (*e.g.*, Cedar, Pine, Larck, Douglar fir etc.) are used as wood.
- Many gymnospermous plants (*e.g., Cycas revoluta*, *Cryptomeria*, *Araucaria*, *Thuja* etc.) are cultivated as ornamental plants in gardens. *Araucaria* (monkey puzzle) is form Australia and South America.
- **Tannins** (complex phenolic substance) from the bark of ***Tsugo candensis.***
- Many gymnosperms yield essential oils which are used in perfumery and as flavouring agent.
- *Pinus roxburghii* (chir) is the principal source of methyl alcohol, terpentine and resin.
- *Gnetum montanum* have piscicidal properties.
- *Gnetum ula* seeds are edible, produces cooking oil. The oil is also used for massage in rheumatism and for illumination.
- Red cedar wood oil is obtained from *Juniperus virginiana.*

Some Gymnosperms with their common and scientific name

COMMON NAME	SCIENTIFIC NAME
Sago palm	*Cycas revoluta*
Monkey puzzle	*Araucaria*
Maidan Hair tree	*Ginkgo biloba*
Chir pine	*Pinus roxburghii* (= *P. longifolia*)
Chilgoza pine	*Pinus gerardiana*
Cedar	*Cedrus deodara*
Firs	*Abies* spp.
Spruce	*Picea smithiana*
Douglas fir	*Pseudotsuga taxifolia*
Red cedar or Juniper	*Juniperus virginiana*
Jointed fir	*Ephedra*
Silver fir/Blue pine/Kail	*Pinus excelsa* (*P. wallichiana*)

SOME IMPORTANT FACTS

- **Cycads** referred as **"reptiles of plant kingdom"** or **"panda of vegetable kingdom.**
- Gymnosperms originated during late **Palaeozoic era** and flourished well during **mesozoic era.**
- **World tallest tree :** ***Sequoia sempervirens*** (giant red wood) about 125 metre in height, 30 metres in girth, about 4,000 years old and found in **Red-wood park of California.**
- Largest gymnospermous tree (in girth) : ***Sequodendron*,** about 13-16 metres in diamter.

- Smallest gymnosperm : ***Zamia pygmia*** possess underground tuberous stem and reaches only upto 25 cm in height.
- Coralloid roots of ***Cycas*** are symbiotically associated with algae whereas mycorrhizal roots of *Pinus* are symbiotically associated with fungus.
- Largest ovule in plant kingdom : ***Cycas thouarrii,*** 6-7 cm in diameter.
- Largest egg in plant kingdom : ***Cycas circinalis,*** about 0.5 mm in diameter.
- Largest sperm in plant kingdom : ***Cycas revoluta*** (200-300 μ wide).
- Longest (oldest) gymnospermous tree (in age) : **Pinus longavaea,** about 4900 years old.
- **Cycadofilicales or pteridosperms :** A group of fern like fossil plants bearing seeds commonly on the edges of leaves.
- **Gnetales** : Vessels in xylem *e.g., Ephedra, Gnetum, Welwitschia.*
- *Welwitschia* : It possess only two large leaves with basal meristems and showing limited growth (only 45 cm tall).
- **Zoidiogamy :** Fertilization involves motile or ciliate male gamete or sperm. *e.g.,* ***Cycas*** (it also shows **siphonogamy** *i.e.,* fertilization through pollen tube).
- **Living fossil :** ***Ginkgo biloba*** and ***Cycas*** because possess traits of extinct pteridosperms and other gymnosperms.
- Bisporangiate strobili : ***Ephedra intemedia.***
- Unbranched stem gymnosperm : ***Cycas.***
- Connecting link between gymnosperms and angiosperms is ***Gnetum.***
- Mano and monoxylic wood : *Cycas*.
- Pycnoxylic wood (hard & compact) : ***Pinus.***
- Medicinally most important gymnosperms : ***Taxus*** and ***Ephedra.***
- Cleavage polyembryony : Pinus.
- Simple polyembryony : Feature of gymnosperms.
- ***Gnetum*** (only gymnosperm) lacks haploid endosperm.
- The number of needles are 1, 2, 3, 4, 5 in a spur of ***Pinus monophylla, P. sylvestris, P. roxburghii, P. quadrifolia*** and ***P. wallichiana,*** respectively.
- All gymnosperms have **unitegmic, orthrotropous ovules.**
- In gymnosperms **endosperm** is haploid and develops before fertilization.
- Germination of ***Cycas*** seeds is **hypogeal.**
- Linoleum and plastic is made from saw dust of conifers.
- In ***Pinus,*** four tiers in proembryo starting from base are embryo tier, suspensor tier, rosette tier and upper tier (or open tier).

ANGIOSPERM

Introduction

- Most successful group on the earth.
- Term **angiosperm** means **enclosed seed** because the ovules or potential seeds are enclosed within a hollow ovary.

- More than 2,50,000 different species which occupy a very wide range of ecological habitats.
- They include trees, shrubs, vines and herbs adapted to almost every kind of environment. Some **hydrophytes** (*Hydrilla* – water lili etc.) have taken water secondarily and even in shallow seas (*e.g.* eel grass–*Zostera*). Some are **epiphytes** (*e.g.* Vanda), many are xerophytes.
- Leaves exhibit reticulate or parallel venation forming **areoles.**
- The libriform fibre and true vessels in xylem and companion cells in phloem are present.
- Sporophytic plant bears **flowers** (site of sexual reproduction) which is a modified shoot. Flowers consists of 4 whorl of appendages – sepals, petals, stamen and carpels which arise from **thalamus. Sepals (calyx)** and **petals (corolla)** are two outer accessory reproductive structures while, **Stamen (androecium)** and **carpel (gynoecium)** constitute the two inner essential parts of a flower.
- Each stamen (microsporophylls) consists of stalk like **filament** and flattened globoid top called **anther**. Anther produces tectate pollen grains with exine differentiated into rod-like **columellae** covered by a **tectum**. Stamens are **bilaterally symmetrical.**
- Each carpels (megasporophylls) exhibit upper terminal **stigma,** middle elongated **style** and basal swollen **ovary**. Ovules borne on placentae are present in ovary.
- Female gametophyte is highly reduced and consists of **single egg cell, two synergids, three antipodals** and **two polar nuclei.** Archegonia absent.
- Pollination takes place by wind, insects, birds, water, human and other animals. Pollination may be self or cross. **Entomophilus** (insect pollinated plants) are generally colourful and showy, possess nectar and scent etc.
- The pollen grain germinates on stigma and form a pollen tube which carries tube nucleus.
- The most characteristic feature of angiosperms is **double fertilization** *i.e.,* one of the male gamete fuses with the egg and produce diploid zygote which develops into embryo or new sporophyte and the other male gamete fuses with **two polar nuclei (triple fusion)** and form triploid **primary endosperm nucleus.**
- The sepals, petals, stamens, style, stigma wither at the time of fruit formation. The ovules ripen into **seeds** and ovary ripens into **fruits.**
- The seed possess **dormant embryo along with food material** in endosperm or cotyledons.
- They have wide nutritional modes *e.g.* **autotrophs** (most of the green plants), **saprophytes**. (*Monotropa, Corallorhiza*), **parasites** (*Cuscuta, Rafflesia*) and **insectivorous plants** (*Nepenthes, Drosera*) etc.
- According to **Warming** (1895), plants are divided into 5 major groups *i.e.,* **hydrophytes** (*Hydrilla, Wolffia* etc.), mesophytes (*Brassica*, sunflower etc.), **xerophytes** (*Cynodon, Asparagus* etc.), **halophytes** (*Spartina, Portulaca* etc.) and **epiphytes** (*Vanda*).
- Plants are divided into 4 categories on the basis of duration of life *i.e.,* **Ephemerals** (*e.g. Arabidopsis*), **annuals** (*e.g. Wolffia, Triticum* etc.), **binnials** (*e.g.* sugar beet) and **perennials** (*e.g. Agave*, Bamboo etc.)
- Plants may be herbs (*e.g., Brassica, Canna*), shrubs (*e.g.* Rose), trees (*e.g.* Palms), climber, twiner, trailer and creeper etc.
- Bentham and Hooker classified seed plants (angiosperms) into three classes *i.e.,* **dicotyledons, gymnospermae** and **monocotyledons.**

DIFFERENCES BETWEEN DICOTS AND MONOCOTS

PARTS OF PLANT	DICOTS	MONOCOTS
1. Cotyledons	Two	One
2. Leaves	Mostly with reticulum venation (exception ***Callophylum*** and ***Eryngium***)	Mostly with parallel venation (exception ***Smilex***, ***Colocasia*** and relatives).
3. Stem	Open vascular bundles arranged in a ring with central pith *i.e.*, **dictyostele.**	Scattered closed vascular bundles.
4. Root	Tap root or adventitious root or both. Vascular bundle in **polyarch** condition.	Primary tap root is replaced by adventitious roots. Vascular bundles are **diarch** to **hexarch.**
5. Floral parts	The number of flower parts mostly in fours *i.e.*, **tetramerous** or fives *i.e.*, **pentamerous.**	Mostly in threes *i.e.*, **trimerous.**

Economic importance of Angiosperms

- Plants are divided into 4 categories on the basis of duration of life *i.e.*, **Ephemerals** (*e.g. Arabidopsis*),
- Major source of food, produce **cereals, pulses, fruits, vegetables** and nuts.
- Plants are divided into 4 categories on the basis of duration of life *i.e.*, **Ephemerals** (*e.g. Arabidopsis*),
- Flowering plants are main source of edible oils used for cooking *e.g.* groundnut, sunflower, coconut, mustard etc.
- Various parts of flowering plants are used as spices *e.g.* coriander, *chillies*, cloves, black pepper, fennel, caraway, cinnamon etc.
- Common beverages are tea, cocoa, coffee.
- Timber from mainly dicotyledons which yield valuable hard wood *e.g.* Teak, sal, oak, sandalwood, sisham etc.
- Fibres from various species of angiosperms *e.g.*, cotton, flax, sunhemp, hemp, jute etc.
- Medicines are also obtained from various angiosperms. The medicinal plants are aconite, quinine, asgandh, belladona etc.
- There are many useful and valuable articles which are obtained from angiosperms. They may be ornamental plants.

SOME IMPORTANT FACTS

- Smallest angiosperm : ***Lemna*** (duck weed)
- Smallest flower : ***Wolffia microscopia***
- Longest flower : ***Rafflesia arnoldi*** (1m in diameter and 15 kg weight)
- Spanish moss (***Tillandria***) is an epiphytic angiosperm
- Angiosperm begins terrestrial life but becomes epiphytic at maturity is ***Scindapsus afficinale.***
- Leafless inflorescence : ***Balanophora dioica***
- Largest inflorescence of the world : ***Puya raimondii*** (32 ft.) and the second largest is ***Amorphophallus*** (8 ft.)
- *Cuscuta reflexa* : Dicot without cotyledons

- **Hydrophytes :** May be submerged (*e.g., Hydrilla*), free floating (*e.g., Wolffia*), attached floating (*e.g. Nymphaea*), and amphibious or partly emerged hydrophytes (*e.g., Sagittaria*).
- Total stem parasite : ***Cuscuta*** or dodder
- Total root parasite : ***Orobanche, Rafflesia*** etc.
- Insectivorous plants (partly autotrophic and partly heterotrophic) : Pitcher plant (***Nepenthes***), butter wort (***Pinguicula***) venus's fly trap (***Dionaea***), sundew (***Drosera***), bladder wort (***Utricularia***) etc.
- Tallest angiosperm : ***Eucalyptus*** upto 100 metres or more.
- In parasitic plants, **haustoria** are present.
- Total saprophytic angiosperms having mycorhizae : ***Monotropa*** and *Sarcodes*.

FUNGI

Introduction

- **Mycology** (Gk. *mykes*–mushroom) or **Mycetology :** Study of fungi.
- **Father of plant pathology :** de Bary
- **Father of Indian Mycology and Indian Plant Pathology :** E.J. Butler
- **Father of mycology :** Pier Antonio Micheli (1729)
- **Fungal Pathology :** Study of fungal diseases.
- Division fungi comprises more than 1,00,000 species, **Cosmopolitan.**
- **Ubiquitous** *i.e.*, found in almost every available habitat on earth.
- **Achlorophyllous** (absence of chlorophyll), **Thallophytic** (not differentiated into stem, axis and leaves) and **heterophytic** organisms.
- Based on their habitat, fungi are **coprophilous** (dung inhabiting), **keratinophilous** (on hair, horns), **corticolous** (bark), **epixylic/xylophilous/lignocolous** (on wood) etc.
- Exhibit symbiosis with algae to form **lichens** and symbiotic association with roots of higher plants called **mycorrhiza.**
- Body is made up of fine tubular, colourless filaments called **hyphae** which form complex network called **mycelium.**
- Nutrition is **heterotrophic** and **absorptive,** may be parasites or saprophytes. They possess special absorbing organs **(haustoria)** to obtain nourishment from host.
- Food reserve is glycogen (animal starch) and oil globules.
- Eukaryotic cell possess all cell organelles except **plastids.** Cell wall is made up of **fungus cellulose** or **chitin.**
- Hyphae can be **septate** or **aseptate (multinucleate** and **coenocytic).**
- Vegetative reproduction by fragmentation, fission, budding, gonidia, rhizomorphs, sclerotia etc.
- Asexual reproduction through conidia, oidia, ascospores, endospores, chlamydospores, pycniospores, basidiospores, teleutospores, uredospores etc.
- Sexual reproduction may be isogamous, anisogamous to oogamous.
- Perrenating structures are **rhizomorphs and sclerotia.**
- Life cycle may be **haploid** (*e.g.*, phycomycetes and ascomycetes), **haploid-dikaryotic** cycle (*e.g.*, basidiomycetes), **haploid-diploid** cycle (*e.g.*, yeast) and **diploid** cycle (*e.g.*, oomycetes of phycomycetes).

CLASSIFICATION OF FUNGI

- Proposed by **Ainsworth** and **Sussman** (1972–73)

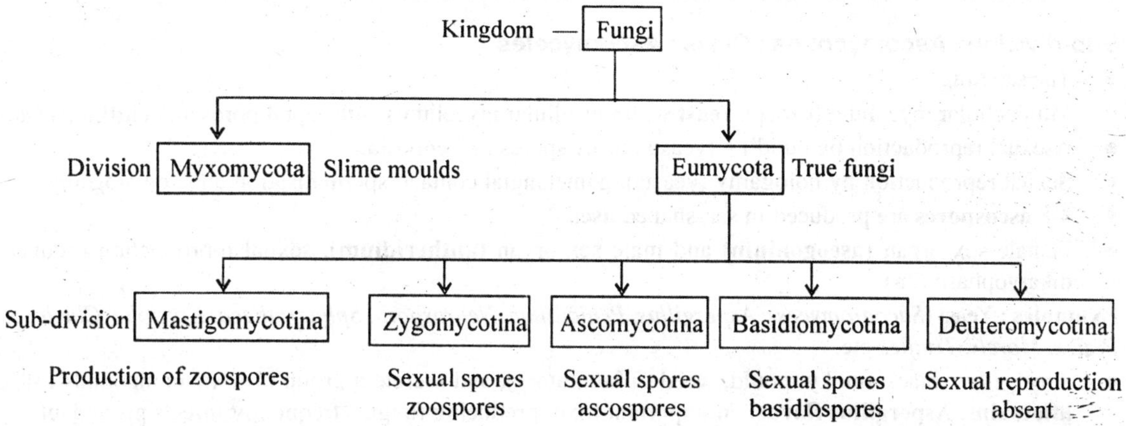

Sub-division : Mastigomycotina : Algal fungi or egg fungi : Class : Oomycetes

- Mycelial thallus, coenocytic hyphae, hyphal wall may contain **chitin** or **cellulose**.
- Asexual reproduction by formation of spores in sac-like **sporangia**. Terrestrial species produces **aplanospores** and aquatic species produces **zoospores** (**heterokant** flagellation *i.e.*, one smooth and one tinsel).
- Sexual reproduction may be **isogamous** or **oogamous** (male-sex organ-**antheridia** and female sex organ-**oogonia**.
- Gametangial contact type sexual fusion.
- Sexual reproduction leads to the formation of resting **oospores**.

Examples *Phytophthora, Albugo (= cystopus), Phythium. Scherospora, Perenospora, Plasmopora* etc.

- *Phytophthora infestans* causes late blight of potato and tomato.
- Potato femine (1843-1846) in Europe due to epidemic caused by *P. infestans.*
- Zoospores : biflagellate, reniform, uninucleate.
- Oogamous sexual reproduction, results in formation of oospores.
- *Albugo (= cystopus) candida* causes **white rust of crucifers** and **hyper trophied** inflorescence of *Brassica.*
- Asexual reproduction by formation of **conidiosporangia**.

Sub-division : Zygomycotina : Class : zygomycetes : conjugation fungi

- Mycelial **thallus, coenocytic hyphae, chitinous** or **fungal cellulosic** cell wall, absence of motile cells.
- Asexual reproduction by thinwalled, non-motile **sporangiospores** (aplanospores) produced inside the sporangium.
- Sexual reproduction by **gametangial copulation** (conjugation) forming a **gametes**.
- Each zygospore forms a **germ sporangium** at the tip of a hypha called promycelium which produces neiospores called **germ spores**.

Examples *Pilobolus, Rhizopus, Mucor etc.*

- *Pilobolus crystallinus* grows on dung, also called as **squirting fungus.**
- *Rhizopus solonifere (= nigricans)* causes **leak and soft rot of sweet potatoes and apple**. It is called as "*bread mould*"

- *Mucor pusillus* causes **bronchomycosis disease in man.**
- *Mucor caninus* is dung mould.
- *R. stolonifer* and *M. Caninus* (= mucedo) are called **Pin moulds.**

Sub-division : Ascomycotina ; Class : Ascomycetes

- The sac fungi.
- Multicellular mycelium (except **Yeast** with unicellular mycelium) with septal pores and **chitinous** wall.
- Asexual reproduction by budding (yeasts) or by spores *i.e.,* **conidia.**
- Sexual reproduction by hologamy (yeasts), gametangial contact, spermatisation and somatogamy.
- 4-8 **ascospores** are produced in sac-shaped **asci.**
- Female sex organ **(ascogonium)** and male sex organ **(antheridium)**, sexual reproduction produces dikaryophase (2n).

Examples : Yeast (*Saccaromyces*), *Aspergillus, Penicillium, Neurospora, Sphaerotheca, Erysiphe, Claviceps, Peziza, Morels, Truffles* etc.

- *Aspergillus* (black smoky mould, weed of laboratory), and secrete a group of toxic compounds called **aflotoxins. Aspergillus flavus,** an important toxin producing fungus, frequently infects groundnut.
- *A. fumigatus* causes **pulmonary aspergillosis** and ear infection.
- *Penicillium* **(green mould)**, production of antibiotic **penicillin.**
- *P. italicum* causes **blue mould** and *P. digitatum* causes **green mould** of citrus fruits in storage.
- Some species causes respiratory diseases **penicillosis** in animals, and human being.
- Some yeast causes serious diseases in plants. *e.g., Nematospora lycopersici* (on tomato fruits), *N. phaseoli* (on garden beans) and *N. gossypii* (on cotton).

Sub-division : Basidiomycotina ; Class : Basidiomycetes

- Club fungi
- Most advanced, best decomposers of wood, mycelium is filamentous,branched and septate hyphae.
- 3 types of mycelia :
  (*a*) **Primary mycelium**—Developes from uninucleate haploid basidiospores, it is uninucleate.
  (*b*) **Secondary mycelium**—Long lived and dikaryotic, produced by fusion between two monokaryotic cells or spores, cell division accompanied by clamp connection. Dikaryophase may multiple by spores like uredospores, aecidospores and teleutospores. Karyogamy and meiosis takes place in club-shaped **basidia.** Each basidia produces four exogenous meiospores or basidiospores. Motile structures are absent.
  (*c*) Some higher forms produces fruiting bodies called **basidiocarps.** The body of basidiocarp comprises of complex secondary mycelium known as **tertiary mycelium.**

Examples — *Agaricus, Puccinia, Ustilago, Amanita*

- *Agaricus* – mushroom
  A. campestris (= *Psalliota campestris*) also called as **field mushroom or gilled mushroom.**
- *Puccinia* – rusts
- *Ustilago* – Smuts

Sub-division : Deuteromycotina ; Class : Deuteromycetes

- Fungi imperfecti
- Saprotrophs in soil and on decaying organic matter.
- Well developed, branched, septate hyphae.
- Multinucleate cells, septate. Clamp connection absent.

- Asexual reproduction by **conidia** which are produced on **conidiophores** or **sporodochia, pycnidia, acervuli** and **synnemata**. Sometimes by the formation of oidia and chlamydospores.
- Sexual reproduction absent or not known.

Examples : *Cercospora, Pyricularia, Alternaria, Colletotrichum, Helminthosporium, Fusarium* etc.

SOME FUNGI WITH THEIR COMMON NAMES

COMMON NAME	FUNGI OR GROUP
Squirting fungus	*Pilobolus crystallinus*
Bread/Pin/Black mould	*Rhizopus*
Yeast (sugar fungus)	*Saccharomyces*
Black smoky mould	*Aspergillus*
Morels, sponge mushroom or gucchi	*Morchella*
Cup fungi	*Peziza*
Pink bread mould	*Neurospora*
Blue/Green mould	*Penicillium*
Toad stools	*Amanita*
Bracket/shelf fungi	*Polyporus* and *Fomes*
Puff balls	*Lycoperdon*
Sacred mushroom	*Psilocybe*
Honey mushroom	*Armillaria* (= *Armillariella*)
Laboratory weed	*Aspergillus*
Tooth fungus (hedgehog fungi)	*Hydnum*
Algal or Lower fungi	Phycomycetes
Late blight fungus	*Phytophthora*
Conjugation fungi	Zygomycetes
Pin bread mould	*Mucor*
Sac fungi	Ascomycetes
Dung mould	*Mucor mucedo*
Pigmented moulds	*Aspergillus and Penicillium*
Truffles	*Tuber*
Club fungi	Basidiomycetes
White button mushroom or dhingri	*Agaricus campestris*
Wood fungi	*Ganoderma, polyporus*
Gill fungi (mushroom)	*Agaricus*
Sink horns	*Phallus*
Death cup	*Amanita palloides*
Fly Agaric	*Amanita muscaria*
Caesar's mushroom	*Amanita caesarea*
Honey mushroom	*Armillaria mellea*
Khumb	*Podaxon podaxis*
Fairy ring mushroom	*Marasmius oreades*
Jelly fungi/Trembling fungi	*Tremella*
Coral fungi	*Clavaria*
Bird's nest fungus	*Cyanthus*
Jew's ear	*Auricularia polytricha*
Paddy straw mushroom	*Volvariella volvacea*
Shiitake mushroom	*Lentius edodes*
Oyster mushroom	*Pleurotus edodes*
Guinea pig of plant kingdom	*Aspergillus flavus*

Some important plant diseases with their causal organisms

NAME OF DISEASE	CAUSAL ORGANISM	CROP
1. White rust of crucifers	*Albugo candida* or *Cystopus*	Family cruciferae
2. Damping off of seedlings	*Pythium debarynum*	Various seedlings
3. Late blight of potato	*Phytophthora infestans*	Potato
4. Early blight of potato	*Alternaria solani*	Potato
5. Brown rust of wheat	*Puccinia recondita*	Wheat
6. Black rust of wheat	*Puccinia graminis-tritici*	Wheat
7. Yellow rust of wheat	*Puccinia striiformis*	Wheat
8. Loose smut of wheat	*Ustilago tritici*	Wheat
9. Grain smut of jowar	*Sphacelotheca sorghi*	Jowar
10. Whip smut of sugarcane	*Ustilago scitaminea*	Sugarcane
11. Flag smut of wheat	*Urocystis tritici*	Wheat
12. Flag smut of oat	*Ustilogo avenae*	Oat
13. Covered smut of barley	*Ustilago hordei*	Barley
14. Blast of rice/paddy	*Pyricularia oryzae*	Rice
15. Powdery mildew of wheat	*Erysiphe graminis*	Wheat
16. Powdery mildew of peas	*Erysiphe polygoni*	Peas
17. Powdery mildew of cucurbits	*Erysiphe cichoracearum*	Cucurbits
18. Red rot of sugarcane	*Colletotrichum falcatum*	Sugarcane
19. Ergot disease of rye	*Claviceps purpurea*	Rye
20. Wilt of gram	*Fusarium orthaceras*	Gram
21. Tikka disease of groundnut	*Cercospora personata*	Groundnut
22. Leaf spots of oat	*Helminthosporium avenae*	Oats
23. Leaf curl of peach	*Taphrina deformans*	Peach
24. Wart disease of potato	*Synchytrium endobioticum*	Potato
25. Downy mildew of grapes	*Plasmopara viticola*	Grapes
26. Club rot of crucifers	*Plasmodiophora brassicae*	Cabbage
27. Bakanae disease and food rot of rice or foolish seedling of rice	*Gibberella fujikuroi*	Rice
28. Brown leaf spot of rice	*Helminthosporium oryzae*	Rice
29. Covered smut of oat	*Ustilago kolleri*	Oat
30. Downy mildew of cereals	*Sclerospora graminicola*	Cereals
31. Rot of ginger	*Pythium debaryanum*	Ginger
32. Brown rot	*Sclerotinia fruticola*	Peas, plum, peach
33. Smut in corn	*Ustilago maydis*	Corn
34. Wilt of pigeon pea	*Fusarium oxysporum*	Pigeon pea
35. Powdery mildew of cucurbits	*Sphaerotheca fuliginea*	Cucurbits
36. Green ear disease of bajra	*Sclerospora graminicola*	Bajra
37. Leaf spot of turmeric	*Taphrina*	Turmeric

SOME ANTIBIOTICS OBTAINED FROM FUNGI

ANTIBIOTICS	FUNGAL SOURCE(S)
1. Penicillin	*Penicillium notatum, P. chrysogenum*
2. Citrinin	*Penicillium citrinum*
3. Griseofulvin	*Penicillium griseofulvum, P. nigricans*
4. Patulin	*Aspergillus clavatus*
5. Fumigatin	*Aspergillus fumigatus*
6. Proliferin	*Aspergillus proliferans*
7. Jawaharin	*Aspergillus niger*
8. Trichothecin	*Trichothecium roseum*
9. Cephalosporin	*Emericellopsis minimum*
10. Viridin	*Gliocladium virens*
11. Ramycin	*Mucor ramannianus*
12. Campestrin	*Agaricus campestris*
13. Chaetomin	*Chaetomium cochliodes*

COMMERCIAL PRODUCTION OF ORGANIC ACIDS FROM FUNGI

ORGANIC ACIDS	FUNGAL SOURCE
Citric acid	*Aspergillus niger, Citromyces pfefferiaur*
Oxalic acid	*Aspergillus niger*
Itaconic acid	*Aspergillus terreus*
Gluconic acid	*Aspergillus niger, Penicillium purpurogenum*
Fumaric acid	*Rhizopus stolonifer*
Kojic acid	*Aspergillus flavus*
Gallic acid	*Aspergillus gallomyces*
Lactic acid	*Rhizopus oryzae*

SOME MYCOTOXIN (TOXINS SECRETED BY FUNGUS) WITH THEIR FUNGUS

MYCOTOXIN	FUNGUS
Amatoxins	*Amanita phalloides* (death cup)
Phallotoxins	*Amanita phalloides* (death cup)
Coprine	*Coprinus atramentanius* (edible mushroom)
Ochratoxins	*Aspergillus ochraceus, Penicillium viridicatum*
Aflatoxins	*Aspergillus flavus*
Zearalenone	*Fusarium*
Trichothecenes	*Fusarium, Cephalosporium, Trichoderma*

SOME HUMAN DISEASES CAUSED BY FUNGI

DISEASES	FUNGUS
1. Athletes foot	*Tinea pedis, Epidermophyton, Trichophyton*
2. Aspergillosis	*Aspergillus fumigatus*
3. Candidosis	*Candida albicans*
4. Barber's itch	*Trichophyton*
5. Onchomycosis	*Microsporum* and *Trichophyton*
6. Dermatomycosis (ring worm)	*Microsporum audouini, Trichophyton, Epidermophyton*
7. Cryptococcosis (Torulosis)	*Cryptococcus neoformans*
8. Histoplasmosis	*Histoplasma capsulatum*

Lichen

- Term **Lichen** was coined by **Theophrastus** (371-284 BC).
- Murison (1699) called such plants as **Musco-fungus**.
- **Composite** or **dual organism** which are formed by a fungus partner or **mycobiont** generally **ascomycete** and an algal partner or **photobiont** or **phycobiont** mostly blue-green alga (*Gloeocapsa*, *Nostoc*, *Scytonema*) or green algae (*Trebouxia* etc.)
- **Lichenology :** Study of lichens.
- Worldwide in distribution, pioneer colonizers of barren rocks and mountains.
- Constitute dominant vegetation of **Tundra region** forming food of animals like **reindeer.**
- Lichens may be–**Corticolous** (bark of trees *e.g., Usnea*), **Lignicolous** (wood directly *e.g., Cyphelium*), **Saxicolous** (rocky substrata *e.g.,Porina*), **Terricolous** (on the ground e.g., *Lecidea, Cladonia*), **Marine** (siliceous rocky shore of sea *e.g., Caloplaca, Verrucaria*) and **Fresh water** (hard siliceous rocks in fresh water *e.g., Hymenelia*).
- Morphologically lichens may be–**Crustose lichen** (closed attached to the substratum and look like crusts *e.g., Graphis, Rhizocarpon* etc.), **Foliose lichen** (leaf like with irregular margins, attached to substratum by rhizoid-like structures called **rhizines** *e.g., Physcia, Peltigera, Parmelia* etc.), **Fructicose lichen** (more or less bushy, may be erect or pendent and attached to substratum by means of basal ends *e.g., Usnea, Ramalina, Alectoria* etc.), **Leprose lichen** (as minute scales *e.g., Lepraria*), and **Filamentous lichen** (phycobiont is filamentous and covered by fungal hyphae *e.g., Racodium*).
- Possess a carbohydrate **lichenin** or **lichen starch** (in fungal cell walls).
- Lichen thalli may be **homoiomerous** (throughout) or **heteromerous** (restricted to small gonidial layer) on the basis of distribution of alga in the body of lichen.
- Asexual repoduction by fragmentation, soredia, isidia and conidia. Isidia are superficial outgrowths having both partners. Soredia are microscopic propagules that develop in sori. Soredia are composed of algal cells clasped and surrounded by fungal hyphae.
- Sexual reproduction is exhibited exclusively by the mycobiont. The **ascolichens** (*e.g., Cladonia, Lecidia*) produce **asci** and **ascospores** in the fruiting bodies whereas the **basidiolichens** (*e.g., Cora*) produce **basidia** and **basidiospores.**

Economic importance of Lichens

- Early or pioneer colonisers of barren areas and acids produced by these lichens disintegrate rock surface.
- Sensitive to SO_2 so **bioindicator of air pollution.**

- *Certraria islandica* (Iceland moss), *Lecanora esculenta* (bread of Heaven/Manna by Jews), *Umbilicaria*, *Parmelia* (Rock flower) and *Dermatocarpon miniatum* are used as food.
- *Certraria islandica* and *Cladonia rangiferina* are used as fodder.
- Dye **Orceil** and **Litmus** solution are obtained from *Roccella tinctoria.*
- *Peltigera* (dog lichen), *Parmalia* and *Lobaria* are useful to cure **hydrophobia, epilepsy** and **tuberculosis,** respectively.
- *Cladonia rangifera* (Reindeer moss) is staple food of Reindeer, Caribou or musk ox and other arctic animals.
- *Lobaria* (**Lungwort**) is used in medicine, brewing, perfumery and tanning.
- *Usnea* (old man's beard) can yield drugs (*e.g.,* usnic acid) but in highly inflammable and causing **forest fires.**
- *Ramalina* and *Evernia* are used to prepare dhup, cosmetic soaps, antiseptic creams and samagri.
- Species of *Evernia* and *Remalina* are the sources of essential oils which are used in soaps and other cosmetics.
- *Lobaria* and *Evermia* yields delicate perfumes.
- *Letharia vulpina* (wolf moss) is known for its poisonous effect.

Mycorrhizae

- Term mycorrhiza (*mykes* = mushroom + *rhiza* = root which means **fungus root**) was coined by Frank (1885).
- It is an association (**mutualistic symbiosis**) between a fungus and the roots of higher plants.
- It is an infected root system arising from the rootlets of a seed plant.
- Mycorrhizae are of 2 types – **ectomycorrhizae** and **endomycorrhizae.**
- **Ectomycorrhizae** – Fungus partner in basidiomycete which lives in intercellular spaces of cortex.
- **Endomycorrhizae** – Fungus partner is commonly a zygomycete. The tips of fungal hyphae pass into cortical cells producing swollen **vesicles** or finely branched **masses** called **arbuscules**. They are also called on **VAM** or **Vesicular arbuscular mycorrhiza.**
- Mycorrhizae enhance mineral absorption by green plants. The plants, inturn, provides essential growth substances to the fungus.

SOME IMPORTANT FACTS

- Beadle and Tautam put forward *one-gene-one enzyme theory* through their experiments on *Neurospora* (Ascomycete).
- *Neurospora crassa* is called *Drosophila* of plant kingdom because used widely in genetic research.
- **Yeast :** *Saccharomyces cerevisiae* (Beer or Baker's yeast) and *S. ellipsoidens* (wine yeast) are useful in **Brewing** and **Baking industry.** Yeasts are source of various vitamins and enzymes, rich in digestible compounds specifically fats and proteins, used in curing cocoa beans etc.
- *Aspergillus* **:** Source of enzyme **diastase.**
- *Claviceps purpurea* (ergot fungus) : LSD (Lysergic Acid Dimethyl Amide) is a narcotic obtained from sclerotium.
- **Heterothallism :** According to **Blackslee** (1904) unisexual or dioecious forms were called as **heterothallic** whereas monoecious or bisexual types were designated as **homothallic.** It means existence of two different types of physiological strains in which one thallus is of (+) strain and other of (–) strain. This phenomenon was confirmed first on *Mucor* and *Rhizopus.*
- **Endophytic fungi :** Fungi growing inside host tissues.

- **Xerophillic fungi :** Fungi which tolerate very dry atmospheric conditions.
- **Predacious fungi :** Develop a number of structures called **traps** to capture their preys *e.g.*, Protozoa, Nematodes etc. *e.g., Dactylaria, Arthrobotrys.*
- Some Indian Mycologists : K.C. Mehta, T.S. Sadasivan, C.V. Subramanian, B.B. Mundkur etc.
- **Ascocarp :** Fruiting bodies of ascomycotina. 4 types—**Cleistothecium** (completely closed *e.g., Penicillium*), **Perithecium** (flask shaped with a pore or ostiole *e.g., Pyronema*), **Apothecium** (cup or saucer–shaped with an exposed **hymenium** *e.g., Peziza*) and **Ascostroma** (*e.g., Pleospora*).
- The fruiting bodies (basidiocarps) of *Agaricus* arise in concentric rings (**fairy rings** or **fungal flowers**) from the mycelium spreads centifugally.
- **Torula :** Budding of oidia in sugary solution.
- **Bessey** defined fungi as chlorophylless, non-vascular plants.
- *Penicillium roqueforti* and *P. camemberti* are used in cheese to give flavour and shining to butter.
- Fruits of *Agaricus, Pleurotus* and *Volvariella* are used as nutritious food.
- **Single cell protein :** Produced from yeast and some fungi.
- Some fungi causes spoilage of food and stored grains *e.g., Aspergillus, Penicillium, Rhizopus* etc.
- *Aspergillus* causes spoilages of valuable items *e.g.,* glass, wood, cloth etc.
- **Poisonous fungi :** *Amanita phalloides* and *A. verna.*
- **Aflatoxin :** Produced by *Aspergillus niger* and *A. flavus* as toxin.
- *Ericaceous mycorrhizae* : Forming a dense intracellular coils of hyphae in the outer cortical cells. The fungus is mainly *Pezizella ericae.*
- *Orchidaceous mycorrhizae* : Associated with orchid roots. Fungus *Rhizoctonia* coils inside the cell which later breaks up into nutrient rich **peletons** on which orchid depend.
- Relation of *Conifer-Boletus-Monotropa* : *Boletus* froms **ectomycorrhiza** with *Monotropa* and **endomycorrhiza** with conifer. It form mycorrhizal association between conifer (green plant) and *Monotropa* (non-chlorophyllous plant grows near the roots of conifer).
- **Holocarpic :** Entire cell converted into reproductive structure *e.g., Synchytrium.*
- **Eucarpic :** Only a part of thallus is converted into reproductive structure *e.g., Rhizopus.*
- **Largest fungus : Giant Puff-ball** (Clavatia) is 90-120 cm across. Lignocolous shelf fungus/Bracket fungus (*Ganoderma applanatum*) fruiting body 60 cm across.
- **Smallest fungus :** Yeast (3-15 μm × 2-10 μm).
- **Most complex fungi :** mushrooms.
- **Zymologist :** Scientist dealing with yeast.
- **Zymology :** Branch dealing with yeast.
- **Zymosis :** Formerly used for fermentation.
- **True yeasts :** Develop ascospores, 3 types-**budding yeast** (*e.g., Saccharomyces*), **fission yeasts** (*e.g., Schizosaccharomyces*) and **helobial yeasts** (*e.g., Saccharomycodes*).
- **False yeasts :** Donot produce ascospores *e.g., Mycoderma, Candida, Torula* etc.
- Ascomycetes are our worst fungus enemies.
- Millardet discovered fungicide **Bordeaux mixture** (quick lime and $CuSO_4$ mixture).
- Irish Famine (1845-1847) due to Late blight of potato (*Phytophthora infestans*) destroying potato crop of Ireland.
- Bengal Famine (1942-1943) due to Brown or Sesame leaf spot of rice (*Helminthosporium oryzae*) destroying rice crop of Bengal.

- **Luminescent fungi :** Pileus part of *Panus* and *Pleurotus* species and fruiting body and mycelium in *Clitocybe illudens.*
- Diplanetic fungus : *Saprolegnia* (water mould).
- Parasexuality reported by **Pontecorva** and **Roper** in fungus (*Aspergillus nidulans*).
- Basidiomycetes are most commonly seen fungi.
- Emperor **Claudius Caesar** was murdered by his wife by giving him extract of a **toad stool fungus** (*Amanita phalloides*) which stops mRNA synthesis.
- Father of Systemic Mycology : **E.M. Fries** (1794-1878) wrote **Systema Mycologicum** in 3 volumes.
- P.A. Micheli (1729) wrote *Nova Genera Plantarum* in which 900 fungi were described.
- **Biobleaching :** *Phanerochaete chrysosporium* fungus or its enzyme **cartazyme** is used to bleach the paper pulp.

ALGAE

Introduction

- Kingdom plantae includes multicellular photoautotrophic organisms, *i.e.*, green algae,brown algae, red algae, bryophytes, pteridophytes, gymnosperms and angiosperms.
- **Eichler** (1883) divided kingdom plantae into two subkingdoms.
  - (*a*) **Phanerogammae** (seed plants) or **Spermatophyta**–two divisions
    - (*i*) Gymnospermae
    - (*ii*) Angiospermae
  - (*b*) **Cryptogammae** (seedless plants)–three divisions
    - (*i*) **Thallophyta** (bacteria, fungi and algae)–Now bacteria and fungi are excluded.
    - (*ii*) **Bryophyta**
    - (*iii*) **Pteridophyta**
- **Embryophyta :** Plants with embryo formation *e.g.*, all plants except algae and fungi.
- **Tracheophyta :** Plants with tracheary system *i.e.*, vascular supply *e.g.*, pteridophytes, gymnosperms and angiosperms.
- **Cormophytes :** Plants with distinct root, stem and leaves.

Algae

- **Linnaeus** (1753) introduced the term **algae.**
- **Phycology :** Study of algae.
- **Father of Indian Phycology :** M.O.P. Iyengar.
- Chlorophyll bearing, nonvascular, aquatic forms having accessory spores for asexual multiplication and nonjacketed gametangia for sexual reproduction.
- Absence of embryo stage.
- According to **Whittaker,** algae included under kingdom plantae are **chlorophyceae, phaeophyceae** and **rhodophyceae.**
- **F.E. Fritsch** (1935) divided algae into the following 11 classes on the basis of number and mode of attachment of flagella in motile cells, thallus structure, chemical nature of pigments, reserve food material, method of reproduction and varieties in life cycle– Chlorophyceae (green algae), Xanthophyceae (yellow-green algae), Chrysophyceae, Bacillariophyceae (Diatoms), Cryptophyceae, Dinophyceae (Dinoflagellates), Chloromonadineae, Euglenieae (Euglenoids), Phaeophyceae (brown algae), Rhodophyceae (red algae) and Myxophyceae or Cyanophyceae (blue-green algae).

Green Algae – Chlorophyta

- Cosmopolitan in distribution. They may be–**Terrestrial** (*Ulothrix, Zygogonium*), **Epiphytes** (*Protococcus, Trenteopohlia*), **Endophytes** (*Coleochaete nitellum*), **Epizoic** (*Cladophora, Characium*), **Endozoic** (*Zoochlorella, Chlorella*), **Parasites** (*Cephaleuros*), **Thermophilic** (*Chlorella*), **Cryophytes** (*Chlamydomonas, Scottiela*) and **Lichens.**
- Thallus organization ranges from–**Unicellular flagellate forms** (*e.g., Chlamydomonas*), **unicellular nonflagellate forms** (*Chlorella*), **colonial flagellate form** (*Volvox*) **colonial nonflagellate coenobia** (*Hydrodictyon*), **coenocytic** (Caulerpa), **filamentous unbranched** (*Oedogonium*), **filamentous branched** (*Cladophora*), **pseudoparenchymatous** (*Ulva*), **Siphenaceous** (Caulerpa). *Aetabularia* (Umbrella like) considered as largest unicellular plant, has a holdfast (with nucleus), stalk and an umbrella like cap.
- Cellulosic cell wall.
- Cell possess one or more chloroplasts which may be **cup shaped** (*Chlamydomonas*), girdle shaped (*Ulothrix*), star shaped (*Zygnema*), spiral (*Spirogyra*), reticulate (*Chlamydomonas*), parietal reticulate (*Oedogonium*), parietal band shaped (*Hydrodictyon*) or disc-shaped (*Chara*). Chloroplasts have 2-20 thylakoid lamellae. **Pyrenoids** are present to store starch.
- Motile forms, zoospores, gametes and other motile cells are flagellated (2 or 4 or even more at the anterior end, whiplash type and equal in size).
- Vegetative reproduction by cell division, fragmentation, stolons and tubers.
- Asexual reproduction by formation of zoospores (*Ulothrix*), daughter coenobia (*Volvox*), aplanospores (*Oedogonium*), akinetes (*Pithophora*), hypnospores and autospores.
- Sexual reproduction by isogamous (*Ulothrix*), anisogamous (*Chlamydomonas*) and oogamous (*Volvox*) methods.
- Regular alternation of haploid gametophytic and diploid sporophytic generations. which may be **isomorphic** (*Ulva*) or **heteromorphic** (*Stigeoclonium*).
- Embryo stage absent, gametangia non-jacketed, vascular system absent.

COMPARISON OF RED, BROWN AND GREEN ALGAE

BASIS	RED ALGAE	BROWN ALGAE	GREEN ALGAE
(1) Habitat	Mostly marine	Mostly marine	Mostly fresh water
(2) Organisation	Few unicellular forms	Unicellular forms absent	Many unicellular forms present
(3) Chloroplast (Thylakoids or lamellae,	Not stacked	Stacked in group of three	Stacked in group of 2-20
(4) Chlorophyll	Chl. *a* and chl *d* present	Chl *a* and chl *c* present	Chl *a* and chl *b* present
(5) Fucoxanthin	Present	Present	Absent
(6) Phycobilins	Present	Absent	Absent
(7) Reserve food	Floridean starch	Laminarian	Starch
(8) Motility	Absent	Present	Present

Chlamydomonas

- Free living, aquatic, **unicellular,** biflagellate green alga (10-30 μm), found in **ammonium** rich fresh water (some species are marine). These are **snow dwellers** called **cryophytes.**
- Sometimes, the cells occur in large number to impart a **green colour** to the water. *Chlamydomonas nivalis* grows in polar regions and hypnospores impart red colour to the surface of ice and snow called **red snow** (due to presence of a red pigment **haematochrome**).

- Cell wall is made up of glycoproteins instead of cellulose.
- Spherical or ovoid or pyriform or ellipsoidal in shape, **papilla like** outgrowth at the anterior end. Two **whiplash** flagella of **equal length** arise from basal granules (blepharoplasts).
- Uninucleate cells with two contractile vacuoles (excretory and osmoregulatory) at the anterior end.
- A single massive cup shaped chloroplast in each cell associated with a prominent pyrenoid. An eye spot (red and photosensitive) on the anterior side of chloroplast is present.
- Asexual reproduction by **zoospores, aplanospores, phypnospores** and **palmella** stage. Aplanospore formation takes place in *Chlamydomonas caudata.*
- Sexual reproduction may be **isogamous, anisogamous** and **oogamous.** The compatible gametes fuse to produce a diploid zygote which secretes a thick wall to form resting diploid spore called **zygospore** (zygote) which produce 4 haploid zoospores.
- Hologamy in *C. media, C. snowiae* ; isogamy in *C. debrayana* (homothallic) or *C. reinhardii* (heterothallic) and oogamy takes place in ***C. coccifera.***

Spirogyra

- Unbranched filamentous algae, free floating ; bright green coloured, silky masses in stagnant fresh water bodies.
- Slimy due to mucilagenous covering, called as **water silk, pond silk** or **Pondscum.**
- Thalloid, filamentous, large number of green cylindrical cells placed end to end in a single row.
- Each cell contains 1–16 **spirally coiled ribbon shaped** chloroplasts. Each chloroplast contains several **equidistant pyrenoids** and has smooth or wavy margins.
- Vegetative reproduction by fragmentation.
- Asexual reproduction by the formation of akinetes, aplanospores and azygospores (parthenospores).
- Sexual reproduction by **conjugation (scalariform** or **lateral).**
- **Scalariform (dioecious) conjugation** takes place between cells of two filaments of different physiological strains (+/–). The protoplasts of cells function as gamete. One gamete is more active. The gametes show amoeboid movement. It results in **zygospore.** *e.g, S. tuwensis.*
- **Lateral (monoecious) conjugation :** Between cells of the same filament, may be **direct** or **indirect.** It results in **zygospore.**
- **Direct lateral conjugation :** Through a **pore** in the septum between two cells *e.g.,* ***S. jogensis*** (discovered by M.O.P. Iyengar).
- **Indirect lateral (chain) conjugation :** Through lateral outgrowth or papillae on either side of the septum.
- *S. sahni* forms azygospores or parthenocarp.
- *S. jogensis, S. affinis* show terminal conjugation.

Ulothrix

- Unbranched filamentous, fresh water, long, unbranched, multicellular form.
- Unbranched filament consists of a row of short rectangular (broader than longer) cells joined end to end. Each filament have a dome shaped **apical** cell, a basal long colourless **holdfast** and rectangular **intercalary cells.**
- Green due to presence of single girdle shaped or **collar shaped** chloroplast with one or many pyrenoids. **Eye spot** absent. The cytoplasm encloses a large central vacuole.
- Vegetative reproduction by fragmentation.
- Asexual reproduction by formation of flagellated zoospores (all cells except holdfast are capable of producing zoospores) and non-motile aplanospores, hypnospores, akinetes and palmella stage.
- Sexual reproduction is **isogamous** *i.e.,* fusion of two similar biflagellate gametes. A mother cell produces 8–32 isogametes which form diploid zygote and develops into **zygospore.**
- The life cycle is **haplontic** type.

IMPORTANCE OF GREEN ALGAE

- Green algae (*Chlorella, Ulva, Enteromorpha, Caulerpa* etc.) are used as food.
- *Chlorella* (unicellular) contains 50 protein which possess all the amino acids essential for human nutrition. It also contains vit. A, vit. B, vit. C, vit. K and various other essential elements.
- *Ulva lactuca* formerly used in salad and soup in Scotland.
- *Chlorella* yield first algal antibiotic **chlorellin,** used against Gram + ve and Gram – ve bacteria. *Caulerpa* also yield antibiotics.
- *Chlorella* and *Chlamydomonas* are used in sewerage disposal ponds.
- *Chlorella* used to provide O_2 during space flight trips.
- *Cephaleuros virescens* (parasitic) causes red rust on the leaves of tea.
- *C. coffeae* causes red rust on the leaves of coffee.

BROWN ALGAE–PHAEOPHYTA

- Mostly marine (except *Pleurocladia, Heribaudiella* and *Bodanella* which are fresh water.
- Grow in tidal and sub-tidal regions of cooler seas. However, **Ectocarpales, Dictyotales** and *Sargassum* grow in warmer waters.
- No unicellular, colonial or unbranched filamentous forms.
- Thallus organisation may be branched filamentous heterotrichous forms (*Ectocarpus*), multiaxial construction forms (*Myriactula pulvinata*), uniaxial pseudoparenchymatous forms (*Hecatonema*) and parenchymatous form (*Laminaria, Fucus*).
- Some highly advanced forms *e.g., Fucales,* **Laminariales** (*Laminaria*) differentiated into **holdfast, stipe** and **lamina** or **blade.**
- Possess **air-bladders** to provide buoyancy.
- Internal differentiation of thallus in higher forms into outermost photosynthetic **meristoderm,** middle **cortex** and **central medulla.**
- **Trumphet hyphae** or conducting tubes present.
- Cell wall is made up of inner layer of cellulose and outer mucilaginous layer of a mixture of polysaccharide collectively known as **phycocolloids** which are non-sulphated mucosaccharides–**alginic acid, fucoidin** and **fucin.**
- More than one **parietal chromatophores** in each cell, may be ribbon shaped, plate like or discoid. Chromatophore possess chlorophyll *a,* chlorophyll *c,* b and C-carotenes and xanthophylls. Large amount of brown coloured xanthophyll **fucoxanthin,** which dominates over the green colour of the chlorophyll.
- Reserve food material is **laminarin starch** and **D-mannitol.**
- Fucosan vesicles (small vacuoles and refractive bodies) present in cytoplasm which contain **fucosan** which is colourless inside the water but turns black or brown on exposure to air.
- Vegetative reproduction by **fragmentation,** stolons, adventitious branches and specialised nests of cells called propagules.
- Asexual reproduction by formation of motile zoospores and non-motile neutral-spores, tetraspores and monospores. Zoospores are pyriform, biflagellate (heterokont flagellation *i.e.,* one whiplash and other tinsel shaped) and possess contractile vacuoles, chromatophore and eye spot.
- Sexual reproduction is isogamous (in *Ectocarpales*), anisogamous (in *Cutleriales*) and oogamous (in *Fucus, Laminaria, Dictyota*). Life cycle is **diplohaplontic.** (*Dictyota*) or **diplantic.**
- Internal fertilization, **no zygotic** meiosis, Alternation of generation may be **isomorphic** (*Ectocarpus, Dictyota*) and **heteromorphic** (*Laminaria*).
- **Giant Kelp** or **Trees of Seas :** Some brown algae are of massive sizes and called as Giant kelp *e.g., Laminaria* (2-9 metres); *Nereocystis* (45 metres) and *Macrocystis* (60-90 metres).

- **Sea Palm :** *Postelsia palmaeformis* appear like palm tree.
- **Sea Weeds :** A large number of brown algae are called as sea weeds.
- **Lithophytes :** Most of the brown algae are attached to rocks and stones. Few are epiphytes and endophytes.
- **Sargasso Sea :** *Sargassum* (brown algae) grow in warm water and cover thousands of hectares in the parts of North Atlantic ocean.

IMPORTANCE OF BROWN ALGAE

- Many brown algae used as food *e.g., Laminaria, Macrocystis, Sargassum,* and number of kelps.
- *Laminaria saccharina* is called as **Kombu** or Devils' Apron rich in carbohydrates.
- *Alaria* produces **Sarumen** in Japan.
- As fodder for cattles and poultry *e.g., Laminaria, Fucus, Sargassum* etc.
- **Alginic acid** from giant brown algae or kelp (*Laminaria, Macrocystis, Lessonia, Fucus* etc.). In India, it is obtained from *Sargassum.* It is used in preparation of emulsions, security glass, sizing textiles etc. It is used as agent to stop bleeding.
- **Soda, Potash and Iodine** obtained from brown algae **(Laminarales or kelps). Iodine** is important constituent of thyroid hormones and used in treatment of thyroid and goitre.
- **Sodium laminarin sulphate** from *Laminaria* is effective blood anticoagulant.
- *Durvillea* extract is an effective vermifuge.
- *Ascophyllum* and *Laminaria* yields antibiotic like substances.
- Some brown algae are **bifuelers.**

RED ALGAE–RHODOPHYTA

- Mostly marine, possess bright red or red colour due to the presence of biliproteins **(r-phycoerythrin** and **r-*phycocyanin*)** along with chlorophyll and carotenoid tetraxanthin. Red pigment absorbs the blue-green wavelength in visible spectrum easily.
- *Batrachospermum* is not red in colour and not marine.
- Motile stages absent, eucaryotic cells with true nuclei.
- Thallus varies from microscopic unicellular (*e.g., Porphyridium*-terrestrial), palmelloid (*Asterocystis*), uniaxial filamentous branched forms (*Grimelia*), multiaxial filamentous branched forms (*Polysiphonia*) to multicellular pseudoparenchymatous thallus (*Gelidium*).
- Generally lithophytes, some are calcareous (calcium carbonate) and form lime stone and coral reefs (*Corallina, Lithothamnion*).
- Cell wall consists of cellulose, pectic compounds and certain mucopolysaccharides *i.e.,* phycocolloids (agar, carrageenin and funori).
- Reserve food material is **floridean starch, galactoside and floridosides.**
- Chromatophores with monothylakoid lamellae. Photosynthetic pigments are chlorophyll *a,* chlorophyll *d,* α–β-carotenes, xanthophylls and biliproteins.
- Some red algae *e.g., Harveyella* is heterotrophically (*i.e.,* parasite) on other autotrophic photosynthesizing red algae.
- Vegetative reproduction by fragmentation.
- Asexual reproduction by monospores, neutral spores, carpospores, tetraspores.
- Sexual reproduction by advanced type of oogamy.
- Female sex organ **(carpogonia)** is flask shaped with egg base and elongated **trichogyne.** Male sex organ **(antheridia** or **spermatangia)** produce non-motile male gametes **(spermatia).**
- External fertilization, zygote may produce **carpospores** or **corposporophyte.**
- Alternation of generation of gametophytic (haploid) and sporophytic (diploid) generations.

IMPORTANCE OF RED ALGAE

- Many red algae are edible *e.g.*, ***Rhodymenia*** (Dulse or sheep's weed), *Chondrus* (Irishmoss), *Porphyra* (Laver).
- **Agar** obtained from *Gelidium, Gracilaria, Ceramium, Chondrus*, etc. and used in microbiological work and used as a **laxative** and employed for the manufacture of pills and ointments.
- **Carrageenin** from *Chondrus* used as emulsifier in chocolates, ice-creams, toothpaste etc. also used as clearing agent in liquors and in leather finishing.
- **Funori** from ***Gloiopetis*** used as adhesive.
- **Bromine** from *Rhodomella* and *Polysiphonia.*
- Vegetative reproduction by fragmentation.
- *Porphyra* is used as an important ingrediant in soups and also cooked as flavouring agent with meat.
- *Corallina* extract used for the treatment of bladder, lung and kidney diseases.
- *Polysiphonia* (lithophytic, marine alga) possess antibacterial properties.

COMMON NAME OF SOME ALGAE

COMMON NAME	SCIENTIFIC NAME
Stone wort	*Chara*
Sea lettuce	*Ulva*
Pond scum or water silk	*Spirogyra*
Rolling alga	*Volvox*
Gulf weed	*Sargassum*
Frog-spawn	*Batrachospermum*
Water-net	*Hydrodictyon*

SOME IMPORTANT FACTS

- Sea weed ***Ulva pertusa*** is eaten by Japanese under the name **ao-nori**
- **Cryophytes :** Algae grow on snow and ice at low temperature which produces specific colours.
  e.g., Red snow–*Chlamydomonas nivalis*
  Red-snow ball–*Haematococcus*
  Yellow-snow–*Chlamydomonas flavovirens*
  Blue snow–*Dactylococcopis caucasica*
  Purple snow–*Ancylonema nordenskioldii*
  Black snow–*Raphidonema*
- Spores–Cells germinate **without fusion**
  Aplanospores–Non-motile spores
  Hypnospores–Thick walled aplanospores
- **Gametes**–Cells which fuse to form **zygote.**
  Planogametes–Motile gametes
  Aplanogametes–Non-motile gametes.
- Swarmer–Any motile cell.
- **Akinete**–Vegetative cell with thick walls, possess food serves and are resistant to unfavourable environmental conditions.

- **Agar-Agar** is also known as **Japanese Isinglass,** Japanese gelatin or **kanten** is dried, hydrophilic and phycocolloidal substance present in the cell wall of *Gelidium cartilagineum* and other red algae.
- The isomorphic alteration of generation is found in *Ulva.*
- The heterotrophic (heterologous) alteration of generation is found in *Stigeoclonium suspinosum.*
- The ancestors of land plants are **green algae**.
- In green algae–3 types of life cycles.
  (1) **Haplontic life cycle** : *e.g., Chlamydomonas* (Zygotic meiosis takes place), *Spirogyra, Ulothrix.*
  (2) **Diplontic life cycle** *e.g., Caulerpa* (gametic meiosis).
  (3) **Diplohaplontic life cycle** *e.g., Ulva, Cladophora.*

DIVISION – BRYOPHYTA

Introduction

- **Bryophyta** (Gk. *Bryon* : moss ; *phyton* : plants.
- Term **Bryophyta** was first used by **Robert Braun** (1864). He included algae, fungi, lichen and mosses under it.
- **Bryology :** Study of bryophytes.
- Intermediate position between algae and pteridophyta.
- Simplest and primitive land plants.
- Found in tropical and temperate habitats of the world. Very commonly grow on damp soils, rocks, walls, bark of trees etc.
- Includes **liver worts and mosses.**
- The **amphibians of the plant kingdom** because also require water for dehiscence of antheridia, liberation of antherozoids, transfer of antherozoids from antheridia to archegonia, opening of archegonial neck and movement of antherozoids into the archegonial neck.
- They may be aquatic, (*Riccia, Riella, Ricciocarpus*), epiphytes (*Dendroceros, Radula*), saprophytes (*Buxbaunia, Cryptothallus*) and in dry habitats *i.e.,* (*Polytrichum juniperinum* (dry heaths), *Tortula desertorum* (deserts) and *Porella platyphylla* (dry rocks).
- Vascular tissues and roots are absent, rhizoids present which may be unicellular or multicellular.
- Life cycle with two phases :
  (*i*) **Gametophytic** (haploid) phase – Dominant, long-lived, green and independent.
  (*ii*) **Sporophytic** (diploid) phase – Short lived, dependent upon the gametophyte (parasitic over gametophyte).
- Gametophytes may be **thalloid** or **leafy shoot** (stem like central axis and leaf like appendages).
- Xylem-like **hydroids** (conduct water) and phloem like **leptoids** (conduct the assimilates) present.
- Accessory spores (mitospores) not formed.
- Asexual (vegetative) reproduction by fragmentation, tubers, adventitious branches, gemmae, buds, formation of innovations and secondary protonema.
- **Oogamous** sexual reproduction. Sex organs jacketed (with sterile jacket) and multicellular.
- The male reproductive organs **(antheridia)** and female reproductive organs **(archegonia)** present.
- Antheridia produce biflagellated male gametes (sperms or antherozoids) for which an external layer of water is essential for the swimming.
- Internal fertilization, produces an embryo which grows into a **sporophyte** or **sporogonium.**
- Sporogonium is protected by **calyptra** (produced by wall of venter). It is responsible for the production (asexual) of haploid spores (meiospores).

- The spores are first cells of gametophytic generation. It germinate directly or through a juvenile filamentous stage called **protonema.**
- **Heterologous** or heteromorphic alternation of generation.

Classification of Bryophytes

- According to Rothmaler (1951) - 3 classes
  (1) **Hepaticopsida –** Popularly called as **liver worts.**
  e.g. – Riccia, Marchantia, Pellia, Porella etc.
  (2) **Anthoceratopsida –** Commonly called as **horn worts.**
  e.g. – Anthoceros, Megaceros, Notothylos etc.
  (3) **Bryopsida –** Commonly known as **musci**, largest class of bryophyta.
  e.g. Funaria, Sphagnum, Andreaea etc.

Marchantia–Liver wort

- Grows in moist and shady terrestrial environment.
- **Thalloid, flat, dichotomously branched, dorsiventral** with a distinct midrib.
- An apical notch at the apex of each lobe, leaves absent, **rhizoids** unicellular, unbranched and of 2 types – **Smooth walled** and **tuberculate, scales multicellular** as 2-3 rows on either side of the midrib and are of 2 types – **ligulate** and **appendiculate.**
- Thallus differentiated into upper green **photosynthetic** and lower colourless **storage** regions.
- Upper epidemis with well developed **barrel-shaped pores** (each pore with 4-8 superimposed tiers of cells, each tier has 4-5 cells) projected partly above the surface of the thallus.
- Photosynthetic region–with **air chambers** which has simple or branched **photosynthetic** filaments.
- Storage region – colourless parenchymatous cells, consituted by ventral part of the thallus.
- Vegetative reproduction by death and decay, adventitious branches, gemmae etc.
- **Mostly dioecious, oogamous** sexual reproduction.
- Male sex organ **(antheridia)** borne on the lobes of the **terminal peltate** disc of **antheridiophores**. Each antheridium is stalked, oval or conical structure with **single-layered** jacket. Curved and biflagellated antherozoids are liberated by the disintegration of antheridial jacket. Antheridia arranged in **acropetal** manner.
- Female sex organ **(archegonia)** develop on the dorsal surface of the **terminal discs** of archegoniophores. Neck is made up of 6 vertical rows of neck cells. Neck canal cells 4-6 in number. A rosette of 4 cover cells lies at the apex of the neck. **Archegonia** hang in **centrifugal** fashion.
- The **sporophyte** is differentiated into **foot, seta and capsule. Foot** is well developed and parenchymatous. **Seta** is small when sporophyte is young, but elongates rapidly when it matures. **Capsule** is oval, one layered capsule wall, archisporium develops from **endothecium. Elaters** (diploid) long, hydroscopic, spindle shaped with two **spiral thickening band,** no columella. Elaters help in dispersal of spores.
- The sporophyte possess three protective coverings – **calyptra, perigynium** and **perichaetium** (involucre).
- Life cycle exhibit **heteromorphic** alternation of generations.

Riccia

- Small prostrate, dichotomously branched green fleshy thallus attached to the substratum by thin, unicellular, unbranched rhizoids (two types-smooth walled and tuberculate).
- Scales (amphigastria) on the ventral surface of thallus are unistratose, multicelled membranous and violet coloured.

- Thallus is internally differentiated into upper photosynthetic region and lower storage region.
- On the dorsal surface, sex organs are embedded. May be **monoecious** (*R. gangetica, R. billardieri*) or **dioecious** *R. discolor, R. pearsonii*).
- Sporogonium consists of mass spores enclosed with the capsule (spore sac). Foot and seta absent.
- Haploid spores directly grow in the flat branching thalli.
- Sporophyte is **most primitive**, parasitic and embedded.
- *Heteromorphic* alternation of generation and *diplohaplontic* life cycle.

Funaria

- A typical moss plant.
- Found mainly in **damp** habitats forming dense cushions on trunks of trees, damp ground during mainly rainy season.
- Gametophyte or **gametophore** is small, green coloured main plant body (3-5 cm in height), consists of stem like **axis** and branches (extra axillary). **Spirally** arranged **phylloids** on the axis. Plant is attached to substratum by **rhizoids** which are **multicellular, branched** and have oblique cross walls.
- Axis with **single layered epidermis** containing chloroplasts, stomata absent, parenchymatous cortical cells and conducting tissue **(hadrome)** in central cylinder **(medulla).**
- Leaves are one celled thick with many celled midrib.
- Vegetative reproduction by fragmentation, death and decay, regeneration, secondary protonema, bulbils, gemmae, aposory etc.
- **Monoecious,** main axis acts as male shoot **(antheridiophore)** possess **antheridia** which is surrounded by **perigonial leaves** so male branch looks like a flower **(male flower).** Young antheridia are of **green** colour but when fully mature they become **orange brown** in colour.
- Lateral branch acts as female shoot **(archegoniophore)** possess many archegonia at its tip which is surrounded by **parichaetial leaves.**
- Each **antheridium** with a **stalk** and a **club-shaped** body surrounded by a single layered wall or jacket. It is filled with **cubical cells (candrogonial cells)**, each of which **obliquely** divided to form two **triangular androcyte** which metamorphose into elongated, spirally coiled, biflagellates (equal and at anterior end) **antherozoids.**
- Each **archegonium** (flask shaped) with short multicellular **stalk,** lower swollen portion (venter) and upper **neck** (tube like). **Venter** with two layered wall and possess a large **ovum** or **egg cell** which contains **female gamete.** A **venter canal cell** above the egg present. The jacket of neck consists of a **single layer of cells** arranged in **six vertical rows.** Neck possess 6-9 neck canal cells. All these cells are **haploid.**
- Multicellular, uniseriate sterile **paraphyses** present in between the **antheridia** and **archegonia** which secrete mucilage to hold water.
- Fertilization through rain water or dew. On maturity venter canal cell as well as neck canal cells disintegrate to form **mucilage containing sugars.**
- Male gametes or **antherozoids** liberated by the bursting of antheridium, swim and reach upto archegonium by attraction of sugars **(chemotaxis).** A number of antherozoids enter the archegonium but only one is able to fertilize the egg and form **zygote** (oospore). Syngamy is of **oogamous type.**
- The diploid zygote divides and develops into a **sporophyte** or **sporogonium** which remain attached to parent gametophyte and obtain nourishment from it. The sporophyte produces **asexual spores.** It consists of a bulbous **foot, seta** (forming the stalk) and pear shaped **capsule** (spore containing body). In the capsule, diploid cells undergo meiosis and produces thousands of **haploid single-celled spores.**

- Capsule is a complex structures with **operculum** (2-3 layered thick, circular cup-shaped lid on the top), **annulus** (at the base of the operculum, layer of thickened cells), **peristome** (ring of tooth like projections at the rim of the capsule, 32 tooth, arranged in two rings of 16 each outer **exostome** and inner **endostome**), **columella** (solid sterile central column with water and food), **spore sac** (single barrel-shaped, cylindrical sac, around columella having numerous spores with chloroplasts), **cylindrical cavity** (around **spore sac**), **capsular wall** (wide air space), **trabeculae** (multicellular, uniseriate act as shock absorber) and **apophysis** (sterile solid basal portion of the capsule with chloroplasts in many cells and stomata in epidermis). They synthesize food. It exhibit that **sporophyte is only partially dependent upon gametophyte.**
- In dry conditions, capsule **dehisces** and spores scattered by the wind under favourable environment spores germinate into a **green**, much branched filament **(protonema).**
- Protonema (juvenile stage of moss) consists of some slender **rhizoids** and a number of **chloronemal branches** which bear small **lateral buds** which develop into new plants.
- Regular alternation of generation.

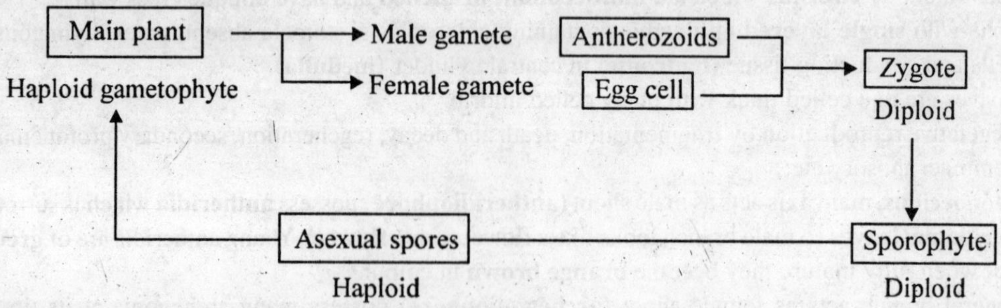

ECONOMIC IMPORTANCE OF BRYOPHYTES

- Bryophytes help in **soil conservation** as they bind soil particles and prevent soil erosion by running water.
- Mosses along with lichen play an important role in the formation of soil and ecological succession.
- *Sphagnum* used in nursery because it can retain water two hundred times more than their own weight.
- *Sphagnune* is also used as fodder and fuel.
- *Sphagnum* plants form a compact dark coloured **peat** (rich in carbon, superior absorptive power and antiseptic properties). Alcohol, peat tar, paraffin, nitrates, tanning material, ammonium sulphate, brown dye etc. are obtained from peat.
- The tea prepared from *Polytrichum commune* is used to dissolve kidney and gall bladder stones.
- Many bryophytes used as **indicator plants** and **antibiotic** substances.

COMMON NAME OF SOME TRUE MOSSES

COMMAN NAME	SCIENTIFIC NAME
Peat /Quacking Bog / Turf moss	*Sphagnum*
Granite moss	*Andraea*
Twisted moss	*Tortula*
Golden or Maiden hair moss	*Pogonatum*
Cord moss	*Funaria*
Hair cap moss	*Polytrichum*
Black moss	*Grimmia*

SOME IMPORTANT FACTS

- **Father of Indian Bryology** – Professor S.R. Kashyap
- **Gold mine of liverworts** – Western Himalayas
- **Liver-wort :** Belongs to class Hepaticopsida (L. *hepatica* – liver) *i.e.*, resemble a liver in shape or because used for the treatment of liver disorders.
- **Horn-wort :** Liverwort like thallus with embeded sex organs while the sporophyte is aerial, elongated and cylindrical.
- **Apospory :** Production of thalloid plant body from diploid cells of sporophyte *e.g., Anthoceros.*
- **Sterile nurse cells :** In *Riccia crystallina*, some cells in capsule fail to form spores and serves as nutritive cells.
- Absorptive foot : *Corsinia*
- Sphagnum extract **(sphagnol)** is used for skin disorders.
- Largest bryophyte : ***Dawsonia*** (70 cm) found in New Zealand and Australia.
- Smallest bryophyte : *Zoopsis argenta* (0.5 mm).
- **Xerochasy** exhibited by elaters of *Marchantia.*
- Aquatic bryophytes : *Riccia fluitans, Riella and Ricciocarpus.*
- ***Marchantia*** can form 3,000,000 spores per capsule.
- ***Sphagnum*** is most economically important.
- Non-green **heteretrophs :** *Buxobaumia aphylla, Cryptothallus mirabilis.*
- *Pogonatum* sporogonium is without as apophysis.
- **Epiphragm :** Flat roof of columella.
- **Calyptra :** Loose cap like portion of capsule.
- Sporogonial cells of mature ***Riccia*** are always haploid.
- According to **Koch, Caulid** and **Phyllid** are stems and leaves of bryophytes, respectively. These are haploid and lacking vascular tissue.
- **Largest archegonium** of plant kingdom : ***Funaria***
- Oldest bryophyte fossil are 350 million years old.
- In ***Funaria,*** gemmae are formed at the tips of chloronemal branches of protonema.
- **Protandry :** Common feature in ***Funaria***.
- Gemmae are found in all groups of bryophyta **except Sphagnidae.**

DIVISION – PTERIDOPHYTA

Introduction

- Pteridophytai (Gk. *Pteron :* feather; *phyta :* plants) : Plants with feather like fronds or **ferns.**
- Term **Pteridophyta** was first introduced by **Haeckel** in 1866.
- Most primitive group which flourished well during **Devonian** and **Carboniferous periods** of palaeozoic era.
- Flowerless, seedless, spore producing vascular plants which have successfully invaded the land.
- Small sized annual or perennials, mostly terrestrial and thrive well under damp and shady conditions. Some grow in xeric climate (*Selaginella lepidophylla*), some are **epiphytes** (*Selaginella oregana, Ophiglossum pendulum*) and some are **aquatic** (*Salvinia, Azolla, Marsilea*).
- **Sporophyte** is **main independent** plant body, differentiated into **true roots, true stem** and **true leaves.**
- Leaves may be **megaphyllous** (large pinnatified leaves *e.g.,* ferns) or **microphyllous** (small simple, uninerved leaves *e.g., Equisetum* and *Selaginella*). Leaves are **scaly** (*e.g., Equisetum*) or small and sessile (*e.g., Lycopodium, Selaginella*) or large, petiolate and compound (e.g., Ferns).

- Vascular system (xylem + phloem) well developed. Cambium absent. True vessels absent in xylem while in phloem, companion cells are absent and sieve cells are present.
- The stele (central cylinder–xylem, phloem, pericycle and sometimes medullary rays as well as pith) is **protostele** (*e.g., Lycopodium, Selaginella*) or **Siphonostele** (*e.g., Equisetum*) or **Dictyostele** (*e.g. Pteris, Dryopteris*).
- Reproduction by **spores** produced inside the **sporangia** (diploid) borne on leaves **(sporophylls)** usually on the ventral surface. In some cases, they are borne in the axil of stem and **leaves** (*e.g., Selaginella*), or in some specialised structure as **fertile spike** (e.g., *Ophioglossum*), **sporangiophores** (*e.g., Equisetum*), **sporocarps** (*e.g., Marsilea*).
- They may be **homosporous** (one type of spores *e.g., Lycopodium, Pteris, Equisetum*) or **heterosporous** (two different types of spores *i.e.,* smaller **microspores** and larger **macrospores** *e.g., Marsilea, Selaginella*).
- A sporangium originates from **a group of superficial** cells *i.e.,* **eusporangiate development** *e.g., Selaginella, Equisetum, Lycopodium* or from a **single initial cell** (*e.g., Pteris, Marsilea*).
- Sporophylls may be **uniformly distributed** (*e.g., Pteris, Adiantum*) or aggregated to **form compact mass** (strobili) at the stem apices (*e.g., Selaginella, Equisetum*).
- The sporangia present in **sporocarps** in aquatic pteridophytes *e.g., Azolla, Marsilea* and *Salvinia.*
- In higher ferns sporangia are either borne singly or in groups called **sori** which may be—**Simple** (all sporangia mature together *e.g., Botrychium*), **gradate** (mature sporangia in centre and immature sporangia on periphery. *e.g.,* Marsilea) or **mixed** (*e.g., Pteris*).
- Spores are produced by **meiosis** so these are **haploid.** Spore germinate to produce **gametophyte** which may be—
  (*i*) In **homosporous** pteridophytes, **exosporic** (outside the spore wall) gametophyte development, prothalli are usually **monoecious.**
  (*ii*) In **heterosporous** pteridophytes, **endosporic** gametophyte development, and gametophytes are **dioecious.**
- Sex organs *i.e.,* male sex organ **(antheridia)** and female sex organ **(archegonia)** are either embedded in the prothallus (*e.g., Lycopodium, Selaginella*) or are projected (*e.g., Pteridium*).
- Antheridium is surrounded by a single **antheridial jacket** and **antherozoids** are unicellular, uninucleate and biflagellate.
- Archegonium is differentiated into **neck** and **venter** (embedded in prothallus). Neck consists of 4 vertical rows of cells and possess **two** neck canal cells which may be more than two (*e.g. Lycopodium*) or only one (*e.g.. Pteridium*).
- Water is required for fertilization, antherozoids are chemically attracted towards archegonium due to **malic** or **fumaric acid.**
- Zygote (diploid) develop into a well developed **sporophyte** with roots, stem and leaves.
- In some pteridophytes gametophyte arise directly from the cells of the sporophyte without meiosis and spore formation *i.e.,* **apospory** while in **apogamy,** sporophytes arise directly from gametophytes without gametes and sexual fusion.
- Extinct group of pteridophytes are—**Club mosses, Horse tails** and **Ferns.**
- The alternation of generation is heterologous **(heteromorphic)** type.

CLASSIFICATION OF PTERIDOPHYTA – FOUR CLASSES

(1) Psilophytes (Psilopsida) (2) Lycopods (Lycopsida), (3) Horse tails (Sphenopsida) and (4) Ferns (Pteropsida).

Ferns

- Big group of pteridophytes, dominated on earth in **carboniferous period** (about 300 million years ago).
- Quite common in tropical rain forests.

- Some of ferns are **giant tree ferns** (18 m in height). Common examples of ferns are *Dryopteris* (Male shield fern), *Pteridium* **(Bracken fern)** and *Adinatum* (Maiden hair fern).
- All are **homosporous, leptosporangiate**, belong to order **Filicales.**
- Dominant plant body is **sporophyte** (consists of mainly **rhizome, leaves** and **roots).**
- **Rhizome**–Underground, horizontally growing stems, produces **roots** on **lower** side and **leaves aerially,** may grow **obliquely upward** through the soil. The older parts of the rhizome are covered with the **remnants** of leaf bases of old and dead leaves.
- Roots are dark coloured **adventitious roots.**
- Leaves may be **simple** (one blade) or **pinnately compound** (may be bi or tripinnately). The leaflets or pinna are borne on the axis called **rachis.** The compound leaf alongwith its stout rachis is **frond. Ramenta** are dry brown scales covering the bases of fronds. **Circinate** is a condition of leaf in which leaves are tightly rolled during young stage but uncoil like a watch spring as these grow.
- Internally **rhizome** is differentiated into **cuticularised epidermis** followed by several layers of **sclerenchymatous hypodermis** followed by **parenchymatous ground tissue** in which many **meristeles** are present. **Concentric** (central xylem surrounded by phloem) meristele. In mature rhizome it is **dictyostelic.**
- Roots with **diarch** xylem. Protoxylem is exarch and pholem is present on both sides of xylem.
- In young rachis, ground tissue consists of 'U' or 'C-shaped' stele but in mature rachis it gets broken into **meristeles.**
- Vegetative reproduction by **fragmentation** of rhizome and development of adventitious buds. In *Dryopteris*, the leaf bud present at leaf base separates and grows into a new plant. In *Adiantum caudatum* and other few species, adventitious buds develop at leaf tips, they form new plants when touch the soil. The process helps in spreading the fern over a large area. Because of this habit *Adinatum caudatum* is commonly called **walking fern** and **maiden hair fern.**
- **Diploid sporophyte** plant body produces haploid spores. On the underside or margins of leaflets small brown or yellow spots **(sori)** are present. Sours is a group of sporangia covered by a protective covering called **indusium.** Each sporangium has 8-16 diploid spore mother cell which produces 64 or lesser haploid spores by meiosis. Leaves having sporangia are called sporophylls.
- Sporangium consists of a **stalk** (multicellular) and a **capsule** (biconvex). Capsule filled with spores. The one layered wall of the capsule is thin and has a conspicuous strip of cells **(annulus).** The thin walled cells constitute **stomium** on maturity of spores, the **indusium** shrivels. The exposed sporangia dehisce in the region of stomium due to differential contraction of annulus. Spores are thrown away and dispersed by air currents. Spore germinate to form the gametophyte generation called **prothallus.**
- Gametophyte (haploid) *i.e.*, prothallus is very small ($\approx$1 cm), thin, green, heart-shaped plate of cells and photosynthetic, attached to soil by **unicellular rhizoids,** bears **gametes** and reproduces sexually. It produces simple **archegonia** and **antheridia** on its under surface **(Homothallic).**
- Antheridium is **sessile, spherical** or **oval,** has a 3-celled (2 are ring cells basal and middle and one is upper lid cell or cover cell) jacket and about 3 sperm mother cells, each of which produces **spirally coiled** (2-3 coils) **multiflagellated antherozoid** (male gamete).
- Archegonium (flask shaped) with a swollen basal portion **(venter)** and a slender like upper position **(neck). Neck** is **short** and **curved** with a **binucleate neck canal cell** surrounded by a wall of **four vertical** rows of cells. Venter is embedded in prothallus and possess a single large egg cell with a female gamete in it. In mature state, the venter canal cell and the neck canal cell **gelatinise.** Sperms swim through the film of water to the opened archegonia by **malic acid.** An antherozoid fuses with an **oosphere** (egg cell) to form a diploid **oospore** (zygote). It divides vertically to give rise to two cells (*i*) **Hypobasal cell** (towards the prothallus) forms foot and root and (*ii*) **Epibasal cell** (towards the soil) produces cotyledons and stem. Another vertical division results in the formation of **quadrant.**

- Young embryo develops into a **young sporophyte.** The prothallus dies meanwhile.
- Heteromorphic alternation of generation in which diploid sporophyte alternates with haploid gametophyte.

Selaginella

- Commonly called as **"Spike moss"** or **"little club moss".**
- Xerophytes (*e.g., S. lepidophylla*) and **resurrection plants** *i.e.,* roll up to form **ball-like** structure during dry season but spread out and revive when sufficient moisture is available.
- Plant body is **evergreen sporophyte herb,** differentiated into root, stem and leaves.
- Stem is prostrate and dichotomously branched. Rhizophores are leafless, positively geotropic structures which develop **exogenously** from **angle meristem.**
- Leaves are sessile, small called **microphylls.** These are **ligulate.** The bulbous basal region of the ligule made up of larger cells is called **glossopodium.** All of these possess vascular system.
- Stem is **polystelic** (1-16 steles). Each stele is a **protostele** and surrounded by **air space.** Xylem is **diarch, exarch** and made up of tracheids.
- Roots has **monarch** stele with **exarch** xylem. Phloem is **horse-shoe** shaped. Pith absent.
- Rhizophore has **monarch** stele. It was regarded as **organ suigenesis** (organ of independent origin by Bower and Globel).
- Leaves with cup-shaped chloroplast.
- Vegetative reproduction by **fragmentation, bulbils** (*e.g., S. subdiaphana*) and **stem tubers** (*e.g.,* ***S. chrysocaulos***).
- Asexual reproduction by spores (heterosporous-2 types-micro and megaspores) produced in **microsporangia** (producing numerous microspores) and **megasporangia** (producing usually only 4 megaspores) which are borne on **microsporophylls** and **megasporophylls** respectively. Sporangia are **eusporangiate.**
- Microsporangium with multicellular **stalk** and round or oval body covered by **two** layered jacket. Single layered tapetum present beneath the jacket provides nourishment for developing spores. Microspores are produced by meiosis in microspore other cells.
- Megasporangium is large, four-lobed (one megaspore per lobe) with **two** layered jacket and a **multicellular stalk.** Megaspores are formed by meiosis in megaspore mother cells. In *S. monospora* only one megaspore survive while in *S. rupestris* two megaspore survive.
- Microspore produces an endosporic male gametophyte which is highly reduced. Growth of gametophytes is **precocious.** The microspore liberated at **13-celled stage** (1 prothellial cell + 12 cells of antheridium (8 jacket cells + 4 primary androgonial cells). Primary androgonial cells divide repeatedly and form **128-256 androcytes** which metamorphoses into **oval, biflagellated** antherozoid (sperm).
- Megaspore produces a partially exosporic, autotrophic, multicellular female gametophyte (female prothallus). After release of megaspores, a few superficial cells act as **archegonial initials,** each of which develops into an **archegonium** (short projecting **neck** with one cell thick jacket and is made up of two tiers of four cells each and **venter** embedded).
- Fertilization takes place with the help of water which produces diploid zygote **(oospore)** that divides to form an **embryo** and a suspensor. **Meroblastic** embryo development. Suspensor helps in pushing the embryo into food laden storage tissue.
- **Heteromorphic** or **heterologous** alternation of generations.
- In some species of ***Selaginella*** (*e.g., S. rupestis*) megaspore is not released from the megasporium. Fertilization and embryo development takes place while the megaspore is still inside **megasporangium** *i.e.,* **viviparous.**

ECONOMIC IMPORTANCE OF PTERIDOPHYTES

- The sporocarp of ***Marsilea*** are rich in starch and used for its nutritive value.
- The rhizomes and petioles of fern ***Dryopteris*** is used to produce an antihelminthic drug.
- Some ferns are grown in gardens for their ornamental value as they have showy, large and graceful foliage.

SOME PTERIDOPHYTES WITH THEIR COMMON AND SCIENTIFIC NAME

COMMON NAME	SCIENTIFIC NAME
Spike moss	*Selaginella*
Creeping pine or Club moss	*Lycopodium*
Bird's nest moss	*Selaginella rupestris*
Scouring rushes or Horse tail	*Equisetum*
Male shield fern	*Dryopteris*
Walking fern or maidan hair fern	*Adiantum*
Braken fern	*Pteridium*
Golden fern	*Onychium*
Adder's tongue fern	*Ophiglossum*

SOME IMPORTANT FACTS

- Mosses (bryophytes) and ferns (pteridophytes) are commonly called as amphibians of the plant kingdom.
- **Cryptogams :** Coined by **Linnaeus** (1737), meaning is plants without seeds.
- Pteridophytes have only **tracheids** in their xylem and only **sieve tubes** in their phloem.
- **Ramenta :** Brown scales.
- **Caudex :** Unbranched erect axis.
- **Indusium :** Soral covering in ferns.
- **Annulus :** Strip of thickened cells on capsule.
- **Stomium :** Area on sporangial wall from which spores dehisce.
- **Psilophytales :** The earliest known vascular land plants includes extinct vascular plants *e.g., Cooksonia, Rhynia* etc.
- ***Azolla* :** An aquatic **water fern** used as biofertilizer.
- ***Salvinia* :** An aquatic pteridophyte **weed.** It is rootless pteridophyte.
- **Smallest pteridophyte :** *Azolla.*
- **Largest pteridophyte :** *Cyathaea/Alsophila* (Tree ferns).
- **Tallest fern :** *Alsophila.*
- **Heterosporous pteridophytes :** *Selaginella, Isoetes, Marsilea, Salvinia, Azolla, Pitularia* etc.
- **Quadrifoliate fern :** *Marsilea.*
- **Hieronymus** (1902) : Genus ***Selaginella*** divided into two subgenera *e.g.,* **homeophyllum** and **heterophyllum.**
- Pteridophytes are first tracheophytes to appear on earth and called **vascular cryptogams** (seedless, flowerless vascular plants).
- Pteridophytes, are **snakes of plant kingdom.**
- **Apogamy** in *Pteris cretica* was reported by Farlow (1874).
- **Apospory** in *Arthyrium* was reported by Druery (1884). Polyploidy is common in ferns due to apospory.
- **Carboniferous coal :** Mainly from ferns and other pteridophytes.

- **Tree fern :** Fern with upright aerial stem *e.g., Cyathaea, Alsophila.*
- First tracheophytes : Psilotales like *Rhynia* named after the place **Rhynie** in Scotland.
- Telome (Zimmermann, 1930) : Ultimate terminal part of a dichotomous axis that has given rise to all parts of land plants including leaves.
- **Xerophytes :** *Selaginella lepidophylla* and *S. pilifera*, sold in market as novelties.
- **Walking fern :** *Adiantum*, due to vegetative propagation by its leaf tips. Some species of *Adiantum* are xerophytes.
- **Epiphytes :** *Selaginella oregana, Lycopodium squarrosum, Asplenium nidus.*
- **Halophyte :** *Acrostichum aureum.*
- ***Marsilea*** found as terrestrial, amphibious as well as aquatic plant.
- **Pyrenoids** present in chloroplasts of *Selaginella.*
- **Distelic** condition present in stem of *Selaginella kraussiana.*
- ***Selaginella*** and ferns exhibit diplohaplontic life cycle.
- Protostele is simplest and dictyostele is advanced type of stele in pteridophytes.
- **Cespitose habit :** Under dry conditions the xerophytic species of ***Selaginella*** roll on brown balls.
- Rhizophore absent in ***Selaginella cuspidata.***
- **Organ *Sui generis*** (a sturcture of unknown origin) is used for rhizophore of ***Selaginella.***
- Holoblastic development : ***Dryopteris.***
- ***Selaginella rupestris*** exhibit a near approach to seed habit.
- ***Rhynia*** discovered by Makkie (1913) from red sand stones of devonian period.
- **Trophopod :** Food storing leaf base in many ferns *e.g., Asplenium platyneuron, Dryopteris fragans, Onoclea.*
- **Fruit Bodies :** Only formed by aquatic ferns *Azolla, Marselia and Salvinia.*
- **Secondary growth** is present in some pteridophytes *e.g., Isoetes, Ophioglossum, Botrychium.*
- ***Ophioglossum*** possess **largest chromosome number** in biological kingdom.
- **Stelar theory** was given by **Tiegham** and **Douliot.**
- **Megasporophylls** of pteridophytes are equivalent to carpels of angiosperms.
- *Equisetum* (Sphenopsid) is **homosporous** while *Selaginella* is **heterosporous.**

---

2. Structural Organisation in Plants and Animals

(I) STRUCTURAL ORGANISATION IN ANIMALS

Cells are the basic units of structure and function in all living organisms. The branch of Zooloogy which deals with the basic structure of organs and tissues is called Histology. Histology is the study of tissues. The word histology was coined by Mayer. The founder of general histology is F.X. Bichet. Marcello Malpighii is the "father of animal histology". A group of more or less similar cells of common origin specialised to perform a specific function or functions is known as tissue. The formation of tissues from germinal layers is termed as histogenesis.

Four types of tissues are seen in animals, they are:

1. Epithelial tissues
2. Conncctive tissues
3. Muscular tissues
4. Nervous tissues

1. Epithelial Tissues

The epithelial tissue forms a covering on the surface of the body and also lines the ducts, vessels and body cavities. Here, the cells are held together by a viscous intercellular substance. The cells rest on a supporting connective tissue called the basement membrane in all cases, whether in a single layer or many layers. The origin of epithelial tissue varies depending upon their function. The free surface of the cells may not contain projections when it is called smooth or may have protoplasmic projections like cilia, stereocilia or microvilli. These projections have a granule at their base.

On the basis of structure, epithelial tissues can be classified into two major groups:

I. Simple epithelia: formed of a single layer of cells.

II. Stratified epithelia: composed of several layers of cells.

Simple epithelia can be further classified as:

1. Squamous epithelium: Here the cells are thin and flat. It is seen in the peritoneum of frog, alveoli of lungs and endothelium of blood vessels.

2. Columnar epithelium: Cells are tall column like and have distinct elongated nuclei which are situated at the base of the cells. This epithelium is found in digestive system and urogenital organs.

3. Cuboidal epithelium: They appear like cubes and are found in many glands, ducts and in certain kidney tubules.

4. Pseudo-stratified epithelium: Cells lack uni formity, found in trachea and olfactory chambers.

On the basis of function the simple epithelial can be classified as follows :

1. Glandular epithelium: It is a modified columnar epithelium, specialised for secretion, found in inner lining of intestinal mucosa, liver, pancreas, salivary glands *etc.* Some glands are unicellular (goblet cells of intestine), others multicellular (*e.g.,* Salivary gland). The secretion from glands is poured out through ducts, whereas glands may be devoid of ducts thus called ductless glands or endocrine glands. (e.g., Pituitary gland).

2. Ciliated epithelium: The cells sometimes simple cuboidal or simple columnar consist of cilia (fine thread like structures) on their surface and are found in oviduct, kidney tubules, trachea and respiratory passage.

3. Sensory epithelium: These are specialised cells for the reception of stimuli as they are innervated at their bases by sensory nerve fibres. They are found in olfactory lining, taste buds and retina.

4. Endothelium: It is simple squamous epithelium lining the blood and lymph vessels including the heart.

5. Mesothelium: Simple squamous epithelium covering the surfaces of all body cavities and mesenteries.

6. Pigmented epithelium: Cells consist of pigment cells as in pigment cells of retina.

7. Germinal epithelium: It forms a lining in the ovary, consisting of stratified epithelium.

Stratified epithelium consists of many layers of cells arranges one above the other. They are found in places of wear and tear *i.e.,* tongue, skin, buccal cavity, nasal chambers.

Stratified epithelia can be classified on the basis of structure into four groups.

1. **Stratified columnar epithelium** *e.g.*, in ducts of salivary and mammary glands.
2. **Stratified cuboidal epithelium** *e.g.*, in Graffian follicle, seminiferous tubule.
3. **Stratified squamous epithelium** *e.g.*, seen in epidermis of skin, oesophagus, anus.
4. **Stratified transitional epithelium cells** can change their shape, *e.g.*, renal pelvis ureter, bladder.

Epithelial glands

1. These glands are those which secrete their materials through ducts. On the basis of their shape, they are—

(a) Simple tubular gland (*e.g.*, intestinal glands)
(b) Simple coiled tubular (*e.g.*, sweat glands)
(c) Simple branched tubular (*e.g.*, gastric glands)
(d) Simple alveolar (*e.g.*, mucous glands in skin of frog)
(e) Simple branched alveolar (*e.g.*, sebaceous gland)
(f) Compound alveolar (*e.g.*, Salivary and mammary glands)

Method of Secretion: The modes of secretion form a basis of dividing exocrine glands into three types—

(a) **Apocrine glands:** The apical part of cell where the secretion has accumulated is cut off to release the secretion, *e.g.*, mammary glands.
(b) **Merocrine glands:** Product is released by exocytosis, *e.g.*, salivary glands.
(c) **Holocrine glands:** When the cell as a whole is shed, which is abundant in secretion, *e.g.*, sebaceous glands.

An Epithelium has usually no direct blood supply, but obtain its nourishment from the fluid in the inter cellular spaces. An exception is stria vascularis of cochlea. All epithelia show marked regenerative power.

2. Connective Tissues

Connective tissues consist of a group of cells which remain embedded in an extra-cellular material called matrix. They originate from the mesoderm only. The inter cellular substances are the homogenous ground substance and intercellular fibres.

Types of connective tissue:

(a) Connective tissue proper - fibrous binding tissues
(b) Supporting tissues - rigid tissues like cartilage and bone
(c) Fluid tissue - blood and lymph.

Connective tissue proper

The matrix here is less rigid and contains many polysaccharides including hyaluronic acid:

The Cell types:

(i) **Fibroblasts:** Form fibres and matrix
(ii) **Adipose cells:** Occur singly or in groups and store fat.
(iii) **Plasma cells:** Synthesize antibodies, found in sersous membranes, lining of respiratory and intestinal tracts and in inflamed areas.
(iv) **Mast cells:** Produce histamine involved in inflammatory and allergie reactions, serotonin: constricts blood vessels, heparin: inhibitor of blood clotting.
(v) **Reticular cells:** Associated with reticular fibres.
(vi) **Pigment cells:** Seen in epidermis and choroid coat of the eye. They help in absorbing light rays.
(vii) **Macrophages:** Wandering cells or histiocytes which engulf loose blood, bacteria, cell debris and foreign bodies.

(viii) **Lymphocytes:** Migrate from blood into connective tissue and are abundant in respiratory and gastro-intestinal tracts.

(ix) **Reserve mesenchyme cells:** They are like embryonic cells.

Fibrous component: The fibres are of three types they are—

(i) **Collagen fibres:** The most common, whitish, nonelastic and opaque. Tannic acid makes them hard and tough. The bundles of fibres branch are easily stainable.

(ii) **Reticular fibres:** They form a fine network by branching and uniting. In wound healing, they are the first to develop.

(iii) **Elastic fibres:** They are seen singly or in sheets.

Amorphous ground substance

It is the inter cellular substance which permits diffusion of nutrients, water, gases over considerable distances.

Classification of connective tissue proper

I. Loose connective tissue

1. **Mucous connective tissue:** Found in the embryo. In adult it is found in the vitreous humour of the eye. In mammlian embryo, the example is the umbilical cord.
2. **Reticular connective tissue:** Fibroblasts and reticular cells are embedded in its matrix. Seen in lymphnodes, bone marrow, liver. It occurs in stomach, intestine, trachea and bronchi forming basement membrane below epithelia.
3. **Areolar connective tissue:** Appears spongy and consists of collagenous fibres. It is found in mesentrics, in omenta of alimentary canal and in subcutaneous tissue. It is a supportive and protective skeleton for many organs.
4. **Adipose connective tissue:** It is a highly specialised form of areolar tissue. It consists of fat cells. Brown fat is a special type of adipose tissue of brownish colour occurring in foetus of human beings.

II. Dense connective tissue

1. **Inter woven dense connective tissue:** Fibres are arranged in an irregular manner so as to withstand tensions exerted on it.
   It is found in dermis of the skin, protective capsule of spleen, testis and periosteal part of bone.
2. **Parallel dense connective tissue:** Fibres are abundant, regularly oriented, flexible but resistant to a pulling force. *e.g.*, Tendons and ligaments.

Supporting connective tissue forms internal skeleton in vertebrates. They are:

(1) Cartilage made up of chondrocytes.
Cartilages are of three types—
(a) Hyaline *(b)* Elastic *(c)* Fibrous

(2) Bone: It is a specialised hard connective tissue. The matrix has hard, calcified collagenous substance. The central cavity of the bone encloses a bone marrow, which forms blood cells.

The bones are of different types-Spongy bones, compact bones, investing bones and replacing bones.

Bone marrow is divided into yellow bone marrow and red bone marrow, the latter produces red blood corpuscles and is seen in mammals only.

Fluid tissues

These include blood and lymph.

Blood: The tissue has a liquid matrix called plasma in which float the blood corpuscles. The blood proteins in plasma are fibrinogen, albumin, globulin and prothrombin.

Blood corpuscles in vertebrates are erythrocytes, leucocytes and thrombocytes.

Lymph : It is a modified form of tissue fluid. The lymphoid organs are lymph nodes, spleen, tonsils and thymus.

Blood cells are formed in the bone marrow of the long bones and lymph nodules by a process termed haemopoiesis.

Erythrocytes have haemoglobin in them which is used in oxygen transport. They are nucleated and oval in shape.

3. Muscular Tissue

This tissue is responsible for movement of the body and its various parts. The cells become elongated called muscle fibres and are highly contractile. The cells have well defined nuclei, cytoplasm is known as sarcoplasm and contains fibrils called myofibrils which run parallel. The sarcolemma surrounds the myofibres. Sarcoplasmic reticulum is a specialized type of endoplasmic reticulum of muscle tissue.

On the basis of their structure muscles are classified as—

(i) Smooth muscles
(ii) Skeletal muscles
(iii) Cardiac muscles

(i) Smooth muscles: They have spindle shaped cells without sarcolemma. Show slow contraction by involuntary factors. These muscles are innervated by branches of the autonomic nervous system. The fibrous proteins, actins and myosin are present in the smooth muscle cell.

They are found in walls of many glands, walls of urinogenital ducts, alimentary canal, blood vessels and respiratory passages.

(ii) Skeletal muscle (Striated muscle) : The muscles attached to skeleton are skeletal muscles. The cells are elongated, multinucleated and constant in number after birth. The increase is seen due to enlargement of myofibrils present in the cells. Sarcolemma is vivid. In some muscles, the muscle fibres unite together into bundles with the help of connective tissue (fasciculli) e.g., Biceps. The connective tissue sheath called epimysium covers the muscle as a whole. In a longitudinal section all myofibrils exhibit alternate dark and light segments in uniform pattern, thus the name Striated muscle.

The fine structure of a muscle fibre is made up of long, thin elements called myofibrils. A muscle is made up of myofibres and a myofibre is made up of myofibrils. In a resting myofibril there are fine darkly staining lines (the 'Z' lines) running through middle of light band - the 'I' bands. The darker middle band is 'A' band and its lighter middle area 'H' band. — A single unit consists of 'Z line' an 'I band', an 'A band' and then the next I band and finally the next Z line. This structure from one Z - line to next is termed sarcomere - the functional subunit of myofibrils. Sacromeres are made up of myofilan:tents - thick ones are made up of myosin, the thin ones of actin, Z lines of tropomyosin.

Sliding filament theory describes muscle contraction as a sliding of actin filaments in between thick myosin filaments. Muscles attached to the skeleton, upper one-third of oesophagus, diaphragm, tongue, muscles attached to the eye-ball are examples of striated muscles. The red muscles contain fibres which are in constant action, whereas white muscle fibres are not in constant action.

(iii) Cardiac muscle: This is a modified striated muscle in which fibres are short and branched. The contraction is involuntary and rhythmical. Nuclei per cell is one or two, placed centrally. The branches of fibres unite to form a network or syncitiym. Intercalated discs are present, which are localized specializations of the sarcolemma of abutting cells.

4. Nervous tissue

This is a specialised tissue which is responsible for receiving, transmitting and discharging various types of stimuli. Nervous system in man has two parts 1. Central nervous system, (CNS), and 2. Peripheral nervous system-(PNS). CNS consists of brain ad spinal cord and PNS of ganglia and both afferent and efferent nerves. The afferent fibres receive stimuli from external surface and transmit impulses to CNS. The efferent fibres, originate from CNS and their axons connect with the effector organs. Thus, the bodies functions become coordinated.

Nerve tissue is made up of neurons and nerve fibres. The nerve cells (neurons) form the structural and functional units of nervous tissue. Neuron consists of a cell body with a nucleus, cytoplasm, Nissl's granules and dendrites. The longest dendrite called axon carry impulses away from cell body, whereas dendrites carry impulses towards the cell body. Neurofibrils present in cytoplasm transmit impulses. The ends of axon may branch up called axon-endings or temporal arborisation.

Types of neurons:

1. **Unipolar neurons:** Have only a single process from the cell body, which divides to give dendron and axon.
2. **Bipolar neurons:** A single dendrite and a single axon are seen on opposite ends of the cell. They are. seen in the retina of the eye, olfactory epithelium and ganglia of auditory' nerve.

3. **Multipolar neurons:** There is only one axon and a number of dendrons. The cell bodies of multipolar neurons are located in the grey matter of the brain and spinal cord.

On the basis of function, neurons can be classified as follows:

(i) **Sensory neurons:** Carry impulses from different parts of the body to the brain and spinal cord, *e.g.*, Neurons in dorsal foot of spinal cord.

(ii) **Association neurons:** Also called as intercalated neurons. They are present only in the brain to form special circuits for nerve conduction.

(iii) **Motor neurons:** Conducting impulses from CNS to different parts of the body or effector organs. They are seen in motor area of cerebral cortex.

Nerve fibres : A nerve fibre consists of a centrally placed axon which is bound by a sheath called neurolemma or sheath of Schwann. If the nerve fibre is surrounded by a myelin sheath, it is said to be myelinated or medullated, whereas in the absence of myelin sheath the nerve fibre is called non-medullated fibres. Myelin sheath lies between axolemma and the neurolemma, and is interrupted at regular intervals by constrictions, the nodes of Ranvier. Schwann cells are needed for formation of myelin fibres. The peripheral nerves consist of myelinated fibres.

The non-medullated fibres are seen in autonomic nervous system. The nerve fibres which conduct impulses at fast rates are covered with thick myelin sheaths. There is a sort of jumping of action potentials from one node to another which is termed as saltatory conduction.

Histology of mammalian organs

1. Stomach: Outermost layer is composed of squamous epithelium and is called serosa. Muscle coat consists of rather ill-defined layers, outer longitudinal, a middle circular and an inner oblique layer. The middle coat is regular and is greatly thickened at the pyloric sphincter. Between the muscle groups are found nerve cells and fibres.

The submucous coat consists of loose connective tissue, large number of blood vessels, nerves and lymphatics. The mucous coat is thrown into ridges in the empty organ. The epithelium here is simple columnar with gastric glands which are simple branched tubules. There are three types of glands—

(i) **Cardiac gland:** They are in the form of simple tubules.

(ii) **Fundic glands:** Found in the fundus of stomach. The gastric cells are of three types - peptic, oxyntic and mucoid cells.

(iii) **Pyloric glands:** The glands are coiled and branched in pyloric region of stomach.

2. Intestine: There are no oxyntic and peptic cells here. Serous coat is made up of mesothelial cells. The muscular coat is well differentiated into external longitudinal and internal circular coats, with blood vessels, lymphatics and nerve plexus lying between them. The submucous coat consists of connective tissue. The mucous coat is thrown into finger like folds called villi which are covered by simple columnar epithelium with scattered goblet cells. At the base between villi are seen crypts of Lieberkuhn which lead into Bruners glands.

3. Liver: It is composed of polygonal lobules containing a central vein in the centre and portal canals at the corners. The liver cells are polyhedral and arranged in long chains extending from the central vein to the periphery of the lobule. Liver is a derivative of mesoderm and endoderm. Liver is covered by a connective tissue Glisson's capsule, which on reaching hilum penetrates into liver, giving off septa.

Trabeculae from these septa and capsule pass into lobes dividing them into lobules. Lobule is the unit of liver structure. The central vein running in middle of each lobule (intralobular vein) drains away into sub-lobular vein of the hepatic venous system. At the periphery of lobule the interlobular vein is seen which is a tributary of portal vein, along with hepatic artery interlobur bile ducts and lymphatic vessels. The whole system is termed portal canal.

4. Spleen: It is encapsulated by a capsule made up of fibrous connective tissue. Spleen is composed of lymphatic tissue which is distinguished into white and red pulp. From inner surface of capsule extend trabeculae carrying blood vessels. The space between trabeculae is filled with lymphatic tissue. The white pulp is distributed as rounded areas, consists of ordinary lymphoid tissue. The red pulp occupies the space between large terminal venous sinuses. All cellular elements are present here.

5. Lung: The surface is covered by a serous membrane, the visceral pleura. Septa of connective tissue pass from the pleural covering into the organ dividing it into lobules. A pulmonary unit consists of bronchiole, alveolar passages, air sacs, with blood vessels, lymphatics, nerves and connective tissue between them. Alveoli form clusters which open in an alveolar duct.

6. Kidney: It is surrounded by a dense connective tissue capsule. The glandular part of the kidney is made up of outer cortex and inner medulla. The cortex contains many uriniferous tubules, Malpighian capsules having Bowman's capsules and glomerulus. The medulla is composed of many real pyramids, medullary rays, columns of Bertini, tubules and connective tissue.

The functional unit of kidney is the nephron which consists of glomerulus and its tubule. Blood supply is extremely rich and the vessels are in close association with the tubules.

7. Pancreas: It is a tubulo-racemose gland, the exocrine portion opens through a duct into the duodenum. The endocrine part secretes insulin and glucagon. The exocrine part consists of a series of lobules bound together by connective tissue and secrete digestive enzymes. The endocrine part is constituted by Islets of Langerhans with alpha and beta cells.

8. Gonads: *(a)* Testis is surrounded by fibrous connective tissue, the tunica albuginea. It is composed of coiled seminiferous tubules in which spermatogenesis occurs. The intertubular connective tissue contains blood vessels and. interstitial cells of Leydig which produce androgens, the male hormones. In between these germinal cells are seen Sertoli cells which are large and contribute in nutrition.

(b) Ovary: Ovary is a solid organ attached by its antero-lateral border to the broad ligament. The tissue of broad ligament continuesinto ovary as troma. The ovary is lined by germinal epithelium. Beneath this is the tunica albuginea.

Stroma has connective tissue cells and spindle-shaped cells. The ovum grows in a follicle from where it is shed into peritoneal cavity after which this follicle is called corpus luteum. Ovary is also an endocrine organ producing female hormones like progesterone and estrogen.

(II) STRUCTURAL ORGANISATION IN PLANTS

The angiosperms are the dominant vegetation today. They are flowering, seed and fruit bearing plants. The morphology includes study of leaves, seeds, flowers, stems, roots with their modifications, inflorescence, pollination fertilization and type of embryo formation. Angiosperms have dominant sporophytes and are broadly classified into herbs, shrubs and trees. The herbs are more advanced than trees and monocots are more advanced than dicots. The tap roots develop from radicle and adventitious roots arise from any part of the plant except the radicle.

The angiosperms may be annuals, biennials and perennials.

The accessory structures seen are :

(i) Bud : It is embryonic shoot. The biggest bud is cabbage.

(ii) Accessory buds : When more than one bud arises in axil of leaf, it is termed as accessory bud; *e.g., Cuciurbita* species.

(iii) Adventitious buds : When buds grow in places except axil or terminal; *e.g.* Leaf buds on margin of *Bryophyllum.*

(iv) Bulbil : These are axillary buds, which store food material, detach from parent plant and grow into new plants; *e.g.,* Pine apple, Cacti.

(v) Stipule : Any two emergences at the base of petiole are called stipules.

(vi) Bracts : A leaf like structure at the base of pedicel is called bract.

(vii) Thorns : Sharp straight pointed energetic structures arising exogenously and in the axils of leaves; *e.g., Citrus.*

(viii) Prickles : Sharp, straight or curved pointed structures which arise on stem and branches; *e.g.,* Rose

Erect herbs and trees are of different types based on stem nature:

1. Scape : Leafless peduncle arising in between radical leaves seen in most monocotyledons; *e.g., Allium cepa* (Onion).
2. Caudex : Leafless erect stem; *e.g.,* Palm tree.

3. **Culm** : Plants will jointed type of stem; *e.g.*, Bamboo
4. **Excurrent**: Pyramidal shape of tree; *e.g.*, *Pinus.*
5. **Deliquescent**: The erect growth of tree is aided by lateral buds; e.g.. Banyan tree.

Weak stem forms :

1. Creepers : Have soft stems, which creep on ground.
2. Twines : Twist around some support; *e.g.*, Bean.
3. Climbers : Stems climb over other objects:

(*a*) Rootlet climbers : They have adventitious roots for support; *e.g.*, Betel.

(*b*) Hook climbers : They have special thorns and spines which act as hooks to get support for the plant; *e.g.*, Spines act as hooks in rose, in *Bougainvillea* throns act as hook.

(*c*) Tendril climbers : Tendrils are thin, slender, leafless structures which can be modifications of stem, leaf, petiole *etc.*
Stem-climbers : *e.g.*, Passion flower, balloon wine.
Petiole - tendril; *e.g.*, Smilax. Leaf-tendril; *e.g.*, *Lathyrus* (wild Pea).
Leaflet tendril; *e.g.*, *Gloriosa.* Axillary bud tendril; *e.g.*, Passiflora.
Apical bud tendril; *e.g.*, *Vitis vinifera.*

(*d*) Leaf climbers : as in above examples.

(*e*) Lianes : Thick woody twiners in dense forests; *e.g.*, Hiptage.

The stem

Stem develops from plumule, has nodes and internodes, buds and leaves. It is positively phototropic and negatively geotropic. Apex has terminal bud. It is branched and undergoes various modifications to perform special functions - food storage, vegetative reproduction, defense *etc.*

I. Underground stem modifications

Underground stems are seen in unfavourable conditions in some perennial herbs. They have buds which help in vegetative propagation. Stems have nodes and internodes, scale leaves and axillary and terminal buds. The various types of modifications are as follows :

(*i*) *Rhizome* : Rhizome is a thick, prostrate, non-green, branched underground stem bearing nodes and internodes. Rhizome grows in a horizontal direction, but when grows vertically it is called a root stock; *e.g.*, *Alocasia.* Rhizomes are seen in ginger, turmeric, banana *etc.*

(*ii*) *Bulb* : It has a very reduced stem with scale or fleshy leaves around it. Adventitious roots are borne on the lower side.
The food in usually starch except onion. The two kinds of bulbs are:

(*a*) Tunicated bulb : The stem is enclosed by concentric rings of scale leaves, thus the bulb is said to be coated; *e.g.*, onion, tulip *etc.*

(*b*) Scaly bulb : It has partly overlapping scale leaves; *e.g.*, lilies.

(*iii*) *Tuber* : The stems are non-green, oval or spherical swellings with stored food at the ends of underground branches or stolons. This reserve food is transferred to them from the aerial leaves. The stems bear axillary buds at the nodes (eyes); *e.g.*, Potato (*Solanum tuberosum*).

(*iv*) *Corm* : This is very much thickened, fleshy, underground stem which grows vertically. The corm has nodes, internodes, axillary buds and scaly leaves; *e.g.*, Colocasia, Zamikand (*Amorphophallus*).

II. Sub-aerial stem modifications

These are horizontal branches found just above the surface (sub-aerial) or just below the surface (sub-terranean) of the soil. They are meant for vegetative propagation and are produced by lower axillary buds of weak plants. The different modifications are as follows :

(*i*) *Runner* : These are horizontal sub-aerial branches, prostrate and grow very long but remain fixed to soil with the help of roots from their nodes. Leaves are born on upper side. They have long internodes; *e.g.*, *Oxalis* (wood-sorrel), grasses.

(*ii*) *Stolen* : It is a sub-terranean stem, running horizontally, with short internodes and nodes bearing aerial leaves and root; *e.g.*, Peppermint *(Mentha peperita)*, Colocasia.

(iii) *Offset* : It is seen in aquatic plants, arises from one of the lower axillary buds and produces few nodes and internodes. Offset is thick and bears a tuft of leaves and a cluster of roots; *e.g.*, Water hyacinth *(Eicchlornia)*, Water lettuce *(Pistia)*.

(iv) *Sucker* : Sub-terranean location; short thick fleshy branches arise from under- ground bud, grow obliquely and form new plants at the surface; *e.g.*, *Mentha* (garden mint).

III. Aerial stem modifications

(i) *Stem-tendril* : Thin, leafless coiled structure for climbing, modification of buds (*Passiflora*), floral buds (*Antigonon*) or terminal buds *(Vitis)*.

(ii) *Stem thorn* : Hard, pointed, straight structures which arise from axillary branches. They bear leaves and flowers in Duranta; *e.g.*, Citrus, Bougainvillea.

(iii) *Bulbils* : It is a condensed axillary bud, meant for vegetative propagation; *e.g.*, Pineapple, Dioscorea *etc.*

(iv) *Phylloclade* : Seen in Xerophytes, stem becomes flat and green for photosynthesis as leaves are absent or modified into spines; e.g., Opuntia cocoloba. Phylloclade is also known as cladophyll.

(v) *Cladode :* The phylloclade is short with one or two internodes only; *e.g.*, *Asparagus*, *Ruscus aculeatus.*

Branching of stem : It is of two main types;

I. Axillary lateral branches arise from successive axillary buds. They are of the following types:

(a) *Racemose :* Apical bud grows indefinitely and the lateral branches are from auxiliary buds in acropetal fashion; *e.g.*, *Eucalyptus.*

(b) *Cymose :* Apical bud grows definitely and stops growth; lateral buds grow and stop and this is repeated.

(i) Uniparous : Only one branch below each successive apex; *e.g.*, *Vitas.*

(ii) Biparous : Two branches arise below each terminal bud; *e.g.*, *Mirabilis.*

(iii) Multiparous : *e.g.*, Kasner *(Nerium)*.

II. Dichotomous branches are a result of vertical division of apical bud into two parts which form equal branches, repeated at each successive branch tip; *e.g.*, *Riccia, Marchantia.*

Roots

The root system, generally forms the underground part of the plant body. It is made of the main root and its lateral branches. The main root is a descending organ, formed by radical, positively geotropic and hydrotropic with root cap at the top. The various types of roots are as follows:

(A) Tap root : A growth from radicle, endogenously produces lateral roots. Its modifications are :

1. Fusiform; *e.g.*, Radish *(Raphanus sativus).*
2. Napiform; *e.g.*, Turnip.
3. Conical; *e.g.*, Carrot.
4. Nodulated, *e.g.*, Pea.
5. Pneumatophores (breathing roots) which are negatively geotropic; *e.g.*, *Cycas.*

(B) Adventitious roots : These are roots which develop from any part of the plant other than the radicle. Their modifications are of the following types:

1. Climbing roots : Arise from nodes and internodes for climbing; *e.g.*, Betel.
2. Tuberous roots : Swollen, food storing roots; *e.g.*, Sweet potato.
3. Annulated roots : They have a ring like swelling; *e.g.*, *Cinchona.*
4. Assimilatory roots : They have chloro-plasts and assimilate carbon; *e.g.*, *Tinospora.*
5. Epiphyllous roots : They arise from the leaf margin of buds; *e.g.*, *Bryophyllum.*
6. Epiphytic roots : They are hanging spongy roots surrounded by velamen, and absorb moisture from air; *e.g.*, Orchids.
7. Stilt roots : Arise from lower nodes of main stem; *e.g.*, Maize.
8. Sucking roots : Usually found in parasitic plants; *e.g.*, *Cuscuta.*
9. Respiratory roots : Seen in water plants; *e.g.*, *Pistia.*
10. Fasciulated roots : Cluster of tuberous roots at the base of stem; *e.g.*, Dahlia.

11. Moniliform roots : They have a beaded structure because of swellings at regular intervals; *e.g.*, *Vitis.*

12. Nodulose roots : *e.g.*, Mangoginger (*Curcumma amada).*

Leaves

Leaves are the lateral, green, flat outgrowth of nodes which bears auxiliary bud, has vascular system. They arise in acropetal fashion.

1. Foliage : The green wide leaves meant for photosynthesis.
2. Scaly leaves : (Cataphylls) : These are thin, non-green, stalkless and dry.
3. Radical leaves : Leaves crowded together and growing on reduced stem; *e.g.*, carrot.
4. Cauline leaves : Leaves inserted on stem; *e.g.*, Sunflower, Rose.
5. Ramel leaves : Leaves growing on branches; *e.g.*, *Acacia.*
6. Bracts : Found at the pedicel.
7. Prophylls : First leaves on a branch.
8. Ligule: Outgrowth on adaxial side of leaf base usually in grasses.
9. Sporophylls : Spore and sporangia bearing leaves.
10. Floral leaves : Sepals, petals, stamens, carpels in a flower.
11. Cotyledons : First leaves in embryo with seed.

Leaves have three parts : *(a)* Leaf base or hypopodium, *(b)* Petiole or mesopodium

(c) Leaf lamina or epipodium.

Leaf base when swollen is called pulvinus, a sheathing base covering on stem; *e.g.*, grasses and monocots; stipules in dicots. Leaves may be petiolate and sessile (without a petiole).

Stipules are outgrowths at leaf base and a stipule is at the leaf base of compound leaves. Stipules are of various types:

(i) Freelateral; *e.g.*, Cotton.

(ii) Adnate : Stipules fused on petiole on both sides; *e.g.*, Rose.

(iii) Interpetioler stipules are placed alternate to leaves; *e.g.*, Ixora.

(iv) Intrapetiolar : Both stipules of a leaf fuse and occur at axillary angles; *e.g.*, *Gardenia.*

(v) Foliaceous; *e.g.*, Pea.

(vi) Tendrillar; *e.g.*, Similar.

(vii) Spiny; *e.g.*, *Acacia arabica.*

Petiole may be modified as follows :

(i) Winged; *e.g.*, Lemon.

(ii) Bulbous; *e.g.*, *Eichornia.*

(iii) Tendrillar; *e.g.*, Nepenthes.

(iv) Phyllode; *e.g.*, *Acacia.*

Leaf apex may be modified as :

(i) Acute; *e.g.*, Mango.

(ii) Obtuse; *e.g.*, Banyan.

(iii) Acuminate : The apex is long and pointed; *e.g.*, *Ficus religiosa* (Peepal).

(iv) Retuse : The apex is broad but notched as in pistia :

(v) Emarginate : The apex is deeply notched as in *Bauhinia.*

(vi) Cupsidate; *e.g.*, date palm where the apex is spinelike.

(vii) Cirrhose : The leaf apex is tendril like; *e.g.*, *Gloriosa.*

Leaf margins may be of the following types :

(a) Entire : No incision seen.

(b) Repand : Wavy leafs margins; *e.g.*, Ashoka tree.

(c) Serrate : *e.g.*, Rose.

(d) Dentate : *e.g.*, Ladies finger.

(e) Spiny.

Leaf venation

Veins are composed of vascular tissues and their branches spread in the leaf.

(a) Reticulate venation : Network of veins seen; *e.g.*, Most dicots, some monocots; e.g., *Smilax.*

(i) Unicostate : One mid-rib has lateral veins upto margins; *e.g.*, Mango.

(ii) Multicostate : Several main veins from base to margins. It may be convergent; *e.g.*, Tejpat or divergent; *e.g.*, Papaya.

(b) Parallel venation : Mostly in monocots, some dicots; *e.g.*, *Calophyllum.*

(i) Unicostate; *e.g.*, Musa : One main vein with parallel lateral veins.

(ii) Multicostate - Several parallel veins divergent; *e.g.*, palm or convergent; grasses.

Leaf type

(a) Simple has one lamina with bud in axil; *e.g.*, Mango.

(b) Compound has lamina dissected into leaflets which lack axillary buds. Compound leaves may be—

1. Pinnate : *(i)* Unipinnate; *e.g.*, Rose.

(ii) Bipinnate- Pinnae are divided into pinnules; *e.g.*, *Mimosa, Acacia arabica.*

(iii) Tripinnate : Pinnules divided into tertiary leaflets; *e.g.*, Drum stick.

(iv) Decompound : Tertial leaflets divided many times; *e.g.*, Coriander.

2. Palmate : Leaflets formed as a result of incision from leaf margin to base.

(i) Unifoliate : One leaflet only; *e.g.*, Orange.

(ii) Bifoliate : Two leaflets; *e.g.*, Begonia.

(iii) Trifoliate : *e.g.*, Clover.

(iv) Quadrifoliate : *e.g.*, *Marselia.*

(v) Multifoliate; *e.g.*, *Bombax ceiba* (Silk cotton tree).

Leaves may be modified as :

1. Leaf spines; *e.g.*, Date palm.
2. Leaf tendrils; *e.g.*, Gloriosa.
3. Leaf hooks; *e.g.*, Begonia.
4. Leaf pitcher; *e.g.*, Nepenthes.
5. Leaf bladder; *e.g.*, Bladderwort.
6. Phyllode : Petiole is leaf like; *e.g.*, *Acacia.*
7. False stem : *e.g.*, Banana.

Phyllotaxy

1. Alternate : Successive nodes have a single leaf at different angles.
2. Opposite : Each node has two leaves at 180° angle. These may be decussate-leaf pairs at successive nodes are the right angles; *e.g.*, Guava.

   Superposed : Leaf pairs of successive nodes are in same line; *e.g.*, Jamun.
3. Whorled : Each node has many leaves on different sides; *e.g.*, Hydrilla.

Seed

Seed is a fertilized and mature ovule in which the dormant embryo exists. On the basis of the number of cotyledons in a seed, the plants are classified into monocotyledonous and dicotyledonous types. Dicot seeds have epigeal germination and are usually exalbuminous; whereas monocot seeds have hypogeal germination and are albuminous. Dicotyledonous albuminous seeds; *e.g.*, Castor, Poppy, Mirabilis. Dicotyledonous with hypogeal germination; *e.g.*, Gram, Pea, Mango. Monocotyledonous exalbuminous seeds -Water plantain *(Alisma).* Monocotyledonous with epigeal germination - Liliaceae.

These are exceptions to the usual monocot and dicot seeds. Viviparous germination is seen in *Rhizophora* when seed germinates inside the fruit. Caruncle is outgrowth of outer integu-ments at one end of seed; *e.g.*, *Ricinus communis.* Epidermal hairs; *e.g.*, *Gossypium* sp. Ruminate endosperm; *e.g.*, *Areca* nut; arils are outgrowths of funiculus part of seed; *e.g.*, Litchi.

3. Structural and Functional Organisation of Cell

MEMBRANE STRUCTURE AND FUNCTION

Cell is a unit of biological activity made of an organised mass of protoplasm surrounded by a protective and selectively permeable covering.

Living beings or organisms are made of one or more cells. Cell is a basic unit of structure and function of organisms. It was discovered by Robert Hooke (1665). He wrote a book 'Micrographia' and coined the term *cell*. Leeuwenhoek (1672) was the first to see *free cells*. He observed bacteria, protozoa, red blood cells, sperms etc. under his microscope. In 1809, Lamarck came to the conclusion that all living beings are formed of cells. Dutrochet (1824) believed in individuality of cells. Living substances was first observed by Corti (1772) and was named *sarcode* by Dujardin (1836). Robert Brown (1831) discovered nucleus while Von Mohl (1838, 1846) & Purkinje (1839) named the jelly-like living substance or sarcode of the cell as *protoplasm*.

CELL THEORY

In 1838, Schleiden found that all plant cells have essentially similar structure. Schwann (1838) working independently observed that animal cells do not have cell wall but are otherwise similar amongst themselves. He put forward cell hypothesis bodies of animals and plants are made up of cells and their products. Schleiden and Schwann (1839) compared their findings and formulated *cell theory* which states that :

(*i*) Living beings are made of one or more cells

(*ii*) A cell is a mass of protoplasm having a nucleus.

(*iii*) Cells are similar in basic structure and metabolism.

(*iv*) The functions of an organism are due to activities and interactions of its cells.

However, there are several **short comings** in Cell Theory :

(*a*) Viruses do not have cellular structure

(*b*) Monerans and protistans are not divisible into cells. They are *acellular.*

(*c*) Certain organisms are multinucleate.

(*d*) A typical nucleus is absent in procaryotes

(*e*) Connective tissues have a lot of non-living material as compared to living matter.

(*f*) Certain cells lose their nuclei in the mature state, e.g. RBC, sieve tube elements.

Cell theory was first modified in the light of Virchow's findings (1855, 1858) that cells develop from pre-existing cell-*Omnis cellula-e-cellula.* It is known as law of other modifications were carried out in the cell theory. The modern cell theory is called 'cell principle'.

Protoplasm Theory

It was proposed by Max Schultze (1861) which states that living matter of an organism in protoplasm and the cell is simply an accumulation of protoplasm limited by an outer membrane and containing a nucleus.

Organismal Theory

Sachs (1874) proposed that the whole organism functions as a single entity which is made of a continuous mass of protoplasm incompletely divided into cells.

Cellular Autonomy and Multicellularity

Cells are autonomous or self contained units because

(*i*) They obtain or manufacture food

(*ii*) All cells require energy for overcoming entropy, performing body activities and biosynthesis. For this they oxidise food materials in respiration.

(*iii*) Cells convert nonliving materials into components of living protoplasm.

(*iv*) Worn out parts are replaced by news ones.

(*v*) There is exchange of gases.

(*vi*) Cells discard waste materials.

(*vii*) They are able to regulate their activities through flow of energy and information.

(*viii*) Cells maintain their own internal physico-chemical environment

(*ix*) They may divide and form daughter cells.

(*x*) There is a definite life span. Cells of unicellular organisms lead independent existence with no dependent on others for any function, material or information. They depend upon their own intrinsic information. Irritability is, of course present. Cells of multicellular organisms possess autonomy but show various interactions and specialities.

Multicellularity is more advantageous then unicellularity because it

(*i*) Increases survival

(*ii*) Induces specialisation

(*iii*) Ensure uninterrupted activity

(*iv*) Provides for division of labour

(*v*) Outer cells became specialised to protect internal cells.

(*vi*) Internal cells develop their own environment

(*vii*) Keeps the cells small except where they take part in conduction and support.

(*viii*) Death of a few cells or reproduction does not kill the organisms. Rather some dead cells are functionally important, e.g. tracheary elements.

(*ix*) Differentiated cells may take over the function of division through the process of *dedifferentiation* e.g. plant cells.

(*x*) In some cases differentiation leads to loss of some basic activities like :

(*a*) RBCs do not have aerobic respiration, DNA replication and RNA synthesis since nucleus is lost towards maturity.

(*b*) Sieve tube cells become enucleate

(*c*) Nerve cells posses nuclei but are unable to differentiate.

(*d*) Liver and muscle cells do not divide normally but retain the ability to do so.

Cellular Totipotency and Survival

Somatic nucleated cells are totipotent or able to produce a complete organism. This is especially so in case of plant cells. It was first suggested by Haberlandt (1902) and proved by Steward *et al* in 1957, through tissue or cell culture experiments. For its survival and proper functioning, a cell always requires :

(*i*) *Flow of Energy* for overcoming entropy (tendency for disorderliness) and performing various life activities.

(*ii*) *Flow of Information* which is of two types, *intrinsic* or genetic and *extrinsic* through nerves and hormones. Intrinsic or genetic information is contained in DNA. Specific triggers activate DNA segments to transcribe m RNAs which then help synthesise specific polypeptides/proteins/enzymes, etc. Stimulated nerves secrete chemicals to activate certain cells. Hormones are recognised by either membrane receptors or intracellular receptors. The complexes allow particular activities.

Surface Volume Ratio

Metabolically active cells are small since small cells have higher nucleo-cytoplasmic ratio for better control and higher surface-volume ratio for quicker exchange of materials. Larger cells can be efficient only if they are elongated, branched or possess membrane extensions like microvilli. Large sized animals do not possess large sized cells but more numerous small cells.

SIZE & SHAPE OF CELLS

The diameter of most of the cells ranges from 0.5 μ to 20μ (1 μ = 0.001 mm). The largest known cell is the egg of an Ostrich which can be as long as 170 mm. The smallest cell is perhaps yet to be discovered. The shape also is varied and depends upon the environmental conditions; surroundings, function and need of the organism. Simple bacteria can be rod shaped, spiral, oval, round etc. The shapes of desmids and diatoms are varied. Amoeba keeps on changing its shape. The body of unicellular marine alga, *Acetabularia* is differentiated into a rhizoid like base, a long and slender stalk and an umbrella like cap. The RBCs of human beings are round, whereas, the muscle cells are long and with pointed ends. Animals cells are capable of changing their shapes; but the shape of plant cell is fixed due to the presence of cellulose cell-wall.

Cell Type	*Cell Size*
Smallest Virus (no cellular structure)	7.0×10^{-7} μm^3
Smallest Bacterium	2.0×10^{-2} μm^3
Human Sperm	1.7×10^1 μm^3
Hen Egg (60 × 45 mm)	5.0×10^{13} μm^3
Mycoplasma	1.0×10^{-3} μm^3
Largest Bacterium	7.0×10^0 μm^3
Human Egg	(diameter 100 μm)
Ostrich Egg	(170 × 150 mm)
RBC	7 μ
E. coli	1.5 × 0.7 μ
Influenza Virus	100 μm
TMV	300 × 15 μm
T_3 Bacteriophage	45 mμ

Nerve cells are the longest cells of the human body, reaching 90 cm. Certain plant fibres are similarly very long, e.g. Jute (30-90 cm); Ramie (55 cm), Hemp (1m).

PROKARYOTIC AND EUKARYOTIC CELLS

Basically cells are of two types, procaryotic and eucaryotic.

A **prokaryotic** cell has one envelope system with no membrane lined internal organelles, except thylakoids, if present. A nucleus is absent, instead, a nucleoid made of naked and folded DNA lies freely in cytoplasm. Internal compartments are absent. Respiratory enzymes are located on the cell membrane. Cytoplasm does not show streaming. Sap vacuoles are absent. Gas vacuoles may occur-cell wall, if present, contains peptidoglycan or mucopeptide. Flagella, if present are single stranded and made of flagellin.

An **eukaryotic** cell has internal compartments and double envelope system, that is, besides cell membrane, the cell organelles are also covered by membranes. Mitosis and meiosis occurs in the life cycle. Cytoplasm show streaming, sap vacuoles occur. Flagella if present are double-stranded and made of tubulin.

Comparison of Cell Organisation in Prokaryotic and Eukaryotic cells

Cellular Component	*Prokaryotic Cells*	*Eukaryotic cells*
1. Nuclear Envelope	Absent	Present
2. DNA	naked	combined with proteins
3. Chromosome	Single	Multiple
4. Division	amitosis	mitosis or meiosis
5. Ribosomes	70 s (50 s + 30 s)	80 s (60 s + 40 s)
6. Endomembranes	Absent	Present
7. Mitochondria	Absent, Respiratory & photosynthetic enzymes in the plasma membrane	Present
8. Chloroplast	Absent	Present in plant cells
9. Cell wall	non-cellulosic	Cellulosic, only in plants.
10. Exo & Endocytosis	Absent	Present
11. Locomotion	Single fibril flagellum	Cilia and flagella
12. Examples	Bacteria, blue green algae mycoplasma (PPLO)	Protozoa, other algae, metaphyta & metazoa.

General Organization of the Eukaryotic Cell

Main Component or components	*Subcomponent or subcomponents*	*Main Function*
1. Cell Membrane	Cell wall Cell coat Plasma membrane	Protection cell-cell interaction permeability, endocytosis, exocytosis
2. Nucleus	Chromatin & chromosomes	Genetic information system
	Nucleolus	Synthesis of Nucleoplasm, Ribosomes
3. Cytoplasm matrix, cytosol, cytoskeleton	Soluble Enzymes Microfilaments Microtubules	Glycolysis, Cell motility, Cell shape & Motility,
	Ribosomes	Protein Synthesis.
4. Endomembrane System	Nuclear Envelope	Nuclear permeability,
	Endoplasmic reticulum, rough & smooth	Synthesis and transport of materials, Secretion
	Golgi complex	Secretion
5. Membrane organelles	Mitochondria Chloroplast Lysosomes Peroxisomes	Cell respiration Photosynthesis Digestion Peroxidation
6. Microtubular organelles	Centroioles & spindle basal bodies, cilia and flagella	Cell division Cell motility

PLANT AND ANIMAL CELLS

Both plant and animals posses eucaryotic cells. A plant cell is characterised by a cell wall, central vacuole, plastids and anastral spindle (centrioles are generally absent). Golgi apparatus consists of separate units called dictyosomes. Lysosomes are rare. Glyoxysomes and crystals may occur.

Animal cells are bathed by tissue fluid. They are covered by cell membranes only. Vacuoles are small. Plastids are absent. Spindle is amphiastral (centrioles present). Due to absence of wall, animal cells will burst if placed in hypotonic solution, Glyoxysomes and crystal are absent. Lysosomes are present.

A typical plant cell consists of cell wall and protoplast. Cell wall is absent in animal cells. Protoplast (Hanstein, 1880) is made of a plasmalemma, cytoplasm, nucleus and vacuoles.

STRUCTURAL ORGANIZATION AND FUNCTION OF INTRACELLULAR ORGANELLES

CELL WALL

It is the outer rigid protective covering of plant cells and some procaryotes. Cell wall has a matrix of hemicellulose, pectin, glycoprotein and water in which are embedded microfibrils. Microfibrils are made up of cellulose in plant cells, chitin or fungus cellulose in fungi and peptidoglycan (mucopeptide) in bacteria. Plant cell wall may have lignin for strength (e.g. woody tissue), silica for stiffness and protection (e.g. epidermal cells), *cutin* for preventing loss of water (e.g. epidermal cells), suberin for impermeability (e.g. cork cells, endodermal cells), etc.

The cell wall gives a definite shape and provides protection to the protoplasm. It is nonliving in nature and is permeable. Adjacent cells in the plant body remain interconnected by plasmodesmata. A cell wall may have upto three parts-middle lamella, primary wall, secondary wall.

(i) Middle lamella

It is the outermost region which functions as a cementing layer between two cells. It is absent on the outer free surface. It ruptures to create intercellular spaces. It is formed of calcium and magnesium pectate. Pectic acid is long polygalacturonic acid compound in which α-D-galacturonic acid units are joined together by glycosidic linkages in (1 : 4). It is hydrophilic in nature.

(ii) Primary wall

It is thin (0.1 - 3.0 μm), elastic, first wall layer. It contains microfibrils oriented variously, commonly forming a loose network. Cellulose content (5% dry weight basis), hemicellulose (50% dry weight basis), lipid content (5-10% dry basis) are high. An association of about 100 cellulose chains is termed as a micelle, 20 micelles constitutes a microfibril while an aggregation of 250 microfibrils is called fibril. Lignin, hemicellulose, some pectic substances and proteins present altogether form **amorphous matrix**.

(iii) Secondary wall

It is laid inner to primary wall. It is less hydrated i.e. less hydrophilic in nature (30-40%) as compared to primary wall. Cellulose content is high with long closely arranged straight and parallel microfibrils. Hemicellulose content is 25%. Protein is very little while lipid is nearly absent. Lignin deposit is quite common. Secondary wall is often made of three layers—S_1, S_2, & S_3. In each layers, microfibrils lie straight, parallel to one another but at an angle to longitudinal axis. Orientation is different in different layers. It is more pronounced in dead cells such as tracheids and sclerenchyma.

In gymnosperms tension wood, the innermost layer contains xylan and is called 'tertiary wall'. Filler substance of wall matrix is *pectin*. It has methylated and polymerised galacturans, glucouronic acid and neutral sugars.

Hemicellulose is made of polymerised arabino-galactans, xylans, mannans, etc. It binds microfibrils with matrix.

Lignin is formed from coniferyl and coumaryl alcohols and aldehydes through dehydrogenation and polymerisation. Lignin reduces hydration and increases hardness of wall.

Cell wall possesses minute cytoplasmic bridges between adjacent cells. They are called 'plasmodesmata' (Strassburger, 1901). Plasmodesmata produce a continuum of living material called *symplasm* cell walls and intercellular spaces constitute a nonliving component of plant body known as *apoplasm*. Certain thick cell walls possess unthickened areas called *pits*.

In some animal cells, a *cell coat* is present outside the cell membrane, made up of 'glycocalyx' alongwith deposition of silica & calcium salts.

Comparison of Primary and Secondary wall

Primary wall	*Secondary wall*
1. Extensible layer	Non-extensible layer
2. Dispersed texture of microfibril	Parallel texture of microfibrils (to long axis)
3. Smallest cellulosic unit micelle or microfibril	Smallest cellulose unit microfibril or fibril
4. Cellulose 5.2%	Cellulose 50-94%
5. Lipid contents 5-10%	Normally no lipid
6. Protein 5%	Normally very little
7. Hemicellulose 50%	Hemicellulose 25%

CELL MEMBRANES

(Biomembranes, e.g. Plasmalemma) Cell membranes or biomembranes are quasifluid film like partitions of about 75 A° thickness. They are selectively permeable. Plasmalemma or plasma membrane lies on the outside of protoplast and separates it from external environment. *Tonoplast* occurs around vaculoles. Most of the eucaryotic cell organells have their own membrane coverings. Under electron microscope, a cell membrane appears *trilaminar* or *tripartite* with a middle electron transport layer and electrons dense layer on either side. Chemically, it has proteins (60-70%), lipids (20-40%) and carbohydrates (1-5%). Proteins are both structural and enzymatic. Lipids are generally phospholipids with polar hydrophilic heads and nonpolar hydrophilic tails (amphipathic or amphiatic).

Overton (1900)

He was the first scientist to propose that cell membranes are made of lipids.

Deniell & Davson Model (1935)

States that a double phospholipid layer is surrounded on either side by a layer of hydrated globular proteins or P-L-L-P. The hydrophobic or nonpolar tails of the two lipid layers are towards the centre.

Robertson Model (1959)

States that a lipid bilayer is surrounded on either side by extended or β-protein with a difference in their type for outer and inner side. Robertson also gave UNIT MEMBRANE CONCEPT, which proposed that all biomembranes have a trilaminar structure with an electron transparent lipid bilayer (35 A°) lying sandwitched between electrons dense protein layers (20 A° each).

Both the above given models are lamellar models.

Fluid Mosaic Model

(Singer & Nicolson, 1972). Cell membranes are quasifluid with viscous lipid bilayer having proteins at places (mosaic) both on the surface and inside. Singer & Nicolson have described cell membranes as protein icebergs in sea of lipids. External proteins are called EXTRINSIC or PERIPHERAL (30% of total) while internal proteins are named INTRINSIC or INTEGRAL (70% of total). Membrane proteins may function as enzymes, permeases, carriers, receptors etc. Proteins extending from outside to inside are called 'tunnel proteins' or 'transmembrane proteins'. They function as channels. At places the external proteins and lipid molecules bear oligosaccharides forming glycoproteins and glycolipids for recognition; attachment and antigenic properties. They make the cell membrane asymmetric.

Lipid nature of the cell membrane can be destroyed with benzene. Benzene treated beet roots leak out anthocyanin pigment while the pigment is retained in untreated roots. Fluidity of cell membranes can be tested by mixing two types of animal cells treated with green and red fluorescent dyes in the presence of polyethylene glycol. They will initially show half green and half red surface. The cells kept at 0°C do not show further mixing while the lot kept at 37°C exhibits complete mixing.

According to Selby (1959) plasma membrane often exhibits certain specialised structures which are as follows :

(*i*) *Microvilli.* The plasma membrane at its surface, has certain narrow elongated projections called *microvilli*. The function of microvilli is to increase its absorptive surface.

(*ii*) *Plasmodesmata :* There are fine strands of cytoplasm through which the adjacent cells remain inter-connected in the plant body. The plasmodesmata were first of all observed by Tangel (1879) and finally by Strasburger (1882).

(*iii*) *Caveolae :* These are the hair like invaginations of plasma membrane. It was first reported by Yamada (1955). The function of caveolae is to increase the absorptive area of the cell.

(*iv*) *Desmosomes :* In certain cells, the plasma membrane of adjacent cells become thicker in certain regions and from these thickened areas arises many fine filaments known as 'tonofibrils'. Such thickened areas of the plasma membrane are called **desmosomes.** The intercellular space between desmosomes contain a coating material which provides cellular adhesion to the cell.

Plasmalemma

It is the outer membrane covering of the protoplast which was called cell membrane by Nageli and Crames (1855). It was given the present name by Plowe (1931). Plasmalemma is both protective and selectively permeable. Antigenic, recognition, attaching and receptor sites occur over it. The membrane may show *microvilli* (0.6 - 0.8 μm long and 0.1 μm diameter). Plasma infoldings occur in bacteria and fungi. They are called *mesosomes* in bacteria (Fitz. Jammes, 1960) and *lomasomes* is fungi (Moore and McLean).

In animals the plasmalemmae of adjacent cells may show tight junctions, desmosomes, gap junction, interdigitations or intercellular bridges.

(*i*) *Desmosomes* (Macular Adherantes; singular Macula Adherans). Adjacent membranes are thickened with disc shaped adhesive material in between and *tonofibrils* radiating out from the adhesive regions, e.g., epithelia subjected to disruption. In *hemidesmosome*, the thickening is present on one membrane. *septate desmosomes* possesses parallel septa in between the two membrances.

(*ii*) *Tight Junction* (Zonulae Occludentes). Plasmalemmae of two cells fused to form impermeable or occluding junctions e.g., epithelial cells of capillaries and brain cells.

(*iii*) *Terminal Bars* (Zonulae Adherantes). Both plasmalemma and adjacent cytoplasm are thickened.

(*iv*) *Gap Junctions*. They have intercellular gaps and allow movement of substances in betweeen two cells. Hence, communicating junctions. Very common.

(*v*) *Interdigitations* : They are intercellular bridges formed by membrane infoldings and contacts for rapid conduction of stimuli.

Cytoplasm

(Strasburger, 1882). It is the bulk of protoplasm excluding nucleus. Cytoplasm is differentiated into cytoplasmic matrix, cell organelles and cell inclusions. Cytoplasmic matrix, or cytosol is jelly-like semifluid that exist in both sol and gel states. Cytoplasmic matrix is often differentiated into outer gel part called 'ectoplast' (plasmagel) and inner sol part called 'endoplast' (plasmasol). Endoplast is usually in perpetual motion called **cyclosis,** cytoplasmic or protoplsamic streaming (Amici, 1818). In **rotation** type of cyclosis, cytoplasmic matrix continuously flows in one direction. (e.g. young cells of *Hydrilla* leaf). In *Circulation* type of cyclosis, matrix flow in different directions in the same cell (e.g. cell of staminal hair of Tradescantia = Rhoea).

ENDOPLASMIC RETICULUM (ER)

(Ergastoplasm of Garnier, 1897). E.R or EPR was discovered by Porter *et al* (1945). It was given the present name by Porter (1953). According to Dallmer (1966) E.R. originats from the plasma membrane by invagination. According to De Roberties (1970), ER originates from the nuclear envelope. E.R. is a system of membrane lined channels found in all eucaryotic cells except ova, embryonic cells and mature erythrocytes. It constitutes more than 50% of total cell membranes. In muscle cells it is called SARCOPLASMIC RETICULUM. *Mycloid bodies* (granulls at base of retinal pigment cells) and *Nissl granules* are believed to be formed from E.R. It is less developed in meristematic cells. It is made of a few tubules in adipose tissue, few vesicles in spermatocytes but is best developed in cells of liver, pancreas and fibroblast. Endoplasmic reticulum has three parts

(*i*) Cisternae (parallel interconnected flattened sacs)

(*ii*) Tubules (often branched network)

(*iii*) Vesicles (round or oval)

Membranes of E.R. may bear ribosomes when E.R. is called granular/rough endoplasmic reticulum or R.E.R. Attachment between ribosome and endoplasmic reticulum is through glycoprotein called ribophorin. The union is actually between 60 s ribosome subunit and E.R. by means of two types of glycoproteins : ribophorin I (mol. wt.-65000) and ribophorin II (mol. wt. 64000). R.E.R. often contains minute pores below ribosomes to pass synthesied polypetide into its lumen for transport. E.R. without attached ribosomes is called agranular/smooth endoplasmic reticulum or S.E.R. It takes part in synthesis of glycogen, fats and sterols, and detoxification. S.E.R., therefore, occurs in adipose cells, muscle cells, liver cells, steroid synthesising cells, etc. R.E.R. is abundant in cells engaged in production and excretion of protein, e.g. plasma cells, goblet cells, pancreatic cells, certain liver cells. Broken pieces of endoplasmic reticulum appear as microsomes (Claude, 1941). Transitional E.R. is R.E.R. without ribosomes. Glycosylation of newly synthesized proteins occurs within the cisternae through activity of glycosyl transferase located in the E.R. membrane.

Function of ER

(*i*) The endoplasmic reticulum divides the cell into separate compartments, making it possible for the cells different chemical products and activities to be segregated from each other.

(*ii*) Many of the enzymes that carry out there activity from a part of the lipoprotien structure of the membrane forming the endoplasmic reticulum.

(*iii*) According to Sjostrand (1964), the tubules and vesicles have surfaces which may play role in enzymic reactions.

(*iv*) In addition to site of protein synthesis, it is also thought to function as a transport and storage system.

(*v*) E.R. also plays important role in lipid metabolism and glycogen synthesis.

RIBOSOMES (PROTEIN FACTORIES, PALADE GRANULES)

They are submicroscopic polypeptide manufacturing naked nucleoprotein organelles which were discovered by Robinson and Brown (1953) in plant cells and palade (1955) in animal cells. Palade (1955) also gave them the present name, ribosomes. Ribosomes are of two types, cytoplasmic & organelle. **Organelle ribosomes** are 70 s (Svedberg or sedimentation units). They occur inside mitochondria and plastids. Organelle ribosomes do not occur in procaryotes. Instead, their cytoplasmic ribosomes are 70 s. **Cytoplasmic ribosomes** of eucaryotes are 80 s. They may occur freely or attached to E.R. Ribosomes are subspherical in outline with a diameter of 150-250 A° and are not bounded by any membrane. Each ribosome has two parts, smaller avoid or cap like and larger dome-shaped. The smaller subunit has a platform, cleft, head and base. The larger subunit has a protuberance, a ridge and a stalk. On the basis of sedimentation coefficient, the larger and smaller subunits are respectively 60 s and 40 s (50 s & 30 s in 70 s ribosomes). The larger subunit has 28 s, 5.8 s and 5 s r RNA (23 s and 5 s in 70 s ribosomes). While the smaller subunit has 18 s r RNA (16 s r RNA is 70 s ribosome's smaller unit). Besides r RNA, ribosomes has a number of protein molecules like core and split proteins, structural and enzymatic proteins. As compared to r RNA, protein content is higher in 80 s ribosomes (40 : 60) while reverse is true is 70 s ribosomes (60 : 40). A groove is present in between the two ribosomes subunits for m RNA. The larger subunit also has a channel for the passage of synthesized polypeptide. Magnesium ion is essential for binding the ribosome subunits. Smaller subunit has peptidyl transferase, binding site for t RNA and A-site. P-site is jointly formed by the two subunits. Ribosomes may occurs in helical or rosette group linked by m RNA. Such a group is called *polyribo-some* (Rich, 1963) or *polysome*. It is useful in producing a number of copies of the same polypeptide. The ribosomes remain attached with the membrane of endoplasmic reticulum by 60 s subunits. The 40 s subunit occurs on the larger subunit and forms cap-like structure. Peterman (1964) reported several kinds of RNA from ribosomes on the basis of analysis of purine and pyrimidine bases.

Ribosomes are not attached to membranes in prokaryotes, chloroplasts and mitrochondria but are commonly membrane bound is eukaryotic cells (specially actively secreting ones), forming rough endoplasmic reticulum, as well as being attached to outer surface of outer nuclear membrane. The origin of r RNA is the nucleolus.

GOLGI APPARATUS (GOLGI COMPLEX)

It is complex organelle made of membrane lined stack of cisternae, network of tubules, vesicles and vacuoles which was first seen by George (1867) but studied by Camillo Golgi in 1898 in nerve cells of Barn Wol and cat through metallic impregnation technique (osmium chloride + silver salts). Due to metallic impregnation artefacts, the apparatus was once called internal reticular apparatus/canalicular system/*apparato reticolare*. The concept changed after observation of the apparatus under electron microscope by Dalton and Felix (1954). Golgi apparatus is presented in all eucaryotic cells except RBC and sieve tube elements. It is also absent in procaryotes and sperm cells of seedless embroyphytes. A unit of Golgi apparatus is called *Golgisome*. In palnt cells, Golgi apparatus consists of a number of isolated units called *dictyosomes* while in animal cells it occurs as single compact or loose complex. The number of Golgi bodies/ dictyosomes in generally 9-10 in a plant cell but is very high in cells engaged in secretory activity (e.g. root cap cells) and rapid division. Golgi apparatus has a central stack of 3-10 curved but parallel membrane-lined narrow sacs called *cisternae*, cisternae are interconnected. Unicisternal dictyosomes occur in fungi. Golgi apparatus has two faces, maturing and forming (Mollenhauer and Whaley, 1963). The convex *forming face* (cis-face) receives materials from endoplasmic reticulum (GER = Golgi associated E.R.) and cytosol while concave *maturing face* (trans-face, normally towards plasma membrane) gives out large Golgian vacuoles and small vesicles having transformed materials. Vesicles develop from the tubules as well. They are of two types, smooth and coated. Golgi apparatus produces materials for secretion, takes parts in transformation of membranes, formation of number of products like glycoproteins (e.g. mucin from goblet cells), complex hetero-polysaccharides (e.g. mucilage from root cap cells), hormones, melanin, matrix of connective tissue, middle lamella, acrosome and lysosome.

Animal cells usualy contain one. In granular cells, the golgi bodies are usually situated close to the nucleus and has according to Grasse (1957), definite polarity. There are also known as *Lyphochondria.* The membrane of G.C. or apparatus are of lipoproteins and are supposed to be originated from the membranes of endoplasmic reticulums. In plant cells, scales, both organic and inorganic, are formed in the G.C. before being transported to the periphery. In diatoms, the golgi body gives rise to translucent vesicles which collect beneath the plasmalemma where they fuse to form a *silicalemma* in which the siliceous cell wall forms. Two types of vesicles are budded from the golgi body :

Coated vesicles (about-50 nm diameter) and the larger **secretory vesicles** (about 100 nm diameter), which tend to leave from the trans-surfaces. It has a system of outer flattened cisternae which appear as roughly parallel membranes enclosing a space 60-90 A° with a distance of about 200 A° between them. Cisternae and vesciles are associated with the inner cisternae particularly in glandular cells. It is also considered as the source of primary lysosomes membrane bounded particles containing hydrolytic enzymes and also functions as packing centre of the cell.

LYSOSOMES (SUICIDE BAGS, DISPOSAL UNITS)

These are small vesicles (0.2 - 0.8 μm) containing hydrolysing enzymes and surrounded by single membrane. They were discovered by Christian de Duve in 1955 but were named and observed under electron microscopes by Novikoff (1956). They are formed by golgi apparatus and contain some 40 types of *acid hydrolases* for digestion of various materials (e.g. nucleases, proteases, phosphatases, sulphatases). Therefore, they can hydrolyse almost all types of organic substances except cellulose. Lysosomes are most abundant in phagocytic cells (WBC) and osteoclasts. Lysosomes show polymorphism: primary lysosomes, secondary lysosomes (digestive vacuoles = heterophagosomes, primary lysosomes + phagosome); residual (lysosomes having undigested materials, undergo ephagy) and *autophagic* vacuoles (performing autophagy or autolysis of degenerate and useless parts). In many plant cells the function of lysosome is performed by spherosomes and vacuoles. Lysosome membrane is strengthened by cortisome, cortisol, antihistamise, heparin, chloroquine and a type of cholesterol. It becomes fragile in the absence of oxygen or presence of excess vitamin A, vitamin E, progesterone, testosterone, bile salts and high energy radiations. Failure of exocytosis or absence of some hydrolytic enzymes causes accumulation of residual bodies in the cells producing various diseases like hapatitis, polynephritis, Hurler's disease (deformed bones due to accumulation of mucopoly saccharide glucosaminoglycan as its hydrolytic enzyme is absent). Fruit rotting can be however, checked by slowing down the action of rotting enzyme *polygalactouronase.*

MITOCHONDRIA (POWER HOUSE)

Mitochondria were discovered by Kolliker (1880) in striated muscles of insects and given the present name by Benda (1897). Mitochondria were called *sacromeres* by Kolliker (1880), *flia* by Flemming (1882) and *bioblasts* by Altman (1890). Other names are *chondriosomes, chondriomites* and *plastochondria. Chondriome* includes all the mitochondria of a cell. They can be stained by Janus Green. Mitochondria are absent from anaerobic cells and RBCs. A single mitochondrion occurs in *Microsterias, Trypanosoma* and *chlorella.* The number is 5,00,000 per cell in flight muscles. They are 1-10 μm long and 0.5 - 1.0 μm broad with spherical to cylindrical shape. Each mitochondrion is covered by a double membrane envelope.

Intermembrane shape of outer chamber is present in between the two membranes. Innner memberane is thrown into various types of folds called *cristae* (cristae mitochondriale, Palade, 1952). The inner membrane bears oxysomes (10^4-10^5) and Electron Transport Chains (flavoprotein, *cyt.b, cyt. c, cyt. a, cyt. a_3). Oxysomes take part in ATP synthesis (oxidative phosphorylation). They are, therefore, functional units of mitochondria. Each oxysome (= elementary particle = EP = F_0 – F_1 or Fernandes Moran particle, Fernandes-Mòran, 1961) has a flat base of F_0 subunit, a stalk and a head of F_1 subunit.

The inner chamber or matrix of a mitochondria contains DNA (Nass and Afzelius, 1965), RNA, ribosomes (70 s), lipids, granules and enzymes of Kreb's cycle. DNA can be circular and linear. It is naked or without association with histones. Mitochondria are semi-autonomous. They multiply by division (Luck & Rich, 1964). As mitochondria are centres of Kreb's cycle or respiration, they liberate the maximum amount of energy. They are, therefore, called 'power houses' of the cell (Seeckevitz). In prokaryotes, where mitochondria are absent, the site for oxidative phosphorylation and electron transport including dehydrogenases is plasma membrane.

Ordinarily mitochondria are evenly distiributed in the cytoplasm. In columnar or prismatic cells, mitochondria are oriented parallel to the long axis of the cell. Mitochondria may move freely in some cells, carrying ATP wherever required, or may be localized in a particular region. Movement is less in animals than in plants. Often movements are rhythmical.

In one respect the mitochondrion is a part of the eucaryotic cell, in another, it is an independent organism. Mitochondrial genetic code differs from both 'nuclear' and bacterial codes in that the triplet UGA codes for tryptophan and is not a stop codon. Other codons may also have different meanings; even between mitochondria from different organisms Mitochondria of most C_3 plants of temperate latitudes do not engage in aerobic respiration during daylight, this being restricted to the hours of darkness. Instead these plants engage in the seemingly wasteful process of photorespiration, which is greatly reduced or absent is C_4 plants of tropical region.

* cyt = cytochrome).

PLASTIDS

Plastids (Haeckel, 1866) are semiautonomous cell organelles which are surrounded by double membrane envelope, take part in storage and synthesis of organic compounds which occur in plants and some protistans. Plastids develop from colourless precussors called 'proplastids'. Plastids are of three main types (Schimper, 1883). Leucoplasts, chromoplasts, chloroplasts.

(*i*) *Leucoplasts :* They are colourless plastids of various shapes. These are found in storage organs where light is not available, e.g. underground stem and roots. They are found in parenchymatous cells, embryonic cells, sex cells and meristernatic cells. These get specialised into :

(*a*) *Amyloplasts :* Large plastids containing starch.

(*b*) *Elaioplasts* (oleosomes). They store fats and are found in seeds.

(*c*) *Proteinoplast* or *Aleuroplasts.* They store protein and are found in seeds.

(*ii*) *Chromoplasts :* These plastids are coloured other than green due to presence of carotenoids but lack chlorophylls, e.g. red chillies, tomatoes. Chromoplasts attract animals and insect to flowers and fruit for performing pollination and fruit dispersal. They are responsible for the bright colours of not only fruits & flowers but also leaves and vegetables.

They are also of various types including :

(*a*) *Phaeoplasts :* These plastids are present is Brown algae, Diatoms and Dino-flagellates. Brown coloured pigment Fucoxanthium is the main pigment along with chlorophyll. However chlorophyll b is replaced by chlorophyll c.

(*b*) *Rhodoplasts :* These are found in Red algae. The red pigment R-phycoerythrin and R-phycocyanin, are present alongwith chlorophyll a, however chlorophyll b is replaced by chlorophyll d.

(c) *Chromatophores of blue green algae :* These are found in blue green algae (BGA). They have C-phycocyanin, C-phycoerythrin and chlorophyll a.

(d) *Chromatophores of photosynthetic bacteria:* These are found in purple and non-purple photosynthetic bacteria. These bacteria have purple red carotenoid pigments. Special type of chlorophylls bacteriochlorophyll and bacterioviridin are also found in these bacteria.

(iii) *Chloroplasts*. (Autoplasts of Meyer, 1883) They are green plastids which take part in photosynthesis and temporary or permanent storage of starch. In green algae, chloroplasts are of various shapes and sizes but chloroplasts of higher plants are disc-shaped with diameter of 4 - 6 μm and thickness of 2 - 4 μm . The number is small in algae but numerous in higher plants. Each chloroplast is surrounded by a double membrane envelope. Internally it contains matrix or stroma and thylakoids. Thylakoids (Menlee, 1961) or baggy trousers are *structural elements* of chloroplasts. They are membrane lined flattened sacs. At places they form stacks called **grana.** A chloroplasts may have 40-60 grana with each granum having 10-100 thylakoids. Thus there is differentiation of granal and stromal (intergranal) thylakoids. Space present in a granal thylakoid is called *loculus* while that of stromal thylakoid is termed as *Fret channel.* Photosynthetic pigments are located in the membranes of thylakoids in specific areas (according to Park and Biggins, 1963) called *quantasomes* (20 × 10 nm). Photosynthetic pigments of higher plants include *chl a, *chl b, carotenes and xanthophylls. A quantasome is believed to have 230 chlorophyll (160 a + 70 b) and 50 carotenoid molecules. The matrix or **stroma** contains naked DNA (Ris & Plant, circular as well as linear), RNA, ribosomes (70 s), plastoglobuli (lipid/fat globuli) and enzymes of carbon assimilation.

* chl = chlorophyll

Unlike isolated plant cells, isolated cell organelles like chloroplasts and mitochondria cannot be kept in distilled water as they would burst. They can be maintained only in solutions of specific concentrations e.g. 0.25% sucrose. Each quantasome contains 250 molecules of chlorophyll. The evolutionary origin of chloroplasts is currently explained in terms of 'Endosymbiosis'.

SPHEROSOMES

(Perner, 1953). Spherosomes or sphaerosomes are single membrane covered small spherical organelles (10.5-1.0 μm) which synthesise and store fats.

Microbodies

They are single membrane covered small cell organelles which take part in oxidation reactions other than those of respiration. Microbodies often posses a crystalline core and granular matrix. They are two types—peroxisomes & glyoxisomes/glyoxysomes.

(i) *Peroxisome :* (Rhodin, 1954). The microbodies have enzymes for peroxide biosynthesis. They include (*a*) Peroxide, producing oxidative enzymes like peroxidase, urate oxidase (hence uricosome), amino acid oxidase and (*b*) peroxide destroying enzymes like catalase. In mesophyll cells, peroxisomes interact with chloroplasts and mitochondria to take part in 'photorespiration' (Tolbert *et at*, 1969). For this they have glycolate oxidase for metabolism of glycolate. Their number can be 70-100 per mesophyll cell. Other enzymes found in dense granular matrix of peroxisome of both plant and animal cells are D-amino acid oxidase and α-hydroxy acid oxidase. Peroxisome is involved in purine metabolism and in the conversion of fat to carbohydrate.

(ii) *Glyoxysomes :* (Briedenbach, 1967, Beevers, 1963). The microbodies occur only in fat rich plant cells where they take part in β-oxidation of fats and perform glyoxylate cycle. Glyoxysomes possess catalase.

CYTOSKELETAL STRUCTURES

They are fibrous or fine tubular structure which constitute the supportive structures of the cell. Cytoskelatal structures are of three types—

(*i*) microtubuls.

(*ii*) microfilaments.

(*iii*) intermediate fibres.

(*i*) ***Microtubules :*** (Robertis & Franchi, 1953). They are unbranched tubules of indefinite length, 25 nm of thickness with 15 nm core and formed of 13 helically arranged *protofilaments* of α and β, tubulins. Lateral projections occur for establishing cross-bridges. Microtubules grow from nucleating regions. Their tips can grow and shorten quickly. They are basic structures of spindle apparatus, centrioles, basal bodies, cilia and flagella. They play important role in cell division, and transport of ions, water and small organic and inorganic molecules.

(*ii*) ***Microfilaments :*** (Paleviz *et al*, 1974). They are cylindrical rods or filaments of actin-like material with a diameter of 5-6 nm and that of indefinite length. Microfilaments can form hexagonal bundles and three dimensional microtrabecular lattice, take part in cytoplasmic streaming, membrane undulations, microvilli cleavage.

(*iii*) ***Intermediate Fibres :*** They are solid, unbranched protein fibrils of about 10 nm thikness which are made up of noncontractile protein like keratin, desmin, vimetin etc.

CENTRIOLES

They are minute, submicroscopic subcylindrical structures of 0.3-0.5 μm length and 0.15 μm diameter which usually occur in pair (diplosome) inside a specialised cytoplasm called centrosphere or kinplasm. The complex is called *centrosome* (Boveri, 1888) or central apparatus. Each centriole has whorl of **nine triplet fibrils** of tubulin with interconnections amongst adjacent triplets (C-A linkers) as well as with a central *hub* through spokes. Centrioles are surrounded by *massules* or pericentriolar satellites for formation of new centrioles in G_2 phase. (Typical replication is absent). ATPase activity is present. Centrioles are required to form basal bodies, cilia, flagella and astral spindle poles. They occur in most animal cells except some protozoan protists. Amongst others they are found in flagellate forms or forms having flagellate stages (e.g. many green algae, bryophytes, pteridophytes and cycads). Many visual receptor cells and retinal rod cells are originated from centrioles and cilia like bodies. Centrioles in some way can initiate and control the formation of fibrous protein structures.

Basal granules or kinetosomes

The plant or animal cells which are having locomotary organelles such as the cilia and flagella, contain spherical bodies called basal granules at the base of cilia and flagella. These are found embedded in the ectoplasm below plasmalemma and are composed of nine fibrils. Each fibril consists of, three microtubules, out of which two enter in the cilia or flagella. The basal granules may contain both DNA and RNA.

CILIA AND FLAGELLA

They are vibratile hair-like narrow protoplasmic processes which are made of four parts—basal body, rootlets, basal plate and shaft. Shaft consists of an external membrane (extension of plasmalemma), a semifluid matrix and an axoneme. Axoneme has nine peripheral doublet fibrils and two central singlet fibrils. Adjacent peripheral doublet fibrils are interconnected (B-A linkers of protein *nexin*). They also give out nexin spokes which bear transition junctions near the central proteinanceous sheath around the central fibrils. Subfibre A of each doublet has two bent arms, the outer one with a hook. The central fibrils and side arms of subfibre A are made of *dynein* protein with ATP-ase activity. Cilia are shorter (5-10 μm as compared to 150 μm for flagella), more numerous (number of flagella 1-4) have, sweeping or pendular movements (flagella have undulatory motion) and beat in a coordinated rhythmic movement (flagella show independent movements). In both cilia & flagella, the entire assembly is sheathed by a unit membrane which is simply a part of the plasma membrane.

Many animals have cells, the cilia of which serve simply to move materials part the cells.

VACUOLES

They are noncytoplasmic sacs which are separated from cytoplasm by a membrane or tonoplast*. In young cells the vacuole is absent. Mature cells may have a large central vacuole. The vacuoles are filled with a watery solution of many inorganic and organic substances and gases and is known as cell-sap. The cell-sap is responsible for maintaining osmotic relations of the cell. Colours of vast majority flowers are chiefly due to the presence of anthocyanin pigments dissolved in the cell sap which determines the particular colour in fruits and vegetables. Vacuoles are absent from cells of bacteria and blue green algae.

(*i*) *Sap vacuoles :* They enclose sap or water with dissolved inorganic and organic substances. A sap vacuole is surrounded by TONOPLAST. Plant cells have usually a single large central vacuole. Animal cells have numerous smal sap vacuoles. Sap vacuoles maintain osmotic pressure for turgidity and osmosis. They also store useful as well as waste substances.

(*ii*) *Contractile vacuoles :* They occur in some simple fresh water forms (e.g. *Amoeba, Paramecium, Chlamydomonas*. Contractile vacuoles are surrounded by a few feeding canals. They pick up water from surrounding cytoplasm, expand (diastole) and collapse (systole) to throw water to the outside. Contractile vacuoles perform osmoregula-tion and excretion.

(*iii*) *Food vacuoles :* It is a complex of lysosomes & phagosome. Digestion occurs inside them.

(*iv*) *Gas Vacuoles :* (Pseudovacuoles). They occur in some procaryotes. Each gas vacuole is made of a large number of submicroscopic hexagonal gas vesicles. A gas vesicle is surrounded by a thin protein membrane. Gas vacuoles store metabolic gases and take part in buoyancy regulation.

CELL INCLUSIONS (ERGASTIC/ DEUTOPLASMIC, PARAPLASMIC SUBSTANCES)

They are non-living substances of four categories: reserve, excretory, pigment and mineral. Due to their presence, a cell may become different from other surrounding cells. It is then called IDIOBLAST.

(*i*) *Reserve Food :* It can be starch (plant cells) glycogen (animal cells, fungi & bacteria), fat droplets and aleurone grains. Aleurone grains are storage proteins developed inside aleuroplasts. They can be amorphous, with crystalloid alone (aleurone grains of Maize, Wheat), with globloid alone and with both crystalloid and globloid (e.g. castor seed). Crystalloid is protein carbohydrate while globloid has lipid and phytin.

(*ii*) *Excretory/secretory products :* They include mucus, gums, tannins, resins, alkaloids, latex, glucosides, essential oils, nectar etc.

(*iii*) *Pigments :* The major pigments dissolved in cell sap are anthocyanins (bluish or reddish depending upon pH) and anthoxanthins (yellowish).

(*iv*) *Mineral Crystals :* Calcium carbonate occurs as a mass of crystals around a cellulose core to form CYSTOLITH (leaf hypodermis of Banyan, epidermis of *Momordica*). Cystolith is like a bunch of grapes but is worn like in *Justicia*. Calcium oxalate forms needle-shaped *raphides* (e.g. *Lemna, Eichhornia*), prismatic crystals (e.g. scales of Onion), star shaped sphaeraphide or druse (e.g. *Colocasia, Chenopodium*) or powdery mass named *crystal sand* (e.g. *Atropa*).

* **Tonoplast :** It forms the inner most boundary of the cytoplasm and surrounds the vacuoles and hence also known as vacuolar membrane. Tonoplast is selectively permeable and Lipo-Protein in nature. It acts as barrier between cytoplasm and vacuole.

NUCLEUS

(Discovered by Robert Brown, 1831). It is a double membrane covered protoplasmic body that contains hereditary information. With the help of grafting experiments on *Acetabularia,* Hammerling, (1913) proved that nucleus is a store-house of hereditary information. A cell usually contains a single nucleus. However, binucleate (e.g. *Paramecium*) and multinucleate forms also occur. Multinucleate forms is called *Plasmodium* in slime moulds. It is *syncytium* in animal cells (also by fusion of cells) and *coenocytic* in plant cells. Nucleus is commonly rounded but can be oval, disc shaped, lobed or irregularly branched. A typical nucleus is 5 - 25 μm in diameter. It is the largest amongst cell components. Nucleus has four parts—nuclear envelope, nucleoplasm, chromatin and nucleolus.

(i) Nuclear Envelope (Karyotheca)

It is made up of two membranes, separated by 10-70 nm perinuclear space. The outer membrane may have ribosomes and interconnections with E.R. Nuclear envelope has a large number (1000-10000) of pores with diameter of 200-800 A° (100-1000 A°). Nuclear pores may have diaphragms, septa, annuli, blebs or micropores with a central micropore surrounded by peripheral micropores. The central micropore or channel has *nucleoplasmin* for movement of substances.

(ii) Nucleoplasm (Nuclear Sap)

It is a colloidal complex that fills the nucleus. Its outer part is firm with fibrous protein network. It is called *fibrous lamina*. Nucleoplasm contain raw materials for synthesis of DNA and RNA.

(iii) Chromatin (Discovered by Flemming, 1879)

It is a fibrous hereditary material formed by DNA-historic complex. Chromatin fibres are of two types, narrow, elongated lightly stained *euchromatin* and broader darkly stained granular *heterochromatin* (Heitz). Chromatin is actually folded nucleosome (DNA + histone) containing DNA chains. During nuclear division, chromatin fibres fold variously to produce chromosomes.

(iv) Nucleolus

It was originally discovered by Fontana (1781) and given the present name by Bowman (1840). It is *naked* (without covering membrane), roughly rounded, darkly stained structure that is attached to chromatin at specific spot called NUCLEOLAR ORGANISER REGION or NOR. It is the area of synthesis of r RNA. It contains four parts, *amorphous, fibrillar, granular* and *chromatin*. Both fibrillar and granular parts are formed of RNA and protein. Nucleolus is the site for elaboration of r RNA and synthesis of ribosomes. Ribosomal protein is synthesised in the cytoplasm.

(Nucleus carries the hereditary information and regulates the ongoing activities of the cell, ensuring the complex molecules the cell requires are synthesized in the number and of the kind needed which are involved in various activities and also in forming organelles & other structures).

NUCLEOID

In prokaryotes, DNA is circular and folded variously to form a nearly compact structure called *nucleoid* or genophore. There is no membrane, no nucleolus and no nucleoplasm. The anionic charges present on internucleotide phosphate are balanced by polyamines. Histone are absent. DNA is, therefore, naked.

Osmosis

Bulk flow of water through semiperimeable membrane into another aqureous phase containing a solute in higher concentration.

Osmotic pressure generated by the osmotic flow of water through a membrane into aqueous phase containing a solute in higher concentration.

Plants are able to absorb water through osmosis.

Active Transport

It is the energy-dependent process. A membrane protein acts as carrier that binds and transports the molecule or ion in a specific direction across the membrane. It even takes place against-electro-chemical gradient. In sodium-potassium-exchange pump, Na^+ –K^+ ATPase actively transports three molecules of Na^+ outwards and two molecules of K^+ inwards.

Flow of Materials

To perform the various life activities, the cell must exchange certain substances with environment. It is necessary that metabolic-essentials such as oxygen, mineral salts and nutrients must set into cell and waste products such as NH_3, CO_2, Calcium crystals and other metabolites, must passout the cell. All these exchanges can take place only through the cell membrane by many processes as under:

(*i*) Passive transport < Diffusion / Osmosis
(*ii*) Facilitated diffusion
(*iii*) Active transport
(*iv*) Na^+ and K^+ exchange pump
(*v*) Endocytosis < Phagocytosis / Pincytosis
(*vi*) Exocytosis.

ORGANIZATION OF GENES AND CHROMOSOMES

REGULATION OF GENE EXPRESSION

Gene : The term gene was coined by Johanssen (1909) for mendelian *factor* or particulate elementary unit of inheritance which takes part in expression of a trait. Morgan (1911) called gene as the smallest segment of a chromosome which determines a trait as well as undergo crossing over. Beadle & Tatum (1948) proposed *one gene-one enzyme* hypothesis.

Yanofsky *et al* (1965) proposed *one gene/cistron one polypeptide* hypothesis. Berzer, distinguished three structural units of DNA—*cistron* (unit of function, determines synthesis of polypeptide), *recon* (unit of recombination or crossing over) and *muton* (unit of DNA that can undergo mutation). A *muton* can be as small as a nitrogen base. Cistron is commonly used as a synonym of gene. A gene can be structural or regulatory in nature. *Regulatory gene* is the one which controls the functioning of structural genes, e.g. regulator genes are repressor, promoter & operator types. *Structural gene* in the one which produces a biochemical molecule required for cellular machinery—*t* RNA, *r* RNA, *m* RNA. *m* RNA is involved in synthesis of structural proteins, enzymes, transport proteins, proteinaceous hormones, toxins, antigens etc. A structural gene normally codes for only a single polypeptide but a few produce POLYPROTEINS which are later broken to produce individual proteins. There is colinearity in the arrangement of nitrogen bases (in triplets) of a structural gene and amino acid sequence of polypeptide synthesized by it. A change in even a single nitrogen base may change the amino acid specified by its triplet. Eucaryotes possess split genes where the coding bases are not continuous but are interrupted by non-coding sequences. The two are respectively called *exons* and *introns*. Intron portions are also called *spacer* DNA or intervening sequences (IVS). Functional eucaryotic *m* RNA is formed by SPLICING—removal of intron portions and fusion of coding parts or exon portions. Split genes are also known from prokaryotes, e.g. thymidylate synthetase gene, ribonucleotide reductase gene of T_4. A few eucaryotic genes are without introns. They are called *exonic genes* (= nonsplit genes), e.g. histone genes and interferon genes. Certain eucaryotic exonic gens are called **processed genes.** Processed genes lack both introns and promoters. They are, therefore, nonfunctional. Processed genes are believed to have been formed by reverse transcription. In some viruses, the genetic material has *overlapping functions* with a segment of genetic material participating in two or more genes **(overlapping genes)**, e.g. D within E and B within A in ϕ 174.

In a cell, hardly 10% of the genes are active, (90% being inactive). Different genes are active in different types of tissues/cells. *Constitutive* or *house keeping* genes are those genes which are always in action because their products are always in action because their products are always required for cellular activities, e.g. ATPase, enzymes of glycolysis. *Nonconstitutive genes* are those genes which can be switched on or off as per requirements. They are of two kinds, *inducible* (remain repressed but are switched on in the presence of an inducer chemical) and *repressible* (remain active till switched off by a chemical).

60-70% of functional genes are a *single copy genes* as they are represented only once in the whole genome. The genes having more than one copy in the same genome are called *repeated genes,* e.g. histone gene, *t* RNA genes, *r* RNA genes, actin genes. *Multigenes* or multiple gene family is a group of nearly similar products, e.g. globin gene family *Pseudogenes* are nonfunctional genes. They are unable to produce functional products due to inactivation of promotoer region, presence of intervening nonsense codons, insertions or deletions, e.g. several sn RNA genes.

Transposons or **jumping genes** are those DNA segments which can pass from one place to another in the genome. At their ends, transposons have similar or inverted repetitive DNA sequences. The sequences can be cleaved by an enzyme **'transposase'.** Most common human transposon is Alu-family (so called as has a site for restriction endonuclease Alu-I). Transposons may take strong promoters to new sites or cause reshuffling of gene segments which lead to change in gene expression, e.g. protooncogene → oncogene.

GENE EXPRESSION IN VIRUSES

The shape of viruses can be **cylindrical/helical** (e.g. TMV), **polyhedral/cuboidal** (e.g. Adeno-Virus, Herpes Virus, Mumps Virus) and binal with polyhedral head and **helical coil** (e.g. T_2, T_4). Holmes (1948) has differentiated viruses into 'phytophagineae' (plant viruses), 'Zoophagineae' (animal viruses) and 'phagineae' (microbe viruses). Phagineae includes **'bacteriophages'** (bacterial viruses, e.g. T_2, T_4, Lambda Phage) and **cyanophages** (Blue Green Algae Viruses, e.g. LPP-1, SM-1).

VIRAL COMPONENTS

A virus is made of two parts—nucleoid and capsid. Additionally, it may have an envelope. Enzymes are rare.

1. *Nucleoid/Viral Chromosome :* It is made up of a single molecule of either DNA (Deoxyviruses or RNA (Riboviruses). DNA is generally double stranded (e.g. T_2, T_4) and rarely single stranded (e.g. coliphage *fd*, ϕ174). RNA of riboviruses is commonly single stranded (e.g. TMV, Polio Virus, Influenza Virus) while rarely double stranded (Reovirus, Rous Sarcoma Virus). It may be even fragmented (e.g. Influenza Virus). Depending upon the mode of replication of RNA genome, riboviruses are of two types, RNA-RNA (negative strand RNA) and RNA-DNA (positive strand RNA). Nucleoid contains a few genes, e.g. 100 in T_4. Nucleic acid is coiled by means of polyamines. Some viruses possess enzyme lysozyme (e.g. T_2) and transcriptase (Retroviruses).
2. *Capsid :* It is a protein covering around nucleoid and other parts.
3. *Envelope :* It is a loose membranous covering in some zoophagineae (e.g. HIV). Envelope often possesses surface spikes.

Cryptogram

It is symbolic representation of various traits of viruses which was proposed by Gibbs *et al* (1966) and adopted by ICNV. A cryptogram has four parts:

(*i*) Nucleic acid type, (D or R) and number of strands (1 or 2).

(*ii*) Molecular weight of nucleic acid in millions/percentage of nucleic acid of total particle.

(*iii*) Outline of particles like S or E or X (complex)/outline of nucleocapsid like S.

(*iv*) Host/vector like seed plant (S), invertebrate (I), vertebrate (V), bacterium (B), fungus (Fu) dipera (Di), Coleoptera (Cl), aphid (Af), nil (Zero or 0), unknown*.

Based on cryptogramic representation, below are given few examples of description of viruses.

1. Influenza Virus (*Myxovirus influenzae*)
   R/1, 2-3/10, S/E, V/O
2. Pox Virus (Poxvirus variolae)
   D/2, 160/5-7-5, X/*, V/O
3. T_4, D/2, 130/40, X/X, B/O
4. Polio Virus (Poliovirus primus)
   R/1, 2.5/30, S/S, V/O

VIRAL REPRODUCTION

(A) Lytic cycle

T_4 bacteriophage is binal virus which attaches to the surface of bacterium *E. coli* by its tail fibres. Lysozyme creates a hole in the host cell wall. The tail sheath contracts and ejects the viral chromocome/DNA into the bacterium. Viral DNA controls the metabolic machinery of the host cell. It produces nucleases. Nuclease degrade DNA and *m* RNAs of the host. Viral DNA is not affected as its cytosine bases are methylated (huydroxy methylated cytosine or HMC). A number of copies of viral DNA are produced followed by synthesis of capsid proteins, polyamines and lysozyme. The components assemble and form phage particles or viruses. The hose cell ruptures or releases.

(B) Lysogenic Cycle

Lambda phage (λ) attaches to the surface of *E. coli* by means of tail, which produces a hole in host cell wall and injects the phage DNA. Phage DNA produces a repressor (CI), becomes nonvirulent or temperate and attaches to bacterial chromosome at a specific site (e.g. galctose locus in λ phage) by means of enzyme **intergrase**. The viral genome is now called **prophage/provirus**. It multiplies alongwith bacterial genome and is passed on to the progeny. The phenomenon of existence of nonvirulent prophage in the host is called *Lysogeny*. The host cell is called *Lysogenic* cell. Occasionally the synthesis of repressor is stopped. The temperate/ nonvirulent phage is now changed to lytic/virulent phage.

The single strand DNA of $\phi \times 174$ or coliphage *fd* is known as *'plus strand'*. It forms its complementary or *'negative strand'*. The double strand or 'replicative' DNA takes over the metabolic machinery of host of synthesise plus strand DNAs and proteins for assembly of new phages.

(C) Pinocytic Reproduction

The whole virus enters the host cell except the envelope. It is quite common in RNA viruses which are of two types :

(*a*) **RNA-RNA Viruses :** DNA has no role in their multiplication. After entering the host cell, the viruses produce enzyme *replicase* which helps in producing more genetic RNA genome. The latter also produces *m* RNAs for synthesis of viral proteins.

(*b*) **RNA-DNA Viruses :** They are also called *retroviruses* (Temin, 1970) e.g. Tumour/Cancer Viruses, HIV. The viruses possess enzyme *reverse transcriptase* (Temin & Baltimore, 1972, in Rous Sarcoma Virus or RSV of Mouse). The enzyme builds DNA over RNA genome. The phenomenon is called reverse transcription or *teminism*. The *copy DNA (c DNA)* builds its complementary strand. The double strand copy DNA attaches to host DNA/chromosome and is now called *provirus*. It produces chemicals which disturb cellular machinery. The cell with provirus may dedifferentiate and start dividing leading to cancer (uncontrolled growth forming tumour which sends branches/roots to invade different parts). Some **20 viral oncogenes** (genes that trigger cancer) have been recorded. However, no virus has been definitely proved to cause cancer in humans. Humans have some proto-oncogenes (similar to viral oncogenes) which take part in growth but under certain circumstances they get changed to *cellular oncogenes*. Jumping genes/transposons can also cause cancer. There are a number of chemicals, physical factors and some viruses (i.e., Hepatitis B, Herpes, Papiloma, Epstein-Barr Virus) which promote Cancer. HIV (Human Immuno-deficiency Virus) destroys immune system of the body and causes AIDS. The provirus ultimately dissociates, transcribes viral RNA genomes, produces reverse transcripture and viral proteins. Different parts assemble to form retroviruses. The latter come out through exocytosis or pass out to other cells through protoplasmic connections.

GENE EXPRESSION IN PROKARYOTES

Bacterial Chromosome

A circular double strand or duplex DNA is folded variously with the help of RNA and polyamines to form bacterial chromosome, nucleoid, or genophore. It has 1/1000 DNA content of a eukaryotic genome. DNA of *E. coli* has a length of 1100 μm with some 2500 genes. Nucleoid is connected by γ-shaped forks to a membranous body/mesosome that develops over the plasmalemma.

Plasmids

A bacterial cell contains one to several circular extrachromosomal DNA segments called *plasmids* (Hoyes and Lederberg, 1952). They are capable of replication like nucleoid. At times the plasmid integrates with bacterial chromosome. It is then called *episome*. A plasmid carries a few genes, e.g. fertility factor (F^+), R-factors (resistance factors against common antibiotics like chloroamphenicol, tetracycline, streptomycin, sulphonamide), *Nif* (Nitrogen fixation) or colicinogenic factors (for synthesis of bacteriocidal and bacteriostatic chemicals).

Genome Replication

Bacteria multiply by binary fission. Generation time is 20 minutes in *E. coli* to 15-20 hours in *Myxobacterium tuberculosis*. Nucleoid replicates while attached to mesosome. It behaves like a single replicon (Cairns, 1963). Mesosome divides alongwith replication of nucleoid so that each daughter nucleoid is attached to its own mesosome.

GENE RECOMBINATION IN BACTERIA

Sexual reproduction and **haploid-diploid alternation** are absent in bacteria. However, one way gene reshuffling or recombination **(mesomixis)** can occur by three methods-conjugation, transformation & transduction.

(1) Conjugation

It was discovered by Lederberg and Tatum (1946) in *E. coli*. They found that mixing of two different double (Bio^-, Met^-) and triple (Thr^-, Leu^-, Thi^-) auxotrophs over minimal medium produced occassional prototrophs. Cell contact was required. Anderson (1957) observed conjugation sare dimorphic, male donor having fertility factor (F^+) and *sex pili* while female or recipient is without both fertility factor (F^-) and sex pili. Contact between the two types cause development of 'conjugation tube' by means of a pilus of donor.

Meromixis occurs by two methods.

(*a*) **Sterile Male Method :** No gene of the male chromosome is transferred to the recipient cell. Fertility factor replicates. One plasmid passes into recipient/female cell through the conjugation tube to make it donor as well. The phenomenon is called *sexduction*.

(*b*) **Fertile Male Method :** The plasmid of fertility factor gets integrated to bacterial chromosome and is called *episome*. The donor F^+ cell with episome is called Ffr (High frequency of recombination) or **super male** as recombination frequency increases to some 1000 times. The integrated F^+ factor breaks bacterial chromosome at the end of its attachment. The freed chromosome end (zero end) becomes linear and passes into recipient cell. The whole male chromosome is rarely transferred (it takes some two hours). The fertility factor is the last to migrate. Conjugation is generally interrupted any time. A few to several genes of male/donor are transferred to female/recipient cell. The latters is now called *merozygote* or *partial zygote*. The donor cell generally dies after conjugation. Some donor genes get integrated to recipient genome while others degenerate.

(2) Transformation

It is the picking up of genes from DNA of the dead relatives. Transformation was discovered by Griffith (1928) in *Diplococcus pneumoniae* (transfer of gene for virulence from dead bacteria to nonvirulent bacteria). Avery *et al* (1944) found transferring material to be segment of DNA. Transformation is quite common as DNA is released into the medium after death of cells. *Competence* or ability to pick up foreign DNA is present for a brief period towards the end of active growth. Additionally calcium chloride in required by *E. coli*. A competent cell has many receptor sites for attachment of foreign DNAs but only a specific DNA segment gains entry. It attaches to fork of mesosome and gets integrated to host DNA during its replication. The competent recipient cell now becomes recombinant.

(3) Transduction

Transfer of genes from one organism to another with the help of a virus/vector is known as transduction. It was discovered by Zinder & Lederberg (1952) in case of *Salmonella typhimurium* (typhoid in mice). Later it was reported in a number of other bacteria. Bacteriophages have two types of multiplication, **lysogenic** and **lytic**. In lysogenic/nonvirulent/temperate phase, the virus genome is integrated to bacterial genome and called **prophage**. At times the prophage dissociates from the bacterial genome, becomes virulent and performs lytic cycle. However, the bacterial DNA is not destroyed completely so that some of the phage particles come to have segments of bacterial genome. They are called 'transducting phages' as they transfer some genes of the previous host to the new host. (the new host is not harmed as the phage becomes deficient in some of its own genes). Transduction is of two types, 'generalised' (genes not fixed) and 'restricted' (same gens, e.g. *lac* or *bio* gene in case of lambda phage in *E. coli* K-12, because the phage genome attaches between the two). Donor gene may integrated between the two. Donor gene may integrate with genome of recipient (becomes recombinant, hence complete transduction) or fails to get associated with recipient DNA and degenerate (*abortive* transduction.)

OPERON CONCEPT

Operons are segments of genetic material which function as regulatory units or units or units that can be switched on and off. Operon concept was given by two French scientists, working at Pasteur Institute, Francois Jacob and Jacques Monod (1961). While studying lactose utilisation in mutants of *E. coli*. An operon consists of one to several structural genes (three in lac operon and five in tryptophan operon of *E. coli*, nine in histidine or operon of *Salmonella typhimurium*), one operator gene, a promoter gene, a regulator gene, a repressor and inducer/or corepressor. Operons are of two types, inducible and repressible.

Inducible Operon System/Lac Operon System

An inducible operon system is that regulated genetic material which remains regulated genetic material which remains switched off normally but becomes operational in the presence of an inducer. It occurs in *catabolic pathways*. The components are :

(1) ***Structural Genes :*** They are genes which produce *m* RNAs for forming polypeptide/proteins/enzymes. Lac operon of *E. coli* has three structural genes-Z (produces enzyme β-galactosidase for splitting lactose/galactoside into glucose and galactose), Y (produces enzymes galactoside permease required in entry of lactose/galactoside) and A (produces enzyme galactoside acetylase/transacetylase without any function in *E. coli*). The three structural genes of *lac operon* produce a single polycistronic *m* RNA. The three enzymes are, however, produced in different concentrations.

2. *Operator Gene :* It gives passage to RNA polymerase when the structural genes are to express themselves. Normally it is covered by a repressor. Operator gene of the *lac operon* is small, made up only of 27 base pairs.

3. *Promoter Gene :* It is recoginition centre/initiation point for RNA polymerase of the operon.

4. *Regulator Gene (i Gene) :* It produces a repressor that binds to operator gene for keeping it nonfunctional to pass from promoter to structural genes).

5. *Repressor :* It is a small protein formed by regulator gene which binds to operator gene and blocks passage of RNA-polymerase towards structural enzymes. Repressor has two allosteric sites, one for attaching to operator gene and second for binding to inducer. Repressor to *lac operon* has a molecular weight of 160,000 and 4 subunits of 40,000 each.

6. *Inducer :* It is a chemical which attaches to repressor, changes the shape of operator binding site so that repressor no more remains attached to operator. Lactose/galactose is inducer of *lac operon*. As soon as the operator gene becomes free, RNA polymerase is recognised by promoter gene. This process requires c AMP. RNA polymerase passes over the operator gene and then reaches the area of structural genes. Here it catalyses transcription of *m* RNAs.

REPRESSIBLE OPERON SYSTEM/ TRYPTOPHAN OPERON SYSTEM

A repressible operon system is that regulates genetic material which normally remains active/operational and enzymes formed by its structural genes present in the cell till the operon is switched off when concentration of an end product crosses a threshold value. Repressible operon system usually occurs in *anabolic pathways*, e.g., *tryptophan operon*, *arginine operon*. Each has the following parts:

(1) *Structural Genes :* They are genes which take part in synthesis of polypeptide/proteins/enzymes through the formation of specific *m* RNAs. **Tryptophan operon** has five structural genes-E, D, C, B and A.

(2) *Operator Gene :* It provides passage to RNA polymerase moving from promoter to structural genes. Operator gene of repressible operon is normally kept swtiched on as **aporepressor** formed by regulator gene is unable to block the gene.

(3) *Promoter Gene :* It is initiation/recognition point for RNA polymerase.

(4) *Regulator Gene :* The gene produces an apropressor.

(5) *Aporepressor :* It is a proteinaceous substance formed through the activity of regulator gene. It is able to block operator gene only when a corepressor is also available.

(6) *Corepressor :* The nonproteinaceous component of repressor which can be end product (feed back inhibition/repression) of the reaction mediated through enzyme synthesized by structural genes. Corepressor of tryptophan operon is tryptophan. It combines with apropressor, forms repressor which then blocks the operator gene to swtich off operon.

MULTIGENE FAMILIES

Multigene family is a group of similar or nearly similar genes that help in forming multiple copies either for meeting higher demand or time/tissue specific products. The former are called repeated genes. Globin gene family is an example of time/ tissue specific multigene family.

Repeated Genes : There are genes occurring in multiple copies or having variant repetition are called repeated genes, e.g., histone genes, *t* RNA genes, Ss RNA genes, actin genes, Sn RNA genes, heat shock protein genes.

Globin Gene Family in Humans : In early embryo, haemoglobin consists of $\zeta_2\in_2, \zeta_2\gamma_2$ and $\alpha_2 \in_2$ claim. In foetal stage haemoglobin is $\alpha_2\gamma_2$. In adult, 97% of haemoglobin in $\alpha_2\beta_2$, 2% $\alpha_2\delta_2$ and 1% $\alpha_2\gamma_2$ (foetal form). $\in, \delta, \beta$ and γ genes are located on chromosome 11 while ζ and α genes occur on chromosome 16.

Sn RNA : Small nuclear RNA. Uridine rich, seven types, named U_1 to U_7. They are stable and ubiquitous. Each Sn RNA combines with 7-8 molecules of molecules of protein to form ribonucleoprotein or Sn RNP. Sn RNPs are involved in splicing (U_1 and U_2), *r* RNA processing (U_3) and *m* RNA processing.

CELL DIVISION AND CELL CYCLE

MECHANISM OF CELL DIVISION (MITOSIS & MEIOSIS)

Cell division was first studied by Prevost and Dumas (1824) when they described cleavage in fertilized egg of Frog. Rudolf Virchow (1855, 1859) *gave cell lineage theory* that new cells arise by division of pre-existing one—*omnis cellulae cellula*. Strasburger (1873) found that new nuclei develop from pre existing ones. The details were worked out by Strasburger (1875) and Flemming (1879). The term of *mistosis* was coined by Flemming (1882). Meiosis was studied by Sutton (1900) and to some extent by Strasburger (1888) and Winiwater (1900). The term meiosis was coind by Farmer and Moore (1705). The agents which stimulate cell division are called mitogens e.g. cytokinins and some steroids. There are some agents which inhibits cell division. They are called *mitotic poisons*. e.g. *azides, cyanides, colchicine etc.*

(*i*) *Cell Cycle :* Cell cycle is a series of cyclic changes through which a cell passes during its growth and divisions. Time interval between two successive divisions is called *generation time*. Cell cycle has two parts: long nondividing I-phase and short dividing M-phase.

INTERPHASE (I-phase) : It is complex of changes that occur in newly formed cell before it is able to divide. Interphase has three stages

(*a*) *G_1-Phase*. In this, first growth or post mitotic gap phase, the cell and its nucleus grow in size. RNA and protein (including histone) synthesis occurs.

(*b*) *S-Phase*. Chromosomes replicate. Therefore it is called invisible stage of M-phase.

(*c*) *G_2-Phase*. It is the second growth or pre-mitotic gap phase where macro-molecules including protein tubulin are synthesised for cell division. A new centriole pair is formed.

M-Phase. It is the phase of cell division. Cell division consists of nuclear division of *karyokinesis* and protoplast division or *cytokinesis*. Cell division or M-phase is of three types-amitosis, mitosis, meiosis.

(*ii*) *Amitosis :* (Direct Division, Robert Remark, 1841). During amitosis, nucleus elongates, constricts in the middle divides directly into two daughter nuclei. This is followed by division of cytoplasm through constriction, e.g. cartilage cells, degenerate cells.

(*iii*) *Mitosis :* It is also called somatic division, because it occurs during formation of somatic or body cells. Mitosis is studied in plants in the regions of meristems, e.g. stem tip, root tip (onion $2n = 16$). In animals it is studied in bone marrow, skin, base of nails etc. Mitosis is equatiorial division in which a parent cell divides into two identical daughter cells; each of which contains the same number and kind of chromosomes as are present in the parent cell. Mitosis occurs in two steps, karyokinesis & cytokinesis.

(A) Karyokinesis

It is the stage of nuclear division (indirect nuclear division) which is continuous but is divided into four stages for the sake of convenience—prophase, metaphase, anaphase and telophase.

(*a*) *Prophase :* In early prophase, the chromatin fibres condense to form elongated chromosomes. The nucleus appears as ball of wool. Centrosome has already divided. The daughter centrosome begin to move away from each other. In *mid prophase*, chromosomes shorten and become distinct with each having two chromatids attached to narrow point called CENTROMERE. The centrosomes develop astral rays and migrate farther. In *late prophase*, the centrosome reach the poles, form asters and begins to develop spindle fibres. Nucleolus degenerates and nuclear envelope starts breaking. In plant cells, centrosomes are absent, spindle fibres develop without them.

(*b*) *Metaphase :* A bipolar spindle is produced. It is anastral (without asters) in plants and *amphiaster* in animals. Spindle is observable with the help of polarising microscope. Spindle has three types of fibres (I) Continuous (pole to pole) (II) Discontinuous (come out of one pole but do not reach the other pole, (III) Chromosome Fibre (Fibres that attach chromosomes to spindle poles. Each spindle fibre is made of 4-20 microtubules. The middle part of spindle having the maximum diameter is called *equator*. Chromosomes move to the equatorial plane and form equatorialor *metaphasic plate* with their centrosomes attached to both the poles by chromosomal fibres. *Colchicine arrests cell division at metaphase stage. Metaphase is the best time to see chromosomes.*

(*c*) *Anaphase :* The centromere of each chromosome divides. This converts the two chromatids into daughter chromosomes each being attached to the spindle pole of its side by independent chromosomal fibre. The chromosomes move towards the spindle poles. The two pole-ward moving chromosomes of each type remain attached to each other by *interzonal fibres*. Ultimately, two groups of chromosomes come to lie at the spindle poles. The spindle fibres shorten one third to one fifth of the original length.

(*d*) *Telophase :* Chromosome again unfold, elongate forming chromatin fibres. Nucleolus, nucleoplasm and nuclear envelope appear form ER so that two daughter nuclei are formed.

Dinomitosis is the type of nuclear division found is dinoflagellates in which the nuclear envelope persists. Microtubular spindle is not formed. Chromosome move while attached to inner membrane of nuclear envelope.

Karyochorisis : Intranuclear spindle is formed with spindle pole bodies (SPBs) developing at the two ends.

(B) Cytokinesis

It is the process of separation of the cytoplasm. In animal cells, there is constriction at the equator that finally results in the separation of the daughter cells. It is of two types.

(*a*) *Cleavage Cytokinesis :* The cell membrane constricts and develops a centripetal furrow or cleavage in the middle. The furrow deepens and divides the parent protoplast into two uninucleate protoplasts or cells. Cleavage is the usual method of cytokinesis in animal. It also occurs in some lower plants where wall material is deposited in the furrow between the two daughter protoplasts.

(*b*) *Cell Plate Cytokinesis :* It occurs in plants vesicles having pectic compounds and other wall materials appear in the middle of persisting spindle called 'Phragmoplast'. They fuse and form a film or *cell plate* with membrane on either side. This divides the parent binucleate cell into two daughter uninucleate cells. Cell plate grows centrifugally and functions as middle lamella. Primary wall is deposited on its either side by the two daughter protoplasts.

(*iv*) *Meiosis :* Meiosis is a special type of cell division present in germ cells of sexually reproducing organisms. Sexual reproduction occurs by way of sexual cells or gametes (eggs & sperms), which after fertilization constitute the Zygote. Meiosis consists of a single duplication divisions. In animals and lower plants, meiosis is *terminal* or *gametic* (i.e., it occurs before the formation of the gametes). In the male, four haploid sperms are produced, in female, one ovum and three polar bodies are produced. In most plants, meiosis is *intermediary* or *sporic* i.e. it occurs sometime between fertilization and the formation of gametes). Cells in meiosis are called *Meiocytes.*

Meiosis is divided into division I and II. In division I, there is a long prophase of which the stages are preleptonema and leptonema, zygonema, pachynema, diplonema and diakinesis.

(A) Meiosis I

Meiosis I is the actual reduction division which is also called heterotypic division (the two chromatids of a chromosome often become different due to crossing over.)

(*a*) *Prophase I :* It is longest phase which is complex and divisible into five stages-leptotene, zygotene,pachytene, diplotene and diakinesis.

(*i*) *Leptotene :* (Leptonema). Chromatin fibres condense and form chromosomes. The chromosomes often show chromomeres. They may also develop baset like arrangement called *bouquet* stage (diverging from a common point lying near centrosome). Chromosome number is diploid where there are two chromosomes of each type called 'homologous chromosomes'. Their chromatids are not clear because of the development of nucleoprotein core between them.

(*ii*) *Zygotene :* (Zygonema). Homologous chromosomes join laterally in the process of synapsis (Montgomery, 1901)/*syndesis* to form bivalents. The two chromosomes of a bivalent are held together by nucleoprotein core. The whole structure is called 'Synaptonemal Complex' (Moses, 1956). SC is composed of two lateral arms (which appear in each homologous at the end of leptonema) and a medial element. At the time of paring the packing of DNA is 300/1 and there is only 0.3% matching between homologous DNA. Pairing starts at random, but telomeres are generally inserted at the nuclear envelope. The 0.2 μm space between homologous chromosomes is occupied by the SC. This may have the appearance of a ladder, with bridges crossing the medial element. The main component of this complex is protein. The macromolecular organization of meiotic chromosomes is similar to that of mitotic ones with a 20-30 nm chromatin fiber composed of nucleosomes. In early prophase, the fibres make discrete loops that coalesce in dense foci, where the lateral arms of SC are deposited. The packing of there loops increases throughout meiotic prophase, and some RNA transcription may be seen in certain loops corresponding to active nucleolar genes.

(*iii*) *Pachytene (Pachynema) :* The nonsister chromatids of a bivalent may exchange segments in the process of crossing over. However, individual chromatids are not clear. In this pairing is complete and chromosomes become shorter & thicker. The number of chromosomes have been halved (i.e. bivalents or tetrads). Each tetrad has four kinetochores (two homologous and two sister). During pachynema, two homologous chromatids exchange segments at a molecular level (recombination). The SC appears to stabilise the pairing thus enabling the interchange. At pachynema the SC may show the recombination nodules or bars, which may be actual sites of crossing over.

(iv) *Diplotene* : (Diplonema). During diplotene the paired chromosomes begin to separate, but they are held together at the *chiasmata* (points of interchange or crossing over). Chiasmata (first seen by Johanssen, 1909) or nucleoprotein attaching points occur at places between the homologous chromosomes. There is at least one chiasma per bivalent chromosome. At diplonema, the SC is shed from the bivalents. At each chiasma, there is a piece of SC that ultimately disappears and is replaced by a chromatin bridge. Diplonema may last for months or years. In this the chromatids become clear. Each bivalent now appear as tetrad.

(v) *Diakinesis* : Chiasmata shift towards the chromosome ends (terminalisation). Nucleolus degenerates. Nuclear envelope breaks at places. A spindle begins to develop with centrioles in animals & without centrioles. There is reduction in the number of chiasmata and further contraction. This is followed by prometaphae, metaphase I, anaphase I, telophase I.

(*b*) *Metaphase I* : A bipolar fibrous spindle appears in the area of nucleus. It has asters at the two poles in animal cells (amphiaster) while the same are absent in plant cells (anastral). The chromosome pairs shift to the equator of spindle forming two or double metaphasic plate with the help of their centromeres. Each chromosome gets attached to spindle pole of its side by a chromosome fibre.

(*c*) *Anaphase I* : Chiasmata disappear completely and the homologous chromosomes separate. The process in called *disjunction*. The separated chromosomes (univalents) show divergent chromatids and are called *dyads*. They move towards the spindle poles and ultimately form two groups of haploid chromosomes.

(*d*) *Telophase I* : Chromosomes elongate. Nucleolus, nucleoplasm and nuclear envelope appear over each chromosome group forming nuclei.

During the interphase between the two meiotic divisions there is no replication of the chromosomes, and division II is very similar to mitosis, by the end of which each nucleus has a haploid number of chromosomes composed of single chromatids.

The fact that in meiotic division I there is separation of homologous kinetochores (and chromatids) and in division II the sister kinetochores (and chromatids) are separated, can be explained by the orientation of kinetochores, which determines nucleation and preferential polarization of microtubules.

(B) Meiosis II

It is homotypic or equational division which is meant for maintaining the haploid number and separating the two chromatids of a chromosome which have become different due to crossing over. DNA replication is absent.

(*a*) *Prophase II* : The chromatin fibres shorten to form chromosomes. Nucleolus and nuclear envelop break down. Spindle in formed in the area of each nucleus. Both telophase I and prophase II are omitted in some organisms where anaphase I directly leads to metaphase II; e.g. Trillium.

(*b*) *Metaphase II* : Chromosomes come to lie at the equator of the spindle forming a single metaphasic plate. The centromere of each chromosome gets attached by both its surfaces to the spindle poles of their sides by distinct chromosome fibres.

(*c*) *Anaphase II* : Centromere of each chromosome divides into two. This separates the two chromatids of a chromosome into two independent daughter chromosomes. Each daughter chromosome is attached to spindle pole of its side by a chromosome fibre. Chromosomes move towards the spindle poles forming two groups. Since there were two spindle, a total of four groups are formed.

(*d*) *Telophase II* : The four groups of chromosomes organise themselves into four haploid nuclei.

(C) Cytokinesis

Cytokinesis may occur after each division (successive type) or simultaneously at the end of meiosis. It is generally through cleavage. In case of plants, wall material is deposited in the furrows. Cytokinesis give rise to four haploid cells.

(D) Significance of Meiosis

In all organisms 'Meiosis' takes place at the time of gamete formation. 4 haploid cells are produced as a result of meiosis in a diploid cell. The product of meiosis gives rise to gametes after metamorphosis, some of them may be viable or nonviable.

The object of reduction division is as follows:

(*a*) To keep the chromosome number same in daughter cells.

(*b*) To keep the parental characters in daughter cells.

(*c*) This division enables the cells to pass from one generation to another.

(*d*) In the sporophytic generation, the number of chromosome is 2*x* i.e. diploid and passes into gametophytic generation, reduction in number of chromosomes take place so that each of the gametophytic generation has got only *x* number of chromosomes. So this phenomenon is most essential for completing a life history of a plant.

(*e*) Fertilization duplicates the chromosome number but meiosis halves it to maintain the chromosomal balance in all organisms.

(*f*) At the time of chiasmata formation, the exchange of chromatid material causes a combination of new characters. Thus meiosis helps in bringing about variation in population.

Meiosis may last for 50 years in human female as the number of oocyte in a new born female is about one million. By the age of 07 years, there are some 300,000 oocytes left while only 400 reach maturity between 12 & 50 years. Thus meiosis may last upto 50 years. This may explain the increase in incidence of chromosonal aberrations with the increasing age of mother. While in human male, meiosis starts after puberty.

THE ESSENTIAL DIFFERENCES BETWEEN MITOSIS AND MEIOSIS

The essential differences between mitosis and meiosis are as follow :

(*a*) Mitosis occurs in all somatic cells while meiosis is limited to germinal cells only.

(*b*) In mitosis, one replication cycle of DNA is followed by one division, resulting in diploid cells. In Meiosis, one replication of DNA is followed by two divisions, resulting in haploid cells.

(*c*) In mitosis DNA replication occurs in the 'S' phase, which is followed by G_2. In meiosis there is a premeiotic DNA synthesis, which is very long and followed immediately by meiosis.

(*d*) In mitosis, each chromosome behaves independently, while in meiosis there is pairing of homologous chromosomes.

(*e*) Mitosis last 1 to 2 hours and meiosis lasts longer; in the male it may last 24 days and in the female, several years.

(*f*) In mitosis, the genetic material remains constant, and in meiosis there is genetic variability.

The essential processes of meiosis are

(*a*) pairing of homologous chromosomes;

(*b*) Formation of chiasmata with underlying genetic recombination;

(*c*) Segregation of the homologous chromosomes.

MICROBIAL PHYSIOLOGY

CELL DIFFERENTIATION

Cell differentiation is the process by which stable differences arise between cells. All higher organisms develop from a single cell, the fertilized ovum, which gives rise to various tissues and organ. Cell differentiation leads to distinguish-able cell types whose character and properties are determined by their pattern of gene activity and the *proteins* they produce. Transplantation of nuclei from differentiated animal cells into fertilized eggs and cell fusion studies show that the pattern of gene expression in the nucleus of a differentiated cell can often be reversed, implying that it is determined by factors supplied by the cytoplasm and that no genetic material has been lost. Although the differentiated state of an animal cell *in vivo* is usually extremely stable, some causes of differentiation are reversible. Transdifferentiation of one differentiated cell type into another type has been shown to occur during regeneration and in cells in tissue culture. In many cases, the pattern of gene activity is under continuous control. Maintenance and inheritance of a pattern of gene activity may involve several mechanisms, including the continued action of gene regulatory proteins; changes in the packing state of chromatin, and chemical modifications to the DNA.

(A) *Cytoplasmic determinants :* Nuclear transplantation experiments in frog have shown that the genome remains constant during cell differentiation. Cytoplasm contains substances called 'determinants' that become unequally distributed among embryonic cells and cause them to follow a particular differentiation pathway.

The best example of cytoplasmic determinants is provided by the granules present in germ cells. When they are centrifuged or transplanted into different positions, they will induce the formation of germ cells in a different position.

In early embryos, rate of cell division is very fast and during this period there is no RNA synthesis, but when the 4000-cell stage (called-mid-blastula transition) is reached, synthesis of most types of RNA starts simultaneously.

(B) *Molecular Differentiation :* How is a gene expressed in certain tissues and not in others? It seems that not one but multiple mechanisms are used. Activation of *transcription* is probably the most common one, used in many protein-coding genes, e.g. globin in red blood cells, ovalbumin in oviduct & silk fibroin in the silk gland. Exactly how this is achieved is not known. Chromatin structure and DNA methylation have been explored as possible mechanisms. *Translational* control is known to occur is some eggs that have "marked" m RNAs that are translated only after fertilization. The best example of translational control is provided by the heat shock m RNA of *Xenopus* oocytes, which are stored but not translated unless the temperature is raised.

Differentiation establishes a pattern of gene activity

⇓

Pattern of gene activity is passed onto daughter cells by various mechanisms.

⇓ Positive feddback control of gene expression and interaction with other gene

⇓ DNA methylation

⇓ Changes in chromatin state (e.g. in inactivated X-chromosome)

Pattern of gene activity is reversible

⇙ Transfer of nucleus of differentiated cell to egg support embryonic development

⇘ Transdifferentiation e.g. lens retinal pigment cells.

In *gene amplification* specific genes are selectively replicated to attain a higher level of expression. Gene amplification happens with r DNA in some oocytes, the DNA puffs of *Rhynocosciara*, and with the chorion (egg shell) genes of *Drosophila*. It is a rare event, and in all cases the amplified DNA is not passed on to future cell generations.

Transposition of genes form a 'silent' site in the chromosome into an 'expression site', where they are actively transcribed, occurs in the yeast mating type switch and in trypanosomes that change periodically their surface antigens as a defense against the host's immune system. Transposition is known not to occur for globin, ovalbumin and many other genes.

The production of antibodies by B-lymphocytes is the best example of how intricate the control of cell differentiation might be. Initially, variable region DNA is brought close to a constant region by a DNA deletion. A membrane-bound antibody molecule is initially produced but upon stimulation with antigen, the cell starts secreting antibody by a mechanism controlled at the RNA processing level. Finally another DNA deletion might bring the same variable region closer to a new type of constant heavy chain, producing different types of immunoglobulins (IgG, IgE, IgA).

It is possible in adult tissue mechanisms similar to those of cytoplasmic determinants in embroyes might operate. For example, when cytoplasmic components become unequally distributed among daughter cells, one cell may become differentiated while the other remains as a *stem cell.*

The differentiation of the various lineages seems to depend on external signals, although there is evidence for autonomous diversification, and external factors are essential for survival and proliferation of specific cell types. Similar processes also occur in the diversification of neural crest. Before migration, single crest cells have a broad developmental potential, and environmental signals can both direct the pathways of neural crest differentiation and promote survival of particular cell types. Programmed cell death is common fate for cells, especially during development and there is evidence that positively acting signals are generally required to prevent programmed cell death and allow cells to continue to survive.

CELL-CELL INTERACTION

(A) Differentiation of the Cell Membrane

The cell membrane may present regional differentiations that are related to specialized functions such as absorption, fluid transport, electrical coupling. Microvilli are found at the apical surface of the intestinal epithelium and form the brush border of the kidney tubules. They increase the absorption surface and are covered by a coat of glycoproteins.

Intercellular attachments comprise tight junctions, belt desmosomes, and spot desmosomes. **Tight junctions** serve to seal the intercellular spaces and to maintain the intercellular environment. They form a network of sealing strands below the apical regions of the cells. **Belt desmosomes** have a system of action and intermediate filaments and are situated below the zone of tight junctions. These belt desmosomes represent the terminal bars or intermediary junctions of the old literature. **Spot desmosomes** are localized circular areas of mechanical attachment having two dense plaques with keratin tonofilaments. The number of spot desmosomes is correlated with the degree of mechanical stress that the tissue has to support e.g. epithelium of vagina is rich is spot desmosomes.

Hemidesmosomes are found at the base of certain epithelia. Therefore similar to desmosomes in fine structure, but represent only half of them, the outer side frequently substituted with collagen fibrils.

Tight junctions are also known as *zonula occludens,* belt desmosomes as *zonula adherens* & spot desmosomes as *macula adherenes.*

(B) Gap Junctions & Intercellular Communications

Cellular interactions are essential for the coordination of activities, and furthermore, the propagation between cells of signals for growth and differentiation is indispensable for development. It is now known that most cells in an organized tissue are interconnected by *junctional channels* and that they share a common pool of many small metabolities and ions that pass freely from one cell to another. Their individuality, however, is maintained by macromolecules that are not exchanged between cell.

The so called *gap junctions* (nexus) are essential in intercellular communications. They represent regions in which there are junctional channels through which ions and molecules can pass from one cell to another. Cells having gap junction are electrically coupled i.e. there is a free flow of electrical current carried by ions. At the gap junction the membranes are separated by a space of only 2 to 4 nm, and there is a hexagonal array of 8 to 9 nm particles. At the centre of each particle there is a channel 1.5 to 2 nm in diameter. The macromolecular unit of the gap junction is called the **connexon**, which appears as annulus of six subunits surrounding the channel. It is thought that the sliding of the subunits causes the channel to open & close.

Gap junction provides direct intercellular communication by allowing the passage of molecules upto a limiting weight of 1300 to 1900 daltons (in chironomous salivary glands). The permeability is regulated by Ca^{++} , if the intracellular Ca^{++} level increases, the permeability is reduced or abolished. Through the gap junction, metabolities (i.e., labeled nucleotides) can pass from one cell to another. In several strains of cancer cells, there is no coupling as seen in normal cultured cells. Coupling is genetically determined, and probably genes linked to one chromosome can correct the cancerous growth and the channel defect. Junctional communication may convey electrical signals between certain neurons (i.e. electrical synapses) and between cardiac cells, however, most neurons and skeletal muscle lack electrical coupling. Gap junctions are also used in the transfer of substances that control growth and differentiation in cells.

(C) Cell Coats and Cell Recognition

Most cell membranes have a coat, sometimes referred to as *glycocalyx*, made of glycoproteins or polysaccharides. The cell coat is negatively charged and may bind Na^+ and Ca^{++}. Several cytochemical techniques are used to reveal the cell coats (e.g. PAS & ruthenium red). The oligosaccharides may be visualised by the use of *lectins*. The cell-coat is a kind of secretion product that undergoes an active turnover.

Extracellular materials lie outside the cell coat proper and the fuzzy layer of certain cells. In these extracellular materials collagens and glycosaminoglycans are the main components. There are polysaccharzides, such as *hyaluronic acid* and *chondroitin sulfate*, in which there is a repeating disaccharide unit. These acidic molecules are associated with proteins forming proteoglycans.

Many functions are attributed to the cell coat, like filtration, diffusion, protection of membrane. The cell coat makes a kind of microenvironment for the cell. It contains enzymes involved in the digestion of carbohydrates and proteins.

Molecular recognition between cells may depend on a molecular code made up of the individual monosaccharides such as galactose, hexosamine, mannose, fucose and sialic acid. The classical ABO blood groups are based on specific antigens of the red cell coat, which are specified by their terminal carbohydrates. Several other antigens are found on the cell-coat. Molecular recognition reaches maximum expression in the nervous tissue. Cell adhesion and cell dissociation and reassociation are dependent on cell coat. Cells are able to recognize similar cells in a tissue. In all cell recognition phenomena, the presence of specific carbohydrates at the membrane is essential. From embryonic and adult animal tissues, low molecular weight proteins that act as plant lectins have been isolated. These animal lectins recognize saccharides on the cell surface and cause a β-galactoside hemoagglutination. Cells can also interact through diffusible substances acting at a distance. One such example is the life cycle of *Dictyostelium discoideum*, a slime mold in which the single amoeba may aggregate by the long range action of c AMP.

(D) Cell Surface in Cancer Cells

Cancer cells are characterized by uncontrolled growth, invasion and dissemination (metastasis). In a tumour all cancer cells are monoclonal. They may show changes in karyotype, increased glycolysis, and disorganization of cytoskeleton.

In cancer cells, there are many changes in the cell membrane and cell coat, such as the disappearance of gap junctions, loss of coupling, changes in glycolipids and glycoproteins and a reduction in gangliosides. There is also more mobility of surface receptors, increased transport of sugars, and growth of new antigens.

While in normal cells, the transport of iron and trace metal ions involves transferrin and transferrin receptors, in transformed cells there is an alternative mechanism. Transformed cells secrete siderophore like growth factors (chelating agents that trap the metal ions), which compete with transferrin and transport the iron inside the cell.

In the cell coat, **fibronectin,** a large glycoprotein found in "footprints" of moving cultured cells is reduced in cancer cells. A major characteristic of cancer cells is the combined loss of contact inhibition, motility and growth control, which is characteristics of normal cells in culture. Cancer cells are "immortal" and tend to pile up, while normale cells die after a number of divisions and tend to form monolayers.

A normal cell can be converted into a cancerous cell by a number of transforming agents, all of which affect the DNA and cause mutations. Different DNA and RNA viruses can produce transformation. Among the DNA viruses, polyoma and SV 40 are extensively used in experiments. Adeno and Herpes virus (DNA) may also be involved. The RNA retroviruses are natural agents in animal tumors and can be transmitted to the offspring through the mother's milk. In all these cases the viral genome becomes, integrated in certain regions of the host's genome and is expressed in cancerous cells.

4. PLANT PHYSIOLOGY

SOLUTE TRANSPORT AND PHOTOASSIMILATE TRANSLOCATION

WATER

- Most important constituent of the protoplasm.
- 80 - 90% of the fresh weight of most herbaceous plants and over 50% of the fresh weight of woody plants.
- Acts as solvent, reactant or reagent and maintains turgidity.

WATER POTENTIAL (Ψ, PSI)

Ditference between the free energy of water in a system and free energy of pure water at atmospheric pressure.

- The measurement unit of water potential is pascal (Pa).
- 1 mega pascal, MPa = 10 bars.
- Water potential is influenced by 3 factors - concentration, pressure and gravity.

  Water potential $\psi W = \psi s + \psi p + \psi g$

  where,

  ψs = Solute potential or osmotic potential (the amount by which the water potential is reduced as a result of the presence of solutes).

  ψp = Pressure potential or hydrostatic pressure (is positive in contrast to negative value of water potential and solute potential and operates in plant cell in the form of wall pressure).

  ψg = Gravity potential (the component of water potential influenced by the effect of gravity on water potential). The gravity potential depends on the height of water above the reference state of water, the density of water and the acceleration due to gravity. When vertical length is less than 5 metres, value of ψg is negligible and the modified equation is–

$$\psi w = \psi s + \psi p$$

- Theoretically ψw of the pure water = **zero**, so ψW inside plant cells is negative.

ABSORPTION AND MOVEMENT OF WATER

- Water is mainly absorbed through the roots, especially **at the tips in the region of the root hairs.**
- **Pathways of water movement in root**

  (1) Apoplast pathway: Water moves exclusively through the cell wall without crossing any membranes. Apoplast or outer space is a non-living continuous system made up of water-filled **cellulosic cell wall** and **inter cellular spaces** from epidermis to xylem.

Ions ⟶ Cell wall of epidermis ⟶ Cell wall of cortex ⟶ Cytoplasm of endoermis ⟶ Cell walls of Pericycle ⟶ Accumulate in xylem vessels

  (2) Symplast pathway: Water moves from one cell to another cell through **plasmodesmata**. Symplast or inner space is a living continuous system formed by cytoplasm and plasmodesmata from epidermis to xylem, parenchyma.

Ion ⟶ Cytoplasm of epidermis ⟶ Cytoplasm, cortex endodermis, pericycle through plasmodesmata ⟶ Xylem vessel

(3) **Transmembrane pathway :** Water after passing through cortex is blocked by casarian strips (deposition of wax like substance **suberin**) present on endodermis. Water crosses at least two membranes from each cell in its path. These two plasma membranes are found on entering and exiting of water. Here, water may also enter through tonoplast surrounding the vacuole *i.e.,* also known as **vacuolar pathway**.

DIFFUSION

The net movement of molecules or ions of a given substance from a region of higher concentration to lower one by virtue of their kinetic energy. The rate of diffusion of molecules is affected by temperature, density of diffusing molecules, medium in which diffusion takes place and concentration gradient.

- **Diffusion pressure:** The potential ability of a substance to diffuse from an area of its greater concentration to an area of lesser concentration is called diffusion pressure.

PERMEABILITY

The degree of diffusion of gases, liquids and dissolved substances through a membrane. It depends on the membrane composition, as well as the chemical nature of thesolute.

- It can be measured readily by determining the rate at which solute passes through a membrane under a specific set of conditions.
- Membranes may be permeable, impermeable and semipermeable.

OSMOSIS

Migration of solvent from a hypotonic solution (lower concentration) to hypertonic solution (higher concentration) through a semi-permeable membrane to keep the concentration equal.

- **Exosmosis :** Water moves out of the cell due to hypertonic solution (of higher concentration).
- **Endosmosis :** Water enters the cell due to hypotonic solution (of lower concentration).
- **Osmotic pressure :** The pressure needed to prevent the passage of pure water into an aqueous solution through a differentially permeable membrane thereby preventing an increase in the volume of the solution.
- Osmotic pressure depends upon **concentration** of solute particle, **ionisation** of solute particles, hydration of solute particles and temperature.
- **Reverse osmosis :** By applying additional pressure, water can be made to move out of solution from thistle funnel into water. This process can be used for removing salts from saline waters.
- **Osmosis is driven by two factors :** Concentration of dissolved solutes in a solution and pressure difference.
- **Osmotic potential or solute potential** (ψs) **:** Negative of osmotic pressure, since they are equal but opposite forces

$$\psi s = -\pi$$

e.g., Osmotic pressure of a plant is 200.5 atms but an osmotic potential of –200.5 atms.

PLASMOLYSIS

The phenomenon of shrinkage of protoplasm from the cell wall under the influence of some hypertonic solution is called as plasmolysis. As plasmolysis begins (incipient plasmolysis) the protoplasm is no more pressed against the cell wall, and the cell wall is said to be in a flaccid condition. However, further loss of water results in more shrikage of protoplasm and the cell is called **plasmolysed.**

- Continuous loss of water from plant cells results in wilting and drooping of leaves and stems.
- Plasmolysis is helpful in killing weeds from 'tennis courts', preservation of meat, jelly etc., to determine the osmotic pressure of cell, to know the living nature of cell, explains the phenomenon of osmosis etc.

IMBIBITION

A physical process by which solvent is adsorbed by certain substances making them swell. The solid particles which adsorb water or any other liquid are called imbibants and the liquid which is imbibed is known as **imbibate.**

- **Imbibition pressure (matrix potential) :** The potential maximum pressure that an imbibant will develop if it is submerged in pure water.
- Inbibition depends upon the affinity between imbibant and imbibed (*e.g.*, Rubber does not imbibe water, but imbibes kerosene oil and swells) and the water potential gradient between the surface of the adsorbant and the liquid imbibed.
- Dry seeds have a highly negative water potential.
- Both living and dead plant cells possess large amounts of **carbohydrates, proteins** and **polypeptides** etc. which are **hydrophilic colloids** and therefore, have very strong affinity for water.

TURGIDITY AND TURGOR PRESSURE

If a plant cell is placed in a **hypotonic solution** or pure water, water starts moving into the cell by osmosis. As the volume of the protoplast increases, it begins to exert pressure against the cell wall and stretches it. The pressure exerted by the protoplast against the cell wall is called turgor pressure (TP).

- **Wall pressure (WP) :** The cell wall being rigid, exerts an equal and opposite pressure on the protoplast which is called wall pressure.
- The two pressures are equal and opposite in direction.
- As a result of this interplay of forces, the plant cell under these conditions is said to be **turgid**.

DPD, OP AND TP

- DPD (diffusion pressure deficit) or SP (suction pressure) is the amount by which diffusion pressure of a solution is lower than that of its pure solvent. DPD was coined by B.S. Meyer (1938).
- The greater the concentration of a solution, the greater is its DPD.
- When a flaccid cell was placed in pure water, the suction pressure or DPD is roughly equal to the osmotic pressure of cell.

$$\boxed{\text{SP or DPD} = \text{OP}}$$

But when the cell became turgid, the turgor pressure resisted the entry of water into the cell and in that condition

$$\boxed{\text{SP or DPD} = \text{OP} - \text{TP}}$$

- Cell to cell movement of water depends upon the DPD and not on osmotic pressure and turgor pressure.

THEORIES OF WATER TRANSLOCATION

- The upward movement of water through stem is called ascent of sap (water with dissolved minerals).
- Goldlewski proposed **relay pump theory** and J.C. Bose proposed pulsation theory to explain the vitalistic view of ascent of sap.
- The three most prominent theories are-

(1) Root pressure theory

Stocking (1956) defined the root pressure "a pressure developed in the tracheary elements of xylem as a result of metabolic activities of the root.

- The development of root pressure is an active process which depends upon active secretion of salts or other solutes into the xylem sap, thereby lowering its osmotic potential.
- This theory can not account for water movement up the xylem in tall trees.

(2) Capillarity

In capillarity, water moves upward in narrow tubes due to the force of surface tension in small sized plants.

Boehm (1809) proposed that xylem vessels are narrow and ascent of sap occurs through capillarity further supported by atmospheric pressure.

- According to this theory, water is first taken in due to the force of adhesion between water and the wall of thin xylem vessels. As the water flows upwards along the wall, strong cohesive forces between water molecules come into play to pull the water upward. This continues until the forces of adhesion and cohesion are balanced by the downward force of gravity.

(3) Cohesion theory

Given by Henry Dixon in 1914. This depends upon the force of cohesion between water molecules. The important points are:

(i) **Cohesion force :** Water molecules are held together by strong cohesion force (due to hydrogen bonds). Another force of adhesion holds water to the walls of xylem channels.

(ii) **Continuous water column :** Present in the xylem channels of plant.

(iii) **Transpiration pull :** Transpiration from aerial parts causes a suction pressure in the water column of the plant. It is known as transpiration pull which lifts the water upwardly.

- Water column is continuous and cannot be pulled away from xylem walls due to cohesive and adhesive properties.
- The value of cohesive force for plant sap has been calculated to be 47 – 207 atm. by Dixon and Jolly.
- Cohesive force is also called as **tensile strength**.

TRANSPIRATION

The loss of water in the form of vapours from the living tissues of aerial parts of the plant is called transpiration.

- About 98% of water absorbed by land plant is transpired.

Types of transpiration

(1) **Cuticular :** Cuticle provides a relatively impermeable covering. If cutilcle is thin and green, about 20% of the total transpiration takes place through it, but if its thickness is increased, the extent of water vapour loss is significantly reduced.

(2) **Lenticular :** Lenticels are small regions on bark etc. and possess small loosely arranged cells called as complementary cells.

According to Huber, this loss through lenticels is only 1.0 per cent of the total transpiration.

(3) **Stomatal :** Stomata are tiny pores present on the epidermal surface of leaves, young stems and in certain truits. Nearly 97 per cent of the total transpiration takes place through these stomata.

STOMATA

Help in aseous exchange at the time of respiration and photosynthesis.

- There are two kidney shaped guard cells which bound a minute elliptical pore in a stoma. Guard cells are modified epidermal cells. The wall of guard cells near the pore is thick. The outer wall is thin, elastic and semipermeable.
- Loftfield classified stomata on the basis of their daily movement into four main types-

(a) **Alfalfa type :** Open throughout the day and closed all night *e.g.,* radish, mustard, turnip, apple, pea.

(b) **Potato type :** Open throughout the day and night except few hours following sunset *e.g.,* cabbage, pumpkin, onion.

(c) **Barley type :** Open only for a few hours in day *e.g.,* barley, maize, oat, wheat.

(d) **Equisetum type :** Always open throughout day and night *e.g., Equisetum.*

Distribution of stomata on the leaves

1. **Apple or mulberry type :** On the under surface of leaves only *e.g. apple.*
2. **Potato type :** More on under surface than upperside. *e.g. Potato, brinjal.*
3. **Oat type:** Equally distributed on both the surfaces. *e.g. rice, wheat.*
4. **Water lily type :** Only on the upper surface. *e.g. water lily.*
5. **Potamogeton type :** Either absent or if present, they are functionless, present mostly in submerged aquatic plants. *e.g. Potamogeton.*

Significance of transpiration

- Removal of water in the form of vapours has a cooling effect on the leaves. So it does not allow the leaf temperature to rise to detrimental levels.
- It helps in movement of xylem sap which simultaneously increases the absorption of mineral nutrients by the roots from the soil. It enhances extensive development of root system that supports the heavy aerial growth against wind.
- Curtis (1926) called transpiration as necessary evil.

FACTORS AFFECTING TRANSPIRATION

(A) External factors

1. **Atmospheric humidity :** If atmosphere is humid, it reduces the rate of transpiration. When the air is dry, the rate of transpiration increases.
2. **Wind :** A high wind speed or a dry breeze will greatly increase transpiration.
3. **Atmospheric pressure :** Low atmospheric pressure increases the rate of transpiration.
4. **Soil temperature :** Plants growing in warm regions exhibit less transpiration at a temperature lower than 5 - 8°C.
5. **Air temperature :** The rate of evaporation doubles with every rise in temperature by 10°C. High temperature affects the closure of stomata, reduces transpiration.
6. **Water :** Less amount of soil water decreases the rate of transpiration. If the rate of transpiration exceeds the rate of absorption, the stomata get closed and plant wilts.

(B) Internal Factors

1. **Leaf structure :** Presence of thick cuticle and sunken stomata reduces the rate of transpiration.
2. **Leaf orientation :** Transpiration is low in north-south orientation as compared to other orientation.
3. **Leaf area :** Directly proportional to the transpiration rate.
4. **Plant age :** Germinating seeds exhibit a slow rate of transpiration. It becomes maximum at maturity and decreases at senescence stage.
5. **Root shoot ratio :** The increase in ratio of root and shoot enhances the rate of transpiration.
6. **Water contents of the leaves :** Directly proportional to the rate of transpiration.

STOMATAL OPENING AND CLOSING

Opening and closing of stomata takes place due to turgor changes in guard cells. Solutes are taken in by the guard cells from the neighbouring epidernal and mesophyll cells so both osmotic potential and water potential of the guard cells are lowered. This create a water potential gradient between the guard cells and the neighbouring cells and make the water move into the guard cells. The guard cells become turgid and swell in size, resulting in stomatal opening.

- With a decline in guard cells solutes, water moves out of the guard cells, making them flaccid to stomata close.
- Levitt (1974) proposed active potassium theory. He observed that proton (H^+) uptake by guard cells. chloroplasts takes place with the help of ATP. This leads to increase in value of pH in guard cells. Rise in pH converts starch into organic acid (like malic acid).

Starch ⟶ Phosphoglyceric acid $\xrightarrow{\text{Carboxylase}}$ Phosphoenol pyruvic acid + CO_2

↓

Malic acid ⟵ Oxaloacetic acid

Malic acid further dissociates to form H^+ and malate anion.

- The uptake of K^+ ion in balanced by one of the following: uptake of Cl^-, transport of H^- ion from organic acid or by negative changes of organic acid when they lose H^+ ions. Thus all these factors lead to the opening of stomata.
- The stomata closure is due to excretion of K^+ from guard cells surrounding epidermal and subsidiary cells.

Factors affecting stomatal movement

1. **Light :** Stomata open in the presence of light and close in darkness. Light intensity required to open the stomata is very low, as compared to the intensity required for photosynthesis. In CAM (Crassulacean Acid Metabolism) plants, stomata open during dark and remain closed during the day. Even moonlight is sufficient to keep the stomata open in some plant species.

2. **Temperature :** Rise in temperature induces stomatal opening while fall in temperature causes closure. At 38°–40°C, stomata open even in darkness. In some plant species. stomata remain closed even under continuous light at 0°C.
3. **Carbon dioxide :** Low CO_2 concentration induces stomatal opening and vice versa. In closed stomata, external CO_2 concentration has no effect.
4. **Oxygen :** Essential for stomatal opening.
5. **Water availability :** Water stressed (less water available to plant and high transpiration rate) plants induces stomatal closure, due to formation of ABA and lowering of water potential in epidermal cells.
6. **Potassium :** Influx of K^+ causes opening of stomata while efflux of K^+ from guard cells causes closure of stomata.
7. **Mechanical shock :** Causes stomatal closure.
8. **Hormones :** Abscisic acid brings about closure of stomata. Cytokinins are required for keeping the stomata open.

GUTTATION

The loss of water in the form of liquid is called guttation. It generally occurs from tips and margins of leaves during night or early morning when there is high atmospheric humidity as during wet seasons.

- **Hydathodes** or **water pores** are special pores on the leaves in the region of guttation which are permanently open pores as their guard cells are immobile.
- Gutted water possess minute quantities of both inorganic and organic substances.

SOME IMPORTANT FACTS

- DPD can become zero (fully turgid cell). TP can also become zero (flaccid cell) but O.P. of a cell can never be zero.
- **Cryoscopic osmometer :** Measures osmotic potential of solution by measuring its freezing point.
- **Tensiometer :** Instrument for measuring soil water tension.
- **Psychorometer :** To mearene relative humidity as well as transpiration.
- **Manometer :** To measure pressure like root pressure.
- **Barometer :** To measure atmospheric pressure.
- **Porometer (F. Dawin, 1912) :** To measure the size of stomata.
- **Potometer :** To measure the rate of transpiration.
- **Atmometer :** To measure pull caused by evaporation of water from a porous pot.
- Term **guttation** was coined by Bergerstein (1887).
- **$CoCl_2$ Paper Method** (Hygrometric method, Stahl, 1894)-Used to compare the rates of transpiration.
- **Blue light** of visible light promotes stomatal opening.
- Plants growing at high altitudes exhibit xeromorphy *i.e.*, adaptation to minimise transpiration.
- **Transpiration ratio :** The amount of water lost per unit of dry matter produced during the growing season of a plant.
- **Stomatal frequency :** Number of stomata per unit area of leaf Its value is 1000 - 60,000/cm^2 or 10 - 600/mm^2.
- **Permanent wilting coefficient (PWP or PWC):** Amount of soil water at which the plants growing in it show first signs of permanent wilting.
- **Antitranspirants :** Chemicals which have been found to reduce the rate of transpiration without affecting CO_2 uptake. They may be **metabolic inhibitors** (*e.g.*, ABA-Abscissic acid, PMA - Phenyl mercuric acetate and Aspirin) **or film forming anti-transpirants** (*e.g.*, silicon emulsions and some low viscosity waxes).
- **Selectively or differentially permeable membrane :** Membrane which is normally semipermeable but allows selective transport of certain solutes.
- **SPAC (Soil Plant Atmosphere Continuum) :** Plants function as living connecing system between soil water and atmospheric water.

- **Stephen Hales (1676 -1761)**-Father of Plant Physiology, coined the term **root pressure**.
- **Yon Mohl :** Gave diagrammatic representiation of size of stoma at different times of the day.
- **Transpiration flux:** The quantity of water transpired by a unit area of leaf surface in a unit time.
- **Pfeffer :** Proposed term **'osmotic pressure'**. **Nollet :** Coined term **"osmosis"**.
- TP = 0 in plasmolysed cell.
- **Deplasmolysis :** A plasmolysed cell regains normal condition if placed in a hypotonic solution.
- **Slatyer and Taylor :** Proposed concept of water potential.
- Cohesive force of attraction between water molecules is upto **300 bars**.
- In *Saxifraga-Rate* of guttation is high during flowering.
- Active hydathode lack cuticle over specialized cells.
- *Lactuca scariola* and *Sylphium laciniatum* are called **compass plants** as their leaves lie vertically in north-south direction.
- In *Colocasia antiquorum,* guttation is a normal process.
- Transpiration is old stems and fruits takes place through lenticels.
- Osmotic pressure can be calculated by following relationship OP = cRT (where c = molar concentration of solution, R is gas constant and T is absolute temperature –273°C).
- Root pressure is absent in Gymnosperms.
- When the transpiration pull is exerted, a negative pressure or tension is generated in the xylem.
- **Isotonic solution :** Solution which has concentraton similar to that of cell sap.
- **Steward (1964) :** Proposed starch sugar hypothesis.

NITROGEN METABOLISM

INTRODUCITON

- **Mineral Nutrition :** The study of source, mode of absorption, distribution and metabolism of various inorganic substances or minerals by plants for their growth, development, structure, physiology and reproduction.
- **Autotrophs :** Organisms which use inorganic source of carbon *i.e.,* CO_2, Two types:
  - *(a)* **Photoautotrophs (photosynthetic) :** Use light energy *e.g.,* all green plants, blue green algae, green and purple sulphur bacteria.
  - *(b)* **Chemoautotrophs (chemosynthetic) :** Use chemical energy *e.g., Nitrosomonas, Nitrosococcus* and some other nitrogen cycle bacteria.
- **Heterotrophs :** Organisms which depend upon organic sources of carbon. Two types-
  - *(a)* **Photohetrotrophs :** Use light energy *e.g.,* some purple nonsulphur bacteria.
  - *(b)* **Chemoheterotrophs :** Use chemical energy *e.g.,* all animals, fungi, most bacteria and some flowering plants.

ESSENTIAL MINERAL ELEMENTS

- Such elements without which the plant cannot complete its life cycle.
- Arnon and Stout (1939) proposed criteria of essentiality of an element *i.e.,* the element must be directly involved in the nutrition of plant, must be absolutely necessary for supporting nornlal growth and reproduction and the requirement must be specific and not replaceable by another element.
- Based on the quantity in which they are required by plants:
  - *(a)* **Macro nutrients (major elements):** Required by plants in quantity of more than 1 milligram/gram dry matter. Total 9 in number-C, H, O, N, P, K, S, Mg and Ca.
  - *(b)* **Micro nutrients (Micro or minor or rare or trace elements):** Required by plants in quantity less than 1 milligram/gram of dry matter. Total 8 in number-Fe, Mn, Zn, Cu, Mo, B, Cl and Ni.

Sources of essential elements for plants

- **Carbon:** As atmospheric carbon dioxide
- **Hydrogen:** Mainly in the form of water.

- **Oxygen:** From the air or water or in the form of inorganic ions.
- **Nitrogen:** Absorbed by plants is the form of nitrate from the soil. Nitrogen fixers (organisms) convert nitrogen gas (N_2) to anionic forms such as nitrate (NO_3^-) or nitrite (NO_2^-) or a reduced cationic form such as ammonium (NH_4^+). These compounds enter plants through the root and are assimilated as organic nitrogen.
- **Other elements:** Absorbed from the soil e.g., phosphorus as phosphates and sulphur as sulphate etc.

ROLE OF MACRO-AND MICRO-NUTRIENTS

Element	Obtained in the form of	Specific role in Plants	Deficiency symptoms
1. Nitrogen	NO_2^-, NO_3^- or NH/	Consituent of proteins, vitamins, hormones, nucleic acids, coenzymes, ATP, chlorophyll etc.	Stunted growth, chlorosis, development of anthocyanin
2. Phosphorus	HPO_4^-	Constituent of nucleic acids, phospholipids, coenzymes, nucleotides, NAD^+, $NADP^+$ etc.	Poor growth, leaves dull green, premature fall of leaf and flower buds and delayed seed germination.
3. Potassium	K^+	Involved in protein synthesis in opening and closing of stomata, activates enzymes and helps in maintenance of turgidity of cells.	Yellow edges of leaves, inward curving of leaves, premature death.
4. Calcium	Ca^{2+}	As calcium pectate in the middle lamella of the cell wall, activates certain enzymes involved in selective permeability of cell membranes.	Stunted growth, disintegration of apical meristems and chlorosis.
5. Magnesium	Mg^{2+}	Constituent of chlorophyll, maintains ribo-some structure, activates enzymes in phosphate metabolism	Interveinal chlorosis
6. Sulphur	SO_4^{2-}	Constituent of amino acids (methionine, cysteine and cystine), vitamins, ferredoxin etc.	Chlorosis, rolling oftips and leaf margins.
7. Iron	Fe^{3+}	Constituent of ferredoxin, çytochromes, activates catalase, required for synthesis of chlorophyll	Chlorosis
8. Manganese (trace)	Mn^{2+}	Activates some enzymes necessary for O_2 evolution in photosynthesis.	Chlorosis, grey spots on leaves
9. Molybdenum (trace)	Mo^{3+} or Mo^{4+} or MoO_2^{2+}	Activates certain enzymes in nitrogen meta-bolism ascorbic acid synthesis.	Slight retardation of growth, whiptail in crucifers, loosening of cauliflower head.
10. Boron (trace)	BO_3^{3-} or or $B_4O_7^{2-}$	Calcium metabolism, pollen germination, cell differentiation, carbohydrate translocation	Suppression of flower formation, leaves becomes coppery in texture, heart rot or brown heart of Sugar beet and Turnip.
11.Copper (trace)	Cu^{2+}	Constituent of several oxidising enzymes, plastocyanin, cytochrome oxidase	Dieback, brown heart disease, blackening of potato tuber, reclamation of leguminosae
12. Zinc (trace)	Zn^{2+}	Activates various enzymes especially carboxy-lases, part of carbonic anhydrase and various dehydrogenases involved in synthesis of growth hormone auxin (IAA).	Little leaf disease, mottle leaf disease of apple and citrus, white bud, stunted growth, interveinal chlorosis.
13.Chlorine (trace)	Cl^-	Photolysis of water, with Na^+ and K^+ helps in maintaining solute concentration and anion-cation balance in cells, activator of amylase.	Wilting, stunting of roots and swollen root tips, flower abscission, reduced fruiting bronze coloured leaves.

MECHANISM OF ABSORPTION OF ELEMENTS

- **Flux :** Movement of ions
- **Influx :** Movement into the cell
- **Efflux :** The outward movement

Two ways:

1. Passive absorption

Movement of mineral ions into root cells as a result of diffusion. Three theories:

(a) **Donann's equilibrium (Donann, 1911) :** Entry of ions into the cell across the plasma membrane to maintain equilibrium is called **Donann's equilibrium.**

(b) **Ion exchange theory (Jenny and Overstreet, 1938) :** Exchange of anions and cations absorbed to the root surface with similarly charged ions of soil solution is called as ion exchange.

(c) **Mass flow/Bulk flow theory Hylmo (1955) :** Movement of ions takes place through root alongwith the stream of water under the influence of transpiration.

2. Active absorption

Uptake of mineral ions against concentration gradient. Metabolic energy is utilized for this. This energy is derived from respiration and is supplied through ATP.

- **Carrier concept (Van den Honert, 1937) :** Some organic substances (carriers) transfer ions from outer surface to the inner surface of plasma membrane by forming **carrier-ion complexes.**
- **Cytochrome pump hypothesis** (Lundegardh, 1954) explains the absorption of anions only.

ION TRAFFIC INTO THE ROOT

1. **Apoplastic pathway :** Occurs due to diffusion and bulk flow of water from cell to cell through spaces between cell wall polysaccharides.

Ions → Cell wall of epidermis → Cell wall of cortex → Cytoplasm of endodermis → Cell walls of pericycle → Xylem Vessels

2. **Symplastic pathway :** Active transport of mineral nutrients.

Ions → Cytoplasm of epidermis → Cytoplasm → Cortex → Endodermis of pericycle through plasmodesmata → Xylem vessels

TRANSLOCATION OF SOLUTES

- Stout and Hoagland (1939) proved that mineral salts are translocated through xylem.
- The rates at which inorganic solutes are translocated through the xylem vessels, correspond closely with the rates of translocation of water.
- Some of the minerals are transferred radially from xylem to the phloem mainly through parenchymatous cells.

NITROGEN METABOLISM

- **Nitrogen Cycle :** Regular circulation of nitrogen amongst living organisms, reservoir pool in the atmosphere (78% of atmosphere is N_2) and cycling pool in lithosphere. Plants obtain nitrogen from soil as nitrate, ammonium nitrite and urea.
- The atmospheric nitrogen is fixed into oganic combinations such as amino acids, protenis, nucleic acids etc. in living organisms via inorganic forms such as NH_4^+.
- **Ammonification :** The dead remains of animals and plants are decomposed through microbial activities to produce ammonia.
- **Nitrification :** Ammonia is rapidly converted first to nitrites and then to nitrates by the process of nitrification.

$$\text{Ammonia} \xrightarrow{\textit{Nitrosomonas}} \text{Nitrite} \xrightarrow{\textit{Nitrobacter}} \text{Nitrate}$$

- **Denitritication :** Nitrate is converted to nitrogen gas by the micro-organisms *e.g., Pseudomonas.*
- **Biological nitrogen fixation:** Nitrogen gas fixed in the form of NH_4^+ by both free living and symbiotic bacteria.
- Freeliving nitrogen fixing bacteria includes cyanobacteria, *Azotobacter* and *Clostridium.*
- **Symbiotic N_2 fixation :** Symbiotic bacteria are found in the root nodules of the members of family Leguminosae, they have the ability

to take up atmospheric N_2 through a process called **Symbiotic N_2 fixation**. *Rhizobium (e.g., R. leguminosarum, R. meliotii)* present root nodules of fabaceae *e.g., Cajanus, Cicer, Glycine, Lens, Phaseolus, Vigna, Pisum* etc.

- Root hair of legume secrete flavonoids and betaines which attract bacteria of *Rhizobium* species *(e.g., R. leguminosarum, R. melilotii)*.
- Bacteria release nod factors that cause curling of root hair, degeneration of cell wall, passage into root hair where infection thread carrying bacteria is formed.
- Finer branehes of infection thread pass into cells where bacteria stop dividing and form irregular, polyhedral bodies called bacteroids. These bacteroids present in groups or vesicles surrounded by host membrane.
- A pinkish pigment *i.e.*, **leg haemoglobin** (Lb) develops around each vesicle which is related to blood pigment haemoglobin. In root nodules, it found as **oxygen scavenger**, protecting enzyme nitrogenase from oxygen.
- Symbiotic nitrogen fixation requires **Nod** genes of legume, **nod, fix** and **nif** gene clusters of bacteria.
- Nitrogen fixation requires an enzyme **nitrogenase**, ATP, a source of hydrogen (NADPH, FMNH) and organic acids to trap ammonia produced through nitrogen fixation.

$$N_2 + 2H \xrightarrow[\text{Nitrogenase}]{\text{ATP}} N_2 + H_2 \xrightarrow[\text{Nitrogenase}]{\text{+4H, ATP}} 2NH_3$$

$$NH_3 + \alpha - \text{ketoglutarate} + NAD(P)H$$

$$\xrightarrow{\text{dehydrogenase}} \text{Glutamate} + NAD(P)^+ + H_2O$$

From this other amino acids and nitrogenous substances of different types are formed.

- Amino acids are translocated to other parts of the plant, which act as building blocks for the synthesis of various types of proteins.

SYNTHESIS OF AMINO ACIDS

- Amino acids are the main building blocks of proteins and in plants they act a number of additional functions in regulation of metabolism and the transport and storage of nitrogen.
- Amino acids are the initial products of nitrogen assimilation.

1. **Reductive amination**

$$\alpha - \text{ketoglutaric acid} + \underset{\text{ammonium}}{NH_4^+} + NAD(P)H$$

$$\xrightarrow[\text{Dehydrogenare}]{\text{Glutamate}} \text{Glutamate} + H_2O + NAD(P)$$

2. **Transamination :** Involves transfer of amino group from one amino acid to the keto group of keto acid. From glutamic acid other 17 amino acids are formed through transamination in the presence of enzyme **transaminase**.

- **Amides :** Amino acids, glutamic acid and aspartic acid takes part in the formation of amides **asparagine** and **glutamine**. The hydroxyl part of the acid is replaced' by any other NH_2 radical and this takes place in the presence of enzyme **glutamine synthetase or asparagine synthetase.**
- **Protein synthesis :** Proteins are nitrogenous compounds containing C, H, O and N. Sometimes P and S are also associated with protein. The amino group of one amino acid attaches to the carboxyl group of its neighbour amino acid. In this process a molecule of water is eliminated and peptide bond (NH–CO–) is formed.
- Proteins consist of one or more chains called **polypeptide chains** each of which consists of hundreds of amino acids.

HETEROTROPHIC NUTRITION

Some plants are incapable of photosynthesizing and obtain water, mineral and certain organic compounds from other autotrophs are called heterotrophs and the nutrition is called heterotrophic nutrition.

1. Parasitic nutrition

Parasites obtains their nutrition from living plants or animals which are called hosts. Parasites may be obligate (total parasite) or partial (semi-parasites).

(A) Obligate parasites : Without chlorophyll, take whole of their nutrition from host.

- Total stem *parasite-Cuscuta*
- Total root *parasite-Orobanche, Balanophora, Raffesia.*

(B) **Partial parasites :** Green, manufacture their own food but depend upon other plants for minerals and water.

- Partial stem *parasite-Viscum album, Loranthus*
- Partial root *parasite-Santalum, Thesium, Striga.*

2. Saprophytic nutrition

Saprophytes obtain their nutrition from dead and rotting organic matter *e.g.,* Many bacteria, fungi mosses, some pteridophytes etc.

- *Neothia* (Bird's nest orchid) : Grows on **humus rich soil**. Roots are associated with ectotrophic mycorrhiza.
- *Monotropa* (Indian Pipe) : Grown on humus rich soil of pine forests, under ground part is associated with endotrophic mycorrhiza.

3. Symbionts

Symbiosis is an association of dissimilar organisms to their mutual advantage *e.g.,* Lichen (association of algae and fungi), a coralloid root of *Cycas,* Mycorrhiza etc.

- **Mycorrhiza :** An association between a fungus and roots of higher plants. Fungus supplies the water and salts to the higher plants and in return obtain the prepared food from the green plants. Such association may be endotrophic or ecto-trophic.

4. Insectivorous plants

Such green plants which obtain their nourishment partly from soil and atmosphere and partly by catching and digesting small insects, the decomposition products of which are rich in nitrogen. The leaves of such plants are modified in various ways for capturing insects. *e.g., Drosera. (sundew), Utricularia* (bladder wort), *Dionaea* (venusfly trap), *Pinguicula* (butterwort), *Nepenthes* (pitcher plant), *Aldrovanda* (water flea trap) etc.

SOME IMPORTANT FACTS

- **Most abundant element :** Oxygen on fresh weight basis and Carbon on dry weight basis.
- **Frame work elements :** Constitute the carbohyrates which form the cell wall *i.e.,* C, H and O.
- **Balancing elements :** Ca, Mg, K -Counteract the toxic effect of other minerals by ion balancing.
- **Protoplasmic elements :** Form part of protoplasm alongwith C, H, O. These are N, and S.
- **Functional elements :** Occur in the range of micro nutrients. These are cobalt, vanadium and aluminium.
- Micronutrients are as important as macro nutrients in plant nutrition.
- Pungent smell of onion and garlic is due to sulphur compounds.
- Deficiency of Mo causes : Whiptail of *Brassica,* scald of beans, water core in turnip.
- Deficiency of Zn causes : Exanthema of fruit trees, mottle leaf of *Citrus,* white bud of maize, sickles leaf or cocoa.
- Deficiency of S causes : Tea yellows.
- Deficiency of Bo Causes : Heart rot of sugarbeet, Corky Core of apple, Water core in turnip, Celery stem crack, Top sickness of tobacco.
- Deficiency of Mn causes : Speckled yellows of beet, marsh spots of peas, gray specks of oats.
- Some plants require other essential elements *e.g.,* silica (grasses and diatoms), sodium (Halophytes and plants rith Cu pathway) **Cobalt** (algae and microbes), Aluminium (ferns and *Lycopodium)* and Iodine (marine algae).
- **Hydroponics :** Solless growth or tank farming or water or solution cutlures. Various scientists suggested suitable media for hydroponics are Sach (1860), Knop (1865), Pfeffer (1900) and Crone (1902). The pH of medium should be 5 - 6. This helps in knowing the essentiality of mineral element, dificiency symptoms developed due to nonavailability of particular nutrient, toxicity to plant when element is present in excess,. role of essential element is the metabolism of plant etc.

- **Aeroponics :** Grouping plants in stands provided with five mist of solution having all the required inorganic nutrients.
- **Liebig's Law of minimum** (Liebig, 1840, father of Biochemistry) Productivity of soil depends upon the proportionate amount of that essential element which is deficient in that soil.
- Deficiency symptoms are also known as **hunger signs.**
- *Aulosirafertilissima : Most* active nitrogen fixer in rice fields.
- **Vanadium** is essential for alga *Scenedesmus.*
- **Rubedium** has chemical properties similar to potassium.
- **Selenium :** Absorbed and accumulated in relatively high concentration by *Astragalus* species.
- **Nickel :** Essential part of enzyme **Urease** which catalyzes hydrolysis or urea to CO_2 to NH_4.
- Most mobile element-**Potassium.** Most immobile element-**Iron.**
- **Phytotran :** Place or laboratory where plants can be maintained and studied under a wide range of controlled conditions.
- **Molybdenum :** Required by plant in least quantity.
- **Gold :** Reported to occur in stem *of Equisetum.*
- **Plant ash :** The ash which is left on heating a dry plant or plant part at 600°C in a crucible which contain oxides and carbonates of elements.
- **Holophytic nutrition :** Photoautotrophic nutrition.
- **Phyllosphere association :** Ruiner (1954-61) observed considerable variety of micro-organisms occurring abundantly on the surface of the leaves of many trees and strubs under humid tropical conditions and suggested that these organisms might fix nitrogen. The environment provided by the wet leaf surface for microbial development was termed by her as **phyllosphere.**
- *Rafflesia : Plant* grows as total root parasite on the roots of figs. Flowers are red in colour, unisexual, borne singly and the largest flowers is plant kingdom (measuring 3 feet in diameter, with 3/4" thickness and 5lb weight.

PHOTOSYNTHESIS

- Synthesis of organic compounds (carbohydrates) from inorganic raw materials (CO_2 and Hydrogen donor) by green plants in the presence of light (solar energy)

$$CO_2 + 2H_2O \xrightarrow[\text{Green plants}]{\text{Light energy}} (CH_2O)_n + H_2O + O_2$$

This equation was given by **C.B. Van Niel** for photosynthesis.

- Only 0.2% of the light energy falling on earth is utilised by photosynthetic organisms.
- **Cyanobacteria:** Where photosynthesis was first appeared.

HISTORY

1. **Aristotle (320 BC) :** Plants get their food only from the soil.
2. **Von Helmont (1648) :** All the substance of the plant was produced from water and none from the soil.
3. **Stephen Hales (1727) :** Air and light are important for nourishment of plants.
4. **Joseph Priestley (1772) :** Plants have ability to take up CO_2 from the atmosphere and release O_2.
5. **Jan Ingenhousz (1779) :** Recognize importance of sunlight and chlorophyll.
6. **Senebier (1782) :** Rate of purification of air depends upon concentration of foul air.
7. **Theodore de Saussure (1804) :** Water also participate in photosynthesis.
8. **Pelletier and Caventou (1818) :** Discovered chlorophyll due to which leaves are green in colour.
9. **Von Mayer (1845) :** Solar energy is changed into chemical energy.
10. **Sachs (1862) :** Starch is formed as a reserve product of photosynthesis.
11. **Engelman (1888) :** Plotted the action spectrum of photosynthesis.
12. **Blackman (1905) :** Proposed law of limiting factors and possibility of two phases of photosynthesis.

13. **Emerson and Arnold (1932) :** Light reaction consists of two distinct photochemical reactions.
14. **Robert Hill (1937) :** Evolution of oxygen does not require carbon dioxide; photolysis of water; light produces assimilatory power.
15. **Ruben, Hassid and Kamen (1941) :** Oxygen evolved in photosynthesis comes from water by using heavy isotope of oxygen *i.e.,* $H_2{}^{18}O$.
16. **Calvin (1954) :** Calvin cycle/C_3 cycle/Calvin Benson cycle with the help Of $^{14}CO_2$ discovered cycle involved in carbon assimilation.
17. **Arnon, Allen and Whatley (1954) :** Demonstrated fixation of CO_2 by chloroplast using $^{14}CO_2$, discovered photophosphorlylation.
18. **Emerson *et.al.* (1957) :** Emerson effect, proposed two photosystems.
19. **Hatch and Slack (1965) :** C_4 cycle for CO_2 fixation.
20. **Huber *et.al.* (1985) :** Crystallised photosynthetic reaction centre of bacterium *Rhodobacter* and got Nobel Prize in 1988.

SITE FOR PHOTOSYNTHESIS

- Mainly leaves, though all green parts containing chloroplasts have the potential to carry on photosynthesis.
- Chlorophyll (green pigment) is present in chloroplasts *i.e.,* localised.

PHOTOSYNTHETIC PIGMENTS: 3 TYPES

(1) Chlorophyll

- Total 9 types; **chlorophyll 'a'** and **chlorophyll 'b'** are important types of chlorophyll.
- **Chlorophyll :** Molecule consist of a porphyrin ring (hydrophilic) and a **phytol** tail (lipophilic).
- **Porphyrin ring :** Flat, square structure having smaller **pyrrole** rings with a magnessium atom at the centre. Chiorophyll ***a*** ($C_{55}H_{72}O_5N_4Mg$) possess a **CH_3 (methyl)** group and chlorophyll ***b*** ($C_{55}H_{70}O_6N_4Mg$) possess a **- CHO (aldehyde)** group. The head is joined to a long' hydrocarbon tail *i.e.,* **Phytol**.
- **Chlorophyll *a* :** most abundant, only pigment in all photosynthetic plants.
- Chlorophyll absorbs light near both ends of the visible spectrum *i.e.,* blue and red light and transmit or reflect green light *i.e.,* why looks green in colour.
- Chlorophyll synthesis in flowering plants require **light** and **iron**.
- Algae, bryophytes, pteridophytes and gymnosperms develop chlorophyll even in absence of light.
- Raw materials for chlorophyll synthesis are glycine (amino acid) and succinyl co-A.
- **Fluorescence :** Isolated chlorophyll a in pure form emits red colour. It is known as fluorescence.
- **Phosphorescence :** The delayed emission of long wave radiation from an activated molecule is called phosphorescence.

(2) Carotenoids

- Yellow to orange pigments, absorb light strongly in the blue-violet range.
- Called shield pigments because protect chlorophyll from photo oxidation by light of high intensity and also from oxygen produced during photosynthesis.
- Absorb light and transfer' it to chlorophyll for use in photosynthesis.
- Two types: ***(a)* Carotenes :** (Orange coloured) - hydrocarbons (tetrapenes)
  ***(b)* Xanthophylls :** (Yellow) - contain oxygen

(3) Phycobilin

- Water soluble, open tetrapyrrole pigments found in red algae and blue green algae.
- Found in phycobilisomes attached to thylakoids and transform light energy to chlorophyll. 3 types *i.e.,* **Phycocyanin** (blue), Allophycocyanin (blue) and Phycoerythrin (red).

Quantasome

- Present as small units on the membranes of thylakoids.
- This term coined by **Park and Biggins** (1964) for a group of pigment molecules required for carrying out a photochemical reaction.

- Each quantasome consists of about **250-300 chlorophyll** molecules, carotenoids, quinone compounds, sulpholipids, phospholipids, proteins etc.

ABSORPTION AND ACTION SPECTRA

- **Action Spectra :** Graph exhibiting the rate of photosynthesis at different wavelengths of light.
- **Absorption Spectra :** Graph depicting amount of light of different wavelengths absorbed by a pigment.
- Close similarity between action spectrum of photosynthesis and absorption spectrum of chlorophyll exhibits that chlorophylls are responsible for absorption of light in photosynthesis.

MECHANISM OF PHOTOSYNTHESIS

Two-phases *i.e.,* light reaction and dark reaction.

(A) Photochemical phase (light reaction or Hill reaction)

- Takes place in thylakoids of grana.
- Solar energy is trapped by chlorophyll and is stored in form of chemical energy (ATP) and as reducing power (NADPH)
- **Photosystems :** Groupings of photosynthetic units which possess photocentres and are surrounded by specific light harvesting pigment molecules. 2 types.
  (a) **Photosystem-I (PS I) :** Present in stroma thylakoid and non-appressed parts of granal thylakoid.
- Photocentre P_{700} along with accessory pigments which absorb at or below 700 nm constitute the PS-I.
  (b) **Photosystem-II (PS II) :** Present in appressed part of gra..al thylakoids.
- Possess chlorophyll ***a,*** chlorophyll ***b*** and carotenoids.
- The cluster of pigment molecules which transfer their energy to P_{680} absorb light at or below the wavelegnth of 680 nm.
- **Light reaction :** in which light energy is transformed by photophosphorylation into chemical energy in the form of the energy source ATP and $NADPH_2$ which is used to reduce CO_2, Takes place in following steps.
  1. Excitation of pigments by light so, that excited pigments lose electrons and become oxidised.

$$\text{Chlorophyll} \xrightarrow{\text{Light energy}} \underset{\text{oxidised}}{\text{Chlorophyll}^+} + \underset{\text{electron}}{e^-}$$

  2. The electron is captured by an electron acceptor. This represent the conversion of light energy into chemical energy. Depending upon whether the electron lost by chlorophyll molecule is returned to it or not, the further events may be cyclic or non-cyclic.

Non-cyclic photophosphorylation (Hill and Bendall proposed Z-scheme for electron transport)

- Light energised ATP synthesis in which the electron expelled by excited photocentres does not return to them.
- Both PS I and PS II are involved.
- Coordinate their activities to produce assimilatory power (ATP and NADPH).
- Oxygen is released during photolysis of water.
- Takes place at one place only.

Cyclic photophosphorylation

- Light energised ATP synthesis in which the electron expelled by excited photo centre is returned to it after passing over a chain of electron carriers.
- It is related to photo act I (PS I) only.
- Electron released from chlorophyll return back.
- There is no photolysis of water and release of oxygen.
- NADP is not oxidised.
- Takes place at two places.
- It occurs under low light conditions, wavelength longer than 680 nm and when CO_2 fixation is being inhabited.

(B) Biosynthetic phase (Dark phase or Blackman's reaction)

- Independent of light and studied by **Blackman** in following steps:
  (a) **Carboxylation** *i.e.,* acceptance of CO_2 by

RuBP - CO_2 receptor, carboxylation of RuBP is catalysed by the enzyme **RuBP carboxylase** or **Rubisco** (most abundant protein on earth).

(b) **Glycolytic reversal :** The 6 molecules of PGA (3 phosphoglyceric acid) utilises 6 ATP molecules to form 6 molecules of 1,3-diphosphoglyceric acid. These, in turn, utilizes 6 NADPH supplied by the light reactions and get converted to a 3-C glyceraldehyde phosphate.

(c) **Regeneration of RuBP :** RuBP is regenerated through the formation of 4-C, 5-C and 7-C intermediates. Five molecules of triose phosphate (TP) and three molecules of ATP are involved in the regeneration of RuBP.

- Dark reaction takes place in stroma. It comprises a series of reactions controlled by enzymes. The sequence of these reactions was determined in *Chlorella* and *Scendesmus* by **Calvin, Benson** and **Bassham** using radioactive carbon ^{14}C and techniques like chromatography and autoradiography. This is also known as **Calvin Cycle** or **Calvin-Benson Cycle** or **C_3 Cycle or Reductive Pentose Pathway or Photosynthetic Carbon Reduction or PCR.**

PHOTORESPIRATION (DICKER AND TIO, 1959)

- Respiration which is initiated in chloroplasts and takes place in light only is called **Photo respiration.**
- The enzyme Rubisco catalyses the carboxylation reaction where CO_2 combines with RuBP, called **oxygenation.**
- Also called **Photosynthetic Carbon Oxidation Cycle** and involves an interaction of three organelles *i.e.,* **chloroplast, peroxisome** and **mitochondria.**
- The function of photorespiration is to recover some of the carbon from the excess glycolate. However, there is a **wasteful loss of carbon** as **CO_2** and **loss of energy.**
- It is stimulated by high light intensity, high temperature, ageing of leaf and high oxygen concentration.
- Two molecules of phosphoglycolate (2C) produced by oxygenation of RuBP are changed into one molecule of phosphoglycerate (3C) and one molecule of CO_2.
- 75% of carbon lost to oxygenation is recovered by PCO cycle.

HATCH-SLACK PATHWAY OR C_4-PATHWAY OR DICARBOXYLIC ACID PATHWAY

- C_4 plants possess a characteristic leaf anatomy **(Kranz anatomy)**. In which vascular bundles are surrounded by two rings of cells *i.e.* **inner ring (bundle sheath cells** having starch-rich chloroplasts lacking grana) and **outer ring (mesophyll cells).**
- It C_4 plants CO_2 is picked up by phosphoenol pyruvate (PEP - 3 Compound) in the **cytoplasm of mesophyll cells** and form **oxaloacetate** (4C) which is converted to malic acid or aspartic acid (4–C) for transport to bundle sheath cells.
- In bundle sheath cells, CO_2 is released and is assimilated through Calvin cycle. Pyruvate is released which passes back into mesophyll cells where PEP is regenerated.
- The C_4 Pathway is more eftlcient than the C_3 pathway due to the absence of photorespiration.

CRASSULACEAN ACID METABOLISM (CAM)

- Takes place in succulents *(e.g.,* Cactus, *Bryophyllum, Kalanchoe, Sedum* etc.) and other plants that normally grow in dry conditions. Such plants have a photosynthetic pathway similar to C_4 plants.
- CO_2 taken up by the leaves on green stems through open stomata during night and fixed as malic acid with the help of **phosphoenol pyruvate.**
- Calvin cycle takes place during the day when stomata are closed. Fomation of malic acid

during dark is called acidification (Phase I) and the release of CO_2 for actual photosynthesis during day is called deacidification (Phase II).

- CAM is a type of adaptation that allows certain plants *(e.g.,* pineapple) to carry out photosynthesis without much loss of water which is inevitable in plants with C_3 and C_4 mechanisms.

FACTORS AFFECTING PHOTOSYNTHESIS

Blackman (1905) Proposed Law of limiting factors which states that "When a biological process is conditioned as to its rapidity by a number of separate factors, the rate of the process is limited by the pace of the slowest factor".

1. Light

Provides energy for photosynthesis.

(i) **Light quality:** Photosynthesis successfully takes place only in the visible light (3800 Å - 7600 Å wave length). Rate of photosynthesis is maximum in red light, average in blue light and minimum in green light.

(ii) **Light intensity :** It has a direct relationship with the rate of photosynthesis. As the intensity of light (μ mol. $m^{-2}s^{-1}$) increases, the rate of photosynthesis increases. At higher light intensities, the rate of photosynthesis decreases.

(iii) **Light duration:** Long continuous periods of light increase the rate of photosynthesis.

2. Carbon dioxide

As the CO_2 concentration increases upto 0.9%, the rate of photosynthesis also increases. At the same time very high concentration of CO_2 becomes toxic to plants and inhibit photosynthesis.

3. Temperature

Generally, the rate of photosynthesis increases by increase in temperature upto 40°C. High temperature results into the deactivation of enzymes and so, the dark reaction is affected. The effect of temperature varies from plant to plant. C_4 plants have higher optimum temperature than C_3 plants. 25-30°C is the optimum temperature for photosynthesis.

4. Water

It rarely act as a limiting factor because less than 1 % of the water absorbed by a plant is used in photosynthesis. Electrons in the photochemical phase are supplied by the water but its availability for photosynthesis depends upon the closure of stomata. However, lowering of photosynthesis has been observed if the plants are inadequately supplied with water.

5. Nutrient supply

Nitrogen has a direct relationship with photosynthesis since it is a basic part of chlorophyll and all enzymes involved in carbon reactions, so any reduction in nitrogen supply leads an adverse effect on photosynthesis. Deficiency of mineral elements *(e.g.,* Mg, Fe, Cl, Cu, Mn, P etc.) ultimately reduces photosynthesis.

6. Chlorophyll

Emerson (1929) found the direct relationship between the chlorophyll content and the rate of photosynthesis.

Willstatter studied **assimilatory number** *i.e.,* **Photosynthesis/chlorophyll unit** in leaves of different ages of plants and the effect of amount of chlorophyll on the rate of photosynthesis. Assimilatory number decreases with the age of the leaf.

7. Leaf Factors

i.e., leaf age, leaf angle and leaf orientation etc. have effect on photosynthesis. Leaf age has the most prominent effect on photosynthesis. Rate of photosynthesis is maximum in just matured leaves but declines with age. In a senescence leaf there is deactivation of enzymes and degeneration of chlorophyll.

TRANSLOCATION OF PHOTOSYNTHATES

- The transport of photosynthates or photoassimilates (energy rich carbon compounds) formed during photosynthesis from the production centres (leaves) to the consumption centres (non-photosynthetic organs *i.e.,* apices, roots, tubers, fruits etc.)

through phloem is called translocation of organic solutes or long distance transport.

- Translocation may be upward, downward and radial in directions from the source to the sink *i.e.,* fruits, tubers, roots, apices etc.) through phloem.
- Photosynthates provides energy to the non-photosynthetic tissues through respiration.

SIGNIFICANCE OF PHOTOSYNTHESIS

- Helps in conversion of solar energy into organic matter.
- Consumes atmospheric carbon dioxide and yields carbohydrates and molecular oxygen.
- Evolves molecular oxygen for use by other living organisms and maintains the level of atmospheric oxygen which is continuously consumed by plants and animals during respiration.
- Produces carbohydrates and used by plants and animals to synthesize organic acids, proteins, fats, nucleic acids, pigments, hormones, vitamins, alkaloids and other metabolites.

CHEMOSYNTHESIS

Such reactions in which reduction of carbon dioxide to carbohydrates does not require light and takes place in presence of energy obtained from oxidations of inorganic substances is called **chemosynthesis** *e.g.,* **Nitrifying bacteria** *(Nitrosomonas, Nitrosococcus)* obtain energy by oxidising ammonia to nitrites), sulphur bacteria *(e.g., Beggiatoa* convert H_2S to sulphur), Carbon monooxide bacteria *(e.g., Carboxydomonas* convert CO to CO_2), **methane bacteria** *(e.g., Methanococcus* oxidise methane into CO_2 and HzO) etc.

SOME IMPORTANT FACTS

- **Compensation point :** The light intensity at which rate of photosynthesis is equal to the rate of respiration *i.e.,* in morning, in evening.
- **Photosynthesis :** Anabolic, endergonic, oxidation - reduction process.
- **NADP :** Acts as hydrogen acceptor during photosynthesis in plant cells.
- **Rubisco :** RuBP carboxylase enzyme, is a large protein molecule and constitute about 16% of the chloroplast protein and is the most abundant protein on the earth.
- Grass Alloteropsis semi-alata possess both C_3 and C_4 ecotypes.
- **Fret membranes:** Membranes of thylakoids.
- Plastidome: Plastid complex of a cell.
- **Keilin (1925) :** Coined the term cytochrome.
- Electrons accepted from reaction centres by the acceptors are passed down hill through the electron transport chain.
- The reaction centre of PS II is P_{680} (or chlorophyll a_{680}) and that of PS I is P_{700} (or chlorophyll a_{700}).
- **Assimilatory power :** NADPH + H^+ produced in light reaction constitute assimilatory power *i.e.,* reducing power.
- **Redox potential :** The tendency of an atom/molecule to give or take up electrons. Electrons move from substances having low redox potentials to those having high redox potentials.
- In C_3 plants, more CO_2 is released in light than in dark (due to photorespiration).
- **Solarisation :** Destruction of chlorophyll due to high light intensity.
- **Carbon dioxide :** Most common limiting factor for photosynthesis.
- Only 0.2% of the light energy falling on the earth is utilised by photosynthetic organisms.
- The reaction centre in bacteria is B-890.
- The size of quantosome is about 180 × 155 × 100 Å.
- DCMU (Dichlorophenyl dimethyl Urea) – a herbicide which inhibits PS II and oxygen release in light phase.
- Calvin cycle is exhibited by *A triplex rose us* whereas Hatch-Slack cycle is exhibited by *A. hastata.*
- In bacteria only one ATP molecule is generated during cyclic or non-cyclic electron transport.
- **K^+ ions :** Helps in the translocation of solutes.
- Annually, about 75 × 1012 kg of carbon (in the form of CO) is fixed through

photosynthesis, producing about 1700 million tonnes of dry matter. About 90% of it is carried out in the oceans (mostly by the phytoplanktons and algae).

- **Photosynthetic material :** 264 g of CO_2 and 216 g of water give rise to 108 g of water, 192 g of O_2 and 180 g of glucose.
- **PEP or Phosphoenol pyruvate :** Primary CO_2 acceptor in C_4 and CAM plants. Combination of CO_2 and PEP is called **initial fixation.** It takes place in me ophyll cells and the enzyme is pepco.
- **RuBP or ribulose biphosphate :** Secondary/ final, CO_2 acceptor in C_4 and CAM plants. The phenomenon is called final fixation. It takes place in bundle sheath chloroplasts of C_4 plants and mesophyll cells in CAM plants and the enzyme is **rubisco.**
- **C.G. Strokes (1864) :** first to separate pure fractions of Chlorophyll ***a*** and Chlorophyll ***b***.
- Protochlorophyllide *a* is reduced to chlorophyllide a in presence of light and then esterified with phytol group to form chlorophyll.
- Orange wavelength (586-647 nm) are least absorbed and also least effective.
- T.W. Englemann (1880) determined the approximate action spectrum of photosynthesis.

RESPIRATION AND PHOTORESPIRATION

INTRODUCTION

Respiration

It is an energy liberating enzymatically controlled multistep catabolic process of stepwise breakdown of organic substances inside the living cells.

Respiratory Substrates

The organic substances which can be catabolised to liberate energy inside the living cells *e.g.*, carbohydrates, fats and proteins.

Type of respiration

1. **Aerobic :** Takes place inside the mitochondria in the presence of molecular oxygen in most of plants and animals called aerobes. Divided into 4 phases-Glycolysis, oxidative decarboxylation, Krebs or TCA cycle and Electron Transport system.
2. **Anaerobic (Fermentation) :** Involves the production of energy from the food nutrients in the absence of oxygen.

Respiratory Ratio or quotient (RQ)

The ratio of the volume of carbon dioxide released to the volume of oxygen taken in respiration in the given period of time at standard temperature and pressure.

$$RQ = \frac{\text{Moles of } CO_2 \text{ produced}}{\text{Moles of } O_2 \text{ absorbed}}$$

It provides the nature of the substrate being respired by a particular tissue.

(1) Carbohydrate RQ = 1 or unity
(2) Fats RQ = 0.7 *i.e.,* less than one
(3) Proteins RQ = less than unity (usually 0.5 to 0.9)
(4) Fermentation RQ = ∞ or infinity
(5) Succulents RQ = 0 or zero
(6) Maturing fatty seeds RQ = more than one
(7) Organic acids RQ = more than one
(8) Germinating fatty seeds RQ = less than one

MECHANISM OF RESPIRATION

- Glycolysis (splitting of sugar) results in the break down of glucose molecules into pyruvic acid.
- Completed in the **cytoplasm** of the living cells.
- Also known as **Embden-Meyerhof-Parnas** (EMP) pathway.
- 3 steps.
  1. **Phosphorylation of Glucose :** Initial, 6-carbon sugar is transformed into 6-carbon sugar diphosphate. This addition of phosphate groups is called phosphorylation, it activates the sugar and preventing it from getting out of the cell.
  2. **Splitting of fructose-I, 6-diphosphate :** Fructose-l, 6-diphosphate is broken down into two molecules of 3-carbon sugar phosphates *i.e.,* dihydroxy acetone

phosphate and glyceraldehyde-3-phosphate (undergoes further glycolysis). Both the molecules are interconvertible.

3. Formation of Pyruvic acid-3-phosphoglyceraldehyde in combination with one inorganic phosphate and coenzyme NAD is converted into 1, 3-diphosphoglyceric acid which is dephosphorylated to 3-phosphoglyceric acid and further changed to 2-phosphoglyceric acid. On dehydration 2-phosphoglyceric acid forms phosphoenol pyruvate or PEP which transformed to pyruvic acid.

- In glycolysis, a molecule of glucose is broken down to two molecules of pyruvic acid. There is gain of 2NADH and 2ATP or equivalent to 8 ATP.

Fate of pyruvic acid during aerobic respiration

Each pyruvic acid molecule enters a **mitochondrion** where its oxidation is completed. Pyruvic acid molecule undergoes oxidative decarboxylation *i.e.*, removal of CO_2 from pyruvic acid and oxidation of pyruvic acid by dehydrogenation. The 2-carbon fragment combines (7.64) with coenzyme **A** and form Acetyl coenzyme **A**. During this process, two molecules of NADH are produced and results in a net gain of6ATP molecules.

Fate of pyruvic acid during anaerobic respiration

- When oxygen is limiting, NADH and pyruvic acid begin to accumulate.
- Under anaerobic conditon plants carry out **fermentation** and leading to the formation of CO_2 and either ethanol or lactic acid.
- Pyruvic acid releases one molecule of CO_2 to produce acetaldehyde which reoxideses NADH and itself reduced to ethanol.
- These reaction are catalysed by **pyruvic acid decarboxylase and alcohol dehydrogenase enzymes.**
- Net yield of ATP in anaerobic respiration is of only 2 molecules of ATP that too during glycolysis is anaerobic respiration.

CITRIC ACID CYCLE

(Tricarboxylic acid or TCA cycle or Kreb's cycle).

- Sir Hans Krebs (1937) discovered the second phase in the aerobic oxidation of pyruvic acid. Got Nobel prize in 1953 (Fig. 1).

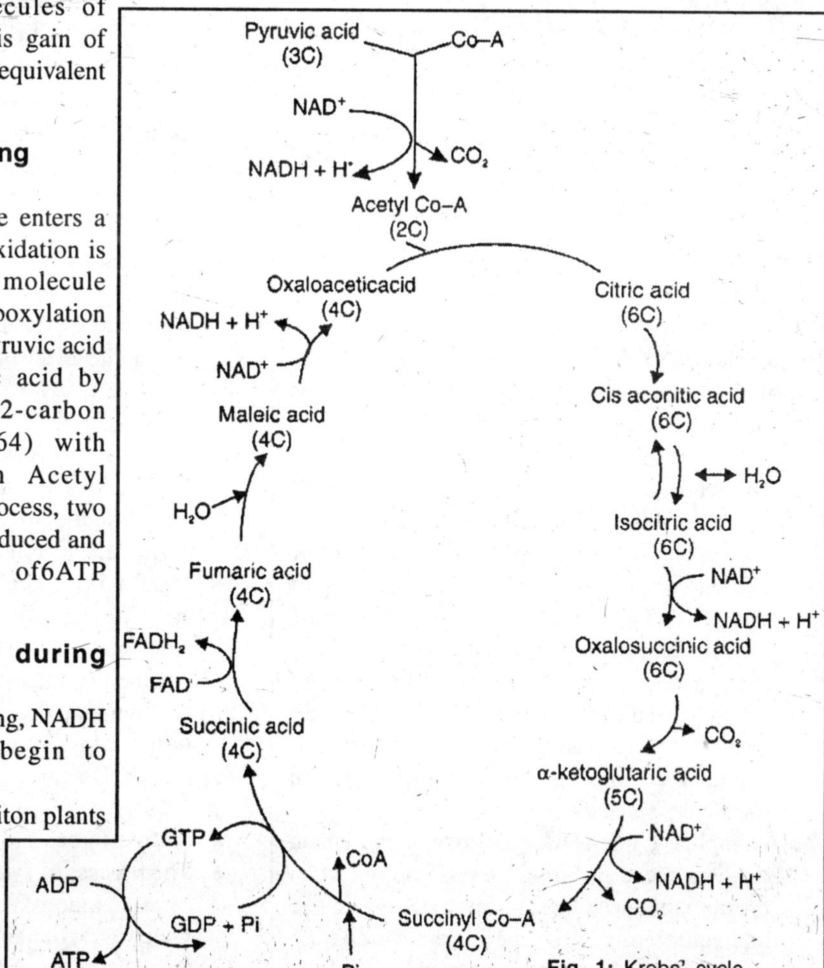

Fig. 1: Krebs' cycle

- It takes place in the matrix of mitochondria.
- Acetyl Co-A is a common intermediate of carbohydrate and fat metabolism, it is a substrate entrant of Kreb's cycle or connecting link between glycolysis and Krebs' cycle.
- Acetyl CoA produced not only from pyruvic acid but also that produced as a result of β-oxidation of fatty acids undergoes TCA cycle.
- Enzymes required for cycle are present in the matrix of mitochondria.
- In total there are five oxidations and three decarboxylations (one decarboxylation and one oxidation outside Kreb's cycle)
- The net products from two pyruvates are 8NADH, 2FADH2 and 2ATP *i.e.,* 30 ATP/15 per pyruvic acid or in Krebs' cycle 24 ATP/ 12 per acetyl Co-A.
- Krebs' cycle is also called amphibolic (both catabolic and anabolic) because a number of Krebs' cycle intermediates are used in anabolic pathways.

ELECTRONS TRANSPORT SYSTEM (ETS) AND OXIDATIVE PHOSPHORYLATION

- Terminal oxidation takes plae is two steps *i.e.,* electron transport and oxidative phosphory-lation.
- **Electron transport system (ETS) :** Through which the electron passes from one carrier to another and takes place in the inner mitochondrial membrane. ETS consists of flavins, FeS complex, quinones (Ubiquinone or CoQ) and cytochromes (cyt b, cyt c, cyt c] cyt a and cyt a). Cytochromes possess iron which can undergoes $Fe^{2+} \rightarrow Fe^{3+} \rightarrow Fe^{2+}$ change during passage of electrons. cyt a_3 additionally contains copper which helps in transferring electrons to oxygen.
- **Complex I : NADH dehydrogenase** which oxidises electrons from NADH produced in the mitochondrial matrix, during Kreb's cycle and electrons are then transferred to ubiquinone in the inner membrane.
- **Complex II : Succinate dehydrogenase** – Ubiquinone receives electrons from NADH and also by reducing equivalents via $FADH_2$ which is generated during oxidation of succinate, through the activity of the enzyme succinate dehydrogenase.
- **Complex III : Dihydroubiquinone, cytochrome** oxidoreductase and two forms of **cytochrome b and cytochrome c_1** The reduced ubiquinone (ubiquinol) is oxidised with the transfer of electrons to cytochrome c via this complex.
- **Complex IV : Cytochrome c, Cytochrome oxidase, cytochrme a, cytochrome a_3 and two copper centres :** Electrons are handed over to cyt C_1 → cyt c → cyt a → cyt a_3. Both cyt a and cyt a_3 fuction as cytochrome oxidase and handover electrons to oxygen. Reduced coenzyme NADH + H^+ helps is pushing out 3 pairs of H^+ to outer chamber while $FADH_2$ sends two pairs of H^+ to outer chamber.
- Cytochrome c acts as mobile carrier for transfer of electrons between complex III and IV.
- **Complex V : ATP synthase**–Electrons pass from one carrier to another via complex I to IV in the electron transport chain, they are coupled to ATP synthase for the production of ATP from ADP and inorganic phosphate.
- 3 pairs of protons ($6H^+$) are transported from mitochondrial matrix to outer side of the inner mitochondrial membrane. The energy released during electron transfer is used for this work.
- **Oxidative phosphorylation:** The accumulation of protons outside the inner membrane results in their higher concentration outside the inner membrane than in the matrix creating a **proton gradient** (Δ.pH) and **electric potential** (Δ.ψ) across the membrane.
- Energy liberated during electron transport in used is building a proton gradient or proton motive force (PMF) in the outer membrane.
- The process of synthesis of ATP at the expense of proton motive force is called chemiosmosis which is explained by Mitchell (1961, Nobel Prize 1978).

- Protons can not diffuse back into the matrix across the membrane but can enter the membrane via a proton channel established by the membrane bound **adenosine triphosphatase** (ATPase).
- ATPase is a multienzyme complex containing two parts F_0 and $F_1.F_1$ (acting as ATP sythethase) catalyses the synthesis of ATP from ADP. For each pair of protons flowing back into the matrix, one molecule ofATP is synthesized.
- F_0 is an integral membrane protein complex that forms the channel through which protons cross the inner membrane.
- $FADH_2$ donates its electrons to CoQ and not to FMN, only 4 protons are transported outside the membrane. Therefore, the back flow of these 4 protons through $F_0 - F_1$ complex results in the formation of only 2 ATP molecules.
- Total 38 ATP molecules are yielded during aerobic respiration of glucose. In most eukaryotic cells, 2 ATP molecules are expended in transporting the NADH produced in glycolysis into the mitochondrion for further oxidation in such cells, the net gain of **36 ATP** molecules instead of 38.

Pentose pathway (Pentose phosphate pathway (PPP) or Hexose monophosphate (HMP) shunt or Warburg Dickens pathway

- Takes place mainly in liver, lactating mammary glands, adipose tissues, adrenal cortex, gonads and erythrocytes.
- Takes place in the cytoplasm like glycolysis.
- This starts with a 6-carbon sugar, **glucose 6-phosphate** formed by phosphorylation of simple glucose with the help of hexokinase and ATP, and produces **5-carbon sugar, ribose 5-phosphate.**
- Six molecules of glucose produce via HMP shunt as much energy as produced by one glucose molecule via glycolysis and Kreb's cycle.
- Ribulose 5-phosphate formed in this pathway is of major importance in reaction involved in photosynthesis.

COMPENSATION POINT

- At given low concentration of CO_2 and non-limiting light intensity, the photosynthetic rate of a given plant will be equal to the total amount of respiration.
- **CO_2 compensation point :** The atmospheric concentration of CO_2 at which photosynthesis just compensates for respiration
- CO_2 compensation point is reached when the amount of CO_2 uptake is equal to that generated through respiration at a non limiting light intensity.
- The CO_2 compensation point is usually much higher in C_3 plants (25-100 $\mu l.l^{-1}$) as compared to C_4 plants (less than 5 $\mu l.l^{-1}$).

FACTORS AFFECTING RESPIRATION

1. **Temperature :** Affecting the activity of enzymes. $Q_{10} = 2$ or 3. Optimum temperature is 20 – 30°C. At high temperature the rate of respiration declines with time and at very low temperature, the respiration rate is insignificant.
2. **CO_2 :** Increase in CO_2 concentration and absence of O_2 adversely affect the rate of aerobic respiration.
3. **Light :** Control respiration by raising the temperature of an organism.
4. **O_2-Extinction point :** *i.e.,* minimum oxygen concentration at which aerobic respiration takes place which is 3 - 10% of oxygen. In some cases a direct relation between the respiration rate and oxygen concentration has been reported.
5. **Water :** Very low water content in dry seeds and stored tubers is responsible for very feeble rate of respiration. In wilted tissues the stored starch converted into sugars which increase the rate of respiration while in well hydrated plants the rate of respiration is not likely to be affected much by slight changes in the water content.
6. **Respiratory substrates :** Higher availability of respiratory substrates increases the rate of respiration upto a certain limit.

7. **Stimulation :** Mechanical disturbance, injury or infection increases respiration. Hopkins (1927) found that in wounded plant tissue the sugar content is suddenly increased which is responsible for temporary increase in the respiration rate.
8. **Climacteric fruits :** Such fruits have high rate of respiration during their ripening *e.g.*, Banana, Apple.
9. **Inhibitors :** A number of chemicals inhibit respiration *e.g.*, azide, cyanide, malonate, carbon monoxide etc.
10. **Protoplasmic factor :** Young growing cells exhibit high rate of respiration as compared to mature cells.

SOME IMPORTANT FACTS

- **Floating respiration :** Carbohydrates and fats are used as respiratory substrates.
- **Protoplasmic respiration (Blackman) :** Proteins are used as respiratory substrates.
- The energy present in one gran1 of different respiratory substrates is-
  Carbohydrates: 4.4 kcal or 18.4 kJ.
  Fats: 9.8 kcal or41 kJ.
  Proteins: 4.8 kcal or 20 kJ.
- **Lohmann** discovered ATP in 1929 and coined it in 1931.
- **Lipmann (1941) :** discovered ATP cycle.
- **Gaylussac :** To measure rate of respiration.
- Viruses do not exhibit respiration.
- **Pasteur effect (Louis Pasteur) :** A sudden change from anaerobic to aerobic respiration due to availability of oxygen.
- **α-Ketoglutaric acid :** An organic acid, undergoes both dehydrogenation and decarboxylation and is first dicarboxylic acid formed during Kreb's cycle.
- **Mercury (Hg) :** Used in anaerobic respiration experiments because it does not react with CO_2.
- **Oligomycin :** Inhibits oxidative phosphorylation *i.e.*, energy transfer inhibitor.
- **Meldrum :** Wrote book **"Cellular Respiration"**.
- **Glyoxylate cycle :** Takes place in seeds that contains tissues rich in fat and enable stored fat to be converted into carbohydrates. Enzymes for the cycle are present in glyoxysomes.
- Cyanide resistant respiration is characteristic of plants and very useful for **climacteric action** (*i.e.*, helpful in fruit ripening.)
- **Red or dark muscles :** Store myoglobin and hence oxygen for meeting the gap between supply and consumption during continuous activity.
- **White or pale muscles :** Do not store much myoglobin.
- **Lactic acid fermentation :** In muscles, pyruvic acid is reduced by NADH to form lactic acid which is catalysed by enzyme lactic dehydrogenase. Net gain is 2 ATP molecules per glucose molecule.
- **Zymase :** Enzyme complex present in yeast which helps in fermentation (zymosis)
- Some of the energy liberated during respiration is wasted as heat.
- **Proton motive force :** Proton gradient + electric potential.
- **Dinitrophenol (DNP) :** Inhibits ATP synthesis *i.e.*, uncoupling of oxidative phosphorylation.
- Mammalian RBCs are usually without mitochondria, so these show glycolytic pathway.
- **Cardiac muscles :** Fatigueless because have enzyme which can convert lactic acid into pyruvic acid to bel used in aerobic respiraton.
- **Robinson's ester :** Glucose - 6 - P.
- **Newber's ester :** Fructose- 6 - P.
- **Harden and Young ester :** Fructose - I, 6-DiP.
- **Fermentation :** 2 types *i.e.*, **Homofermentative** (when only one end-product) and **Heterofermentive** (when two or more than two types of end-products).
- **Kostychev (1902) :** gave term anaerobic respiration.
- Respiration is regulated by : Regulatory enzymes of cell respiration (phospho fructokinase) ; inhibited by ATP build up. while activated by excess of ADP ; Allosteric inhibition or negative feed back by

accumulation of $NADH_2$ and decreased in dark and by high sugar solution (osmotic effect).

- Cut surfaces of apple becomes dark as tannins are oxidised to polyphenols in the presence of iron of knife. which is prevented by ascorbic acid (vitamin C) as it acts as anti-oxidant.
- In bacteria, mesosomes are sites of ATP synthesis.

SENSORY PHOTOBIOLOGY

INTRODUCTION

- **Plant growth** : A vital process which brings about a slow, permanent and irreversible increase in size or volume or mass accompanied by an increase in dry weight.
- **Development** : A process in which there is sequence of qualitative changes, towards a higher or more complex state. Plants exhibit a regular sequence of seed germination, growth, differentiation, maturation, seed formation and senescence.
- The growth of a multicellular organism can be divided into 3 phases *i.e.,* cell division, cell expansion and cell differentiation.

DORMANCY AND SEED GERMINATION

- Internal inhibition of germination of an otherwise viable seed even when it is placed in most favourable external conditions is called as **dormancy.**
- The suspension of growth of a viable seed may be due to exogenous control such as a change in environmental conditions and is called as **quiescence.**
- **Dormancy of seed** may be due to : Tough seed coats (*e.g., Capsella, Lepidium*), rudimentary embryos (*Eranthis hiemalis*), impermeable seed coat (*Chenopodium, Brassica, Xanthium*), mechanically resistant seed coats, excess salts (*Atriplex*), after ripening (Oat, Barley, Wheat/and even by the presence of germination inhibitors *e.g.,* abscisic acid, phenolic acids, short-chain fatty acids and coumarin).
- **Natural breaking of seed dormancy** : Leaching of inhibitors and salts ; development and after-ripening of embryo ; development of growth hormones ; destruction of inhibitors by heat, cold, light and oxidation ; weakening of impermeable and tough seed coats by mechanical abrasions, microbial activity and digestive eyzymes of the alimentary canal of animals.
- **Artificial breaking of seed dormancy** : By mechanical scarification (machine threshing, chipping or filing), chemical scarification (hot water, fat solvents, mineral acid etc.), vigrous shaking, pressure (about 2000 kg for 5-20 min), chilling treatment, light (red light breaks domancy and induces seed germination in Lettuce and Tobacco), counter acting inhibitors (soaking seeds in KNO_3, thiourea, ethylene chlorohydrin, gibberellin etc.).
- **Seed germination** : This is the first step towards plant growth. After seed dormancy and necessary conditions for growth are present, the dormant embryo resumes metabolic activities and growth. This process is called **seed germination.**
- **Water, oxygen and temperature** are the essential condition for seed germination. **Red region** of visible spectrum is most effective for the onset of seed germination.
- **Internal factors** for seed germination are completion of after-ripening, completion of seed-dormancy, maturity of embryo, presence of sufficient food and viability.
- **Vivipary** : Phenomenon of producing young ones in advanced state of development. Seed germinate inside the fruit, while still attached to the parent plant. It is found in mangrove plants *e.g., Rhizophora, Sonneratia* and *Heritiera,* such plants grow in marshy land. The seedling of such plant is heavy and falls down into salt rich marshy water with plumule remaining outside.

CHARACTERISTICS OF GROWTH

- **Primary growth** : Formation of primary permanent tissues and organs which is caused by activity of apical and intercalary meristems.
- **Secondary growth** : Initiated by cambium, which are essentially lateral meristem (vascular cambium and cork cambium) *i.e.,* increase in girth.

- **Limited growth** : Growth which stops after some time *e.g.,* leaves, flowers, fruits.
- **Unlimited growth** : Growth that continues throughout life as in case of root and stem.
- **Efficiency index** : is the rate of growth which can be measured by an increase in size or area of an organ of the plant, like leaf, flower and fruit in a unit time.
- The supply of nutrients, water, oxygen, suitable temperature and light are necessary for proper growth.
- The force of gravity and light determines the direction of root and shoot growth.
- Salt, mineral deficiencies and stress factors also influence the rate of growth.

PHASES OF GROWTH

- In plants, the growth in length is due to enlargement and elongation of cells at the apical regions and in thickness due to the activity of lateral and intercalary meristems.
- In unicellular organisms growth consists of a single step while in higher plants, growth involves three steps or phases *i.e.,* **phase of cell division** (formative phase), **phase of cell enlargement** (elongation phase) and **phase of cell maturation** (maturation phase). The phases are also known as **regions.**
- **Grand period of growth** : time internal from the formative phase to maturation phase.
- **Growth curve** : The mathematical curve which represents the variation in growth rate, it is somewhat flattened S-shaped curve (sigmoid growth curve). It is differentiated into three phases :
  (A) Lag phase (slow phase)
  (B) Logphase (exponential phase)
  (C) Stationary phase (steady state)

MEASUREMENT OF GROWTH

- **Horizontal microscope** : Used to measure growth in length of a potted plant and herb/ seedling.
- **Auxanometer** : Devised to measure the growth in length of a plant.
- Growth in plants can be measured in terms of
  (*i*) Increase in the length of girth (in case of stem and root).
  (*ii*) Increase in fresh or dry weight.
  (*iii*) Increase in area or volume (in case of fruits and leaves) or
  (*iv*) Increase in number of cells produced.
- **Growth regulators** : In all plant, minute quantities of some chemical substances (plant growth regulators or phytohormones) are present which regulate growth and differentiation. These are organic compounds and are capable of influencing physiological activities leading to promotion, inhibition and modification of growth.

Major types of Growth substances

1. Auxins : related to cell enlargement and differentiation.
2. Gibberellins : related to cell enlargement and differentiation.
3. Cytokinins : related to cell division.
4. Ethylene : related with senescence.
5. Abscisic acid : related to resting states like lateral buds.

Other related growth regulators are Jasmenic acid, Salicylic acid and Brassinosteroids.

PLANT HORMONES

AUXIN

- Weak organic acids with the acidic group.
- Indole-3-acetic acid (IAA) and other natural or synthetic growth regulating substances having structures and functions similar to IAA are called **auxins.**
- **First plant growth hormone** to be discovered.
- First indication of their existence came from the work of **Darwin** (1880).
- **F.W. Went** (1928) proved that the coleoptile tips contained a substance **auxin** and found that the degree of curvature of coleoptile is proportional to the amount of active substance in the agar blocks. This test is known as **avena curvature test.**

- Maximum concentration of auxins are found in the growing tips of the plant. From tip, it is transported **towards the base.**
- Same concentration of auxin exhibit different responses in different parts of the plant.

Functions

Cell elongation (stimulate the cell walls to stretch in more than one directions) ; **cell division** (in the vascular cambium that results in secondary growth); **phototropism ; geotropism** (high concentrations of auxins are stimulatory for stem *i.e.,* negatively geotropic, on the other hand, higher concentrations of auxins are inhibitory for roots *i.e.,* positively geotropic) ; **apical dominance** (auxins in apical bud inhibit the development of lateral buds) ; **prevention of abscission layer** (leaves and fruits have to produce auxin continuously to prevent the formation of abscission layer) and **root initiation** (very low concentration of auxins promote the growth of root).

Uses of Some Synthetic Auxins

Type of Auxin	Examples	Uses
Indoles and Napthyls	NAA (Naphthalene acetic acid)	1. Flower initiation in litchi and pineapple 2. Root initiation in cuttings. 3. Help in natural fruit setting. 4. Methyl ester of NAA is used to prevent sprouting of potatoes.
	IBA (Indole butyric acid)	1. Induces rooting of cuttings.
	IPA (Indole propionic acid)	1. Induces rooting of cuttings. 2. Help in natural fruit setting.
Phenoxyacetic acids	2, 4–D (2, 4-dichlorophenoxyacetic acid)	1. Flower initiation in litchi and pineapple 2. Prevents fruit drop (abscission) 3. Selective weed killer *i.e.,* kills broad leaved plant (dicots) but does not affect mature monocots
Benzoic acids	2, 3, 6-trichlorobenzoic acid 2, 4, 6-trichlorobenzoic acid	Powerful weed killers

- Auxin treated plants have been found to develop fruits even in the absence of pollination and seeds.
- Auxins stimulate the activity of enzymes. They exhibit inhibitory effect on isoenzymes like peroxidase in tobacco.
- **Auxin precursors** : Compounds which can be converted into auxins.
- **Anti-auxins** : Compounds which inhibit the actions of auxins.
- **Free-auxins** : Auxins which can easily be extracted. Active form.
- **Bound-auxins** : Auxins which are hard to extract and need the use of organic solvents. Inactive in growth.
- **Auxin bioassays** : The *Avena* curvature test and root growth inhibition test are the bioassays for examining auxin activity.

GIBBERELLINS (GA)

- The discovery of gibberellin (GA) was based upon the observations made in Japan in early 1800s on the **bakane** or **foolish seedling disease of rice.**
- Widely distributed in nature particularly in angiosperms.
- Chemically, all GA are **terpenes** and weak acids.
- Found in abundance in young, expanding organs; being synthesised especially in embryos, young apical leaves, buds seeds and root tips.

Functions

Overcoming genetic dwarfism (help in stem elongation) ; **bolting (elongation of intermodes to floweing in hosette plants) and flowering** (*e.g.*, Cabbage) ; **breaking of dormancy and germination of seeds** (after imbibition of water, the embryo secretes gibberellin which diffuses to the aleurone layer, stimulating the synthesis of several enzymes including amylase, proteases, lipases) ; **breaking of bud dormancy ; control of flowering** (promote flowering in some long days plants even under short day conditions, **control of fruit growth; promoting growth** (in both stems and leaves) ; **overcoming vernalisation; stimulate maleness** (*e.g.*, cucurbits and *Cannabis*) ; **increases fruit yield** etc.

- Gibberellin bioassay is performed through **dwarf maize/pea test** and **cereal endosperm test.**
- **Yabuta** (1935) coined the term gibberellin.
- About 100 different types of gibberellins have been isolated. They are denoted as GA_1, GA_2, GA_3 and so on.
- Antigibberellins like **maleic hydrazide, phosphon D** and **chorocholins chloride** (CCC) are also called **antiretardants.**

CYTOKININS

- **Skoog** (1954 – 1956) found that coconut milk contained a substance which stimulated cell division in **tobacco pith cultures.**
- Miller and his colleagues isolated and purified the substance in crystalline form from **herring sperm DNA.** This substance was identified as **6-furfuryl aminopurine.** They named this compound **kinetin** because of its property to activate cell division (cytokinesis).
- First naturally occurring cytokinin to be chemically identified was from young maize (*Zea mays*) grains in 1963, and was called **zeatin.**
- Cytokinins are quite abundant wherever rapid cell division occurs, especially in growing tissues such as embryos, developing fruits and roots. In mature plants, these are frequently synthesized in the **roots** and move to the shoots through xylem.
- **Functions : Cell division and differentiation** (in the presence of auxins, cytokinin promote cell division even in non-meristematic tissues) ; **control of apical dominance** (cytokinin stimulate the growth of lateral buds) ; **delaying senescence** (by controlling protein synthesis and mobilisation of resources) ; **induce flowering ; breaking the dormancy of seeds** and **initiation of interfascicular cambium.**
- The common bioassays for cytokinins include promotion of cell division in tobacco pith culture, expansion of excised radish cotyledons, delay in senescence etc.

ETHYLENE

- Crocker *et. al.* (1935) identified ethylene as natural plant hormone.
- Ethylene is formed from amino acid **methionine.**
- **Auxin IAA** is known to stimulate ethylene formation.
- **Only gaseous** natural plant growth regulator.
- It does not generally move through the air spaces in the plants. Rather, it escapes from the plants surface.

Functions

Apical dominance (in pea seedlings and suppresses the growth of apical buds) ; **stem swelling** (transverse expansion of stem) ; **leaf abscission** (formation of abscission zone is leaves, flowers and fruits) ; **epinasty** (leaf bending) ; **fruit growth and ripening** (a rise in the rate of respiration) ; **accelerates flowering ; sex expression** (increases the number of female flowers and fruits in cucumber plants) and **graviperception** (reduces sensitivity to gravity, seeddlings develop tight epicotyl hook).

- Commercial compound **"Ethaphone** (2-chloroethyl phosphoric acid) breaks down to release ethylene in plants.

ABSCISIC ACID (ABA)

- Fredericle Addicott (1963) and P.F. Wareing (1964) discovered this hormone.
- Liu and Crans (1961) isolated ABA from mature cotton fruit.

- It is slso called stress hormone or dormin because the production of hormone is stimulated by drought, water logging and other adverse environmental condition.
- Chemically, ABA is a **Terpenoid.**
- ABA synthesized in the leaves, stems, fruits and seeds and distributed through the vascular system especially phloem.
- Isolated chloroplasts can synthesize it either from mevalonic acid or xanthophyll like violoxanthin.

Functions

Growth inhibitor (antagonistic to all the three growth promoters) ; **bud dormancy** (by inhibiting growth processes) ; **senescence** (of leaves) ; **abscission** (of leaves, flowers and fruits in plants) ; **stomatal closure ; hardiness** (promotes cold hardiness and inhibits growth of pathogens) ; **promotes flowering** (in some short day plants) etc.

- It is a **stress hormone** *i.e.,* helps the plants to cope with adverse environmental conditions.
- ABA is sprayed on tree crops to regulate fruit drop at the end of the season.

VITAMINS

- Heterogenous group of organic compounds, needed in very small quantities for different metabolic processes.
- Plant store the vitamins in different plant organs.
- Most of the vitamins function as coenzymes and prosthetic groups of various enzymes connected with protein, fat and carbohydrate metabolism.
- Some important examples of vitamins are : vitamins A, B, C, D, E and K.
- Some vitamins are essential in maintaining cell membranes and acting as antioxidants.

PHOTOPERIODISM

- The response of plants to the relative lengths and alternations of light and dark periods with regard to the initiation of flowering is called photoperiodism.
- The effect of photoperiods on flowering was discovered by **Garner** and **Allard** (1920) in case of Maryland Mammoth variety of Tobacco (an SDP).
- On the basis of length of photoperoid requirements of plants, the plants have been classified into :
  - (A) **Short-day plants (SDP)** : Plants requiring light for a shorter period than their critical period *e.g., Xanthium, Glycine max,* Rice, Potato, Tobacco etc.
  - (B) **Long-day plants (LDP)** : Plants requiring longer exposure to light than their critical period *e.g,* Lettuce, Radish, Sugarbeet, Oat, Wheat etc.
  - (C) **Day-neutral or intermediate day plants (DNP)** : Plants which would flower irrespective of the photoperiod, once they are mature *e.g.,* Cucumber, Tomato, Maize, Cotton etc.
  - (C) **Short-long day plants (SLDP)** : Plants requiring first short days and then long days *e.g., Trifolium repens, Campanula medium* etc.
  - (E) **Long-short day plants (LSDP)** : Long photoperiods for initiation of flowering and short photoperiods for blossoming *e.g., Bryophyllum, Cestrum* etc.
- **Critical dark period** : It is actually the length of dark period which is critical.
- **Critical day length** : Continuous duration of light which must always be exceeded in long day plants and must not be exceeded in short-day plants.
- **Short-night plants (SNP)** : Long day plants do not require any continuous dark period.
- **Long-night plants (LNP)** : Short-day plants and any interruption of critical dark period even by a flash of light prevents flowering. The reaction is called **light break reaction.**
- **Photoperiodic induction** : Phenomenon of perceiving approriate light periods and obtaining the stimulus of flowering.

- **Flowering hormone** : Chailakhyan (1937) proposed the view that flower hormone namely **florigen** in synthesized in the leaves under favourable photoperiodic conditions. This hormone is transmitted to the growing point where the flowering takes place.

VERNALIZATION

- Term **Vernalization** was coined by **Lysenko** (1928) to refer to the method of accelerating the flowering ability of biennials or winter annuals, by exposing their soaked seeds to low temperature for a few weeks.
- The various requirements of vernalization are:
  (*i*) Actively dividing cells
  (*ii*) Proper nourishment
  (*iii*) Proper hydration
  (*iv*) Continuous low temperature for a few days
  (*v*) Aerobic respiration.
- The site of vernalization is believed to be **shoot apical meristem.**
- Vernalisation effect is reversible and the reverse process is called **devernalization.**
- The vernalisation stimulus can be transmitted between plants by grafting hence the stimulus is believed to be a hormone called **vernalin.**
- **A. Lang** discovered that during vernalization, the levels of gibberellins increase and also that the application of gibberellins to unvernalised plants can substitute for vernalization.

SENESCENCE

- The sum of deteriorative processes which naturally terminate that functional life of an organism.
- Ageing is a sum total of changes in the total plant or its constituents while senescence represents degenerative and irreversible changes in a plant.
- Senescence may be **whole plant senescence** (*e.g.,* monocarpic plants) ; **shoot senescence** (some perrennials *e.g.,* banana, gladiolus) ; **sequential** or **progressive senescence** (perrennials *e.g.,* mango, *Eucalyptus*) and **simultaneous** or **synchronous leaf senescence** (perrennial polycarpic deciduous plants *e.g.,* maple, elm, poplar etc.).
- Senescense can be delayed by removing flowers from the plants.

ABSCISSION

- Shedding of leaves, foliage branches, floral parts, fruits etc. without causing any injury is called abscission.
- It generally occurs due to change in the hormonal balance.
- Abscission zone is usually located at the base of petiole which is made up of two distinct layers *i.e.,*
  (*i*) The **abscission** (or separation) **layer** where breakdown of cells takes place and
  (*ii*) **The protective layer,** which develops next to abscission layer to protect the exposed surface.
- Abscisic acid is known to play an important role in abscission.

PLANT MOVEMENT

- Plant movement is change in position and these are not as much apparent as in case of animals.

SOME IMPORTANT FACTS

- **Hitchcock** and **Zimmerman** exhibited that flowering in *Nicotiana* can be enhanced by auxins.
- **Auxins** are synthesised mainly in apices and exhibit **polar transport.**
- **Crescograph** : Used for recording plant growth in seconds.
- Plants having **deliquescent** stem **have poor apical dominance** while plants having **excurrent** habit (palms, conifers, polyalthia) have **greater apical dominance.**
- **IPA** (Isopentenyl adenine) : Most widely occurrinng cytokinin, isolated from *Pseudomonas tumefaciens.*
- **IAA** : Promotes the liberation of a water soluble **xyloglucan** from the cell wall.
- **Mowing of grass** : removes apical bud,

Plant Movements

Vital
(Shown by living cells)
Movements of locomotion
(movements in whole plant body cell or cytoplasm)

(A) Autonomic
(not induced by external stimuli)

1. **Ciliary/ flagellar movement**
   e.g. *Chlamydomonas. Paramecium, Volvox,* zoospores etc.
2. **Amoeboid movements**
   e.g., Protistans, slime molds etc.
3. **Cyclosis movements**
   e.g., leaf calls of Hydrilla, staminal hair of Tradescantia, chara, moss etc

(B) Paratonic (Tactic)
(induced by external stimuli)

1. **Phototactic**
   (in response to direction and intensity of light)
   e.g., zoospores of algae
2. **Chemotactic**
   (in response to chemical)
   e.g., antherozoids.
3. **Thermotactic**
   (in response to temperature)
   e.g., *Chlamydomonas*

Hygroscopic
(Shown by dead plant parts)
Movements of curvature
(bending in some plant parts)

(A) Autonomic

- **Variation movement**
  (temporary bending)
  e.g., Telegraph plant
- **Paratonic movement** of curvature

(B) Paratonic

- **Growth movement**
  (permanent bending)

1. **Hyponastic**
   (greater growth on abaxial side) *e.g.*, closing of Cycas and ferns.
2. **Epinastic**
   (greater growth on adaxia side)*e.g.*, opening of flowers, fern leaves when mature
3. **Nutation**
   (autonomic side ways movements of shot apex and tendril) *e.g.*, trailers and creepers
4. **Circumnutation**
   (spiral movement or bending in all direction) *e.g.*, stem tips of twiners.

Tropic
Growth movements
(due to differential growth)

1. **Geotropic** (in response to gravity stimulus)
   (a) Positive geotropism (roots)
   (b) Negative geotropism (stem)
   (c) Diageotropic (rhizomes of certain grasses)
   (d) Plageotropic (leaves, lateral shoots etc.)
   (e) Ageotropic
2. Phototropic (in response to external unilateral light)
   (a) Positively phototropic (stem tips)
   (b) Negatively phototropic (roots)
3. **Thigmotropic** (in response to touch) *e.g.*, tendrils in the members of family cucurbitaceae
4. **Hydrotropic** (in response to water)
   e.g., roots are positively hydrotropic
5. **Chemotropic** (in response to chemicals)
   e.g., fungal hyphae and movement of pollen tube
6. **Thermotropic** (in response to temperature)
   e.g., seedlings curve towards warm side.

Nastic
Variation movement
(due to turgor changes, not necessarily directed towards or away from stimulus)

1. **Photonastic** (due to changes in intensity of light)
   e.g., Flowers of Oxalis open in morning and close at night
2. **Nyctinastic** (due to alternation of day and night)
   e.g., flowers of *Gerbera, Portulaca*
3. **Thermonastic** (due to variation in temperature)
   e.g., flowers of *Oxalis* open quickly when temperature rises
4. **Seismonastic** (due to mechanical stimuli *e.g.*, touch etc.)
   e.g., *Mimosa pudica* (sensitive plant, touch me- not).

stimulates axillary buds and intercalary meristem.

- **Double sigmoid curve** : Growth curve present in some fruits *e.g.*, Grape, Plum etc.
- **Agent orange** : A mixture of 2, 4-D and 2, 4, 5-T (Trichlorophenoxyacetic acid) was used in Vietnam war by U.S. to defoliate the forests under the name 'Agent orange'.
- **HDT** : Hormone directed transport. It is believed that cytokinin promotes movement of nutrients towards apical bud. So, lateral buds do not sprout near it.
- **Morphactins** (Zeigler, 1970) : Synthetic growth regulator having a skeleton of 9-hydroxy-fluorine 9-carboxylic acid. It reduce cell division, shorten internodes, cause

dwarfism, inhibit seed germination and seedling growth, overcome apical dominance, break bud dormancy, reduce leaf growth and curvature movements, stimulate growth of primary root but inhibit growth of lateral roots. They affect flowering, fruiting and sex expression.

- **Ephemeral movements** : Once in life *e.g.*, expansion of leaf.
- **Clinostat/Klinostat** : Instrument which can eliminate the effect of gravity and allow a plant to grow horizontaly by slowly rotating it.
- **Perceptive region** : The area of perception of stimulus.
- **Responsive region** : The area of response.
- **Presentation time** : The minimum time required for a stimulus to become effective.
- **Reaction time** : The period required for a stimulus to exhibit response.
- **Relaxation time** : Time required for the effect of a response to disappear.
- **Weber-Fechner law :**
  (*i*) Within limits, the equal relative differences between two stimuli of the same type are equally perceptible.
  (*ii*) There is a tendency of the intensity of sensation to vary as logarithm of the stimulus.
- **Richmond-Lang effect** : Cytokinin prevent chlorophyll degradation, hence ageing.
- **Sleep disease** (in rolling of petals in opened flowers) is caused by ethylene. Even 1 ppm of ethylene prevents the opening of flower buds.
- **Tromatropism** : Movement induced by injury.
- **Photomorphogenesis** : The control of development of form (*i.e.*, morphogenesis) by light.
- **Phytochrome** : Proteinaceous pigment. The sensitivity of seeds to the effect of red and far-red wavelengths of light is due to the presence of phytochrome. It is a regulatory pigment which regulates several light-dependent developmental processes in plants.
- **ABA** : Inducing synthesis of carotenoids and turns green organges into yellow.
- **Automatic or Pfeffer's auxanometer** : Register total growth, rate of growth at specific time and overall pattern of growth. An improved auxanometer over the arc auxanometer.
- **Phenology** : The different aspects or appeare-nces of plants in different seasons of a year.
- **IAA destruction** : Takes place due to photo-oxidation by blue light and dark oxidation by IAA oxidase.
- **IAA-aspartic acid, IBA-alanine** : More effective in bound state.
- **Human Urine** : Also natural source of auxins.
- **DCMU** (Dichlorophenyl dimethyl urea) : Strong inhibitor of photosystem II.
- **Impaction** : Treatment given to seeds when they are shaken vigorously.
- **Antiauxins** : Compounds which compete with the auxins for the reactive site *e.g.*, TIBA, 4-chlorophenoxy isobutyric acid, 2, 6-dichlorophenoxy acetic acid, 2, 4-dichloroanisole.
- *Gibberella fujikuroi* : A fungus, causes **"Foolish seedling"** disease in rice plant in Japan. Gibberellin (a growth hormone) was first extracted from this fungus.

5. Human Biology

BLOOD AND CIRCULATION

INTRODUCTION

Circulatory System or Internal Transport

Includes blood vascular system (blood, heart and blood vessels) and lymphatic system (lymph and lymph vessels). It helps in transportation of water, heat, hormones, nitrogenous waste, nutrients, respiratory gases, intermediate metabolites etc.

- Circulation of body fluids can be of following types :
  1. **Intracellular circulation** : Takes place inside the individual cells through cyclosis or cytoplasmic streaming *e.g., Amoeba, Paramecium.*
  2. **Extracellular circulation** : Fluid circulation outside the cells. It can be extra organismic circulation (outside water circulates in the body of an organism) or intra organismic circulation (involves circulation of body fluid). It includes parenchymal circulation *(e.g.,* in flatworms), coelomic circulation *(e.g.,* in round worms, arthropods etc.) and blood vascular system *(e.g.,* in higher invertebrates and all chordates).

TYPE OF BLOOD VASCULAR SYSTEM

A. Open Circulatory System

Found in arthropods and most molluscs (except cephalopod and tunicates). The main blood vessels arising from the heart pour the blood into tissue spaces called sinuses. In arthropods and molluscs, these sinuses join to form a body cavity with blood called the haemocoel.

Blood flows at a very low velocity and at low pressure due to absence of smooth muscles; direct contact *i.e.,* direct exchange of materials: respiratory pigment (if present) is dissolved in the blood plasma etc.

B. Closed Circulatory System

Formed in some annelids *e.g., Pheretima, Sepia* and all vertebrates. The blood flows around the blood through the specific blood vessels (arteries, veins and capillaries).

- Blood flows at high pressure due to the presence of smooth circular muscles in the walls of arteries and arterioles; there is no direct contact between the blood tissues and blood.
- Annelids are the simplest animals to have closed circulatory system.

CIRCULATORY SYSTEM OF COCKROACH

Open type, consists of heart (dorsal blood vessel), sinuses and the haemolymph.

Haemolymph/Blood

Colourless, no haemoglobin, made up of clear plasma and numerous haematocytes (Proleucocytes and phagocytes).

Haemocoel or body cavity

Pseudocoel filled with blood, divided into 3 sinuses by two fenestrated diaphragms *i.e.,* **Dorsal** or **pericardial diaphragm** and ventral or sternal diaphragm. Three sinuses are dorsal **pericardial sinus** (encloses hemt and alary muscle), middle **perivisceral sinus** (largest, encloses various viscera) and ventral **perineural sinus** (encloses nerve cord). Head possess small sized spaces called **head sinsuses.**

Heart

Straight, elongated, tubular, 13 – chambered (3 in thorax and 10 in abdomen), lies in the pericardial sinsus below terga. At the posterior end of each chamber, except the last, there is a pair of small holes (the **ostia**) are on either side. First chamber of heart continues into a small and tubular **anterior aorta** which extends into the head. Ostia are guarded by **auricular valves** which allow the blood to enter the heart from the dorsal sinus. Each chamber of the heart opens into the one in front of the opening is guarded by a pair of ventricular valves which allows flow of blood only in forward direction.

Circulation of Blood

Contraction and relaxation of **alary muscles** (paired and lie in the pericardial sinus on either side of heart) straighten and arch the dorsal diaphragm. Heart contracts postero-anteriorly (blood also flows posterio-anteriorly) at the rate of 50 times per minutes. Blood circulation is completed in 5-6 minutes.

Dorsal diaphragm ⟵ Heart ⟵ Aorta

↑ Pericardial sinus ↑ ... Head sinus ↑ / ↓

Ventral diaphragm ⟵ Perivisceral sinus ⟵ Legs sinus ⟵ Perineural sinus

BLOOD VASCULAR SYSTEM OF HUMANS

Closed type with a muscular heart, blood (fluid plasma + blood corpuscles) and blood vessels (arteries + veins).

Human Blood

Forms about 6–10% of the body weight, volume of blood in an adult about 6.8 litres complex connective tussue, consists of two components: 1. Plasma 2. Blood corpuscles

1. Plasma

Faint yellow coloured non-living fluid, forms about 55 - 60% of the blood volume, alkaline in nature, contain 91-92%, water, 7% proteins, 0.9% inorganic constituents, 0.1 % glucose and rest includes various other organic and inorganic substances. Plasma proteins mainly include albumins (4%, provides the colloid osmotic pressure in plasma), globulins (2.5%), fibrinogen (0.3%), properdin and prothrombin (0.03%). These proteins act as enzymes, coagulatin factors and antiboidies. The dissolved mineral ions are Na^+, K^+, Ca^{++}, Mg^{2+}, HPO_4^{2-}, PO_4^{3-}, Cl^-, HCO^{3-} etc. which maintain the pH of blood by buffering action. It helps in transportation of food components, metabolic wastes, hormones, nurition, excretion, respiration and homeostasis; helps in homeothermy pH constancy; blood clotting; immunity; osmotic tension; as a middleman; properdin; erythropoiesis etc.

2. Blood Corpuscles

Cell which float freely in the plasma, form 40 – 45% of blood plasma. 3 types:

1. ***Erythrocytes or red blood corpuscles (RBCs):*** Biconcave disc shaped, enucleate, reddish coloured cells, 7-8 mm is diameter, most abundant of blood corpuscles, 5.5 ± 1. 0 million/mm^3 in men, 4.8 ± 10 million/mm^3 in women, lifespan 120 days, contain haemoglobin (helps in transport of O_2) and enzyme carbonic anhydrase (required for formation of bicarbonate from CO_2), Moving RBCs tend to adhere with one another to form rows called *rouleaux.*

Haemocytometer : Instrument used to determine RBC count.

Anaemia : RBC count decreases.

Polycythemia : RBC count increases much more than the normal level.

Erythrocytopenia : Decrease in the number of RBCs which leads to hypoxia *i.e.,* O_2 deficiency in the body tissues.

Erythropoeisis : Formation of red blood cells form the organs *(erythropoeitic organs).*

Spleen (blood bank of body) : Stores excess of erythrocytes.

The RBCs due to the presence of haemoglobin carriers out the most important function of blood. *i.e.,* transport of gases.

2. ***Leucocytes or white blood corpuscles (WBCs) :*** Rounded or amoeboid, nucleated, non-pigmented cells, wandering cells, larger than RBCs, 8–15 mm (may be 20 mm) in size, much less in number than RBCs (1 : 600), colourless, average WBC count is **7,000 per cubic millimetre.**

Leucocytosis : Rise in WBC count.

Leucopenia : Fall of WBC count below 4000.

Leukaemia : Pathological increase in number and denotes one type of neoplastic disease (blood cancer).

Leucopoiesis : Formaton of leucocytes takes place in bone marrow, Peyer's patches, lymph nodes, thymus, spleen etc.

On the basis of **cytoplasmic granules** leucocytes are of 2 types *i.e.,* **granulocytes** (with granules, polymorphic nucleus, produced in myeloblasts of red bone marrow, form 65% of total leucocytes) and **agranulocytes** (non-granular, non-lobulated nuclei, forms 35% of total leucocytes).

GRANULOCYTES

(*a*) **Neutrophils :** 62% of total number of white cells, most abundant subtype, 4900 per mm^3 of blood, 2 – 7 lobulated nucleus, vary in size from 10 – 12 mm, life span 10 – 12 hours, soldiers of body (engulf microbes by phagocytosis), act as **shock troops,** do not take colour when exposed to acidic as well as basic dyes, helps in **sex-differentiation** as the neutrophils of female exhibit a **'drum stick'** or **barr-body** attached to one of the nuclear lobes.

(*b*) **Eosinophils (Acidophils) :** About 2 – 4% of the total leucocyte cells, coarse granules that get stained with acidic dyes (bright red with eosine), 10 – 15 μm in size, bilobed nucleus, 14 hours life span, increase in number in allergic diseases like **asthma** or **hay fever** and is parasitic infections *e.g.,* **Ascariasis,** helps in healing of wound, play an important role in detoxification.

(*c*) **Basophils :** About 0.5 – 2% of the total leucocyte cells, least in number 8-10 μm in size, coarse cytoplasmic granules, stained with basic dyes *e.g.,* methylene blue, nucleus S-shaped and 3 lobed, life span 8 – 12 hours, secrete heparin and histamine and helps in local anticoagulation and formation of ground substance.

AGRANULOCYTES

(*a*) **Lymphocytes :** About 30% of total leucocyte count, 1,500 – 2,700 per cubic mm of blood, 8 – 12 μm in size, large and rounded nucleus, 2 types-small (7 μm) and large (20 μm) lymphocyte, formed in the thymus and lymphoid tissues; non-motile and non phagocytic, produces antibodies and opsonins.

(*b*) **Monocytes** : Largest sized leucocytes, 12 – 15 μm in diameter (may be 20 μm), forms about 5.3% of total leucocyte count, 100-400 mm^3 of blood, oval excentric and horse shoe-shaped formed in the lymph-nodes and spleen from the monoblasts highly motile and phagocytic in action, second line of defence (engulf the bacteria), act as macrophages or scavenger cells (remove the damaged and dead cells).

3. Blood platelets (Throbocytes)

Smallest sized blood corpuscles, 2-3 mm in diameter, found only in the blood of mammals, colourless, oval shaped discoidal cytoplasmic fragment formed from giant cells *i.e.,* megakaryocytes of bone-marrow, non-nucleated. 2.5 – 3.5 × 10^5 per cubic mm of blood: secrete a vasoconst or (serotonin) which causes construction of blood vessels to reduce the blood loss; release a number of platelet factors and an enzyme thromboplastin which causes the coagulation of blood and clot formation to prevent excessive bleeding.

CARDIOVASCULAR SYSTEM

HUMAN HEART

Mesodermal in origin; hollow; muscular structure; situated behind the sternum and between the lungs in the thoracic cavity, with its apex resting on the diaphragm; looks like a blunt cone, which is 12 cm in length and 9 cm in width at the broadest point;

automatic pumping organ; heavier in man (average 280-340 g) than in woman (average 230 – 280 g; form about 0.45% of body weight in males and about 0.4% of body weight in females.

Pericardium

Thin, transparent, two layared serous sac around the heart, outer non-distensible fibrous layer (parietal pericardium) and inner serous layer (visceral pericardium). A narrow cavity (pericardial cavity) between two layers, is filled with fluid (pericardial fluid) which allows frictionless movements of heart and protects the heart from mechanical shocks.

On the surface of heart

Two grooves on the ventricle *i.e.,* **anterior interventricular** sulcus and **posterior interventricular** sulcus; a transverse groove between atria and ventricles is coronary sulcus **(atrio-ventricular groove)**. These sulci house coronary arteries, through which the heart receives blood.

Internally human heart is four chambered-Two auricles (atria) and two ventricles and there is a complete separation of oxygenated and deoxygenated blood.

Atria or Auricles

Thin walled, push blood only upto ventricles, situated at the broader end, both auricle separated by a thin vertical **interatrial or interauricular/ septum** (prevents mixing of oxygenated and deoxygenated blood); right atrium is larger in size. Both auricles are smooth walled except a low network of ridges called **musculi pectinati**. Interatrial septum has an oval-shaped depression *i.e.,* **fossa ovalis** which is a vestige of an oval aperture *i.e.,* **foramen ovale**, present in the foetus and connecting two auricles.

Right auricle (RA) receives deoxygenated blood by 3 large veins *i.e.,* **superior vena cava (pre-caval)** from head. fore-limbs and upper part of chest; inferior vena cava (post-caval) from lower part of trunk and hind limbs and coronary sinus from wall of heart. Opening of inferior vena cava and coronary sinus are guarded by *a* **valve of Eustachus** and **valve of Thebesius**, respectively. Right auricle open in right ventricle (RV) by **right auriculoventricular aperture** guarded by **right auriculoventicular valve** which is formed of three flaps called **cusps (tricuspid valves)**. It regulates unidirectional flow of blood from RA to RV but prevents the back flow of blood with the help of **chordae tendineae** (whitish elastic threads) which extends from tricuspid valve to wall of RV.

Left Auricle (LA)

Receives oxygenated blood from lungs by four pulmonary veins (two from each lung), has no valve. LA opens in left ventricle (LV) by **left auriculoventricular aperture,** guarded by left auriculoventricular valve, formed of two flaps or cusps **(bicuspid or mitral valve)**. It regulates the flow of blood from LA to LV but prevents backflow of blood with the help of chordae tendineae similar to those in RV.

Ventricles

Thick walled, LV is much thicker than RV because LV has to push the blood to all the body parts while RV has to push the blood to closely lying lungs only. Both ventricles are rough walled and have two ridges *i.e.,* **columnae or trabeculae carneae** and **papillary muscles or musculi papillaes** (to which chordae tendineae are attached) and grooves. **Interventricular septum** separates the both ventricles and prevent mixing of deoxygenated and oxygenated blood in ventricular part of heart.

Right ventricle (RV)

From left anterior corner of right ventricle, there originates the **pulmonary arch** or **pulmonary aorta** which carries deoxygenated blood to the lungs.

Left ventricle (LV)

From right anterior corner of left ventricle, there originates aortic (systemic) arch which carries oxygenated blood to various body parts.

Pulmonary valve and aortic valve are present at the base of each of pulmonary and aortic arches respectively. Each valve is formed of three semilunar valves which are directed away from the ventricle which allow blood to enter the great artery from ventricle, but present the back flow of blood into the ventricle.

In adult, two arches are inter-connected by a yellow fibrous band called ligamentum arteriosum which is vestige of ductus arteriosus or duct of Botalli present in the embryonic heart.

Histologically heart wall is made up of 3 coats *i.e.,* **endocardium** (innermost layer of squamous epithelium), myocardium (middle coat formed of cardiac muscle fibres) and **pericardium** (visceral coelomic epithelium of flat cells).

PUMPING ACTION OF HUMAN HEART

Initiation of heart beat in under three special bundles of cardiac muscles (nodal tissues) which are :

1 .SA node-Sinu-auricular or sino-atrial node

Lies in the right wall of RA, below the opening of superior vena cava, small, flattened and ellipsoid strip of muscle fibre of 0.3 mm size, also called **right sided structure.** It has a rest potential of only–**55 to 60 m V.** Also called pacemaker as it is first to originate the cardiac impulses and determines the rate of heart beat. So the atrial contraction preceeds the ventricular contraction. It has highest degree of autorhythmicity (70-80 times/minute) but least conductivity. The fibres of SA node have high concentration of sodium ion in the extracellular fluid and negative charge inside the nodal fibres. Due to this high concentration and presence of open channel, sodium ion always tend to enter inside. This results is the rise of membrane potential and the generation of the action potential, causing the excitation of the SA node. The fibres of the sinus node remain closely associated with the muscles of auricles. Due to this the action potential generated at SA node very soon travels throughout the auricles at a velocity of **0.3 m/sec.**

2. AV Node : Atrio-ventricular node

Also called Pace setter lies in the right atrium near the junction of interauricular and interventricular septum close to opening of coronary sinus. It is stimulated by the waves of contraction initiated by SA node. It generates the cardiac impulses which are conducted to the muscles of the ventricles through **bundle of His** and **Purkinje fibres** at the rate of 1.5-4 metres second.

3. Bundle of His

Also called **AV bundle,** arises from AV node, descends in the inter ventricular septum and divides into two branches which descend along two sides of interventricular septum and supply the wall of ventricle of their own side by Purkinje fibres which bring about synchronous contraction of the ventricles form the apex of heart which force the blood into the pulmonary arch and aortic arch.

SA node, AV node, bundle of His (A.V. bundle) and Purkinje fibres collectively form the conducting system of hean and is responsible for auto rhythmicity of heart.

CARDIAC CYCLE

The period between end of one heart beat to the end of next heart beat. During this cycle, blood flows through the cardiac chambers in a specific manner and direction, the backflow is prevented by the valves. It involves alternate contraction (systole) and relaxation (diastole) of heart at the rate of 70-72 times per minute at rest. Cardiac cycle is formed of following steps :

1. **Atrial systole:** Involves contraction of atria from anterior to posterior side which pushes blood to respective ventricle. It takes 0.l/second.
2. **Ventricular filling :** As soon as the atrioventricular valves open 70% of the atrial blood passes into ventrcles passively. Rest of the ventricular filling takes place during the contraction of the atria.
3. **Ventricular systole :** Involves simultaneous relaxation of atria (atrial diastole) and contraction of ventricles (ventricular systole). Due to ventricular systole, the pressure on the blood in the ventricles is increased compared to that in the atria. The auriculoventricular valves close rapidly to prevent the backflow of blood from ventricular to auricles. The blood does not pass back into atria due to closure of tricuspid and bicuspid valves. It produces "Lub" or first heart sound or systolic sound. It takes 0.3 second.

4. **Ventricular diastole :** There is fall in ventricular pressure. The semilunar valves close to prevent back flow of blood trom aortas. At the same time, the AV valve opens to allow the flow of blood from both the atria to the respective ventricles. The blood sent into great arteries cannot come back due to closure of semilunar valves called **"dub"**. Atria require 0.7 sec for their diastole while ventricles require 0.5 sec. **Dub is second heart sound or diastolic sound.**

HEART BEAT AND PULSE

The rhythmic contraction and relaxation of the heart to pump out and receive blood to and from the body parts is called heart beat. In an adult healthy person, the normal rate of heart beat at rest is about 70 – 72 times per minute. The human heart contracts more than 2.5 billion times in a life time. In newly born baby heart rate is 40 times per minute. A wave of distension passess *(arterial pulse)* along the arteries which can be felt by placing a fingertip on the artery near the wrist. Factors like exercise, rise of body temperature, shock and tension, rise in blood pressure, vaso-constrictor decrease in pH value increase the rate of heart beat.

Heart Sound

Produced due to closure of valves :

1. **First sound (Lubb) :** Longer duration (0.16 – 0.90 sec), louder one, created by the closure of the atrioventricular valves immediately after the start of the ventricular systole.
2. **Second sound (Dubb) :** Shorter duration (0.10 sec), created by the closure of the semilunar valve at the end of the ventricular systole.

   The pause between the end of the second sound and the beginning of the first sound coincides with ventricular diastole.

BLOOD VESSELS AND COURSE OF CIRCULATION OF BLOOD

The blood flows strictly through a fixed route via the arteries and veins which consists of 3 layers.

1. **Tunica intima or interna :** Innermost lining of squamous endothelium.
2. **Tunica media :** Middle layer of smooth muscle and elastic fibre.
3. **Tunica externa or Tunica adventitia :** External layer of fibrous connective tissue with collagen fibres. It is less developed in an artery.

Mammalian heart has **complete double circulation** *i.e.,* blood passes twice through the heart to supply once to the body. It involves two circulations:

1. **Systemic or Greater Circulation :** Blood completes its circulation from left ventricle to right auricle through body organs.
2. **Pulmonary or Lesser Circulation -** Blood completes its circulation form right ventricle to left auricle through the lungs.

CORONARY CIRCULATION

Involves the blood supply to the heart walls and also drainge of the heart wall. It is made up of coronary arteries (one pair, arise from aortic arch just above the semilunar valves, supply oxygenated blood to the heart wall) and *coronary veins* (collects blood from heart wall. most of the veins join to form a coronary sinus which open in the right auricle. Opening is guarded by a valve of Thebesius.

PORTAL SYSTEM

A portal vein (special type of vein which collects blood from some organs by a system of capillaries, but divides into a second capillary system in some intermediate organ before the blood finally returns to the heart) with its branches is called a portal system. The flow of blood through the portal system is called portal circulation. 2 types :

1. **Hepatic portal system :** Hepatic portal veins carries food ladden blood from alimentary canal and associated glands like pancreas, spleen etc. to the liver which acts as an intermediate organ. It helps in removal of glucose, amino acids and other nutrients; deamination of extra amino acids and conversion of harmful ammonia to urea; separation of toxic chemical and their toxification G and direct pouring of liver products into venous blood.
2. **Hypophyseal portal system :** Hypophyseal portal vein collects the blood from

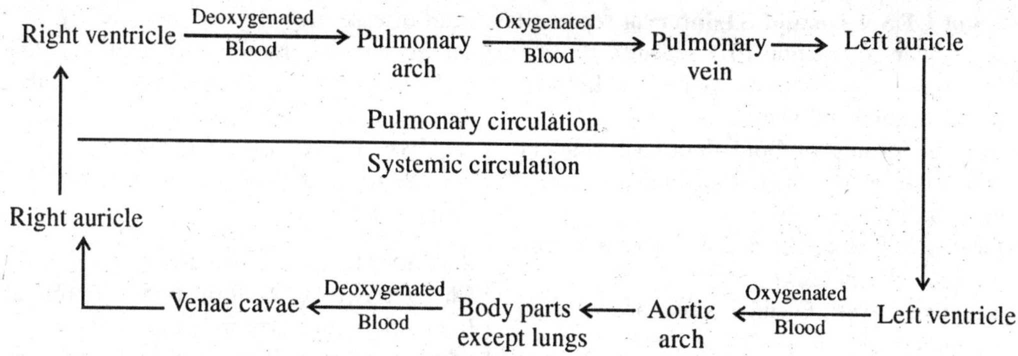

hypothalamus of the brain and forms second set of capillaries in anterior lobe of pituitary gland. It transfers the releasing hormomes of the hypothalamus to anterior lobe of pituitary to stimulate or inhibit the secretion of trophic hormones like TSH, ACTH etc.

LYMPHATIC SYSTEM

1. **Lymph :** Transparent fluid derived from blood and other tissues which accumulates in the interstitial spaces as the interstitial fluid. It contains leucocytes mainly lymphocytes, water content 94%, protein content is less (3 - 4.5% instead of blood plasma with 6 - 8%), Albumin globulin ratio is 1 : 5 instead of 1 : 1 in blood. It maintains balance of blood and tissue fluid; picks up hormones from endocrine glands; adds lymphocytes etc.
2. **Lymph capillaries :** Small, thin walled, present in nearly all the tissue spaces, lined by an **endothelium** of thin and flat cells. Special milky coloured lymph capillaries called **lacteals** (present in villi of the small intestine).
3. **Lymphatic vessels :** Thinner walls, numerous valves which give them a beaded appearence, join and rejoin and finally form two main lymphatic ducts.
   (*a*) **Thoracic duct :** The lymphatic vessels from the lower body parts extend upward to form the left **thoracic duct** which receives the vessels from left arm, left side of head and partly from throacic region. It opens into the vein near the junction of left internal jugular vein and the subclavian vein.
   (*b*) **Right lymphatic duct :** Shorter and collects lymph from the right side of thorax, right upper limb and right side of neck. It finally opens into the venous system at the junction of right subclavian and right internal jugular veins.
4. **Lymph nodes :** Small, oval or bean like bodies placed in the course of the lymphatic vessels, acts as filters and are the sites of formation of the lymphocytes, mainlly present in the neck, axilla, thorax, abdomen and groin. Lymphnodes are maximum in armpit and groin. Each lymph node receives one or more afferent lymph vessels. These are the sites of formation of lymphocytes which form antibodies to provide immunity.

ELECTROCARDIOGRAM (ECG)

A graphic record of the electrical variations produced by the beating of the heart. An instrument used to observe the working of the heart is called electrocardiograph which was discovered by **Einthoven** (1903) commonly called "Father of Electrocardiography" . ECG is formed of a series of ridges and furrows. A normal electrocardiogram is composed of a P Wave, QRS complex and a T wave.

- **P Wave** (small upward wave) indicates the depolarisation of the atria or the spread of impulse from the sinus node throughout the atria.
- **QRS** wave indicates the spread of impulse of contraction from A. V. node of the wall of ventricles causing ventricular depolarization. . Interval PQ represent atrial contraction (0.1 second).

- **RS of QRS wave and ST interval** represents ventricular contraction (0.3 second).
- **T wave** represents the relaxation (repolarisation) of ventricles.
- ECG is formed of both depolarisation and repolarisation waves. It also indicates rate of heart beat.
- **Positive waves :** P, R and T waves are above the base line of ECG.
- **Negative waves :** Q and S waves are below the base line of ECG.

PACE MAKER

The heart beat is triggered into action by the pacemaker. The pacemaker region in called sinoatrial (SA) node. It is present in the right auricle between the precaval and the former. The SA node causes rhythmic depolarisation which are conducted via auricles to auriculo-ventricular (AV) node. SA node controls the heart beat and it is the natural pacemaker of the heart. Failure of atrial impulse to pass into ventricles for a few seconds to few hours is called ventricular escape (Stokes-Adams syndrome). In such cases an artificial pacemaker is connected to the right ventricle for controlling the rhythm. The artificial pacemaker consists of a pulse - generator containing cell (solid state lithiilm cell) to produce electrical impulse, the lead in the form of a wire (transmits the impulse) and an electrode which is connected to the portion of the heart, where impulse is to be transmitted. Pacemaker are however, liable to be influenced by microwave ovens, metal detectors, diathermy, electric showers, automobile ignition, cellular phones etc.

DISORDERS RELATED TO THE CIRCULATORY SYSTEM

1. Hypertension

Presistent high blood pressure. In a healthy individual the normal arterial systolic and diastolic pressure is 120 mm Hg and 80 mm Hg, respectively. But an increase in the blood pressure beyond 140 mm Hg (systolic) and 90 mm Hg (diastolic) is referred to as high blood pressure. It can potentially harm the heart, brain and kidneys. It compels heart to work excessively due to which the congestive heart disease may set is at an early age. In brain, it causes **haemorrhage** or **infarctions,** leading to various disabilities. In the long run it also affects kidneys, leading to renal failure.

Hypertension is commonly called **silent killer** because it may be present for years with no distinct symptoms.

2. Atherosclerosis (Atheroma)

Characterised by the formation of fibrolipid plague (angina) in the arterial intima especially in the coronary arteries. It results into the reduction of the lumen size of the artery and consequently, the flow of blood is also reduced. The proliferation of smooth muscles takes place due to these plaques provide a rough surface to the platelets causing the release of platelet derived growth factor (PDGF). In myocardial infarction, the patient suffers from severe chest pain, breathlessness, restlessness, nausea and vomitting. Vasodilator drugs like nitroglycerin give immediate relief from pain.

3. Arteriosclerosis

Caused by deposition of calcium salts or cholesterol in the walls of blood vessels or increased fibrous tissue in their walls. The arteries become hard, narrow and less elastic and is referred to as the **"hardening of the arteria"**. It leads to hypertension which sometimes causes haemorrhage of blood vessels of brain or visceral organs causing *cerebral haemorrhage or* **visceral haemorrhage.**

SOME IMPORTANT FACTS

- **Cardiac output (minute volume) :** The amount of blood ejected by either ventricle/min.
  Cardiac output = stroke volume × Number of cardiac beats/min. = 70 × 72 = 5.041/min.
  It is directly proportional to size of the organism, amount of blood entering into the heart (called venous return), metabolic rate, age etc. but is inversely proportional to age and total peripheral resistance.
- **Myogenic heart :** Found in vertebrates. The cardiac impulse originate in the cardiac muscle fibres and not brought to the heart by the nerve fibres.

- **Neurogenic heart :** Found in most crustaceans, some insects (*e.g.,* cockroach) and annelids. The excitation waves of the heart beat originate from nerve ganglion cells present on the dorsal surface of the heart.
- **Period of isovolumic contraction :** Period during which ventricles contract (0.02 – 0.03 seconds) but no blood is ejected from the ventricles.
- **Period of isovolumic relaxation :** Period during which ventricles relax (0.03 – 0.06 seconds) but there is no filling of ventricles.
- Amphibians and most of reptiles have **partial double circulation** while birds and mammals have **complete double circulation.**
- Left ventrticle of human heart is about three times thicker than right ventricle.
- **Angiology :** Study of blood vessels.
- **Coronary angiography :** Radio-autograph of coronary arteries of heart.
- **Bradycardia :** Low rate of heart beat, usually less than 60 times/mt.
- **Tachycardia :** High rate of heart beat. usually more than 100 times/mt.
- **Pericarditis :** Inflammation of pericardium of heart.
- **Endocarditis :** Inflammation of endocardium of heart.
- **Blue baby :** A baby born with atrial or ventricular septal defects.
- **Fibrillation :** When muscles of atria or ventricles or both undergo rapid but uncoordinated contraction.
- **Cardiomegaly :** Enlargement of heart.
- **Haemotomeris :** Presence of blood in vomiting.
- **Patent ductus arteriosis :** A congenital heart defect in which ductus arteriosus between two arches remains open.
- **Rheumatic heart disease (RHD) :** Defects in heart valve due to toxins produced by throat infection caused by *Streptococcus* leading to rheumatic fever.
- **Marley's law of heart :** An increase relationship between the rate of heart beat and blood pressure.
- **Cardiac index :** Cardiac output per square metre surface area of body per minute. The body surface area of a nornlal young adult is 1.7 metres so cardiac index in 3 litres/min./sq.m.
- **Auriculo-Ventricular node** was discovered by His.
- **Sinu-auricular node :** Pace maker or Keith and Flock Node. It was first discovered by Sir Arthur Keith and Martin Black.
- Syphilis and Rheumatic fever causes **murmur.**
- **Aplastic anaemia :** Due to fall in rate of erythropoeisis in bone-marrow.
- **Ramanowski stain :** Used to differentiate three types of granulocytes.
- **Critical count of platelets :** If the platelet counts falls below 40,600/μl.
- Mammals have **left systemic** while birds have **right systemic.**
- **Angiogram :** Film showing radio-autograph of blood vessels.
- **Haemotoma :** Blood collected in an intercellular space.
- **Haemodialysis :** Separation of nitrogenous wastes from blood with the help of an artificial kidney.
- **Oedema :** Swollen body parts due to blockage of lymph vessels.
- **William Harvey :** First to study blood circulation in human heart. Wrote a book Decardiomotu. Father of modern physiology.
- **Corotid labyrinth :** A swollen part at the base of internal carotid and has base receptors to note changes in blood pressure.
- Heart is the *busiest* organ of human body which is a modified blood vessel.
- **Angina :** Heart pain for a short period usually in the front of the chest.
- **Myocardial infarction :** An acute heart attack in which a part of heart muscle becomes dead due to cessation of blood supply to it.
- **Ischaemia :** An inadequate flow of blood to a part of the heart due to obstruction of its blood supply.
- Earthworm has 4 pairs of pulsating hearts; frog has two pairs of lymph hearts; Blue whale has the largest heart.

- **Largest artery :** Systemic aorta in human body.
- **Larget vein :** Inferior vena cava in human body.
- **Slowest blood flow :** Blood flow is slowest in the capillaries to allow enough time for the exchange of materials.
- **Spindle cells :** Found in amphibian blood, help in blood clotting like the mammalian platelets.
- **Blood letting :** Bleeding a person for therapeutic purpose.
- **Negative blood pressure** is recorded in great veins.
- **Phonocardiogram :** Instrument used to magnify and *record* the heart sounds.
- **Lymphatology :** The study oflymphatic system.
- **Venal cordis minimal -** Very fine coronary veins which open directly in right auricle.
- **Coronary sclerosis :** Narrowing of coronary arteries leading to severe chest pain and called angina pectoris.
- **Coronary thrombosis :** Formation of a blood clot in coronary arteries of heart. It causes death of heart tissues and leads to heart attack or **myocardial infarction.**
- **CVA or Cardiovascular Accident or Stroke :** Reduce or stoppage of blood supply to brain due to sclerosis or thrombosis or haemorrhage of carotid artery. It leads to paralysis.
- **Vasa vasorum :** Blood vessels in coats of larger blood vessels.
- Osmotic pressure of blood = 5900 mm of Hg, 7.8 atm.
- Malpighi (1661) : Discovered blood capillaries.
- Halls (1732) : Measured blood pressure for the first time.
- **Stokes-Adams syndrome :** Delayed pick up of heart.
- **Ectopic pacemaker :** Shifting of pacemaker to some *other* part of heart.
- **Arrythmia :** Irregular heart beat due to damage to S.A. node.
- Antarctic icefish, *Chaenocephalus,* has colourless blood and is without RBCs.

RESPIRATORY SYSTEM

INTRODUCTION

Respiration

Catabolic process which involves exchange of environmental oxygen and body's carbon dioxide through a liquid medium to utilitize the oxygen for the oxidation of glucose in the mitocondria to produce the energy.

- Respiration is a **physico-chemical process.**
- Respiration may be direct or indirect.

Direct respiration

Exchange of gases takes place on the principle of diffusion through **moist body surface.** Found in unicellular organisms like aerobic bacteria protists and metazoans like sponges, coelenterates, flatworms, round worms etc.

Indirect respiration

A respiratory surface is present for exchange of gases. In this the transportation of gases between the respiratory organs and the body cells is brought about by the blood of the circulatory system *e.g.,* through skin (annelids and amphibians), gills (most of crustaceans, molluscs, all fishes and some amphibians); lungs (snails, some amphibians, all reptiles, birds and mammals).

Aerobic respiration

Takes place in the presence of molecular oxygen. It involves intake of oxygen and liberation of carbon dioxide.

Anaerobic respiration

Takes place in the absence of molecular oxygen, also called as fermentation. In muscles, lactic acid is formed as a product which is later oxidised aerobically in muscles and liver. Mammalian RBCs exhibit anaerobic respiration as these lack the mitochondria.

Internal respiration or tissue respiation

The uptake of oxygen by tissue cells, oxidatiion of respiratory substrate (cellular respiration), liberation of energy and elimination of carbon dioxide evolved.

External respiration

Intake of oxygen by the blood from water or air in the respiratory organs and elimination of carbon dioxide.

Breathing or ventilation

Refers to the bringing in of fresh air and taking out of foul air. Rate of breathing is 12 – 14 (14 – 18 in adolescents) times per minute in human adults and 18 - 22 times/min in children (40 - 60/min in neonates).

VARIOUS RESPIRATORY PIGMENTS

- **Haemoglobin :** Oxygenated blood is red in colour; found in REC of vertebrates and blood plasma of invertebrates; metal base is ferrous ions.
- **Haemoerythrin :** Colourless; oxygenated red or brown in colour; found in annelida; metal base is iron.
- **Haemocyanin :** Colourless; oxygenated blue in colour; metal base is copper; found in phylum arthropoda (except insecta) and in mollusca.
- **Echinocbrome :** Red in colour; metal base is iron; found in echinodermata.
- **Vanadium :** Metal base is vanadium; found in coelomic fluid of protochordates.
- **Chlorocruorin :** Green in colour; oxygenated blood red in colour, metal base is iron; formed in annelida *e.g., Sebella.*

GASEOUS EXCHANGE IN ANIMALS

- Free living acellular protists and multicellular animals exchange gases with their surrounding environment.
- **Body Surfaces :** Protozoans, poriferans and cnidarians obtain oxygen dissolved in water through diffusion by their general body surface. CO_2 follows the opposite path and is released through body surfaces.
- **Gills :** Most of the higher aquatic invertebrates and fishes have developed gills for aquatic mode of respiration.
- **Lungs :** Terrestrial animals *e.g.,* amphibians, reptiles, birds and mammals have well developed lungs for aerial mode of respiration.

RESPIRATION IN EARTHWORM

Respiratory organs are absent. They exchange O_2 and CO_2 between their looped epidermal blood capillaries and moist skin. They keep their body moist by glandular secretion from the epidermis and coelomic fluid exuded via dorsal pores. The O_2 dissolved in thin film of fluid over the skin has greater concentration than in the blood flowing in the skin capillaries. Therefore, it diffuses from the fluid film into the blood. There is absence of red blood corpuscles to carry oxygen molecules. The blood carries the respiratory pigment haemoglobin dissolved in the blood plasma; the oxygen tension, or partial pressure of oxygen in blood, is low relative to the moist skin. The dissolved oxygen binds with haemoglobin of the plasma contraction of some blood vessels facilitate the passage of blood and dissolved gases round the body.

RESPIRATION IN COCKROACHES

The respiratory system consisting of tubules forming the tracheal system. There are 3 pairs of **longitudinal tracheal trunks** interconnected by **transverse tracheae.** Each trachea is connected to outside by the respiratory opening, **spiracle (stigmatum).** Each spiracle has valves (to regulate its opening and closing) and **bristles** (filtering apparatus). Main trachea divides and redivides to form a fine network called tracheal intercom. The finest branches of this intercom are called tracheoles which are intracellular structures and directly end into the body cells. Terminal parts of the tracheoles are filled with a tissue fluid called tracheolar fluid. Trachea has cuticular lining called intima while tracheoles have a lining of protein called trachein. Trachea and its branches are supported by chitinous rings called taenidia. When abdominal muscles (tergosternal muscles) relax, the air is drawn into the tracheal system and finally diffuses through the tracheolar fluid to reach the cells. When the abdominal muscles contract, the air with some CO_2 is forced out via the spiracles as most of CO_2, produced is lost through the permeable cuticle.

In cockroach expiration is an active process while inspiration is a passive process. During active respiration, tracheolar fluid is with drawn from the tracheoles into the cells. So the air reaches directly into the cells which increases the efficiency of respiration.

First thoracic and first abdominal spiracles remain open all the time while other eight pairs of spiracles open during inspiration and close during expiration.

RESPIRATION IN HUMANS

Respiration brings about inspiration (breathing in), expiration (breating out), exchange of gases in lungs and transport of gases between the lungs and tissues.

Human Respiratory System

Consists of respiratory tract (conducting portion) and respiratory organs.

(A) Respiratory Tract

Consists of nostrils or external nares (one pair, oval apertures present at the lower end of nose and just above the mouth); nasal chambers (a pair, enclosed in the nasal capsules, above the palate, separated by nasal septum, divided into 3 parts. *i.e.,* vestibular part, respiratory part or conditioner region and olfactory part); **internal nares** (openings of nasal chambers in the roof of nasopharynx); **laryngopharynx** (possess slit like aperture **glottis** which is closed by a leaflike bilobed cartilage, **epiglottis**): **larynx or voice box** (supported by four cartilages *i.e.,* one cricoid, one thyroid and two arytenoids; lined by stratified columnar ciliated epithelium); **trachea or wind pipe** (supported by 16 – 20 dossally incomplete, C–shaped contilaginous tracheal rings; lined by **pseudo-stratified ciliated epithelium** with mucous secreting goblet cells')and primary bronchi (one pair, formed by the division of trachea. each primacy bronchus enters the lung of its own side through the hilus and forms a bronchial intercom.

(B) Respiratory organs

Provide the surface for the exchange of gases. In man respiratory organ are one pair of lungs.

LUNGS

A pair, soft, elastic, spongy organs, present in an air tight **thoracic** or **pleural** cavity one on either side of heart. Each lung is enclosed in two membranes *i.e.,* inner layer (**visceral pleuron**) and outer layer (**parietal pleuron**). Between these layers, there is a narrow **pleural cavity** filled with a watery **pleural fluid**. Its outer convex, posterior semilunar-shaped and inner concave surfaces are called **costal, diaphragmatic** and **mediastinal** surface. Mediasternal surface possess a triangular shaped area. *i.e.,* **hilum or hilus** through which blood and lymph vessels, primary branches and nerves enter the lung. Each lung is a lobulated organ, divided externally into the lobes by transverse and oblique grooves called **fissures.**

Left Lung : Two lobes–superior and inferior lobes, has a **cardiac** notch along its anteromedian border to accomodate the heart, 567 gm weight.

Right lung : Three lobes – superior, middle and inferior lobes, 25 gm weight, slightly lárger and broader in size.

Right bronchus divides into 3 smaller branches *i.e.,* **lobar** or **secondary bronchi** inside the lung which further divide into smaller branches called **tertiary bronchi**. Each tertiary bronchus divides into **branchioles** which further divides into minute branches *i.e.,* **terminal branchioles**. Each terminal branchiole divides into **respiratory branchioles** which further divides into **alveolar ducts** each of which opens into an **alveolar sac** or **infundibulum** or **atrium**. Each alveolar sac is made up of 6 to 8 pocket like outgrowths called **alveoli or airsacs**, these are the **sites of respiration**. Each alveolus is lined by **squamous epithelium** which is highly glandular and vascular; blood and air are separated by only two layers *i.e.,* **alveolar epithelium** and **capillary endothelium.** Each alveolus called as a miniature lung.

MECHANISM OF RESPIRATION

1. Breathing or pulmonary ventilation
2. Exchange of oxygen and carbon dioxide
3. Transport of gases in blood.

Breathing or pulmonary ventilation

i.e., inspiration or inhalation or breathing in and elimination or *exhalation* or breathing out. These are respiratory movements. Lungs are expanded or contracted in two ways.

(*i*) Downward and upward movement of the diaphragm to expand or contract the chest cavity.

(*ii*) Raising and depression of the ribs to increase or decrease the diameter of the chest cavity.

Inspiration

Active process, brought about by diaphragm muscles and external intercostal muscles (**inspiratory muscles**). Peripheral muscles contracts and lower the diaphragm making it flat and enlarges the thoracic cavity. External intercostal muscles, contracts and pulls the ribs and sternum upward and outward. Abdominal muscles relax and allow compression of abdominal organs by the diaphragm.

Expiration

Passive process, involves relaxation of the inspiratory muscles *i.e.*, peripheral muscle of diaphragm and external intercostal muscles. Diaphragm pushes upward and become convex. The contraction of *abdominal muscles* presses the *abdominal* viscera against the diaphragm, bulging further upward. Contraction of *internal intercostal muscles* move the ribs downward and inward. These two muscles are called *expiratory muscles.*

LUNG AIR VOLUMES

1. **Tidal volume (TV) :** Volume of air inspired or expired in relaxed or resting position. It is 500 ml (150 ml of dead space volume + 350 ml of alveolar volume).
2. **Inspiratory reserve volume (IRV) or complemental air** : The extra volume of air that can be inspired beyond the normal tidal volume. It is about 2500 – 3000 ml of air.
3. **Expiratory reserve volume (ERV) or supplemental air :** Volume of air in excess of tidal volume which can be exhaled due to forceful expiration. It is 1000 ml to air.
4. **Residual volume (RV) :** After forceful expiration, air left in lungs and dead space. It is about 1500 ml of air. It is useful for lungs in uninterrupted gaseous exchange.
5. **Inspiratory capacity (IC):** Amount of air that a person can inhale to the maximum level
   IC = IRV + TV = 2500 to 3000 ml + 500ml = 3000 to 3500 ml.
6. **Vital Capacity (V.C) of lung :** Maximum amount of air which can be breathed out through forceful expiration after a forceful inspiration.
   V.C. = TV + IRV + ERV = 3400 – 3800 ml.
7. **Total lung capicity (TLC) :** Maximum amount of air the lungs can hold after forceful inspiration:
   TLC = VC + RV. It is about 5600 – 6000 ml.
8. **Minute respiratory volume (MRV) :** Total amount of air which is moved into the respiratory passage *per* minute. It is equal to the product of tidal volume and the respiratory rate.
   Normal tidal volume = 500 ml
   Normal respiratory rate = 12 times/minute
   MRV = 6000 ml/minute.
9. **Functional residual capacity (FRC) :** Sum total of expiratory reserve volume (ERV) and residual volume (RV). It is about 2500 – 3000 ml.
10. **Pulmonary capacity (PC) :** Obtained through summation of two or *more* values.
11. **Dead space :** Part of respiratory tract not involved in gaseous exchange *i.e.*, nose to terminal bronchi. Volume 150 ml.

EXCHANGE OF OXYGEN AND CARBON DIOXIDE

In the alveoli of lung, oxygen of the inspirated air is taken by the blood and carbon dioxide is released into the alveoli for expiration. Alveolar air is separated from blood present in surrounding blood capillaries by a very thin partition of 0.2 11m thickness (average 0.6 μm). It is called **respiratory membrane. Diffusing capacity** of a gas across a membrane is the volume of gas that diffuses per minute for a pressure difference of 1 mm Hg. The rate of diffusion of CO_2 is 20 times faster than that of oxygen while oxygen diffuses twice as fast as nitrogen. The process of diffusion is directly proportional to the pressure caused by the gas alone.

Partial pressure

The pressure exerted by an individual gas is called partial pressure. Partial pressure of O_2, *i.e.*, PO_2, in alveolar air is about 100 – 104 mm Hg, while that of deoxygenated blood in alveolar capillary is 40 mm Hg. So, O_2 diffuses into blood and combines with haemoglobin to form oxyhaemoglobin. PO_2 of oxygenated blood is 95 mm Hg. PCO_2 of alveolar capillary blood is 46 mm Hg while in fresh alveolar air it is 40 mm Hg. As the diffusing capacity of CO_2 is 20 times higher than that of O_2, CO_2 of blood rapidly passes out into alveolar air. Its partial pressure in oxygenated blood is 40 mm Hg (equal to that of fresh alveolar air).

Gaseous exchange takes place in the tissues between tissue cells and capillary blood through the intestinal fluid. PO_2 in respiring cell is 20 mm Hg, tissue fluid 40 mm Hg while it is 95 mm Hg in capillary blood. Therefore, O_2 diffuses from blood into tissue fluid and from there into cells. Blood leaving the tissue capillaries has a Po_2 of about 40 mm Hg, PCO_2 of blood capillaries is 40 mm Hg, tissue fluid 46 mm Hg and that of cells 52 mm Hg. Therefore, carbon dioxide diffuses out of cells into tissue fluid and then blood. Blood leaving the tissue capillaries has a PCO_A, of 46 mm Hg.

TRANSPORT OF GASES IN BLOOD

- The **pulmonary artery** supplies oxygenated blood to the left atrium, from where it is pumped into left ventricle and ultimately, to the different tissues of the body.
- About 3% of oxygen travels as its solution in the plasma. Bulk of oxygen (about 97%) diffuses from the plasma into the red blood corpuscles. It loosely joins with the Fe^{++} ions of haemoglobin to form bright red oxyhaemoglobin (HbO), process is called oxygenation.

$$Hb_4 + 4O_2 \underset{\text{In tissue}}{\overset{\text{In lungs}}{\rightleftharpoons}} Hb_4\,O_8$$

- In the tissue capillaries low Pc_2 and high Pco_2 favour dissociation of oxyhaemoglobin to darker purplish red deoxygenated haemoglobin (reduced haemoglobin) and molecular oxygen.
- Oxygen diffuses from the blood into the tissue fluid and into the cells where it is used in oxidation. Haemoglobin returned to the lungs for reuse in oxygen transport.
- The relationship between the percentage saturation of the haemoglobin in the blood and the oxygen tension Po_2 of the blood depicts **oxygen dissociation curve of haemoglobin**. It is sigmoid and dependent on Po_2 Pco_2, temperature and pH. Increase in these factors brings rightward shift of the curve there by decreasing the affinity of haemoglobin for oxygen.
- **Bohr effect :** CO_2 reacts with water to form carbonic acid that lower the pH in active tissue and induces oxyhaemoglobin to give up more of its O_2. This phenomenon is called **Bohr effect**.
- In a normal and healthy person, the measurement of haemoglobin is approximately 15 g per 100 ml. 1 g of haemoglobin combines with oxygen is 1.34 ml. Thus on an average, 100 ml of blood carries about 20 ml (19.4 ml exactly) of oxygen.
- Carbon dioxide is carried by the blood in three forms:
  (*a*) **Physical solution :** About 7% of CO_2 transported by blood as carbonic acid which is formed by the dissolution of CO_2 in water. Each decilitre of blood transports about 0.3 ml of CO_2 in the dissolved form.
  (*b*) **Bicarbonate ions :** About 70% of CO_2 transported as sodium and potassium bicarbonates. CO_2 combines with water to form carbonic acid. The reaction is catalyzed by a zinc containing enzyme *carbonic anhydrase*. Carbonic acid dissociates into bicarbonate (joined by bases Na^+, K^+ to maintain pH of the blood) and hydrogen ions (picked up by proteins).
- **Chloride shift or Hamburger's phenomenon:** Exit of most of the bicarbonate ions considerably changes ionic balance between the plasma and the erythrocytes. To restore the ionic balance, the chloride ions diffuse from the plasma into the erythrocytes. This movement of chloride ions is known as chloride shift or Hamburger's phenomenon.
  (*c*) **Carbaminohaemoglobin :** About 23% of CO_2 entering the RBCs loosely combines

with the amino group ($-NH_2$) of the reduced haemoglobin (Hb) to form carbaminohaemoglobin.

$$HbO_2 + CO_2 \rightleftharpoons HbCO_2 + H^+ + O_2$$

- **Haldane effect :** Oxyhaemoglobin behave as a strong acid. As more and more oxyhaemoglobin forms in the lungs, it releases more and more H^+ ions that are formed thus increasing the acidity of blood.

Release of CO_2 in the Alveoli of Lung

- In the pulmonary capillaries, the CO_2, dissolved in plasma diffuses into alveoli.
- Carbaminohaemoglobin splits into CO_2 and haemoglobin. The same passes out of a erythrocytes and diffuses into alveolar air.
- The haemoglobin in the pulmonary blood takes up oxygen, the H^+ is released from it.
- The Cl^- and HCO_3^- ions are released from KCl in blood and $NaHCO_3$ in the RBC, respectively.
- HCO_3^- reacts with H^+ to form H_2CO_3 which splits into CO_2 and H_2O in the presence of carbonic anhydrase enzyme and CO_2 is released into lungs.

REGULATION OF RESPIRATION

Respiratory centres

A number of groups of neurons located bilaterally in the medulla oblongata control the respiration. Three respiratory centres are identified.

(*i*) **Dorsal Respiratory Group :** Present in **medulla oblongata**. stimulates the inspiratory muscles to control the normal rhythm of respiration, mainly causes inspiration.

Respiratory cycle (5 seconds) = Inspiration (2 seconds) + Expiration (3 seconds)

(*ii*) **Ventral Respiratory Group :** Nervous located **anterolateral to the dorsal respiratory group**, sends signals for both inspiration and expiration.

(*iii*) **Pneumotaxic centre :** Located in the dorsal part of **pons varolii,** transmits signals to the **inspiratory** area, primarily controls the switch off point of inspiration. During weak pneumotoxic signal, inspiration lasts for 5 seconds or more, resulting into complete filling of lungs. Strong signal causes increased rate of breathing because inspiration as well as expiration is shortened.

The concentration of CO_2 and H^+ causes increased strength of inspiratory as well as expiratory signal. However O_2 has no such direct effect.

RESPIRATORY DISORDERS

1. **Bronchitis :** Inflammation of the bronchi.
   - Characterised by **hypertrophy and hyperplasia** of the sero-mucous gland and goblet cells lining of the bronchi.
   - **Symptoms :** Regular coughing with thick greenish yellow sputum indicating infections and excessive secretion of mucus.
   - Caused due to cigarette smoking and exposue to air pollutants like carbon monooxide.
   - **Prevention and cure :** By avoiding smoking, irritating chemicals and pollutants. Bronchodilator drugs provide symptomatic relief. Intake of suitable antibiotics cure infection.
2. **Bronchial asthma :** Due to narrowing of bronchi and spasms in bronchial muscles (smooth).
   - Generally caused due to the hypersensitivity of the bronchiole to the foreign substances present in the air passing through it.
   - **Symptoms :** Coughing, or difficulty in breathing, mainly during expiration. Mucous glands become overactive producing a lot of mucus that clogs bronchioles and bronchi.
   - **Prevention and cure :** Avoiding exposure to the foreign substance or allergens; hypersensitisation; treatment includes antibiotic therapy, bronchodilator drugs as well as inhalers for symptomatic relief.
3. **Emphysema :** Inflammation or abnormal distension of the bronchiole or alveolar sac which results into the loss of elasticity of these parts.
   - Caused due to cigarette smoking and chronic bronchitis.

- Lung size increases but ventilation is poor.
- **Prevention and cure :** By avoiding exposure to cigarette smoke and pollutants. its a chronic lung disease resulting in irreversible distension and loss of elasticity of alveoli which can not be cured permanently.
- Symptomatic treatment involves use of branchiodilators, antibiotics and oxygen therapy.

4. **Pneumonia :** Acute infection due to inflammation of the alveoli of the lung.
   - Caused mainly due to infection of the bacteria, *Streptococcus pneumoniae.*
   - Infants, elderly persons and immuno compromised individuals are susceptible to it.
   - In this disease, most of the air space of the alveolar sac is occupied by the fluid with dead WBC.
   - **Prevention and cure :** By proper and timely vaccination, can be cured by the use of antibiotics, symptomatic treatment like bronchodilator drugs.
5. **Occupational lung disease :** Due to exposure of potentially harmful substances such as gas, fumes or dusts, present in the work place.
   - **Silicosis and asbestosis** occur due to chronic exposure of silica and asbestos dust in the mining industry.
   - Characterised by fibrosis (*i.e.,* proliferation of fibrous connective tissue) of upper part of lung, causing inflammation.
   - **Prevention and cure :** Symptoms appear after chronic exposure of 10–15 years or more. These are incurable. Preventive measures include-to minimise the exposure of harmful dust at the work place, harm of the exposure to such dusts to the workers should be preinformed, regular health checkup, protective gears and cloths, brief holiday from duty at short intervals for such workers.
   - Symptomatic treatment involves use of branchiodilators and antibiotics to remove underlying secondary infection.
6. **SARS** (Severe acute respiratory syndrome)- Typical pneumonia, caused due to a variant of common cold *Corona* virus which spreads by droplet and other methods.
7. **Whooping cough (Pertussis) :** Cough with inspiratory whoop caused by *Bordetella* (*Haemophilus*) *pertussis.*
8. **Asphyxia (Suffocation) :** The O_2 content of blood falls while the CO_2 content rises and paralyses the respiratory centre. Breathing stops and death takes place.

SOME IMPORTANT FACTS

- **Stick test :** A sensitive test to diagnose *Diphteria.*
- **Mantoux test :** A specific test for the presence of tuberculin in sputum inTB cases.
- **Word T B day :** 24th March.
- **Respiratory disorders**
  Apnoea : Temporary stopping of respiration.
  Acapnia : Stopping of respiration due to very low CO_2 in blood.
  Apneusis : Prolonging of respiration during inspiration.
  Atelactasis : Collapsing of lung alveoli.
  Eupnoea : Normal respiration rate.
  Hypopnoea : Decreased rate of respiration.
  Hyperpnoea : Increased rate of respiration.
  Dyspnoea : painful respiration.
  Hypercapnia : Increased CO_2 in blood.
- **Respiratory quotient (RQ) :** Ratio of CO_2 released to O_2 consumed in unit time. It is one (for glucose), 0.71 (for fats), 0.85 (for proteins), more than one for organic acids, infinity for anaerobic respiration etc.
- **Panting effect :** Controlled by pneumotaxic centre of pons varoli.
- **Cartilage of Santorini :** A nodule like cartilage at the upper end of each arytenoid cartilage.
- **Sternohyal and petrohyal muscles :** Help in buccopharyngeal and pulmonary respiration in frog.
- **Respiratory organ *e.g.,* book lungs** (in scorpions and most of spiders); **book gills** (in aquatic arachnids *e.g., Limulus*). **pulmonary sac** (in molluscs *e.g., Pila, Limax* etc.); dermal

branchiae (in echinoderms), pouched gills (in agnathans *e.g., Cyclostomes etc.*). Mediastinal space – Space between two pleura.

- **Ludwig** (1872) : Described gaseous exchange in blood.
- **Sleep apnoe syndrome (SAS) :** Persons with snoring habit seem to suffer from sleep apnoe syndrome because their respiratory tract closes on inhalation.
- **Spirogram :** Graph exhibiting pulmonary volumes and pulmonary capacities during different conditions of respiration.
- Mammalian RBC and skeletal muscles in exercise exhibit anaerobic respiration.
- **Positive chloride shift :** Shifting of Cl^- ions into RBC at cellular level.
- **Negative chloride shift :** Shifting of Cl^- ions into blood plasma from RBC at the lung level.
- **Coefficient of ultilization :** Percentage of oxygen used by the body tissue and it is 25%.
- **Spirometer or respirometer :** Apparatus to measure the amount of air exchanged during breathing.

DIGESTIVE SYSTEM

INTRODUCTION

Nutrition : Sum of processes involved in taking of all the nutrients required by the body, their internment, distribution and utilization for obtaining energy, repair and growth materials and body protection.

Nutrients : Materials required by the living organisms to sustain their life, they include oxygen, water and food.

Dietetics : Science of study and regulation of diet for specific requirements.

Dietetist or dietition : Specialist associated with the needs and problems of nutrition.

On the basis of mode of nutrition, the organisms are classified as **autotrophs** and **heterotrophs.** Autotrophs synthesise their own organic food from inorganic raw material (autotrophic nutrition). Heterotrophs are unable to manufacture their own food (heterotrophic nutrition).

TYPES OF NUTRIENTS

May be organic or inorganic in nature.

- **Organic nutrients** include carbohydrates, lipids, proteins and vitamins.
- **Inorganic nutrients** constitute minerals and water.
- **Macronutrients or Proximate principles of food :** Carbohydrates, lipids and proteins. These constitute the energy sources for the production of heat and different organic functions.
- **Micronutrients or Protective principles of food :** Minerals, vitamins and water. These donot provide energy but their deficiencies are related to specific diseases and abnormalities in man.
- **Macroelements (about 21 minerals) :** Essential for human nutrition, required in more than 100 mg per day *e.g.* Na, Ca, S, K, Mg, Cl.
- **Microelements** or **Trace elements :** Required in very small amounts *i.e.*, less than 100 mg per day e.g. Fe, I, Zn, Co, Cu, Mn, Mo etc.
- About 20 vitamins are thought to be required in small amount in human nutrition.

MODES OF NUTRITION IN ANIMALS

1. **Holozoic nutrition :** Engulfment of the whole or part of a plant or an animal, either in solid or in liquid state. *e.g.*, most of the free-living protozoans and animals.
2. **Saprozoic nutrition :** Organisms obtain food from dead and decaying organic food by first pouring digestive juices over the same and then sucking the digested food. *e.g.* spiders, horse-fly etc.
3. **Parasitic nutrition :** A smaller organism (parasite) draws food from another organism (host). *e.g. Plasmodium, Taenia,* Trypanosoma, Ascaris etc.
4. **Symbiotic nutrition or mutualism :** Two organisms or animals live in association and derive nutrition from each other. *e.g. Escherichia coli* and human. *E.coli* synthesize vitamin B_{12} for humans which human provide food to bacterium.

TYPES OF HOLOZOIC NUTRITION (INGESTIVE NUTRITION)

1. **Herbivores :** Consume only algae or plant material e.g. cow, horse and rabbit.
2. **Carnivores :** Flesh eating animals *e.g.* lion, tiger and dog.
3. **Omnivores :** Feed both plants and animals *e.g.* cockroach, rat, crows, man etc.

Others are:

4. **Cannibals :** Eat upon the members of their own species *e.g.* some fishes, cockroach, certain snakes etc.
5. **Predators :** When the larger animals feed upon the smaller animal species *e.g.* birds like eagle, kite etc.
6. **Piscivores :** Feed on fishes *eg.* crocodile, penguins, kingfisher etc.
7. **Insectivores :** Feed upon insects *e.g.* frog, lizards, small bats etc.
8. **Scavengers or Carrian eaters :** Feed up other dead and decaying material *e.g.* vultures, crow, hyena etc.
9. **Grainivorous :** Feed upon grains *e.g.* pigeon.
10. **Coprophagous :** Feed upon faeces *e.g.* dung beetle, pigs etc.
11. **Detritivores :** Feed chiefly upon dead organic matters present in the mud *e.g.* earthworms.
12. **Myrmecophagous :** Take ants as prey *e.g.* spiny ant eater, scaly ant eater.
13. **Larvaevorous :** Feed on larvae *e.g. Gambusia* fish.
14. **Sanguinivores :** Suck blood of other animals *e.g.* leeches, mosquitoes, fleas etc.
15. **Folivorous :** Eat leaves *e.g.* sheep, goat etc.
16. **Frugivores :** Eat fruits *e.g.* birds, monkey etc.
17. **Fluid feeders :** Feeding on plant fluids *e.g.* butterflies, male mosquitoes etc.

STEPS OF HOLOZOIC NUTRITION

1. **Ingestion :** Method of feeding on the basis of gross size of food, ingestion is of 2 types :
   (*a*) **Microphagy :** Feeding on microscopic organisms *e.g, Amoeba, Paramecium.*
   (*b*) **Macrophagy :** Feeding on larger form of organisms *e.g.* majority of non – chordates and some chordates.
2. **Digestion :** Breaking down of the covalent bonds in the organic food molecules (carbohydrates, lipids, proteins and nucleic acids) by hydrolysis. In heterotrophs, two types of digestion *i.e.*,
   (*a*) **Intracellular digestion :** takes place inside the individual cells with the help of lysosomal enzymes, found in unicellular protozoans. (*e.g. Amoeba, Paramecium)* and sponges.
   (*b*) **Extracellular digestion :** Digestion takes place outside cells within a cavity *e.g,* sac like coelenteron or *gastrovascular cavity* in cnidarians (*Hydra, Aurelia etc,)* Gastrovascular cavity is lined by endobderm cells which secrete their enzymes into cavity and digest the food extracellularly. The partly digested tragmented food particles are digested by nutritive cells for intracellular digestion. *i.e.*, Cnidarians perform both intra- and extracellular digestion.
   - Free living platyhelminthes or flat worms (*e.g. Planaria)* employ both types of digestion.
   - In most non – chordates and chordates a develped complete digestive tract (with two openings) present. The entire alimentary canal and its associated glands, together constitute alimentary or digestive system.
3. **Absorption :** The digested food is absorbed. The absorbed food is circulated in the body through blood vascular system for meeting the needs of cell living cells. The absorbed food is used for energy liberation and anabolic processes.
4. **Egestion :** Elimination of undigested food through food vacuole (exocytosis) in protozoans, single opening in cnidarians and **anus** in most non – chordates and chordates.

DIGESTIVE SYSTEM OF COCKROACH

Omnivorous, devour any kind of organic molecules as food.

Alimentary canal complete, three parts:

(*i*) **Foregut or Stomodaeum :** Ectodermal in origin, internally lines with cuticle, made up on pre-oral cavity (bounded by mouth parts, tongue-like hypopharynx hangs in it), mouth, pharynx, oesophagous, crop or ingluvius (largest, acts as reservoir, stores the food) and gizzard or proventriculus (**armerium** with six chitinous teeth, six cushion like pads or pulvilli, acts as strainer and **stomodael valve** which secrete a protective peritrophic membrane around the food).

(*ii*) **Mid gut or Mesenteron or Ventriculus :** Endodermal in origin, 7 or 8 tubular finger like hepatic caecae at the anterior end and 60 – 150 fine yellow coloured, thread – like **malpighian tubules** at the posterior end.

(*iii*) **Hindgut or Proctodaeum :** Ectodermal in origin, lined with cuticle like foregut, made up of ileum, colon and rectum (possess six longitudinal folds *i.e.*, **rectal papillae**). It finally opens out by a slit like aperture **anus** at the end of abdomen below the 10th tergum.

DIGESTIVE GLANDS

(*i*) **Salivary glands :** A pair, present in the thorax, one on either side of crop, made up of a biparfite and lobulated **glandular part** and a long sac-like **reservoir** or **receptacle**. Saliva is secreted by glandular part and contains starch splitting amylase enzyme.

(*ii*) **Hepatic caecae**

(*iii*) **Midgut lining**

Digestion is completed by the enzymatic secretions of hepatic cae cae and midgut lining which possess **Trypsin and Erepsin** (to hydrolyse protein into amino acids); **lipase** (to digest fats into fatty acids and glycerol); and **invertase, maltase** and **lactase** (to digest the carbohydrates like sucrose, maltose and lactose).

- Most of the absorption takes place in midgut. The lining cells of the caeca absorb the glucose only. Water and minerals are absorbed in hindgut.
- The undigested food or faeces finally expelled out through the anus in the form of almost solid pellets.

DIGESTIVE SYSTEM OF HUMAN

Consists of alimentary canal or gut and some accessary digestive organs.

- **Alimentary canal :** Coiled, muscular tube, extending from mouth to the anus, complete, about 6–9 metres long, consists of many specialised sections.
- Arranged sequentially, these are mouth, oral or buccal cavity, pharynx, oesophagus, stomach, small intestine, large intestine, rectum and anus.
- **Buccal or oral cavity :** Has two lateral walls (**cheeks**), an anterior roof (hard palate), a posterior roof (soft palate) and a pair of jaws the upper maxilla and lower mandible.
- **Tongue or lingua :** A thick, musculo-sensory organ, present on the floor of buccal cavity, greatly protrusible, posteriosly attached to the floor of buccal cavity by a soft ligamentous fold (*frenulum*). *Dorsum* is lined by a **straitified squamous epithelium** posses a median groove and three types of lingual papillae

  (*i*) **Circumvallate or Vallate papillae :** 8 – 12 in number, largest in size, in a Λ – shaped manner, at the the back of the tongue.

  (*ii*) **Fungiform papillae :** Numerous, mushroom-shaped, red coloured, present on the tip and sides of the tongue.

  (*iii*) **Filiform papillae :** Most abundant, smallest size, conical-shaped, present on anterior two-third part of the tongue.

  (*iv*) **Foliate papillae :** 4–5 transverse fold, at each border of the tongue near the base.

  - **Different areas for different taste *i.e.*, sweet (tip), salt (tip and sides), sour (sides) and bitter (base).**
  - Basal region of tongue possess two tonsils or **lingual tonsils**. Other types of tonsils are **pharyngeal** (adenoids) or **palatine** (posterolateral walls).

TEETH (DENTENES)

Each half of the jaw holds four types of teeth.

Incisors or cutting teeth

Chiesel shaped, present in anterior part of buccal cavity, used for cutting, chopping or gnawing.

(ii) Canine or tearing teeth

More pointed, dagger shaped, used for tearing or ripping or shredding.

***(iii)* Premolars and molars (cheek or grinding teeth)**

Broad, have 2 – 4 cusped crown, located in the posterior part of the buccal cavity, used for shearing, crushing and grinding.

Dental formula *i.e.,* arrangement of teeth, I^{12}, $C^{1/1}$, $PM^{2/2}$, $M^{3/3}$ or 2123/2123 = 32

Teeth are developed in two sets i.e. **milk** (or temporary or deciduous teeth and permanent (or successional) teeth. Dental formula of milk teeth is $I^{1/2}$, $C^{1/1}$, $PM^{0/0}$. $M^{2/2}$ or 2102/2102 = 20

(iv) Wisdom teeth

Third pair of molars of permanent set erupt between the eighteenth and twenty-fifth year and sometimes never erupt.

Human teeth are **the codont** (embeded injaw sockets i.e. alveoli), diphyodont (milk teeth are replaced by permanent teeth in the adult), heterodont (four types of teeth).

Structure of tooth

Made up of three parts *i.e.* **crown** (exposed part of tooth, made up of shining, whitish and hard substance *i.e.* **enamel** which is mainly formed of calcium phosphate, forms chewing surface of tooth), **neck** (covered by fleshy skin *i.e.,* **gum** or **gingiva**) and **root** (embedded in the socket of jaw bone and is fixed by a bone like cementum and a thick fibrous peridontal membrane).

Internally, a tooth is made up of a hard, bone-like substance *i.e.* **dentine** which encloses the **pulp cavity** (contain soft, gelatinous and vascular connective tissue *i.e.,* **pulp** that enters via **pulp canal** at the base. The pulp cavity is lined by dentine – forming cells *i.e.,* **odontoblasts.**

Stomach

Most distensible part, thick, muscular, J-shaped organ present on the left side of upper part of abdominal cavity, suspended by a mesentery *i.e.,* **mesogaster.** Four parts *i.e.,*

(*i*) **Cardiac stomach :** Broad upper part, receives oesophagous through **cardiac aperture** guarded by cardiac sphincter which prevents **regurgitation** of food

(*ii*) **Fundus :** Apex of stomach, contains gas or air.

(*iii*) **Body :** Main part, dome shaped.

(*iv*) **Pyloric entrum :** Lower, narrow part, opens in the duodenum by pyloric aperture or **pylorus** which is guarded by ***pyloric*** sphincter, it regulates passage of food into intestine.

Stomach helps in mechanical churning and chemical digestion of food. It acts as food reservoir.

Small Intestine

Longest part, about 20ft or 6 metres, narrow, tubular, divided into three parts.

(*i*) **Duodenum :** Widest, shortest (about 25 cm), most flexed part, forms a C-shaped curve, receives bile pancreatic duct.

(*ii*) **Jejunum :** Middle part, about 8 ft long

(*iii*) **Ileum :** Longest part (12 ft), opens into the large intestine, the opening is guarded by an **ileo-caecal valve.**

Small intestine is the main region where digestion and absorption of food takes place.

Large intestine or colon

About 5 feet (1.5 metres) long, shorter but wider than small intestine, forms an arc around the small intestine. Three parts.

(*i*) **Caecum :** Small, pouch like, ends into a tubular structure (13 cm long) called **vermiform appendix.** Caecum and vermiform appendix are **vestigial** as they are not involved in cellulose digestion.

(*ii*) **Colon :** Long sized, sacculated structure, differentiated into four regions *i.e.,* ascending colon (extending upto liver on the right side); transverse colon (crosses the abdominal cavity below the pancreas); descending colon (running downward on the left side and sigmoid or pelvic colon (S-shaped), enters the pelvis and joins the rectum). It is related with conservation of water, sodium or other minerals and formation of faeces.

(*iii*) **Rectum :** Slightly dilated part, about 13 cm long and related to temporary storage of faeces, leads into and canal (3-8 cm long), opens out by anus and guarded by two anal sphincter muscles.

HISTOLOGY OF HUMAN GUT

Four major layers of different cell types are :

(*i*) **Mucosa :** Inner most layer, moist and friction resistant lining epithelium, contains secretory and absorptive cells and some smooth cells at the base of mucosa.

(*ii*) **Submucosa :** Just outside mucosa, soft connective tissue layer with blood and lymph vessels and nerve supply.

(*iii*) **Muscularis externa :** Made up of a circular inner layer and a longitudinal outer layer of smooth muscle.

(*iv*) **Serosa :** Outer most layer, fibrous coat.

Villi : Millions of microscopic folds or finger like projections from mucosa, supplied with a network of blood capillaries and also a network of lymph vessels. Largest villi is **central lacteal.**

Microvilli or **brush border :** Numerous microscopic bristle like projections from the cells of surface of villi, help in absorption of nutrients.

Mucous or goblet cells : Present on surface of mucosal epithelium, single cell mucous glands, mainly secrete mucus that acts as a lubricant and protects the epithelial surface from excoriation and digestion.

Crypts of Leiberkuhn : Pits of intestine in the submucosa, contain specialised secretory cells.

Tubular glands : Besides stomach and upper duodenum.

THE ACCESSORY DIGESTIVE ORGANS

A. Tongue

Gustatory receptors, located in the buccal cavity, muscular organ with bony attachments (styloid process and hyoid bone).

B. Digestive glands

1. Salivary glands

(*i*) **Parotid glands :** largest, present just below the external ear, saliva is carried by the parotid ducts to the second upper molar tooth.

(*ii*) **Submaxillary glands :** lie beneath the jaw angles, secretion is carried by sub-maxillary or Wharton's ducts which open below the tongue.

(*iii*) **Sublingual glands :** Smallest sized, lie beneath the tongue and open at the floor of buccal cavity by a number of small **sublingual** or **Bartholin's ducts** or *ducts* of Rivinus.

Saliva = 95% water + 0.2% minerals + 0.3% organic compounds like mucin and a starch splitting enzyme **ptyalin** (salivary amylase).

2. Liver

Largest sized, weighs about 1.5 kg, reddish brown gland, present in the posterior concavity of the diaphragm in the right upper part of abdomen, multilobulated gland, Two main (larger **right** and smaller **left lobe**) and two smaller lobes (**quadrate** and **caudate** lobes).

Gall bladder : Present on the lower surface of right liver lobe, thin walled, pear shaped sac, stores bile secreted by the liver. Bile is drained from the liver by a bile duct which is made by the joining of a cystic duct from the gall bladder and a common hepatic duct from different liver lobes.

Bile duct and pancreatic duct (from pancreas) join to form **hepatopancreatic** duct just near the duodenum. This duct opens in duodenum which is guarded by a **sphincter** of **oddi.**

3. Pancreas

Second largest gland, yellow coloured, 12–15 cm long, **compound racemose gland,** present in the loop of duodenum, made up of **head, body** and **tail, heterocrine gland,** glandular cells secrete the **pancretatic juice** which is drained by a **pancreatic duct** which joins bile duct. Liver and pancreas act as **endocrine** and **exocrine** glands, whereas the gall bladder acts as a **storing organ.**

MOBILITY OF HUMAN GUT

The ability of alimentary canal to undergo movements through contraction and expansion of parts. It is required for propelling food, churning food, mixing food with digestive secretions, absorption and egestion.

The food is tasted in the oral cavity and mixed with saliva which is a mixture of water and electrolytes, derived from the blood plasma, mucus salivary amylase or ptyalin enzyme and lysozyme (antibacterial agent), all secreted by the salivary glands.

Swallowing

Mixture of food and saliva *i.e.* **bolus** pushed inward through the pharynx into the oesophagus. It involves coordinated activity of tongue, soft palate, pharynx and oesophagus.

Peristalisis

A wave of progressive contraction and distension which is useful in propelling food through the digestive tract. It is produced by involuntary contraction of circular muscles, which is preceded by a simultaneous contraction of the longitudinal muscle and relaxation of the circular muscle lining the gut. Sphincter muscle, guarding the junction of the oesophagus and stomach, normally remains closed and does not allow contents of the stomach to move back. In both small and large intestine it keeps the food moving forward.

GASTROINTESTINAL SECRETIONS AND DIGESTION

Exocrine tissues : Salivary glands, secretory cells in the stomach and intestinal epithelium, and the secretory cells of the liver and pancreas.

Exocrine secretion : Consists of aquedus mixtures of substances *i.e.*, water, ions, mucus and enzymes.

Role of digestive enzymes in digestion in mammals (Humans)

Gland	Enzyme	pH	Site of action	Substrats	Products of action
Salivary	Salivary amylase	6.7	Buccal cavity,	Starch	'Limit' dextrins, maltose, isomaltose
Gland	or ptyalin		Oesophagous,		
(Saliva)			Parts of stomach		
Gastric Gland	(*i*) Pepsinogen → Pepsin	1,2 – 8	Stomach	Protein casein (milk)	Peptones paracasein (curd)
(Gastric Juice)	(*ii*) Proprennin → Rennin (calf)		Stomach	Casein	Paracasein
	(*iii*) Hydrochloric acid		Stomach	Pepsinogen	pepsin
	(*iv*) Gastric lipase (infants)		Stomach	Milk fat	Fatty acids and glycerol
Pancreas (Pancreatic	(*i*) Pancreatic Amylase	8.8	Small intestine	Starch glycogen	'Limit' dextrins, maltose, Isomaltose
juice)	(*ii*) Trypsinogen $\xrightarrow{\text{enterokinase}}$ (Trypsin)		Protein	Peptides	
				Chymotryp-sinogen	Chymotrypsin
				Percarboxy Peptidases	Carboxypeptidases
	(*iii*) Elastase			Elastin	Large peptides
	(iv) Lipase			Fat	Fatty acids, monoglycerides, Glycerol
	(*v*) Chymotrypsinogen → Chymotrypsin			casein (milk)	Paracasein (curd)
	(*vi*) Carboxypeptidases			Larger peptides	Smaller peptides
	(*vii*) Amino peptidases			Larger	Oligopeptides
	(*viii*) DNAase			DNA	Deoxy ribonucleotides
	(*xi*) RNAase			RNA	Deoxy ribonucleotides

Gland	Enzyme	pH	Site of action	Substrats	Products of action
Small Intestine (Intestinal) (juice)	(*i*) Enteropeptidase or Enterokinase	8.3	Small Intestine	Trypsiogen	Trypsin
	(*ii*) Aminopeptidases			Peptides	Smaller peptides, amino acids
	(*iii*) Dipeptidases			Dipeptides	Amino acids
	(*iv*) Nucleotidases			Nucleotides Phosphoric acid	Nucleosidases, inorganic phosphate
	(*v*) Nucleosidases			Nucleosides	Sugars, purines
	(*vi*) Isomaltase			'Limit' dextrin Isomaltose	2 Glucose
	(*vii*) Maltase			Maltose	2 Glucose
	(*viii*) Sucrase (Invertase)			Sucrose	Glucose, fructose
	(*ix*) Lactase			Lactose	Glucose, galactose
	(*x*) Lipase			Triglycerides	Monoglycerides, fattyacids
Liver Bile	Bille Salts, no enzymes	8.0	Dueodenum	Fats	Fat droplets

HORMONAL CONTROL OF DIGESTION IN HUMAN

The activities of **gastrointestinal (GI) tract** are coordinated by **nervous** and **endocrine** systems of the body. **Gastrointestinal peptide hormones** are the hormones secreted by the endocrine cells found scattered in the mucosa of stomach and intestine, These hromones regulate the digestive activities. Most of the gastroinestinal hormones are **"local hormones"** as act upon the same part of gut which secrete them.

Hormone	Source	Stimulus	Target/Action
1. Gastrin	G-cells or Argentaffin cells of Pyloric stomach	Vagus nerve activitiy; peptides and proteins stomach	(*i*) Stimulates secretion of gastric juice. (*ii*) Constricts cardiac sphincter. and duodenum
2. Secretin	S–Cells of mucosa of duodenum and jejunum	Acidic chyme entry into duodenum	(*i*) Release of sodium bicarbonates in pancreatic juice (*ii*) Steps up secretion of bile (*iii*) Inhibits secretion of gastrin
3. Cholecystokinin (CCK)	I-cells of mucosa of	Presence of fats in duodenum	(*i*) Release of enzymes in pancreatic juice (*ii*) Release of bile from gall bladder
4. Gastric Inhibitory peptide (GIP)	**Upper part of small intestine *i.e.*, duodenum**	**Monosaccharides** and fats **(fatty) chyme in duodenum**	**(*i*) Inhibits** gastric mobility and secretion.
5. Enterogastrone	**Duodenum**	**Chyme entry** into duodenu	**(*ii*) Slows gastric contractions to delay its emptying** **(*iii*) Stops secretion of gastric** juice
6. Duocrinin	Duodenum	Acidic chyme **in intestine**	Activates **Brunner's glands** for producing **mucus** and HCo_3

Hormone	Source	Stimulus	Target/Action
7. Enterocrinin	Duodenum	Acidic chyme in intestine	Release of enzymes from Lieberkuhn's crypts
8. Motilin	Duodenum	Food/acidity	Mobility of stomach and intestine.
9. Villikinin	Intestinal epithelium	Food in duodenum	Accelerates movement of villi

ABSORPTION AND ASSIMILATION OF DIGESTED PRODUCTS IN HUMAN

Absorption

The digested food passes from the alimentary canal into the blood and lymph through its mucous membrane. This is called absorption. Absorption takes place by two types of processes *i.e*, **passive** and **active** absorption.

(A) Passive absorption

Takes place by physical processes like simple diffusion, osmosis and facilitated diffusion.

(*i*) **Simple diffusion :** Small and water soluble molecules takes place via concentration gradient across the apical membrane of the brush border of the cells lining the intestinal villi. They include fatty acids, monoglycerides, cholesterol and other fat soluble substances.

(*ii*) **Osmosis :** Water is absorbed by osmosis, Absorption of any solute raises the osmotic pressure of the blood and brings about absorption of an equivalent amount of water. Water is absorbed partly in the small intestine and mostly in the large intestine.

(*iii*) **Facilitated diffusion :** Hydrophilic lipid insoluble sugar such as fructose are carried down their concentration gradient by facilitated diffusion which is facilitated by specific transporter proteins present in the absorptive cell membrane.

(B) Active absorption

The nutrients are absorbed through the intestinal mucosa against concentration gradient. By active absorption, the nutrients can be absorbed completely from the intestinal lumen. There are two processes.

(*i*) **Active transport :** Involves the carrier molecules called permeases or translocases which are generally proteinous in nature. Glucose, galactose, amino acids, Na^+ etc. are absorbed by active transport. For active absorption of Na^+, a sodium pump operates in the cell membrane,

(*ii*) **Endocytosis :** Large sized liquid or solid nutrients are taken in some vesicles through the plasma membrane.

The end products of fats are a mixture of mono glycerides, fatty acids and glycerol. In the intestinal lumen, fatty acids, monoglycerides and the bile salts aggregate to form water-soluble molecules *i.e.*, **mixed micelles** which are taken by the intestinal mucosal cells generally by the process of pinocytosis.

The intestinal absorptive cells then, collect the reconstructed triglycerides, combine them with phospholipids and cholesterol, and release into the lymph in the form of protein-coated water soluble fat globules or droplets *i.e.,* **chylomicrons.**

Chylomicrons are transported to blood via the **central lacteal** of the lymphatic system for distribution throughout the body.

EGESTION OR DEFAECATION

- The waste material discharged from the alimentary canal is called **faeces** *or* **stool.**
- Faeces is made up of 75% water and 25% solid matter which is further made up of undigested roughage (30%), fats (20%)), inorganic matter (15%), proteins (3%) and bacteria (3%).
- Brown colour of faeces is due to **stercobilinogen** and **stercobilin** (formed from

bile pigments by the fermentive action of colon bacteria).

- Odour of faeces is due to skatole, indole, mercaptans, H_2S and CH_4.
- Faeces are given out through the anus by the process of **defaecation or egestion or evacuation.**
- Egestion is partly voluntary and partly involuntary process.

Nutritional Requirements of Humans

The food is mainly formed of six kinds of components *i.e.*, carbohydrates, proteins, lipids, vitamins, water, minerals etc. Carbohydrate, lipids and proteins are macro-nutrients or proximate principles of food which serve the energy sources. Vitamins and minerals are called micro-nutrients or protective principles of food which are non-provider of energy.

ENERGY YIELDING NUTRIENTS

Primarily carbohydrates are used as sources of chemical energy, metabolised into glucose, stored as glycogen. Living cells receive carbohydrates from blood mostly as glucose (**blood sugar**). Normal content of glucose in blood is 80–100 mg/ 100 ml. The process of synthesis of glycogen is called **glycogenesis.** The liver can store enough glycogen to maintain blood glucose level for several hours. Under acute starved conditions, the liver cells begin to convert amino acids and the glycerol into glucose. Such production of new glucose is known as **gluconeogenesis.**

Proteins are the most abundant organic biomolecules found in the living cells. These are polypeptide chains of amino acids. Animal proteins are called **first class proteins** because they provide all the amino acids required for building various proteinaceous substances. The amino acids, which cannot be formed by human from other amino acids are called **essential amino acids** which are 8 (10 in children) in number. Two amino acids are slow to be formed which are known as semi-indispensible *e.g.* arginine, histidine.

Lipids or fats or esters of fatty acid are the source of concentrated energy. Fat is major stored food kept in adipose tissue (fat depot). Subcutaneous fat not only provides body form but also functions as insulating layer. Some hormones require fat for their synthesis. Vitamins A, D, E and K require fat for their absorption and transport. Triglycerides are used as fuel. Human body is able to synthesize most of the fats in enough quantity except three polysaturated fats (linoleic, linolenic and arachidonic acids). These essential fatty acids are provided through diets.

The gross calorific values (*i.e.*, amount of energy liberated during complete combustion of 1 gm of substance in bomb calorimeter) of carbohydrates, proteins and fats are 4.1 k cal/g, 5.65 k cal/g and 9.45 k cal/g, respectively, where as, physiologic vallies (*i.e.*, amount of energy made available during complete oxidation of 1 gm of a substance inside the body) are 4.0 k cal/g, 4.0 k cal/g and 9.0 k cal/g, respectively.

MINERALS AND VITAMINS

Minerals are the elements which are present in small amounts (4% of body weight) and regulate various metabolic functions in our body. There are about 25 types of elements found in intracellular cytoplasm and extracellular fluids which are major or principal elements (about 95% of cellular pool. only 4 in number *i.e.*, C, H, O and N), **minor elements** (about 5% of cellular pool, 9 in number *i.e.*, Ca, Na, K, Mg, Fe, S, C1 and I) and **trace elements** (less than 1 % of the cellular pool, 12 in number *i.e.*, Co, Cu, Zn, Si, Mn, F, Va, Mo, B, Cr, Sn and Al).

On the basis of amounts, elements are *macro-elements* (required in amounts more than 100 mg per day, include Ca, Mg, Na, K, P, Cl) and *micro-elements* (often required in very small amounts *i.e.* less than 100 mg per day, include Cu, Co, Zn, Cr, Mn, Fe, Mo, Se, F, I etc.)

Some Important Minerals and their Functions

Mineral	Functions
1. Calcium	Component of bones and teeth; required for blood clotting, muscle contraction, ATP-ase, nerve impulse transmission, heart functioning etc. Deficiency causes **tetany** and **rickets.**
2. Chlorine	Chief anion of extracellular fluid, involved in HCl synthesis and acid-base balance.
3. Copper	Synthesis of haemoglobin; co-factor for enzymes *e.g.* oxidases, component of **haemocyanin**. Causes **anaemia**.
4. Iodine	Metabolic control as part of thyroid hormone thyroxine. Deficiency produces *goitre.*
5. Iron	Formation of Hb and myoglobin, respiratory enzymes *e.g.* cytochromes and, O_2 transport enzymes. Deficiency causes **anaemia**.
6. Phosphorus	Bone and teeth formation, part of nucleic acids, energy metabolism, phosphorylation, maintain normal blood pH (buffer action). Deficiency reduces growth, metabolism and causes **rickets** in children.
7. Potassium	Osmotic balance; muscle contraction; nerve-impulse conduction. Deficiency causes rickets among children.
8. Sodium	Osmotic balance; acid base balance; muscle contraction; nerve impulse conduction, bile salts.
9. Sulphur	Components of hormones (*e.g.* insulin), necessary for normal metabolism. Deficiency causes skin patches.
10. Zinc	Component of at least 70 enzymes *e.g.* carbonic anhydrase and some peptidases.
11. Flourine	Maintain enamel and prevents dental caries. Deficiency causes dental caries.
12. Magnesium	Co-factor of enzymes *e.g.* Hexokinase. Causes heart and vascular irregularities.
13. Manganese	Normal reproductive function, co-factor for enzymes. Deficiency causes **reproductive failure.**
14. Molybdenum	Co-factor for nitrogenase enzyme. Causes **whiptail disease** in cauliflower.

Vitamins are organic compounds, always taken from outside the body along with food in small amounts (mg or mg/day) so called **micro-nutrients** and are vital for certain metabolic activities of life.

- Absence or deficiency causes **avitaminosis or deficiency disease** while excess causes **hypervitaminosis** and metabolic disorders.
- Term **vitamin** coined by C. Funk (1911) who discovered vitamin B_1.
- On the basis of solubility vitamins are of two types :

  (i) **Fat soluble vitamins :** Derived from 5-carbon hydrocarbon – **Isoprene** soluble in organic solvents. *e.g.* vitamin A, D, E, and K.

  (ii) **Water soluble vitamins :** Vitamin B and C.

Some Important Vitamins

Vitamins Functions	Some important Vitamins	Deficiency Symptoms
(A) Fat Soluble Vitamins		
1. Vitamin A (Retinol) epithelial tissue.	**Body growth, principal component of retinal pigments; promotes normal vision, growth of bones and teeth, and maintenance of Night blindness, Keratomalacia, Retarted growth**	**Xerophthalmia,**

Vitamins Functions	Some important Vitamins	Deficiency Symptoms
2. Vitamin D (Calciferol)	Antirachitic, absorption and retention of Ca and P, growth and maintenance of bone	Rickets in children, Osteomalacia in women
3. Vitamin E (Tocopherol)	Prevents oxidative breakdown of vitamins, also for normal functions of gonads.	Reversible sterility in rats, Erythrocyte breakdown.
4. Vitanlin K (Phylloquinone)	Prothrombin formation in liver	Haemorrhage
(B) Water Soluble Vitamins		
1. Vitamin C (Ascorbic acid)	Absorption of iron, formation of dentine collagen and bone matrix, amino acid oxidation, anti-oxidant, recovery from toxicity and burns	Scurvy
2. Vitamin B complex		Beri-Beri
(*i*) Vitamin B_1 (Thiamine)	Formation of cocarboxylase enzyme involved in decarboxylation (citric acid cycle) –	
(*ii*) Vitamin B_2 (Riboflavin)	Maintenance of skin and oral mucosa, component of FMN and FAD	Cheilosis, glossitis
(*iii*) Vitamin B_3 (Pantothenic acid)	Participates in metabolism as coenzyme A	Dermatitis in chicken, Early ageing in man
(*iv*) Vitamin B_5 (Niacin)	In oxidation-reduction reactions as coenzyme NAD or NADP	Pellagra
(*v*) Vitamin B_6 (Pyridoxine)	Component of coenzyme pyridoxal phosphate	Anaemia, convulsions, impairment of antibody synthesis
(*vi*) Vitamin H or B_4 (Biotin)	Involved in carboxylation and decarboxylation	Dermatitis, muscular pain, growth failure
(*vii*) Folic acid	Formation and nucleoturation ofRBCs	Macrocytic anaemia
(*viii*) Vitamin B_{12} (Cyanoco-balamine)	Important for nucleoprotein synthesis and formation of RBCs, Myelin formation	Pernicious anaemia

NUTRITIONAL DEFICIENCIES AND DISORDERS

- **Malnutrition :** Impairment of health due to improper intake of food or nutrients. It covers problems of undernutrition and overnutrition.
- **Undernutrition :** Taking a diet deficient in calories. It may also result from inability to digest, assimilate or utilize the necessary nutrients.
- **Overnutrition :** Intake of excess food and nutrients which are stored as increased body mass, may produce overweight and obesity (excessive accumulation of fat in tissues).
- **Hypercholesterolemia :** Blood cholesterol content becomes abnormally high, ultimately leading to cardiac disorder, mainly due to excess intake of saturated fats like butter, ghee, vegetable oils, red meat, eggs etc.

Nutritional Disorder

Nutritional	Disorders	Deficiency symptoms
1. Protein	Kwashiorkor (Protein energy malnutrition, PEM)	**Stunted growth in the children; loss of appetite; anaemia; bulging eyes; protruded belly; darkening of the skin; repeated diarrhoea; atrophy of muscles, oedema of hands, feet and face**
2. Protein and Calorie	Marasmus	**Shrieveled appearence, subcutaneous fat used, ribs prominent, skin dry and wrinkled, stunted growth and repeated diarrhoea, extreme thinning of limbs (emaciation).**

Nutritional	Disorders	Deficiency symptoms
3. Iron	Anaemia, failure to mature RBC	Reduced number and size of RBC, reduced haemoglobin content, reduced learning ability, increased risk of infection and even death during child birth.
4. Iodine	Goitre	Enlargement of thyroid gland, cretinism in childhood causes retarded physical, mental and sexual growth.
5. Flouride	Dental caries	Appearence of cavities in the teeth due to acids produced during anaerobic respiration of bacteria.
6. Vitamin C (Ascorbic acid)	Scurvy	Bleeding gums, loosening and falling of teeth, pain in muscles and joints, loss of weight and poor wound healing.
7. Vitamin A (Retinol)	Xerophthalmia, Night blindness (Nyctalopia)	Non-functioning of lacrymal glands; dryness and keratinization of conjunctiva and cornea. Inability to see at night
8. Vitamin D (Calciferol)	Rickets in children Osteomalacia in adult	Weak and soft bones, distorted skeleton, poor muscular development.
9. Vitamin B_{12} (Cyanocobalamin)	Pernicious Anaemia	Enlarged size but reduced number of erythrocytes.
10. Vitamin K	Haemorrhage (Menadione)	Deficiency of prothrombin in the blood, deficiency of factor VII, IX and X required for blood coagulation.
11. Vitamin B_1 (Thiamine)	Beri-beri	Muscular dystrtophy (dry beri-beri), heart enlargement, indigestion nervous disorder, polyneuritis (wet beri-beri)
12. Folic acid	Macrocytic anaemia	Impairment of antibody synthesis, stunted growth.
13. VitaminB_5 (Niacin)	Pellagra (4 – D syndrome)	Dermatitis, dementia, diarrhoea and death.
14. VitaminB_6	Marasmus	Convulsions, dermatitis, impairment of antibody synthesis
15. VitaminB_2	Cheilosis	Cracking of skin at corners of mouth and base of nose
16. Vitamin E (Tocopherol)	Sterility	In adult female, foetus is resorbed in the uterus after sometime. Atrophy of seminiferous tubules of testes in adult male.
17. Vitamin B_3	Ageing	Poor growth, early ageing and greying of hair.

SOME IMPORTANT FACTS

- **World food day :** 16th October.
- **Basal Metabolic Rate (BMR) :** Amount of energy required by a person to maintain vital functions at rest or sleep. It increases with decrease in size of organism. It is about 1600 k cal/day.
- **Active Metabolic Rate (AMR) :** Amount of energy required daily by a person to maintain its high metabolic rate during heavy physical work. It is about 6000 k cal/day.
- **Routine Metabolic Rate (RMR) :** Daily energy requirement in a moderately active person. It is 2800 k cal/day for/adult man and 2200 k cal/ day for a woman.
- **IDD : Day** (Iodine Deficiency Disorder Day) : 21st October.
- **Senile-dementia :** Neurological problem usually after 65 years.
- **Presenile-dementia :** Neurological problem at younger age, also called Alzheimer's disease.
- **Balanced diet :** Which provides materials for all the metabolic requirements of body. Carbohydrates, proteins and fats should be in 5 : 1 : 1.
- **Dentition :**

1. **Polyphyodont :** Replaced many times during life span ego fish, amphibia and reptiles.
2. **Diphyodont :** Appearence of two sets of teeth in the life span *e.g.* mammals.
3. **Monophyodont :** Replaced only once during life span *eg.* molar and premolar teeth of mammals, duck billed platypus and toothed whale.
4. **Acrodont :** Teeth are direct extension of the bone, not embedded in sockets ego reptiles (except crocodiles), amphibians.

5. **Thecodont:** Embedded in sockets *e.g.* mammals and crocodiles.
6. **Homodont or Isodont :** All teeth are similar *e.g.* amphibians, reptiles and toothed whale.
7. **Heterodont :** Teeth are of different types *i.e.* ,more than one type *e.g.* incisors, canines, molars, premolars in mammals.
8. **Pleurodont :** Teeth fixed by sides to lateral. surface on jaw ridge *eg.* snakes.
9. **Bunodont :** Round cusps *e.g.* primate mammals (man).
10. **Lophodont :** Raised transverse ridges on teeth *e.g.* elephant.
11. **Solenodont :** Crescent shaped cusps where teeth appear as single plate *e.g.* Horse and pig.
12. **Carnassial teeth or secondont :** The cusps are pointed *e.g.* carnivore mammals.

- **Dental Formula of Some Mammals :**
  Cow =I 0/3, C 0/1, Pm 3/3, M 3/3 = 32
  Sheep = I 0/3, C 0/1, Pm 3/3, M 3/3 = 32
  Bat = I 2/3, C 1/1, Pm 0/0, M 4/5 = 32
  Man = 12/2, C 1/1, Pm 2/2, M 3/3, = 32
  Rabbit = I 2/1, C 0/0, Pm 3/2, M 3/3 = 28
  Dog= I 3/3, C 1/1, Pm 4/4, M2/3 = 42
- Ruminants mammals have specialised stomach called as **compound stomach** made up of : **Rumen** (largest part, 60 – 70% of cellulose is digested by bacteria in this region), **Reticulum** (internally highly folded, rich in water cells which store metabolic water), **Omasum** (amylase digest starch) and **Abomassum** (true stomach where digestive juices are released).
- Erythrocyte maturing factor (EMF) - Vitamin B_{12}.
- **Gaucher's disease :** Abnormal fat deposition or lipidosis in liver, lymph nodes, spleen, alveolar capillaries and bone marrow due to deficiency of enzyme glucocerebrosidase. It causes enlargement of spleen and liver, impairment of various body functions and leads to death.
- **Diastema :** A space in jaw where canines are absent *e.g.* rat and squirrel.
- **Tusks of elephant :** Evergrowing upper incisors while **tusks of walrus** are modified canines.
- In **sloths** and **Armadilloes :** Teeth are without enamel.
- **Stomach** absent in *Labeo,* Lamprey and Hagfish.
- **Duct of Wirsung :** Main pancreatic duct. Accessory duct is called **duct of Santorini.**
- **Caries :** Decay of teeth due to degeneration of enamel and formation of cavities.
- **Pyorrhoea :** Infected gums and tooth sockets.
- **Maximum number of teeth : Opossum** – 50, Horse and Pig – 44.
- **Salivary glands absent in Human :** Infra orbital glands.
- **Hepatopancreas :** Digestive glands of crustaceans (prawn) and molluscs.
- **Protein Energy Metobolism (PEM) :** Deficiency of proteins as well as food calories.
- **Vitamin L : 'Lactation vitamins'** from liver and yeast that promote milk secretion.
- **Hunger pangs :** Stomach churns every 20 seconds. When an empty stomach churns, hunger pangs are felt.
- **White revolution :** Increased milk production.
- **Blue revolution :** Increased fish production.
- **Silver revolution :** Increased egg production.
- **Yellow revolution :** Increased oil production.
- Surgical removal of tonsils, gall bladder and vermiform appendix is called **tonsillectomy, cholecystectomy and appendictomy,** respectively.
- **Choleresis :** Process of bile secretion.
- **Vitamin B_{17} :** Recently discovered vitamin with anti-cancer properties.
- **Vitamin Q :** Helps in blood clotting. Discovered by A. J. Quick.
- Egg white contains **avidin** protein which interferes the absorption of Biotin.
- **Philtrum :** A depression on upper lip and below the nose.
- **Frenulum :** A fold which connects the inner lining of lip to the gum.

- **Hump of camel** has stored fats. Chemical breakdown of these fats provides water for metabolism during deficiency of water.
- **Odontology** : Study of teeth
- **Goblet cells :** In the gastric glands and mainly located in their neck part.
- Viral infection of **parotid** salivary glands results in **mumps** characterised by painful jaw movements.
- **Peyer's patches :** Lymphoid masses in submucosa of ileum and are involved in the production of B-lymphocytes. Also called as **abdominal tonsils.**
- **Zymogenic cells** are mainly present in the basal part of fundic gastric glands.
- **Trypsin** is called **universal enzyme** because found from protozoans to mammals.
- **Jaundice :** Yellowing of skin and eyes due to presence of increased level of bile pigments especially **bilirubin** in blood. It may be due to increased hepatitis or liver cirrhosis (fatty liver syndrome).
- **Pendular movements** ring like contractions moving backward and forward over short lengths of intestine to churn and mix the food and digestive secretions.
- **Tartar :** Hard deposit of calcium phosphate on the teeth.
- **Vitamin P** (Citrin, Permeability vitamin) – Reduces permeability and fragility of capillaries.
- **Oedema :** Accumulation of intestinal fluid in the tissues, takes place due to acute kidney failure.
- **Vitaminer :** Different forms of some vitamin *e.g.* A_1 andA_2
- **PABA** (Para – Amino Benzoic Acid) acts as coenzyme and is converted with folic acid by bacteria.
- Among the diet, carbohydrates and fats acts as **energy sources;** proteins, salts and water act as **body builders,** while **vitamins** and **hormones** acts as **regulators.**

THERMOREGULATION

INTRODUCTION

Homeostasis : Maintenance of the constant internal environment of the body. Both osmoregulation and excretion help in maintaining chemical and fluid homeostasis *i.e.,* nearly uniform and beneficial physiological state in the body.

Osmoregulation : The regulation of water content and salt concentration in the body of an organism.

Osmosis : Type of diffusion where the movement of water takes place from a dilute solution **(hypotonic)** to a strong solution **(hypertonic)** across a semipermeable membrane. No water movement takes place when two solutions have same molarity and are called **isotonic.**

Osmolarity : Total solute concentration of a solution, indicates number of moles of solute per litre of a solution. Unit is milliosmole per litre(mosm L^{-1}).

Osmoconformers : Animals which have wide range of osmolarity of their body fluids and change their osmolarity according to that of surrounding medium. *e.g.,* all marine invertebrates, some fresh water invertebrates and a single vertebrate *i.e.,* **hagfish.**

Osmoregulators : Animals which can maintain an internal osmolarity different from the surrounding medium *e.g.,* many aquatic invertebrates (**strict or limited osmoregulators**). and most vertebrates (**strictosmoregulators**) except *Myxine* (hagfish – a marine cyclostome) and elasmobranchs (sharks and rays). Osmoregulators maintain their osmolarity by taking water in or out of their bodies.

Euryhaline : Organisms that can tolerate a wide range of salinity.

Stenohaline : Organisms that can live within a narrow range of salinity.

WATER AND SOLUTE REGULATION

1. In Fresh Water Environment

Fresh water vertebrates have hypertonic body fluids (osmolarity about 200–3000 mosmol per litre) than the surrounding water (less than 50 mosmol per litre). Such animals encounter two problems *i.e.,* gain of water due to osmotic gradient and continuous loss of body salts. Fresh water animals prevent the net gain of water and net loss of body salts by several means –

(*i*) Protozoans like *Amoeba. Paramecium* etc. possess contractile vacuole to pump out excess water.

(*ii*) By excreting large volume of very dilute urine.

(*iii*) Fresh water fishes do not drink water.

(*iv*) Presence of impermeable covering over the body (subcutaneous fat layer of scaleless fish and scales over the body of fish or crocodile).

(*v*) Active absorption of ions against concentration gradient (less than 1 mM NaCl in water and 100 mM NaCl in body fluids) with the help of specialised cells *e.g.*, ionocytes or chloride cells in the gill membrane.

2. In Marine environment

Body fluids of marine vertebrates is hypotonic (about 300 mosmol per litre) to sea water (osmolarity about 1000 mosmol per litre). They have the problem of water loss from their body fluids through their permeable surface of gills, mouth and anal membranes. Water loss is prevented by :

(*i*) Drink sea water.

(*ii*) Expel excess of monovalent ions *e.g.*, Na^+, K^+, Cl^- etc. from their body fluids to sea water with the help of ionocytes or chloride cells of membrane of gill lamellae.

(*iii*) Eliminate divalent ions *e.g.*, Mg^{2+} and SO_4^{2-} with faeces.

(*iv*) Hilsa, Salmon and other fish migrate between sea water and fresh water when in ocean, drink and excrete excess salt through the gill membrane. A number of hormones play a key role in this switching over process.

(*v*) Elasmobranch fishes (shark and rays) and coelacanth (*e.g.*, lobe finned fish) prevent loss of water by accumulating organic osmolytes like urea and trimethylamine oxide (TMAO). It makes the fishes rather hyperosmotic but hypoionic to sea water.

3. In terrestrial Environment

Land animals are airbreathers which constantly lose water through their respiratory surfaces *e.g.*, Man loses nearly 400 ml of water per day through its lungs in normal resting condition :

(*i*) Animals utilize various means to minimise this water loss *e.g.*, waxy coated **chitinous plates** in insects, **calcareous shell** in molluscs; a water proof and multi-layered epidermis of skin in the tetrapods etc.

(*ii*) By drinking water and taking moist food.

(*iii*) To avoid the day heat and to reduce water loss, many desert animals have become nocturnal *e.g.*, behavioural adaptation.

(*iv*) **Camels** (ship of desert) minimize water loss by producing dry faeces and concentrated urine, when plenty of water they can drink upto 80 litres of water in 10 minutes, reduce the chances of overheating by orienting themselves in such a way that minimum surface area is exposed to direct sunlight; In case of water scarcity they do not produce urine, store urea in tissues and solely depend on metabolic water.

(*v*) Desert mammals have special adaptations to reduce water loss *e.g.*, **Kangaroo rat** does not drink water but can recover 90 per cent of the water loss by using **metabolic water. Nasal counter current mechanism** is also present to conserve the water from the expired air.

EXCRETORY SYSTEM

ELIMINATION OF NITROGENOUS WASTES

Nitrogenous waste materials are formed as the end product (mainly) of protein metabolism and small amounts by metabolism of nucleic acids.

Nitrogenous wastes are produced in two ways :

(*i*) Deamination of excess and unwanted amino acids present in the food taken **(exogenous source)** and

(*ii*) Breakdown of body's own proteins and nucleic acids **(endogenous source).**

On the basis of nature of nitrogenous end products, there are three types of excretion.

1. Ammonotelism

Main nitrogenous end product is **ammonia**; animals with such excretion are called ammonotelic animals.

Readily soluble in water and highly toxic (because of high pH). *e.g.*, many aquatic animal groups like protozoans *(e.g.. Amoeba. Paramecium);* sponges (*e.g., Scypha*); Coelenteratas (*e.g., Hydra*); Crustaceans *(e.g., Palaemon);* echinoderms (*e.g., Asterias*); bony fishes (*e.g.*, Teleosts); Tadpole larva and some aquatic amphibians *(e.g.*, salamanders).

2. Ureotelism

Main nitrogenous waste is **urea**, animals are called **ureotelic** animals; 1,00000 times less toxic than ammonia, water soluble but can be concentrated to some extent (100 times in human, several hundred times in camels, sharks and kangaroo rat). *e.g.*, cartilagenous fishes, adult amphibians, aquatic reptiles(like turtles), mammals etc. Urea is produced in liver from ammonia and CO_2 through ornithene or urea cycle.

3. Uricotelism

Main nitrogenous waste is **uric acid** animals are called **uricotetlic** animals, least soluble nitrogenous waste, least toxic adaptation to terrestrial mode of life. *e.g.*, in birds, land reptiles (*e.g.*, lizards and snakes); insects (*e.g.*, Cockroach); land snails (*e.g., Helix)* and some land crustaceans (*e.g., Oniscus).* The white part of the faecal matter dropped by lizards and birds made up of insoluble crystals of uric acid and urates. The faceal matter is called **guano.** In human being main sources of uric acid are purines. Uricotelism is particularly advantageous to the land vertebrates those lay shelled eggs.

Tadpole and aquatic amphibians excrete ammonia while their terrestrial adult forms and excrete urea.

Most terrestrial reptiles excrete uric acid, but crocodiles excrete ammonia in addition to uric acid.

Aquatic turtles excrete both urea and ammonia.

Some tortoise can even modify their nitrogenous wastes when their environment is changed.

EXCRETORY ORGANS AND PRINCIPAL N_2 WASTES

Phyla/class	Excretory /osmoregulatory organ/organelles	Principal N_2 waste	Example
(A) Invertebrates			
1. Protozoa	Contractile vacuole	Ammonia	*Amoeba, Paramecium*
2. Porifera	General body surface	Ammonia	*Sycon, Leucon*
3. Coelenterata	General body surface	Ammonia	*Hydra*
4. Platyhelminthes	Flame cells (solenocytes) form the protonephridial system	Ammonia	*Taenia. Fasciola, Planeria*
5. Nematoda	H-shaped excretory system, Rennett cells	Ammonia	*Ascaris*
6. Annelida	Nephridial system, metanephric various types	Ammonia	*Pheretima*
7. Arthropoda			
(*a*) Class-Insecta	Malpighian tubule	Uric acid	*Periplaneta*
(*b*) Class-Crustacea	Antennary (green) gland	Uric acid	*Palaemon*
(*c*) Class-Arachnida	Coxal glands	Uric acid	*Spider*
8. Mollusca	● Kidney (organ of Bojanus)	Aquatic form Ammonia	*Pila*
	● Keber's organ	Terrestrial form Uric acid	Pulmonate mollusc *Limax*
9. Echinodermata	Dermal branchiae, tubefeet, body surface	Ammonia	*Cucumeria, Asterias*
B. Vertebrates			
1. Class-Cyclostomata	Pronephros (archinephros)	Urea	*Petromyzon*
2. Class-Pisces	Mesonephros	Urea	All fishes
3. Class-Amphibia	Mesonephros	Urea	Amphibians
4. Class-Reptilia	Metanephros	Uric acid	Reptiles
5. Class-Aves	Metanephros	Uric acid	Aves
6. Class-Mammalia	Metanephros	Urea	Mammals

HUMAN EXCRETORY SYSTEM

One pair of kidneys, one pair of ureters, a urinary bladder and a urethra.

1. Kidney

Primary or major excretory organ, one pair, large sized, 10 cm long × 5 cm broad x 3 cm thick, bean shaped, dark red 125-170 gm in weight in adults, slightly flattened structure, present in upper part of abdominal cavity along dorsal body walt one on either side of vertebral column. Concavity of kidney **(hilum or hilus renalis)** is always inward directed. Each kidney is embeded in **renal fat. Asymmetrical** in position, right kidney is slightly posterior in position and is probably pushed by well developed liver. There are **extra-coelomic, retroperitoneal** and **metanephros** in position. Each kidney is made up of about **one million uriniferous or renal tubules** or nephrons.

2. Ureters

One pair, long, 25 – 30 mm, muscular tubular, narrow, arising from the **hilum** of kidney by its upper broader part **(renal pelvis)**, open in dorsal wall of urinary bladder, lined by **transitional epithelium.**

3. Urinary bladder

Large, thin walled distensible, pear shaped sac, present in pelvis region of abdominal cavity, wall lined with smooth muscles (*detrusor muscles*), temporarily stores urine, lined by **transitional epithelium.** *Upper broader part* (body *of bladder*) is concerned with storage of urine, **lower narrow part** is neck of bladder. **Internal urethral orifice** (at narrow part) guarded by *two sphincters;* inner **smooth muscle fibres** and outer **striated muscle fibre.** Trigone – Small triangular area in the wall of bladder, formed of 3 openings (2 openings of ureters and 1 internal urethral orifice at the lower most end of trigone).

4. Urethra

Muscular, tubular, extends from neck of bladder to outside. In female about 4 cm long and opens out directly by external urethral orifice above the vaginal orifice in vulva. In male urethra (20 cm long) joins the ejaculatory duct to form urinogenital canal which passes through the penis and opens by urinogenital aperture at the tip of penis and is differentiated into 3 parts – **prostatic** (about 2.5 cm through prostate gland and receiving sperm ducts), *membranous* (about 2.5 cm, free) and **penile** (about 15 cm and inside penis).

STRUCTURE OF A NEPHRON (URINIFEROUS TUBULE OR RENAL TUBULES)

One million per kidney, more convoluted in peripheral part *i.e., renal cortex* and is central part there tubules run straight *i.e., renal medulla. 2 types of nephrons.*

(*a*) **Cortical nephron** (about 80 – 90%) in human kidney but less in other placentals.

(*b*) **Juxta medullary** (10 – 20%).

Cortical nephron

About 3 cm long, 20 – 60 mm is diameter, formed of two parts :

1. Bowman's capsule with glamerulus (renal corpuscles)

Double walled cup present in the renal cortex, lined by a thin and semipermeable squamous epithelium formed of flat cells. Inner layer is **visceral layer** and outer layer is **parietal layer**. Visceral layer is made up of **podocytes** or **foot cells** (special epithelial cells) having millions of minute pores called slit pores to pass ultrafiltrate. In the cavity of Bowman's capsule, about 50 capillaries called *glomerulus present. The glomerlus is* made up of branches of afferent arteriole which interconnect to form tuft of capillaries capped by Bowman's capsule. Glomerular capillary endothelium has numerous minute pores called **fenestrae.**

A basement membrane (between visceral epithelium and glomerular capillary endothelium) acts as **dialysing membrane.** The visceral layer, basement membrane and glomerular endothelium collectively form a filtering membrane which acts as **ultrafilter** and responsible for **ultrafiltration.**

Bowman's capsule and glomeralus, both collectively called **malpighian** body (first reportered by M. Malpighi, 1966) or renal corpuscle of Pygmalian corpuscle and is about 150 mm is diameter.

2. Nephric tubule

Long, coiled and formed of

(i) **Proximal convoluted tubule** (PCT) : Continuous with Bowman's capsule, lined by brush bordered **cuboidal epithelial cells** with numerous microvilli, cells have numerous mitochondia for active transport and selective reabsorption of sodium, calcium, glucose, amino acids etc. from nephric filtrate. 75% of filtrate is absorbed, remaining is isotonic with blood. Some waste products present in the blood of peritubular capillaries pass into lumen of PCT through tubular secretion across the intestitial fluid. The phenomenon is called **tubular secretion** *e g*., H^+, NH_3 drugs, toxic substances.

(ii) **Loop of Henle** : Runs straight in renal medulla, U-shaped, formed of thin descending (lined by **squamous epithelium**) and thick ascending limb (lined by cuboidal epithelium). Descending limb is permeable to water but not to NaCl, while ascending limb is absolutely impermeable to water but permeable to NaCl.

(iii) **Distal convoluted tubule (DCT)** : Convoluted part, present in cortex, opens in the collecting tubule, lined by cuboidal epithelum with a few microvilli. DCT is permeable to both Na^+ and K^+.

(iv) **Collecting tubule (CT)** : Drains a number of ducts of DCT is the cortex, descends to the tip of medulla to form the collecting ducts of Bellini which empty via calyces into renal pelvis. The highly **columnar cells** of CT respond to circulating titers of ADH (antidiuretic hormone) which affects their permeability and size of intercellular space.

Juxtamedullary Nephrons

Glomeruli are placed close to the inner margins of the cortex, and long loops of Henle are placed deep into the medulla and are associated with vasa recta. The blood first passes through the capillaries of glomerulus, and then, flows through the hair pin loops of the vasa recta of the loop of Henle. It operates when there is shortage of water and more concentrated urine is to be formed.

MECHANISM OF URINE FORMATION

1. Glomerular filtration (Ultrafiltration)

Glomerulus obtains blood from an **afferent arteriole** (broader) and is drained out to form an **efferent arteriole** (narrow). Blood present in glomerulus is put to a great pressure. The walls of Bowman's capsule and glomerular capillaries are closely applied and extremely thin so that pressure of the blood causes the plasma to filter out a fluid into lumen of Bowman's capsule (Richards and Other, 1924). This filtration is very fine and is caused by pressure it is called as **ultrafilteration.** The force of ultrafiltration or effective *filtration pressure* (EFP) is 10 – 25 mm Hg (pressure in glomerular capillaries 75 mm, osmotic pressure of plasma in glomerular capillaries 30 mm osmotic pressure of glomerular filtrate 10 mm hydrostatic pressure of interstitial fluid 10 mm). Filtration takes place through tiny spaces amongst the cells of capillary walls and filtration slits of podocytes in the wall of Bowman's capsule. The process of ultrafiltration depends on :

(a) Net hydrostatic pressure difference between the lumen of the capillary and the lumen of Bowman's capsule favours filtration

(b) The colloidal osmotic pressure of plasma opposes filtration.

About 1300 ml of blood flows through kidney per minute. About one fifth of blood plasma flowing through kidneys is filtered out as *glomerular or nephric filtrate.* The glomerular filtration rate (GFR) is about 125 ml min^{-1} or about 180 L day^{-1} in human kidneys. GFR is autroregulated by 2 factors.

(a) **Myogenic mechanism** : Increase in blood pressure tends to strecth the afferent arteriole which responds by contraction, reducing the diameter and hence blood flow.

(b) **Juxtaglomerular Apparatus (JGA)** : Responds to low blood pressure by **secreting renin.** At high blood pressure renin secretion is inhibited. Extrinsic neural control is also known to regulate GFR.

Extrinsic neural control also regulates the filtration rate.

2. Tubular Reabsorption

Selective transport of substances across the epithelium of the excretory tubule from the ultrafiltrate to the interstitial fluid is called **reabsorption.**

- **PCT** actively reabsorbs almost whole of glucose, 75% of amino acids and vitamin C, about 90% of inorganic buffer bicarbonate (HCO_3^-), about 70% of Na^+ about 75% of K^+ and a large amount of Ca^{2+} from the glomerular filtrate. So PCT reabsorbs about 65 – 80% of the filtrate.
- **Descending limb of Henle's loop :** Permeable to water but not to salt, helps to concentrate NaCl in the filtrate.
- **Ascending limb of Henle's Loop :** Actively reabsorb about 25% of K^+ and some Cl^-, some Na^+ (by diffusion), permeable to NaCl, transfers NaCl from filtrate to interstitial fluid, but here the transport is by active transport.
- **DCT and CT :** Actively reabsorb some Na^+ from nephric filtrate in exchange with K^+ of the interstitial fluid. Some Cl^- is reabsorbed by back diffusion.
- Reabsorption helps in maintenance of homeostasis.

3. Tubular Secretion (Augmentation)

Highly selective process by which the glandular cells of nephron, especially of PCT and DCT, extract the wastes like uric acid, creatinine, hippuric acid, K^+, H^+, ammonia etc. from the blood in the peritubular capillaries by active transport and secrete them in the nephric filtrate.

- PCT controls the controlled secretion of H^+, NH_3 creatine, hippuric acid and drugs.
- DCT and CT secrete most of K^+ eliminated in urine in exchange with reabsorbed Na^+. DCT secretes K^+, NH_4^+, H^+ and HCO_3^- ions in the nephric filtrate by active transport.

WATER CONSERVATION AND PRODUCTION OF CONCENTRATED URINE

Loop of Henle (LH) and Capillary loop (vasa recta) play an important role in this mechanism. Glomerular fluid in the LH and blood in the vasa recta flow in opposite directions in the two limbs of the loops, toward the renal medulla in the descending limb and toward the renal cortex in the ascending limb. These two counter-current systems help in concentrating the urine.

1. Loop of Henle

When filtrate passes through the ascending limb it loses to the interstitial fluid in the renal medulla NaCl by diffusion in its narrow region and Na^+ and Cl^- ions by active transport in its wide region of the limb. It draws out water by osmosis from the narrow region of the descending limb and also from the collecting duct (both are permeable to water). The urine leaving the collected duct is nearly as concentrated as the interstitial fluid deep in the medulla. It is 4 times as concentrated at the blood plasma in humans.

2. Vas Rectum

Its endothelial cells are freely permeable to ions, water and urea. In its increase descending capillary toward the renal medulla, water is drawn out from the blood plasma by osmosis due to a progressive increase in the concentration of the interstitial fluid and Na^+ and Cl^- ions and urea enter the plasma by diffusion. In the ascending capillary toward the renal cortex, the reverse takes place, water reenters the plasma and Na^+ and Cl^- and urea leave it due to progressive decrease in the concentration of the interstitial fluid.

Some urea diffuses from the last (urea permeable) part of the collecting duct into the interstitial fluid to further raise the latter's density for increasing water reabsorption from the collecting duct as well as from the bottom of the loop of Henle.

Counter current mechanisms operating in the Henle's loops and vasa recta concentrate the urine by maintaining high salt concentration around the nephrons and collecting duct. Production of hypertonic urine conserves body's water.

REGULATION OF KIDNEY FUNCTION BY FEEDBACK CIRCUITS

Two main hormonal controls of the kidney function by negative feed back circuits are:

1. Control by Antidiuretic Hormone (AD H)

In DCT, collecting tubules and connecting tubules, membrane permeability of water depends upon **antidiuretic hormone (ADH)** or **vasopressin.** ADH is produced in the hypothalamus of the brain and released into the blood stream from the pituitary gland, enhances fluid retention by making the kidneys reabsorb more water. The release of ADH is triggered when osmoreceptors in the hypothalamus detect an increase in the osmolarity of the blood above a set point of 300 mosmL^{-1}. In this situation, the osmoreceptor cells also promote thirst. Drinking reduces the osmolarity of the blood, which inhibits the secretion of ADH, thereby completing the feed back circuit. In the absence of ADH, water is not absorbed by the medullary brew fluid and hence hypotonic or dilute urine passes out. This is a mechanism to regulate water balance in the body.

2. Control by Juxta glomerular apparatus (JGA)

It operates **renin-angiotensin aldosterone system** (RAAS). It responds to a decrease in blood pressure of blood volume in the afferent arteriole of the glomerulus and releases an enzyme, **renin** into the blood stream. In blood renin converts plasma protein **angiotensinogen** to a peptide called **angiotensin** II. **Angiotensin**-II. increases blood pressure by causing arterioles to constrict, increases blood volume through causing reabsorption of NaCl and water by stimulating the release cf adrenal hormone **aldosterone**. Aldosterone induces the DCT to reabsorb more Na^+ and water. This leads to an increase in blood volume and pressure, completing the feedback circuit by supporting the release of renin.

Atrial Natriuretic Factor (ANF)

Opposes the regulation by RAAS when there is higher blood volume and pressure. The walls of the atria of the heart release ANF which inhibits **renin** secretion by JGA and ADH by pituitary gland. It inhibits NaCl reabsorption and concentration of urine.

ADH, RAAS and ANF provide an elaborate system of checks and balance that regulate the kidney functioning, to control body fluid osmolarity, salt concentrations, blood pressure and blood volume.

MICTURITION (URINATION)

The urge for micturition takes place when 400 – 500 ml of urine has collected in urinary bladder. The release of urine is accomplished by the simulataneous contraction of the smooth muscle of the urinary bladder wall and the relaxation of the skeletal muscle sphincter around the opening of the bladder. Micturition can also be performed voluntarily.

CONSTITUENTS OF URINE

Pale yellow coloured (due to **urochrome** pigment), slightly acidic (pH = 6.0, range 4.5 – 8.0), 1.03 – 1.04 specific gravity, faint aromatic odour (due to bad smelling substances **urinod**), daily urine output in a normal adult person is 1.5 – 1.8 litres. Chemically, 95 – 96% water and 2% urea.

ABNORMAL URINE

Normal urine contains no sugars or ketonic bodies or proteins or blood cells but there are certain pathological conditions in which urine may have abnormal constituents *e.g.* :

- **Glycosuria :** Urine with sugar *e.g.*, glucose is diabetes mellitus.
- **Ketonuria :** Urine with ketonic bodies like acetoacetic acid, β-hydroxybutyric acid etc.
- **Hematuria :** Urine with blood cells in disorders like renal tuberculosis.
- **Haemoglobinuria :** Presence of haemoglobin in urine.
- **Uraemia :** Presence of excess urea in urine.
- **Albuminuria :** Urine with albumin proteins in conditions like nephritis.
- **Proteinuria :** Excess protein level in urine.
- **Jaundice :** Presence of bile pigments in urine in conditions like obstructive bileduct, hepatitis etc.
- **Pyuria :** Presence of pus cells in urine.
- **Alcaponuria :** Presence of alcapton in urine which turns black when comes in contact with air (Black urine disease).

HAEMODIALYSIS

An artificial kidney is used for removing excess urea from the blood of the patient by a process called **haemodialysis.** Artificial kidney performs dialysis (separation of micromolecules and ions from colloids/macromolecules) of blood or haemodialysis of waste products (urea, uric acid, creatinine, phosphate, sulphate etc.). So as to prevent toxicity that may lead to death.

Blood is taken out from an artery of the patient, cooled to 0°C, mixed with an anticoagulant (heparin) and then pumped into the apparatus called the **artificial kidney.** The blood coming out of the artificial kidney is warmed, mixed with antiheparin to restore its normal coagulability and returned to a vein of the patient.

KIDNEY TRANSPLANTATION

Grafting a kidney from a compatible donor to restore kidney function in a recipient suffering from kidney failure is called kidney or renal transplantation. The donor may be anonymous or a living person usually a relative. The kidney should be perfectly match for the recipient inviting least reaction form the immune system. The kidney must be healthy, with well preserved ends and properly flushed with cold preserving solution to minimize tissue injury. Immunosuppressant drugs are used to prevent the kidney rejection.

ROLE OF LUNGS IN EXCRETION

Human lungs exhales about 18l of CO_2 per hour and about 400 ml of water per day in normal resting condition. The rate of ventilation as well as breathing through nose or mouth (breathing pattern) affect the water loss through the lungs. The quantity of water loss increases in dry climates. Different volatile materials are also readily eliminated through the lungs. They have access to abundant O_2 and oxidise foreign substances thus causing detoxification

ROLE OF SKIN IN EXCRETION

Mammalin skin retains a minor excertory role by way of its sudoriferous or sweat glands and sebaceous or oil glands.

Sweat glands

Pass **sweat.** Sweat consists of water containing some inorganic salts (NaCl mainly) and traces of urea, lactic acid, amino acids and glucose. The volume of sweat varies from negligible to 14 l a day, rising with activity and temperature. Its principal funcion is evaporative cooling of the body surface. Excessive sweating may lead to **muscular cramps** due to loss of sodium chloride.

Sebaceous glands

Pass **sebum.** It is a waxy protective secretion to keep the skin oily and this secretion eliminates some lipids, such as waxes, sterols, other hydrocarbons and fatty acids.

In many aquatic animals such as *Hydra* and starfish, excrete ammonia into the surrounding water by diffusion through the body wall or integument.

ROLE OF LIVER IN EXCRETION

It decomposes haemoglobin of worn out RBC to bile pigments, bilirubin, biliverdin and urochrome. Urochrome is eliminated via urine. Bilirubin and biliverdin are excreted through bile along with cholesterol and inactivated derivaties of steroid hormones, certain vitamins, drugs, alkaline salts. Infected or damaged liver does not remove bile pigments which accumulate in the blood and cause **jaundice**. Liver deaminates the excess and unwanted amino acids, producing ammonia, which is quickly combined with CO_2 to form urea in **urea** or **ornithine cycle**.

- **Large Intestine :** Cells of colon transfer some inorganic ions such as calcium, magnesium and iron from the blood into the cavity of the colon for removal with the faeces.
- **Saliva :** Heavy metals and drugs are excreted in the saliva.
- **Gills :** Remove CO_2 in aquatic animals, also excrete salt in many bony fish.
- **Salt glands :** Removes salts of marine birds and reptiles.

SOME IMPORTANT FACTS

- **Renal Plasma Flow (RPF) :** Amount of blood plasma which passes through glomerular capillaries of all the nephrons of both the kidneys in one minute and is about 650 ml.

- **Filteration coefficient (Kf) :** Glomerular filtration per mm Hg of GFP and is about 12.5 ml per mm Hg.
- **Renal Threshold :** Upper limit of kidneys upto which a high threshold substance can be reabsorbed *e.g.,* 180 mg/100 ml of nephric filtrate for glucose.
- **Compensatory Hypertrophy :** Enlargement of a kidney to compensate damaged other kidney.
- **Renal Fraction :** Part of cardiac output (5600 ml/min.) which passess through the kidneys (1200 ml/min.) and is about 12 per cent (Range is 12 – 30 %).
- **Urography :** Radio X-ray photograph of urinary tract.
- **Aminotelism :** Expelling of amino acids as nitrogenous wastes *e.g., Pila, Unio, Asterias, Holothurion* etc.
- **Ptosis :** Displacement of kidneys from normal position.
- **Oedema :** Increased volume of intestinal fluid.
- **Urethritis :** Inflammation of urethra.
- **Unilobar kidney :** A kidney with a single pyramid *e.g.,* in Rabbit.
- **Multilobar Kidney :** A kidney with many pyramids *e.g.,* in humans.
- **Urinometer :** An instrument for estimating the specific gravity of urine.
- **Neural gland :** An excretory structure of urochordates *e.g., Herdmamia.*
- **Kidney Types :**
  1. **Pronephros** (Anterior kidney) : Functional kidney of some adult cyclostomes (*Myxine*) and some bony fishes (*Fierasfer*).
  2. **Mesonephros** (Middle kidney) : Function in adult lampreys, most fishes and amphibians.
  3. **Metanephros** (Posterior kidney) : Functional kidney of adult reptiles, birds and mammals.
- **Nocturia :** Urinating at night, often because of increased secretion of urine at night.
- **Uriposia :** Urine drinking.
- **Uropoiesis :** Production of secretion of urine.
- **Nephrectomy :** Surgical removal of kidney.
- **Noctural Enuresis :** Bed-wetting during sleep.
- **Dysuria :** Difficult or painful micturition.
- **Polyuria :** Excretion of an exessive amount of urine.
- **Oliguria :** Deficient urine excretion.
- **Anuria :** Absence of urine formation by the kidneys.
- **Nephritis :** Inflammation of kidney, usually caused by bacteria.
- **Walter Cannon :** Coined the term homeostasis.
- **Guanotelic :** Excretory product is *guanine e.g.,* spiders, scorpions.
- **Gout :** Painful great toe, due to of deposition of uric acid.
- **Cystitis :** Inflammation of urinary bladder caused due to bacterial infections causes painful urination with burning sensation.
- **Glomerulonephritis :** Inflammation of glomeruli due to Streptcoccal infection. Proteins and RBCs pass into filtrate.
- **Bright disease :** Characterised by nephritis.
- **Diabetes insipidus :** Characterised by diuresis (10 litres urine output per day) due to deficiency of ADH.
- **Diabetes mellitus :** Disorder characterised by high blood sugar level and excretion of sugar in urine due to lack of insulin.
- **Pygmolion corpuscles :** Discovered by Marcello Malpighi.
- **Ornithine Cycle :** Takes place in mitocondria of liver cells.
- **Bidder's canal :** Inside the kidney of male frog and carries the sperms only.
- **Trimethylamine oxide (TMO) :** Nitrogenous waste of many teleosts (bony fishes).
- Each kidney has about **sixteen renal pyramids.**
- **Columns of Bertini :** Conical projections of renal cortex into renal medulla between the renal pyramids.
- **Incomplete loop of Henle :** Found in birds.
- **Complete loop of Henle :** Found in mammals.
- **No loop of He :** Found in nephrons of fishes, amphibians and reptiles.
- **Urate cells :** Excretory cells of fat body of insects. These store the nitrogenous waste permanently calle **excretion by storage.**

- **Desert mammals** have long loop of Henle for more conservation of water.
- **Hepatic vein** is with maximum amount of urea, while **renal vein** is with minimum amount of urea.
- **Pyelolithotomy :** Removal of a stone from renal pelvis.
- **Lithotripsy :** Surgeryless treatment of renal stones. It is bloodless, painless and low costing. In this, renal stones are broken with radiations.
- **Creatinine** is formed from muscle proteins so is more in amount in urine of persons taking protein rich diet.
- **Renal stone (renal calculus) :** Stone formation in renal tubules or renal pelvis due to mainly sodium oxalates and some phosphates.
  It causes severe painful condition called **renal colic**. It is more common in men than women. It may lead to anuria and haematuria.
- **Hagfish** (*Myxine*) : Only vertebrate osmoconformer.
- **Bi-directional transport :** K^+ in urine formation.
- **Ornithine cycle :** Five steps :
  1. Formation of carbamyl phosphate from ammonia and carbon dioxide.
  2. Synthesis of citrulline from ornithine and carbamyl phosphate.
  3. Synthesis of arginosuccinic acid from citrulline and ammonia.
  4. Decomposition of arginosuccinic acid forming fumarate and arginine.
  5. Hydrolysis of arginine to form urea and ornithine.
- **Compensatory Hypertrophy :** Enlargement of a kidney to compensate damaged other kidney.
- **Filtered load :** Amount of a substance present in the glomerular filtrate per day *e.g.*, of 575 gms/day for Na^+.
- **Botryoidal tissue :** Excretory tissues of leeches.
- **Founder of comparative physiology :** Marcello Malpighi (1628 – 1694).
- **Normal level of urea in human blood :** About 4gm/litre of blood or 17 – 38 mg/100 ml of blood.
- **Nephrology :** Study of the structure, working and disorders of the kidneys.
- **Urology :** Study of the female urinary tract and the male urogenital tract.
- The total length of all tubules of both kidneys is estimated to about 110 km (70 miles).
- **Hippuric acid** is formed by combination of benzoic acid and glycine, found in urine of mammals including man.
- **Holonephros or ancestral kidneys or Archinephros :** From it different types of kidney have evolved. Found in larvae of **hagfishes** (*Myxine*) and **Caecilians.**
- **Juxtaglomerular cells :** Smooth muscle cells of tunica media of afferent arteriole. These secrete *renin enzyme* which is formed of 340 amino acids with 41,000 mol. wt.
- Both glucose and amino acids exhibit **symport** (= Co-transport) along with Na^+ by active transport.
- **Diluting segment of nephron :** Ascending limb of loop of Henle.
- In adult man, urge for urination can be suppressed upto 1–1.5 litres of urine in urinary bladder.
- **Uric acid :** Produced by degradation of purines (*e.g.*, guanine) in liver and kidneys to some extent.
- **Nasal glands :** Present in sea birds for salt excretion.
- **Pyelitis :** An inflammation of the renal pelvis and its calyces.
- **Pyelonephritis :** An inflammation of one of both kidneys, involves both the nephrons and the renal pelvis.
- **Gravidex test :** Occurrence of human chorionic gondotropin (HCG) indicates pregnancy.

STRESS AND ADAPTATION

INTRODUCTION

- **Movement:** The act of changing place or position by the entire body or by one or more of its parts is called movement.
- **Kinesiology :** Study of movements.
- Movement may occur at the **cellular level** (*i.e.*, cyclosis in cells); at the organ level (*e.g.*,

rotation of eye ball); at the organism level (*e.g.*, walking by man) etc.

- Plants exhibit phototropic, geotropic, nastic and other movements.
- **Locomotion :** It is the movement of an animal as a whole from one place to another *e.g.*, Walking, creeping, flying, running, hopping, swimming etc. In multicellular organism locomotion takes place by means of muscles with or without skeleton and its joints. Non-muscular locomotion takes place in protists and individual cells of multicellular organisms *e.g.*, Amoeboid, protoplasmic or cytoplasmic, streaming, flagellar and ciliary.

BASIC TYPES OF MOVEMENT

Basic mechanisms are :

1. Amoeboid/Pseudopodial movement

By means of temporary protoplasmic outgrowths called pseudopodia; involves change in shape of the cell body and streaming movement of cytoplasm helps in food capture and change of place as well; found in leukocytes like phagocytes and macrophages of the human lymphatic system for engulfment of antigen and migration in the circulatory fluid. *Amoeba* and its relatives creep by means of pseudopodia.

2. Ciliary Movements

Paramecium and other ciliates swim by means of cilia. *Paramecium* use the cilia of the cytopharynx to drive water and food in their gullet. Cilia set up water currents that pass over the gills of bivalve molluscs (*e.g., Lamellidens*) for feeding; drive water through the water vascular system of echinoderms (*e.g., Asterias*) for locomotion. The cilia of the cells lining of trachea, oviducts and vasa efferentia propel by their lashing movements dust particles, eggs and sperms, respectively in specific directions in these organs. This movement take part in propulsion of excretory product in urinary tubules and flame cells.

3. Flagellar movements

Perform locomotion is euglenoids and other flagellate protists, *Chlamydomonas* and other unicellular colonial motile green algae, sperms etc. Flagellate choanocytes bring about circulation of water in the canal system of sponges.

4. Protoplasmic or cytoplasmic streaming (cyclosis)

It has been seen in most of the cells such as leukocytes, Amoeba and other unicellular organisms. Cyclosis helps in circulation of materials in the cells.

5. Muscular movements

Found in majority of vertebrates; including humans; brought about by sliding of myofilaments past each other in the muscle fibres. This is the ability to exert a force by alternate contraction and relaxation. Most multicellular animals have muscle fibres for movement of different organismic attaining locomotion .

Locomotion in Humans

Locomotion in humans depends on the movements of muscle fibres or muscle cells which causes movements of limbs and internal organs and thus coordinate locomotion in humans. It depends on the contractile capacity of the muscle fibres.

TYPES OF MUSCLES

Myology or Sarcoglia

Muscle system is made up of muscle tissue which consists of long, narrow, highly specialised cells muscle fibres possessing the property of contractility, electrical excitability, extensibility and elasticity.

Human body has some 639 separate muscles, which make up about half of the body weight. Three types:

1. Skeletal muscle or Striated muscle or Striped muscle or Voluntary muscles

Causes limb movements and locomotion in the vibrates; mostly attached to bones; possess transverse striations or dark bands; innervated by voluntary nervous system; can be moved at will.

2. Cardiac muscles

Found in the **myocardium of the heart;** striated muscle; not under voluntary control *i.e.* **Involuntary** innervated by autonomic nervous system. Cardiac muscle cell is cylindrical, uninucleated striated and branched.

3. Smooth muscles or Visceral muscles or Involuntary muscles or Non-striated muscle

Innervated by autonomic nervous system; found inside the wall of the hollow internal organs e.g., alimentary canal, reproductive tract, blood vessels *etc.*, help in the movement of materials through the tubular organs.

STRUCTURE OF SKELETAL MUSCLE

Skeletal muscles are striated muscles in which the muscle fibres are arranged in bundles called fasciculi and are held together by connective tissue. Each muscle fibre is covered by a thin connective tissue sheath (endomycium), while earth fasciculus and whole muscle are covered by sheath called **perimycium** and **epimycium,** respectively.

The two ends of a skeletal muscle are typically attached to two different bones and the contraction of the muscle draws one bone toward the other like a lever. The joint between the two bones acts as the *fulcrum* of the lever.

The skeletal muscle fibre is a cylindrical, unbranched, long cell with a diameter of 10-100 μm, multinucleated **(syncytial)** cell, which is bounded by plasma membrane **(sarcolemma)** and contains in its cytoplasm **(sarcoplasm)** well developed endoplasmic reticulum (sacroplasmic reticulum) which is specialised for calcium storage.

The skeletal muscle fibre exhibit alternating dark and light cross bands, **(striations** or **stripes)** under the microscopes.

A dark anisotropic band **(A-band)** is present in the centre of sarcomere. Adjacent to this lies a light isotropic band (*I-band*). Alternate arrangement of dark and light bands gives the striatedly appearance to a skeletal muscle.

All the centre of the A-band, a comparatively less dark zone (H-zone) is present. In the centre of H-zone (contains only thick filaments), M-line is present, formed by threads that connects the myofilaments. I-band (contains only thin filaments) is crossed through its centre by a dark membrane (Z-line).

The part of the muscle fibre between two successive Z-lines functions as a contractile unit termed sarcomere which consists of the A-band and half of each adjacent I-band.

Invaginations (T-tubules) of sarcolemma extend into the muscle fibre adjacent to Z-line. Each sarcomere is a bundle of fine longitudinal myofilaments of two types :

1. **Primary myofilaments :** Thicker, confined to **A-band** only, formed of the protein myosin, free at both the end, and bear globular heads (formed of light meromyosin L-MM, sticking off to the side from a long tail (fanned of heavy meromyosin H-MM).
2. **Secondary myofilaments :** Thinner, present in I-band but extend for some distance into the **A-band** between the primary myofilaments; made up of protein **actin,** *having with it two regulatory proteins i.e.,* tropomyosin (rod-shaped, fibrous protein, the rods link end to end to form two helical strands, which are wrapped around the F-actin) and troponin (small globular protein molecule, marks the active sites on the F-actin); have smooth surface; and are attached to Z-lines by one end, being free at the other more numerous than the primary myofilament.

A thin myofilament consists of two strands of actin and are strands of tropomyosin coiled around one another. Partial overlapping of the primary myofilaments by the secondary myofilaments imparts dark appearance to the **A-bands.**

THE MECHANISMS OF MUSCLE CONTRACTION

Most satisfactory theory of muscle contraction is sliding filament theory proposed by A. F. Huxley, H. E. Huxley and J. Hansen (1954). This is based on structural changes in the banding pattern of the sarcomeres of the myofibrils of the striated muscle fibres.

Physical changes

Contractile units are sarcomeres. During contraction, the actin and myosin filaments slide part each other to reduce the length of the sarcomeres by 60-70%. A sarcomere lies between two Z-lines **(membranes of Krause)** and consists of **A-band** in the middle and half I-bands on either side. The actin filaments move inwards towards the centre of the sarcomere *i.e.*, deeper into the **A-bands.** The region of **A band** possesses thick rough primary myosin filaments. The heads of the myosin operate as "hooks"; attracting to the **F-actin** they form cross-bridges, then change their relative configuration and pull the actin filaments further deep into the **A-band.**

As a result, Z-lines limiting the sarcomeres, are drawn closer together. The length of A-band remains unchanged. I-bands reduce in length. However, the net result is the shortening of the sarcomere. The actin filaments slide out from the A-band, resulting in the lengthening of the sarcomere.

Biochemical and Electrical events

Muscle contraction involves a number of biochemical changes which were explained by **Albert Szent-Gyorgyi** (1942) and **R.E. Davis** (1963). The membrane is polarised with a positive charge on the outside due to operation of a Na^+ – K^+ exchange pump. The resting potential of sarcolemma is + 50 to + 100 mV. Normally a nerve impulse arriving at the neuromuscular junction initiates contractile response. A neurotransmitter (acetyl choline) released at the neuro-muscular junction, enters into the sarcomere through its membrane channel. This depolarises the sarcolemma and develops an action **potential** with the reversal of flow of ions-more Na^+ towards interior than K^+ pass out. Due to which sarcolemma is negative on the outside and positive on the inside. It results in release of Ca^{++} ions from sarcoplasmic reticulum which binds with the specific sites present on the troponin component of the thin filament. As a result active sites present on the F-actin molecules are exposed. These sites are specific to the myosins head, which exhibits Mg^{++} dependent ATpase activity. During relaxation of muscle, the Ca^{++} is pumped back into the sarcoplasmic reticulum. As a result, the troponin component becomes free to mask the active sites for the myosin head. The cross-bridge breaks and the thin filament occupies it normal position. The muscle relaxes.

RED AND WHITE MUSCLES

Skeletal muscle are of 2 types–Red and white muscles :

1. Red (Slow, Tonic) muscle fibres

Thin, dark red, slow contracting muscle fibre, contains a high content of a hemoprotein pigment called myoglobin. Excess of mitochondria, low glycogen content. Poorly formed sarcoplasmic reticulum. Myoglobin combines with oxygen to form oxyhemoglobin which speediness oxygen supply to the mitochondria. They can perform slow sustained work over long periods without getting fatigued due to nonformation of lactic acid and undertaking aerobic contractions. *e.g.*, extensor muscles of back in man, flight muscles of birds.

2. White (Fast, Twitch) Muscle Fibres

Much thicker, lighter in colour, fast contracting muscle fibres, low content of myoglobin, few mitochondria, abundant glycogen granules, well formed sarcoplasmic reticulum. They can perform fast strenuous work for short duration, consume oxygen quickly, perform anaerobic oxidation and accumulate lactic acid. As a result these muscle fibres get fatigued quickly *e.g.*, eyeball muscles, flight muscles of sparrow etc.

THE SKELETAL SYSTEM

Human endoskeleton is made up of bones and cartilage of various types.

- **Bone** : Hard connective tissue, very hard ground substance. Contains calcium salts. Ground substance has enormous irregular spaces (lacunae) in which the osteocytes are present.
- **Cartilage** : Firm, elastic skeletal connective tissue with large number of chondrocytes embedded in the matrix.

Skeleton may be exoskeleton or endoskeleton.

(a) Exoskeleton

Present on the outer surface of the body, generally formed of nonliving elements. It can be epidermal/ectodermal exoskeleton (found in mammals, birds and many reptiles) or mesodermal/dermal exoskeleton (found in fishes and some reptiles like crocodiles, turtles and tortoises). Exoskeleton may be as calcareas shell in the molluscs. Chitinous and sclerotized in the arthropodos, epidermal scales on the skin in reptiles. dermal scales on the skin in fish, claws and feathers in the birds and hair, nails, claws and hoofs in the mammals.

(b) Endoskeleton

Hard parts present beneath the skin. *e.g.*, Bones and cartilaginous in vertebrates. It may be replacing or cartilaginous bones, membranous or dermal bones and sesamoid bones.

Functions of skeleton

Provide mechanical protection, supporting framework, production of sound (in larynx), stores fats (marrow cavity of long bones), reservoir of minerals (Ca. P, Mg salts), help in breathing movements and hearing, hemopoiesis or formation of blood cells, attachment of muscles, providing shape etc.

HUMAN SKELETON

206 bones in adult man and some cartilage, categorised into **Axial skeleton and Appendicular skeleton.**

(A) Axial Skeleton

Skull + vertebral column + ribs + sternum; present along the longitudinal axis of the body. Made up of 80 bones (87 bones in children).

1. Skull

29 bones, endoskeleton of head, heaviest part of body.

(*i*) **Cranial bones :** 8 bones (1 frontal + 2 parietals + 1 occipital + 2 temporal + 1 sphenoid + 1 ethmoid) large, hollow part, encloses and protects the brain in its cranial cavity, forms helmet for protection of brain, cranial cavity size ranges from 1450-1600 cm in adult man. Occipital possess foramen magnum for passage of spinal cord and two *occipital condyles* for fixation with atlas vertebra. Upper jaw fused with cranium while lower jaw remains connected with the cranium by muscles.

(*ii*) **Facial bones :** 14 bones (2 nasals + 2 inferior turbines or chonchae + 1 vomer + 2 larymalse + 2 zygomatics or molars - 2 palatines - 2 maxillae - 1 mandible or lower jaw).

- **Craniostylic jaw suspension** : Mandible of lower jaw is suspended from squamosal bone of upper jaw.
- **Alveoli :** Sockets in maxilla and mandibles bone in which teeth embedded.

(*iii*) **Hyoid bone :** Bone placed at the floor of the buccal cavity.

(*iv*) **Bones of middle ear :** 6 bones (2 malleus + 2 incus + 2 stapes). Stapes is smallest bone of human body.

2. Vertebral column or Backbone

Long (70 cm), curved bony rod present on dorsal side of neck and and trunk; articulates with skull, pectoral girdle, pelvic girdle and the ribs; centrally hollow so makes the vertebral column a hollow tube through which the spinal cord coming out of the foramen magnum of the cranium possess and thus remain protected. Vertebral formula of vertebral column of human being is C7 Th12 L5S(5) Co(4) = 33

(*a*) Cervical (7)–curve directed forward.
(*b*) Thoracic (12)–curve directed backward.
(*c*) Lumbar (5)–curve directed forward.
(*d*) Sacral (5)–curve directed backward,
(*e*) Coccyx (4). Sacral and coccyx are two triangular fused bones.

3. Sternum or breast bone

Thorax supported by sternum on the ventral side and the thoracic vertebrae on dorsal side, flat, narrow bone about 15 cm in length, dagger like, formed on parts-Manubrium or prosternum (upper handle like), Body or mesosternum (middle largest part) and xiphoid cartilage or xiphisternum or metasternum (lower small cartilaginous plate).

4. Ribs

12 pairs of semi-circular bones present in the thorax. Each rib is made up of posterior bony vertebral part and anterior cartilaginous sternal part. The bony part of each rib is double headed (Tubercular and capitular head)-3 types on the basis of their sternal parts.

(*i*) **True ribs** : First seven pairs whose sternal parts are directly attached to the sternum through small sized costal cartilages

(ii) **False ribs or Vertebro-chondral ribs** : Three pairs of ribs (8th, 9th and 10th pair) whose bony vertebral parts are attached to vertebrae while sternal part are attached on that of the 7th pair of ribs and not to the sternum directly.

(*ii*) **Floating ribs :** Last two pairs (11th and 12th pair) whose sternal parts remain free and do not even reach the sternum.

- **Rib cage :** Formed of thoracic vertebrae, sternum and ribs.
- **Gorilla rib** : An extra rib in some individuals, it is normally present in gorillas.

(B) Appendicular Skeleton

List along the transverse axes of body and includes two types of girdles and limb-bones. Total 126 bones.

1. Limb Bones

2 pair (1 pair forelimb or arm bones + 1 pair hindlimb or leg bones).

(*a*) **Forelimb (arm) 30** : bones (1 Humerus + 2 Radiusulna + 8 carpals + 5 metacarpals + 14 phalanges).

- **Humerus (upper arm or Brachium):** 3 parts (head, shaft and trochlea). Head articulates with glenoid cavity of pectoral girdle by a ball and socket joint has greater and lesser tuberosity. Shaft with V-shaped deltoid ridge. Trochlea with two epicondyles and a capitulum, has coronoid fossa on anterior side and olecranon fossa on posterior side.
- **Radius ulna (fore arm or Antebrachium):** 2 bones lower arm inner (radius) and outer (ulna). Ulna has an olecranon process for forming elbow joint by a hinge joint (uniaxialjoint).
- **Hand or Manus :** 3 parts (8 wrist or carpus) + 5 palm or metacarpus + 14 fingers or digits, phalangeal (14 bone) formula of hand of man is 2,3,3,3,3. **Thumb** (great finger of hand) = **pollex,** opposable to the fingers for grasping. Second index of hand = **index.**

(*b*) **Hindlimb (leg)** : Longer than arms, strengthen the legs to support body weight and help in locomotion. 30 bone (1 femur + 2 tibia fibula + 7 tarsals + 5 metatarsal + 14 phalanges + 1 patella).

- **Femur (thigh bone)** : Largest bone of human body, cylindrical with head, shaft and condyle. Head-rounded; articulates into acetabulum of pelvic girdle by a freely movable ball and socket joint; with greater and lesser trochanter. Lower end of thigh with two *condyles* and an intercondylar groove for the articulation of a sesamoid bone called knee cap or patella.
- **Tibia and fibula** (shank or skin bones). Tibia-inner, longer, thicker with tibial tuberosity at upper end and medial malleolus at distal end.
  Fibula : Thinnest bone of the man body, outer, lower end with lateral melleolus, articulates with lower end of tibia. Knee joint lies at the junction of tibial tuberosity and condyles of femur.
- **Foot bones :** 3 parts (7 ankle or tarsus + 5 instep or metatarsus + 14 toes or digits or phalanges). Phalahgel formula of foot of man is 2, 3, 3, 3, 3.
- Thumb (great toe) of foot - Hallux.

2. Girdles

(*a*) **Pectoral or shoulder girdle** : 2 in number. Each half is conists of **clavicle** or **collar bone** (narrow, rod-like, S-shaped, extending between sternum and acromion process of scapula bone) and scapula or shoulder bone (flat, triangular bone present at the back of shoulder as shoulder blade). At the junction of these bones, there is a cup-like depression called **glenoid cavity,** in which the head of the humerus fits in. Scapula is produced into a scapular spine which ends into a triangular acromion process.

(*b*) **Pelvic or Hip girdle** : Present in lower part of trunk and are two in number. Each half is formed of single and semicircular innominatum or hip bone formed of fusion of ilium upper side, broadest part), ischium *(below the pubis)* and pubis (inner side). Two pubic bones are joined by a cartilagenous slightly movable joint called pubic symphysis to enclose an arch like pelvis.

- At the juncion of these three bones, there is a cup-like depression, the *acetabulum.* in which the head of femur bone of thigh fits in.
- Between the pubis and ischium bones, there is a large oval opening *obturator foramen.*

JOINTS

Meeting place of two bones. 3 main types :

1. Immovable or Fixed or Fibrous Joints

No space between bones, union of bony elements by continuous intervening fibrous tissue. 3 types :

(*a*) **Sutures** : Present amongst skull bones and innominate bones.

(*b*) **Syndesmosis** : Ligament joints as betwen radio-ulna, tibio-fibula.

(*c*) **Gomphosis** : Peg and socket joint as between tooth and jaw bone.

2. Slightly movable or cartilaginous joints (imperfect)

Adjoining bones are joined by thick elastic pads of fibro-cartilage, permits only slight movements between the bones 2 types : *Synchondrosis* and *symphysis e.g.,* between centra of two vertebrae public symphysis, ribs and sternum.

3. Freely movable or synovial joints (perfect)

One bone forms a knob-like swelling while other bone forms a depression. The ends of both bones are covered by smooth *articular-cartilages.* In such joints,a space between the bones is present, called **synovial** cavity which remains filled with a viscous and slippery **synovial fluid.** These can be :

(*a*) **Ball and Socket joint** *e.g.,* **shoulder joint** (head of humerus and glenoid cavity of pectoral girdle) and hip joint (head of femur and acetabulum of pelvic girdle).

(*b*) **Hinge joints** : One bone is movaple or another bone in only one plane *e.g,* inter phalangeal joints, elbow joint, ankle joint, knee joint

(*c*) **Pivot Joints** : One bone exhibits the rotatory movement on another bone which remains fixed. *e.g.,* atlas and axis in humans.

(*d*) **Gliding joints** : One bone can slide upon each other *e.g.*. carpels in wrist, tarsals in ankle, zygapophyses of adjoining vertebrae and between clavicle and sternum.

(e) **Ellipsoidal joints or angular joints** : One articular end is oval and convex while the other end is elliptical and concave. *e.g.,* wrist or radio-carpal joint of humans, toes and sole.

(*f*) **Saddle joints** : Imperfectly developed ball and socket joint in which one bone is movable on another fixed bone in many direction *e.g.,* carpo metacarpal joint of human.

ROLES OF MUSCLES AND BONES IN MOVEMENT

Movement of an organ takes place due to the pulling of the bones caused by the force generated by contracting muscles. Movement takes place along the joints which act as fulcrum of the lever while bones and joints function as lever. There are three types of levers.

1. First order lever

Joint between the first vertebra (atlas) and occipital bone of skull. In this fulcrum or joint lies between weight and power.

2. Second order lever

Raising of body (weight) on toes by means of leg muscles. In this fulcrum lies at the joints between proximal phalanges and metatarsals.

3. Third order lever

Lifting of weight by hand with elbowjoint functioning as fulcrum and muscles attached to fore arm acting as power. In this power lies between fulcrum and weight.

DISORDERS OF BONES

1. Arthritis (Arching joints)

Inflammation of joints, characterised by pain and stiffness in the joints. 3 types :

(*a*) **Rheumatoid arthritis** : Painful inflammaion of synovial membranes. It is followed by its thickening and secreting of extra-synovial fluid resulting in increased pressure and pain. The abnormal granules or pannus is produced which accumulating on the surface of the cartilage, causes erosion of cartilage, ossification of fibrous tissues, stiffening and nonmovement of joint.

(*b*) **Osteoarthritis (degenerative arthritis) :** Characterised by the degeneration of the articular cartilage and proliferation of new bones usually affected joints are of spine, knee and hands.

(*c*) **Gouty arthritis or gout :** Caused either due to excessive formation of uric acid or inability to excrete it. It generally attacks the **great toe.**

2. Osteoporosis

An age dependent systemic disorder characterised by low bone mass, micro architectural deterioration of the bone, increased fragility and proneness or susceptibility to ftacture. It is caused due to deficiency of calcium or vitamin D in diet, lack of vitamin C, lack of physical stress, deficiency of estrogens, old age or cushing's syndrome. The elderly men and women are most susceptible.

3. Bursitis

Bursae or fluid filled spaces nearjoints swell up which may be due to deposition of calcium in the underlying tendons. *e.g.*, tennis elbow, miner's elbow, baker's cyst, ischiogluteal bursitis, house maid's knee,

4. Osteomyelitis

Inflammation of bony due to pus producing or pyogenic organism; may remain localised or spread inside involving various parts including bone arrow.

SOME IMPORTANT FACTS

- **Poliomyelitis :** A viral disease which causes weakening of muscles and generally leads to paralysis.
- **Myaesthemia gravis :** Autoimmune disease of the muscles.
- **Myalagia :** Pain in muscles.
- **Cori's cycles :** Exhibits relationship between muscle glycogen and liver glycogen.
- Only ciliary muscles and iridial muscles of eye are ectodermal in origin.
- **In human body :**
  Largest muscle : Gluteus maximus (Buttock muscle)
  Smallest muscle : Stapedius muscle (middle ear)
  Longest muscle : Sartorius
  Strongest muscle : Jaw muscles
- Voluntary muscle of tongule and upper part of oesophagus are not attached to bones.
- **H-zone=Hansen's zone of A-band** or **Heller's line** or *Micellar* or *Mesogramme line.*
- **Z-line on-band** : Krause membrane or Dobber's dot.
- **Rigor mortis** : Rigidity of muscles offer deaths first seen in jaw muscles, start second hour after death.
- **Vigor mortis :** Rigidity of muscles due to deficiency of ATP in muscles.
- Growth ot cartilage is **unidirectional** while growth of bone is **bidirectional.**
- **Chondrology** : Study of bones.
- Number of bones is newly born baby is **306.**
- **Arthrology** : Study of joints.
- **Sprain** : Injury to joint due to over stretching or tearing of ligament or tendon takes time and rest to heal.
- **Sella turcica** : Depression in sphenoid of skull that lodges pituitaly body.
- **Kymograph or myograph** : Instrument used to record single muscle twitch while its record is called single muscle curve or myogram.
- Largest smooth muscles are found in the wall of uterus of a pregnant female.
- Contraction period of voluntary muscle fibre is 0.1 second, while it is 3-180 seconds for smooth muscles. Contraction period for cardiac muscle is 0.8 second.
- **Cancellous or Tubecular bone** : Spongy bone while Periosteal bones : compact bone.
- **Osteogenesis or ossification** : The process of bone formation.
- **Calcination** : Process of burning of bone till it becomes white.
- **Strongest cartilage** : Fibro cartilage due to collagen fibres.
- **Osteoid :** Uncalcified matrix of bone.

- **Diploid bones** : Partly spongy and partly compact bones *e.g.*, ribs and flat bones of skull.
- **Osteoblasts** : Bone forming cells.
- **Osteocytes** : Bone maintaining cells (control respiration, nutrition and excretion of bone cells).
- **Osteoclasts** : Bone dissolving cells, with large amount of acid phosphatase enzyme.
- Red bone marrow (present in spongy part *i.e.*, epiphyses of bones)-Involved in the formation of erythrocytes and granular leucocytes.
- **Yellow bone marrow** (Present in the shaft or diaphyses of long bones) : Involved in the fat storage.
- **Sesamoid bones : Cotyloid** of pelvic girdle; **Fabella** bone.

NERVOUS SYSTEM

INTRODUCTION

Comprises highly specialised cells (neurons), nerves and nervous organs that coordinate and control the activities of different parts of an animal body by receiving sensory input from internal and external environment, processing the input information and responding by sending motor commands to various body parts and cells.

FUNCTIONS OF NERVOUS SYSTEM

(*i*) Controls and coordinates the body functions.

(*ii*) Coordiantes visceral functions to maintain a homeostasis in the body fluids.

(*iii*) Receives sensory impulses from the sensory organs through afferent nerve fibres, analyses, processes and integrates these informations and initiates the motor impulses which are carried to effector organs to show response.

(*iv*) Keeps the previous stimuli as the experience or memory which guide the animal in future.

(*v*) Producing sensations like pain, pleasure, smell taste, touch, vision, hearing etc, with the help of special sense organs.

(vi) Taking immediate remedial action for harmful sensations without consulting will of the animals.

- **Invertebrates** have relatively simpler nervous system than the vertebrates.
- **sponges** (Porifera) lacking.
- ***Hydra*** (Coelenterata) : All neurons alike and fused to form a nerve net or nerve plexus between epidermis and astrodermis.
- **Planaria (Platyhelminthes)** : Two nerve cords converge to form a rudimentary brain.
- **Earthworm** (Annelida) : A central nervous system consisting of a single ventral nerve cord and paired segmental ganglia has evolved.

NERVOUS SYTEM OF COCKROACH

1. Central Nervous System

Consists of a prominent **brain** or supraoesophageal ganglion or cerebral gangalion (whitish, bilobed mass, located on the oesophagus in head), a **suboesophageal ganglion** (reletively small, whitish mass beneath the oesophagus in the head), a pair of **circumoesophageal connectives** (connecting the supraoesophageal and suboesophageal ganglia in head) and **a nerve cord** develops from the suboesophageal ganglion as a double longitudinal chord, lies in the perineural haemocoel, bears **three thoracic ganglia** in the thorax, one in each thoracic segment and **six abdominal ganglia** in the abdomen, one to seven segment except the fifth. The *thoracic* ganglia and the last abdominal ganglia are larger than others.

2. Peripheral Nervous System

Consists of nerves which arise from CNS and innervate the various body parts. **Brain** gives off three pairs of nerves *i.e.*, **optic** (eyes), **antennary** (cantennae) and **labrofrontal** (labrum) nerves. *Suboesophageal ganglion* gives off four pairs of nerves *i.e.*, **mandibular** (mandibles), **maxillary** (maxillae), **labial** (labium) and cervical (neck) nerves.

Segmental Ganglia : Several pairs of nerves arise from each thoracic ganglion and one pair from each abdominal ganglion (except the last which gives off 3 pairs). These nerves innervate thoracic and abdominal regions.

3. Autonomic or Sympathetic Nervous System

4 ganglia : **frontal** (ahead of brain), **hypocerebral** or **occipital** (below brain), **ingluvial** (over the crop)

and **proventricular** (over proventriculus). These ganglia are joined together and with the brain by connectives and send nerves to gut, heart and endocrine glands.

NERVOUS SYSTEM OF HUMANS

A. Central nervous System (CNS)

Dorsal, hollow and non-ganglionated. 2 parts :

1. **Brain :** Upper, broader part in the head
2. **Spinal cord :** Lower, long, narrow part, running from beginning of neck to trunk.

B. Peripheral Nervous System (PNS)

All the nerve pathways of the body outside the brain and spinal cord, includes the sensory or afferent pathways (transmit information to the CNS) and motor or efferent pathways (transmit commands from the CNS). It mainly controls the voluntary activities of the body. It includes

1. Cranial nerves
2. Spinal nerves

C. Autonomic Nervous System (ANS)

Consists of nerves which control the visceral receptors and effectors with the CNS through the cranial and spinal nerves, controls the involuntary activities of the body. Two systems:

1. Sympathetic nervous system
2. Parasympathetic nervous system

- **Neuroendocrine System** : A network of endocrine glands whose hormone production is controlled by commands form the CNS.
- **Nuclei :** Mass of neurons clustered inside the CNS.
- **Ganglia :** Mass of neurons clustered inside the PNS.
- **Tracts :** Bundles of nerve fibres within the CNS.
- **Nerves :** Bundles of nerve fibres within the PNS.

A nerve consists of several bundles of nerve fibres commonly called fasciculi. A fascicle contains connective tissue (**endoneurium**). surrounded by connective tissue sheath (**perineurium**). Each nerve is surrounded a dense layer of connective tissue called **epineurium.** Each nerve has its own supply of small blood vessels.

The functional unit of nervous system is nerve cell or neuron, which have a special structure but vary greatly in size and shape. Each neuron has a cell body (encloses cytoplasm and a nucleus, usually a single axon a variable number of dendrites. 3 types of neurons :

1. **Multipolar neuron :** One long axon with many dendrites, most common type *e.g.*, pyramidal cells is cerebral cortex.
2. **Bipolar neuron :** Neuron has two processes, an axon at one end and a dendrite at the other end. *e.g.*, bipolar neurons in the retina of eye.
3. **Paurounipolar or Unipolor neuron :** The cell body on a side branch of the main axon *e.g.* cells of dorsal root ganglion.

Neuroglia or Glial cells or Glia

Packing and supporting cells found in the brain and spinal cord. They perform many house keeping functions, provide nutritional support to neurons and consume waste products. They may be astrocytes, oligodendrocytes and **microglia.**

Schwann cells

In the PNS, they wrap around the axons of neurons, covering the axon with concentric layers of insulating plasma membrane.

THE NERVE IMPULSE

Prosser defined the nerve impulse as the sum of mechanical, chemical and electrical disturbances created by a stimulus in a neuron.

The most accepted mechanism of nerve impulse conduction is **ionic theory** proposed by **Hodgkin** and **Huxley.** According to this theory nerve impulse is an electrochemical event governed by differential permeability of neurilemma to Na^+ and K^+ which in turn is regulated by electric field.

A neuron is surrounded by extracellular interstitial fluid having Na^+ and K^+ ions. Its membrane has voltage gated (regulated) ion channels for Na^+, K^+, Cl^-, Ca^{++} and $Na^+ - K^+$ **active transmembrane transport or pump** with the help of carrier. Ion channels open only when a minimum or threshold amount of stimulus is applied. The stimulus can be mechanical pressure, touch, chemicals, light, sound or even just voltage applied.

In the condition of rest, neuron membrane is **polarised** with outer surface **positively charged** and inner surface **negatively charged**. The **resting membrane potential** (electrical potential difference across the plasma membrane) is about –40 m V to –90 m V with an average of –70 m V (1 millivolt = 1/1000 volt). It can be measured by a **dual beam cathode ray oscilloscope** which acts as a sensitive voltmeter. It has two electrodes, one inside (**intracellular electrode**) and one outside (extracellular electrode) in an unstimulated axon. Its maintenance requires more energy than during impulse conduction. It is maintained by:

(*a*) Operation of **Na^+ – K^+ ion transmembrane pumps** (expels three Na^+ ions for every two K^+ ions imported). Such pumps are **electrogenic**. As a result K^+ concentration is 30 times higher inside the neuron than outside' while Na^+ concentration is 10 times greater in the outside tissue fluid,

(*b*) Resting nerve membrane is 40 times more permeable to K^+ than Na^+ and Cl^-.

(*c*) Immobile negatively charge protein ions occur inside.

CONDUCTION OF NERVE IMPULSE ALONG THE AXON

1. Initiation of the impulse
2. Its transmission along a nerve fibre
3. Its transfer to a target muscle or nerve, and
4. Its effect on the target tissue.

The trigger zone for a particular neuron is the place on the membrane where voltage-gated channels are clustered most densely. The stimulus causes the opening of voltage gated Na^+ channels. There is a rapid inflow of Na^+ ions which wipes out the local electrical potential difference. This is called **depolarisation.**

Depolarisation causes the Na^+ ion channels in the membrane to close so that no more Na^+ ions can enter the cell. After about 0.5 ms, permeability to K^+ ion increases because the build up of positive charge inside the cell opens voltage gated K^+ channels. The exodus of K^+ ions lowers the number of positive ions within the cell, and the potential falls back toward the resting potential. This is called as repolarisation. The whole process of depolarisation and repolarisation is very fast and takes only about 1 to 5 milliseconds (ms). The sodium pump starts working once again transferring sodium ions out of the fibre and potassium ions back in.

ACTION POTENTIALS

A rapid change in membrane permeability results in depolarisation. The stimulus required to open enough Na^+ channels to initiate depolarisation is called threshold stimulus. Threshold stimulus for opening of Na^+ channels is generally –55 to –60 mV (about 10 m V less than resting potential).

Due to rapid inflow of Na^+, the potential increases first to zero, then rises to + 45 to + 50mV and this newly developed potential difference is **called action** potential or reverse potential or reverse polarisation. Its value is 20–30 m V (+), occasionally + 60 m V.

Change in membrane potential exhibits spike like variation and it is also called spike potential. Because different neurons possess different densities of Na^+ ion channels, different neurons exhibit different action potentials. The stimulus "**fire**" the neuron as an electric current is created due to depolarised region becoming charged differently than the polarised part.

Refractory Peroid

The propagation of each impulse is followed by a period of inexcitability during which the stimulus cannot produce a second impulse, by closing of Na^+ gates, opening of K^+ gates and operation of Na^+ – K^+ pump. It is 1–5 milliseconds.

Saltatory Conduction

The vertebrates have evolved a different mechanism for quick conduction of nerve impulse. They have myelinated nerve fibres which carry impulse about 20 times faster than the non-myelinated ones. Fatty or myelin sheath of medullated nerve fibre acts as insulating covering that prevents flow of ions between exracellular fluid and axoplasm. The ionic flow and reversed polarity occur only at the nodes *of Ranvier;* where the insulating myelin sheath is absent and the voltage-gated ion channels are concentrated. Because the action potential jumps from node to node, transmission of impulse is more rapid in myelinated fibres. This is called the saltatory conduction of nerve impulse. It is more rapid than smooth conduction in non-myelinated fibres (50 : 1), more than 120 m/sec for large diameter neurons. Such conduction is also economical as there are fewer sites of depolarisation. The intensity of stimulus is recognised by frequency of impulses.

SYNAPSE : TRANSFERRING INFORMATION FROM NERVE TO TARGET CELL

Synapse is the close proximity of the axon of one neuron and the dendrite or cyton of another neuron with a gap of just about 200 Å in between. Over 1000 synapses may occur on the dendrites and cell body of motor neuron of spinal cord. In a synapse, the transmitting cell is called the pre-synaptic cell and the receiving cell is called the post-synaptic cell. A narrow gap, called *synaptic cleft,* separates the presynaptic cell from the post-synaptic cell. The pre-synaptic knob may gror in post-synaptic neuron forming a sort of sub-sytnaptic web, *e.g.*, brain cortex, retina.

On the basis of nature of transfer of information across the synapse. Two types of synapse:

1. Chemical synapse
2. Electrical synapse

1. Chemical synapse

Commonest type of synapse, consist of a bulbous expansion of a nerve terminal, called *synaptic knob* or *bouton terminaux,* lying in the close proximity to the membrane of a dendrite. It has large number of mitochondria and many synaptic vesicles. Each synaptic vesicle is about 50 nm in diameter and contains about 2000-1 0000 neuro-transmitter chemical molecules *e.g.,* Ach.

2. Electrical synapse

Specialised for rapid signal transmission, the cells are separated by a gap, *the synaptic cleft,* of only 0.2 nm, so that an action potential at arriving at the pre-synaptic side of cleft, can sufficiently depolarise the post-synaptic membrane to directly trigger its action potential. However, more than 20 nm gap of most synapses is too great a distance for such direct electrical coupling'.

When a wave of depolarisation reaches the *pre-synaptic membrane* (membrane of the synaptic knob on the axon side, thickened as a result of cytoplasmic condensation), voltage gated calcium channels, concentrated at the synapse open. Ca^{2+} ions which are 10,000 more concentrated in outside medium diffuse rapidly into the knob. It potentiates the synaptic vesicles to move to the pre-synaptic membrane, fuse with it and discharge neurotransmitter into synaptic cleft. Magnessium inhibits the release. Neurotransmitters combine with specific **receptor molecules** on the membrane of the target cell, which is called the **post-synaptic membrane**. The latter is excited causing opening of ion channels and creation of action potential. Some neurotransmitter molecules are asbsorbed by pre-synaptic knob while others are broken down by enzyme (cholinesterase for acetyl choline, monoamine oxidase for noradrenaline). The products are absorbed to reform the neurotransmitter inside synaptic vesicles. Chemical synapse is better than electrical synapse as there is a large variety of neurotransmitters *i.e.,* 30 biochemicals (**biogenic amines and derivatives of amino acids**) and over 60 neuropeptides which can bring about different types of responses.

- **Neuromuscular junction** : Synapse between an axon of a motor neuron and a muscle fibre.
- **Neuroglandular junction** : Synapse between an axon of a motor neuron and a glandular cell.
- **Neuroreceptor junction** : Synapse between a sensory neuron and a sensory receptor.

CENTRAL NERVOUS SYSTEM

Brain (Encephalon)

Situated in the cranial cavity of the skull, 98% of the weight of whole CNS, average human brain weight from 1200-1400 gm, possess about 100 billion neurons, protected by meninges.

In lower vertebrates *(e.g.,* amphibians) there are two meninges, **durameter** and **piaarachnoid membrane.**

In mammals three meninges :

1. **Piameter :** Innermost layer, close to the brain, highly vascularised and nutritive, at two places it is fused with roof of brain to form

choroid plexus for secreting *cerebrospinal fluid* (CSF).

2. **Arachnoid :** Middle layer, very thin sheet of delicate connective tissue, porous and serous membrane. A narrow subarchnoid space is present between archnoid and piameter which contains cerebrospinal fluid and connective tissue strands.
3. **Durameter :** Outer layer, thick double layer of fibrous tissue, can resist the movement of the brain that may stretch and break the blood vessels.

Adult brain is pinkish grey, wet and wrinkled like a walnut. It has three parts :

1. **Forebrain or Prosencephalon :** Rhinencephalon (olfactory lobes), Telencephalon (cerebrum) and diencephalon.
2. **Mid brain or Mesencephalon :** Cerebral peduncles (crura cerebri), corpora quadrigemina.
3. **Hind brain or Rhombencephalon :** Metencephalon (cerebellum and pons) and myelencephalon (medulla).

FORE BRAIN

Forms anterior two third to brain. It has three parts:

1. Olfactory lobe

One pair, completely covered by cerebral hemisphere dorsally. Each is differentiated into **olfactory bulb** and **olfactory tract**, control the smell.

2. Cerebral Hemisphere

One pair, 80% of weight of brain, demarcated by a median or cerebral fissure. Two cerebral hemispheres are collectively called cerebrum, which are interconnected by thick band of transverse nerve fibres called corpus callosum.

- Left half of brain controls the right side of body and viceversa.
- **Pallium :** Roof of each cerebral hemisphere and highly folded to form ridges **(gyri)** and depressions **(sulci)**.
- **Corpora striata :** Ventrolateral walls of cerebrum, thick.
- **Cerebral cortex :** Peripheral portion of each cerebral hemisphere, formed of grey matter.
- **Cerebral medulla** deeper part of each cerebral hemisphere, formed of white matter.
- **Basal ganglia** (basal nuclei) are **subcortical nuclei** (grey masses) present lateral to thalamus in the interior part of each cerebral hemisphere. They help cortex execute at the subcontinuous level, learned pattern of movements, planning multiple parallel and sequential patterns of movement like slow or rapid writing, typing, throwing a ball etc.
- **Corpus striatum :** Largest nucleus, regulates planning and execution of stereotyped movements.
- Some sulci (depressions) are well developed and form three deep and wide fissures which divide each cerebral hemisphere into four **lobes**:
  (1) Anterior **frontal lobe**
  (2) Middle **parietal lobe**
  (3) Posterior **occipital lobe**
  (4) Lateral **temporal lobe**

  Fissures are : Central fissure (between frontal and parietal lobes), **parietooccipital fissure** (between parietal and occipital lobes) and **lateral** or **sylvian fissure** (demarkating frontal and parietal lobes from the temporal lobe).
- **Lateral ventricle or paracoel** : Fluid filled cavity in each cerebral hemisphere.
- **Frontal lobe : Each has motor area** (controls voluntary movements of muscles), premotor area (centre of involuntary) movements of muscles and for autonomic nervous system; association area (controls sensation and movements; motor speech area or Broca's area (controls speech), expressions of emotions will power, personality and intelligence.
- **Parietal lobes :** Somaesthetic area (general sensations like pains, touch, pressure, temperature), sensory speech area, taste area (gustation), to follow direction, of map, reading a clock or dressing yourself.
- **Temporal lobe :** Auditory or Acoustic area (hearing), Wernicke's area (understanding speech, decoding and interpretation of sound etc.
- **Occipital lobe :** *Visual area* (visual sensation), *i.e.,* decoding and interpretation of visual information etc.

- **Silent areas :** Areas of cerebrum which regulate intellect, memory, fore sight imagination, mood, emotions etc.

3. Diencephalon

Completely covered by cerebral hemisphere, forms less than 1 % of brain volume.

(*i*) **Thalami :** One pair, masses of grey matter, present in cerebral medulla of cerebral hemisphere, act as relay centres, relays sensory impulses except those of smell and regulates smooth muscle activity.

(*ii*) **Hypothalamus :** Floor of diencephalon, formed of one pair of masses of neurons present in cerebral medulla below thalami inner to basalganglia, controls the involuntary functions, secretes neurohormones (releasing hormones) which control secretion of trophic hormones from anterior lobe of pituitary gland *i.e.*, hypothalamus is an important link between *nervous* and endocrine systems. On the inferior surface hypothalamus possesses :

(*a*) **Optic chiasma** (cross of two optic nerves).
(*b*) **Pituitary gland** or hypophysis with a base called *infundibulum* and
(*c*) Two mammillary bodies or corpora mammillares.

- **Limbic system :** Wish bone or fork like nucleus present close to hypothalamus, connected with both cerebrum and the brain stem, controls the behaviour patterns like feeding habits, sexual behaviour and emotional behaviour etc.
- **Amygdala :** Almond shaped nucleus, attached to the internal tips of fork of limbic system, controls emotional behaviour like aggresion and fear.
- **Hippocampus area :** Associated with swollen lower tip of limbic system, converts information from short term to long term memory especially in learning.
- **Third ventricle or diocoel :** A narrow cavity inside diencephalon, connected anteriorly with lateral ventricles (paracoels) of cerebral hemispheres (called **first and second ventricle**) by a common aperture called **foramen of Monro** and it is connected posteriorly with fourth ventricle of medulla oblongata through a narrow longitudinal canal called **iter** or **aqueduct of sylvius** or **cerebral aqueduct.**
- **Epithalanus :** Roof of diencephalon, anterior part froms **anterior choroid plexus** (secretes cerebrospinal fluid), posterior part forms *pineal body* (vestigial third eye) at the tip of a pineal stalk. Pineal body act as an endocrine gland, secretes **melatonin** hormone.
- **Septum :** Linked to the hypothalamus, medial part on either cerebral hemisphere which has olfactory, hippocampal and hypothalamic connections. It is a emotion centre for sexual arousal.

MID BRAIN

Completely covered by cerebral hemisphere. It has 2 parts :

1. Optic lobes

One pair, present on dorsal side, each divided transversely into upper and larger **superior coliculus** and lower and smaller **inferior coliculus** *i.e.,* there are 4 optic lobes *(Optic quadrigemina* only in mammals). Controls visual (superior coliculi) and auditory (inferior coliculi) reflexes.

2. Cerebral peduncles (Crura cerebri)

A pair of thick bands of longitudinal nerve fibres present on the floor of mid brain act as coordination centres between hind and forebrain.

Iter (Cerebral aqueduct) : Narrow canal that connects third and fourth ventricles.

HIND BRAIN

It has 3 parts:

1. Cerebellum (Metencephalon)

Present below the occipital part of cerebral hemisphere, three lobes :

(*i*) **Cerebellar hemispheres :** One pair, large sized lobes present on lateral sides.

(*ii*) **Vermis** small, worm like median lobe between two hemispheres.

- **Cerebellar cortex** : Peripheral part formed of grey matter.

- **Cerebellar medulla :** Central part formed of white matter.
- **Cerebellar peduncle** : 3 pairs, connects cerebellum to other parts of brain, act as communication pathways. These are :
  (*a*) Superior cerebellar peduncle–between cerebellum and midbrain.
  (*b*) Middle cerebellar peduncle–between cerebellum and pons.
  (*c*) Inferior cerebellar peduncle–between cerebellum and medulla oblongata.
- Arbor vitae– A tree like branching of white matter.
- Cerebellum coordinates voluntary movements, controls equilibrium, controls rapid musclar activities etc.

2. Medulla Oblongata (Myelencephalon)

Posterior part of brain, located beneath the cerebellum.

- Fourth ventricle or Myelocoel : A cavity of medulla oblongata, continuous with central canal of spinal cord.
- Posterior choroid plexus-thin, non-nervous, roof of medulla oblongata.
- It controls involuntary functions, have a number of centres like cardiac centres (heart beat); respiratory centres (rate of respiration); vasomotor centres (contraction of blood vessels); salivary centres (secretion of saliva) etc. Also controls coughing, sneezing, vomiting, urinating, blood pressure, swallowing of food, defaecation, gut peristalsis etc.

3. Pons varolii

Thick band of transverse nerve fibres present at floor of upper part of medulla oblongata, coordinates two cerebellar hemispheres so coordinates muscles of two sides of body, Acts as neuronal link between cerebrum and cerebellum.

- **Brain stem** : Formed collectively by diencephalon, midbrain, pons varolii and medulla oblongata.
- **Histologically :** Brain is made up of 2 types of matter *i.e.,* **grey matter** (cytons and non-medullated nerve fibres) and **white matter** (medullated nerve fibre and large amount of myelin).

In medulla oblongata and pons varolii-Grey matter is internal and white matter is external, while in other parts of brain, grey matter is external and white matter is internal.

SPINAL CORD (MYELON)

Long, soft, whitish, slightly flattened, cylindrical rod present in the neural canal of vertebral column, about 45 cm long, 2 cm thick, about 35 gm in weight, exists from the skull (atlas) through formen magnum and extends as a taper to a point (conus medullaris) upto first lumbar vertebra. Conus medullaris is connected to coccygeal end of vertebral column by fibrous connective tissue derived from piameter and called filum terminale.

It has two longitudinal fissures *i.e.,* **dorsal sulcus** (deep) and **ventral sulcus** (shallow).

The diameter is not uniform, has two swellings *i.e.,* **upper cervical** and **lower lumbar** swelling.

Neurocoel or central canal : Narrow longitudinal canal of spinal cord, connected anteriorly with fourth ventricle of **medulla oblongata** but is **closed posteriorly.** It is lined by a single layered cuboidal epithlium called ependyma.

Central canal is tilled with cerebrospinal fluid. **Dorsal septum** is a thin sheet of connective tissue which extends from dorsal fissure to inward.

Two types of matter *i.e.,* **grey matter** (internal), butterfly shaped in mammals, produced into white matter as the dorsal and ventral **horns** or **columns** or **roots**, also has **lateral columns** (horns) only in the thoracic, upper lumbar and sacral segments of spinal cord, formed of association neurons and cell bodies of motor neurons, present behind and in front of the central canal, respectively called **posterior (dorsal)** and **anterior (ventral) grey commissure)** and **white matter** (external, divided into three **columns** or funciculi on either side respectively called–dorsal, lateral and **ventral funiculus**. These funiculi have bundles of nerve fibres which descend or ascend and are called **nerve tracts** and are divisible into two, **ascending** (conducting sensory impulses towards brains in dorsal funiculi) and **descending** (conducting motor impulses from brain through lateral and ventral funiculi).

Spinal cord conducts sensory and motor impulses to and from the brain *i.e.*, acts as link between brain and the peripheral nerves and also controls reflex actions of the body.

CEREBROSPINAL FLUID (CSF)

Clear, colourless fluid, similar to blood plasma except that it has a much lower proportion of protein and cholesterol. The entire CNS possess 80-150 ml of CSF, produced by membranes in the roof of the ventricles. It contributes to homeostasis, protection of the delicate brains and spinal cord, medium of transport of hormones in the brain, providing buoyancy to the brain, excretion of waste products, reduction in net weight of brain from 1.4 kg to about 0.18 kg which reduces pressure at the base.

PERIPHERAL NERVOUS SYSTEM

Formed of a number of long, thin, whitish threads called nerves extending between CNS and body tissues. 2 types of nerves :

A. Cranial or Cerebral Nerves

Either arise from or end into brain; 12 pairs; 3 pairs of sensory (I, II and VII), 5 pairs of motor (III, IV, VI, XI and XIII) and 4 pairs of mixed (V, VII, IX and X) nerves.

Cranial nerves

Name	Nature	Origin	Innervation	Function
1. Olfactory	Sensory	Olfactory mucous membrane or nasal chamber	Olfactory lobe	Smell
2. Optic	Sensory	Retina of eyes	Optic chiasma	Sight
3. Occulomotor	Motor	Cerebral peduncles of mid brain	Four eye muscles, muscles of ciliary body, iris and tear glands	Movement of eye ball, pupil size, accomodation
4. Pathetic or trochlear	Motor	Near cerebral peduncle	Superior oblique eye muscle	Rotation of eye ball
5. Trigeminal (Dentist's nerve)	Mixed	From anterolateral side of medulla oblongata swells and forms *Gasserian ganglion* and divides into 3 branches		
(a) Ophthalmic	Sensory		Skin receptors of nose, forehead, eyelids	Tactile and lower jaw movements
(b) Maxillary	Sensory		Lower eyelid, cheek, upperlip upper Jaw	Sensations
(c) Mandibular (largest nerve)	Sensory		Lowerlip, buccal cavity, earpinna, lower teeth	Sensations, tongue movement
			Muscles of lower jaw	Mastication
6. Abducens	Motor	Midventral side or medulla oblongata	External rectus eye muscle	Rotation of eye ball
7. Facial	Mixed	Anterolateral side of medulla oblongata behind Vth, swells and forms geniculate ganglion	Sensory fibres to taste bends on posterior 2/3 part of tongue Motor fibres to muscles of face, salivary gland, neck etc.	Tasting of food, facial expression, saliva secretion Movement of neck.
8. Auditory	Sensory	Internal ear	Anteriolateral side of medulla oblongata behind VIIth	Hearing and equilibrium,
9. Glossopharyngeal	Mixed	Lateral side of medulla oblongata	Sensory fibres to taste budson anterior 1/3 part of tongue motor fibres to muscles of pharynx and parotial salivary gland	Tasting of food, salivation, swallowing

Name	Nature	Origin	Innervation	Function
10. Vagus or pneumogastric *(a)* Superior laryngeal *(b)* Recurrent laryngeal *(c)* Cardiac *(d)* Pneumogastric *(e)* Depressor	Mixed	Lateral side of medulla oblongata behind IXth	Sensory fibres to receptors present in wall of visceral organs. Motor fibres to muscles in the wall of visceral organs like alimentary canal, heart, blood vessels, trachea, lungs kidneys, genital tracts etc.	Sound production breathing, cardiac slowing, vasomotor and visceral reflexes gastric and pancreatic secretions; gastrointestinal movements
11. Accessory spinal	Motor	Lateral side of medulla oblongata behind Xth	Muscles of larynx, pharynx, neck and shoulder	Movement of larynx, pharynx, neck and shoulder
12. Hypoglossal	Motor	Ventral side of posterior part of medulla oblongata	Hypoglossal muscles below tongue	Movement of tongue

(B) Spinal nerves

Arise from spinal cord, 31 pairs in man (37 pairs in rabbit), mixed, divided into 5 groups-

(1) **Cervical :** 5 pairs-In neck region

(2) **Thoracic :** 12 pairs-In thoracic region

(3) **Lumbar :** 5 pairs-Upper part of abdomen

(4) **Sacral :** 5 pairs-Lower part of abdomen

(5) **Coccygeal :** 1 pair-Represents the tail nerves

Spinal formula in man is $\boxed{C_8Th_{12}L_5S_5Co_1}$

These nerves exit via **intervertebral foramen.**

Each spinal nerve arises from spinal cord by two roots :

(1) **Dorsal or Posterior or Afferent or Sensory Root :** Continuation of dorsal horn, formed of grey matter, presents a ganglionic swelling in middle called dorsal root ganglion, transmit sensory nerve impulses from the sense organs to spinal cord to initiate sensations like touch, temperature and pain, or involuntary spontaneous activities like reflexes.

(2) **Ventral or Anterior or Efferent or Motor Root :** Continuation of ventral root, formed of grey matter, absence of ganglion, formed of only efferent nerve fibres, transmit motor nerve impulses to effect or organs like muscles and glands.

Each spinal nerve has three branches:

(1) **Ramus dorsalis :** Supplies muscles and skin of dorsal or posterior side.

(2) **Ramus ventralis or lateralis :** Supplies to skin and muscles of ventral (anterior) and lateral sides and also to upper and lower limbs.

(3) **Ramus communicans :** Joins sympathetic ganglion of ANS.

The main spinal nerves or anterior/ventral branches of spinal nerves are joined at places to form plexuses-5 types of plexues.

(1) **Cervical :** First to fourth cervical-nerves to neck and diaphragm.

(2) **Branchial :** Fifth cervical to first thoracic-nerves to chest and arm.

(3) **Lumbar :** First three lumbar and a branch of fourth lumbar for leg-to leg.

(4) **Sacral :** First three sacral, fifth lumbar and a branch of fourth lumbar-to hip joint and parts of pelvis.

(5) **Coccygeal :** Fourth and fifth sacral and coccygeal-to skin and part of pelvis.

AUTONOMOUS NERVOUS SYSTEM

Auto functioning or self governed, maintains homeostasis, controlling the smooth muscles, cardiac muscles and certain glands by both feedback loops and antagonistic control. Formed of two systems.

A. Sympathetic nervous system

B. Parasympathetic nervous system.

Autonomous Nervous System

Features	Sympathetic Nervous system	Parasympathetic Nervous System
1. Composition	Sympathetic trunk, preganglionic sympathetic fibres, post-ganglionic sympathetic fibres, collateral ganglia. fibres	Pre-ganlionic parasympathetic fibres, parasympa thetic ganglia, post-ganglionic parasympathietic
2. Ganglia	Sympathetic trunk is formed by interconnected 21 lateral or **chain ganglia** (3 cervical, 12 thoracic, 5 lumbar and 1 sacral).	Ganglia remain isolated and to not form a chain.
3. Preganglionic sympathetic	Small sized axons of neurons present in lateral funiculus of the spinal cord. ● Form syanapse with dendrites of thoracic and upper three lumbar chain ganglia and form the **thoracicolumbar outflow.**	Long sized neurons which emerge from cranial as well as spinal nerve form **cranio sacral outflow** ● From synapses with neurons of the parasympa thetic ganglia.
4. Post-ganglionic sympathetic fibres	● Long sized axons of the neurons of chain of ganglia ganglia and supply to smooth muscles and glands visceral organ. ● They supply to viscera *e.g.,* heart, ciliary muscles, iris of eyes, lungs, liver, gut, urinary and reproductive systems	● Small sized axons of neurons of parasympathetic ● Form a network in the wall of the visceral organs **Aurebach plexus.**
5. Collateral ganglia	(1) Coeliac (2) Superior mesentric and (3) inferior esentric ganglia, Post-ganglionic fibres extend from neurons of collateral ganglia to visceral organs	— —
6. Post-ganglionic fibres	Mostly adrenergic	Mostly cholinergic

ANS regulates the function of involuntary visceral organs so also called visceral nervous system. Auonomic ganglia act as relay centers. Pre-ganglionic nerve fibres of both sympathetic and paraympathetic nervous system are cholinergic.

Sympathetic and parasympathetic systems function in an antagonistic manner and facilitates in maintaing homeostasis.

Antagonistic role of sympathetic and parasympathetic nervous system

Organs	Sympathetic Nervous system	Parasympathetic Nervous system
1. Gut peristalsis	Decreases	Increases
2. RBC count	Increases	Decreases
3. Hair	Contraction of arrector pilli muscles so the hair stand erect causing "goose flesh"	Relaxation of arrector pilli muscles
5. Blood supply to skin	Constricts the cutaneous blood vesels so reducing blood supply and skin appears pale	Dilates the blood vesels to increase blood supply to the skin
6. Saliva secretion	Decreases	Increases
7. Secretion of tears	Increases	Decreases
8. Blood clotting period	Decreases	Increases
9. Gall bladder	Relaxes	Contracts
10. Anus	Contracts anal sphincters to close anus	Relaxes the anal sphincters to open anus
11. Gastric gland secretion	Inhibits	Stimulates
12. Pancreatic secretion	Inhibits	Promotes
13. Intestinal gland secretion	Inhibits	Promotes
14. Liver	Promotes glycogenolysis	Promotes glycogenesis
Inhibits bile secretion	Promotes bile secretion	Promotes bile secretion
15. Sweat gland secretion	Increases	Decreases

Organs	Sympathetic Nervous system	Parasympathetic Nervous system
16. Trachea and bronchi	Dilation	Constriction
17. Peripheral arteries	Constrict	Dilate
18. Blood pressure	Becomes higher	Lower
19. Adrenals	No action	Stimulated
20. Penis	Induces ejaculation	Stimulates erection

Reflex Action : Rapid and Automatic Responses

Reflex action

An involuntary response to a stimulus, a stereotype reaction which has conscious control *e.g.*, knee jerk, withdrawl of hand on touching a hot object, blinking of eyes, yawning, sneezing, coughing etc.

Reflex pathway or arc has the following components.

1. **Sensory receptor :** Present in dorsal ganglion which lies outside the spinal cord, tissue or organ or cell which receives an external or internal stimulus *e.g.*, skin, ear, eye.
2. **Sensory neuron :** Conducts sensory impulse from receptor organ to spinal cord.
3. **Spinal cord :** Acts as modulator and changes sensory impulse into the motor impulse.
4. **Motor/Efferent nerve fibre :** Conducts motor nerve impulse from spinal cord to the effectors *e.g.*, leg muscles.
5. **Effector organ :** May be organ/muscle/gland which on being activated by a motor impulse produces work or substance to suitably deal with the stimulus.

There are more than 200 reflexes "wired" into our nervous system.

Reflexes are of two types :

1. **Unconditioned or Inborn or Inherited reflexes :** Specific, predictable, purposeful, have survival value, shown by all individuals of a species without training. *e.g.*, simple reflex, compound reflex, chain reflex etc.
2. **Conditioned or acquired reflexes :** Not present at birth but develop later in life through learning,habit, experience or regular association of an indifferent stimulus with unconditioned stimulus. According to Pavlov (1929) conditioned reflex is only acquired and noninheritable property.

Reflexes may be **protective reflex, antigravity reflex** and **righting reflex** on the basis of anatomy and physiology.

On the basis of control, reflexes may be spinal reflexes (controlled by spinal cord) and cerebral reflexes (controlled by brain).

SENSORY RECEPTION AND PROCESSING

- **Sense organ or receptor :** A group of highly specialized cells which receive the stimuli.
- **Sensation :** The conscious or unconscious awareness of an external or internal stimulus with the help of sensory receptors.
- **Perception :** The conscious awareness and interpretation of sensations.

According to Sherrington receptors in terms of their position are :

1. **Exteroreceptors :** Respond to changes in the external enviroment, includes **photoreceptors** (for light in eyes), **phonoreceptors** (for soundwaves in the organ of corti of internal ear), **olfactoreceptors** (for smell in nasal chambers), **gustatoreceptors** (for taste in taste buds on tongue), **tangoreceptors** (for touch, pain, pressure etc. in skin), **rheoreceptors** (for currents of water or air), **thermoreceptors** (for temperature *i.e.*,caloreceptors for heat and frigidoreceptors for cold in skin), **georeceptors** (for gravity), **teleoreceptors** (for distance), **electroreceptors** or **galvanoreceptors** (for electric currents in skin of some fishes) etc.

2. **Proprioreceptors :** Present in the muscles, tendons and joints.

3. **Interoreceptors :** Located within the body and detect the changes in the internal environment of body, includes **statoreceptors** (for equilibrium in cristae and maculae of internal ear), **visceroreceptors** (for changes in visceral organs and stimuli) and **baroreceptors** (for changes in blood pressure present in the wall of carotid bodies in carotid sinus).

6. Sexual Reproduction

GAMETOGENESIS, FERTILIZATION AND EARLY DEVELOPMENT

INTRODUCTION

- Gametogenesis is the process of formation of haploid gametes (sperms or ovum) from diploid gonads (Testis or ovaries).
- Gametes are formed by specialized division *i.e.,* meiosis/reductional. Although sperm and ova are very dissimilar yet both comprise similar phases of sequential changes.
- Gametogenesis is of two types as
  I. Spermatogenesis II. Oogenesis

SPERMATOGENESIS (STUDY–SPERMATOLOGY)

- It is the process of formation of haploid, microscopic and functional sperm/ spermatozoa from diploid spermatogonia. It is under the control of FSH and androgens. Sperm formation occurs in different steps as:

(a) **Multiplicative phase:** At sexual maturity the undifferentiated, diploid, germ cells divide several times mitotically to produce *spermatogonia* A and B type. Type A cells act as stem cell and type B serve as precursor of sperms *i.e.,* which enter the growth phase.

(b) **Growth phase:** During this phase spermatogonia increase in size by obtaining nourishment from the nursing cells. These cells are also spermatocyte and the process is called *spermatocytogenesis.* Nurse cells are also called sertolicells.

(c) **Maturation phase:** Now each primary spermatocyte Undergoes two successive divisions as maturation divisions. The first division is meiosis and *i.e.,* reductional division which yields two haploid daughter cells called *secondary spermatocytes.* Now secondary spermatocytes undergo second maturation division *i.e.,* meiosis II (equational division). This it produces four haploid spermatids.

(d) **Differentiation:** The differentiation of non motile, rounded spermatids into functional, motile spermatozoa is called *spermiogenesis / spermioteliosis.* This metamorphosis includes following changes:

- The nucleus of spermatid shrinks by losing its RNA and most of the water from its nucleoplasm.
- Chromosomes of nucleus become compact.
- Golgi body of spermatid form acrosome.
- Proximal centriole plays important role in cleavage of zygote.
- Distal centriole produce axial filament.
- Cytoplasm of spermatid form thin layer around the different parts of sperm. This is known as *manchette/cytoplasmoic droplet.* Mitochondria called *Nebenkern* form a spiral ring behind the neck around the distal centriole and proximal part of axonema. *Ring centriole/annulus Jansen's ring* is present and differs from the centriole in its structure and their function is still not known.
- The plasma membrane extends to surround the acrosome, nucleus, middle piece and main portion of axial filaments of the tail.

Structure of sperm/spermatozoa

- Sperm consists of head, neck, middle piece and tail. The details of different contents are given under heading spermiotoleosis.

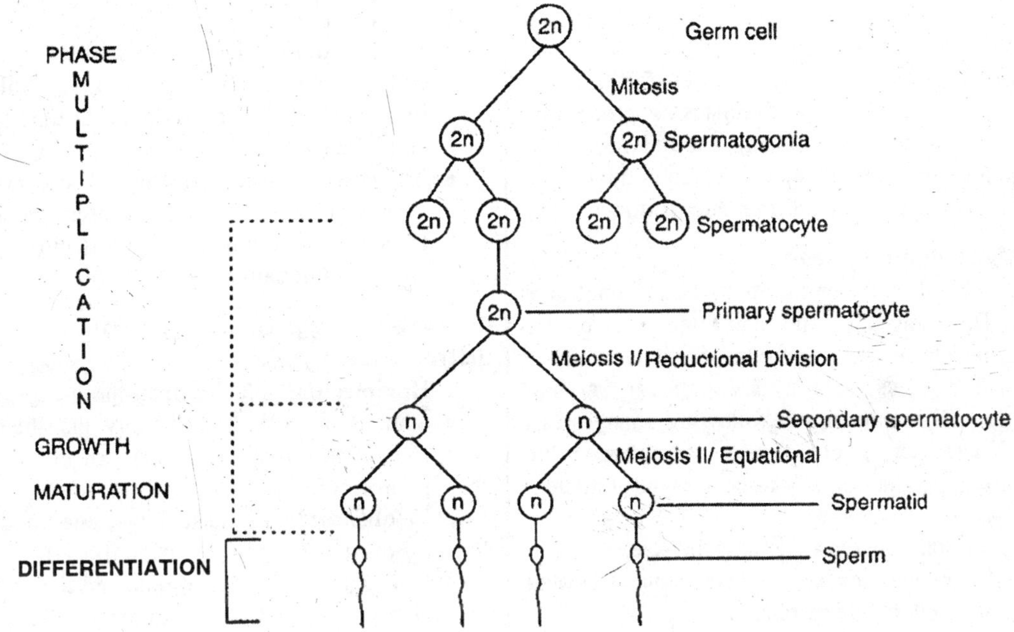

Stages in spermatogenesis

OOGENESIS

It involves the formation of haploid ova/ovum from the diploid egg mother cells, oogonia of the ovary. It occurs in various organisms so it support the evidence of basic relationship of the organisms. It involves two biological processes as genetical programming and packaging. Period of oogenesis is different in different animals. It usually starts before birth and completed only after the onset of puberty. Only one out of 500 cells is stimulated by FSH to mature. So oogenesis is a discontinuous process.

Oogenesis occurs in the follicles of ovaries as follows:

(a) Multiplication phase

The primary germ cells of germinal epithelium of ovary undergo repeated mitotic divisions to form oogonia (2N). These oogonia perfect into stroma as a cord and later on form egg nest. This phase lasts only till the time of birth. Only one cell of egg nest will grow and form primary oocyte and other cells form regular layer around it.

(b) Growth phase

Oogonia grows into a large primary oocyte by taking food from the surrounding follicle cells (usually happens after puberty). Vitellogenesis occurs in this phase whose formation is controlled by mass of mitochondria and golgi body near the nucleus called *balbiani body/ yolk nucleus.*

(c) Maturation phase

Each primary oocyte undergoes two maturation divisions *i.e.,* meiosis I and II. The primary oocyte forms unequal haploid daughter cells after meiosis I *i.e.,* secondary oocyte and first polar *body/polocyte.* In the second meiotic division, oocyte again divide into unequal daughter cells as *ootid* and second polar body. First polar body also divide in two polar bodies.

These polar bodies disintegrates fast due to the lack of cytoplasm so they provide food during development of zygote to form embryo. Usually secondary oocyte does not proceed beyond metaphase until sperm enter in it. Therefore second meiotic division is completed after fertilization. Sperm entry into the ovum stimulates the production of MPF (M-phase promoting factor) and APC (Anaphase promoting complex) which complete the meiosis and it form undifferentiated ootid.

(d) Differentiation phase

Ootid undergo differentiation to form functional ovum. Thus only one ovum and three polar bodies are formed from one oogonium. So it is a highly wasteful process. Ovum is much larger than oogonium. Ootid undergoes following changes as :

- Nucleus of the oocyte becomes enlarged due to the production of a large amount of nuclear sap.
- Nucleolus increases greatly in size.
- The number of mitochondria increases and form mitochondria clouds.
- Golgi complex disappears completely.
- The membranes offer is usually perforated.
- In mature oocytes, formation of cortical granules with acid mucopolysaccharide takes place.
- Vitellogenesis occurs in the primary oocyte either in mitochondria or in the liver cells and then transported to oocyte.
- Ribosomes become very numerous as they actively participate in the synthesis of protein required for yolk formation.

OVUM/EGG

Ovum are always larger than all the other cells of the body. They are nearly spherical and non motile. The large size of ova is mainly due to their high food reserve in the cytoplasm. Ova are without centrioles during the second maturation division, the centrioles are taken away by the second polar body.

(A) Types of eggs on the basis of amount of yolk

- **Alecithal:** These are the eggs without yolk *e.g.* Eutheria.
- **Microlecithal/Oligolecithal:** These are small sized eggs with very small amount of yolk *e.g. Hydra.* tunicates sea urchin, *Amphioxus,* marsupials etc.
- **Mesolecithal:** These eggs contain moderate amount of yolk *e.g.* Annelids, molluscs, *petromyzon,* lung fishes (Dipnoi) and amphibians.
- **Macrolecithal/polylecithal:** These contain very large amount of yolk or reserve food e.g. Insects, elasmobranchs, reptiles, birds and prototherians.

(B) Types of eggs on the basis of distribution of yolk

- **Homolecital/Isolecithal:** In these eggs, small amount of yolk is uniformly distributed in the cytoplasm *e.g.* all animals with microlecithal eggs.
- **Telolecithal:** In these eggs, the moderate amount of yolk is distributed in one hemisphere *i.e.,* vegetal pole and the opposite side of egg is called animal pole. *e.g.,* It is found in mesolecithal, polylecithal and meiolecithal eggs. In meiolecithal eggs, cytoplasm is confined in a disc like area at animal pole called blastodiscs.
- **Centrolecithal:** In these eggs yolk is confined at the centre of the egg surrounded by a peripheral cytoplasm. e.g. Insects.

(C) Types of eggs on the basis of their covering

- **Non cledoic :** These are the eggs without shell and do not contain sufficient amount of nutritive material for the development the embryo and does not have extra embryonic membranes *e.g.* fish, amphibian.
- **Cledoic:** These eggs are fully laden with yolk and are surrounded by albumen and water proof calcium shell. *e.g.* reptiles, birds and prototherians. In the developing embryo, the foetal membranes (allantois, chorion, amnion and yolk sac) are formed.

EGG ENVELOPES

- **Primary membrane:** Secreted by ovum *e.g.* vitelline membrane of human egg.

- **Secondary membrane:** Secreted by ovarian follide *e.g.* zona pellucida, corona radiata of human.
- **Tertiary membrane:** Secreted by oviduct e.g. Albumen, shell membrane of reptiles, birds and jelly layer in frog.

FERTILIZATION / SYNGAMY

- Fertilization is the fusion of haploid male and female gametes to form diploid zygote. The type of fertilization varies in different animals but the basic facts remains the same.
- Fertilization is highly species specific *i.e.,* eggs produce a chemical, fertilizin (Glycoprotein + amino acid + Monosaccharide) and sperms has on its surface antifertilizin (acidic amino acids). This interaction of fertilizin with antifertilizin makes the egg and sperm stick *i.e.,* it results in agglutination.
- The fertilization may be :
- **External:** It takes place outside the body of the parents since gametes can remain alive in water for a short period; fertilization begins immediately after amplexus generally shortly before swelling of albumen into jelly occurs. So the purpose of amplexus in such organisms is to ensure simultaneous discharge of male and female gametes at the same place in water. e.g. All aquatic animals.
- **Internal fertilization:** In this case male deposit sperms during copulation either in the oviduct (veretebrates) or into spermathecal off female (earthworm, insects, spiders) so that fertilization takes place inside the body of female. The sperms are made capable of fertilizing the egg by secretions of the female genital tract and the phenomenon is called *capacitation.*

The various physical and chemical events of fertilization are:

- For penetration, sperm dissolves the vitelline and plasma membranes of the oocyte cell by means of a proteolytic enzymes called sperm lysins (*e.g.* hyduronidase, acrosin) secreted by acrosome. *i.e.,* sperm undergo acrosomal reaction. In certain species, a small conical protubrance called *cone of reception* forms in the oocyte at the place of sperm entrance and is immediately withdrawn simultaneously with sperm penetration. Optimum pH, Ca^{+2}, Mg^{+2} ions and temperature are essential for acrosomal reaction. Ca^{+2} plays major role in acrosomal reaction and in its absence no fertilization occurs.
- Binding of the spern to the secondary oocyte induces depolarization of the plasma membrane of oocyte, that prevents polyspermy and ensure monospermy. Additional sperms usually disintegrate in the cytoplasm of oocyte. When the blocking system is weak, more sperm may enter into the oocyte.
- As the sperm punctures the vitelline membrane of the oocyte, some water oozes out from the oocyte cytoplasm and collects between its vitelline and plasma membrane. So vitelline membrane gets separated from the main cell by fluid filled perivitelline space. Cortical granules of egg cortex are extruded in the perivitelline space by exocytosis. Some of these are attached along the inner surface of vitelline membrane which now thickens and becomes impervious to any other sperm entry. This membrane is called *fertilization membrane.*
- The sperm entry stimulates the secondary oocyte to undergo meiotic - U division which produces the ovum and second polar body. Inside the ovum, the sperm nucleus takes a definite path called *copulation path,* that sets the axis of division.
- The centrioles of middle piece of sperm form a spindle to initiate the cleavage of zygote.
- The nuclear membrane of the gametic nuclei degenerates and two sets of chromosomes initially lie on two poles of the spindle but later these sets of chromosomes mix up and the process is called *karyogamy amphiniuxis.* It combines the characters of two parents and introduces variations. So helps in evolution.
- Metabolic activities as cellular respiration and protein synthesis are increased as more mitochondria are available.

- The fertilized egg is now called zygote.
- The enzyme adenyl cyclase becomes activated in the plasma membrane by sperm entry.

MORPHOGENESIS AND ORGANOGENESIS IN ANIMALS

EARLY EMBRYONIC DEVELOPMENT CLEAVAGE/SEGMENTATION/ CELLULATION

- Cleavage is a series of rapid mitotic divisions of the zygote which convert the single celled zygote into multicellular structure called *blastula.*
- Cleavage results in decrease in cell size and unlike mitosis it is not followed by growth of blastomere so is called fractionating process. There is more consumption of oxygen and more synthesis of DNA during cleavage. Therefore nuclear to cytoplasmic ratio goes on increasing as cleavage progresses.
- Blastomeres show synchronous division in early stages but later this synchrony is lost.

TYPES OF CLEAVAGE

(A) According to potentialities of early blastomeres

- **Indeterminate:** When early blastomeres are equivalent in their potentialities and if any of them is separated it will give rise to a complete normal embryo. *e.g.* All chordates.
- **Determinate/Mosaic cleavage:** In this type of cleavage each early blastomere is destined to become a particular portion of embryo. In this form, embryo is formed only if all the blastomeres remain together *e.g.* Annelid eggs, some tunicates etc.

(B) According to the furrow

- **Radial:** Here furrows line up in successive tyres. *e.g.* Echinoderms, chordates.
- **Spiral:** Here furrows are at right angles to each other. e.g. Annelids, molluscs.
- **Biradial:** When the cleavage furrows of first three divisions do not cut straight the axis of the egg and are not laid down at the right angle to each other *e.g. Ctenopaora. Acoela.*

(C) According to the amount of yolk

- **Holoblastic:** This cleavage divide the zygote (Alecithal, homolecithal and mesolecithal) to two complete blastomeres. Blastomeres are either of equal size (*e.g.* Rabbit, humans) or unequal size (*e.g.* fish, amphibian). This types of division produce stereoblastula (Blastula without blastocoel) and coeloblastula.
- **Meroblastic:** It is a characteristic of poly lecithal eggs where cleavage furrow divide the yolk free part more actively then yolky part the cleavage is confined to cytoplasmic disc at animal pole, cleavage is *discoidal* type and it produces *discoblastula e.g.* reptile, birds and prototherian mammals. Sometimes the divisions are confined to peripheral yolk free cytoplasm and blastocoel is filled with yolk *e.g. centrolecithal* eggs of insects. This type of division leads to *superficial blastula/ periblastula.*

(D) According to the plane of division

- **Meridional plane:** When median axis runs between centre of animal and vegetal pole *e.g. Amphioxus,* frog, *lepidostous.*
- **Vertical plane:** When cleavage furrow passes through axis other than median axis from animal pole towards opposite pole. *e.g. Amia. Calva. Chick.*
- **Equatorial plane:** In this, line of division runs at right angle to median axis *e.g. Ambystoma.*
- **Longitudinal plane:** Cleavage runs through the cytoplasm on either side of equatorial plane *e.g. Amphioxus.*

MORULA

Cleavage produces a solid ball of small blastomeres and the embryo now looks like a mulberry and is called morula. Blastomeres remain in contact with one another of compression. True morula is absent in vertebrates of immediate appearance of blastocoel.

BLASTULATION

As the cleavage proceeds, the number of blastomeres undergo rearrangement. It results in hollow mass of cells with a cavity inside called blastocoel segmentation cavity. The single layer of cells is called blastoderm. The hollow spherical embryo at this stage is called *blastula.* The amount of yolk present in the egg affects the way blastula is formed.

Blastula in different types of eggs is as

- **Isolecithal eggs:** Blastomeres tend to anange in a single layer on the periphery and have central cavity blastocoel. The cells towards vegetal pole are of large size *e.g. Amphioxus,* echinoderms. This type of blastula is called coeloblastula.
- **Moderately Telolecithal eggs** (yolk is unequally distributed): The distribution of yolk causes fast cleavege in animal pole and slow cleavage in vegetal pole which results in macromere and micromere formation in the respective poles. So the blastocoel in such cases is eccentric and blastomeres form 2-3 layers *e.g.* Frog. This kind of blastula is *amphiblastula.*
- **Heavily Telolecithal eggs/Megalecithal eggs:** In such kind of heavily yolky eggs, the cleavage is restricted to the germinal disc as 'a result multilayered central part separates from yolk and those at the margin of the yolk form a continuous layer. So they develop as clear subgerminal cavity whose roof has *epiblast layer* and those forming floor is *hypoblast layer.* This kind of blastula is called *Discoblastula. e.g.* fishes, reptiles, birds.
- In mammals, a peripheral layer of blastomere form trophoderm/trophoblast and consists of an innercell mass attached to one side by the blastocoel. This blastula is called *blastocyst.*

FATE MAP

In all organ grade metazoans, various parts of the body are derived from three basic embryonic cell layers called primary germ layers viz. ectoderm, mesoderm and endoderm.

These area are referred to as presumptive or prospective areas forming a sort offate map on the surface of blastula. It is done by using certain vital stains like neutral red, nile blue sulphate, bismarck brown etc. It was first prepared by W. Vogt (1929).

Major tissues and organs derived from following germ layers are:

1. **Ectoderm:** Epidermis and epidermal glands epithelium, pituitary gland, pineal gland, adrenal medulla, nervous system, enamel of teeth, retina of eyes, optic nerve, internal ear, fore gut and hind gut.
2. **Mesoderm:** Dermis, muscles, connective tissue, coelom, dentine, notochord, skeleton, heart, blood, blood vessels, lymph, spleen, excretory system, adrenal cortex, sclerotic and choroid of eyes and reproductive system.
3. **Endoderm:** Mid gut, digestive glands, tongue, middle ear, eustachian tube, urinary bladder, thyroid, parathyroid, thymus, respiratory tract, liver and pancreas.

GASTRULA

It is the process by which blastocyst is changed into three layered gastrula and the new cavity formed in it is called *archenteron* which opens out through *blastopore.* The most important features of gastrulation are:

- It is a complex, orderly, irreversible, morphogenetic movement of mass of cells.
- The rhythm of cellular division is slowed down.
- Growth if any is insignificant, nuclei become more active.
- Archenteron formed is surrounded by endoderm.
- Chemodifferentiation starts by synthesis of new proteins.
- Cell movements involve processes like emboly, epiboly, delamination, invagination, involution, ingression etc.

ORGANOGENESIS

It is the final phase of embryonic development where cell changes their form and give rise to morphologically recognised tissue and organs of new individuals.

EXTRA EMBRYONIC MEMBRANES IN MAMMALS

The growing mammalian embryo develops four extra embryonic membranes which perform different functions. These foetal membranes are:

1. **Amnion :** Inner side - Trophoblast
   Outer side - Mesoderm
   The space between the embryo and the amnion is called amniotic cavity filled with amniotic fluid. Embryo is suspended in amniotic cavity by means of umbilical cord. The amniotic fluid prevents dessication of the embryo and act as protective cushion against infections and shocks.
2. **Chorion:** Inner side - Somatopleuric mesoderm
   Outer side - Trophoblast
   Chorion takes part in the formation of placenta and helps in metabolic exchange between mother and foetus. It acts as an extra embryonic lung.
3. **Yolk sac:** Inner side - Endoderm
   Outer side - Splanchnopleuric mesoderm
   As human ovum is devoid of yolk, the yolk sac develps an evolutionary process *i.e.,* it is a vestigial organ. Initially it act as a gut and a site of blood cell formation till liver becomes functional (6th week)
4. **Allantois:** Inner side - Endoderm
   Outer side - Mesoderm splanchnopleuric
   It is a sac like structure pushed out from gut during third week. It is reduced and non-functional in humans except the formation of umbilical artery vein and earlier it acted as extra embryonic kidney.

PLACENTATION

Placentation is invariably associated with the viviparity of organism. It is the only, organ in animals formed of temporary connection of the tissues derived from two individuals *i.e.* mother and foetus. The part of placenta derived from foetus is called foetal placenta while that derived from mother is maternal placenta. In mammals the placenta is fully formed in about 10 weeks and lasts throughout pregnancy.

TYPES OF PLACENTA

Histologically there are following tissues which form barrier to separate foetal blood from maternal blood.

Foetal placental tissue

1. Endothelium of blood vessels
2. Chorionic connective tissue
3. Trophoblast

Maternal placental tissues

1. Uterine epithelium
2. Endometrial connective tissue
3. Endothelium of blood vessels

Based on the above tissue layers participating in placenta formations the type of placenta are–

(A) Based on the intimacy of embryonic and maternal tissue

Epitheliochorial	Syndesmochorial	Endotheliochorial	Haemochorial	Haemoendothelia
All the six tissue barriers present e.g. Horse, donkey, pig The degree of intimacy is so strong that eventually the blood vessels of the villi are eventually bathed in the blood.	Uterine epithelium is eroded e.g. cattle, sheep, goat	Uterine epithelium and uterine connective tissue are broken e.g. Dog, cat, shrew mole.	Endothelium of maternal blood vessel disappear e.g. Apes, monkeys, humans.	Chorionic epithelium and mesoderm also disappears. e.g. ,rodents, lagomorph.

(B) On the basis foetal membranes involved in the formation of placenta

Yolk sac	Allantoic	Corionic
Derived from yolk sac and chorion *e.g. Opossum, Macropus* (Kangroo)	Formed of allantois and chorion *e.g. Perameles* (Bandicoot) most of the eutherians.	Made up of only chorion *e.g.* Primates including Humans

(C) On the basis of injury caused to uterine placenta during parturition

Non deciduate	Contradeciduate	Deciduate
No part of placenta is shed in after birth It does not show any injury Their villi are simple apposed without contact with foetus and uterine wall. *e.g.* Cattle, horse, pig	Placenta is indeciduate and even foetal placenta is absorbed *e.g. Perameles* (Bandicoot) *Talpa* (Mole)	Some part of uterine tissue is injured and passed out as decidua in after birth *e.g.* rabbits, dogs, humans

(D) On the basis of distribution of Villi

Diffused	Cotyledonary	Intermediate
Villi are scattered on the surface of allantochorion Non deciduate *e.g.* Pig, horse	Villi are arranged as patches Non deciduate *e.g.* Goat, sheep, cow, deer	They have both scattered and patches of villi Non deciduate *e.g.* Camel, Giraffe

Zonary	Discoidal	Metadiscoidal
Villi form girdle around blastocyst *e.g.* cat, dog, elephant, seal	Villi are restricted to circular disc *e.g.* Bat, rat, mouse, rabbit, bear	Villi are initially scattered and than form disc *e.g.* Monkey, ape, humans

FUNCTIONS OF PLACENTA

During placentation foetal and maternal blood are brought very close so that exchange of substances occur from one circulation to the other by diffusion. So it acts as a physiological barrier and ultrafilter between foetus blood and maternal blood.

The important functions performed by placenta are:

- It helps in nutrition of the foetus as the food contents passes from mother to the baby through placenta.
- It acts as a respiratory organ as oxygen diffuses from mother to foetus and CO_2 from foetus to mother's baby.
- Nitrogen wastes are transported from foetus of mother through placenta.
- It stores the food contents as glycogen, fat and minerals as iron before liver becomes functional.
- Trophoblast of placenta break the proteins before passing them to foetal blood.
- Placenta also acts as a endocrine gland as it secretes certain hormones as estrogen, progesterone, human chorionic gonadotrophin (HCG) and relaxin.
- Three to eight weeks embryo is very sensitive to certain chemicals (Teratogens) as nicotine, heroin, cocain, etc. which may cause malformation in the developing foetus. Some infections e.g. rubella, syphilis, HIV etc. may also pass through the placenta and infect the developing foetus.

RECAPITULATION THEORY/ BIOGENETIC LAW

In 1828 Von Baer put forward Baer's Law. It was later on called *Biogenetic law* by Ernst Haeckel in 1866. This law states that "Ontogeny repeats phylogeny". Ontogeny is the life history of an individual animal whereas phylogeny is the evolutionary history of the race of animals. It means that organism repeats its ancestral history during development.

- *e.g.* In the development of the frog, the fish like characters as gills, gill slits, tail with tail fin, lateral line sense organs etc. indicates that frog has been evolved from fish like ancestors.
- Larva of *Herdmania* shows characters of chordates *i.e.,* presence of notochord, tail and well developed dorsally placed central nervous system. However nervous system is reduced, notochord and tail is absent in adult stage which means larva shows its ancestral characters.

However, recapitulation is not a universal phenomenon *e.g.* Absence of aquatic larval stage during the development of tree frog, *Elutherodactylus* so the modified version of biogenetic law is given. It states that "ontogeny is a shortened and modified recapitulation of phylogeny "*i.e.,* during the development of an individual many steps of phylogeny of the group are ommitted, modified as embryo has to adjust itself in the surrounding environment.

7. GENETICS

MENDELIAN PRINCIPLES

Gregor Mendel (1822-1884) is appropriately called **"father of genetics".** Mendel (1865) discovered the laws of heredity by studying crosses between peas having pair of *contrasting* characters (i.e. allelic). In a cross between parents with yellow seeds and parents with green seeds, he found that in F_1 generation, all the hybrid had yellow seeds (dominant gene). In the F_2 generation 75% of the plant had yellow seeds and 25% had green seeds (recessive gene). Mendel postulated that the genes are transmitted without mixing (*law of segregation*). He demonstrated that in F_2 there are 1 dominant homozygous, 2 heterozygous and 1 ressive homozygous offsprings. The 'genotypic' segregation is 1 : 2 : 1 although the "phenotypic" proportion is 3 : 1. The law of segregation can be explained in terms of the behaviour of chromosomes during meiosis. At times there is *incomplete dominance* (i.e. intermediary heredity).

The behaviour of two or more pairs of allelic genes follow the *"law of independent assortment"*. Genes that lie in different chromsomes are independently distributed during meiosis. For the two pairs of alleles, the phenotypic proportion is 9:3:3:.

Mendel was not the first to perform hybridization experiments, but he was the first to consider the results in terms of single traits. Sageret, (1826) had studied the inheritance of contrasting traits. Others of Mendel's predecessors had considered whole organism, which incorporate a nebulous complex of traits, thus, they could observe only that similarity and differences occured among parents and progeny. They missed the significance of individual differences. Employing the scientific method, Mendel designed the necessary experiments, counted and classified the peas resulting from his crosses, compared the proportions with mathematical models, and formulated a hypothesis for there differences. Although Mendel devised a precite mathematical pattern for the transmission of hereditary units, he had no concept of the biological mechanisms involved. Nevertheless, on the basis of his preliminary experiments and hypotheses, he predicted and subsequently verified his predictions with the results of later crosses.

In 1990, Mendel's paper was discovered simultaneously by three botanists :

(*i*) Hugo de Vries in Holland—Known for his *mutation theory* and studies on the evening primrose and maize.

(*ii*) Carl Correns in Germany—who investigated maize, peas, beans.

(*iii*) Eric von Tschermak-Seysenegy in Austria—who worked with several plants, including garden pea.

Each of there investigators obtained evidence for Mendel's principles from his own independent studies. They all found Mendel's report while searching the literature for related work and cited it in their own publications.

William Bateson, an Englishman, gave this developing science the name "GENETICS" is 1905. He coined the term from a Greek word meaning "to generate".

CONCEPT OF THE GENE

Bateson actively promoted Mendel's view of paired genes. He used the word **"Allelomorph",** shortened to *allele* to identify members of pairs that control different alternative traits.

During early 1800s, a Frenchman, Lucien Cuenot, showed that genes controlled fur colour in the mouse.

An American, W.E. Castle related genes to sex and to fur colour and pattern is mammals.

A Dane and W.L. Johannsen, studied the influence of heredity and environment in plants. He began using the word *gene* from the last syllable of Darwin's term "pangene".

The gene concept, however had been implict in Mendel's visualization of a physical element or **factor** that acts as the foundation for development of a trait. These men and their peers were able to build on the basic principles of cytology, which were established between 1865 (when Mendel's work was completed) and 1900 (when it was discovered).

CHROMOSOME THEORY

Wilhelm Roux has postulated as early as 1883 that chromosomes within the nucleus of the cell were the bearers of hereditary factors. The only model he was able to devise that would account for his observed genetic result was a row of lined-up objects duplicated exactly. To explain the mechanics of gene transmission from cell to cell he, therefore, suggested that nuclei must have invisible structures held in rows or chains that duplicated themselves when the cell divided. Constituents of the nuclei that seemed best designed to carry genes and fill there requirements were chromosomes.

In 1900, **Von Winiwarter,** discovered that in the ovary of a half day old rabbit (*Oryctolagus cuniculus*) chromosomes had associated in pairs side by side for a part of their length. This association appeared at what are now call zygotene stage of meiosis, which was very common in rabbits ovary 1½ & 2½ days old.

Montgomery (1901), after a study of meiosis in 42 species of insects came to conclusion that each association of chromosomes in pairs at zygotene involves one paternal & one maternal chromosome.

Sutton (1902) extended Montgomery's observation while studying meiosis in grasshopper. The male grasshopper has 23 chromosomes in somatic cells, and their chromosomes differed very much in size, so that the largest chromosome was 5-6 times as long as the smallest. Sutton observed that apart from one X-chromosome, 11-paired associations were present in each nucleus and showed same size differences as at mitosis. It was also shown that although due to degree of contraction, absolute lengths of paired chromosomes differed at different stages of meiosis, but their relative lengths were constant. This confirmed Montgomery's conclusion that association were brought about only between paternal and maternal chromosomes.

T. Boveri (1902) : Who demonstrated in sea urchin, that different chromosomes of a set possess different qualities and also showed presence of a complete set of chromosomes was important for survival. This observation derives support now from the fact that a **hypodiploid** (chromosome no. < 2) does not survive while a haploid individual may survive. It is also proved by the fact that trisomics involving different chromosomes differed morphologically as in case of *Detura* and many other plant species and also in Human.

Experiments of **T. Boveri & W.S. Sutton** in 1902 brought confirming evidence that a gene is part of a chromosome. The theory of the **gene as a discrete unit of a chromosome** was developed by T.H. Morgan and his associates from studies on the fruit fly, *Drosophila melanogaster*.

H.J. Muller later promoted the merger of the two sciences that had contributed most to the chromosome theory-cytology (the study of cells) and genetics as cytogenetics.

FORMULATION OF CHROMOSOME THEORY

On the basis of findings of Montgomeny and Boveri and on the basis of his own studies, W.S. Sutton for the first time in 1903 formulated **chromosome theory of Mendelian inheritance** in clear terms. He drew attention to following features which suggested that Mendelian factors should be located on chromosomes:

There is a resemblance between separation of homologus chromosomes during anaphase I of meiosis and the postulated separation of character differences at the time of gamete formation.

If each pair of homologous chromosome is so oriented at metaphase I, so that in a pair the orientation of maternal and paternal chromosomes, towards specific poles is independent of the orientation of these chromosomes in the other pair, we expect that 2^n combinations are possible (n = haploid chromosomes number). This is true of Mendelian factors also. This will further suggest that in Sea Urchin with n = 18, n^{18} = 262, 144 possible combinations of maternal and paternal chromosomes will be available. Therefore, there is a parallelism between presumed independent assortment of homologous chromosomes at meiosis and Mendel's prinsiple of independent assortment. Confirmation of random orientation of different chromosome pairs came by use of sex chromosomes.

SEX CHROMOSOME AND CHROMOSOME THEORY

The first definite evidence for chromosome theory came from sex-determination. **C.E. Mc Clung** in 1902 reported two types of sperms in grasshoppers, one containing an X-chromosome and the other lacking it. Since this was the only difference in sperms and since all eggs were similars with respect to X-chromosome it was concluded that x-chromosome must be responsible for determination of sex.

Proof of parallelism between chromosomes and mendelian factors with respect to independent assortment came from **E.E. Carothers** in 1913. She used a particular grasshopper of three pairs of chromo-some could be morphologically distinguished. If these three pairs are designated as AA', BB' & CC', the possible arrangements at metaphase I can be shown as in following figure:

AA' A'A	AA'	AA'
BB' BB'	B'B	BB'
CC' CC'	CC'	C'C
A'A A'A	AA'	A'A
B'B BB'	B'B	B'B
CC' C'C	C'C	C'C

Eight types of combinations in gametes would then be possible in equal proportions from arrangements shown in the above figure. When crosses of thus marked grasshoppers were made with normal grasshoppers, all eight combinations could be identified morphologically through cytological preparations, suggesting an assortment just like that for mendelian factors in a trihybrid cross.

Mendel had fortunately selected those characters which were located on separate chromosomes. Had he selected two chracters located on the same chromosome, independent assortment would not be observed, since chromosomes and not part thereof, will exhibit independent assortment. A very strong cytological evidence for chromosome theory of inheritance came from **C. Stern's** experiment on crossing over & **C.B. Bridge's** experiment on the non-disjunction of X-chromosomes.

Principles of Mendelian Inheritance (Mendelism)

Principle of Unit Characters

An individual is made up a large number of characters, each of which behaves as a unit.

Principle of Paired Factors

A trait or character is represented genetially in an individual by two factors present on the some locus in the two homologous chromosomes. The two factors may represent the same expression of the trait. (TT for tallness, *tt* for dwarfness) or both expressions as in hybrid (T*t* for heigh/tallness) though only one is evident externally. Factors representing the different expressions of a trait are known as *alleles/allelomorphs/allelomorphic* pair. These days, the two similar factors of a trait/gene are also called *alleles.*

Principle of Dominance

In a hybrid, where both the contrasting alleles are present, only one factor/allele called *dominant* is able to express its effect while the other factor/ allele called recessive remains suppressed. In a cross between pure/true breeding red flowered (RR) Pea plant and white flowered (*rr*) Peal plant, the F_1 generation is red flowered though it has received both the factors (R & *r*). It is because of the dominant nature of factor for red flower colour and recessive nature of the factor for white flower colour. On self breeding, the recessive trait reappears in the F_2 generation showing that it is suppressed in F_1 generation and not lost.

Law of Segregation (Principle of Purity of Gametes/First Law of Mendelism)

Mendelian factors or alleles of a trait are particulate entities which keep their identity in the hybrid, separate out at the time of gametogenesis randomly passing to different gametes for random pairing during passage to offspring.

In a monohybrid cross, say between a pure tall pea plant and dwarf pea plant, F_1 or hybrids are all tall. On self breeding them, both tall and dwarf appear in the ratio 3 : 1 (787 tall to 273) dwarf in Mendel's experiment). Further self breeding shows that dwarf plants breed true. Amongst tall, one third are true while two third (one half of total progeny) behave as hybrids. This shows that phenotypic monohybrid ratio of 3 : 1 is genotypically 1 pure tall : 2 hybrid talls : 1 dwarf. Therefore, F_1 plants or hybrids carry both the factors or alleles which separate out in gemetes, one half from each parent having the factor for tallness and the second half the factor for dwarfness.

Male Gametes (♂)		*Female Gametes* (♀)		*Offsprings*	
1/2 T	×	1/2 T	=	1/4 TT	
1/2 T	×	1/2 *t*	=	1/4 T*t*	1/2 T*t*
1/2 *t*	×	1/2 T	=	1/4 T*t*	
1/2 *t*	×	1/2 *t*	=	1/4 *tt*	

Since gametes carry only one factor of a trait, the principle of segregation is also called *principle* of *purity* of *gametes*. It can be proved by taking those expamples in which the gametophytes or pollen grains carry specific genetic traits, e.g. starchy and waxy (= glutinous, lacking starch), pollen in maize and rice. When true breeding starchy pollen bearing variety is crossed with true breeding waxy pollen bearing plant, the offspring or F_1 plants (diploid) produce pollen (haploid) through meiosis of both the types, starchy and waxy in the ratio 1 : 1 indicating that the two mendelian factor segregate in the ratio of 1 : 1 at the time of sporogenesis/ gametogenesis and that a gamete/gametophyte contains single factor of a trait so that 50% of them contain one factor while the other 50% possess the second factor.

Law of Independent Assortment (Second Law of Mendelism)

The two factors of each trait assort at random and independent of the factor of other traits at the time of meiosis (gametogenesis /sporogenesis) and get randomly as well as independently rearranged in the offspring. In monohybrid cross, the F_1 organisms produce two types of male and two types of female gametes, so that there is possibility of four types of gamete combinations. In a dihybrid cross, if the gene/factors are to assort independently, F_1 organism will produce four types of male (2 × 2, e.g. RY, R*y*, *r*Y and *ry*) and four types of female gametes with 16 types of gametic recombinations (4 × 4). Mendel crossed genetically pure yellow round seeded (YYRR) pea plant with green wrinkled seeded (*yyrr*) pea plant. F_1 plants were all yellow and round seeded. In F_2 generation, four types of plants appeared—315/556 or 9/16 yellow rounded, 101/556 or 3/16 yellow and wrinkled, 108/556 or 31/6 yellow rounded and 32/556 or 1/16 green wrinkled. The ratio of seed colour (416/556 or 3/4 yellow : 140/556 or 1/4 green) and seed texture (423/556 or 3/4 rounded : 133/556 or 1/4 wrinkled) or individual traits is 3 : 1 showing that the factors for each trait behave independent of the factors of the other trait.

Law of Independent assortment is applicable to only those factors or genes which are present on different chromosomes. Chromosomes have hundreds of genes which show linked inheritance or linkage. Mendel himself found linkage between flower and seed colour (white flower and white seed, red flower and grey seed) in pea.

Post Mendelian Discoveries

(*a*) Gene Interaction
(*b*) Incomplete Dominance
(*c*) Overdominance (super dominance)
(*d*) Codominance
(*e*) Multiple Alleles
(*f*) Blood group Inheritance
(*g*) Isoalleles

(*h*) Pseudoalleles
(*i*) Lethal genes
(*j*) Suppressor/Inhibitor Gene
(*k*) Epistasis
(*l*) Complementary genes
(*m*) Supplementary genes
(*n*) Duplicate genes
(*o*) Polymeric/Additive Genes
(*p*) Multiple factors
(*q*) Pleiotropic genes
(*r*) Qualitative Inheritance
(*s*) Quantitative/Poly Inheritance
(*t*) Pedigree Analysis

CONCEPT OF GENE

In the 1930s, G.W. Beadle, B. Ephrussi, E.L. Tatum, J.B.S. Haldane and others provided a basis for understanding the functional properties of genes and suggested functional extensions of the **classical gene concept**. The gene was at first characterized as an indivisible unit of structure, unit of mutation and unit of function. A.E. Garrod, had indicated in 1902 that genes in humans function through 'enzymes'.

Early triumphs were the identification of maromolecules carrying genetic information in a bacterium by O.T. Avery and associates and in a virus by A. Hershey and M. Chase. The Avery *et al* experiments showed that a chemical, deoxyribonucleic acid (DNA) could bring about genetic change **(transformation)** in a *Peumococcus* bacterium; **Hershey and Chase** demonstrated that the nucleic acid component (DNA) and not the protein is the genetic material carried by the bacteriophage. **H. Fraenket Conrat & B. Singer** showed that ribonucleic acid (RNA) is the genetic material in tobacco mosaic virus. Thus, RNA performs the function in some viruses that DNA performs in other organisms.

J.D. Watson and **F.H.C. Crick** worked out the double helix structure of the chemical DNA. The central problem of genetics was thus resolved with the discovery that **DNA is the genetic material**. Genetic mechanisms could now be forumlated in biochemical terms. Also, it became clear how do units (genes) of DNA control specific traits in organisms and how do assemblages of DNA units carried in fertilized eggs provide 'blueprints' for development of entire organisms.

Functional Perspective

Genes accomplish their function (*a*) through **replication** that results in more units like themselves & (*b*) through **transcription** and **translation**, whereby, proteins that function as determiners in the metabolism of the cell are synthesized. Although genes are usually stable, they are susceptible to occasional change or **mutation**, which provides altered forms of genes (alleles). Mendel first postulated the existence of genes from their end effects, as expressed in altered characteristics. Now genes have been defined chemically and are know for what they do in directing the formation of traits through the specificity of protein enzymes. Thus, DNA carries the specifications for growth, differentiation & functioning of cells in the organism.

GENE VERSUS ALLELE CONCEPTS (PSEUDOALLELES)

Gene

"Hereditary unit specifying the production of a distinct protein (e.g. an enzyme) or RNA." In modern sense, an inherited factor that determines a biological character of an organism is called a gene. This is a functional unit of hereditary material. In the part, gene was believed to be unit of structure also, but recent knowledge has shown that it is no longer a unit of structure.

Alleles (Allelomorphs)

Alleles, the abbreviated form of the term "allelomorphs" (meaning one form or the other) indicates alternative forms of the same gene. i.e. "One of two genes for a given trait that occurs in a specific position on each homologous chromosome". For instance, 'D' & '*t*' are two alleles of the gene for plant height. In pure tall or pure dwarf plants, same allele is duplicated (DD or *dd*), while in hybrid tall both the alleles will be present (D*d*). An individual having only one allele or in other words, two identical genes, is known as **homozygous** (DD or *dd*). Similarly, an individual, having two different alleles will be called **heterzygous** or **hybrid** (D*d*). In the present usage the term gene and the allele are interchangable, but while gene can be used for any factor, allele is used with reference to another allele. For instance, while 'D' & '*d*' are alleles to each other, they cannot be allelic to any other gene.

Pseudoalleles

Pseudogenes are partial duplicates of structural genes that have incorporated sufficient changes, that they are not biologically active and are usually not transcribed. Pseudogenes are turning out to be quite common in eukoryotes. There are **inactive but stable component** of a genome resembling a gene, apparently derived from active genes by mutation. The pseudogenes, which are relatively frequent in the mammalian genome, can be identified because they have undergone mutations that render them unable to produce functional *m* RNA e.g., a pseudogene might contain premature chain termination codons, (insertions or deletions) that cause the message to be read out of frame. Most frequently the promoters of pseudogenes are inactive. Because there is no selective pressure to maintain a functional gene product, in due course, pseudogenes accumulate multiple mutations and eventually become random sequence DNA.

EXTENSION OF MENDELIAN PRINCIPLES

Experiments of Knight & Goss on Pea

Knight (1799) and Goss (1824) had conducted experiments on edible pea (*Pisum sativum*), much before Mendel, but failed to formulate the law of inheritance, only because they could not give a mathematical treatment of their results. They were more concerned for improvement of peas rather than their concern for understanding the mechanism.

Germplasm Theory and the Genotype Phenotype Concept

A. Weismann (1834-1914) demonstrated that "Pangenesis" could not be verified. His popular experiments consisted of cutting the tails of mice and then studying the inheritance. Repeating such a treatment for 22 generations, he found that complete tail structure was still inhibited. There experiments of mutilation may appear now rather crude, but results can definitely be used as argument against "pangenesis" because one the tail was removed, the 'pangenes' or 'gemmules' for the tail will not be available and therefore this structure should not develop in the next generation if pangenesis holds good.

Weismann also proposed his own *germplasm theory* to account for heredity. According to this theory, the body of an individual can be divided into "germplasm" and "somatoplasm". The somatoplasm was not able to enter the sex cells, consequently the variations present in the somatoplasm will not be transmitted to next generation. The germplasm on the other hand, was meant for the reproductive purpose only, so that any change occurring in germplasm will influence the progeny. This was very significant advancement in understanding of heredity.

In order to make definite distinction between hereditary and environmental variations, Johannsen, 1909, formulated the *genotype–phenotype concept.* According to him, the genotype of an individual represents sum total of heredity.

On the other hand, phenotype represents features which are produced by interaction between genotype and environment.

A genotype can thus exhibit different phenotype under different conditions. This is referred to as individidual's "norm of reaction" to the environment. Therefore similar genotypes may not have the same phenotype. Conversely, similar phenotypes do not necessarily mean some genotype.

GENE MAPPING METHODS

Soon after rediscovery of Mendel's experiments, two main groups of geneticists emerged :

"Mendelians" : Who believed that all evolutionary important heritable differences are qualitative and discontinuous.

"Biometricians" : Who proposed that heritable variation is basically quantitative and continuous and that genes did not exist as separate units.

To prove that both "mendelian" and "biometricians" were only partly correct, **Johannsen (1903)** used the character of seed weight in beans and analysed its breeding behaviour. In a commercial seed lot of a variety, seed weight ranged from 1 cg (cg = centigram) to 90 cg. In the progeny of seed of every weight group, great-variation was observed, and by successive self pollinations for several generations, it was possible to isolate 19 pure lines. Each pure line had a distinct average seed weight, which was maintained in the progeny, although variation did exist in each pure line and was attributed to environmental effect.

Thus by Johannsen's experiment, it could be shown that continuous variation can be heritable, a belief opposed by 'mendelians'. However since differences between 19 different pure lines isolated by **Johannsen (1903)** could not be ascribed to specific genes, genetic basis of quantitative traits still remained disputed and it could not be proved that like qualitative traits, quantitative traits exhibiting continuous variation are also controlled by individual genes comparable to Mendelian factors.

Subsequently, it was **Yule (1906)**, who suggested that quantitative variation may be controlled by large number of individual genes, each having a small effect. Soon after Yule's proposal, **H. Nitsson-Ehle (1908)** and **East (1910)**, demonstrated segregation and assortment of genes controlling quantitative traits, kernel colour in wheat and corolla length in tobacco. Such genes were later called **polygenic systems** and inheritance due to such a system was explained in the form of **"multiple factor hypothesis."**

Alleles that had small but *cumulative effect* with semidominance rather than complete dominance were postulated to behave in a Mendelian fashion. Several to many nonallelic genes were postulated to have cumulative effects on particular traits. An explanation for continuous variation thus emerged in the form of the **'multiple-gene-hypothesis'.** Experimental results and interpretations substantiating this hypothesis were obtained from the classical investigations of H. Nilsson Ehle in Sweden & E.M. East in the United States during the period 1910-1913.

NUMERICAL AND STRUCTURAL VARIATIONS IN CHROMOSOMES AND THEIR SIGNIFICANCE

Changes in the number and structure of the chromosomes may occur spontaneously or experimentally by the action of radiation or chemicals. The number of chromosomes is generally constant for plant and animal species. 'Chromosomal change' in number are of two main kinds : (1) *Euploids :* a change in the number of chromosome sets, the set being kept balanced (2) *Aneuploids :* there is a loss or gain of one or more chromosomes. In exceptional cases there are *haploid* organisms. In plants, *polyploids* (triploid, tetraploid) are rather common. They originate by **reduplication without cytokinesis**. In animals, polyploids are scarce, because sex is frequently determined by a pair of different chromosomes (XY). **Polyploidy** can be induced by colchicine, this substance in used in agriculture to improve certain plant species. *Allopolyploidy* consists of the formation of a hybrid with different sets of chromosomes. Sometimes a diploid gamete fertilizes a normal haploid gamete, producing a new species with a triploid number. Thus there are two main kinds of change in the number of chromosomes. In *euploids* the change is in the haploid number but the entire set of chromosome is kept balanced, whereas, in *aneuploids* there is a loss or gain of one or more chromosome(s) causing the set to become unbalanced. In humans aneuploidy may cause severe alterations of the phenotype. Polyploidy and allopolyploidy are expamples of euploidy.

Among the aneuploid organisms there are the *trisomic* (i.e. with three similar chromosomes instead of a normal pair) and the *monosomic* (missing one member of a pair of homologous chromosomes) conditions. There two conditions are important in humans and may arise by **nondisjunctional** division.

EXTRA CHROMOSOMAL INHERITANCE

Also called **'structural alterations'** involve a change in the molecular organization of the chromosome. One or two breaks are produced at the level of the chromatin fiber, and the effect depends on whether it occurs in the G_1 phase (one chromatid) or in the G_2 (two chromatids). Chromosomal aberration should be differentiated from *gene* or *point mutations*, which occur at molecular level. Ionizing radiations X-rays, γ-rays, β-rays, fast neutrons, slow neutrons and ultraviolet light can produce point mutations or chromosomal aberrations. The number of mutations increases proportionally with the dose of X-radiation. The effect of radiation is cumulative. An exposure of culture cells to 2DR (roentgen units) is sufficient to produce one chromosome break per cell. In contrast to mutations which increase proportionally with the dose, chromosomal aberrations increase exponentially with the dose. Breakage can be followed by "healing" of the broken end (the breaks may be at the chromosome or the chromatid level). Chromatid breaks are produced in cells irradiated after the S-phase. If two breaks are produced, **translocation, inversions,** and **large deletions** may be induced. **Dicentric chromosomes** may be produced, which form a bridge at anaphase. In the human, heavy medical radiation, nuclear accidents or radioactive substances may produce chromosomal aberrations. In the production of new antibiotics and plants, irradiation is being used to economic advantage. *Somatic mutations* are not transmitted from one generation to another, whereas, germ cell mutations may be passed to the offsprings.

Some of the main chromosomal aberrations are

Deficiency or deletion, in which a part (either interstitial or terminal) of the chromosome is missing. The parts of the chromosome lacking the kinetochore are generally lost. Deficiency may be 'heterogygous' (one chromosome normal) or 'homozygous' (both chromosome are deficient). The latter generally does not survive.

Duplication, in which a chromosome segment is represent two or more times (tandem duplication).

Translocation in which there is an exchange of segments between non-homologous chromosomes (reciprocal type) or between different parts of the same chromosome (simple type). Sometime *centric* fusion occurs when the two chromosomes are broken near the kinetochore and form a metacentric (v-shaped) chromosome.

Inversion, in which there is breakage of a segment, followed by its fusion in a reverse position. It is **'pericentric'** if the kinetochore is outside. Isochromosomes may arise from a break at kinetochore, resulting in two chromosomes with identical arms.

Sister chromatid's exchange consists of the interchange of DNA segments between sister chromatids in a chromosome. First described in studies using ^{3}H-thymidine, it was interpreted as the result of radiation from ^{3}H. This aberration can be studied with bromodeoxyuridine (BrdU), which is incorporated instead of thymidine and which produces changes in fluorescence or in the **Giemsa stain.** This technique permits the detection of diseases, characterized by chromosome fragility and enables the study of the action of mutagenic drugs which increase the number of breaks.

SIGNIFICANCE

Cytogenetic studies have provided excellent methods for establishing taxonomic interrelationships and have, thereby, contributed to studies of *evolution* and systematics. One of the most frequent causes of evolution is a change in the order of genes as a result of chromosomal aberrations. In plants, aneuploids and polyploidy are frequent sources of variations, where as in mammals and birds, speciation depends more on chromosomal rearrangement and point mutations.

In the study of evolution, the number of chromosomes, the characteristics of the karyotype, the total chromosomal area, and the content of DNA are investigated. The presence of metacentric chromosomes may, in some cases, result from fusion of two aerocentric chromosomes. The contrasting phenomenon (i.e. dissociation) may lead to an increase in chromosome number. The problem of *evolution* is very complex. Knowledge of cytogenetics is most fundamental to the understanding of this problem of evolution. One example of importance of cytogenetics in evolution is given in a comparison of the chromosome pairs of the primates and humans. Primates have 48 chromosomes (24 pairs) while human have 23 pairs instead of 24 pairs of primates. There comparative studies have demonstrated that (*i*) 13 pairs of chromosome in humans are identical with 13 pairs in the chimpanzee.

(*ii*) Chromosome number 2 in humans has resulted from centric fusion (or **Robertsonion translocation**) of two chromosomes present in hominoid apes.

(*iii*) The other chromosomes differ in the occurrence of nine pericentric inversions and two additions of chromatin material.

MICROBIAL GENETICS

POLYTENE CHROMOSOME

Polytene chromosomes provided the first evidence that eukaryotic gene activity is regulated at the level of RNA synthesis. When ***dipteran*** chromosomes become polytenic, the DNA replicates by ***endomitosis***, and the resulting daughter chromatids remain aligned side by side. There chromatids are visible during interphase and have a characteristic morphology of dark bands and alternating interbands. Within these chromosomes it is possible to osberve the genetic activity of specific loci at local enlargements called **puffs**, which represent DNA undergoining intense gene transcription. Puff distribution varies from one tissue to another and can be induced experimentally, indicating the cell specialization results from variable gene transcription.

Polytene chromosomes constitute a valuable material for the study of gene regulation because their gene transcription can be visualized directly in the microscope. Some cells of dipteran (flies, mosquitoes, midges) larvae become very large and have a high DNA content. The most prominent ones are located in the salivary gland, but other cells from the gut, fat body, and malpighian tubules of the larva also become 'polytenic'. (Polyteny differs from polyploidy, in which there is also excess DNA per nucleus, but in which the new chromosomes are separate from each other). A polytene chromosome of *Drosophila* salivary glands has about 1000 DNA molecules arranged side by side which arise from 10 rounds of DNA replication ($2^{10} = 1024$). Other dipteran species have even more DNA molecules per polytene chromo-some, for example, *chironomus* has 16,000. In polytene cells, the chromosomes are visible during interphase, and the *chromomeres* (regions in which the chromatin is more tighly coiled) alternate with regions where the DNA fibres are folded more loosely. The alignment of many chromosomes gives polytene chromosomes their characteristic morphology, in which a series of dark bands alternates with clear zones called *interbands.* There are about 5000 bands in the *Drosophilla* genome. They have characteristic morphology and positions, which permit detailed chromosome mapping.

An additional characteristic of polytene chromosomes is that the maternal and paternal homologue remain associated side by side, in what is called *'somatic pairing'*. This permits the identification of deletions, inversions, duplications as regions looped out of the chromosomes. The pericentromeric heterochromatin of all the *Drosophila* chromosomes coalesces in a chromocenter, where the chromosomes are joined together. The satellite DNAs of the chromocenter are underreplicated with respect to the rest of the chromosome. (i.e. they undergo fewer rounds of replication). Polytene cells are unable to undergo mitosis and are destined to die. Not all the cells in a dipteran larva have polytene chromosomes. Those destined to produce the adult structures after metamorphosis (***imaginal discs***) remains diploid.

Polytene chromosomes have become even more important with the advent of recombinant DNA techniques because they make it possible to map any DNA segment to specific chromosomal loci by *in situ* hybridization. Polytene chromosomes are very suitable for *in situ* hybridization because their 1000 DNA molecules are aligned side by side, thereby greatly facilitating the detection of single copy genes.

The bands have greatly helped in the mapping of chromosomes in cytogenetics studies. The bands occasionally form reversible "puffs" known as *"chromosome puffs"* or *"Balbiani rings"* which are associated with differential gene activation. A puff can be considered a band in which the DNA unfolds into open loops as a consequence of intense gene transcription. i.e. "puffs are sites of intense gene transcription". In salivary glands, the appearance of some puffs has been correlated with the production of specific proteins which are secreted in large amounts in the larval saliva. e.g. *Chironomous* has at the base of the salivary glands four specialized cells that contain cytoplasmic granules of a special secretory protein. The gene for this protein is located in a distinct puff that appears only in the four specialized cells. These results show that cell specialization results from variable gene transcription.

Puffing is a cyclic and reversible phenomenon. The steroid hormone **'ecdysone'**, which induces molting in insects, will induce the formation of specific puffs when injected into larvae or when added to salivary glands in culture by temperature shock. When *Drosophila* larvae normally grown at 25°C, are exposed to a temperature of 37°C, a series of specific genes is activated while most other genes are represed. Five minutes after the heat shock, nine new puffs are seen on the giant chromosome of the salivary glands. There puffs are active in RNA synthesis as can be demonstrated by ^{3}H-uridine labeling and radioautography. These new RNAs are accumulated in cytoplasm after being released from the puffs and give rise to eight specific heat shock proteins, so the induction of specific proteins is due to an increased transcription of individual genes RNA polymerase II accumulates in the heat shock puffs, while it disappears from other regions of chromosomes.

In D. *melanogaster* the giant chromosomes are found in the form of five long and one short strands radiating from a single more or less amorphous mass known as *chromocentre*. One long strand corresponds to the X-chromosome and the remaining four long strands are the arms of IInd and IIIrd chromosomes. The short strand which is small dot like is IVth chromosome. The centromeres of all there chromosomes fuse to form chromocentre. In the male files, the Y chromosome is also found fused within the chromocentre and is therefore not seen as a separate strand.

LAMPBRUSH CHROMOSOMES

Special kind of chromosomes known as lampbrush chromosomes are found during the prolonged diplotene stage of first meiotic division and in spermatocyte nuclei of *Drosophila*. They are characterized by a remarkable change in structure. The change in structure includes an enormous increase in length. These chromosomes may sometimes become even larger than polytenic giant salivary gland chromosomes. The largest chromosome having a length up to 1 mm have been observed in *urodele* amphibian. The chromosomes seem to have a chromomeric pattern with loops projecting in pairs from a single chromomere. The size of loops varies from an average of 9.5 μ in frog to upto 200 μ in newt. The chromomeres are connected by inter-chromomeric fibres. These pair of loops in these chromosomes give them the characteristic lampbrush appearance. Frequently there loops exhibit a thin axis (which probably consists of one DNA double helix) from which fibres project which are covered with a loop matrix consisting of RNA and protein. The number of pairs of loops gradually increases in meiosis till it reaches maximum in diplotene. As meiosis proceeds further, number of loops gradually decreases and the loops ultimately disappear due to disintegration rather then reabsorption back into the chromomere. (H. Ris., had though that the loops were integral parts of chromonemata which are extended in the form of major coils.) It is also believed that the loops represent the modified chromosome structures at the loci of active genes. It has been observed that, if the activity of there genes is checked by actinomycin D, the loops will collapse. Numerous small nucleoli are commonly formed from the lampbrush chromosomes due to the rings detached from the loops at specific loci.

Lampbrush chromosomes occur at the diplotene stage of meiotic prophase of all animal species. Highly condensed chromomeres form the chromosome axis, from which loops of DNA extend laterally as a result of intense RNA synthesis. Each loop has an axis formed by a single DNA molecule which is covered by a matrix of nascent RNA with hn RNA-binding proteins attached to it. Transcriptional units in oocyte may be extremely long-upto 100 μ. Some experi-ments suggest that the long transcriptional units of lampbrush chromosomes may be due to a failure of transcriptional termination.

Lampbrush chromosomes were first observed by Flemming in 1882 and were described in detail in shark oocyte by Ruckert in 1892. He coined the name because the chromosomes look like the brushes used in those times to clean the chimneys of oil lamps.

Lampbrush chromosomes occur at the diplotene stage of meiotic prophase in oocytes of all animal species, in spermatocytes of several species, and even in the giant nucleus of the unicellular alga *'Acetabularia'*. They are visualized best in *Salamander* oocytes because they have a high DNA content and therefore very large chromosomes.

Because Lampbrush chromosomes are found in meiotic prophase, they are present in the form of 'bivalents' in which the maternal and paternal chromosomes are held together by chiasmata at those sites where crossing over has previously occurred. Each bivalent has four chromatids, two in each homologue. The axis of each homologue consists of a row of granules or chromomeres from which lateral loops extend. The loops are always symmetrical, each chromosome having two ot them, one for each chromatid (two additional symmetrical loops will be found on the homologue because cells in prophase of meiosis have a 4C DNA content—equivalent to a tetraploid cell. The loops can be distinguished by size, thickness, and other morphologic characteristics. Each loop appears at a constant position in the chromosome, and detailed chromosome maps can be drawn. There are about 10,000 loops per chromosome set. Each loop has an axis formed by a single DNA molecule that is unfolded from the chromosome as a result of intense RNA synthesis. About 5 to 10% of the DNA is in the lateral loops; the rest being tightly condensed in the chromomeres of the chromosome axis, which are transcriptionally inactive. Lampbrush chromosomes are very good material for *in situ* hybridization of cloned DNA to RNA because the thousands of nascent RNA molecules aligned side by side along the loop greatly amplify the hybridization signal. Studies with there techniques have shown that in some loops simple sequence satellite DNAs are transcribed; which is unusual because satellite DNA are normally not expressed.

The hybrization results are due to initiation of transcription at a histone gene promoter that then foils to terminate normally. Enormous transcripts are produced which result from read through into the satellite DNA. Eventually transcription stops when the next transcriptional unit is reached. This failure of termination may be generalized throughout the lamp-brush chromosome and may explain the long loops.

TABLE : Size of the Lampbrush Lateral Loops Increases with the Genome Size

	C-value (pg of DNA)	*C-value Increase*	*Lampbrush Loop Size*
Xenopus laevis (South African clawed frog)	3.1	1	5-10μm
Triturus cristatus (Common European newt)	23	7.4	30-50μm
Neiturus maculosus (American "Mudpuppy" Salamander)	78	25.1	>100μm

BACTERIAL CHROMOSOME

Bacterial and blue green algae are designated as the *akaryobionta* as against the *karyobionta* having better differentiated nuclei. However, feulgen positive bodies are seen in bacteria and blue-green algae, a reaction meant for the nucleus of chromosomes. There bodies can be clearly observed with the help of electron microscope. It has also been demonstrated that there bodies consist of a network of fine thread. Further work by a number of workers demonstrated that the network of threads consists of a single chromosome in the form of a ring. However, the exact three dimensional arrangement by which 1100 μ - 1400 μ long DNA chain is packed in a nucleoid is not very clear. The cross sections showed 500-900 strands indicating that a single DNA strand is folded back and forth several hundred times. It is also known that large part of the DNA in bacterial nucleoid is not combined with proteins. It has also been shown that the nucleoid is not combined with proteins. It has also been shown that the nucleoid of *Escherichia coli,* one of the most extensively studied bacterium often has a point of contact with the plasma membrane. This is perhaps the point at which the replication of DNA strand is initiated.

HUMAN GENETICS

DOSAGE COMPENSATION AND MECHANISM OF SEX DETERMINATION

The word 'sex' denotes the idea of differentiation into two opposite and complementary characters of maleness and femaleness. The majority of animals have distinct males and females in natural population. These are called *gonochoristic* organisms. On the other hand, there are organisms which possess the sex organs of both sexes, which are called *hermaphrodites* or bisexual organisms. Environment determines sex in some potentially hermaphrodite animals. Marine moluscs *Crepidula* becomes female when reared alone but produces male in company of an adult. Marine worm *Bonellia* turns female in isolation or when attached to substratum. The newly hatched worm develops into male if it happens to get attached to proboscis of female. Such a male enters the female and stays there as a parasite. Bridges put forward a *genic balance theory of sex* which states that basically the genotype of an individual possesses both male and female characteristics but the type of sex which develops depends upon preponderance of genes of that sex. In bacteria, 'sex' determination is controlled by *fertility factor* located on a plasmid. In several simple organisms, sex is determined by a single gene. In most animals and some plants, sex is determined by *sex chromosome/allosomes*. X-body or X-chromosome was discovered by Henking (1891) when he found that in the testes of male bug, one chromosome has no homologue. Stevens (1902) discovered Y chromosome. Mc Clung (1902) observed that in Squash Bug (Anas), male has 21 chromosomes while female has 22 chromosomes. He showed that X-chromosome has a role in sex determination. Wilson and Stevens (1905) put forward the *chromosome theory of sex* with X and Y chromosome being named as sex chromosomes.

MALE HETEROGAMETY

(a) Protenor type (XX-XO type)

Wilson demonstrated in *Protenor belfragei* (a plant bug) that while the female has 14 chromosome, the male has only 13. In roundworms and certain insects (true bugs, grasshoppers, cockroaches), the females have two sex chromosomes, XX while the males possess a single sex chromosome, X. The females are homogametic (A + X). Amongst angiosperms, *Dioscorea sinuata* has XX-XO sex complement.

$$XX = ♀, XO = ♂$$

(b) Lygaeus type (XX-XY type)

This was shown by Wilson in the plant bug (Hemiptera) *Lygaeus turcicus*. Here the female have 12 autosomes and two X chromosomes, the males have 12 autosomes, one X chromosome and a smaller Y chromosome. It occurs in mammals and many insects with females having homomorphic XX sex chromosomes and males possessing heteromorphic XY-chromosomes. Y is shorter, may be hooked (as in *Drosophila*). Despite differences in morphology, XY chromosomes synapse during zygotene. They have two parts, homologous and differential. Homologous regions of the two take part in synapsis. They carry similar genes, called X-Y linked genes, e.g. Xeroderma pigmentosum, Epidermolysis bullosa. The differential region of Y chromosome is mostly heterochromatic. The euchromatic part of differential region of this chromosome has *holandric* genes like TDF (testis determing factor) or SRY, ZFY (sperm formation), hypertrichosis (excessive hairness) on pinna, porcupine skin, keratoderma dissipatum (thickened skin of extermities) and webbed toes. TDF is the smallest gene (14 base only; Page *et al*, 1987). Holandric genes are transferred directly from father to son. Genes present on differential region of X-chromosome also find expression in males (sex linked traits) whether they are recessive or dominant because males are hemizygous for these genes; e.g. red-green colour blindness, haemophilia; Male is heterogametic (A + Y, A + X, in human beings, 22 + Y and 22 + X) while female is homogamatic (A + X, in human beings 22 + X). The two types of male gametes or sperms are called *androsperms* (22 + Y) and gynosperms (22 + X). Y-chromosome of father is directly transferred to male offspring while its X-chromosome is passed to the female offspring. Male offspring receives its X-chromosome from mother (and hence all the sex linked traits). Female offspring receives its two XX-chromosomes from the two parents, one from each. Because Y-chromosome determines the male-sex, it is also called *androsome*. XY sex determination is found in many bryophytes (females A + X, males A + Y). Amongst angiosperms XY sex determination is found is *Melandrium* (*Lychnis*), *Coccinia*, *Salix*, *Elodea*, etc. Sex is decided at the time of fertilization. It is known as *syngametic sex determination*.

XX = ♀; XY = ♂

MALE HOMOGAMETY

In the homogametic male, the two sex chromosomes are known as Z and Z. If there are two sex chromosomes in female, they are called W & Z, if there is a single sex chromosome, then it is Z.

The types are thus ZZ-ZO, or ZZ-WZ

(ZZ = ♂, Z(O) or ZW = ♀ i.e. Z corresponds to X and W corresponds to Y)

(*a*) *ZZ-ZO* type e.g., *Fumea carta, a moth (Lepidoptera)* : In moths and butterflies, the female have odd sex chromosome (AA + ZO) while males have two homomorphic sex chromosomes (AA + ZZ). The females are heterogametic (A + Z, A + Zero) and the male homogametic (A + Z). The males of *F. carta* have a diploid number 62 chromosomes, 60 autosomes + ZZ) the females have one less, 60 autosomes + Z. Thus, these are eggs with Z (sex chromosome) and without it.

60 AA + ZZ = ♂

60 AA + ZW = ♀

(*b*) *ZZ-WZ or (WZ-WW)* type e.g., *Solenobia triquetrella (Lepidoptera)* : In birds, some reptiles and fishes, the females (hers) have heteromorphic sex chromosomes and are hence heterogametic (A + Z, A + W). W chromosome determines the female sex. The males have homomorphic sex chromosomes (ZZ) and are hence homogametic (A + Z). The condition is just the opposite found in mammals. *Fragaria eletior* is the plant having ZW sex determination. Selier showed in *Solenobia* (moth) the presence of same number of chromosomes in both the sexes.

COMPOUND TYPE OF SEX CHROMOSOMES

There are complicated cases in which the X (or Z) is represented not by one chromosome but by a group of chromosomes which act together as compound X-element during gametogenesis. Similarly, the Y (or W) may also be represented by a group of chromosomes in certain cases.

(a) The X-complex

The number of X-components varies from 2 (e.g., in the Mantis, *Tenodera Superstitiosa*, and *Drosophila miranda*) to 8 (in *Ascaris incurva*). In *Cimex penticularis*, X consists of 13 chromosomes. The male of the animal is $X_{(1\text{-}13)}$ Y the female is $X_{(1\text{-}13)}X_{(1\text{-}13)}$, 26 chromosomes for sex.

(b) The XY complex

Here, both the X & Y chromosomes are represented by multiple chromosomes. The number of components for X & Y may be the same or may vary. The *Myriapod, Otocryptos sexspinosus* has 5 chromosomes for each X and Y. Thus, it has autosomes + $X_1X_2X_3X_4X_5Y_1Y_2Y_3Y_4Y_5$.

(c) The Y complex

In these cases there will be a single X, but many components for Y. Multiple Y-chromosomes occur much more rarely than multiple X-chromosome. The number of Y-components does not exceed 2, i.e. Y_1Y_2.

Example: *Drosophila americana* has XY_1Y_2.

SEX DETERMINATION BY MALE HAPLOIDY

(Haplodiploidy) or (Honey Bee Method). The phenomenon of development of unfertilized egg leading to the formation of an offspring is called *parthenogenesis*.

If the unfertilized egg produces a male, it is called *arrhenotoky*. If a female in produced by partheno-genesis, it is *thelytoky*.

The offspring produced by either types of parthenogenesis will be haploid individuals (with one set of chromosomes). *Rotifera*, *Hymenoptera*, *Thysanoptera*, *Hemiptera* and *Arachnida* have representatives which are parthenogenetic. The wasps and bees are members of order Hymenoptera. The males (drones) in these animals are developed from parthenogenetic eggs—arrhenotoky. The females are diploid, while the males are haploid. The sex chromosomes have not been identified. There are 32 chromosomes in the female and 16 in the males. (the chromosome number is not halved during spermatogenesis. The primary spermatocyte divides unequally into two cells, of which one contains all of the 16 chromosomes; the small polar body like cell is devoid of chromosomes.)

The phenomenon was first recorded on parasitic wasp, *Habrobracon*.

So, one sex is haploid other is diploid. Queen Bee picks up all sperms from a drone during nuptial flight and stores the same in its seminal vesicle. It does not fertilise the eggs which are to develop into drones or males. Workers and queen bee develop from fertilised egg and are sexually female. The difference between the workers and queen bee lies in nourishment and hence level of development. Sex determination is *progamic* in drones and *epigamic* in females. Drones produce sperms directly without meiosis while queen develop haploid eggs, through oogenesis (meiosis).

Gynandromorphs

If both male and female parts are present in an individual, the organism is gynandromorph. (In a sexually dimorphic gonochorist, there are distinct female and male forms, so gynandromorph of such an animal can be distinguished. The distribution of male and female parts are variable. The most striking gynandromorphs are bilateral types in which one longitudinal half is male and the other half female. One in about 200 flies in *Drosophila*, is a *gynandromorph*.

Sex Mosaicism

Mosaics are individuals which have groups of cells that are different in their chromosomal constitution, from other parts of the body. The sex mosaics orginate through non-disjunction or through the loss of the sex chromosomes in early or later stages of development.

QUANTITATIVE GENETICS

In 1949 Barr and Bertman made the important discovery that in the interphase nucleus of females there is a small chromatin body (i.e. chromocenter) which is lacking in males. This was called *sex chromatin* or the *Barr body*, and more recently after 1971 Paris Conference, *X-chromatin*. It is found in different positions within the nucleus, Sex chromatin bodies not only distinguish normal female cells from male cells, they are also useful for diagnosing various kinds of sex chromosomes abnormalities in people. Those who have two or more X-chromosomes have one less chromatin body than the number of X-chromosomes present. Cells of abnormal females with only one X-chromosome *(Turner's syndrome)* have no sex chromatin bodies and cells of males with two XX chromosomes and one Y chromosomes (*Klinefelter's syndrome*) have one sex chromatin body. Abnormal females with three X-chromosomes have two sex chromatin bodies in their cell nuclei. In some cases, females homozygous for genes in the X-chromosomes do not express a trait more markedly than do hemizygous males. Thus there must be a mechanism of **"Dosage Compensation"** through which the effective dosage of genes of the two sexes is made equal or nearly so.

Sex chromatin body and dosage compensation in mammals is determined by the inactivation of one X-chromosome in the normal female. This hypothesis was named after M.F. Lyon, who first formulated it, in detail, from cytological observations and genetic studies on mouse coat colour. The **Lyon hypothesis** was based on the observation that the number of sex chromatin bodies in interphase cells of adult females, is one less than the number X-chromosomes observed in metaphase preparations. It is, therefore, proposed that the sex chromatin body is a heterochromatinized X-chromosome. On this premise, it must be assumed that only one X-chromosome is required for cellular metabolism in the female cell. Any additional X's become positively heteropyknotic (i.e. stain more densely than other chromosomes) and are genetically inactive. Thus the mammalian X-chromosome has the capability of being heterochromatic in some cells and euchromatic in others.

Which X-chromosome becomes inactive is a matter of chance, but once an X-has become inactivated, all cells arising from that cell will keep the same inactive X-chromosome (a sex-chromatin body). In the mouse, the inactivation apparently occurs early in development, and in human embryos, sex-charomatin bodies have been observed by the sixteenth day of gestation. Some human traits could, therefore, be influenced by both X-chromosomes during the first 16 days. Later (after the 16th day), only one X is functional in a body cell. The female is mosaic with some parts having the alternate allele expressed. X-chromosomes inactivation occurs only when at least two X-chromosomes are present. When several X-chromosomes are in the same nucleus, all but one are inactivated. The number of sex-chromatin bodies after the period of inactivation is, therefore, one less than the number of X-chromosomes in the original cell.

The Lyon hypothesis explains certain genetic consequences of genes in mammals, (*i*) the dosage compensation for females with two X-chromosomes that regulates enzymes activity to the level of males with only one X-chromosomes and (*ii*) the variability of expression in heterozygous females because of random inactivation of one or the other X-chromosomes becomes highly condensed early in embryogenesis. Although, it is replicated at each division, it remains transcriptionally inactive. This pattern is preserved through many cell divisions in the individual's lifetime. Inactivation is not irreversible, however, as the inactive X-chromosome is reactivated during germ cell formation. The chromatin in the inactivated X-chromosome is in a different physical state from that in the active one.

During interphase, when the other chromosome become extended threads of chromatin and are no longer visible under the light microscope, the inactive X-chromosome remains condensed into a highly compact form of *chromatin-heterochromatin*-which is not transcribed and is visible is human cells as a *Barr Body*.

VARIOUS STRATEGIES ARE USED FOR DOSAGE COMPENSATION OF X-LINKED GENES

In each of the animals whose sex determination we have looked at these is an imbalance of X-linked genes between the sexes. One sex has two X-chromosomes, whereas, the other has one. This imbalance has to be corrected to ensure that the level of expression of genes carried on the X-chromosomes is the same in both sexes. *The mechanism by which the imbalance in X-chromosomes is dealt with is known as DOSAGE COMPENSATION.* Failure to correct the imbalance leads to abnormalities and arrested development. Different animals deal with the problem of dosage compensation in different ways.

Mammals, such as mice and humans, achieve dosage compensation by inactivating one of tthe X-chromosomes in the females, after the blastocyst has implanted in the uterine wall. One X-inactivation is initiated in female embryos, it is maintained in all somatic cells throughout life. The inactive X-chromosome can be identified in the nucleus as a *Barr body* and X-inactivation provides an important model for the inheritance of gene expression. *Whatever the sex chromosome constitution*, for example, *XY, XX, XXY or XXXY, there is only one active X-chromosome per somatic cell, with all the other X-chromosomes inactivated.* During early cleavage stages, both X chromosomes are active and the first X-inactivation occurs in the extra embryonic tissue when the paternal X is exclusively inactivated. Later at gastrulation, random X-inactivation occurs in the cells of embryo. Inactive X becomes reactivated during germ cell development.

X-inactivation is dependent on a small region of the X-chromosome, the inactivating centre. It contains a proposed switch gene, *Xist*, which produces a non-coding RNA. Inactivation seems to be caused by the chromosomes being coated by *Xist* RNA, which is expressed by the inactive X, but not by an active X chromosome. If the *Xist* gene is introduced into another chromosome, that chromosome becomes silenced. This inactivation is correlated with methylation of DNA. Dosage compensation in *Drosophila* works in the opposite way to that in the mouse, instead of repression of the extra 'X' activity in females, transcription of the X-chromosomes in males is increased nearly two-fold, and there is also an increase in the translation of m RNA derived from the X-chromosome. This increased activity is regulated by the primary sex-determining signal, which results in the dosage compensation mechanism operating when the sex-lethal gene is 'off'. In females, where sex-lethal is 'on', a cascade of gene activity turns off the dosage compensation mechanism.

In *C. elegens*, dosage compensation is achieved by reducing the level of X-chromosomes expression in XX animals to that of the single X-chromosome in XO males.

Y CHROMATIN—THE HETEROCHROMATIC REGION OF THE Y CHROMOSOME

The fluorescence method for the study of Q-banding led to the demonstration that a large protion of the Y-chromosome is heterochromatic and appears, at interphase, as strongly fluorescent body, the so called *Y-chromatin.* While the X chromatin is 1.0 to 1.2 µm in diameter, the Y chromotin is only about 0.7 µm in diameter and generally is not attached to nuclear envelop. The number of Y-chromatin bodies is identical to the number of Y chromosomes. e.g. individuals with XYY have two Y chromatin bodies. The human Y chromosome consists of two segments, one that does not fluoresce and is genetically active and another that fluoresce and is genetically inactive and contains a highly repetitive (satellite) DNA. It is this latter segment that may be polymorphic. The size of the long arm of the Y-chromosome, where this heterochromatic segment is located, may vary considerably among individuals and subpopulations. For example, it is very large in the Arab populations of North Africa and very small in an American sect, the *Amish*, who are descendants of a Swiss and German group that emigrated in the eighteenth century and who have generally intermarried.

MUTATION

MUTATIONS : (BIOCHEMICAL & MOLECULAR BASIS)

There are sudden inheritable/transmissible discontinuous variations which appear in organisms due to permanent change in their genotypes. They are also known as *sports* or *saltations*. The term mutation was coined by Hugo de Vries (1901) who also proposed *mutation theory of evolution*. He observed 834 mutations in a population of 54343 plants of *Oenothera lamarckiana* (Evening Primrose). Most of the mutations observed by de Vries were due to changes in chromosome number and chromosomal aberrations. Genotype can change due to changes in chromosome numbers, chromosome structure and gene mutations.

CHANGES IN CHROMOSOME NUMBER/ GENOMATIC MUTATIONS

They are of two types, *euploidy* and *eneuploidy*. Euploidy is the condition in which chromosome number is exact multiple of a genome, e.g. monoploidy, diploidy, polyploidy.

Polyploidy

It is the phenomenon of having more than two genomes or sets of chromosomes, e.g. 3n (triploid), 4n (tetraploid), 5n (pentaploid), etc. Polyploids with odd number of genomes are sexually sterile e.g. Banana, Pineapple. They are propagated vegetatively. Other polyploids also become genetically distinct because they do not cross-breed freely with diploids. Polyploidy can develop due to:

(*i*) Failure of spindle development
(*ii*) Failure of meiosis I
(*iii*) Fusion between unreduced gametes, unreduced and normal gametes, one egg with more than one sperm, etc.

Polyploidy is induced by

(*i*) Decaptiation
(*ii*) High or low temperatures
(*iii*) Mechanical injury
(*iv*) Infection
(*v*) Irradiation
(*vi*) Chemicals like colchicine, granosan, sulphanilamide, veratrine sulphate etc.

Colchicine ($C_{22}H_{25}O_6N$) is an alkaloid obtained from Autumn Crocus (*Colchicum autumnale*). It is a mitotic poison (Blakeslee, 1937) which inhibits spindle formation without affecting replication of chromosomes.

Polyploidy is of three types-

1. Autopolyploidy
2. Allopolyploidy
3. Autoallopolyploidy.

There is a *gigas effect* with larger size and often higher yield (due to polyploidies).

1. Autopolyploidy : It is the increase in number of same genome e.g. AAA, AAAA-Rice, Gram, Lablab, Maize, Guava, Potato, Groundnut, Coffee, etc. (Banana is autotriploid). Seedless autotriploid variety of water melon has been evolved. Triploid sugarbeet has more sugar content. Colchicine induces autotetraploidy.

2. Allopolyploidy : It is the increase in number of chromosome set due to coming together of genomes of two or more species—hence *interspecific polyploidy*, e.g. AABB, AABBDD. Allotetraploids like AABB are also called *amphidiploids*. Allopolyploidy has occurred in nature due to hybridisation between two species followed by doubling of chromosomes e.g. wheat (Durum AABB, Bread wheat, AABBDD), American cotton, and *Nicotiana tabacum*. *Raphanobrassica* was the first man made allopolyploid developed by Karpechenko (1928) after crossing Radish (*Raphanus sativus*, $2n = 18$) and cabbage (*Brassica oleracea*, $2n = 18$) followed by doubling of chromosome (AABB, 36).

Triticale was formed by Muntzing by crossing Rye (*Secale* cereale, $2n = 14$) and wheat (*Durum*, $4n = 28$, Bread wheat, $6n = 42$) followed by doubling of chromosome so that it can be hexaploid or octaploid. *Brassica juncea* (Rai) is an allopolyploid between *Brassica compestris* (Yellow mustards, $2n = 18$) and *Brassica nigra* (Black mustard $2n = 16$) produced through hybridisation followed by chromosome doubling (AABB = 34)

3. Autoallopolyploidy : It is the increase in chromosome sets due to coming together of different genomes and the occurrence of one genome in more than diploid state, e.g. AAABB (*Helianthus tuberosus*).

Aneuploidy/Heteroploidy

It is the deletion or addition of one or more chromosomes from the original genomes. Aneuploidy develops due to nondisjunction of homologous chromsomes at the time of meiosis so that abnormal gametes develop which are either deficient in chromosomes (e.g. $n - 1$, $n - 1 - 1$) or surplus in chromosomes (e.g. $n + 1$, $n + 1 + 1$). **Hypoploidy** is **aneuploidy** with loss of chromosomes while **hyperploidy** is **aneuploidy** with addition of chromosomes. *Double aneuploidy* is change in number of two homologous chromosome pairs (e.g., $2n - 1 - 1$) while 'triple aneuploidy' is changed chromosome number for three homologous chromosome pairs (e.g. $2n + 1 + 1 + 1$). Organisms having aneuploidy are called **aneuploids.** They are provided with a name corresponding to number of affected chromosomes appended with suffix-*somic*, e.g. monosomic, nullisomic, trisomic, tetrasomic, pentasomic. Aneuploidy is corresponding trisomy, tetrasomy, pentasomy, etc.

Monosomic

It is an aneuploid in which a chromosome is deficient of its homologue causing genetic imbalance resulting in weaker than a normal man. Monosomic is formed by the union of deficient gamete ($n - 1$) and normal gamete. A sex chromosome monosomic in human beings is TURNER's SYNDROM (44 + X). In double monosomic, two different chromosomes are deficient of their homologues ($2n - 1 - 1$).

Nullisomic

It is an aneuploid in which a pair of homologous chromosomes is deficient ($2n - 2$) resulting in absence of certain genes. Nullisomy is lethal in diploid organisms but can survive in polyploidy. It is produced by the union of two gametes deficient in the same chromosome ($n - 1$) × ($n - 1$).

Trisomic

Trisomic is an aneuploid or heteroploid which has one chromosome represented in triplicate ($2n + 1$). It is followed by the union of a normal gamete (n) with a gamete having an extra chromosome ($n + 1$). Trisomics show gigas effect for certain genes and abnormality for others. **'Down's syndrome'** of human beings is due to trisomy of chromsome 21 while **Klinefelter's Syndrome'** is due to additional X-chromosome in otherwise male individual (XY). All the possible trisomics have been studied in *Datura.*

Tetrasomic

It is an aneuploid in which one chromosome is represented in quadraplicate. Tetrasomic is formed by union of two gametes each having the similar extra chromosome, $(n + 1) \times (n + 1)$. Two chromosomes are represented in quadruplicate in *double tetrasomic* $(2n + 2 + 2)$ and three in *triple tetrasomic* $(2n + 2 + 2 + 2)$. Tetrasomic super females (44 + XXXX) are infertile and have mental abnormality. Otherwise, tetrasomics are most stable of all the aneuploids showing gigas effect of many genes.

Pentasomic

An aneuploid with one chromosome represented five times $(2n + 3)$ e.g. a rare super female in human beings (44 + XXXXX).

Mixed Aneuploid

It is an aneuploid with both hypoploidy (deficiency) and hyperploidy (addition), e.g. $2n$ + 1A – 1B.

STRUCTURAL AND NUMERICAL ALTERNATIONS OF CHROMOSOMES

CHROMOSOME ABERRATIONS

They are changes involving chromosome morphology which result in changes in number and sequence of genes without altering ploidy or gene structure. Chromosome aberrations involve breaking of chromosome segments, their loss or union with same (intrachromosomal aberration) or different chromosomes (interchromosomal aberration). The important types are as follows :

Deficiency

It is the loss of chromosome segment. The lost segment may be *terminal* (deficiency or terminal deficiency) or *intercalary* (intercalary deficiency or deletion). The terms deficiency and deletions are also used interchangeably. Terminal deficiency involves a single break near the chromosome end. In intercalary/intrestitial deficiency or deletion, there are two breaks (double breaks), loss of separated segment and the union in the region of breaks. In **heterozygous deficiency** (deficiency in one out of two chromosomes of a homologous pair) the synapsed chromosomes would show difference in length at one end (terminal deficiency) or loop (intercalary deficiency/deletion). **Homozygous deficiency** may be lethal if some vital gene is involved (e.g. sex-linked notch wing deletion in *Drosophila*). Notch wing heterozygous deficiency produces notched wings margins in female *Drosophila*. Even a recessive gene may express if corresponding gene on the other homologous chromosome has become deficient. The phenomenon is called **pseudodominance.**

Duplication

It is the phenomenon of having one or more genes in excess of the normal complement segment :

(*i*) **Tandem/Repeat Duplication :** The duplicating segment gets incorporated next to normal corresponding segment, e.g. ABCDEFGHGH.

(*ii*) **Reverse Tandem Duplication :** The duplicating segment is incorporated next to normal corresponding segment but the order is reversed, e.g. ABCDEFGHHG.

(*iii*) **Displaced Duplication :** The duplicating segment is incorporated away from the correponding segment on the same chromosome.

(*iv*) **Transposed Duplication :** The duplicating segment is incorporated in a nonhomologous segment. Duplication increases the number of genes which increases genetic redundancy, allows development of variations and hence evolution. However, some duplications are harmful, e.g. development of bar eye in *Drosophila.* Presence of single B gene on X-chromosome (both chromosomes in female) produces normal eye with 780 facets. An extra B gene due tc duplication produces smaller and narrow *bar eye* with 350 facets in heterozygous state and 200 facets in homozygous state. If, by chance, there is shifting of one B gene from one chromosome to its homologue, it results in 3 B genes on one and one B gene on second. This produces *double bar eye* which is very small. The change in phenotypic expression when genes are reallocated without altering their number is called **'position effect'**.

Inversion

A chromosome segment having one or more genes gets separated and reinserted in its position but after inversion or rotation by 180° so that the order of genes is reversed. Inversion may include centromere **(pericentric)** or occur beyond centromere **(paracentric).** Chromosomes remain unsynapsed in the region of inversion with crossing over resulting in development of deficiencies, duplications, and bridge formation so that cross-over products are sterile. Therefore, inversion suppresses genetic recombinations. This is helpful in maintaining heterozygosity and balanced lethal systems.

Translocation

It is an aberration in which a chromosome segment separates and gets attached to a non-homologous chrmosome.

(*i*) *Reciprocal Translocation :* Mutual exchange segments between two non-homologous chromosomes.

(*ii*) *Simple Translocation :* One sided translocation. If a chromosome segment gets inserted in interstitial position of a non-homologous chromosome, it is known as '*shift translocation*'. Reciprocal transloca-tion develops multivalents instead of bivalents at synapsis. During anaphase it breaks chromosomes, develops new linkages, produces a large number of sterile gametes, causes position effect (e.g. recessive hairiness to dominant hairiness in *Drosophila*) but is useful in maintaining heterozygosity and balanced lethal sysetem.

(*iii*) *Whole-arm translocation* or *centric fusion* reduces the number of chromosomes. Human chromosome number 2 has been produced by centric fusion of two chromosomes of ape-like ancestors.

GENE MUTATIONS

They are sudden stable changes in the structure of gene or cistron due to change in nucleotide type and/or nucleotide sequence. Most of gene mutations involve a change in single nucleotide. They are called **'point mutations'.** *Ancon Sheep* was the first recorded mutation (Seth Wright, 1791) followed by Hornless (Polled) Cattle (1889). Scientific study of mutations started with the noticing of white eye colour in *Drosophila* (Morgan, 1910). A mutation from wild to a new type is called **'forward mutation'.** The reversal of mutated gene back to its original/wild form is called **reverse/back mutation.** Mutations affecting vegetative cells are called *somatic mutations.* They are not inheritable, and disappear with the death of the individual. Somatic mutations occur in some of the cells from *chimeras*, patches or mosaics, e.g. **variegation.** In plants, somatic mutations can be preserved and passed on to future generations through vegetative propagation & tissue culture. *Germinal mutations* occur in the sex cells and are inheritable. Depending upon the effect, mutations may be *dominant* or *recessive.* The recessive mutations show their effect after a few generations when they become homozygous. A single mutation affecting more than one character is called *pleotropic mutation.* Mutations have helped in development of new varieties of plants and animals, e.g. *Sharbati Sonora* from Sonora-64.

SPONTANEOUS MUTATIONS

They are mutations which develop at random naturally, automatically or spontaneously in an organism due to internal reasons without any relation to any external/environmental factor. The frequency of spontaneous mutations is different for different organisms and their different genes, e.g., 1 in one million in *Drosophila*, 1 in 10 million cell generations in bacteria & 1 in 50,000 in human beings. The genes which mutate frequently are called MUTABLE GENES, e.g. R-gene of colour in maize (1 in 2000 gametes). *Stable genes* do not mutate even once in several million gametes. ***Mutator*** genes increase frequency of spontaneous mutations, while ***antimutator*** genes prevent spontaneous mutations.

Spontaneous mutations may be due to (*i*) Errors in replication (*ii*) Failure of proof reading machinery (*iii*) Presence of tautomeric form of nitrogen bases e.g. imino tautomer instead of amino group (e.g. cytosine, adenine) or enol group instead of keto-group (e.g. thymine, guanine). (*iv*) Slow spontaneous deamination of cytosine to uracil. (*v*) Back ground radiations.

INDUCED MUTATIONS

They are mutations that are produced in response to specific external factors or chemicals. Muller (1927) was the first scientist to produce induced mutations in *Drosophila* with the help of X-rays (upto 150 times the spontaneous sex-lined lethal mutations). He got nobel prize in 1946.

Mutagens

There are physical and chemical factors which bring about new mutations and increase the frequency of spontaneous mutations.

Physical Mutagens

They are physical factors which induce mutations. Physical mutagens are of three types-temperature, ultra-violet radiations and ionising radiations.

(*i*) *Temperature :* Increase in temperature increases the frequency of mutations. Q_{10} being 5 for Rice. Very low temperature is also mutagenic.

(*ii*) *UV Radiations :* (Muller and Altenberg, 1932). They induce hydrolysis of cytosine and formation of thymine dimers. Thymine dimers cause bending and misreplication of DNA. Organisms overcome damage from UV radiations present in normal sunlight by photorepair (photoreactivation), excision repair and post replication repair.

(*iii*) *Ionising Radiation :* They include X-rays (man-made, Roentgen, 1895), cosmic ray (proton and helium nuclei present in space), α-particles (helium nuclei), β-particles (electrons), gamma rays (massless radiations). The latter three are emitted from radioactive elements and radio-isotopes. P-32 is radio-isotope which gets incorporated in DNA but starts decaying and changed to sulphur. DNA develops breaks in there regions. Ionising radiations produce electrically charged particles which ionise biomolecules and bring about several changes in DNA. There is deamination and dehydration of nitrogen bases, formation of peroxides and oxidation of deoxyribose.

Chemical Mutagens

They are chemicals which induce mutations. Most of the mutagens are also carcinogens.

(A) *Nitrous acid :* It deaminates cytosine to uracil, guanine to reanthin and adenine to hypoxanthin. This results in replacement of A-T with H-C, C-G with U-A and C-X. Nitrous acid is a common insustrial chemical and preservative of meat products.

(B) *Alkylating agents :* They bring about methylation and ethylation of nitrogen bases, e.g. methyl guanine, ethyl gaunine. The alkylated base may slip out of DNA duplex or cause change of base pair, e.g. C-G to A-T. Alkylating agents include ethyl ethane sulphonate (EES), ethyl methane sylphonate (EMS), diethyl sulphate (DES), dimethyl nitrosamine dibromide, griseofulvin, endrin, etc. Ethyl dibromide (EDB) is used in food preservation, Griseofulvin is common antifungal medicine while endrin is an insecticide.

(C) *Base Analogous :* e.g., (*i*) 5-bromouracil (Bu), (*ii*) 5-iodouracil (Iu), (*iii*) 5-chlorouracil (Cu), (*iv*) 5-Flurouracil (Fu)

All these replace thymine and pair with guanine. 2-aminopurine is incorporated in place of adenine with its tautomes pairing with cytosine. Thymine in its enol state pairs with guanine.

(D) *Acridines :* Proflavin, acriflavin, euflavin and acridine orange are intercalated in between base pairs leading to their insertion and deletion so as to cause **frame-shift** or **gibberish** mutations.

RECOMBINATION

(*i*) *Inversion :* Base sequence of a segment is reversed.

(*ii*) *Transition Substitution :* One nitrogen base is replaced by another of similar type, e.g A $\rightleftharpoons$ G, C $\rightleftharpoons$ T. It is induced by **tautomerisation** (alternate state due to rearrangement of hydrogen atoms, – NH_2 into –NH or – CO, into – COH), deamination, base analogue and ionisation.

(*iii*) *Transversion Substitution* : One nitrogen base is replaced by another of different type, e.g. C $\rightleftharpoons$ G, A $\rightleftharpoons$ T.

(*iv*) *Insertion Frameshift* : Addition of a nucleotide changes the reading of codons.

(*v*) *Deletion Frameshift* : Deletion of a nucleotide changes the reading of codons.

Gene mutations often change them into inactive, recessive or lethal state.

SAME SENSE, MIS-SENSE AND NON-SENSE MUTATIONS

Due to **wobble** position, a change in one neucleotide of a codon does not change amino-acid specificity. This is called *same sense* (or silent) mutation, e.g. AGA = AGG = AGC. When a nucleotide change in one codon causes the change of one amino acid of a polypeptide, it is called *mis-sense mutation.* If a mutation causes early termination of polypeptide synthesis, it is termed as *non-sense mutation.*

HARDY WEINBERG GENETIC EQUILIBRIUM

A Mendelian population is an interbreeding group of organisms sharing a common *gene pool.* A gene pool is the total genetic information possessed by reproductive members in a population of sexually reproducing organisms. Alleles in the pool have *dynamic relations* with other alleles and with the environment in which the organism reside. Environmental factors that collectively provide selection tend to alter allele frequencies and thus to cause evolutionary changes in local populations.

In 1908, an English mathematician, G.H. Hardy and a German physician, W.Weinberg, independently discovered, the principle concerned with the frequency of alleles in a population, called the ***Hardy-Weinberg equilibrium principles.*** It states that at equilibrium, both allele and genotype frequencies remain constant from generation to generation. This occurs among diploid, sexually reproducing organisms with nonoverlapping generations in which mating is random and no selection or other factors are present for changing the allele frequencies or as long as the following assumptions are met :

1. The population size is very large
2. Random mating is occurring
3. No mutation takes place
4. No genes are input from other sources
5. (No migration takes place)
6. No selections occurs.

Dominant alleles thus do not, in fact, replace recessive ones, Because their proportions do not change, the genotypes are said to be in *Hardy-Weinberg Equilibrium.*

In algebric terms, the H.W. equilibrium principle is written as an equation. Its form is what is known as *bionomial expansion.* For a gene with two alternative alleles, which one will call B and *b*, the equation looks like,

$(p + q)^2 =$	p^2	+	$2pq$ +	q^2
	(Individuals homozygous for allele B)		(Individuals heterozygous with alleles B + *b*)	Individuals homozygous for allele *b*)

In *statistics, frequency is defined as the proportion of individuals falling within a certain category in relation to the total number of individuals under consideration.* Thus, in a population of 100 cats, with 84 black and 16 white cats, the respective frequencies would be 0.84 (or 84%) and 0.16 (or 16%). In the algebric terms of this equation, the letter p designates the frequency of one allele, the letter q designates frequency of alternative allele. By convention, the more common of the two alleles is designated p and rarer q. Because there are only two alleles, p plus q must always equal 1.

If we assume that the white cats are homozygous recessive for a gene designated *b*, and the black cats are, therefore, either homozygous dominant BB or heterozygous B*b*, we can calculate the *allele frequencies* of the two alleles in the population from the proportion of black and white individuals. If $q^2 = 0.16$ (the frequency of white cats), then $q = 0.4$. Therefore, p, the frequency allele B, would by 0.6 (1.0 – 0.4 = 0.6). We can now easily calculate the genotype frequencies, there are $p^2 = (0.6)^2 \times 100$ (the number of individuals in the total population), or 36 homozygous dominant BB individuals. The heterozygous individuals have the Bb genotype, and there would be $2pq$, or $(2 \times 0.6 \times 0.4) \times 100$, or 48 heterozygous B*b* individuals.

Phenotype	*Black*		*White*
Genotype	BB	B*b*	*bb*
Frequency of genotype in population	0.36	0.48	0.16
Frequency of gametes	0.36 + 0.24 = 0.6 B		0.24 + 0.16 = 0.4b

In the absence of factors that alter them, the frequency of gametes, genotypes and phenotypes remain constant genertion after generation.

USING THE HARDY-WEINBERG EQUATION

The H.W. equation is a simple extension of the Punnett squares with two alleles assigned frequencies *p* and *q*. From the table given above, one can trace genetic reassortment during sexual reproduction and sea how it affects the frequencies of the B and *b* alleles during the next generation. In this table, it is assumed that the union of sperm and egg in these cats is random, so that all combinations of *b* and B alleles are equally likely. For this reason, the alleles are mixed randomly and represented in the next generation. Each individual in each generation has a 0.6 chance of receiving a B allele ($p = 0.6$) and a 0.4 chance of receiving a *b* allele ($q = 0.4$).

In the next generation therefore, the chance of combining two alleles is p^2, or 0.36 (that is, 0.6×0.6), and approximately 36% of the individuals in the population will continue to have the BB genotype. The frequency of *bb* individuals is q^2 (0.4×0.4) and so will continue to be about 16%, and the frequency of B*b* individuals will be $2pq$ $(2 \times 0.6 \times 0.4)$, or approximately 48%. Phenotypically, 84 black individuals (with either BB or B*b* genotypes), and 16 white individuals (with *bb* genotype) in the population are seen. The simple relationship has proved extraordinarily useful in assessing actual situations. Consider the recessive allele responsible for the serious human disease *cystic fibrosis*. This allele is present in North Americans of Caucasian descent at a frequency *q* of about 22 per 1000 individuals, or 0.022. What proportion of North American Caucasians, therefore, is expected of express this trait? The frequency of double recessive individuals (q^2) is expected to be 0.022×0.022, or 1 in every 2000 individuals. What proportion is expected to be heterozygous carriers? If the frequency of the recessive allele *q* is 0.022, then the frequency of the dominant allele *p* must be $1 - 0.022$, or 0.978. The frequency of heterozygous individuals ($2pq$) is thus expected to be $2\times 0.978 \times 0.022$, or 43 in every 1000 individuals.

Most human populations are large and effectively random-mating and are, therefore, similar to the "ideal" population envisioned by Hardy and Weinberg. For some genes, the calculated predictions do not match the actual values. The reasons they do not tell us a great deal about evolution.

Why Do Allelle Frequencies Change : According to the Hardy-Weinberg principle, both the allele and genotype frequencies in a large, random-mating population will remain constant from generation to generation if no mutation, no migration, and no selection occurs. The stipulations tacked onto the end of the statement are important. In fact, they are the key to the importance of the Hardy-Weinberg principle, because individual allele frequencies *are* changing all the time in natural populations, with some alleles becoming more common than others. The Hardy Weinberg principle establishes a convenient baseline against which to measure such changes. By looking at how various factors alter the proportions of homozygous and heterozygous in populations (usually expressed as the HETEROZYGOSITY, the likelihood that a randomly selected individual will be heterozygous at the gene locus), one can identify the factors affecting particular situation.

Many factors can alter allele frequencies. Only five, however, alter enough the proportions of homozygous and heterozygous to produce significant deviations froim the proportions predicted by H.W. principle : **mutation, migration** (both immigration into and emigration out of a given population); **genetic drift** (random loss of alleles, which is more likely in small populations), **nonrandom mating**, and **selection** (see table below).

Of there only selection produces adaptive evolutionary change because only in selection does the result depend upon the nature of the environment. The other factors operate relatively independently of the environment, so the changes they produce are not shaped by environmental demands.

AGENTS OF EVOLUTIONARY CHANGE

Factor	Description
1. Mutation	The ultimate source of variation. Individual mutations occurs so rarely that mutation alone does change allele frequency much.
2. Migration	A very potent agent of change. Populations exchange members.
3. Nonrandom mating	Inbreeding is the most common form. It does not alter allele frequency but decreases the proportion of heterozygotes.
4. Genetic drift	Statistical accidents. Usually occurs only is very in very small populations. Genetic drift can result in the permanent loss of alleles from a population.
5. Selection	The only form that produces adaptive evolutionary changes. Only rapid for allele frequencies greater than 0.01.

8. Biology in Human Welfare

BREEDING IN PLANTS

INTRODUCTION

Reproduction : Process of producing offspring and a mean of self-perpetuation.

Asexual reproduction (vegetative reproduction or vegetative propagation) : Plant reproduce without fusion of gametes.

Apomixis : Formation of new individuals through asexual reproduction without involving the formation and fusion of gametes.

Amphimixis : Formation of new individuals through the normal process of sexual reproduction by meiotic formation of gametes and their subsequent fusion during fertilization.

Apomixis takes place by three methods :

1. Agamospermy
2. Spore formation
3. Vegetative propagation

1. Agamospermy

Formation of new individuals by asexual reproduction without involving fusion and formation of gametes. Three types.

(*a*) **Adventive embryony** : One or few extra embryos are formed from a diploid cell of nucellus or integument but never from egg *e.g., Opuntia, Citrus.*

(*b*) **Recurrent apomixis** : Diploid egg grows parthenogenetically into diploid embryo *e.g., Poa, Allium.*

(*c*) **Non-recurrent agamospermy** : Development of embryo from haploid female gamete without fertilization.

- **Parthenogamy** : Union of two incompatible gametes *e.g.,* fusion of two female gametes.
- **Parthenospore or azygospore** : A spore formed directly from a gamete.
- **Parthenoapogamy** : Fusion of vegetative nuclei.
- **Apospory** : Involves development of gametophyte from sporophyte directly may be **somatic apospory** (embryo sac from somatic cell) or **generative apospory** (embryosac from archesporium).
- **Apogamy** : Development of sporophyte from gametophyte without the fusion of gametes.
- **Diplospory** : Diploid embryosac can develop directly from diploid megaspore mother cell.
- **Parthenogenesis** : Development of seed/embryo from a female gamete without fertilization.

2. Spore formation

Spores which take part in asexual reproduction are called **accessory spores** or **mitospores** (produced by mitotic division of a parent cell) *e.g.,* conidia, sporangiospores, aplanospores, akinetes, zoospores etc. They are quite common in algae, fungi, bacteria and protistans.

3. Vegetative reproduction

Occurs naturally in a number of wild and domesticated plants. Two types:

(A) Natural, and (B) Artificial methods.

(A) Natural methods

(*a*) **By stems** : Runners (*Cynodon*, *Oxalis*), stolons (*Vallisneria*), offsets (*Pistia*), bulbs (Onion, Garlic), corms (*Colocasia*, Banana), rhizomes (*Typha*, Ginger), suckers (Mint, *Chrysanthemum*), tubers (Potato) etc.

(*b*) **By roots** : Adventitious buds (*Dalbergia*, Guava), tuberous roots (Topoioca, *Dahlia*) etc.

(*c*) **By leaves** : Adventitious buds (*Bryophyllum*, *Begonia*), buds on the tip of leaves (*Adiantum*).

(*d*) **By bulbils** : *e.g.*, *Oxalis*, *Agave*, *Allium* etc.

(*e*) **By turions** : *e.g.*, aquatic plants (*Utricularia*, *Potamogeton*) etc.

(B) Artificial methods

(*a*) **Cutting** *e.g.*, Sugarcane, rose, cocoa, bougainvillea etc.

(*b*) **Layering** : May be **mound layering** (*e.g.*, Grape vine, strawberry etc.) or **air layering** or **gootee** (*e.g.*, Litchi, orange etc.).

(*c*) **Grafting** : Especially in dicotyledonous plants having vascular cambia *e.g.*, mango, rose, apple, peach, *Citrus*. etc.

(*d*) **Bud grafting or Budding** *e.g.*, Rose, Apple, Peach etc.

(*e*) **Micropropagation** (Propagation by plant tissue culture) *e.g.*, Chrysanthemum, gladiolus, orchids, carnation, ornamental plants etc.

Significance

Quicker, easier, cheaper method of multiplying the plants which have either poor viability or prolonged seed dormancy.

- Helps is removing common infections from the parent plant.
- Grafting helps in getting an economically important plant having useful characters of two different individuals in a short time.

Sexual reproduction

- The sexual reproductive organs are present in the flowers of angiosperms.
- Stamens and carpels represent the male and female sex organs, respectively.
- **Perfect or bisexual or hermaphrodite** : Flower which possesses both the essential organs *i.e.*, stamens and carpels.
- **Male or staminate flower** : Unisexual flower, carpels absent.
- **Female or pistillate flower** : Unisexual flower, stamens absent.
- **Monoecious** : Plant with both male and female flowers *e.g.*, Maize, Castor etc.
- **Dioecious** : Male and female flowers present on the different plants *e.g.*, Papaya, Mulberry etc.

Development of the male gametophyte

- Each stamen consists of a cylindrical, massive thread like **filament** and a broad terminal bilobed **anther.**
- Typical anther is **tetrasporangiate** with four microsporangia **(dithecous)** but sometimes with only two microsporangia (**monothecus**) *e.g.*, Malvaceae.
- In dithecous anther, the two lobes are separated in the anterior side by a deep groove and attached on back side by the **connective.**
- There is a single vascular bundle in the connective.
- In the anther wall of a mature anther, the outer most layer is **epidermis** followed by a single layer of **endothecium,** then one to three middle layers and innermost is single layered **tapetum.**
- Endothecium (radially elongated, fibrous thickening of cellulose) attains its maximum development when the anther is ready to dehisce. The **hydroscopic** nature of endothecial cells help in the dehiscence of the anthers by the means of **slits.**
- **Pollen grain** (haploid) represents the first stage of male gametophyte and may be referred to as **male gametophyte** or **partially developed male gametophyte** or **male gamete.**
- A pollen grain has two layered wall :
  (*i*) An **outer exine** (tough, cuticularised and with spinous out growth) and
  (*ii*) an inner **intine** (thin and made up of cellulose). Exine is made up of **sporopollenin.** Exine possess one or more weak spots known as **germ pores** (usually 3 in dicots and 1 in monocots).
- Development of male gametophyte starts in pollen grain. Microspore undergoes only two

mitotic divisions and produces bigger **vegetative cell** (tube cell) and a smaller **generative cell.** At this stage, dehiscence of the anther takes place and the two celled pollen grains are released.

- After falling of pollen grains on stigma, pollen grains absorb water and nutrients of the stigmatic secretion through its germ pores.
- The intine grows out through a germ pore into a slender pollen tube. The generative nucleus divides to form two male nuclei. Usually generative cell comes down into pollen tubes and then divides to form the male gametes. The male gametophyte in angiosperms is highly reduced.

Development of female gametophyte

- The ovule is technically a **megasporangium** having nucellus (parenchymatous tissue), integuments (one or two covering) and a short stalk-like structure **(funicle)** by which it is attached to the **placenta** and the integuments enclose-an opening *i.e.*, **micropyle.**
- In young ovule, a hypodermal **archesporial** cell is differentiated which forms the **archesporium** of the ovule. Archesporial cell divides by a periclinal division and forms :
  (*i*) an **outer primary parietal cell** (forms nucellus) and
  (*ii*) **inner primary sporogenous cell** (differentiates as **megaspore mother cell).**
- The **megaspore mother cell** (megasporophyte) divides by meiosis and a linear tetrad of four megaspores is produced. The upper three towards micropyle degenerate and the lowermost towards chalaza is functional.
- The fuctional megaspore is the first cell of the female gametophyte. It divides by three mitotic divisions so that eight nuclei are formed : 4 towards the micropyle and 4 towards the chalaza. Out of four nuclei at each pole, one nucleus **(polar nucleus)** moves towards the centre. The two polar nuclei fuse together just at the time and fertilization of form a diploid **secondary** or **definitive** nucleus. Three nuclei towards micropyle form **egg apparatus** (one **egg cell** and **two synergids)** : all haploid. The three nuclei towards chalaza form antipodal cells (haploid and vestigeal). So, the mature or organized embryo sac at the time of fertilization is **7-celled and 8 nucleate.**
- 7-celled, 8 nucleate and monosporic embryo sac is known as **Polygonum** type of **embryo sac** because it was discovered for the first time in **Polygonum** by **Strasburger.**
- In an embryo sac, all the cells are haploid except the secondary nucleus (2n).
- **P. Maheshwari** (1950) classified the female gametophyte into monosporic, bisporic and tetrasporic embryo sac, depending upon the number of megaspore nuclei taking part is the development.

POLLINATION

Transfer of pollen grains from anthers to the stigma.

(A) **Self-pollination** (Autogamy) : Transfer of pollen grains within the same flower *e.g.*, pea, wheat and rice.

(B) **Cross-pollinaion** (Allogamy) : Transfer of pollen grains from one flower to another.

  (1) **Xenogamy** : Transfer of pollen grains from one plant to another of the same species.

  (2) **Gietnogamy** : Transfer of pollen grains from one flower to another on the same plant. Also called **genetically self pollination.**

  (3) **Hybridism** : Transfer of pollen grains from one plant to another related allied species.

Advantages of cross pollination

Heal their progeny of offsprings, better adaptability, production of new varieties, more number of viable seeds etc.

Advantages for self-pollination

(A) **Homogamy** : Anthers and stigmas of a flower mature at the same time *e.g.*, in *Brassica* and *Gardenia florida.*

(B) **Cleistogamy** : Flowers remain closed. They never open throughout their life span *e.g.*, in *Arachis hypogea* (ground nut) and *Commelina bengalensis.*

(C) **Geitonogamy** : Transfer of pollen grain from one flower to another on the same plant *e.g.*, *Triticum aestivum.*

Advantages of cross-pollination

(A) **Dicliny** (unisexuality) : *e.g.*, pumpkin, palm, cucumber.

(B) **Self sterility** : *e.g.*, Tea, *Malva*, Orchids.

(C) **Dichogamy** : Anther and stigma of a flower mature at different times.

- (*i*) **Protandry** : Anthers mature earlier than the stigmas of the same flower *e.g.*, Cotton.
- (*ii*) **Protogyny** : Stigma matures earlier than the anthers of the same flower *e.g.*, *Ficus*.

(D) **Heterostyly** : Stamens, style and stigma are of different heights.

(E) **Herkogamy** : A natural barrier develops between anthers and stigma to check self pollination *e.g.*, *Calotropis*.

Anemophily : Pollination by **wind ;** Flowers are colourless ; pollen grains are produced in**large amount ;** style and stigma are hairy *e.g.*, *Bambusa*, *Saccharum*, grasses, wheat, maize, rice, barley and palms.

Entomophily : Pollination by **insects ;** rough and sticky pollen grains ; insects are attracted by necter/scent/colour. Example of insects are bees, butterflies and moths. The flowers of Asteraceae and Labiatae families are generally pollinated by the bees and butterflies.

Hydrophily : Pollination by **water currents ;** pollen grains are sticky *e.g.*, *Vallisneria*, *Hydrilla*, *Ceratophyllum*, *Zostera* etc.

Zoophily : Pollination by **animals** *e.g.*, in *Bombax* (silk cotton) by *birds* **(Ornithophily)**, in *Anthocephalous*, *Adamsonia* and *Kigelia* by **bats (Cheiropterophily)** ; in *Arisaema* by **snakes (Ophiophily)**, in *Colocasia* by **snails (Malacophily)**.

POLLEN GERMINATION AND FERTILIZATION

Pollen tube enters the ovule through micropyle **(porogamy)**, sometimes it enters through chalaza **(chalazogamy)** or through the base of ovule or through funicle or integuments **(mesogamy)**.

Pollen tube produce enzymes which digest the tissues of the stigma and the style. After entering into the embryo sac, pollen tube liberates the male gametes and disintegrates.

Syngamy : One of the male gamete fuses with the egg resulting in the production of zygote (diploid).

Triple fusion : Second male gamete fuses with the secondary diploid nucleus, producing a triploid primary endosperm nucleus.

The process of fertilization was discovered by **Strasburger** (1884).

Double fertilisation

Takes place in angiosperms only ; discovered by **Nawaschin** (1898) in *Frittilaria* and *Lilium* and later by **Guignard** (1899). It is the fusion of :

- (*i*) One male gamete with the egg cell (**real fertilization** or **syngamy**) and
- (*ii*) Another male gamete with the **secondary** or **definitive nucleus** or **polar nuclei.**

In double fertilization, above all **five nuclei** are involved.

ENDOSPERM AND EMBRYO DEVELOPMENT

- Endosperm (triploid, nutritive tissue) develops after fertilization from secondary nucleus.
- 3 types of endosperm, depending on the development.
  - (A) **Free Nuclear** : Most common ; the first division and many subsequent divisions of primary endosperm nucleus are not followed by wall formation *e.g.*, cotton, maize, wheat, rice, sunflower etc.
  - (B) **Cellular** : Every nuclear division is followed by cytokinesis, making it cellular from the beginning.
  - (C) **Helobial** (Intermediate type)–First division of primary endosperm nucleus results in the formation of a **large micropylar chamber** and a small chalazal chamber. Rest of the divisions are free nuclear.
- **Perisperm** : Remnant of nucellus or persistent nucellus surrounding the embryo.
- **Chalazosperm** : Perisperm like tissue in chalazal region ; subtitute for endosperm.
- In dicots like pea, bean etc. reserves in the endosperm are consumed by the developing embryo and visible only as few cell layers in the mature seed.

- In many other plants *e.g.,* cereals, coconut etc. endosperm enlarges considerably by cell division and is much bigger than the embryo on seed maturation.
- The **first division** of the zygote is **transverse** and a **basal** (hypobasal) cell towards the micropyle and a **terminal** (epibasal) cell is formed towards the chalaza.
- The epibasal cell divides repeatedly to produce a row of 4-8 cells.
- The terminal cell divides in various planes to produce a cluster of cells, called **proembryo.**
- The hypobasal and the remaining cells constitute the **suspensor** which pushes the proembryo into the endosperm to enable the developing embryo to receive nutrition.
- A few cells of the proembryo nearest to suspensor develop into hypocotyl and radicle. The other cells give rise to epicotyl, plumule and cotyledons (two in dicots and one in monocots).
- As the embryo and endosperm develop and mature, the integument of the ovule become hard (seed coat) and lead to the formation of seed.
- **Post-fertilization changes : Ovary** (carpel) : fruit; **Ovule** (megasporangium):seed ; **Nucellus** : perisperm ; **Egg cell** : embryo ; **Secondary nucleus** : endosperm ; **Outer integument** : outer seed coat (testa) ; **Inner integument** : inner seed coat (tegmen) and **Micropyle** : an opening in seeds (micropyle).

INCOMPATIBILITY (INTRASPECIFIC OR SELF-STERILITY OR SELF-INCOMPATIBILITY)

- Inability of certain otherwise viable gametes from the genetically specific individuals to fuse with each other.
- Reported in 66 families of angiosperms.
- Can be morphological or physiological.
  - (1) **Morphological self-incompatibility** : Two or three mating types viz. distyly (*e.g., Primula*), tristyly (*e.g., Lyhrum*).
  - (2) **Physiological self-incompatibility** : Due to physiology. Morphological differences absent. May be :
    - (A) **Gametophytic self-incompatibility** (GSI) : Due to the genotype of the pollen *e.g., in* Poaceae, Solanaceae, Liliaceae.
    - (B) **Sporophytic self-incompatibility** (SSI) : Due to the genotype of the sporophytic/stigmatic tissues *e.g.,* Asteraceae, Brassicaceae.
      - It prevent pollen germination, retardation of growth, deorientation of pollen tube or even failure of nuclear fusion.
      - This incompatibility is due to a single multiallelic gene (S-allele). Usually, in develops with the maturation of stigma.

SPECIAL MODES OF REPRODUCTION

- Cases where propagation without the act of fertilization.
- **Apomixis** : The term opomixis was given by Winkler in 1908. Development without fertilization of fusion of gametes *e.g.,* Citrus.
- **Agamospermy** : Formation of seeds without fertilization.
- **Parthenogenesis** : Formation of embryo from an unfertilized egg.
- **Parthenocarpy** (coined by F. Nou, 1902) : Development of fruit without pollination and fertilizaton. *e.g.,* Pineapple, grapes, apple, pear and banana.
- **Sporophytic budding** : Sometimes takes place in the nucellus and integuments, resulting in the development of an embryo. *e.g.,* orange, opuntia, mango and onion.
- **Polyembryony** : Development of more than one embryos in the same seed ; discovered by Leeuwenhoeck (1719) in citrus; quite common in *Citrus* and *Pinus*.

SOME IMPORTANT FACTS

- **Allergenic** : Pollen grains of many plants including *Parthenium, Chenopodium, Prosopis, Sorghum, Amaranthus* are allergenic.
- **Palynology** : Study of pollen grains.

- **Myrmacophily** : Pollination by ants *e.g.*, many members of family Rubiaceae.
- **Hay fever** : Due to allergic reaction due to the presence of pollen in air.
- **Lever mechanism** or **Turn pipe mechanism :** Pollination in the members of family Labiatae *e.g., Salvia* (sage flower).
- **Flytrap mechanism** *: Aristolochia.*
- **Trap door mechanism** : Present in hypanthodium inflorescence of *Ficus* species which receives Blastophaga for laying eggs and pollination. This is an example of mutualism.
- **Largest pollen tube** *: Zea mays.*
- *In Calotropis* and orchids pollen is packed in **pollinia** (massulae).
- **Absence of endosperm (double fertilization in angiosperms)** : 3 families *e.g.*, Orchidaceae, Podostemonaceae and Trapaceae.
- **Size of pollen-Longest** *: Zostera* (filamentous without exine) = 2500 μm.
  - — **Biggest**—*Mirabilis* diameter 250 mm
  - — **Smallest**—*Myosotis*, 2.5-3.5 μm
- **Panmictic** : Plant reproducting asexually.
- **Apomictic** : Plant multiplying parthenogenetically.
- **Amphimictic** : Plant reproducing sexually.
- *Erythrina* : Pollinated by crows as well as squirrels.
- **P. Maheswari** : Great plant embryologist of India, wrote a book "An Introduction to the Embryology of Angiosperms".
- **G.B. Amici** (1824) : First to observe pollen tube in *Portulaca.*
- **Hanstein** (1868, 1870) : First to study early development of embryo.
- **S. Miller** : Reported importance of **coconut milk** in tissue culture.
- **Guha and Maheswari** : Obtained pollen and anther culture embryos from family Solanaceae.
- **Piston mechanism of pollination** : White **Centaurea.**
- **Edible pollen** *: Rosa, Magnolia, Clematis.*
- **Translator type pollinia** : Family Asclepiadaceae.
- **Sporopollenin** : Present in exine of pollen and preserved during fossilization as it is resistant to decomposition.
- **Prepotency** : In many plants the pollen grains form a flower when present on the stigma of another genetically different flower germinate more quickly as compared to the pollen grains of the same flower so, help in cross pollination *e.g.*, Grape, pear and apple.
- **Primrose** : Two type of flowers based on the length of styles.
- **Pollinium** : In *Calotropis* and orchids, the pollen of each anther lobe form a sac likemass called **pollinium.** Each of which is provided with a stalk called **caudicle** and a sticky base called **disc** or **corpusculum.**
- **Biotransformation/culture products** : Plant product can be more easily obtained from tissue culture *e.g.*, Shikonin (*Lithospermum erythrorhizon*), taxol (*Taxus brevifolia*), digoxin (*Digitalis lanata*), ajmnalicin (*Catharanthus roseus*).
- **Wetraore and Wardlaw** : Successfully cultured shoot tips of pteridophytes *e.g., Selaginella, Equisetum* and ferns.
- **Embryo sac** : Monosporic is *Polygonum* ; bisporic in *Allium* and tetrasporic in *Peperomia.*
- **Heteromorphism** : A single species with flowers of different forms. The length of stamen and style varies in these flowers *e.g., Linum ussitatissimum* and *Primula.*
- **Cleavage polyembryony** : Cleavage of the zygote or proembryo *e.g.*, in Orchidaceae family.
- **Adventive embryony** : Formation of several embryos due to the 'budding' or proliferation of the cells of the nucellus or integuments.
- **In** *Bryophyllum*, plantlets develop along the margin of intact leaves.
- **Gynogenic haploids** : Possible from unpollinated ovules.
- **Rudolph Camerarius** (1694) : First to describe sexual reproduction in plants.

BIOTECHNOLOGY

It is the controlled use of biological agents, such as micro-organisms or cellular components for beneficial use.

Microorganisms were first used to produce some organic compounds like citric acid, following the first World War. Subsequently a variety of products, including antibiotics. In addition, animal and plant cells cultured *in vitro* are used to obtain several valuable products. In some cases, genetic improvements have enhanced the levels of production *e.g.,* Penicillin yield has been improved by a factor of about 1000. However, there has been no change in the type of product. These activities are called as **old biotechnology.**

Modern biotechnology

Use of genetic engineering/recombinant technology to enhance productivity and obtain new products from microorganisms, plant and animal cells.

Recombinant protein

The protein produced by transgenes (expressed in transgenic cells or organisms). These proteins can not be naturally produced by the concerned cells/ organisms.

The first useful commercial product of transgenic microorganisms was the synthesis of human insulin by bacterium *Escherichia coli* with the help of newly inserted human insulin gene.

Application of biotechnology

The products of biotechnology are food (bread, sauce, dosa etc.) dairy products (yoghurt, butter etc.) alcoholic beverages (beer, wine etc.), nonalcoholic beverages (coffee beans, tea leaves etc.), sewage treatment, Biogas (Gobar gas), biofertilizers, organic acids (lactic acid, acetic acid etc.), enzymes, antibiotics, vitamins, hormones/ insulin, growth hormone etc.), tissue culture, vaccines, monoclonal antibodies, transplants, (test tube babies, embryo transplant etc.), genetic engineering (recombinant DNA technology etc.), steroids etc.

GENETICALLY MODIFIED CROPS OR GM CROPS

Such crops are transgenic crops which possess and express one or more useful foreign genes or transgenes.

Two unique advantages are: (*a*) Any gene from any organism or a gene synthesised chemically can be used for transfer and (*b*) Change in genotype is precisely controlled.

This technology is advantageous to breeding programmes because in the breeding activities only the already present genes are reshuffled and that changes would occur in all traits for which the parents are different.

The transgene can perform following functions.

1. **Production of a desired proteins—Hirudin** protein is present in leech which prevents blood clotting. Its gene was chemically synthesised and introduced in *Brassica napus*. The seeds of the *Brassica* come to have hirudin which could be extracted, purified and used as medicine.
2. **Production of a desired phenotype**—Soil bacterium *Bacillus thuringiensis* produces a crystal (cry) protein which is toxic to larvae of certain species. There cry proteins are of various types. Each of which is toxic to a different group of insects. **Cry** gene (gene encoding cry protein) have been isolated and transferred into several crops (*e.g.,* cotton). This Bt cotton is not attacked by boll worm and other insects.
3. **Modify an existing biosynthetic pathway**—Transgenic Golden rice and transgenic potato produce, respectively higher content of vitamin A and protein.
4. **Mask expression of a native gene**—*e.g.,* Tomato variety "Flavr Savr" in which production of polygalacturonase was blocked. This enzyme degrades the pectin and promote the fruit softening. In the absence of enzyme, pectin degradation is stopped and fruit remains fresh for long with a superior taste and increased total soluble solids.

Caution is required in the development of GM crops without proper safe guards because (*i*) Gene transfer from GM crops to weeds would make them more virulent (*ii*) Transgenic crops may become persistent weeds (*iii*) Pollen of transgenic crops may carrying the transgenes to wild relatives (*iv*) Transgenic crops would disturb the balance of nature and damage the ecosystem.

BIORESOURCE AND USES OF BIODIVERSITY

GENETICALLY MODIFIED FOOD OR GM FOOD

The genetically modified food is the produce of genetically modified (transgenic) crops. Technology used during production of transgenic crops involves the use of antibiotic and antibiotic resistance genes. Their persistence is GM food in frought with danger :

(1) GM foods possess transgenic proteins and related metabolites which may cause toxicity and allergies.

(2) Enzyme for antibiotic resistance would cause altergen reactions.

(3) The bacteria present in the alimentary canal of the humans could take up the antibiotic resistance gene that is present in the GM food. It will make the disease resistant to many antibiotics. So these bacteria could become difficult to manage.

SUSTAINABLE AGRICULTURE

Successful management of resources for the purpose of agriculture to satisfy the changing human needs along with maintenance and enhancement of the quality of environment and conservation of natural resources.

Sustainable agriculture would primarily use renewable resources, would cause the minimum pollution and maintain the optimum yield level. Biotechnology is advantageous to sustainable agriculture in following ways—

1. Biofertilizers

Microorganisms which bring about nutrient enrichment of soil enhancing the availability of such nutrients *e.g.*, nitrogen (N) and phosphorus (P).

- Biofertilizers are low cost input, renewable, reduced dependence on chemical fertilizers and donot pollute the environment. Some examples are :
  - (*a*) **Free living nitrogen fixing bateria**—*e.g., Clostridium, Chromatium, Azotobacter* etc.
  - (*b*) **Free living nitrogen fixing cyanobacteria**—*e.g., Anabaena, Nostoc, Tolypothrix* etc.
  - (*c*) **Symbiotic nitrogen fixing bacteria**—*e.g., Rhizobium* in root nodules of legumes.
  - (*d*) **Symbiotic nitrogen fixing cyanobacteria**—*e.g., Anabaena azollae* in small aquatic fan *Azolla pinnata* often inoculated in rice fields.
  - (*e*) **Phosphate bacteria**—*e.g., Bacillus megatherium* var. *phosphaticum.*
  - (*f*) **Phyllosere** and **Rhizosphere nitrogen fixing bacteria**—*e.g., Azospirillum, Beijerinckia.*
  - (*g*) **Mycorrhiza**—Symbiotic association of fungus and plant roots. These are of irregular shapes often coralloid with wooly covering and absence of root hair and root cap. These fungi solubilise phosphorus, produce plant growth promoting substances and protect host plant from soil pathogens.

Biofertilizers donot produce quick and spectacular results but are slow and take time to become effective.

2. Biopesticides

- The biological agents that are used to control weeds, insects and pathogens are called **biopesticides.**
- The biological agents which are used as biopesticides are viruses, bacteria, fungi, protozoa and mites.
- Insect pest can be overcome by the use of **azadirachtin** (from Neem) due to its antifeedant characteristic, predators (*e.g.,* Preying mantis, lady bird beetle), parasites, parasitoids, pathogens of insects, pyrethrin, thurioside etc.
- Weeds are controlled by the use of predator herbivore, smoother crops and mycoherbicides.
- Fungus *Trichoderma* is used in biocontrol of fungal pathogens by its ability to secrete chitinase.
- **Sporeine** was the first bioinsecticide.
- The first bioherbicide was mycoherbicide (based on the fungus *Phytophthora palmivora*) and was developed in 1981. It is used to control the growth of milk weed in citrus orchards.
- The bacterium, *Bacillus thuringiensis* produces protein toxins. One of these, **thurioside** is active

against different groups of insects. The toxins accumulate as crystals inside the bacteria during sporulation. On being ingested by insects, these are converted into active form and kill them by inhibiting ion transport in the midgut.

- Due to use of biopesticides, the application of chemicals to control the diseases, insect pest and weeds is reduced which are the source of widespread pollution.

3. Disease and Insect-Resistant Varieties

Genetic engineering has enabled the development of crop varieties resistant to certain insects and diseases. The disease resistant genes are isolated and transferred to high yielding susceptible plants to produce pathogen-free plants. Several disease resistant somaclones have been identified for resistance to early blight of potato caused by *Alternaria solani*. Progress in engineering insect resistance in transgenic plants has been made through the expression of insect toxin gene of *Bacillus thuringiensis* in plants by transferring the viral genes of coat proteins. The technique has been used to produce a virus-resistant variety of squash.

Development of disease and insect resistant varieties would minimise the use of pesticides, prevent pollution, reduces yield losses due to insects and diseases and enhance agricultural production.

4. Single cell protein (SCP)

Microorganisms (*e.g.*, Algae, filamentous fungi, bacteria, yeast etc.) which can be cultured on a commercial scale in a fermenter, treated in various ways dried and used as food source or as animal feed are called **single cell protein** (SCP). In SCP, biomass is obtained not only from unicellular organisms but also from multicellular organisms. CO_2 produced from industry effluents and materials like saw dust and paddy straw are being used for production of many types of single cell proteins. SCP contain very high amount of proteins with little quantity of fats. Some microorganisms which lend themselves to biotechnological processing belong to—Algae (*e.g.*, *Chlorella, Scenedesmus*); Filamentous fungi (*e.g.*, *Fusarium gramineranum, Chaetomium cellulolyticum*); bacteria (*e.g.*, *Methylopphilus methylatrophus, Brevibacterium* sp. etc.); cyanobacteria (*e.g.*, *Spirulina* sp.) ; yeasts (*e.g.*, *Saccharomyces cerevisiae, Candida utilis* etc.) Processing is required to remove contaminants and excess nucleic acids. Besides providing the much needed proteins, single cell protein is beneficial in reducing environmental pollution by managing industrial and agricultural wastes.

BIOWAR OR BIOLOGICAL WARFARE

It is the international conflict in which viruses, bacteria and other biological agents noxious to or destructive of life are used against enemies.

Bioweapon or biological weapon is a device that carries and delivers to the target organisms a pathological biological agent or a toxin derived from it.

Bioweapon agent

The biological agent or toxin which is kept in a suitable container so that it remains active and virulent during delivery, which in delivered in various ways, including missiles and aircraft. Potential pathogens for bioweapons are *Bacillus anthracis, Vibrio cholerae,* small pox virus, *Pasteurella/Yersinia pestis,* botulinum toxin etc.

Bioweapons are—(*i*) low cost weapons, (*ii*) almost invisible, (*iii*) cause for more casualities than chemical or conventional weapons.

The possible defences against bioweapons include the use of respirator or gas mask, vaccination, administration on of appropriate antibiotics, decontamination and sensitive detection systems.

BIOETHICS

It is a set of perceptions, standards and principles which regulate our activities in relation to exploitation of biological world particularly in view of the latest break through in biotechnology.

The major bioethical concerns related to biotechnology are :

(1) Animals are used for producing pharmaceutical proteins are virtually functioning as factory for human beings.

(2) Use of animals in biotechnology causes great suffering to them.

(3) Transfer of human genes into animals (and vice-versa) dilutes the 'concept of humanness'.
(4) Biotechnology by manipulating genes is producing new genotypes, some of which may be dangerous to the living world.
(5) Transgenics are likely to damage environment.
(6) It would change the crop-weed interaction by the transfer of new genes to weeds and other plants.
(7) It violates integrity of species.

Biotechnologies do these things on a much larger scale and at a much faster rate.

SOME IMPORTANT FACTS

- **Golden rice :** Genetically altered rice with yellow coloured grains, rich in vitamin A.
- **Terminator seeds :** Produced by genetic engineering are in fact seeds that develop into fertile plants which produce nongerminable seeds.
- **Plasticulture :** Use of plastic in agriculture. This technology in being considered as an important tool for evergreen revolution.
- Citizens of Delhi contains the highest level of pesticides is their body fat in the world.
- **Therapeutic cloning :** Used to repair damaged tissues and diseased organs.
- **Reproductive Cloning :** Used to create babies identical in genetic makeup to a given genome. Helps to seek immortality, bypass infertility, triumph over death by recreating a loved one etc.
- **Bioenergy** the energy obtained from biological sources *i.e.,* animal energy and biofuels.
- A transgenic cow has been produced that bears a gene for the production of human lactoferin in cow milk.
- **Bioreactor :** The fermentation tank where fermentation is caried out in the presence of micro-organisms.
- **Hybridomas :** The hybrid cells of same clone.
- **PNA (Peptide Nucleic Acid) :** Nucleotide bases attached to back bone of small peptides stick to RNAs of food poisoning bacteria. The latter fail to produce proteins and die after some time.
- **Biological weapons** convention and Treaty-1972.
- **Broad spectrum antibiotics :** The antibiotics which have the ability to act on several pathogenic species differing from each other in structure and composition of cell wall.
- Department of Biotechnology (DBT)—India.
- Information Centre for Genetic Engineering and Biotechnology (ICGEB) : New Delhi and Italy.
- Central Food and Training Research Institute (CFTRI) : Mysore.
- Central Drug Research Institute (CDRI) : Lucknow.
- Central Institute of Medicinal and Aromatic Plants (CIMAP) : Lucknow.
- Animal energy is available in two forms : **HMP** (Human Muscle Power) and **DAP** (Draught Animal Power).
- **Shikonin :** A red dye used for manufacturing cosmetics.
- **Second generation vaccines :** Those produced by genetic engineering for Hepatitis B and Herpes Virus.
- **Third generation vaccines :** Synthetic vaccines.
- **TPA** (Tissue Plasminogen Activator) enzyme is used to dissolve blood clots particularly in case of heart attacks.
- **Gene bank** : is an institution where valuable genetic material is stored either in the form of seeds or as vegetative material.
- **Germplasm :** The genetic material especially that contained within the reproductive cells.
- **G. Haberlandt** (1854 – 1945) : Father of plant tissue culture, first to have cultured cells which were fully differentiated (on Knop's salt solution + sucrose).
- **Somatic embryogenesis :** Represents the embryo like structures derived from sporophytic or somatic cells of the plant.
- **IPRs :** Intellectual Property Rights (Patents).
- **Humulin :** first genetically engineered human insulin produced by the American firm Eli Lilly.
- **Cellular totipotency :** The ability of somatic cells of a plant to produce a new complete plant.

TRANSGENIC ANIMALS AND PLATNS, MOLECULAR APPROACHES TO DIAGNOSIS AND STRAIN IDENTIFICATION

INTRODUCTION

Domestication

The process of bringing certain plants and animals under human management. Presently, the field of agriculture is the result of continuous and progressive researches in various branches of agricultural sciences.

Genotype

Genotype is the genetic set up of an organism. It is responsible for performance of an organism. The degree of genotype expression depends upon the environment.

Phenotype

Morphology and performance of a crop or domesticated animal is called phenotype which depends upon two factors *i.e.,* genotype/heredity and environment.

The **environment** includes all living and non-living factors with which an individual or the variety interacts. The environmental factors include climatic, edaphic, topographical and biotic factors.

Maximisation of food production would involve the improvement in crop or animal genotypes, as well as the environments under which the crops and animals are raised.

Improved management practices

These practices are undertaken to modify the environment for maximising the yield of crops and animals.

(*a*) **Improved management practices for crops :** *i.e.*, preparation of soil (through ploughing, levelling, manuring etc.), good quality of certified seeds (may be treated with fungicide to check seed borne or soil borne infection), sowing (at proper depth place and time), nutrients (manure, compost, fertilisers etc.), irrigation, weeding, crop protection (from pests and pathogens), multiple cropping, crop rotation etc.

(*b*) **Improved management practices for domesticated animals :** Shelter (well lighted, ventilated and spacious), feed (optimum quality and quantity), drinking water (clean fresh water), washing and grooming (periodically), disinfection (periodically), vaccination, sick animals (should be separated and treated) etc.

IMPROVEMENT IN GENOTYPE

Improvement in genotype is mainly done by improving the genetic potentialities in plants and animals.

- **Trait or Character** : any morpholgical, anatomical, behavioural and biochemical feature of an organism *e.g.,* plant maturity, fruit size, shattering and non-shattering nature, yield, quality.
- **Selection** : the process that leads to different rates of reproduction by different genotypes present in a population.
- **Breeding** : When genotype of an organism is modified to make that organism more useful to humans, the process is called breeding.
- **Plant breeding** : The science of producing improved varieties of crop plants by changing their heredity for one or more traits like higher yield, better quality, shorter duration, suitability to particular environment and resistance to common diseases.
- **Animal breeding** : aims at genetic improvement of domesticated animal species.

IMPROVED VARIETIES

- **Variety** : A variety consists of a group of plants which have the same genotype or similar genotypes and it differs for one or more characters from other varieties of the same crop.
- **Improved Variety** : the race/strain/breed of a species which is superior to all other existing varieties in one or more traits. It is recognized as such by a variety release committee based on its detailed evaluation for yield and other characters.

DEVELOPMENT OF NEW VARIETIES

Consists of the following main steps.

(*i*) Creation of genetic variation,

(*ii*) Selection,
(*iii*) Evaluation and release as a variety and
(*iv*) Seed multiplication and distribution to farmers.

(i) Creation of genetic variation

Two most important steps in plant breeding are to create genetic variation and selection.

Variation means differences among individuals of a population or species for a specific character.

Genetic variation

It is the source of raw material for selection. These are heritable due to genotype and are transmitted from one generation to other. Such variations are useful in selection.

- Success of a breeding programme usually depends on creation of the desired genetic variation. It can be done in following ways *i.e.*, domestication, germplasm collection, plant introduction, hybridisation, polyploidy, mutation and genetic engineering.
- **Hybridisation** : The crossing of two plants differing from each other genotypically in one or more traits.
- **Line** : A group of individuals having a common lineage and similar genotype.
- **Parents** : The individials or lines used in hybridisation.
- **Emasculation** : The removal of male parts or anthers from the future female parent plants in the young state so as to avoid chances of contamination from their pollen. It is essential in bisexual flowers to prevent self-pollination. By doing emasculation, the plant breeder makes a female flower which can be artificially pollinated by the desired pollen grains. This is generally done by hand, through suction pressure, hot or cold water treatment, alcohol treatment or by the use of chemical gametocides.
- **Hybrid or F_1 Seeds** : Seeds produced by emasculated flowers of the female parent are hybrid or F_1 seeds. There will be segregation, independent assortment and recombination in the F_2 and later generations obtained from these F_1 seeds.
- **Single cross** : When a hybridisation is performed between the two plants.
- **Multiple cross** : When a hybridisation is performed between more than two plants.
- **Hybridisation may be**
  (*i*) **Intravarietal** : Between the two plants belonging to same variety.
  (*ii*) **Intervarietal or intraspecific** : Between the two varieties of the same species.
  (*iii*) **Interspecific** : Between the different species of the same genus. *e.g.,* all the sugarcane varieties being cultivated today are interspecific hybrids.
  (*iv*) **Intergeneric** : Between two different genera.

(ii) Selection

During selection, the individual plants or groups of plants having the desired characters are picked up from a population eliminating the undesirable ones. These selected plants are allowed to reproduce for setting their seeds. The seeds are collected and again a new crop is developed. Selection acts on the genetic variation present in a population and produces a new population with improved characters.

- **Selection in self-pollinated crops** : In self-pollinated crops, the amount of cross-pollination is less than 5 per cent. Self-pollination causes a rapid increase in **homozygosity.** Self-pollinated crops gradually becomes **homozygous.** Best homozygous individuals can be easily isolated in such crops. By selection, **pure lines** are produced. Which have identical genotype. Due to self-pollination seeds of such crops can be used year after year.
- **Selection in cross-pollinated crops** : Cross-pollinated crops are **heterozygous** and contains mixture of many genotypes. A cross-pollinated population contains plants of several different genotypes. Some of there genotypes are superior, but many are inferior. Selection in such crops targets at enhancing the frequency of superior genotypes with reducing the heterozygosity.

(iii) Evaluation and release of varieties

A newly developed variety is evaluated for its yield, quality, disease and insect resistance before it is released to farmers. Indian council of Agricultural Research (ICAR) carries out the evaluations in India. In every agro-climatic zone, every crop is evaluated for minimum three years. A new pure line, population or hybrid that is superior to the existing varieties, as well as to other new material may be released as a new variety. Variety release committee recommends the release of improved variety under new name with permission of Government.

(iv) Multiplication of improved seed

Seed means any plant part which is used to grow a crop like grains in wheat, tubers of potato, stems of sugarcane etc. Grains used as food cannot be termed as seed whereas, those used for raising a crop are called **seeds.**

Improved seed : Seed of a varietiy with superior traits which must be of high purity, and have a high germination percentage. These seeds must also be free from weed seeds and diseases.

The quality of seed is often certified by an agency. Such seed is called **certified seed.** National seed corporation (NSC) was established to streamline seed production in India.

GERMPLASM COLLECTION AND CONSERVATION

Germplasm

The sum total of all the alleles of the genes present in a crop and its related species.

Germplasm Materials

(*i*) Cultivated and non-cultivated improved varieties.
(*ii*) Old local/*desi* varieties of different places.
(*iii*) Lines produced by plant breeders, and
(*iv*) Wild species/relatives of the crop plant.

The **first germplasm centre** of the world was established by Vavilov in Leningrad.

International Board of Plant Genetic Resources was established in 1971.

International Crops Research Institute for Semi Arid Tropics (ICRISAT) is located in Hyderabad, which is responsible for conserving germplasm of groundnut, pigeonpea, chick pea, pearl millet and sorghum.

Germplasm is maintained in **gene/germplasm banks.** They are institutes that maintain stocks of viable seeds (seed banks), live growing plants (orchards), tissue culture and frozen germplasm (Cryopreservation).

Orthodox seeds

Partially dehydrated and stored at low temperature of – 10° to – 20°C under anaerobic conditions for long periods *e.g.,* cereals, legumes.

Recalcitrant Seeds

Kept at room temperature under partially humid aerobic conditions for shorter duration *e.g.,* tea, cocoa, jackfruit, coconut etc. All the varieties of trees and plants with recalcitrant seeds are maintained in orchards.

Plant introduction

Shifting of a variety, line or population of a plant species to a new area, where it was not grown earlier. Improved varieties like **"Sonora-64"** of wheat and **"Taichung Native-1"** of rice are examples of plant introduction. These dwarf varieties provided the starting material for "green revolution" in India.

Quarantine

Checking of incoming plants, seeds, fruits, tissues and other organism for any harmful effect the same can cause to the local flora, fauna and humans. Plant quarantine is meant for preventing introduction of exotic pests, weeds and diseases into the country under Destructive Insects and Pests (DIP) Act, 1914. It is applicable to other types of introductions as well like animals and sometimes human beings to reduce the chances of pathogen/pest entry in a country. *Argemone mexicana,* a weed entered India with introduction.

HETEROSIS AND INBREEDING DEPRESSION

Heterosis or Hybrid vigour

Term **Heterosis** was coined by Shull (1914) and in ordinary use hybrid vigour and heterosis are practically synonymous.

Hybrid vigour

The superiority of the hybrid over either parent in one or more traits. When two unrelated individuals or lines are crossed, the performance of F_1 hybrid is often superior to both its parents. Almost all species exhibit heterosis. It is essentially the reverse of inbreeding depression.

Inbreeding Depression

Loss of vigour and appearence of a number of defective traits associated with inbreeding is called **inbreeding depression.** Many cross-pollinated crops and all animals species exhibit inbreeding depression. On the other hand, the self-pollinated crops do not exhibit ill effects of inbreeding because cross-pollination makes the plants highly heterozygous.

Inbreeding is the mating of two individuals of a species which are related to descent.

MUTATION BREEDING

- **Mutation** : Sudden, stable discontinuous and inheritable variations which appear in organism due to permanent change in their genotype.
- **Spontaneous mutation** : Mutations which occur naturally, *i.e.*, both germinal and somatic.
- **Induced mutations** : Mutations produced in response to a treatment with a mutagen. They were first produced by Muller (1927) with the help of X-rays on *Drosophila* and by Stadler in maize.
- **Mutagens** : Rate of mutations is increased by means of certain factors and chemicals called **mutagens.** 2 types :
  (*i*) **Chemical mutagens** : A variety of chemicals like ethylmethane sulphonate (EMS) and sodium azide which induce mutations.
  (*ii*) **Physical mutagens** : Various kinds of radiations *e.g.*, X-rays, gamma rays, ultraviolet rays etc.
- Mutation can arise due to a change in any of the following :
  (*i*) Chromosome structure
  (*ii*) Chromosome number
  (*iii*) Base sequence of the concerned gene.

Mutation breeding

The use of induced mutations in plant breeding to develop improved varieties. In such breeding usually seeds are treated with a suitable mutagen. The treated seeds are grown in the field and self-pollinated. Progeny from these plants are grown during the next crop season. These plants are carefully observed to identify and select mutations of interest. In the end, a desirable mutant line may be obtained which may be good enough to be released as a new variety. Over 200 varieties have been produced from mutation breeding in India.

POLYPLOIDY IN CROP IMPROVEMENT OR POLYPLOID BREEDING

- **Polyploid** : An organism which possesses more than two sets of chromosomes.
- **Polypoidy** : Phenomenon of having one or more genomes in addition to the normal number for the species.
- A polyploid on the basis of number of chromosome set present may be triploid (3N), tetraploid (4N), pentaploid (5N), hexaploid (6N), septaploid (7N), octaploid (8N) etc. The polyploid species are of two types :
  (*i*) **Autopolyploid species/individual** : Contains more than two copies of a single genome.
  (*ii*) **Allopolyploid species/individual** : Contains two or more genomes and each genome is ordinarily present in two copies.

Autopolyploidy

The polyploidy which takes place within a species and results due to multiplication of the same set of chromosomes. It can be induced artificially by the use of a chemical called **colchicine** which arrests and breaks the spindle so that nuclear division is not followed by wall formation. All autopolyploids exhibit **gigas effect** *i.e.*, larger size, more juice, more sugar, more grains etc. Triploids are sexually sterile which are propagated vegetatively *e.g.*, many banana varieties, seedless water melon, triploid sugar beet with more sugar and larger roots, some apple and pear varieties with large sized and more juicy fruits.

An autotriploid (three copies of a single genome) variety of tea has also been developed in India.

Alloployploidy

The polyploids which arise as a result of chromosome doubling following hybridisation of two distinctly different species are called allopolyploids. It is also called **interspecific polyploidy** because increase in number of genomes or chromosome sets is due to pooling from individuals of two or more species caused by hybridisaion followed by chromosome doubling *e.g.*, AABB, AABBCC.

Among artificially produced allopolyploidy *Triticale* is the first man made crop derived by crossing wheat (*Triticum*) and rye (*Secale*). The chromosome number of the resulting F_1 was doubled to produce triticale.

Haploidy

The haploid bears only one set of chromosomes *i.e.*, only one copy of each chromosome. Haploids of higher plants are sterile and generally do not survive. However, they are highly useful in producing pure homozygous lines for breeding programmes. Such plants are developed through a culture technique developed by Guha and Maheshwari (1964). It is called **androgenic haploid culture.** Gynogenic haploids are also developed by using unfertilised ovules.

BREEDING FOR NUTRITIONAL QUALITY

Quality : an important aspect for plant breeders because it determines the suitability of plant produce for various uses. **Qualitative characters** differ from crop to crop and also vary with the use of plant produce *e.g.*, size, shape, colour, milling, baking, malting and cooking in food grains, size, colour, taste, flavour and nutrition in fruits etc.

Nutritional quality of a fruit/crop/vegetable etc. is its value in human/animal nutrition as to number of calories, amount and presence of essential amino acids and fatty acids, vitamins, minerals, roughage and absence of antinutritional factors.

Antinutritional factors are those compounds which badly affect the human/animal growth and development *e.g.*, Glucosinolates in oils and cakes of rapeseed and mustard ; Neurotoxin found in seeds of *Lathyrus sativus* etc.

Protein Quality : The quality of essential amino acids in proteins relative to contents required in human diet represents the **protein quality.** Pulses lack methionine and cysteine (sulphur containing amino acids) Cereals and millets do not possess amino acids lysine and tryptophan. A combination of pulses and cereals are able to provide all essential amino acids.

"Shakti", "Rattan"and "Protina" are the newly developed varieties of maize which are rich in amino acids lysine.

Oil Quality is determined by the presence and relative amounts of saturated and unsaturated fatty acids. Saturated long chain fatty acids like **erucic acid** (22-carbon fatty acid) are not good for health. In contrast polysaturated fatty acids are beneficial to human health. Therefore, oil seed varieties with higher polyunsaturated fatty acid contents are being developed.

BREEDING FOR DISEASE RESISTANCE

There are various physical, chemical and biological methods for disease control but the cheapest and the most convenient method is to produce resistant varieties.

- **Pathogen :** an organism that causes disease in another organism (*i.e.*, host).
- Development of disease in plant depends on (*i*) host genotype, (*ii*) pathogen genotype and (*iii*) the environment.
- **Disease resistance :** the ability of host to inhibit the growth of pathogen so that no or little harm is done to it. It can be mechanical/anatomical feature, protective reaction, antibiosis and non-supply of nutrition by the host which checks pathogen to enter and flourish in the host's body.
- **Susceptible Host :** Term is used for those lines which are not resistant to the pathogen but are attacked and harmed by the pathogen.
- A successful breeding for disease resistance depends mainly on :
  (*a*) good source of resistance, and (*b*) dependable disease test.

- **Disease test :** Is carried out by growing various varieties in an area under conditions in which the susceptible plants would develop the disease.
- Disease resistant varieties provide the cheapest and a hazard-free means of controlling diseases. Is any case, such varieties are very important component of any package designed for disease control. Almost all modern day varieties incorporate in them resistance for important diseases of the crop.

ANIMAL BREEDING

The science of producing improved breeds of domesticated animals by improving their genotypes through selective mating. The chief objectives are :

(*i*) improved growth rate

(*ii*) increased production of milk, meat, eggs, wool etc.

(*iii*) increased productive life,

(*iv*) improved resistance to various diseases,

(*v*) superior quality of milk, meat, eggs, wool etc., and

(*vi*) increased or atleast, acceptable reproduction rate etc.

The main approaches for animal breeding are inbreeding, out-crossing and interspecific hybridisation.

(a) Inbreeding

Due to different males and females in domesticated animals cross fertilization takes place. In inbreeding superior cows and sperior bulls are mated. The progeny obtained from such mating are evaluated and superior males and females are identified for further mating. Progeny is selected for better characters like more milk production in **superior female** cow.

Superior male is that bull which gives rise to superior progeny as compared to those of other males.

Inbreeding increases homozygosity. Harmful recessive geness are eliminated during selection. Other effects of inbreeding are accumulation of superior genes, continuous inbreeding results to reduction in fertility and sometimes production also due to inbreeding depression.

(b) Cross-breeding

Superior males of one breed are mated with superior females of another breed. It allows the desirable qualities of two different breeds to be combined in a single breed. Thus in hybrid, better characters of both the parents appear. Stable breeds may be developed due to further inbreeding and selection. A number of such breeds have been developed.

(c) Inter-specific hybridisation

The cross is made between male and female of two different species. Thus, mule is produced from a cross between male Donkey and female Horse. Mules are adapted to work hard in mountains being more sturdier and hardier. Of course, mules are sterile and are produced everytime through interspecific crosses.

HYBRIDS

A hybrid is a progeny (F_1 generation) that has resulted due to a cross between two genetically unrelated parents (a male and a female parents).

- **Hybrid variety** : When F_1 seed from a cross is used for raising a commercial crop, the F_1 seed constitutes a hybrid variety.
- **Inbrid line** : is a newly homozygous line produced by continuous inbreeding in a cross pollinated crop and is maintained by strict inbreeding.
- **Hybrid varieties** of many cross-pollinated crops *e.g.*, maize, sorghum, pearl millet, cotton, sunflower etc. are in commercial use.
- Differnt steps is the development of a hybrid variety are :
  (*i*) Production of inbred lines by continued inbreeding.
  (*ii*) Evaluation of inbred lines through a series of tests, and
  (*iii*) Large scale production of F_1 seed for distribution among farmers.
- Hybrids have long been used for commercial production in cattle, swine, sheep and poultry.
- The modern practice of hybrid production is

based on inbred stocks. Hybrid varieties are more commonly exploited commercially in case of swine (pig) and poultry.

PLANT DISEASES AND THEIR CONTROL

Disease

Defined as a malfunctioning process that is caused by continuous irritation which results in some suffering producing symptoms.

There are so many agents which cause diseases in plants *e.g.,* **inanimate** (abiotic agents *e.g.,* adverse climatic conditions, adverse soil conditions, nutrient deficiencies, mineral toxicities etc.), **viruses** and **animate** (biotic agents *e.g.,* bacteria, fungi, protozoa, nematodes, mycoplasmas etc.

Diseases reduce the total biomass of the crops by causing : (*i*) death of plants, (*ii*) killing of branches, (*iii*) damage to leaf tissues, (*iv*) general stunting and (*v*)damage to reproductive organs including fruits and seeds.

Plant diseases reduce the quantity and quality of crop produce ; may make the plant produce poisonous to humans and animals and increase the cost of production.

The development of diseases and perpetuation of pathogens take place through a series of events. *i.e.,* (*i*) coming of pathogen in contact with host plants, (*ii*) Entry of pathogen into host through natural openings, wounds or by direct penetration, (*iii*) The pathogen multiplies and spreads in the host tissues (*iv*) pathogen then reproduces and the new individuals so produced spread to new host plants (*v*) Survival on host debris/organic matter or alternate host during periods when the main host plants is not in the field.

PLANT DISEASES CAUSED BY FUNGI

Common pathogens of plants, mostly are **obligate parasites** or **biotrophs** (*i.e.,* true parasites which are restricted only to living host tissues), some are **facultative parasites** (*i.e.,* usually grow saprophytically but under changed circumstances have ability to grow as parasites).

- **Dissemination** : In the form of spores; spread by wind, water, birds, insects and other animals and humans; enter their host by direct peneration through natural openings or through wounds.
- **Symptoms** : Either localised or general symptoms, like tissue death (necrosis), stunting etc. on their host. Other symptoms are tumours, galls, witche's brown, warts, rot, scab, blight, damping off, rusts, smuts, wilts, powdery mildew, downy mildew, leaf curl, leaf spots, cankers etc.
- **Control of fungal diseases** : Use of resistant varieties, destruction of infected plant parts and crop residues, spraying of chemical fungicides or use of biopesticides.

Some fungal diseases

(1) Late blight of potato : *Phytophthora infestans*

(2) Black stem rust of wheat : *Puccinia graminis*

(3) Wilt of Pigeon pea : *Fusarium udum* (*F. oxysporum*).

(4) Fungal/Ascochyta blight of chickpea or gram : *Mycosphaerella racici.*

PLANT DISEASES CAUSED BY BACTERIA

Plant pathogenic bacteria are generally rod shaped, non-spore forming, non-motile or motile by means of one or more flagella and multiply by binary fission.

About 100 bacterial species cause plant disease. Pathogenic bacteria usually do not survive long in soil. They usually multiply and colonise in the intercellular spaces, vascular bundles and spaces formed by dead cells.

Dissemination : Spread by water, insects, other animals and humans ; some bacteria persist in insects and depend on them for their survival and spread; enter through wounds, sometimes through natural openings.

Disease symptoms : Necrosis, excessive growth of tissue, wilting, blight, soft rot, leaf spot, cankers, tumours or galls, vascular wilts, dwarfing of plants, distortion of plant parts, chlorosis etc.

Control measures : Not easily controlled; needed a combination of control measures like use or resistant varieties, use of healthy disease free seed, use of chemical bactericides, biopesticides etc.

Some bacterial Diseases

(1) Citrus canker : *Xanthomonas citri*

(2) Bacterial blight of paddy : *Xanthomonas oryzae*

PLANT DISEASES CAUSED BY VIRUSES

About 1/4th of all known viruses attack plants. Mostly plant viruses have single stranded RNA. Viruses are obligate intracellular parasites made up of proteins and nucleic acids.

Dissemination

Through wounds either made mechanically or by vectors. In almost all cases, viruses ultimately reach phloem and are then transported to long distances within the plant. They spread from one plant to other through (*i*) vegetative propagules (*ii*) mechanically through sap of infected plants, (*iii*) seed, (*iv*) pollen, (*vi*) insect vectors, (*vi*) mites, nematodes, fungi etc.

Disease symptoms

(*i*) **Primary symptoms** : Clearing of veins and local lesions.

(*ii*) **Systemic symptoms** : Mosaic, mottling, distortion, chlorosis, necrosis, stunting, colour break, outgrowths and tumours etc.

Control measures

By using resistant host varieties, disease free propagules, by controlling the insect vectors. They cannot be controlled by chemical methods.

Some viral diseases

(1) Tobacco mosaic : *Tobacco mosaic virus* (TMV)

(2) Yellow vein mosaic of Bhindi-*Hibiscus yellow vein mosaic virus*

(3) Mosaic of Tomato–*Nicotiana virus.*

PLANT DISEASES CAUSED BY NEMATODES

Nematodes are round worms ; free living in the soil, freshwater or marine water. Plant parasitic nematodes lay eggs which hatch into juveniles. Most of them are plant pathogens causing destructive diseases.

- **Dissemination** : by water, animal feet, farm equipments, birds, humans and dust storms. They attack above ground parts either ascend themselves or get splashed by water.
- **Disease symptoms** : They puncture cell wall, inject saliva into the cell and withdraw part of the cell contents. The different symptoms are root knots or root galls, root lesions, excessive root branching, reduced growth of shoot, yellowing etc.
- **Control measures** : Burning of diseased crop refuse, checking of smoking near seed beds, use of properly sterilized tools, use of resistant varieties, weeding out and destroying of diseased plants as soon as the disease appears.

Some nematode's disease

(1) Root knot of Brinjal and Tomato : *Meloidogyne incognita*

(2) Earcockle/Seed Gall of Wheat : *Anguina tritici*

(3) Root knot of Potato and Tomato : *Meloidogyne hapla.*

ANIMAL DISEASES AND THEIR CONTROL

Any condition which impair the health or interferes with the normal functioning of the body due to one or another reason is called a **disease.**

On the basis of occurrence diseases are of two types:

(1) **Congenital disease** (inborn diseases, inheritable, caused by gene or chromosomal mutations) *e.g.*, disease caused by gene mutations, chromosomal mutations, evironmental factors etc.

(2) **Acquired diseases** (only after birth, non-inheritable) : Two types on the basis of communication.

  (*a*) **Communicable** (can be transmitted, infectious diseases) : Bacterial diseases, viral diseases, protozoan diseases, helminth diseases, fungal diseases, rickettsial diseases, spirochaetal diseases etc., **contagious diseases** (spread by contact *e.g.*, STDs, chickenpox, small pox, measles, leprosy etc.), **noncontagious diseases** (taeniasis, cholera, ascariasis, tuberculosis, plague, filariasis etc.).

  (*b*) **Non-communicable** (donot spread) four types :

    (*i*) **Deficiency diseases** : deficiency of some nutrient or some hormone.

(*ii*) **Degenerative or organic diseases** : *e.g.*, cardiovascular diseases, brain diseases

(*iii*) **Allergic diseases** : *e.g.*, asthma, hay-fever

(*iv*) **Cancerous diseases** : tumours.

Infection takes place through skin, digestive tract, respiratory tract, conjunctiva, urogenital tract, placenta, umbilicus, udder, teats and eggs.

General Preventive Measures

(1) Isolation of infected animals.
(2) Disinfection of the animal house and articles used for tending to the animals.
(3) Proper disposal of the carcass and all material that were in contact with the diseased animal(s).
(4) Vaccination of animals against all major diseases.
(5) Injection of antiserum into healthy animals whenever an epidemic is expected.
(6) Use of alternate grazing grounds in case a pasture was being used by diseased animals.
(7) The veterinary authorities should be informed so that they can promptly initiate measures to check the spread of disease.

BACTERIAL DISEASES

e.g., anthrax, mastitis, pneumonia etc.

Anthrax

Caused by bacterium *Bacillus anthracis*, contagious disease ; affects cattle, buffaloes, horse, sheep and goats; spread to human beings also ; spread through contaminated feed, water and pastures.

- **Symptoms and diagnosis** : In very **acute cases :** increased respiration, blood mixed foamy discharge from mouth, nose and anus; infected animals may die within minutes.
- **In subacute and chronic diseases** : high fever, increased pulse and respiration rates; discharge is black, shiny and foamy material from natural openings of animals, the infected animals die within 2-3 days.
- Disease can be confirmed by microscopic observation of the bacterium in the blood of patients or by culturing the bacterium present in the blood on a suitable medium.
- **Treatment** : Suitable antibiotic (ciprofloxacin) in cattle. Anthrax anti-serum can also be used with good results.
- **Prevention and Control** : Healthy animals should be vaccinated, protection by providing antiserum to animals which come in contact with diseased animals.

VIRAL DISEASES

e.g., cattle suffer from rinderpest, foot and mouth disease, cow pox etc.

- **Rinderpest** : Caused by a virus, highly contagious, spreads rapidly by direct contact with patient animals, through contaminated feed, water, workers and their clothes and by flies.
- **Symptoms** : Initially the infected animal develops fever (40.0 to 42.2°C), loses appetite, develops constipation, and passes hard faeces which is generally covered with blood. In the final stages of the diseased animal suffers from loose motions and gives off offensive odours. The animal usually dies in about 7 days.
- **Treatment** : Effective only in the initial stages of the disease. Injection of sulphamethazine sodium is often effective. Rinderpest antiserum injection is highly effective especially when combined with injection of sulphamethazine sodium.
- **Prevention** : To vaccinate animals, it was initiated in India in 1954 and has effectively controlled the disease.

DISEASES CAUSED BY PARASITIC ANIMAL

e.g., tapeworms, flukes, round worms etc. Parasites are of two types :

(1) Ectoparasites : live on the skin *e.g.*, ticks.

(2) Endoparasites : live within the animal body *e.g.*, tapeworm, round worm, liver flukes etc.

- Many parasites transmit pathogens and help in the spread of concerned disease. Some of them also parasitic to human.
- **Ascaris** : Endoparasitic nematode, infects many animals, including humans. Adult

nematode cause wounds in the intestine and interfere with animal digestion. Symptoms—constipation, diarrhoea, anaemia etc. Animal may die is severe cases. Transmitted by grass, the larvae enter alimentary canals of these animals.

- **Treatment** : Administration of specific medicines *e.g.*, piperax, piperazine adipate, wormex etc.

DISEASES CAUSED BY PROTOZOA

Diseases are tick fever, coccidiosis etc.

- **Tickfever** caused by *Babesia* – (protozoan parasite), spread by ticks, caused mainly by *Babesia bigemina* in India. Parasite enters into red blood cells (RBC's) and destroy them.
- **Symptoms** : high fever (41.1 – 41.7°C) in the acute case and stop feeding. In chronic form of tick fever, there is irregular fever and constipation followed by diarrhoea.
- **Diagnostic Feature** : Presence of pear shaped protozoan parasite within the RBCs.
- **Treatment** : Injection of trypan blue, acaprin or berenil, sanitation measures and a suitable insecticide treatment are implimented to eradicate the ticks.
- **Prevention and control** : By effectively controlling the ticks. Insecticide treatments are used to eradicate ticks from animals and from pastures.

SOME IMPORTANT FACTS

- Chickenpox is commonly called **Varicella disease,** while small pox is commonly called **variola disease.**
- Chicken pox, small pox and hepatitis are caused by dsDNA viruses while polio, mumps, measles and rabies are caused by ssRNA viruses.
- **Wander wheat** : Mexico's International wheat and maize improvement centre has developed a new wheat variety with a yield of 18 tonnes per hectare. It has some 200 grains per stalk.
- Crop improvement is possible through judicious combination of selection, introduction and hybridisation.
- Plants can be made disease resistant by breeding with wild relatives.
- Seedless water melon is triploid.
- PV-18, Kalyan. Sona wheat varieties have been developed by selection.
- Most varieties of Sugarcane are aneuploids.
- Chemicals like colchicine, guranoson, viratrine sulphate are able to cause polyploidy.
- High yielding variety of rice was produced in India by introduction dwarfing genes called Dee-goo-woo-gen from Taiwan.
- When fused protoplasms of two cells develops its own wall, they are called somatic hybrid cells.
- New crops are less known, under utilized and under exploited plants.
- Winged bean is an herbaceous legume of Tropical Asia.
- Leucaena's green branches serve as a nutritious food for cattle, buffaloes and goats.
- **Disease Syndrome** : The sum total of all disease symptoms.
- Ringworm of scalp : Caused by *Microsporum* fungus.
- Predisposition Environmental effects which make the plants more susceptible to diseases.
- Tooth decay is the most common disease in the world.
- **Stick test** : A sensitive test to diagnose **diphtheria.**
- **BCG vaccine** : Prepared from Bovine tubercle bacilli of cattle.
- DPT : a triple antigen for 3 diseases : **diphtheria, pertussis and tetanus.**
- MMR vaccine : Triple antigen for **measles, mumps** and **German measles** (Rubella).
- Pampered corn : Maize cannot grow without human effort (removal of grains from cob).
- National Bureau of Plant Genetic Resources (NBPGR) (Established 1976). Keeps control on plant introductions.
- Hybrid breeds : Karanswiss was developed at (NDRI) Karnal while Sunandivi was developed at NDRI Kerala.

GENOMICS AND ITS APPLICATIONS TO HEALTH AND AGRICULTURE, INCLUDING GENE THERAPY

GENE THERAPY

Gene therapy (or **gene replacement therapy**) is the insertion of genes into an individual's cells and tissues to treat a disease, and hereditary diseases in particular. Gene therapy typically aims to supplement a defective mutant allele with a functional one. Gene therapy may be **germ-line** or **somatic cell gene therapy**. Current gene therapy is exclusively somatic gene therapy, the introduction of genes into somatic cells of an affected individual. Germ-line gene therapy involves the permanent transmissible modification of genome of a gamete, a zygote or an early embryo. The prospect of human germline gene therapy is currently not sanctioned.

Gene therapy may be : Classical and nonclassical gene therapy. In classical gene therapy genes are delivered to appropriate target cells with the aim of obtaining optimal expression of the introduced genes. The idea of nonclassical gene therapy is to inhibit the expression of genes associated with the pathogenesis, or to correct a genetic defect and so restore normal gene expression.

Methods for inserting and expressing a gene in a target cell

The genetic material may be transferred directly into cells within a patient *(in vivo* gene therapy), or cells may be removed from the patient and the genetic material inserted into them *in vitro,* prior to transplanting the modified cells back into the patient (*in vivo* gene therapy).

Ex vivo gene transfer

This initially involves transfer of cloned genes into cells grown in culture. Those cells which have been transformed successfully are selected, expanded by cell culture *in vitro*, then introduced into the patient. This approach is only applicable to tissues that can be removed from the body, altered genetically and returned to the patient where they will engraft and survive for a long period of time (*e.g.,* cells of the hematopoietic system and skin cells).

In vivo gene transfer

The cloned genes are transferred directly into the tissues of the patient. This may be the only possible option in tissues where individual cells cannot be cultured in vitro insufficient numbers (e.g., brain cells) and/or where cultured cells cannot be re-implanted efficiently in patients (Fig. 1).

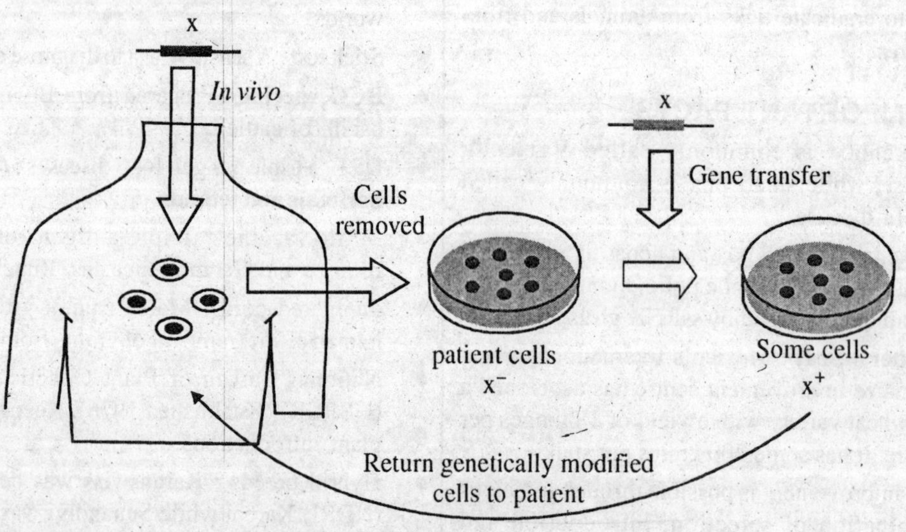

Fig. 1: *In vivo* and *ex vivo* gene therapy.

CLONING OF MAMMALS

In 1997, Ian Wilmut announced that a sheep had been cloned from a somatic cell nucleus from an adult female sheep. This was the first time that an adult vertebrate had been successfully cloned from another adult. He took cells from the mammary gland of an adult (6-year old) pregnant ewe and put them into culture. Culture medium was formulated to keep the nuclei in these cells at the resting stage of the cell cycle (G_0)' They then obtained oocytes (the maturing egg cell) from a different strain of sheep and removed their nuclei. The fusion of the donor cell and the enucleated oocyte was accomplished by bringing the two cells together and sending electrical pulses through them. The electric pulses destabilized the cell membranes, allowing the cells to fuse together. The resulting embryos were eventually transferred into the uteri of pregnant sheep. Of the 434 sheep oocytes originally used in this experiment, only one survived, **Dolly.** Thus, it appeais that the nuclei of adult somatic cells can be totipotent (*see* Fig. 2).

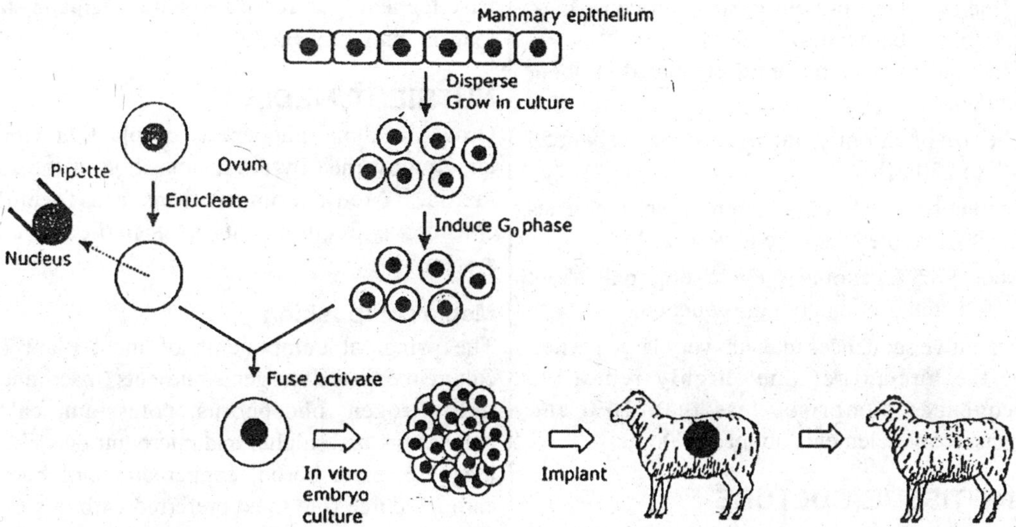

Fig. 2: Cloning sheep by nuclear transfer. The nucleus of an ovum is removed with a pipette. Cells from the mammary epithelium of an adult are grown in culture, and the G_0 state is induced by inhibiting cell growth. A G_0 cell and an enucleated ovum are fused, and the renucleated ovum is grown in culture or in ligated oviducts until an early embryonic stage before it is implanted into a foster mother, where development proceeds to term.

HUMAN GENOME PROJECT (HGP)

The human genome project was a collaborative international, government and private sponsored effort to map and sequence the entire human genome. HGP was formulated by the US. Department of Energy and NIH. The Human Genome Project's ultimate goal was to discover and map all of the approximately 35,000 human genes and make them accessible for further biological study. To facilitate the future interpretation of human gene function, the Human Genome Project also conducted parallel studies on the genetic makeup of other organisms, such as yeast, fruit fly, mice, arabidopsis. After years of multi-billion-dollar research, the Human Genome Project and Celera Genomics (a non-government biotechnology company) jointly announced drafts of the human genome sequence in 2000. By mid-2001, scientists associated with these ventures had presented the true nature and complexity of the digital code inherent in DNA. We now understand that there are approximately 35,000 genes in human nudear DNA, comprised of approximately 3 billion chemical bases arranged in precise sequence.

Salient features of human genome

1. The human genome contains 3164.7 million nudeotide bases.
2. The average gene consists of 3000 base pairs (gene codes for protein dystrophin consists of 2.4 million base pairs).
3. The total number of genes estimated is about 35,000.
4. The size of chromosome is in between about 55 Mb to 250 Mb.
5. Chromosome 1 has maximum number of genes (2968), and the Y has the fewest (231).
6. About 98.5% genome is non-coding (only about 1.5% is the protein coding sequence).
7. Repetitive sequences makeup very large partion of the human genome (highly repetitive sequences comprises less than 10% and transposable elements about 50%).

PLANT TISSUE CULTURE

Cell and tissue culture techniques

Animal or plant cells, removed from tissues, will continue to grow if supplied with the appropriate nutrients and conditions. When carried out in a laboratory, the process is called *Cell Culture*. It occurs *in vitro* (in glass) as opposed to *in vivo* (in life). Plant tissue culture refers to the culture of plant cells and organs such as roots, shoot tips and leaves in artificial. nutrient media aseptically. Tissue culture consists of growing plants cells as relatively on organized masses of cells on an agar medium (callus culture) or as a suspension of free cells and small cell masses in a liquid medium (suspension culture).

Cellular totipotency

The potential of a cell to grow and develop a multicellular or multiorganed higher organism is termed cellular totipotency. Isolated cells from differentiated tissues are generally non-dividing and quiescent; to express totipotency the cells first undergo **dedifferentiation** and then **redifferentiation**. A mature cell reverting to a meristematic state and forming undifferentiated callus tissue is termed dedifferentiation, whereas the ability of a dedifferentiated cell to form a whole plant or plant organs is termed redifferentiation. In animals, the differentiation is irreversible. In contrast to plants where even highly mature or differentiated cells have the ability to regress to a meristematic state as long as they are viable.

NUTRIENT MEDIA

Growth and morphogenesis of plant *in vitro* are largely governed by the composition of the culture media. Media compositions are formulated considering requirements of a particular culture system.

Media composition

The principal components of most plant tissue culture media are inorganic nutrients (macronutrients like nitrogen, phosphorus, potassium, calcium, magnesium and sulphur and micronutrients like iron, magnese, zinc, boron, copper and molybdenum), carbon source (the most preferred carbon source in plant tissue culture is sucrose), organic supplements such as yeast extract, growth regulators, antibiotics such as kanamycin and a gelling agent (agar). The concentration of inorganic and organic constituents in the plant tissue culture media is expressed in mass values (mg/1 or ppm).

Growth regulators

It is namely auxins (such as IAA, 2,4-D, IAA), cytokinins (BAP, 6-benzylaminopurine and kinetin are the most commonly used cytokinin), gibberelins, and abscisic acid. The ratio of auxins and cytokinins is important with respect to morphogenesis in the culture system. For callus root initiation the requisite ratio of auxins to cytokinins is high, while the reverse leads to axillary and shoot proliferation. Gibberellins and abscisic acid occasionally used in tissue culture.

AUXINS

Indole-3-acetic acid (IAA), Indole-3-butyric acid (IBA), 1-naphthaleneacetic acid (NAA), Phenylacetic acid (PAA), 2,4-dichlorophenoxyacetic acid (2,4-D), 2,4,5-trichlorophenoxyacetic acid (2,4,5-T), Picloram, Dicamba, p-chlorophenoxyacetic acid (CPA).

Main effects in tissue culture system

1. Adventious root formation (at high concentration)
2. Adventitious shoot formation (at low concentration)
3. Induction of somatic embryos (in part 2,4-D)
4. Cell division
5. Callus formation and growth
6. Inhibition of outgrowth of axillary buds
7. Inhibition of root growth.

CYTOKININS

Zeatin (Z), Zeatinriboside (ZR), Isopentenyladenine (iP), Isopentenyladenosine (iPA), 6- benzyl-aminopurine (BAP), Kinetin, Thidiazuron (TDZ).

Main effects in tissue culture system

1. Adventitious shoot formation (at high concentration) 2. Inhibition of root formation
3. Cell division
4. Callus formation and growth
5. Stimulation of outgrowth of axillary buds
6. Inhibition of shoot elongation
7. Inhibition of leaf senescence.

GIBBERELLINS

Gibbereilin 1 (GAl), Gibberellin 3(GA3), Gibberellin 4 (GA4), Gibberellin 7 (GA7)

Main effects in tissue culture system

1. Shoot elongation
2. Release seeds, somatic embryos, apical buds and bulbs from dormancy
3. Inhibition of adventitious root formation.

ABSCISIC ACID

It is mostly occurs in angiosperms and gymnosperms. In plants Abssisic acid is from carotenoids.

Main effects in tissue culture system

1. Maturation of somatic embryos
2. Facilitation of acclimatization
3. Bulb and tuber formation
4. Promotion of the development of dormancy.

ETHYLENE

Ethylene is made from methionine its synthesis requires O_2 is inhibited by CO_2.

Main effects in tissue culture system

1. Senescence of leaves,
2. Ripening of fruits
3. Promotion or inhibition of adventitious regeneration (depending on the time of application or on the genotype).

POLYAMINES

Main effects in tissue culture system

1. Promotion of adventitious root formation
2. Promotion of shoot formation
3. Promotion of somatic embryogenesis.

JASMONIC ACID

Jasmonic acid (Ja), Methyljasmonate (MeJa).

Main effects in tissue culture system

1. Promotion of tuber and bulb formation
2. Enhancement of meristem formation.

Solidifying agents

Gelling or solidifying agents are commonly used for preparing semisolid or solid tissue culture media. Agar, a polysaccharide obtained from seaweeds, has several advantages over other gelling agents. First, agar gels do not react with media constituents. Secondly, they are not digested by plant enzymes and remain stable at all feasible incubation temperatures.

Sterilization of nutrient media and plant material

The nutrient media used in tissue cultures are commonly sterlized by autoclaving and filter sterlization. Vitamins, amino acids, plant extracts, hormones and carbohydrates are thermolabile and may decompose during autoclaving. The solutions of these compounds require filter sterlization. In this process the solutions are passed through a bacteria proof membrane-filter under positive pressure. Plant organs or tissues are, only surface-sterilized by treatment with a disinfectant solution at suitable concentrations for a specified period. The most common sterlizing agents are 1-2% sodium hypochlorite, 9-10% calcium hypochlorite and 70% ethanol.

TYPES OF CULTURE

Callus Cultures and Suspension Cultures

Callus is an unorganized, undifferentiated mass of cells. Tissues and cells cultured on an agar media forms callus is known as *callus culture.*

Tissues and cells cultured in a liquid medium produce a suspension of single cells and cells clumps of few to many cells; these are called *suspension cultures.* Liquid cultures must be constantly agitated to facilitate aeration and dissociation of cell clumps into smaller pieces. Suspension cultures grow much faster than callus cultures.

Somatic embryogenesis

A somatic embryo is an embryo derived from a somatic cell, other then zygote. Somatic embryogenesis is the process of a single cell or a group of cells initiating the developmental pathway that leads to reproducible regeneration of non-zygotic embryos capable of germinating to form complete plants *(zygotic embryos* those formed by fertilized egg *i.e.*, zygote and *non-zygotic embryos* those formed by cells other than the zygote). Somatic embryos are bipolar structures in that they have a radicle and a plumule.

Application

- Mass multiplication of elite germ plasm.
- Production of artificial seeds.
- As source material for embryogenic protoplasts.
- For genetic transformation.
- Production of primary metabolites specific to seeds such as lipids in oil seeds.

Meristem culture

Cultivation of axillary or apical shoot meristems, particularly of shoot apical meristem, is known as meristem culture. Meristem culture involves the development of an already existing shoot meristem and subsequently, the regeneration of adventitious roots from the developed shoots. It usually does not involve the regeneration of a new shoot meristem.

Application

- Production of virus free germplasm.
- Mass production of desirable genotypes.

Embryo culture

The embryo of different developmental stages, formed within -the female gametophyte through sexual process, can be isolated aseptically from the bulk of maternal tissues of ovule, seed or capsule and cultured *in vitro* under aseptic condition to grow directly into plantlet.

Application

- Overcoming embryo abortion due to incompatibility barriers.
- Overcoming seed dormancy and self-sterility of seeds.
- Embryo rescue in distant (interspecific or intergeneric) hybridization where endosperm development is poor.
- Production of monoploids.
- Shortening of breeding cycle.
- For development of callus cultures.

HAPLOID CULTURE

Anther culture or pollen culture

Anther culture (called androgenesis) is a technique by which the developing anthers from unopened flower bud are cultured on a nutrient medium where the microspores within the cultured anther develop into callus tissue or embryoids that give rise to haploid plantlets *(androgenic haploid)* either through organogenesis or embryogenesis.

The basic principle of anther and pollen culture is the production of haploid plants exploiting the totipotency of microspore and the occurrence of single set of chromosome (n) in microspore. The first report showing that isolated anthers of *Datura innoxia* were able to form haploid embryos *in vitro* was published by Indian scientists, Guha and Maheshwari.

Application

- Production of haploid plants.
- Production of homozygous diploid lines through chromosome doubling, thus reducing the breeding cycle.
- Production of useful gametoclonal variations.

Ovary/ovule culture

Development of haploid from unfertilized cells of embryosac present in ovary/ovule. It was first reported in Barley by San Noeum.

Application

- Production of haploid plants.
- Recovery of hybrid embryos overcoming embryo abortion at very early stages of development of zygote due to incompatibility barriers.
- Achievement of *In vitro* fertilization.

Somaclonal and gametoclonal variation

Plants derived from tissue culture has been variously referred to as somaclones or calliclones or protoclones and the variations displayed by such plants are simply called somaclonal variation. According to Larkin and Scowcroft (1986), somaclonal variation is the genetic variability which is regenerated during tissue culture. Variations for karyotype, isoenzyme characteristics and morphological variations in somaclones. have been commonly observed. Such variations manifest themselves as heritable mutation and persist in the plant population even after transplantation to the field. **Gametoclonal variation** for variant clones specifically raised from gametic or gametophytic cells.

9. PRINCIPLES OF BIOTECHNOLOGY

RECOMBINANT DNA TECHNOLOGY AND BIOTECHNOLOGY

INTRODUCTION

Recombinant DNA technology (also known as genetic engineering, molecular biology technology or cloning) is the set of techniques that enables DNA from different sources to be identified, isolated, and recombined, so that new characteristics can be introduced into an organism. One of the main technique in recombinant, DNA technology is **DNA cloning** (because it produces an unlimited number of identical copies of a particular DNA segment). It is a technique for artificially and deliberately modifying DNA (genes) to suit human needs. The recombinant DNA technique was engineered by *Stanley Norman Cohen* and *Herbert Boyer* in 1973.

What is DNA cloning?

DNA cloning is the production of large number of identical DNA molecules from a single ancestral DNA molecule. The essential characteristic of DNA cloning is that the desired DNA fragments must be *selectively amplified* resulting in a large increase in copy number of selected DNA sequences. In practice, this involves multiple rounds of DNA replication catalyzed by a DNA polymerase acting on one or more types of template DNA molecule. Essentially two different DNA cloning approaches are used (*see* Fig. 1).

Cell-based DNA cloning

This was the first form of DNA cloning to be developed, and is an *in vivo* cloning method. The first step in this approach involves attaching foreign DNA fragments *in vitro to* DNA sequences which are capable of independent replication. The recombinant DNA fragments are then transferred into suitable host cells where they can be propagated selectively.

Cell-free DNA cloning

The polymerase chain reaction (PCR) is a newer form of DNA cloning Which is enzyme mediated and is conducted entirely *in vitro*.

The essence of cell-based DNA cloning involves following steps.

Cell-based DNA cloning requires attachment of DNA fragments to purified replicons *in vitro* condition and propagation in suitable host cells.

Construction of recombinant DNA molecules

Recombinants are hybrid DNA molecules consisting of autonomously replicating DNA segment plus inserted elements. Such hybrid molecules are also called *chimera*. Construction of recombinant DNA molecules by *in vitro* covalent attachment (ligation) of the desired DNA fragments (target DNA) to a replicon (any sequence capable of independent DNA replication). This step is facilitated by cutting the target DNA and replicon molecules with specific restriction endonucleases before joining the different DNA fragments using the enzyme DNA ligase.

Transformation

The recombinant DNA molecules are transferred into host cells (often bacterial or yeast cells) in which the chosen replicon can undergo DNA replication independently of the host cell chromosome(s).

Selective propagation of cell clones

Selective propagation of cell clones involves two stages. Initially the transformed cells are plated out by spreading on an agar surface *in* order to encourage the growth of *well-separated* cell colonies. These are cell clones (populations of identical cells all descended from a single cell). Subsequently, *individual* colonies can be picked from a plate and the cells can be further expanded in liquid culture.

Isolation of recombinant DNA clones

Isolation of recombinant DNA clones by harvesting expanded cell cultures and - selectively isolating the recombinant DNA.

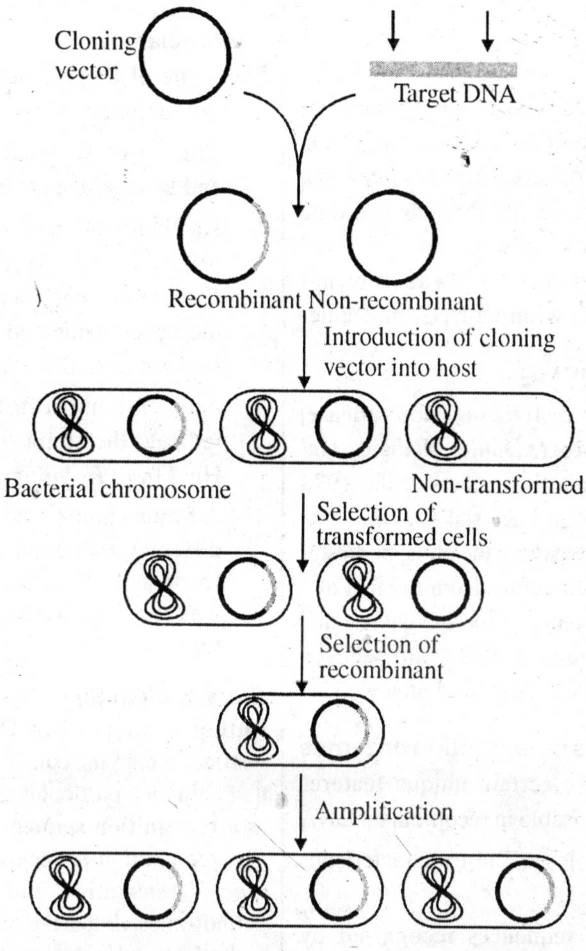

Fig. 1: *An overview of DNA cloning bacteria using a plasmid vector*

TOOLS OF RECOMBINANT DNA TECHNOLOGY

Enzymes For DNA Manipulation

The enzymes used in the molecular biology fall into four broad categories:

Template-dependent DNA Polymerase

DNA polymerase enzymes that synthesize new polynucleotides complementary to an existing DNA or RNA template. Different types of DNA polymerase used in gene manipulation.

DNA polymerase I (Kornberg polymerase) has both the 3' -5' and 5'-3' exonuclease activities and 5'-3' polymerase activity.

Reverse transcriptase, also known as RNA-directed DNA polymerase, synthesizes DNA from RNA.

Reverse transcriptase was discovered by *Howard Temin* at the University of Wisconsin; and independently by *David Baltimore* at about the same time. The two shared the 1975 Nobel Prize in Physiology or Medicine. ***Taq*** **DNA polymerase,**

DNA polymerase derived from a thermostable bacterium (*Thermus aquaticus*). Operates at 72°C and is reasonably stable above 90°C and used in PCR.

Nucleases

Enzymes which degrade DNA molecules by breaking the phosphodiester bonds that link one nucleotide to the next. There are two different kinds of nuclease:

- Exonucleases remove nucleotides one at a time from the end of a DNA molecule.
- Endonucleases are able to break internal phosphodiester bonds within a DNA molecule.

RESTRICTION ENZYME

A restriction enzyme (or **restriction endonudease**, discovered by Werner Arber, Daniel Nathans, and Hamilton Smith, for which they received the 1978 Nobel Prize in Medicine), a bacterial enzyme, cuts double-stranded DNA by cleaving the phosphodiester bonds. The term *restriction* comes from the fact that these enzymes restrict the entry of foreign DNA in the bacteria. Restriction enzymes therefore are believed to be evolved by bacteria to resist viral attack.

Special characteristics of restriction enzymes

Restriction enzymes have certain unique features which make them indispensable in recombinant DNA technology and biotechnology. These characteristics are listed below:

- The restriction site sequences recognized by most restriction enzymes are palindromes.
- Most restriction enzymes are highly specialized to such an extent that they recognize only a single restriction site.
- The restriction site is recognized irrespective of the DNA source.

Nomenclature

The name of any restriction endonuclease consists of four parts.

1. The letter R or M to designate restriction endonuclease or methyl-transferase respectively.
2. An abbreviation of the genus and species of the organism to three letters, e.g. *Econ* for *Escherichia coli* identified by the first letter of the genus name and the first two letters of the specific epithet.
3. A letter, number or combination of the two to indicate the strain of the relevant species e.g. Hind from *H. influenzae* from strain Rd.
4. A Roman numeral to indicate the order in which different restriction modification systems were found in the same organism or strain, e.g., Dsa VI was the sixth restriction modification system found in *Dactylococcopsis salina.*

Sites of cleavage

Rather than cutting DNA indiscriminately, a restriction enzyme cuts only double-helical segments that contain a particular nucleotide sequence, known as a **recognition sequence**-always in the same way. The recognition sequences for the vast majority of *type II* restriction endonucleases are normally palindromes, that is the sequence of bases is the same on both strands when read in the 5' to 3' direction, as a result of a twofold axis of symmetry. Restriction enzymes make either blunt or staggered cut. Thus, restriction fragments may have:

```
              ↓
5′-G-A-T-T-T-C-3′                5′-G-A-T     A-T-C-3′
   |||  ||  ||  ||  ||  |||   EcoRV     |||  ||  ||     ||  ||  |||
3′-C-T-A-A-A-G-5′   ———→     3′-C-T-A     T-A-C-5′
              ↑
        Cleavage site                   Blunt (flush) cut
```

Overhanging ends (the cleavage points do not fall on the symmetry axis, so that the resulting restriction fragments possess so-called 5' *overhangs* or 3' *overhangs.* Overhanging ends generated by cleavage with a restriction nuclease are often described as *sticky ends* or *cohesive termini* because the two overhanging ends of each fragment are complementary in base sequence, and will have a tendency to associate with each other, or with any other similarly complementary overhang, by forming base pairs.

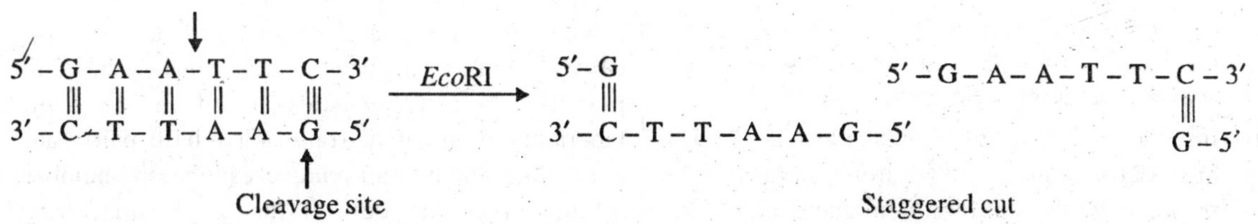

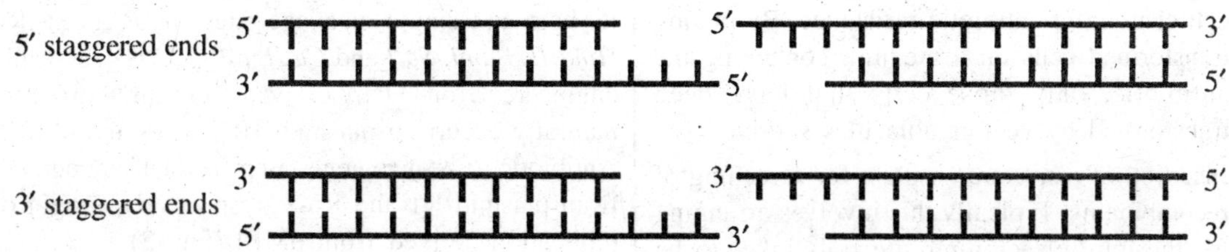

Different fragments with the same sequences in their overhanging ends can be generated by:

1. Cutting with the same restriction nuclease;
2. Cutting with different restriction endonucleases that happen to recognize the same target sequence (isoschizomers); or
3. By cutting with enzymes which have different recognition sequences but happen to produce compatible sticky ends.

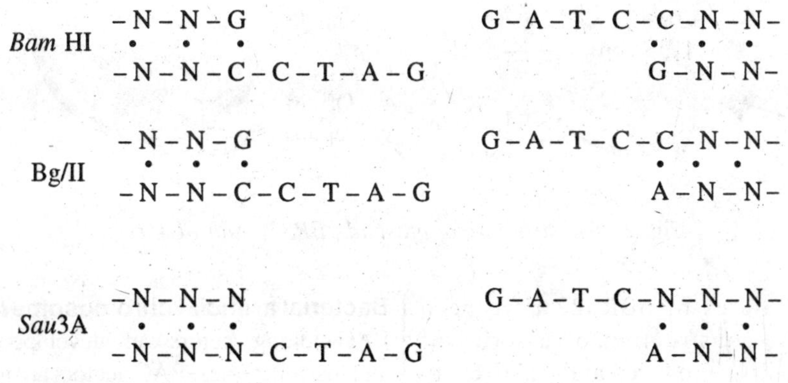

CLONING VECTORS

An autonomously replicating genetic element used to carry a complementary DNA or fragments of genomic DNA into a host cell for the purpose of gene cloning. A viral DNA or plasmid can used as a cloning vector.

CLONING VECTORS FOR *E.coli*

1. Cloning vectors based on plasmid

Plasmids are naturally occurring 'circular, extrachromosomal, autonomously replicating DNA, present in many prokaryotic and few eukaryotic organisms. Plasmid vectors provide a simple way of cloning small DNA fragments in bacterial (and simple eukaryotic) cells. The ideal plasmid cloning vector must have small size, high copy number, own origin of replication, restriction sites for many restriction enzymes and selectable markers. Thus, in order to adapt natural plasmid molecules as cloning vectors, several modifications are normally made:

- Insertion of a multiple .cloning site *polylinker.* This is a short (~30 bp) synthetic sequence which contains unique restriction sites for a variety of common restriction nucleases (pre-existing restriction sites for these enzymes will be deleted from the plasmid if necessary to ensure the presence of unique cloning sites) .
- Insertion of an *antibiotic resistance gene.* The host cells that are used must naturally be sensitive to the antibiotic in question so that any vector molecule which transforms a host cell can confer antibiotic resistance. By plating transformed cells on a medium containing the antibiotic, only those cells that have been transformed by vector molecules survive.
- Insertion of a *selection system* for screening of recombinants. Typically this involves arranging for the multiple cloning site polylinker to be inserted into an expressible gene or gene fragment within the plasmid.

An example of a widely used cloning *'Vector* is pBR322, which replicates in *Ecoli.* In pBR322, p stands for plasmid and BR stands for its developer Bolivar and Rodriguez. '322' distinguishes this plasmid from others developed in the same laboratory. It is small (only 4361 base pairs) and maintain in the host in relatively high copy number, 20-30 copies per cell. It has genes conferring ampicillin resistance and tetracycline resistance on its host and single cleavage sites for *Pst*I; EcoRI, *HindIII, BamI, Sal/I* and *ClaIL* pBR322 is genetically engineered from DNA derived from three different naturally occurring plasmids (R1, R6-S and pMBl). Antibiotic resistance genes amp^R and tet^R are derived from plasmid R1 and R6-S, respectively. Origin of replication derived from pMBl (Fig. 2).

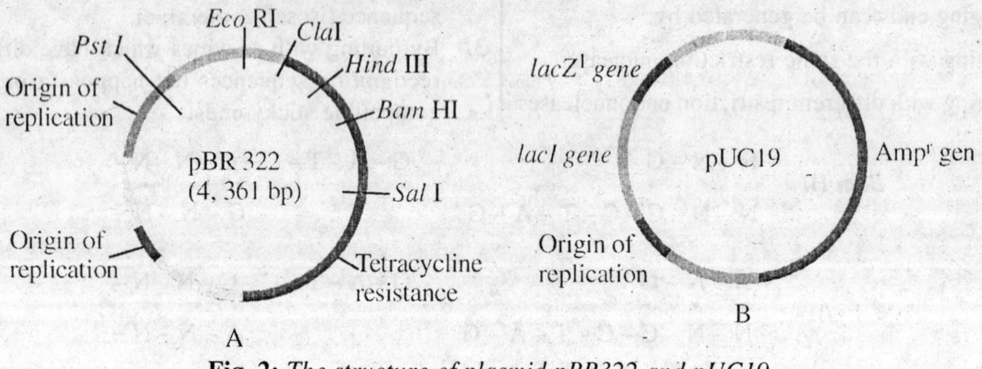

Fig. 2: *The structure of plasmid pBR322 and pUC19*

The valuable features of pBR322 have been enhanced by the construction of a series of plasmids termed pUC (produced at the University of California). The plasmid vector pUC19 (2,686 bp long) contains a polylinker with unique cloning sites "for multiple restriction nucleases and an ampicillin resistance gene to permit identification of transformed cells. In addition, selection for recombinants is achieved by insertional inactivation of a component of the β-galactosidase gene, a complementary portion of this gene being provided by using a specially modified *E. coli* host cell.

Bacterial artificial chromosome (BAC)

BAC cloning vectors were developed by Mel Simon and his colleagues. BAC vectors are maintained in *E. coli* as large single copy plasmids and contain insert of 50-300 kb. BAC vectors contain the F-plasmid origin of replication, F-plasmid genes that 'control plasmid replication and plasmid copy number and the 'bacterial chloramphenicol acetyltransferase gene for plasmid selection.

2. Cloning vectors based on viral DNA

Viral vectors, in which the gene or genes of interest are incorporated into the genome of a virus. Because viruses infect cells with high efficiency, the cloned gene can be introduced into cells at a significantly higher frequency than by simple transformation. Some viral vectors are specialized for producing high levels of proteins encoded by the cloned genes and other viral vectors, such as the bacterial M13-based vectors, are designed to facilitate sequencing and the generation of mutations in cloned genes.

Cloning Vector based on λ phage

Lambda phage infects bacteria *E. coli* and replicates by a *lytic* or *lysogenic* pathway. Its genome is consists of single linear dsDNA of ~48kb. However, at either end of the molecule is a short 12-nucleotides stretch, in which the DNA is single-stranded described as cohesive ends or sticky ends. The lambda cohesive ends are called the ***cos* sites** and they play two distinct roles during the lambda infection cycle. First, they allow the linear DNA molecule that is injected into. the cell to be circularized. The second role of the *cos* sites is rather different, and comes into play after the prophage has excised from the host genome. At this stage a large number of new lambda DNA molecules are produced by the rolling circle mechanism of replication, in which a continuous DNA strand is 'rolled off' the template molecule. The result is a catenate consisting of a series of linear lambda genomes joined together at the *cos* sites. The role of the *cos* sites is now to act as recognition sequences for an endonuclease that cleaves the catenate at the *cos* sites, producing individual lambda genomes.

In the *lytic pathway,* viral functions are fully expressed: viral DNA and proteins are quickly produced and packaged' into virus particles, leading to the lysis of the host cell and release of virus particles, or *virions.* In the *lysogenic pathway,* the phage DNA becomes inserted into the host-cell genome and can be replicated together with host-cell DNA for many generations, remaining inactive. Certain environmental changes can trigger the expression of this dormant viral DNA, which leads to the formation of progeny virus and lysis of the host. Large segments of the ~48-kb DNA of lambda phage are not essential for productive infection and can be replaced by foreign DNA, thus making lambda phage an ideal vector. Several major types of cloning vector have been developed by modifying phage lambda.

REPLACEMENT λ VECTORS

Only DNA molecules from 37 to 52 kb in length can be stably packaged into the λ. particle. The central segment of the λ genome contains genes that are required for the lysogenic cycle but are not essential for lytic function. As a result, it can be removed and replaced by a foreign DNA fragment. Using this strategy, it is possible to clone foreign DNA up to 23 kb in length, and such vectors are normally used for making genomic DNA libraries.

INSERTION λ VECTORS

Lambda vectors used for making cDNA libraries do not require a large insert capacity (most cDNAs are <5 kb long). Design of insertion vectors often involves modification of the lambda genome to permit insertional cloning into the cI gene.

COSMIDS

Cosmids are vectors that are hybrids of lambda phages and plasmids, and their DNA can replicate in the cell like that of a plasmid or be packaged like that of a phage. However, cosmids. can carry DNA inserts about three times as large as those carried by lambda itsef (as large as about 45 kb). The key is that most of the lambda phage structure has been deleted, but the signal sequences that promote phage-head stuffing cos sites remain. This modified structure enables phage heads to be stuffed with almost all donor DNA. Cosmid DNA can be packaged into phage particles by using the *in vitro* system.

The development of cosmid vectors was based on the observation that a about 200 bp DNA sequence in the lambda genome called *cos* is required for lambda DNA packaging into phage particles during lytic infection. Cleavage at *cos* by the lambda terminase protein during phage packaging produces a 12 nucleotide cohesive end at the termini of the linear lambda genome. Recircularization of the lambda genome after bacterial infection is facilitated by base pairing between the complementary cohesive ends. Cosmid cloning vectors with DNA inserts of 30-45 kb can be packaged in vitro into lambda phage particles, provided that the ligated double-strand DNA contains lambda *cos* sequences on either side of the insert DNA. Because the lambda phage head can hold up to 45 kb of DNA, the optimal ligation reaction in cosmid cloning produces recombinant molecules with *cos* sequences flanking DNA segments of about 40 kb. *E.coli* cells infected with cosmid-packaged phage are able to support autonomous replication of circular cosmid plasmids because a ColEl origin of replication and the beta lactamasegene *(amp)* are linked to the cos sequence.

Cosmids contain the F plasmid origin of replication and a l. *cos* site. They are similar to cosmids but have a lower copy number in *E.coli* (Fig. 3).

Cloning vectors based on M13 phage

A very useful vector for cloning DNA, M13 *phage* is especially useful for sequencing the inserted DNA. This filamentous virus contains 6.4-kb single-stranded circle of DNA. M13 enters *E.coli* through the bacterial *sex* pilus, a protein appendage that permits the transfer of DNA between bacteria. The single-stranded DNA in the virus particle [called the (+) strand] is replicated through an intermediate. circular double-stranded replicative form (RF) containing (+) and (–) strands. Only the (+) strand is packaged into new virus particles.

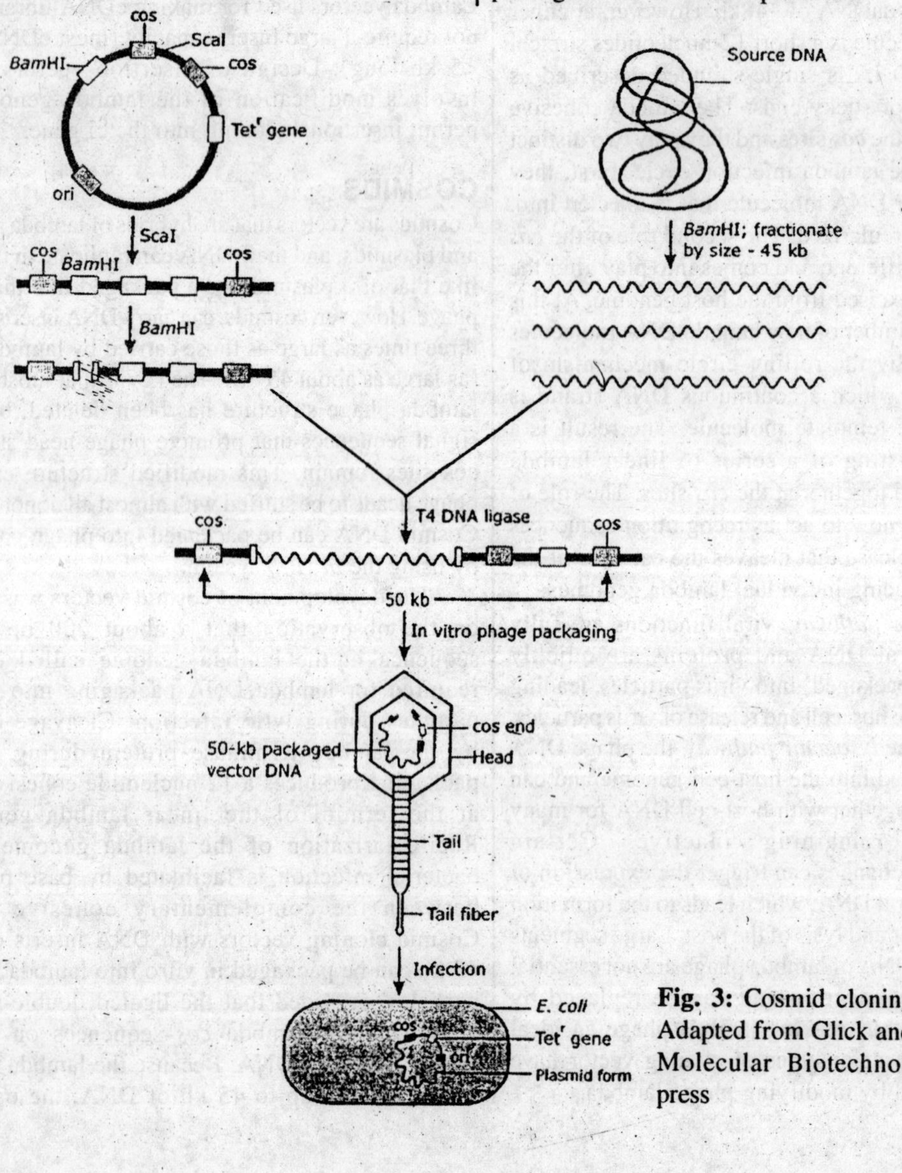

Fig. 3: Cosmid cloning system. Adapted from Glick and Pasternak, Molecular Biotechnology, ASM press

About a thousand progeny M13 are produced per generation. A striking feature of M 13 is that it does not kill its bacterial host. Consequently, large quantities of M13 can be grown and easily harvested (1 gram from 10 litres of culture fluid).

An M13 vector is prepared for cloning by cutting its circular RF DNA at a single site with a restriction enzyme. The cut is made in a *polylinker* region that contains a series of closelv spaced recognition sites for restriction enzymes; only one of each such sites is present in the vector. A double-stranded foreign DNA fragment produced by cleavage with the same restriction enzyme is then ligated to the cut vector. The foreign DNA can be inserted in two different orientations becouse the ends of both DNA molecules are the same. Hence, half the new (+) strands packaged into virus particles will contain one of the strands of the foreign DNA, and half will contain the other strand. Infection of *E.coli* by a single virus particle will yield a large amount of single-stranded M13 DNA containing the same strand of the foreign DNA. DNA cloned into M13 can be easily sequenced (Fig. 4).

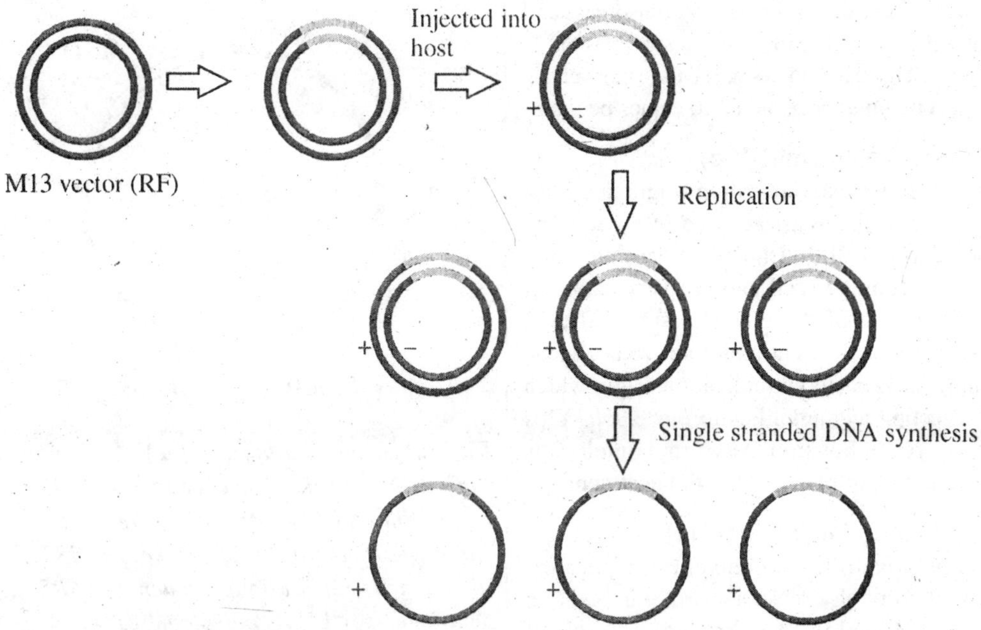

Fig. 4: *Production of single-stranded recombinant DNA using M13.*

PHAGEMID, VECTORS

Phagemid vectors are plasmids DNA which constains a small segment of the genome of a filamentous phage, such as M13, fd or f1. The selected phage sequences contain all the *cis*-acting elements required for DNA replication and assembly into phage particles they permit success ful cloning of inserts several kilobases long (unlike M13 vectors in which such inserts had to be unstable). Following transformation of a suitable *E.coli* strain with a recombinant phagemid, the bacterial cells are *superinfected* with a normal filamentous **helper phage,** such as M13, fl, which is require to provide the coat protein. Phage particles secreted from the superinfected cells will be a mixture of helper phage and recombinant phagemids. The mixed single-stranded DNA population can be used directly or DNA sequencing because the primer for initiating DNA strand synthesis is designed to bind specifically to a sequence of the phagemid vector adjacent to the cloning site.

Bacteriophate P1

Bacteriophage P1 vectors are very similar to λ vectors, being based on a deleted version of a natural phage genome, the capacity of the cloning vector being determined by the size of the deletion and the space within the phage particle. The P1 genome is larger than the λ genome, and the phage particle is bigger, so a P1 vector can clone larger fragments of DNA than a λ vector, up to 125 kb using current technology.

CLONING VECTORS FOR EUKARYOTES

Cloning vectors for Yeast, *S. cerevisiae*

S. *cerevisiae* has a genome of approximately 2×10^7 base pairs contained in 17 linear chromosomes, and some strains possess a type of plasmid known as the **2-micron circle.** This plasmid has 6,318 base pairs and is present in a copy number of about 50 copies per cell.

Yeast Integrative plasmid (YIp)

YIp vectors lack a yeast replication origin and must be integrated into the yeast genome in order to be maintained during cell division. They are normally present at one copy per cell and are very stable. It consists of segment of the *E.coli* plasmid pBR322 containing a selectable antibiotic resistance gene (Ampicillin) and a bacterial replication origin which facilitate selection and amplification in *E.coli.* YIps integrate by recombination between homologous sequences on the YIp plasmid and the host genome.

Yeast Replicating Plasmids (YRp)

YRp vectors contain an Autonomous Replicating Sequence (ARS) of chromosomal origin in addition to the elements found in YIps. YRps are capable of autonomous replication, are present at 3-30 copies per cell.

Yeast Episomal Plasmids (YEp)

YEp vectors are based on the ARS from the endogenous yeast 2μ plasmid which contains genetic information for its own replication and segregation. They are capable of autonomous replication, are present at 20-200 copies per cell.

Yeast Centromeric Plasmids (YCp)

YCp vectors contain both an *ARS* and a yeast centromere. The *ARS* can be either chromosomal or 2μ in origin. YCps are normally present at one copy per cell, can replicate without integration into a chromosome and are stably maintained during cell division.

Yeast artificial chromosomes (YAC)

M. Olsen and colleagues described the first generation of yeast cloning vectors that were based on artificial chromosome. YACs is used for cloning *very* large DNA fragments. These vectors are propagated in S. *cerevisiae* rather than in *E.coli* and are based on chromosomes, rather than on plasmids or viruses (Fig. 5).

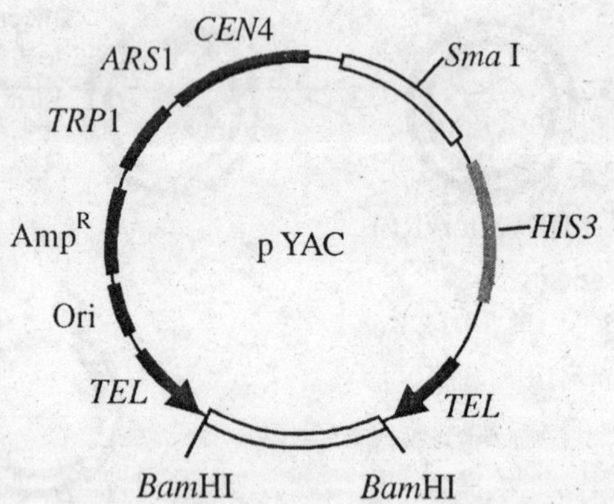

Fig. 5: *Schematic diagram of a YAC cloning vector, indicating prokaryotic gene for resistance to ampicillin (AMP^R), prokaryotic replication origin (ori), yeast auxotrophic markers (HIS3, TRP1), autonomous replicationg sequences (ARS1), yeast centromeres (CEN4), and telomeres (TEL).*

The essential functional components of chromosomes are:

Centromeres, required for disjunction of sister chromatids in mitosis and of homologous chromosomes at the first meiotic division;

Telomeres, required for complete replication of linear molecules and for protection of the ends of the chromosome from nuclease attack;

Autonomous replicating sequence (ARS) elements, acts as origin of replication and *Selectable marker* to select positively for chromosomal maintenance.

SHUTTLE VECTORS

Shuttle vectors are plasmids capable of propagating and transferring (shuttling) genes between two different organism, one of which is typically a prokaryote *(E.coli)* and others a eukaryote (e.g., yeast). Shuttle vectors must have unique origins of replication for each cell type as well as different markers for selection of transformed host cells harboring the vector.

Table: Maximum DNA insert possible with different cloning vectors

Vector	Host	Insert size
M13	*E. coli*	1-4 kb
Plasmid	*E. coli*	1-5 kb
λ phage	*E. coli*	5-25 kb
Cosmids	*E. coli*	35-45 kb
P1 phage	*E. coli*	70-100 kb
PACs	*E. coli*	100-300 kb
BACs	*E. coli*	≤300 kb
YACs	*S. cerevisiae*	200-2000 kb

Source - Principle of gene manipulation by **S.B.Primrose**, **R.M.Twyman** and **R.W.Old** (modified)

CLONING VECTORS FOR PLANTS

Cloning vectors for plants are either plasmid or viral genome based.

- Plasmid based vector
- Viral genome based vector

Ti plasmid based vector

Ti plasmid present in *Agrobacterium tumefaciens. A. tumefaciens* is naturally occurring, gram negative, soil bacteria with two common species, viz. *A. tumefaciens* and *A. rhizogenes.* These are being considered as *natural genetic engineers* for their ability to transform plants. *A. tumefaciens* cause crown gall disease (when *Agrobacterium rhizogenes* infects plants, the production of adventitious roots rather than tumour, is induced at the site of infection) by transferring a defined segment of DNA (called T-DNA) from its tumor inducing (Ti) large sized plasmid of about 200 kb into the nuclear genome of cells in an infected wound on many dicotyledonous plants. T-DNA varies in size between 15 and 30kb depending on the strain. T-DNA carry genes for *phytohormone* (auxin and cytokinin) and opines. The overproduction of phytohormones at the site of infection is responsible for the proliferation of wound cells into a gall (tumour) that can harbour a population of the bacteria. Unusual compound *opines* (octopine, nopaline) are catabolized by *Agrobacterium* (Fig. 6).

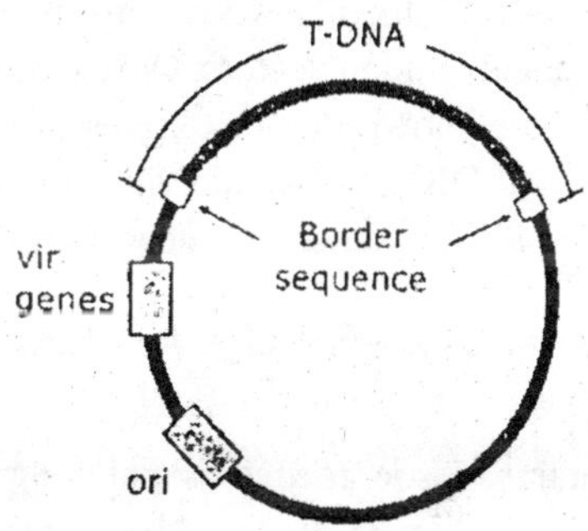

Fig. 6: *Schematic representation of a Ti plasmid. The T-DNA is defined by its left and right borders and includes genes for the biosynthesis of auxin, cytokinin, and an opine; these genes are transcribed and translated only in plant cells. Outside of the T-DNA region, there is a cluster of vir genes, a gene(s) that encodes an enzyme(s) for opine catabolism, and an origin of DNA replication (ori) which permits the plasmidto be stably maintained in A. tumefaciens.*

The movement of the T-DNA is mediated by genes in another region of Ti plasmid called *vir* genes (virulence genes). The virulence genes are not themselves transferred with the T-DNA but mediate the transfer. The *vir* genes. caused T-DNA transfer to plant cell is analogous to transfer of plasmids during bacterial conjugation. Following transfer, T-DNA get integrated with the host genome.

These properties of *Agrobacterium* DNA transfer system are invaluable for developing a powerful vector system for plant transformation. Any genes put in the T-DNA region, gets transferred to the plant genome. The DNA is inherently stable once in the plant genome since neither the border nor the virulence genes are transferred.

The Ri plasmid of A. *rhizogenes* and Ti plasmids are very similar, the main difference being that transfer of the T-DNA from an Ri plasmid to a plant result not in a crown gall but in hairly root disease.

VIRAL VECTORS

The potential of few plant viruses as cloning vectors has been explored. One major problem with vast majority of plant viruses is that they have RNA genome not DNA genome. RNA viruses are not useful as potential cloning vectors. Only two classes of DNA virus are known to infect higher plants, the caulimoviruses (dsDNA) and geminiviruses (ssDNA), and neither is ideally suited for gene cloning.

CLONING VECTORS FOR ANIMALS

For Insects

P element, a transposon, is used as a cloning vector in *Drosophila.* P element are 2.9 kb in length and contain three genes flanked by short inverted repeat sequences at either end of the element. The genes code for transposase, the enzyme that carries out the transposition process. The inverted repeats form the recognition sequences that enable the enzyme to identify the two ends of the inserted transposon. The vector is a plasmid that carries two P elements, one of which contains the insertion site for the DNA that will be cloned. Insertion of the new DNA into this P element results in disruption of its transposase gene. But the second P element carried by the plasmid has an intact version of the transposase gene that provides transposase enzyme to carry out transposition.

Cloning vectors for insects based on viral DNA are not common. However, dsDNA of **baculoviruses** are used as cloning vector for many insects.

For mammal

Genome of many viruses are used cloning vectors for mammal. First cloning vector for mammalian cell was based on SV40 virus genome. SV40 is a small virus that infect monkey (simian). Now genome of many viruses such as adenoviruses, papillomaviruses which have a relatively high insert capacity are used as vectors for cloning genes in mammalian cells. At present, retroviruses are the most commonly used vectors.

SELECTION OF TRANSFORMED CELLS

Identification of cells containing the vector molecule requires the presence of suitable marker gene on the vector molecule whose expression provides a means of identifying cells containing it. Two popularly used marker gene systems are based on:

- **Antibiotic resistance genes :** A host cell strain is chosen that is sensitive to a particular antibiotic, often ampicillin, tetracycline or chloramphenicol. The corresponding vector has been engineered to contain a gene which confers resistance to the antibiotic. After transformation, cells are plated on agar containing the antibiotic to rescue cells transformed by the vector (Fig. 7).

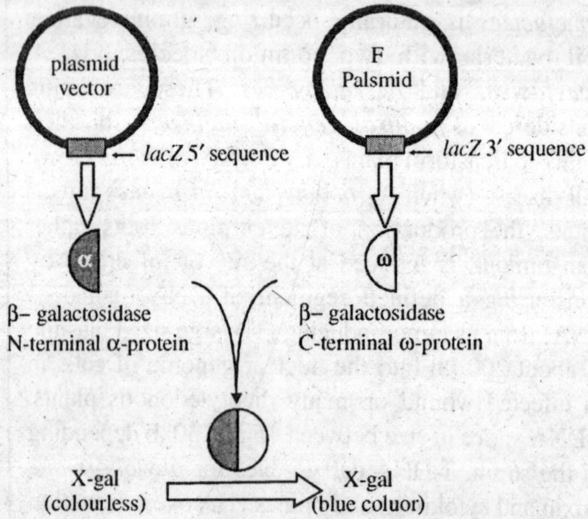

Fig. 7: *Galactosidase activity can be used as an indicator of gene function plasmids that express the N-terminal α-fragment of β-galactosidase can be used in E.coli strains expressing the C-terminal ω fragment of β-galactosidase on an F' plasmid.*

- **β-galactosidase gene complementation :** The host cell is a mutant which contains α-fragment of the β-galactosidase gene but cannot make any functional β-galactosidase. The vector is engineered to contain a different fragment of the β-galactosidase gene. After transformation by the vector, *functional complementation* occurs resulting in active β-galactosidase which can be assayed by acting on a colourless substance, *Xgal* (S-bromo, 4-chloro, 3-indolyl β-d-galactopyranoside), to make a blue product.

RECOMBINANT SCREENING

A selective medium enables transformants to be distinguished from non-transformants. The next problem is to determine which of the transformed colonies comprise cells that contain recombinant DNA molecules, and which contain self-ligated vector molecules. With most cloning vectors insertion of a DNA fragment into the plasmid destroys the integrity of one of the genes present on the molecule. Recombinants can therefore be identified because the characteristic coded by the inactivated gene is no longer displayed by the host cells (called insertional inactivation).

Most commonly the recombinant selection is carried out by insertional inactivation of antibiotic resistance gene. In this case insertion of new DNA fragments (insert) occurs at the site within the gene that confers resistance towards a particular antibiotic.

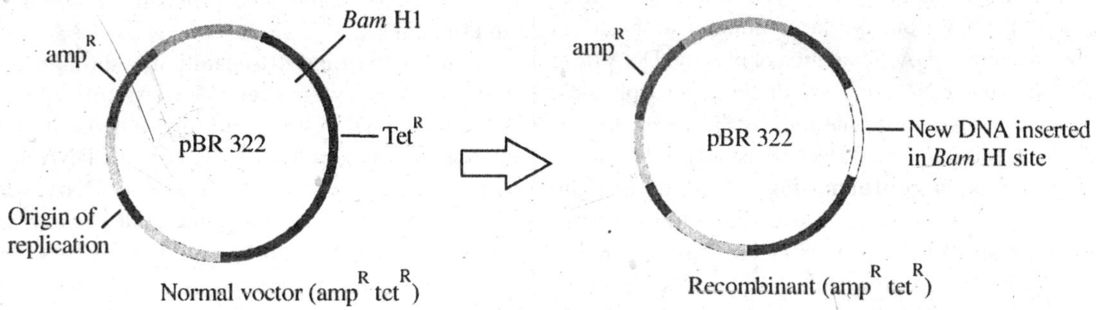

Insertional inactivation does not always involve antibiotic resistance genes. For example in pUC8, gene LacZ′, which codes for part of enzyme β-galactosidase is used for insertional inactivation. Recombinant pUC8 involves insertional inactivation of the lac Z′ gene, canbe identified because of their inability to synthesize β-galactosidase. β-galactosidase, coded by lacZ gene, causes the breakdown of lactose to glucose plus galactose. lacZ′, a modified lacZ gene, codes for the a-peptide portion of b-galactosidase.

BOX: DNA ISOLATION AND PURIFICATION

DNA isolation and purification involve disruption and lysis of the starting material followed by the removal of proteins and other contaminants and finally recovery of the DNA. The cells are lysed using a detergent, and then mixed with 1:1 mixture of phenol and chloroform. These organic solvents precipitate proteins but leave the nucleic acids (DNA and RNA) in aqueous solution. Before the phenol extraction the cell extract is treated with protease like proteinase K for complete removal of proteins. Aqueous solution of nucleic acids can then- be removed.

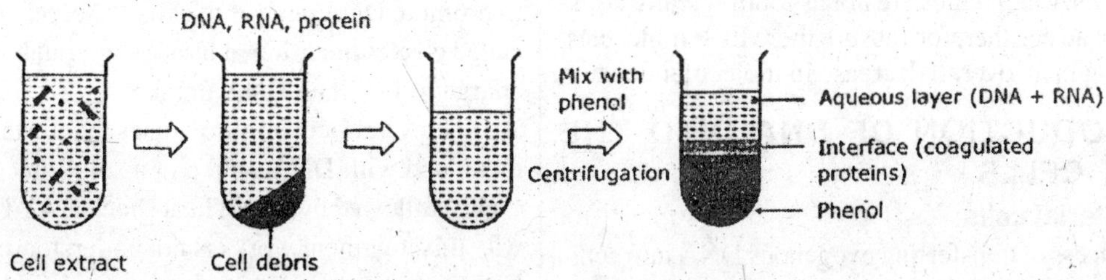

DNA can be purified by centrifugation through a CsCl density gradient. Suspended DNA is mixed with CsCl and ethidium bromide and centrifuged for several hours. The DNA band is collected from the centrifuge tube, extracted with isopropanol to remove the ethidium bromide, and then precipitated with ethanol to recover the DNA.

Plasmid purification

For plasmid purification the bacterial cells extract is deproteinized, the RNA removed, and the DNA concentrated by **ethanol precipitation.** Ethanol precipitation involves the precipitation of nucleic acid by using absolute ethanol in the presence of salt and at a temperature of -20°C or less. In a plasmid purification it is always necessary to separate the plasmid DNA from the large amount of bacterial chromosomal DNA. Separation of plasmid DNA from chromosome DNA are based on the several physical differences like conformation, size, between plasmid DNA and chromosomal DNA. Plasmids and bacterial DNA differ in **conformation.** Plasmids and the bacterial chromosome are circular, but during preparation of the cell extract the chromosome is always broken to given linear fragments. Plasmids are covalently closed circular DNA and present in supercoiled conformation. If one of the polynucleotide strands is broken the double helix reverts to its normal **relaxed** state.

Supercoiled molecules can be easily separated from non-supercoiled DNA. One method of separation is through **alkaline** denaturation. If sodium hydroxide is added to a cell extract containing linear and supercoiled DNA then the hydrogen bonding in linear (non-supercoiled) DNA molecules is broken, causing the double helix to unwind and the two polynucleotide chains to separate. If acid is then added, these denatured bacterial DNA strands reaggregate into a tangled mass. The insoluble network can be pelleted by centrifugation, leaving pure plasmid DNA in the supernatant.

Another method of separation is through **CsCl buoyant density gradient centrifugation** in the presence of DNA intercalating dye EtBr. EtBr intercalation causes local unwinding of DNA helix, which reduces the molecular density of DNA. Large linear genomic DNA (non-supercoiled) molecules can bind more EtBr than supercoiled DNA owing to the difference in their topology.

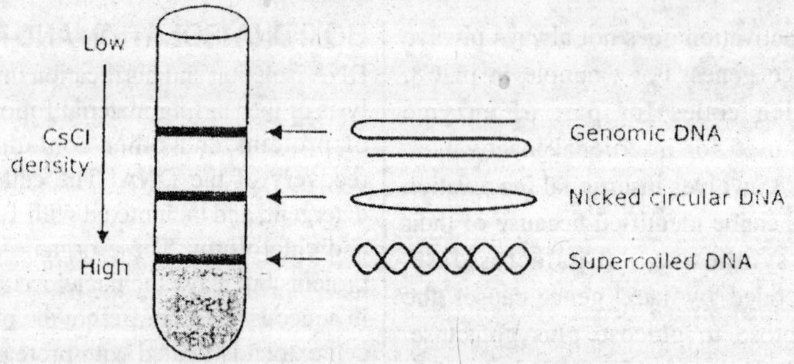

Because supercoiled plasmid DNA cannot be easily unwound, much less EtBr can intercalate. In contrast, linear DNA molecules are not as topologically constrained and can therefore absorb more EtBr molecules, resulting in an overall decrease In molecular density.

INTRODUCTION OF DNA INTO THE HOST CELLS

In bacterial cells

The process of transferring exogenous DNA into cells, called **transformation.** There are basically two general methods for transforming bacteria. The first is a chemical method utilizing CaCl) and heat shock to promote DNA entry into cells. A second method is called **electroporation**, it uses a short pulse of electric charge to facilitate DNA uptake.

The chemical method uses bacteria that are incubated with DNA on ice in a solution containing $CaCl_2$) followed by a brief heat shock at 42°C. Exactly why this treatment works is not understood. Possibly $CaCl_2$) causes the DNA to precipitate onto the outside of the cells, or perhaps the salt is responsible for some kind of change in the cell wall that improves DNA binding.

In plant cells

There are two kinds of gene transfer methods in plants: Direct (vector less) and *indirect* (vector medipted) gene transfer.

Direct gene transfer uses physical, electrical or chemical means to deliver gene of interest in to the host plant cell. These methods are species and genotype independent in terms of DNA delivery. The examples of direct gene transfer are like Liposome encapsidation, Electroporation of protoplasts, Microinjection, Particle bombardment, Physio-chemical uptake of DNA and others.

Physico-chemical uptake of DNA

This method is based on the ability of the protoplast to uptake the foreign DNA from the surrounding solution. Isolated plasmid DNA is mixed with the protoplasts in the presence of polyethylene glycol (PEG). After 15-20 minutes of incubation, the protoplasts are cultured in the presence of appropriate selective agent. Protoplasts are regenerated and putative transgenic plants are further characterized for confirmation.

Liposome encapsidation

Liposome encapsidation procedure was developed to protect the foreign DNA during the transfer process. DNA enclosed in the lipid vesicles penetrates into the protoplasts where lipase activity of the protoplast dissolves the lipid vesicles and DNA gets released for integration into the host genome.

Electroporation of protoplasts

Electroporation involves the creation of pores in the cell membrane using electrical impulses of a high field strength. Reversible breakdown of the membrane allows the entrance of foreign DNA. Generally, protoplasts are used since they have exposed plasma membrane.

Microinjection

Extensively used with the animal cell, microinjection of DNA into plant cells has achieved only a limited success. This is largely because of difficulties in getting the protoplasts immobilized and injecting DNA into the protoplast without damaging the tonoplast, which surrounds the plant cell vacuole.

Particle bombardment

Particle bombardment or microprojectile bombardment or biolistic transformation employs foreign DNA coated high velocity gold or tungsten particles (0.2-0.4 μm) to deliver into plant cells. Different approaches are being used to accelerate the particles. 'Particle gun' accelerated particles penetrates even deep into the tissues. This method is being widely used because of its ability to deliver foreign DNA into regenerable cells, tissues or organs irrespective of the monocots or dicots. Because of the physical nature of the process there is no biological limitation to the actual DNA delivery, thus it is genotype independent.

Vector mediated gene transfer: Among the various vectors used in plant transformation, the Ti and Ri plasmid of *A.,tumefaciens and A. rhizogenes,* respectively has been used extensively. These bacteria are also known as natural genetic engineers of plants since these bacteria have ability to transfer T-DNA of their plasmid into plant genome upon infection of cells at the wound site. Ti and Ri plasmids can be used as gene vectors for delivering useful foreign genes into target plant cells and tissues. The foreign gene is cloned in the T-DNA region of Ti plasmid in place of unwanted sequences.

In animal

There are four general classes of gene transfer methodology that can be applied to cultured animal cells, but *transduction* and *transfection* are the most widely used.

Transduction is virus-mediated gene transfer, in which the foreign DNA is packaged inside a virus particle. **Transfection** involves the use of chemical or physical methods to persuade cells to take up DNA from the culture medium. There are numerous different transfection methods - chemical transfection, liposome-mediated transfection, lipofection, electroporation, receptor-mediated endocytosis.

Direct gene transfer method involves the direct physical introduction of DNA into the cell. The common example is **microinjection**. Microinjection is usually applied to animal eggs, zygotes or early embryos. **Particle bombardment,** which involves the acceleration of high-velocity DNA coated microprojectiles into cells, is another direct transfer method.

BIOPHYSICAL METHODS

POLYMERASE CHAIN REACTION

PCR is a rapid and versatile *in vitro* method for amplifying defined target DNA sequences present within a source of DNA. This technique was formulated in 1985 by *Kerry Mullis.* Usually, the method is designed to permit *selective amplification* of a specific target DNA sequence(s) within a heterogeneous collection of DNA sequences (e.g. total genomic DNA or a complex cDNA population). To permit such selective amplification, some prior DNA sequence information from the target sequences is required. This information is used to design two oligonucleotide primers (amplimers) which are specific for the target sequence and which are often about 15-25 nucleotides long. After the primers are added to denatured template DNA, they bind specifically to complementary DNA sequences at the target site. In the presence of a suitably heat-stable DNA polymerase and DNA precursors (the four deoxynucleoside triphosphates, dATP, dCTP, dGTP and dTTP), they initiate the synthesis of new DNA strands which are complementary to the individual DNA strands of the target DNA segment, and which will overlap each other.

Primer design: To permit selective amplification, some prior DNA sequence information from lhe target DNA is required. The information is used to design two primers (amplimers), which are specific for sequences flanking the target DNA sequence. So, for most PCR reactions, it is very important to reduce the chance of the primers binding to other locations in the DNA than the desired one. Hence certain rules for primer design that are important to consider. These rules follow:

1. **Primer length:** Length of the primers should not be very short or long. If the primers are too short they might hybridize to non-target sites and give undesired amplification products. Similarly, long primer influences the rate at which it hybridizes to the template DNA; long primers hybridize at a slower rate.
2. **Base composition:** The GC content should be betweem 40 and 60% with an even distribution of all four nucleotides.
3. **Nature of sequences:** Inverted repeats or any self-complementary sequences >3bp in length are to be avoided.
4. **Melting temperature:** Tm values for two primers used together should not differ by >5°C and the Tm of the amplification product should not differ from those of the primers by > 10°C.

Reaction cycle

The PCR is a chain reaction because newly synthesized DNA strands will act as templates for further DNA synthesis in subsequent cycles. After about 25 cycles of DNA synthesis, the products of the PCR will include, in addition to the starting DNA, about 10^5 copies of the specific target sequence. PCR consists of a series of cycles of three successive reactions:

- **Denaturation,** typically at about 93-95°C for human genomic DNA.
- **Primer annealing** at temperatures usually from about 50°C to 70°C depending on the T m of the expected duplex (the annealing temperature is typically about 5°C below the calculated T m). Annealing temperature must be low enough to enable hybridization between primer and template, but high enough to prevent mismatched hybrids from forming. This temperature can be calculated by determining the melting temperature or Tm of the primer-template hybrid. The T m can be determined experimentally or calculated from the simple formula:

$$Tm = (4 \times [G + C]) + (2 \times [A + T])\ °C$$

- **DNA synthesis,** typically at about 70-75°C.

These three steps **denaturation, primer annealing** and **DNA synthesis** constitute one cycle of the PCR amplification and can be carried out repetitively just by changing the temperature of the reaction mixture. The thermostability of the polymerase makes it feasible to carry out PCR. Suitable heat-stable DNA polymerases have been obtained from microorganisms whose natural habitat is hot springs. For example, the widely used *Taq* DNA polymerase is obtained from *Thermus aquaticus* and is thermostable up to 94°C, with an optimum working temperature of 80°C. Other thermostable DNA polymerase currently used in PCR are *pfu (Pyrococcus furiosus), Bst E (Bacillus stearothermophilus), Tth (Thermus thermophilus).*

After each cycle, the number of templates doubles, so that if one starts with a single double-stranded DNA molecule, after 20 cycles the number of molecules synthesized by the PCR is 1 x 10^6, and after 30 cycles the number of molecules increases to 1 x 10^9. This number is obtained by applying the following formula:

$$M_f = M_I \times 2^n$$

Where M_I is the initial number of molecules (template), M_f is the final number of DNA segments produced by the PCR, and n is the number of cycles performed.

MODIFICATIONS TO THE PCR TECHNIQUE

Nested PCR

Nested PCR increases the specificity of DNA amplification, by reducing non-specific amplification of DNA. Two sets of primers are being used in two successive PCR reactions. In the first reaction, one pair primers is used to generate DNA products, which besides the intended target, may still consist non-specifically amplified DNA fragments. The product(s) are then used in a second PCR reaction with a set of primers whose binding sites are just downstream of the first primer, or *nested* between the original set of primers. Binding sites are completely or partially different from the primer pair used in the first reaction, but are completely within the DNA target fragment.

Asymmetric PCR

Asymmetric PCR is used to preferentially amplify one-strand of the original DNA more than the other. It finds use in some types of sequencing and hybridization probing where having only one of the two complementary stands is required. PCR is carried out as usual, but with a great excess of the primers for the chosen strand.

RT-PCR

RT-PCR (Reverse Transcription PCR) is a method used to amplify, isolate or identify a known sequence from a cellular or tissue RNA. The PCR reaction is preceded by a reaction using reverse transcriptase to convert RNA to cDNA.

Hot-start PCR

Mixing of all PCR reagents prior to an initial heat denaturation step allows more opportunity for non-specific binding of primer sequences. Hot-start PCR is a technique that reduces non-specific amplification during the initial set up stages of the PCR. The technique may be performed manually by simply heating reaction components briefly at the melting temperature (e.g., 95°C) before adding the polymerase.

Quantitative PCR

Quantitative PCR is used to measure the quantity of a PCR product. It is the method of choice to quantitatively measure starting amounts of DNA, cDNA or RNA. Quantitative PCR is commonly used to determine whether a DNA sequence is present in a sample and the number of its copies in the sample. The method with currently the highest level of accuracy is *Quantitative real-time PCR.* It is often confusingly known as **RT-PCR** (Real Time PCR). Real Time PCR is used to quantify gene expression and also to screen for mutations and single nucleotide polymorphisms.

Touchdown PCR

Touchdown PCR is a method used to increase specificity without compromising yield. The principle is to initiate synthesis at very high annealing temperatures which permit only perfectly matched primer-template hybrids to form. The annealing temperature is dropped in a stepwise fashion with each cycle. Once copies of the target sequence have begun to accumulate over the first few cycles, high temperature annealing becomes much less critical for specificity, as it is previous products which form the major template. These products are unlikely to have any sites for mispriming. The benefit of decreasing the annealing temperature is to increase the probability of stable primer-target interaction.

RACE (Rapid amplification of cDNA ends)

RACE is a PCR based method for locating precise start and end points of gene transcripts. First step in this method is conversion of mRNA into cDNA with reverse transcriptase. One of the primer used during reverse transcription is specific for an internal region close to beginning (5'-end) of the gene under study. Since only a small segment of mRNA is copied, the cDNA so generated will correspond exactly with the start of the mRNA. After synthesis of above cDNA, a short poly(A) tail is attached to its 3' end and it is subjected to normal PCR. The second primer will anneal to this poly(A) sequence and converts the single stranded cDNA into a double stranded molecule, which is subsequently amplified as the PCR proceeds. The sequence of the final PCR product will reveal precise position of the start or 5'-end of the transcript. This is known as 5′-RACE, so called because its results in amplification of the 5'-end of the starting RNA (Fig. 8).

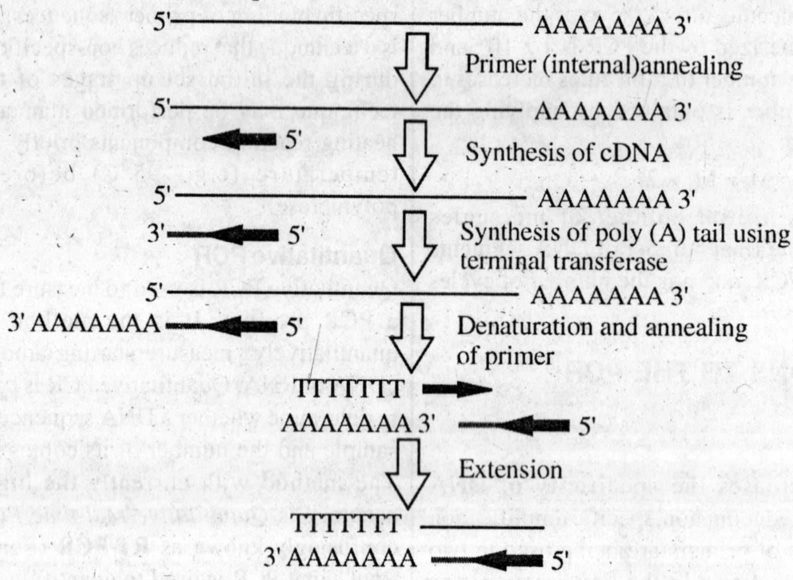

Fig. 8: *5' RACE. An internal primer is used to primer synthesis from a mRNA template. A poly(A) is added to the 3' end of the cDNA using terminal transferase. Second strand synthesis is prime using second primer.*

In 3′-RACE for isolation of 3′-end of an RNA, mRNA is first reverse transcribed to cDNA. PCR amplification of this cDNA is then carried out using a primer specific to known sequence in the mRNA under study (close to its 3'-end) and an oligo U primer. Nested PCR is then performed to improve specificity. These 5' and 3' RACE products can than be used to isolate full length cDNAs in a few days compared to weeks required for screening cDNA libraries.

NUCLEIC ACID HYBRIDIZATION

Nucleic acid hybridization is a fundamental tool in molecular genetics which takes advantage of the ability of individual single-stranded nucleic acid molecules to form double-stranded molecules (that is, to hybridize to each other). For this to happen, the interacting single-stranded molecules must have a sufficiently high degree of base complementarity. Nucleic acid hybridization is used to identify related or identical molecules. Nucleic acid hybridization assays involve a labeled nucleic acid **probe** to identify related DNA or RNA molecules present within a complex mixture of unlabeled nucleic acid molecules, the target nucleic acid. Nucleic acid hybrids can be formed between two strands of DNA, two strands of RNA, or one strand of DNA and one of RNA.

Nucleic acid hybridization provides a means for detecting DNA or RNA sequences that are complementary to any isolated nucleic acid, such as a viral genome or a cloned DNA sequence. Nucleic acid hybridization can be used to detect homologous DNA or RNA sequences not only in cell extracts, but also in chromosomes or intact cells - a- procedure called *in situ* hybridization. In this case, the hybridization of radioactive or fluorescent probes to specific cells or subcellular structures is analyzed by microscopic examination. For example, labeled probes can be hybridized to intact chromosomes in order to identify the chromosomal regions that contain a gene of interest.

Stringency of a hybridization reaction

Stringency is a term that describes the number of mismatched bases that are allowed in a hybridization reaction and still have a double-stranded hybrid. The more stringent the hybridization conditions are, the fewer the mismatched bases that are allowed before the two strands come apart. Stringency is influenced by the *temperature,* the *salt* concentration of the hybridization mixture and the pH of the hybridization reaction. All three of these conditions affect the stability of the double-stranded molecule. High stringency conditions are usually achieved with high temperatures (approaching the melting temperature of the DNA-DNA hybrid) and low salt concentrations (< 0.1 M). High salt concentrations tend to stabilize the double-stranded molecule and allow more mismatches to take place before the two strands come apart. The pH of the solution in which hybridization takes place also effects the stability of hybridizing molecules. Under slightly acidic conditions (pH 6-7), the double-stranded DNA molecule is more stable because the increased H^+ concentration also helps reduce the repulsive forces between the two backbones of the DNA molecule.

Nucleic acid probe

Nucleic acid used to query a complex heterogenous nucleic acid population in a hydridization assay is called **probe.** Nucleic acid probes are segments of DNA or RNA that can bind with high specificity to complementary sequences of target DNA. Probes can be complementary to either DNA or RNA and can be from as few as 20 bases to many thousands of bases long. Nucleic acid probe may be DNA (DNA probes), RNA (RNA probes) or oligonucleotide (oligonucleotide probes).

RADIOLABELING TECHNIQUES

ISOTOPIC AND NON-ISOTOPIC LABELING OF NUCLEIC ACIDS

Isotopic Labeling

Isotopic labeling of nucleic acids has been conducted by incorporating nucleotides containing radioisotopes. Such radiolabeled probes contain nucleotides with a radioisotope (often ^{32}p, ^{33}p, ^{35}S or ^{3}H), which can be detected specifically in solution or, Much more commonly, within a solid specimen (autoradiography). The intensity of an autoradiographic signal is dependent on the intensity of the radiation emitted by the radioisotope, and the time of exposure, which may often be long (one or more days, or even weeks in some applications). ^{32}p has been used widely in Southern blot hybridization, dot-blot hybridization, colony and plaque hybridization because it emits high energy β-particles which afford a high degree of sensitivity of detection.

Autoradiography

It is a technique of recording an image of a sample containing radioactive elements emitting radioactive particles rays, using photographic film, X-ray sensitive film, an emulsion or other radiation sensitive medium. In autoradiography technique samples are placed directly against the film for a period of time to allow radioactive emission from the sample to interact with a film emulsion and create an image. A photographic emulsion is a suspension of crystal of silver bromide embedded in gelatin, when crystals of silver bromide are struck by charged particle or photon radiation; the silver atoms are ionized and form an invisible latent image. After exposure to the sample, the photographic grains in the emulsion are fixed using standard photographic developer, which removes unionized silver bromide. After one emulsion is developed, each small aggregate of reduced silver atoms become a visible dark spot, collectively they make up the photographic image. Autoradiography has large number of practical applications in the biological, chemical and physical sciences, because it provides both qualitative and quantitative information.

Labeling DNA by nick translation

Nick translation is a technique for radioactively labeling double-stranded DNA, making it suitable as a hybridization probe for detecting specific genomic sequences. It involves introdudion of ss break (nicks) in the DNA. The endonuclease DNase I is used to create nicks in a DNA probe fragment. Following DNase I treatment, DNA polymerase I is used to add nucleotide residues to the free 3'-hydroxyl ends created during the DNase I nicking process. As the DNA polymerase I extends the 3' ends, the 5' to 3' exonuclease activity of the enzyme removes bases from the 5' -phosphoryl terminus of the nick. The sequential addition of base onto the 3' end with the simultaneous removal of bases from the 5' end of the downstream annealed strand results in translation of the nick along the DNA molecule. When performed in the presence of a radioactive deoxynucleoside triphosphate (such as [α–^{32}P] dCTP), the newly synthesized strand becomes labeled (Fig. 9).

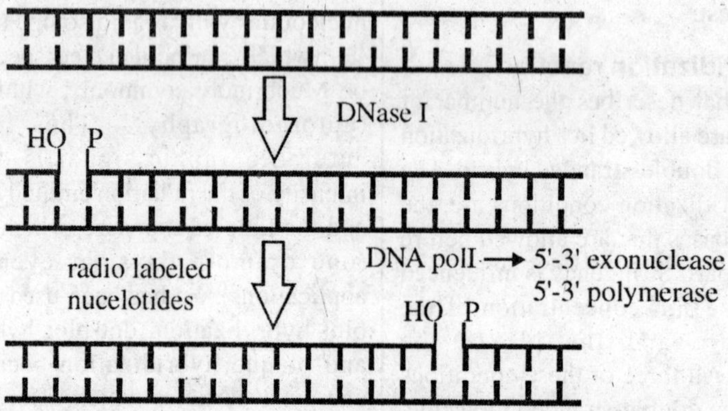

Fig. 9: *Nick translation. DNaseI introduces single-stranded nicks by cleaving internal phosphodiester bonds, generating a 5' phosphate group and a 3' hydroxyl terminus. Addition of DNA polI contributes two enzyme activities - a 5'-3' exonuclease attacks the exposed 5' termini of a nick and sequentially removes nucleotides in the 5'-3' direction and a DNA polymerase adds new nucletotides to the exposed 3' hydroxyl group in the 5'-3' direction.*

End-labeling of DNA

Single-stranded oligonucleotides are usually end-labeled using polynucleotide kinase (kinase end-labeling). Typically, the label is provided in the form of a ^{32}P at the γ-phosphate position of ATP and the polynucleotide kinase catalyses an exchange reaction with the 5'-terminal phosphates. The same procedure can also be used for labeling double-stranded DNA. In this case, fragments carrying label at one end only can then be generated by cleavage at an internal restriction site, generating two differently sized fragments which can be separated by gel electrophoresis and purified.

Nonisotopic labeling

Nonisotopic labeling systems involve the use of nonradioactive probes. Two types of non-radioactive labeling are conducted:

- **Direct nonisotopic labeling,** where a nucleotide which contains the label that will be detected is incorporated. Often such systems involve incorporation of modified nucleotides containing a fluorophore, a chemical group which can fluoresce when exposed to light of a certain wavelength.
- **Indirect nonisotopic labeling,** usually featuring the chemical coupling of a modified reporter molecule to a nucleotide precursor. After incorporation into DNA, the reporter groups can be specifically bound by an affinity molecule, a protein or other ligand which has a very high

affinity for the reporter group. Conjugated to the latter is a marker molecule or group which can be detected in a suitable assay. The reporter molecules on modified nucleotides need to protrude sufficiently far from the nucleic acid backbone to facilitate their detection by the affinity molecule and so a long carbon atom *spacer* is required to separate the nucleotide from the reporter group.

Two indirect nonisotopic labeling systems are widely used:

- The **biotin-streptavidin system** utilizes the extremely high affinity of two ligands: biotin (a naturally occurring vitamin) which acts as the reporter, and the bacterial protein streptavidin, which is the affinity molecule. Biotin and streptavidin bind together extremely tightly with an affinity constant of 10^{-14}, one of the strongest known in biology. Biotinylated probes can be made easily by including a suitable biotinylated nucleotide in the labeling reaction.
- Digoxigenin is a plant steroid (obtained from *Digitalis* plants) to which a specific antibody has been raised. The digoxigenin-specific antibody permits detection of nucleic acid molecules which have incorporated nucleotides containing the digoxigenin reporter group.

HISTOCHEMICAL AND IMMUNOTECHNIQUES

BLOTTING

Blotting is the transfer of nucleic acids and/or proteins from a gel strip to a specialized, chemically reactive matrix called blotting membrane (typically nitrocellulose or activated nylon) on which the nucleic acids/ proteins may become covalently bound in a pattern similar to that present in the original gel.

Southern Blot Hybridization or Southern Blotting

Southern blot hybridizations detect target DNA fragments that have been size-fractionated by gel electrophoresis. This technique was invented in 1975 by E. M. Southern.

In this procedure, the target DNA is digested with one or more restriction endonucleases, size-fractionated by agarose gel electrophoresis, denatured and transferred to a nitrocellulose or nylon membrane for hybridization. During the electrophoresis, DNA fragments, which are negatively charged because of the phosphate groups, are repelled from the negative electrode towards the positive electrode, and sieved through the porous gel. Smaller DNA fragments move faster (Fig. 10).

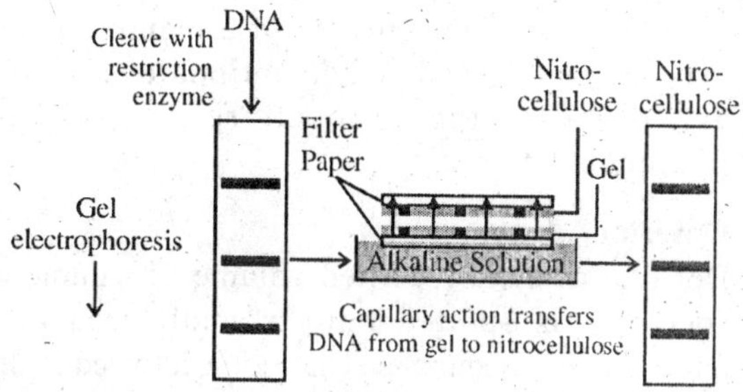

Fig. 10: *The Southern blot technique for detecting the presence of specific DNA sequences. The DNA is denatured and transferred from the gel to a nitrocellulose sheet by capillary action.*

Following electrophoresis, the test DNA fragments are denatured in strong alkali. As agarose gels are fragile, and the DNA in them can diffuse within the gel, it is usual to transfer the denatured DNA fragments by blotting on to a durable nitrocellulose or nylon membrane, to which single-stranded DNA binds readily. The individual DNA fragments become immobilized on the membrane at positions which are a faithful record of the size separation achieved by agarose gel electrophoresis.

Subsequently, the immobilized single-stranded target DNA sequences are allowed to associate with labeled single-stranded probe DNA. The probe will bind only to related DNA sequences in the target DNA, and their position on the membrane can be related back to the original gel in order to estimate their size.

Northern Blotting

Northern blotting or Northern blot hybridization is a variant of Southern blotting in which the target nucleic acid is RNA instead of DNA. In this technique, an RNA extract is electrophoresed in an agarose gel, using a denaturing buffer to insure that the RNAs do not from inter-or intra molecular base pairs. After electrophoresis, the gel is blotted onto a nylon a nitrocellulose membrane, and hybridized with a labelled probe. A principal use of this method is to obtain information on the expression patterns of specific genes.

Western Blotting

Western blotting is a method by which proteins that have been separated and subsequently immobilized on the surface of a membrane are exposed and probed. When antibodies are used as probes, the procedure is called **immunoblotting**.

Dot Blot Assay

Dot blot assay, a specified volume of sample or specimen is spotted onto a small area of a nitrocellulose membrane. The spot is allowed to dry and is then treated with an alkaline solution to break open microbial cells and denature their DNA molecules. A solution of a radioactively labeled probe is added to the membrane and allowed to react. After this, the membrane is washed several times to remove any untreated probe and then allowed to dry. The membrane is covered with a photographic film that is sensitive to radioactivity (e.g., X-ray film) and then placed in a darkroom. The film is developed and examined for the presence of dark spots. A dark spot indicates that the specimen contained DNA sequences that hybridized with the radioactive probe and, therefore, that the sought target DNA is present in the specimen. If no dark spot appears on the film, it can be inferred that no DNA hybridization has occurred.

DNA LIBRARY-GENOMIC LIBRARY

A library encompassing an entire genome. It involves cleavage of the entire genome of a cell with a specific restriction endonuclease and then cloning of each fragment (sometimes called the "shotgun" approach to gene cloning). This technique can produce a very large number of DNA fragments-on the order of a million for a mammalian genome-which will generate millions of different colonies of transfected bacterial cells. Each of these colonies is composed of a clone of cells derived from a single ancestor cell, and therefore harbors many copies of a particular stretch of the fragmented genome. Such a plasmid is said to contain a genomic DNA clone, and the entire collection of plasmids is called a genomic DNA library. But because the genomic DNA is cut into fragments at random, only some fragments contain genes. Many of the genomic DNA clones obtained from the DNA of a higher eukaryotic cell contain only noncoding DNA. The presence of a particular gene is screened by a process of colony or *in situ* hybridization (Fig. 11).

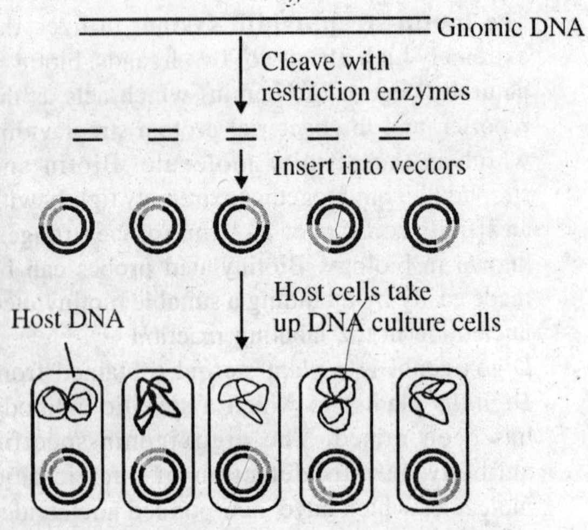

Fig. 11: *A library of genomic clones*

Many clones must be screened to obtain a gene of interest

The number of random cleavage fragments that must be cloned to ensure a high probability that a given sequence is represented at least once in the genomic library is calculated as follows: The probability (P), that some number of clones, *N*, contains a particular fragment representing a fraction, f, of the genome is

$$P = 1 - (1 - f)^N$$

Consequently,

$$N = \ln(1 - P) \ln(1 - f)$$

Thus, to have $P = 0.99$ with fragments averaging 10 kb in length, for the 4639-kb *E. coli* chromosome ($f = 0.00216$), $N = 2134$ clones, whereas for the 180,000-kb *Drosophila* genome ($f = 0.0000606$), $N = 83,000$.

COMPLEMENTARY DNA (cDNA)

cDNA is synthetic DNA made from mRNA with the use of a special enzyme called *reverse transcriptase* originally isolated from retroviruses. With the use of a mRNA as a template, reverse transcriptase synthesizes a single-stranded DNA molecule that can then be used as a template for double-stranded DNA synthesis. Because it is made from mRNA, cDNA is devoid of both upstream and downstream regulatory sequences and of introns. Therefore cDNA from eukaryotes can be translated into functional protein in bacteria (Fig. 12).

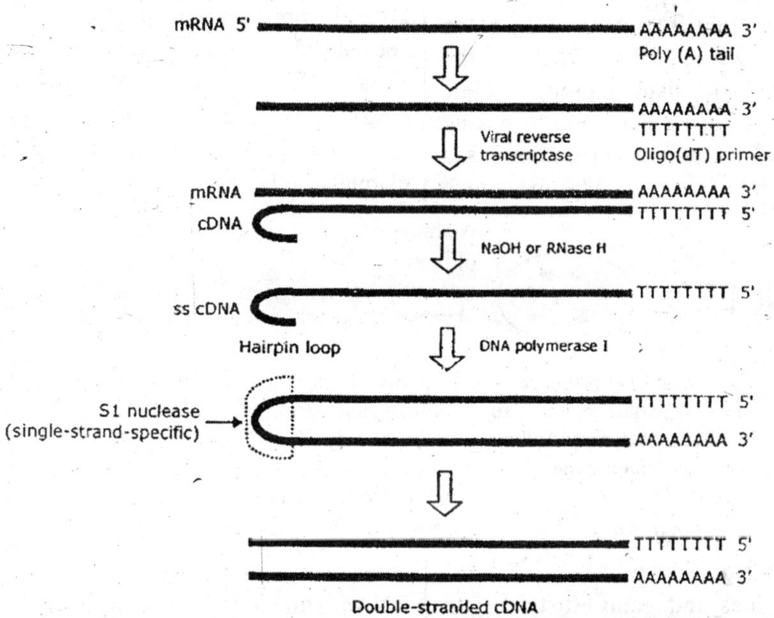

Fig. 12: *The synthesis of double-stranded cDNA from mRNA. A short oligo(dT) chain is hybridized to the poly(A) tail of an mRNA strand. The oligo(dT) segment serves as a primer for the action of reverse transociptase, which uses the mRNA as a template for the synthesis of a complementary DNA strand. The resulting cDNA ends in a hairpin loop. When the mRNA strand has been degraded by treatment with NaOH or RNase H the hairpin loop becomes a primer for DNA polymerase I, which completes the paired DNA strand. The loop is then cleaved by Sl nuclease (which acts only on the single-stranded loop) to produce a double-stranded cDNA molecule. Adapted from J. D. Watson, J. Tooze, and D. T. Kurtz, Recombinant DNA: A Short Course.*

cDNA LIBRARY

The single-stranded DNA molecules synthesized by the reverse transcriptase are converted into double-stranded DNA molecules by DNA polymerase, and these molecules are inserted into a plasmid or virus vector and cloned. Each clone obtained in this way is called a cDNA clone, and the entire collection of clones derived from one mRNA preparation constitutes a *cDNA library.*

There are important differences between genomic DNA clones and cDNA clones. Genomic clones represent a random sample of all of the DNA sequences in an organism and, with very rare exceptions, are the same regardless of the cell type used to prepare them. By contrast, cDNA clones contain only those regions of the genome that have been transcribed into mRNA. Because the cells of different tissues produce distinct sets of mRNA molecules, a distinct cDNA library is obtained for each type of cell used to prepare the library.

METHODS OF CLONE IDENTIFICATION

Once a library has been prepared, a number of procedures can be employed for identification of the desired clone. This is generally achieved by the important technique of *hybridization probing.*

Colony and Plaque Hybridization

Since a genomic library lacks an index, it must be screened for the presence of a particular gene. This is done by a process known as **colony** or **plaque hybridization.** In colony and plaque hybridization, the DNA in plaque or colony is transferred to a nylon or nitrocellulose membrane. The DNA on the membrane is denatured with alkali to produce single strands which are bonded to the membrane by baking or UV irradiation. The membrane is then immersed in a solution containing a nucleic acid probe, which is usually radioactively labeled and incubated to allow the probe to hybridize to its complementary sequence. After hybridization, the membrane is washed extensively to remove unhybridized probe, and regions where the probe has hybridized are then visualized. This is carried out by exposure to X-ray film **(autoradiography)** if the probe was radioactively labeled, or by using a solution of antibody or enzyme and substrate if the probe was labeled with a modified nucleotide. By comparing the membrane with the original dish and lining up the regions of hybridization, the original group of colonies or plaques can be identified (Fig. 13).

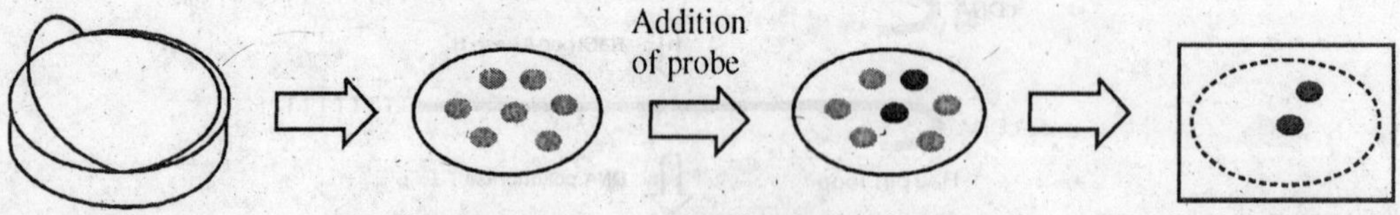

Bacterial colonies are transferred from the surface of an agar culture plate onto nitrocellulose paper.

The filter is treated with detergent to lyse the bacteria and alkali to denature their DNA

The filter is than incubated with nucleic add probe radioactively labeled, ssDNA or RNA which attach by base pairing to complementary DNA present on the filter.

Filter is rinsed and subjected to autoradiography which will make visible only those colonies containing DNA that is complementary in sequence to the probe.

Fig. 13: *Plaque hybridization*

Chromosome Walking

Many eukaryotic genes and gene clusters span enormous tracts of DNA. Some consists of > 1000 kb. With the use of plasmid, phage, or cosmid based genomic libraries, such long DNAs can only be obtained as a series of overlapping fragments. Each DNA fragment that has been isolated is, in turn used as a probe to identify a successive but partially overlapping fragments of that gene. Such a process is known as **chromosome walking** (Fig. 14).

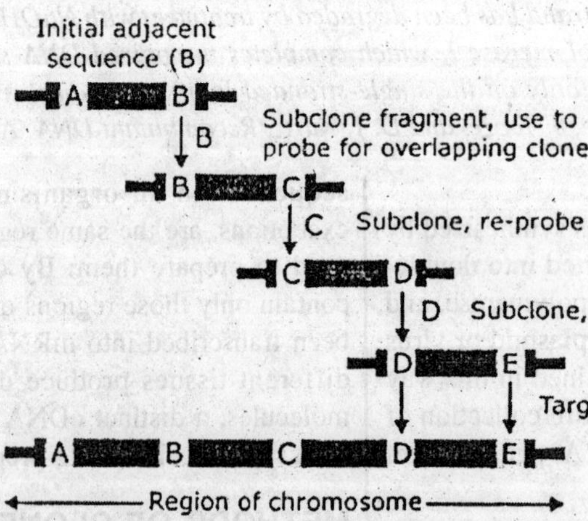

Fig. 14: *Chromosome walking. A subcloned fragment of a linked adjacent sequence recovers overlapping clones from a genomic library*

In this process a DNA segment too large to sequence in one piece is fragmented and cloned. A clone is picked and the DNA insert it contains is sequenced. A small fragment of the insert near one end is subcloned (cloned from a clone) and used as a probe to select a clone containing an overlapping insert, which, in turn, is sequenced. The process is repeated so as to *walk* down the chromosome.

EXPRESSION VECTOR AND GENE EXPRESSION

Expression vectors facilitate the functional transcription of DNA insert and their translation. The production of a desired protein can only be achieved if the cloning vectors have regulatory sites for the initiation of transcription of its gene and translation of its mRNA by the host cell. Expression vectors are vectors that carry a gene that can be efficiently transcribed and translated by the host cell.

For transcription, a *promoter site* and a *terminator site* are necessary. Transcription of the desired gene begins at the promoter site and ends at the terminator site. A *ribosome binding site* upstream from the start codon is also present in many of the expression vectors. This site is required for the efficient initiation of translation in bacteria (Fig. 15).

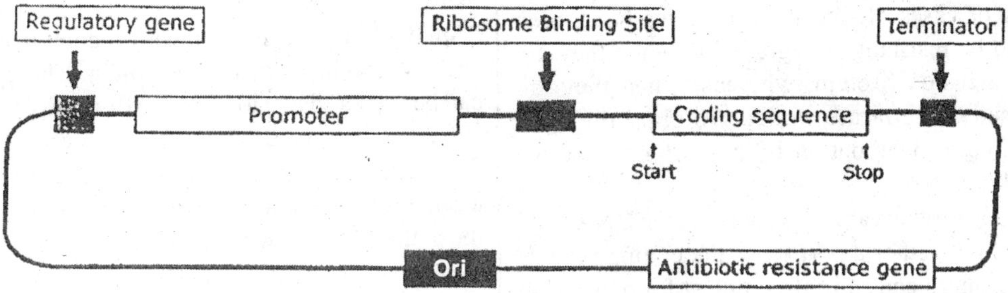

Fig. 15: *Components of a typicl prokarytic expression vector.*

Reporter gene

Reporter gene is a gene producing a protein that can be detected and quantified using a simple assay. They can be used to visualize and measure the efficiency of gene expression, and to investigate intracellular protein localization.

The rate at which a structural gene is expressed depends on its upstream control sequences. Consequently, the rate of expression of a gene can be monitored by replacing its protein-encoding portion with or fusing it in frame to a gene expressing a protein whose presence can be easily determined. Many of the studies to investigate the function of promoters, enhancers and the factors which bind to them have made use of reporter genes. Several reporter genes are used. Most commonly used examples of reporter are the *lacZ* gene of *Escherichia coli,* the *E.coli* gene encoding *chloramphenicol acetyl transferase* (CAT), the firefly gene for *luciferase* and *green fluorescent protein* (GFP) gene. The CAT gene from *E.coli* encodes the enzyme chloramphenicol acetyltransferase, which transfers acetyl groups from acetyl CoA onto the antibiotic chloramphenicol. The *lacZ* gene acts as reporter gene in the presence of X-gal because its level of expression is readily quantitated by the intensity of the blue coluor that is generated. Luciferase catalyzes the oxidation of luciferin with the emission of yellow-green light which can be detected easily and at low levels.

GFP is an autofluorescent protein (238 amino acid residues) of bioluminescent jellyfish *Aequorea victoria.* It acts as a functional fluorophore. It fluoresces with a peak wavelength of 508 nm (green light) when irradiated by UV or blue light (optimally 400 nm). It therefore serve as a unique reporter.

GFP used as a fusion tag for monitoring protein localization. GFP is used as a tag in a fusion protein where it is coupled to the protein whose expression is to be tracked. In such cases, the principal aim is to investigate the subcellular localization of the protein under investigation. Genetic engineering can be used to produce vectors containing a GFP coding sequence into which a coding sequence for an uncharacterized protein, X, can be cloned. The resulting GFP-X fusion construct can be transfected into suitable target cells and expression of the GFP-X fusion protein can be monitored to track the subcellular location of the protein.

Fusion protein

Fusion proteins (also called *hybrid protein, chimeric protein)* are product of two or more coding sequences from different genes that have been cloned together and that, after translation, form a single polypeptide sequence. Fusion protein protects the cloned gene product from attack by host cell proteases. In a number of cases cloned gene proteins have been found to be resistant to degradation when they are part of a fusion protein, whereas, when they are expressed as separate intact proteins, they are susceptible to degradation by proteolytic enzymes (proteolysis).

Fusion proteins are constructed at the DNA level by ligating together a portion of the coding regions of two or more genes. In its simplest form, a fusion vector system entails the insertion of a target gene or gene segment into the coding region of a cloned host gene. Knowledge of the nucleotide sequences of the various coding segments that are joined at the DNA level in necessary to ensure that ligation produces the correct reading frame.

Protein-Protein interaction

Study of interaction between different proteins is very useful as it yields information about the tentative function of a protein through its interaction with well characterized protein with known role or function. Phage display and yeast two hybrid system are two well known and most useful methods for studying protein-protein interactions.

Phage display method was first described by George Smith in 1985. It involves display of a heterologous target protein under study on phage particles. Phage display is a form of expression cloning of foreign genes using phage. Genetic engineering techniques are used to insert foreign DNA fragments into a suitable phage coat protein gene. Initially phage display involved the use of filamentous phages such as fd, f1, M13, where the foreign gene was incorporated into a gene specifying a minor coat protein. The recombinant gene can then be expressed as a fusion protein which is incorporated into the virion and displayed on the surface of the phage which, however, retains infectivity. If an antibody is available for a specific protein, phage displaying the protein can be selected by preferential binding to the antibody.

There are two *main* methods in which phage display can be used to study protein interaction. In one method test protein is displayed and its interaction is sought with a series of purified proteins or protein fragments of known function. In second method a phage display library is prepared. Phage display library made up of many recombinant phage, each displaying a different protein. These libraries can be prepared by cloning a mixture of cDNAs from a particular tissue by cloning genomic DNA fragments. The library consists of phage displaying a range of different proteins and is used to identify those that interact with a test protein (Fig. 16).

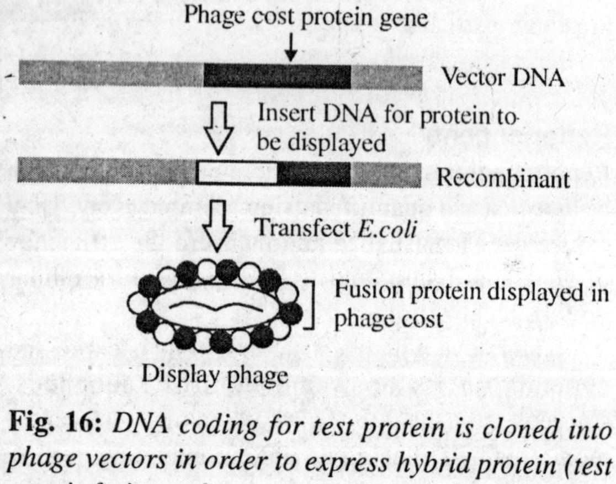

Fig. 16: *DNA coding for test protein is cloned into phage vectors in order to express hybrid protein (test protein fusion to the coat protein) on the phage surface. Phage particles produced by these transformed bacteria therefore display the test protein in their coats.*

Yeast two hybrid assay detects protein interactions in a comparatively more complex way. It is based on the fact that eukaryotic gene expression is promoted by transcription factors called *activators* that contain two distinct domains. One is *DNA binding domain* that binds to regulatory sequences and another is *activation domain* that interacts with

RNA polymerase enzyme and stimulates expression of associated gene. These two domains can be physically separated from each other in which case protein loses its activity but is re-activated when the two domains are brought together.

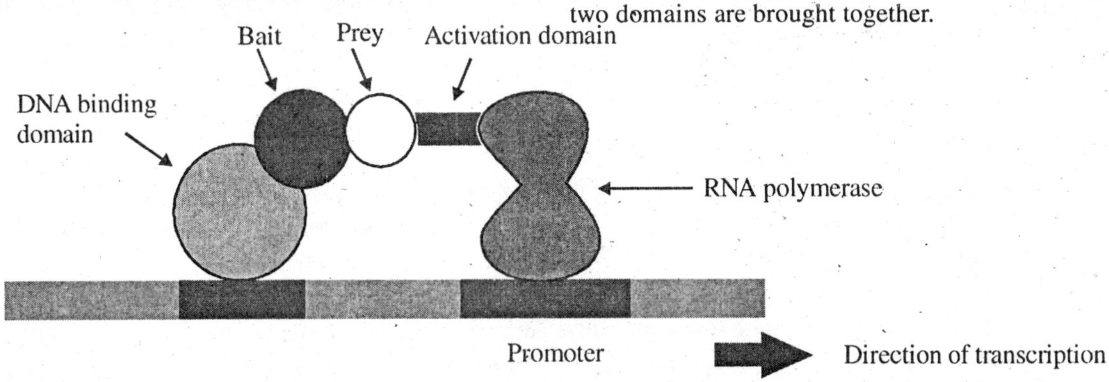

Fig. 17: *Yeast two hybrid system. The activation domain of the yeast transcription factor is fused with a polypeptide called prey. Prey interacts with another polypeptide, bait, which in turn is fused with the DNA1-binding domain of the same transcription factor. Successful transcription of an essential gene is possible only when the bait and the prey interact, bringing together the DNA-binding and the activation domains of the transcription factor.*

Yeast two hybrid system makes use of a *Saccharomyces cerevisiae* strain which lacks activator for a particular reporter gene. Gene for one of the interacting protein called *bait* is fused to the gene coding for DNA binding domain of the activator and specifies synthesis of fusion protein made up of DNA-binding domain and test protein. The recombinant yeast strain is co-transformed with a second construct carrying gene, for the second interacting protein called *prey*, from a c-DNA expression library and gene for activation domain. Reporter gene is expressed only in transformed cells in which *bait* and *prey* genes code for proteins that interact with each other. This given a bait gene its interacting pair the prey can be cloned using a yeast two hybrid system (*see* Fig. 17).

DNA MICROARRAY TECHNOLOGY

Although all of the cells in the human body contain identical genetic material, but the same genes are not active in every cell. Studying which genes are active and which are inactive in different cell types helps scientists to understand both how these cells function normally and how they are affected when various genes do not perform properly. In the past, scientists have only been able to conduct these genetic analyses on a few genes at once. With the development of DNA microarray technology, however, scientists can now examine how thousands of genes express and their product interact at any given time.

A **DNA microarray** (also commonly known as *gene chip*, DNA *chip*, or *gene array)* is a collection of microscopic DNA spots attached to a solid surface, such as glass, plastic or silicon chip forming an array for the purpose of expression profiling, monitoring expression levels for thousands of genes simultaneously.

An *array* is an orderly arrangement of samples. In general, arrays are described as *macroarrays* or *microarrays,* the difference being the size of the sample spots. Macroarrays contain sample spot sizes of about 300 microns or larger and can be easily imaged by existing gel and blot scanners. The sample spot sizes in microarray are typically less than 200 microns in diameter and these arrays usually contain thousands of spots.

A large number of DNA probe, each one with a different sequence, are immobilized at defined positions on a solid surface. The probe can be *synthetic oligonucleotides* (20-25 nt long), short DNA molecules, such as cDNA or PCR products. These can be spotted onto a glass microscope slide or a *piece* or nylon membrane (low density arrays) or on the surface of a wafer of glass or silicon (high density array).

Base-pairing (*i.e.,* A-T and G-C for DNA; A-U and G-C for RNA) or hybridization is the underlining principle of DNA microarray. Microarray technology evolved from Southern blotting, whereby fragmented DNA is attached to a substrate and then probed with a known gene or fragment. To determine which genes are turned on and which are turned off in a given cell, a researcher must first collect the messenger RNA molecules present in that cell. The researcher then labels each mRNA molecule by attaching a fluorescent dye. Next, the researcher places the labeled mRNA onto a DNA microarry slide. The messenger RNA that was present in the cell will then hybridize - or bind - to its complementary DNA on the microarray, leaving its fluorescent tag. A researcher must then use a special scanner to measure the fluorescent areas on the microarray.

If a particular gene is very active, it produces many molecules of messenger RNA, which hybridize to the DNA on the microarray and generate a very bright fluorescent area. Genes that are somewhat active and produce fewer mRNAs, which results in dimmer fluorescent spots. If there is no fluorescence, none of the messenger molecules have hybridized to the DNA, indicating that the gene is inactive. Researchers frequently use this technique to examine the activity of vaiious genes at different times.

Principal application of microarrays

- Expression screening (monitoring of RNA expression levels)
- DNA variation screening (assessing large-scale sequence variation in individuals)

Measuring gene expression using microarrays is relevant to many areas of biology and medicine, such as studying treatments, disease, and developmental stages. For example, microarrays can be used to identify disease genes by comparing gene expression in diseased and normal cells.

SITE-DIRECTED MUTAGENESIS

Site-directed mutagenesis techniques are used to alter the nucleotide sequence of the gene coding for a protein of interest. Conventional mutagenesis is a random process that introduces changes at unspecified positions in a DNA molecule. Hence screening of large numbers of mutated organisms is necessary to find a mutation of interest.

A variety of DNA manipulations can be used to introduce mutations into cloned genes. The simplest are to delete a restriction fragment, to open the DNA at a restriction site and remove a few nucleotides, or to insert new DNA at a restriction site. These are relatively large-scale changes. By the technique called oligonucleotide **directed mutagenesis** one can alter a single nucleotide at a specified position. One version of oligonucleotide directed mutagenesis is described here. First, a single-stranded version of the gene is obtained by cloning in an M 13 vector. A short oligonucleotide is then synthesized, complementary to the relevant region of the gene but containing the desired nucleotide alteration. This oligonucleotide is hybridized to the DNA and used as the primer for a strand synthesis reaction that is allowed to continue all the way around the circular template molecule.

The newly formed heteroduplex is used to transform cells. After introduction into *Escherichia coli,* DNA replication produces numerous copies of this recombinant DNA molecule. Half the resulting double-stranded molecules are copies of the original strand of DNA, and half are copies of the strand that contains the mutated sequence. The double-stranded molecules direct synthesis of phage particles so about half the phages released from the infected bacteria carry a single-stranded version of the mutated molecule. The phages are plated onto solid agar so that plaques are produced, and the mutant ones identified by hybridization probing with the original oligonucleotide. The mutated gene can then be placed back in its original host by homologous recombination or transferred to an *E. coli* vector designed for synthesis of protein from cloned DNA, so that a sample of the mutated protein can be obtained (*see* Fig. 18).

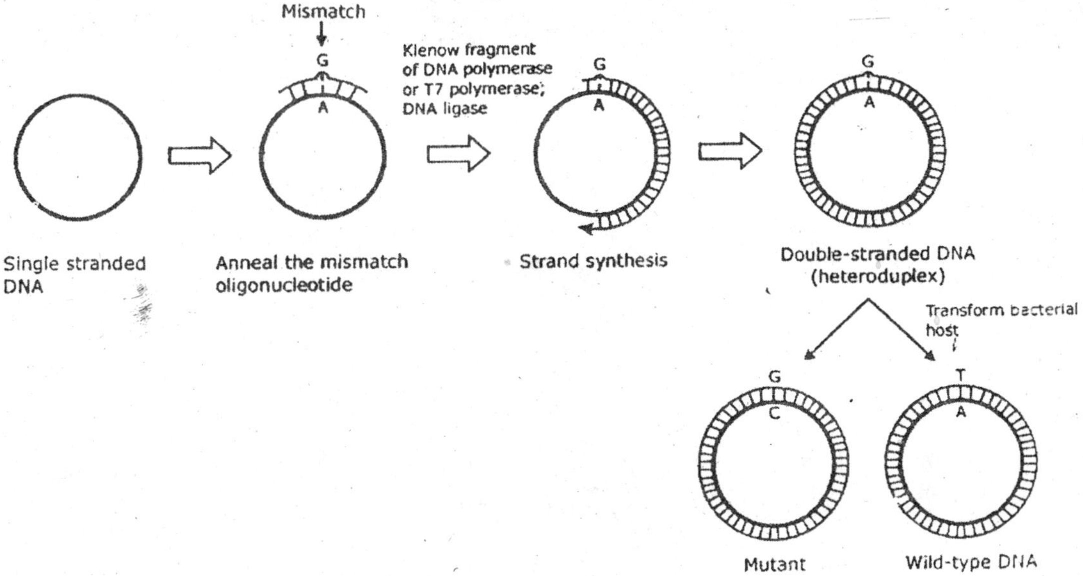

Fig. 18: *Oligonucleotide directed mutagenesis. Typical procedure for site directed mutagenesis using the primer extension method. The mismatch is depicted within the base-pairing region.*

TRANSGENESIS AND TRANSGENIC ORGANISMS

Transgenesis may be defined as the introduction of exogenous DNA into the genome, such that it is stably maintained in a heritable manner. Organisms that have been permanently engineered by either gene insertion, gene deletion, or gene replacement are called transgenic organisms, and any foreign or modified genes that are added are called transgenes. A transgenic animal contains a transgenes in all of its cells usually introduced by microinjection of a fertilized egg cell. The first transgenic animals were produced in 1981 by Ralph Brinster and Richard Palmiter. They succeeded in introducing a gene for rat growth hormone (GH) into the fertilized eggs of mice. The injected DNA was constructed so as to contain the coding portion of the rat GH gene in a position just downstream from the promoter region of the mouse metallothionein gene. Transgenic animals are currently being used to study DNA regulatory elements, expression of proteins during differentiation, tissue specificity, and the role of oncogene products on growth, differentiation and induction of tumorigensis, Such technologies should permit replacing defective genes in the developing embryo.

Mouse transgenesis

Transgenic mice have been produced by injecting DNA into the male pronucleus just after fertilization. Microinjection is done using a microneedle. The microinjected transgene randomly integrates into chromosomal DNA, usually at a single site, and usually as multiple copies. It is more common for the DNA to integrate after one or two cell divisions, in which case the resulting mouse is a **mosaic** containing both transformed and nontransformed cells. The surviving intact eggs after microinjection are implanted into a host female mouse. Three weeks after birth of the pups genomic DNA from mouse are analyzed. Mice that score positive by test are then bred to establish founder transgenic lines (*see* Fig. 19).

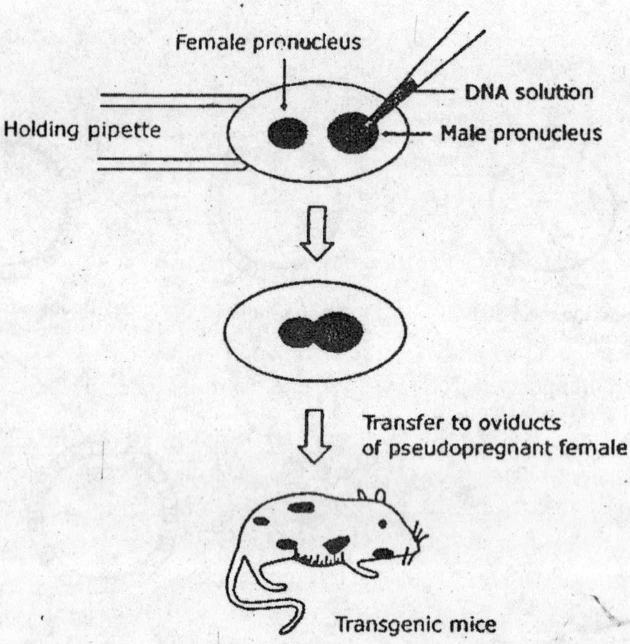

Fig. 19: *Construction of transgenic mice by pronuclear microinjection. A holding pipette which can hold fertilized oocyte in place, while the microinjection pipette is used to pierce the oocyte and then the male pronucleus. An aqueous solution of the desired DNA is then pipetted directly into the pronucleus. The introduced DNA clones can integrate into chromosomal DNA. Surviving oocytes are reimplanted into the oviducts of pseudopregnant foster female (which have been mated with a vasectomized male; the mating act can initiate physiological changes in the female which stimulate the development of the implanted embryos).*

GENE KNOCKOUT

A gene knockout (or simply **knockouts**) is a genetically engineered organism that carries one or more genes in its chromosomes that has been made incoperative. The primary use of this technique has been to replace a normal gene with a mutant allele or a disrupted form of the gene, thus knocking out the gene's function.

Process of developing knockout mouse

Transgenic mice that carry such a disrupted gene, called *knockout mice.* Production of gene-targeted knockout mice involves the following steps:

- Isolation and culturing of embryonic stem (ES) cells from the inner cell mass of a mouse blastocyst.
- Introduction of a mutant or disrupted gene into the cultured ES cells and selection of homologousrecombinant cells in which the gene of interest has been knocked out (*i.e.,* replaced by a nonfunctional form of the gene).
- Injection of homologous recombinant ES cells into a recipient mouse blastocyst and surgical implantation of the blastocyst into a pseudopregnant mouse.
- Mating of chimeric offspring heterozygous for the disrupted gene to produce homozygous knockout mice.

A common approach to inactivate a selected gene is to insert an antibiotic resistance gene, known as *neo,* into the cloned gene of interest. This both inactivates the gene of interest and allows identification of ES cells that have been successfully transfected. The normal gene in a very low percentage of ES cells may be replaced by the neo-disrupted recombinant gene by **homologous recombination** (*see* Fig. 20).

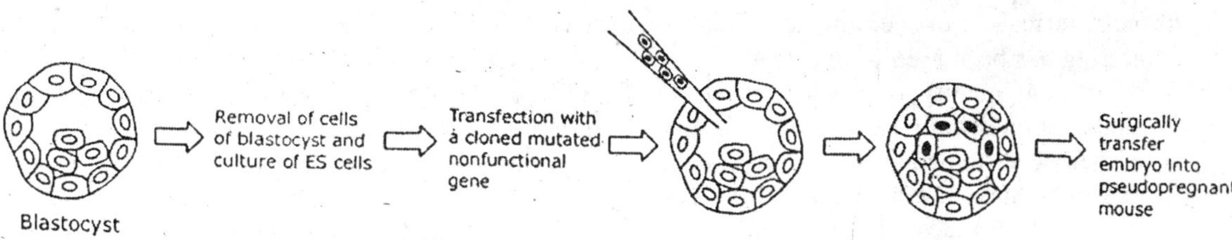

Fig. 20: *Generation of knockout mouse*

TRANSGENIC PLANTS

Transgenic plants are those plants, which carry additional, stably integrated and expressed, foreign gene(s) from transpecies. The whole process involving introduction, integration and expression of foreign gene(s) in the host, is called genetic transformation. The combined use of recombinant DNA technology, gene transfer methods and tissue culture techniques has led to the efficient transformation and production of transgenics, in a wide variety of crop plants. Unlike conventional breeding, only the cloned gene(s) of agronomic importance is being introduced without the cotransfer of other undesirable gene from the donor. The recipient genotype is least disturbed and there is no need for repeated back crosses. This will serve as an effective means of removing certain specific defect of otherwise well adopted cultivars.

General procedure used to make a transgenic plant

The first -step in the process of development of a transgenic plant involves the formation of the recombinant plasmid and its transfer to plant cells. An *Agrobacterium* plasmid that normally carries the T-DNA sequence is modified by substituting a selectable marker (such as the kanamycin-resistance gene) and a desired transgene between the 25-nucleotide-pair T-DNA repeats. *Agrobacteria* that carrying a recombinant plasmid with both a selectable marker and a desired transgene are incubated in culture with plant cells. The wounded plant cells at the edge release substances that attract the *Agrobacteria* and cause them to inject DNA into these cells. Only those plant cells that take up the appropriate DNA and express the selectable marker gene survive to proliferate and form a callus. The growth factors supplied to the callus induces it to form shoots and root and grow into adult plants carrying the transgene.

TRANSGENIC PLANTS: APPLICATION

1. Development of insect, virus, and herbicide resistant plant.

   ***BT* TOXIN:** *B. thuringiensis,* during sporulaltion, forms intracellular crystalline bodies that contain an insecticidal protein called the d– endotoxin. The d– endotoxin protein (cry I, cry II, cry III and others) that accumulates in the bacterium is an inactive precursor. After ingestion by the insect this protoxin is cleaved by proteases, resulting in shorter versions of the protein that display the toxic activity, by binding to the inside of the insect's gut and damaging the surface epithelium. By the process of genetic engineering genes for *B. thurengiensis* toxin canbe expressed in plants.

   Through genetic engineering it is possible to develop crops that are intrinsically resistant to insect. Several different strategies have been used to confer resistance against insect predators. One approach involves a gene for an insecticidal protoxin produced by one of several sub species of the bacterium *Bacillus thuringiensis.* Other common strategies use genes for plant proteins such as alpha amylase inhibitors, protease inhibitors, and lectin that have been shown to be effective against a wide variety of insects.
2. Development of stress tolerant plant like, oxidative stress, salt stress.
3. Modification of plant nutritional content like amino acids, lipids, vitamins, iron.

   The use of genetic engineering techniques allows scientists to develop the plants with improved characteristics. For example, genetic engineering has been used to improve:

I. Nutritional quality of several plants by modification of amino acid content of some of their seed storage proteins. For example rice is extremely low in vitamin A. Potrykus and -Beyer developed genetically engineered rice (popularly known as **golden rice**), which is enriched in pro-vitamin A by introducing three genes involved in the biosynthetic pathway for carotenoids, the precursor for vitamin A.

II. The fatty acid composition of both edible and non-edible oil producing crops.

III. The tests of fruits and vegetables by the introduction of monellin.

4. Plants as bioreactor for production of antibodies, polymers etc.

   Plants are easy to grow and can generate considerable biomass. That is the reason the transgenic plants are used for the production of commercial protein and chemicals. Plants has been used to produce monoclonal antibodies and antibody fragments; the polymer polyhydroxylbutyrate, which can be used to make a biodegradable plastic like material; and a number of potential therapeutic agents like, human protein C (anticoagulant), human hirudin variant 2 (anticoagulant), human erythropoietin (anemia), human alpha interferon (hepatitis C and B), human growth hormone (dwarfism).

5 Synthesis of edible vaccines.

   Commercial vaccines are expensive to produce and package and require trained personnel to administer injections. So, would be advantageous if vaccines could be delivered inexpensively on a broad scale in an edible form, *e.g.*, as part of a fruit or vegetable. An edible vaccine, in contrast to traditional vaccines, would not require elaborate production facilities, purification, sterilization, packaging, or specialized delivery system.

6. Modification of plant yield like, increased iron and oxygen content.

Molecular Farming

It is an application of genetic engineering in which genes, primarily of human or animal origin are intrbduced in to plants or farm animals for cost effective production of therapeutic products such as antibodies, blood products, cytokines, growth factors, hormones, recombinant enzymes and human and veterinary vaccines. Therapeutic compounds so produced are also known as biopharmaceuticals (pharmaceuticals from biological organisms).

The organisms in which genes coding for target therapeutically active compound are introduced are often referred to as expression system. Expression system studied so far include bacteria, yeast, plants viruses, animal cell culture, transgenic plants and transgenic animals. Initially bacteria were the most widely used expression system but due to complexity of the most therapeutic proteins to be produced and simplicity of the bacterial system, new expression systems were explored. As of now plants are the preferred and most widely used expression system in comparison to other systems. The first recombinant pharmaceutical protein produced in plant was human serum albumin, first produced in 1990 in transgenic tobacco and potato plants.

HISTOCHEMICAL AND IMMUNOTECHNIQUES

INTRODUCTION

To possess a healthy mind in a healthy body is every human's desire. But body is a delicately balanced machine and sometimes something may go wrong. The fault may manifest in a disease or may take away the sense of physical well being. We rush to the physician. The physician may prescribe a medicine straight away or recommend some tests such as blood test, urine test, X-ray, NMR etc., before prescribing the medicine. These examination procedures and the equipment used are called diagnostic techniques and tools respectively. In this chapter, you will learn some of the diagnostic techniques that involve examination of blood.

Blood–The Dominant Body Fluid

Our body is full of a variety of fluids. Blood and lymph are the circulating body fluids and transports O_2,salts, vitamins, hormones, food substances etc. to all parts and cells of the body and collects metabolic wastes (CO_2 & NH_3) from them and passes then to the lung and kidneys-respectively for giving OUT. Blood is a fluid connective tissue, which is pumped into blood vessels by the muscular heart to reach all the body organs and back to the heart.

Blood and Diagnosis

Various biochemical reactions occur in the cells of our body during metabolism. As long as normal metabolic processes continue, we remain healthy. Sometimes normal metabolic processes break down due to infection or other reasons. As a result, unusual chemical substances or excessive amount of certain chemicals which are normally synthesized in the body may move out of the cell into blood or urine or some other body fluid. Changes in the body fluids may then manifest as a disease.

Diagnostic tests of the body fluids help the physician to:

(*i*) diagnose, a disease,
(*ii*) confirm an earlier diagnosis,
(*iii*) screen for a disease yet to show its symptoms,
(*iv*) help in prognosis, that is, anticipate the sequence of events of a disease or
(*v*) monitor the course of the disease,

Of all the body fluids, blood is undoubtedly the most important one and is very commonly taken for examination. In this chapter, a few important ,blood tests and the principles involved therein have been discussed.

Blood Tests

Most blood tests are performed on samples obtained from the person in special bottles containing anticoagulant (such as heparin, oxalate, citrate) which prevents blood from clotting.

Some common blood tests are as follows:

(*i*) Haemoglobin Estimation
(*ii*) Blood Glucose
(*iii*) Total Leucocyte Count (TLC)
(*iv*) Differential Leucocyte Count (DLC)
(*v*) Erythrocytic Sedimentation Rate (ESR)
(*vi*) Lipid Profile
(*vii*) Blood Urea
(*viii*) ELISA Test
(*ix*) Widal Test

Haemoglobin Estimation

Haemoglobin (Hb) is the red coloured pigment found in red blood corpuscles of blood It consists of 1 molecule of heme (iron porphyrin and 4 molecules of globulin (protein). It is an oxygen-carrier and hence vitally important for body functioning.

Normal Range of Hb

Men	15.5 ± 2.5 g/dl (dl = deciliter)
Women	14.0 ± 2.5 g/dl
Children, 3 months to 12 years	11.0 ± 1.5 g/dl

Clinical Importance

Haemoglobin is one of the parameters for determination of status of **anaemia** (a condition in which the blood is deficient in the number of red blood cells in haemoglobin content or in total volume of blood). Less haemoglobin than the normal range stated above indicates suspected anaemia.

There are various methods of Haemoglobin (Hb) estimation. The more commonly used method is Sahli's Acid Haematin method.

Blood Sugar-Estimation

The abnormalities of blood sugar *i.e.*, higher or lower glucose levels, reflect disturbances in carbohydrate metabolism. At room temperature, glycolysis in the RBC reduces tho blood glucose at a rate of 5% every hour. To prevent this loss, either the estimation should be performed within half an hour, after collection or an inhibitor of glycolysis such as sodium fluoride (NaF) should be added. More often, the sample is collected in a tube containing a fluoride oxalate mixture.

Techniques

1. Glucose oxidase techniques - specific and representing true glucose.
2. Techniques dependent on the reducing property of glucose. These may, however, over-estimate the blood glucose levels by as much as 5-20%.

Normal Blood sugar range

Whole blood sugar (fasting)	90-120 mg/dl
Plasma/Serum (Fasting)	70-110 mg/dl
Plasma/Serum (Post Prandial)* –PP	up to 140 mg/dl
Whole blood (PP)	up to 180 mg/dl

(*Prandial means "meal", Post prandial = after meals/food/breakfast)

Total Leucocyte Count (TLC)

You know that leukocytes or WBC (white blood corpuscles) remove foreign bodies and micro-organisms entering our body. WBCs remove these either by phagocytosis or by production of antibodies against the antigens of invading microorganisms. In stress, strain, infection and disease, their number is increased as they do phagocytosis and work as organ of offence and defence besides help in healing the wounds. It becomes important, therefore, to determine the total leucocytic count or TLC.

In certain phathological conditions, however, TLC may drop below the normal range.

Normal Range of TLC

Adults	: $7.5 \pm 3.5 \times 10^3$/cu. mm
New Borns	: $18 \pm 8 \times 10^3$/cm. mm
Infants, 1 yr.	: $12 \pm 6 \times 10^3$/cu. mm
Children 4-10 yrs.	: $11 \pm 5 \times 10^3$/cu. mm
Children 8-12 yrs.	: $9 \pm 4.5 \times 10^3$/cu. mm

Differential Leucocyte Count (DLC)

White blood corpuscles are of mainly two types (a) Agranulocytes (20-25%) without azurophilic granules. Monocytes are largest W.B.C. Kidney shaped nucleus. (b) Granulocytes (75-81%) nucleus is lobulated (two or more lopes). They are of three types-Eosinophils (3-4%), Basophils (0.5-2%) and Neutrophils (60-70%). For symptoms of certain diseases, the physician, may recommend a DLC or differential leucocyte count. *e.g.*, increased eosinophil count indicates allergy. Differential leucocyte count means detecting the number of different kinds of leukocytes. For DLC, a blood film is prepared, stained with Giemsa or Leishman stain and the percentage of various kinds of leucoctyes calculated.

PROCEDURE OF MAKING A BLOOD FILM

(*a*) A small drop of blood is placed in the central line of slide about 1-2 cm from one end.

(*b*) The spreader is placed at an angle of 45° to the slide and then moved back to make contact with the drop.

(*c*) The drop should spread out quickly along the line of contact of the spreader with the slide.

(*d*) The moment this occurs, the film should be spread by a rapid, smooth, forward movement of the spreader.

(*e*) The drop should be of such size that the film is 3-4 cm in length.

Qualities of a good film

(*a*) Should not be too thin and the tail of the film should be smooth.

(*b*) There should be some overlap of the red cells diminishing to separate near the tail.

(*c*) The leucocytes in the body of the film should not be badly shrunken.

Staining the Blood Film

Various dyes (stains) are used to stain the blood film for identifying blood cells. Two of them are Giemsa stain and Leishman stain mentioned below in the box with staining procedure.

Normal Differential Leucocyte Count (Adults)

Neutrophils	40-75%
Lymphocytes	20-45%
Monocytes	2-10%
Eosinophils	1-6%
Basophils	0-1%

ERYTHROCYTIC SEDIMENTATION RATE (ESR)

If an anticoagulant is added to the blood and the specimen allowed to stand in a tube, red cells slowly sediment to the bottom of the tube leaving clear plasma as the supernatant. The rate of sedimentation estimated under standard conditions is known as the erythrocytic sedimentation rate (ESR). It is expressed as the fall of RBCs in mm at the end of first hour (starting point-when the tube was filled with blood). Sedimentation takes place in three stages:

(*a*) Formation of rouleaux (red blood corpuscles have a tendency to stack over each other, and such a stack is called rouleaux).
(*b*) Sinking of rouleaux.
(*c*) Packing of the rouleaux

Methods of Estimation

There are two common methods of estimating ESR.

1. Wintrobe method
2. Westergen method

Normal Values of ESR

Wintrobe Method	Men	: 0-9 mm in 1st hour
	Women	: 0-20 mm in 1st hour
Westergen Method	Men	: 0-5 mm in 1st hour
	Women	: 0-7 mm in 1st hour

LIPID PROFILE

Lipids are insoluble in water and hence need to be bound to other molecules to be transported through aqueous medium. Lipids are transported in the blood in small particles called lipoproteins. Lipoproteins are synthesised in the liver and intestine. There are five main types of lipoproteins :

1. Chylomicrons,
2. Very low density lipoproteins (VLDL),
3. Intermediate density lipoproteins (IDL),
4. Low density lipoproteins (LDL) and
5. High density lipoproteins (HDL).

The chylomicrons transport lipids from the intestine via lymph. VLDL particles transport lipids to various parts of the body. LDL and HDL are related to transport of cholesterol. HDL are useful lipoproteins as they remove cholesterol from plasma and cells, transporting it to the liver for processing or removing. LDL are small particles rich in cholesterol. They are the harmful ones as they are directly related to coronary heart disease due to *ATHEROSCLEROSIS*. An atheroma is a p;aque of lipid deposited on large arteries especially at their junctions. Much of this plaque which makes the lumen of arteries narrow, is made of cholesterol. It reduces blood flow and the condition is termed *ATHEROSCLEROSIS*. Cholesterol estimation is thus directly related to evaluation of risk of heart disease.

Some important lipid profile tests

(*a*) Total lipids
(*b*) Serum total cholesterol
(*c*) Serum HDL cholesterol
(*d*) Total cholesterol/HDL-cholesterol ratio

CHOLESTEROL

Cholesterol present in the blood both free and as esters. Most of the cholesterol in synthesized by the liver from acetyl Co A, though all cells are capable of producing it. For lipid tests a fasting sample is obtained to prevent interference by dietary lipids. Normal range of cholesterol is 150-250 mg/dl.

Clinical Significance

(*a*) Elevated levels of serum cholesterol are associated with atherosclerosis (hardening of blood vessels), nephrosis (kidney disease), diabetes mellitus, obstructive jaundice and myxedema.
(*b*) Decreased levels are observed in hyperthyroidism, nutritional malabsorption and anaemia.

Serum High Density Lipoprotein (HDL) Cholesterol

(*a*) *Increased in:*
- Vigorous exercise
- Insulin treatment

(*b*) *Decreased in*
- Stress and recent illness
- Starvation
- Obesity
- Hypothyroidism
- Liver and kidney diseases

Serum Low density lipoprotein (LDL) cholesterol

(*a*) *Increased in*
- Certain genetic conditions
- Diabetes mellitus
- Hypothyroidism

- Kidney disease
- Diet high in cholesterol and total and saturated fats

(*b*) *Decreased in*

- Severe liver cell damage (due to chemicals, drugs; hepatitis)
- Hyperthyroidism
- Malnutrition
- Chronic Anaemia

BLOOD UREA ESTIMATION

Urea is one of the main nitrogenous waste products excreted in the urine. Liver is the sole site of urea formation.

Techniques for Blood Urea Estimation

There are two major techniques. The initial step in both the techniques is same, involving liberation of ammonia from urea by urease.

(*a*) Reaction of NH_3, with Nessler's's reagent.

(*b*) Berthelot's reaction - Liberated ammonia reacts with phenol and hypochlorite to give blue coloured-Indophenol.

ELISA TEST (FOR AIDS, ETC.)

The ELISA TEST (Enzyme linked immunosorbent assay is one of the most widely employed variants of enzyme immunoassay. Enzyme immunoassays have emerged as quantitative techniques for detection of antigens and antibodies. It is the standard technique for the diagnosis and epidemiological studies of important parasitic diseases or hormone assays etc. They all also employ various enzymes linked to either antigen or antibody as a label which can easily, be detected by measurement of enzyme activity.

Principle of ELISA Test

The ELISA assay can be used to measure either antigen or antibody. To measure antigen, the antibody is bound to solid phase, incubated with test serum and then a second enzyme-labelled antibody is added. Substrate is then added and enzyme activity is related to antigen concentration.

Clinical Applications

In detection of Human Chorionic Gonadotropin (HCG) levels in urine or blood and antibodies to bacteria, viruses, DNA and allergens.

ELISA is currently available for the diagnosis of a number of diseases such as

1. Hepatitis
2. STD (Sexually Transmitted Diseases)
3. Infection of Rubella virus
4. Thyroid disorder
5. AIDS (caused by HIV infection)

Widal Test (For Typhoid)

This is a serological test done for diagnosis of typhoid usually in the second week of the disease. In this disease specific agglutinins are usually detectable in the patient's blood after 6 days of fever. Serum from individual vaccinated with TAB/TABC may also show moderately elevated titre of agglutinins.

Interpretation of Widal test

1. Serum from normal individuals may agglutinate these antigens in dilution up to 1:60. The level of normal agglutinin varies in different regions and different communities.
2. Agglutination titres of 1:20 and more are significant and rise in titres on repetition of test after a few hours will confirm the diagnosis of enteric fever.
3. Agglutination titres of 1:240 and above are typically found in case of typhoid (enteric fever).

ELECTRO-PHYSIOLOGICAL METHODS

INTRODUCTION

Man has always been inquisitive to know about the interior of his body. But this inquisitiveness often turned into a pressing need when it was found necessary to know the kind of fault, injury or damage that some times occurred inside the body. The most common examples of such faults are bone fractures or enlarged liver. In this direction, the first revolutionary technique was that of X-ray. It proved to be a boon in detecting bone fractures and in assessing the extent of tuberculosis. Today, techniques are available to get an insight into practically every body organ.

Here, we shall learn about some of the imaging techniques, which provide a pictorial or graphic representation of the body part suspected to be functioning improperly. The techniques covered here are:

(*a*) ECG (Electrocardiography)
(*b*) EEG (Electroencephalography)
(*c*) CT (Computerised tomography)
(*d*) MRI (Magnetic Resonance Imaging) and
(*e*) Ultrasound

Techniques - Invasive and non-Invasive

Some of the techniques used in diagnosis of organ-functioning require some kind of probing or mechanical access to the concerned organs. Such techniques often cause discomfort to the patient and may even damage or injure the tissues. Such techniques are categorized as invasive. Even X-rays are potentially harmful in the sense that as they pass through the body, specially if repeated frequently, the cells and tissues may be adversely affected. But the other techniques listed and described here are known to be free from any kind of risk of injury to body and are thus non-invasive.

Electrocardiography (ECG)

- ECG is electrocardiography.
- It is a display of electrical voltage of the heart muscle.
- ECG has a set pattern in a healthy person. Any deviation indicates faulty heart function.
- ECG is used for detecting several heart diseases.
- It is non-invasive.

What is ECG?

Electrocardiography (ECG) is a graphic display or recording of the electrical voltages produced by heart muscle during a cardiac cycle of contraction (systole) and relaxation (diastole). The activity of the heart creates an electrical field which is conducted through the surrounding body tissues to the surface of the body. When two electrodes are placed on the surface of the body at a distance then the potential difference (*i.e.*, voltage) between the points can be measured. The sequence of events during contraction and relaxation of the heart muscle are graphically presented as voltage displacement on the Y-axis with the time on X-axis. Such a tracing or recording is called **electrocardiogram.** This gives information about the rate and rhythm of the heart and the condition of the heart muscle through three waves called PQRS and T waves.

- The horizontal segment preceding the P wave is designated as the base line or the isopotential line.
- The P-Wave represents depolarization of the atrial musculature.
- The QRS complex is the combined result of the repolarization of the atria and the depolarization of the ventricles, which occurs almost simultaneously.
- The T-wave is the wave of ventricular repolarization whereas the U-wave, if present, is generally believed to be the result of after-potentials in the ventricular muscle.
- The shape and polarity of each of above features vary with the location of the measuring electrode with respect to the heart, and a cardiologist normally bases his diagnosis or readings taken from several electrode locations (*see* Fig. 21).

Uses of ECG

In healthy individuals the ECG remains reasonably constant, even though the heart rate changes with the demands of the body. However, the electrical activity of heart shows changes under the following situations:

(*i*) a change in ionic environment for the heart,
(*ii*) a conduction defect in the heart,
(*iii*) damage to muscle fibres of the heart due to decreased blood supply.

The EGG is used by the cardiologist for diagnosing various diseases and conditions of the heart. Hence, the shape and duration of each feature of the ECG is significant. Fig. C shows the EGG tracing of a person who had a heart attack.

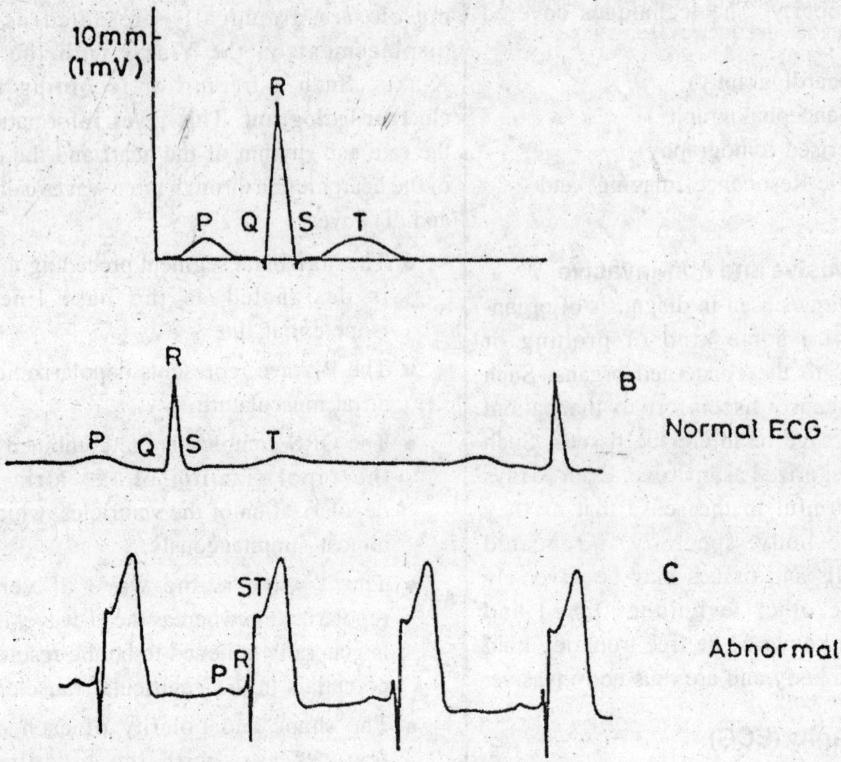

Fig. 21: *Electrocardiogram Tracings. A - The heart waves, B - Normal ECG, C - Abnormal ECG*

ELECTROENCEPHALOGRAPHY (EEG)

- EEG measures the electrical activity of brain.
- It is used for detecting several brain diseases like epilepsy, etc.
- It is non-invasive.

What is EEG?

EEG involves recording the electrical activity of the brain with the help of surface electrodes placed on the scalp. This recording or tracing is called electroencephalogram. The EEG has a very complex pattern compared to EGG. To record an EEG, the electrodes are placed in the frontal (front), parietal (sides), temporal (lower sides) and occipital (back) regions of the head, according to a precisely defined system. The wave form varies greatly with the locations of the measuring electrodes on the surface of the scalp, EEG potentials, measured at the surface of the scalp, actually represent the combined effect of potentials from a fairly wide region of the cerebra cortex and from various points beneath. EEG tracings are affected by the mental activity of a person.

Even though wide variations in EEG among individuals as well as lack of repeatability are noticed, nevertheless certain characteristic EEG wave forms can be observed which are described in terms of frequency, amplitude, and morphology of the signals.

An alert, wide-awake person usually displays an unsynchronized high-frequency EEG. A drowsy person, particularly one whose eyes are closed, often produces a large amount of rhythmic activity in the range of 8 to 13 Hz (alpha wave). As the person begins to fall a sleep, the amplitude and the frequency of the wave form decreases, and in light, sleep, large amplitude and low frequency wave form emerges. Deeper sleep generally results in even higher amplitude and slower frequency waves (delta waves). The various frequency ranges of the EEG have arbitrarily been given Greek letter designations because frequency seems to be the most prominent feature of an EEG pattern (Fig. 22).

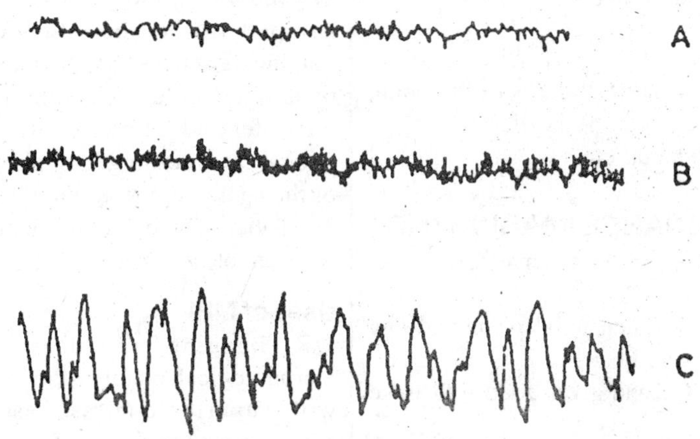

Fig. 22: *EEG tracing (A) Awake with eyes open, (B) Awake with eyes closed, (C) Slow-wave sleep*

USE of EEG

Since normal EEG tracing show certain characteristic features in amplitude and frequency, deviation caused either by brain disease or change in physiological state of the, brain can be detected in terms of changes in the variables. Since EEG is a window to the function of brain, it is most useful, non-invasive and safe investigative technique in the diagnosis of the following:

- Different types of epilepsy,
- Brain infections,
- Metabolic disorders and drug effects on the brain,
- Study of sleep and its disorders and in the determination of brain death.

COMPUTERIZED TOMOGRAPHY (CT)

- Computerized tomography uses X-rays
- Gives excellent image of internal organs of human body
- Very useful in detecting tumours and, other abnormalities
- Repeated exposure is harmful (invasive)

What is CT?

Computerized tomography (CT) is a special type of radiograph and is also called computerized axial tomography (CAT). This technique, which combines X-ray imaging with computer techniques, permits visualization of Internal organs and body structures with greater definition and clarity that could never be attained by conventional X-ray methods. CT uses a movable X-ray tube that is rotated around the patient's body, say for example, the head. Opposite to the tube (*i.e.*, on the other side of the patient's head) are X-ray detectors far more sensitive than conventional film, thereby allowing much shorter exposure times (and less risk of radiation damage). Rather than acquiring a single image as in conventional X-ray picture, a CT scan gathers intensity information from many positions around the patient's head. These data are entered into a computer as a matrix and the radiodensity at each point in the three dimensional space of the head is calculated. With a sufficiently narrow X-ray beam, sensitive detectors and digital signal processing techniques, small differences in radiodensity can be converted into an image. Since the information is gathered for the full volume of the head, the computed matrix contains information about the entire head, it is, therefore, possible to generate "slices" or tomograms (GK, *tomo* means "cut" or "slice") of various planes through the brain, visualizing internal structures at any desired level. A brain CT scan, for example, readily distinguishes gray matter and white matter, differentiate the ventricles (cavities inside brain) quite well and show up many other brain structures, with a spatial resolution of several millimeters.

Uses of CT

CT is useful for diagnosis of diseases of the brain, spine, chest and abdomen. It is also useful in detecting tumours, oedema, etc.

MAGNETIC RESONANCE IMAGING (MRI)

- MRI is completely non-invasive and no X-rays are used.
- It gives 2- and 3-dimensional picture of any organ of the human body.
- It is superior to CT and gives good soft tissue contrast.
- Images of any direction and plane are possible.
- Useful in detecting tumours, cancers, infections, etc.
- It can be used for studying blood flow.
- Useful in the study of functions of brain, heart, etc.

What is MRI?

MRI does not use X-ray or radioactive dyes or material, but can provide clear picture of soft tissues such as muscles, cartilage, ligaments, tendons, blood vessels, bone, etc. MRI is an extension of the more generalized phenomenon called, **nuclear magnetic resonance** (NMR). This technique is superior to CT scanning because it does not employ arising radiations, hence it is free from health hazards. Since its discovery in mid 1940, NMR has played an important role in all branches of science.

Magnetic resonance is the study of interaction molecules (specifically atomic nuclei such as hydrogen) with radio frequency field in the presence of an external magnetic field. Since human body contains nearly 70-80% water (H_2O), and water contains proton (hydrogen, ^1H), it is possible to get the distribution of these protons present in the body, which is shown in the form of an MR image. To take and MRI picture, the patient is positioned at the centre of a machine which has powerful magnets. By using sensitive detectors, the radiofrequency emitted by the ^1H nuclei are received and these are fed into powerful computers similar to those used in CT scanning, to generate extraordinarily detailed images from any part of the body. In short, the MR images obtained are from the abundant and strong signals of mobile protons (atomic nuclei hydrogens) of the water and fat present in the human body. The images are nothing but pictorial representation of the spatial distribution of these mobile protons.

Patients, who have metal implants, pace-makers, etc, cannot be imaged.

Uses of MRI

MR imaging produces a high-resolution morphological picture similar to those of CT but with superior contrast resolution and has an advantage of multiplanar imaging capability, that is, unlike CT, views can be obtained from any angle. MRI is extremely useful for diagnosing tumours), infractions (muscle cell death), haemorrhage, abnormaiities related to spine, etc. MRI is also useful in detecting diseases related to heart such as myocardial infarction (heart attack), myocardial ischemia, coronary artery disease, etc.

MR images of heart can also be put in 'cine-display' mode in the computer's memory, thus enabling the assessment of the several heart functions.

Magnetic Resonance Angiography (MRA) is yet another recent technique of MRI, which is useful in monitoring blood flow.

RADIOLABELING TECHNIQUES

ULTRASOUND IMAGING (US)

- Non-invasive imaging of internal organs
- Very often used for diagnosing defects in internal organs like heart, kidney, gall bladder, etc.

What is Ultrasound Imaging?

Ultrasound (US) is a simple non-invasive imaging technique. Vibrations whose frequency exceeds 20,000 cycles per second (20kHz) are beyond human audible range and hence termed as ultrasonic also called sonography. Diagnostics ultrasound uses 1-15 MHz frequencies. The technique, is very simple. The waves of' ultrasound are produced by a physical phenomenon called piezoelectric effect. It is based on the principle that when an electric potential is applied to certain crystals like lead zirconate, they become excited and start vibrating. These vibrations are source of production of ultrasound.

A piezoelectric crystal housed in a transducer acts both as an emitter and a receptor of sound wave. A transducer is a device which converts one form of variable (for example, energy) into another when a high voltage current is applied to the crystal, it vibrates at a fixed frequency which is beyond human audible frequency. This sound wave traverses through the body and depending upon the acoustic impedance (relative resistance to passage of waves) of the body organs, it is reflected back. This wave is collected by the transducer, reconverted into an electric energy and displayed on a cathode ray oscilloscope. During an ultrasound procedure, gel is applied to a hand-held device that is slid across the skin overlying the area to be imaged. The procedure is not uncomfortable and patients are often able to view a monitor displaying images.

Uses of Ultrasound

The most widely used application of ultrasound in diagnostic medicine involves the non-invasive imaging of internal organs or structure of the body.

Such imaging can provide valuable information regarding the size, location, displacement etc. of a given structure without the necessity of surgery or the use of potentially harmful radiations. Tumours and other regions of an organ that differ in density from surrounding tissues can be detected. It is very useful in diagnosing defects in various internal organs like heart, kidneys, gall bladder etc. In many instances ultrasound techniques have replaced more risky or more traumatic procedures in clinical diagnosis.

10. ECOLOGY

THE ENVIRONMENT

Environment and organism are the two complex and dynamic components of the nature. Place where a species is found in nature and conditions that are present there. The environment simply indicates the surroundings. "Environment is the sum of all physical, chemical, biotic and cultural factors that affect life of an organism is any way."

(A) CLIMATIC AND ATMOSPHERIC FACTORS

These operate in a variety of ways to affect species populations. To begin with, any species has limits of tolerance and some optimum range of tolerance for such factors as sunlight, temperature, humidity, rainfall or wind. If a food climate normally exceeds the limits of tolerance for a species, then the species will not occur in that area, if it exceeds the optimum limits, the species will not thrive there. If the local climate only rarely exceeds the limits of tolerance, then a species may temporarily occupy that area, but will be eliminated in those years when the climate becomes extreme.

Assuming that the climate is favourable to the establishment of a species, then a number of climatic factors may influence population growth. Changes in temperature—years that are warmer or colder than normal—may permit a species to thrive and increase, or they may cause a decrease and permit its survival only in the most favourable sites. Changes in rainfall and humidity, dry years (or cycles) and wet years (or cycles), have major effects. Fluctuations in temperature and rainfall tend to be most severe in areas where temperature or moisture is already near the limits of lowlands where rainfall and temperature are high and near the optimum for the growth of the greatest fluctuation in either factor. In the dry tropics fluctuations in rainfall from year to year may be extreme. In northern temperate regions where winter is cold and the duration of low temperatures restrict the growing season for plants, one finds the greatest variation between temperatures in one year and another.

Climatic and atmospheric factors tend to have their most severe effects upon those introduced populations of plants and animals which man attempts to grow or produce in areas that have climate more extreme than the optimal climate for the species concerned. Native species are adapted to the range of climate in the area they occupy, and although they may be affected by climatic extremes, these effects are usually much less limiting than for a domesticated species introduced outside its normal climatic range. In the African savannas, a drought will be more likely to wipe out a high percentage of the cattle than of the native antelopes. Climatic and atmospheric factors also have more effect of species that are at, or approaching, the level of subsistence density. Well-situated animals or plants, with adequate nutrients, water and other essentials are less likely to be affected by drought than populations which have increased and expanded into marginal areas and are already in poor condition because of nutritional limitations. Certain factors of weather and climate may have catastrophic effects on all populations in an area-hurricanes, torandoes, unusually severe floods or droughts, but usually there are less significant than the more normally occurring changes, except in the case of those species which are highly limited in distribution. With most species, normal fluctuations in climate have their greatest effect when animal population densities are excessive, or when plants are established in sub-optimum environments.

Temperature

Stenothermal : Organisms living at nearly constant temperature cannot tolerate variations.

Eurythermal : Organisms which can tolerate wide variations in temperature.

Megatherm : Living at high temperature.

Mesotherm : High summer temperature and low winter temperature.

Microtherm : Moderate warmth in summer, low temperature in winter.

Hekistotherm : Living with brief summer below 10°C and winter prolonged with very low temperature. Temperature ranges have created different life zones—tropical, subtropical, temperate, arctic/alpine.

Poikilothermal (= Ectothermal = Cold Blooded). Temperature varies with the surroundings.

Homoisothermal : (= Endothermal, Warm Blooded) : Temperature constant due to internal regulation. Excessive subcutaneous fat (blubber) protects whale, seal and polar bear from low temperature. Shivering is a mechanism to increase body temperature. 'Persipration' and 'panthing' reduce body temperature.

Hibernation (= Winter Sleep), aestivation (= Summer Sleep), periodic activity and winter/summer eggs/seeds are adaptations of poikilothermics to avoid unfavourable temperatures. Thick cuticle, corky bark, hair, thick leaves, high solute content, mucilage and tannins are protective mechanisms in plants to tolerate high (55°-73°C) or low (– 20° to – 35°C) temperatures. Generally seeds, spores and cysts tolerate temperature extremes better due to low water content and thick covering.

Thermoperiodicity controls phenology in several cases.

Bergmann's Rule

Bergmann's Rule states that avian and mammalian forms are generally of larger size in colder regions as compared to warmer/hotter regions.

Light

It controls photosynthesis, tissue differentiation, growth, pigmèntation, plant movements, period of activity, reproduction in plants and animals. Depending upon the period of activity, animals are *diurnal* (active during day, e.g. Sparrow, Pigeon, Butterfly), *nocturnal* (active and dusk) and *crepuscular* (active at dawn/dusk, e.g. Rabbit) Depending upon period of breeding, animals and plants are called long day (e.g. Turkey, Ferret, Radish), shortday (e.g. Sheep, Deer, Xantheium, Dahlia) or day neutral (e.g. Guinea Pis, Tomato).

Wind

(Air Current). It determines cloud formation, pollination and dispersal in many organisms. Wind restricts flight animals, nest formation and height in plants. It enhances soil erosion, transpiration and develops flag trees.

Humidy/Precipitation

Epiphytes can be found only in humid areas. Arid areas do not have them. Transpiration in inversely proportional to atmospheric humidity. Low atmospheric humidity produces aridity and xerophytism. Periodicity and amount of precipitation determine type of vegetation—evergreen, deciduous, chapparal, savannah, grassland, desert etc.

(B) SOILS

Here the limiting factors operate directly on plants, and through plants, upon animal populations (other than those of the soil fauna itself, which is often directly limited by soil conditions). The requirements of plants and animals, however, are not identical.

An abundant growth of vegetation does not necessarily mean there will be an abundant food supply for animals, nor that the food supply will have high nutritional value. Certain plants may produce abundant vegetative growth and high amounts of carbohydrates under conditions where certain soil chemicals are in short supply, however, they may produce relatively small amounts of the proteins and vitamins needed to support an abundance of animal life. Thus, a shortage of a trace elements, such as cobalt, in the soil may have little effect on plant growth. However, cattle feeding on there plants may do poorly or do not survive. Addition of a cobalt top-dressing to the soil, which is then taken up by the plants can open up a rangeland to livestock use. For another example, a dense forest may produce an abundance of vegetation, but will support very few ground-dwelling grazing or browsing animals. There is no lack of food for them, but plants growing on a forest floor under dense tree cover are commonly lacking in protein.

Animals grazing of browsing them can receive adequate carbohydrates but not enough protein to thrive or reproduce. Thus, in many areas of dense forest, grazing and browsing animals will only be common around natural or man-made clearings.

The abundance of natural vegetation in an area often has little relation to the inharent fertility of a soil. Thus, the *ferasols* and *acrisols* of the humid tropics are notoriously infertile, yet they support the most luxuriant vegetation to be found on earth. Examination of this situation reveals, however, that virtually all the nutritional elements required for the support of life are tied up in the vegetation and animal life of the area, and recirculate quickly from the dead plant or animal back into a new, living individual. Below the organic surface layer the soil contains few of the elements needed for plant or animal nutrition, and if the vegetation is scraped away with a bulldozer, the soil that remains is often highly infertile. By contrast, some desert soil that support little plant life, because of lack of water, may have a rich supply of soluble mineral elements needed for the support of life. When water can be made available, they will support high levels of productivity, although there may be new ill effects such as salinization, water logging and water borne diseases.

(C) WATER

Water is an obvious limiting factor for plants and animals. Plants are classified in relation to their tolerance for dry medium or wet conditions as *xerophytes, mesophytes* and *hydrophytes*. Most land plants are in the intermediate, mesophytic range, desert plants are usually, but not always xerophytes, hydrophytes grown in water or require an abundance of water in the soil. All plants require water to support their active growth and metabolism. Some plants cannot tolerate even brief periods of moisture deficiency and that will wilt and die when the soil dries out.

Xerophytes have special adaptations that permit them to survive under prolonged drought, but must have some moisture in order to grows and reproduce.

Where present in abundance, water limits the occurrence of terrestrial organisms and provides a habitant for aquatic forms of life. The latter will relate in their diversity and abundance to the quality of the water, its ability of supply oxygen, its salinity, temperature, velocity and other factors. All of these are capable of being affected, usually adversely, by pollution or siltation.

In relation to terrestrial vegetation, an abundance of water or in the soil limits the plant growth primarily by restricting the availability of oxygen. Those plants growing in wet soil or flooded areas have the ability to derive oxygen through special structures, such as PENUMATOPHORES of mangrooves, or the so-called 'Knees' of balt cypresses are good examples. Continuously moist or flooded soils inhibit the bacterial fungal action that would otherwise bring about decay of organic debris and litter—Organic remains will usually accumulate on such soils in the form of organic mucks or peat. Animals, like plants, require moisture for their continued existence, but vary greatly in their ability to endure drought. Apart from purely aquatic animals, amphibious animals such as the crocodile and hippopotamus cannot long survive away from water. Most land animals must drink water regularly in order to continue to live. However, some desert species can exist indefinitely in the absence of free water as long as the food which is eaten contains sufficient moisture and they can find enough shelter to hold the loss of water from their body surfaces to a minimum. A severe drought, bringing an absolute shortage of water to an extensive area, can be fatal to all animals that require water for drinking. Nevertheless, much of the mortality attributed to drought results not from a shortage of water, but from a shortage of food within reach of water.

(D) BIOTIC FACTORS

The greatest number of limiting factors influencing plant or animal growth, abundance and distribution are biotic in nature.

Food supply for animals is one of these, and in the most common factor limiting the growth of animal populations, either directly, through being short of requirements, or indirectly, through behavioural responses to food shortage. The number of plant-eating animals in any area is ultimately limited by the abundance of the plants of which the animals feed. Furthermore, since the plants must survive and reproduce, there must always be a greater abundance of plants than what is actually needed to provide food to the animals. Most plants produce a surplus of vegetative growth and of seed, part of which can be used by animals. However, each plant, in order to survive, must maintain a metabolic reserve—a minimum amount of leaf age to permit it to store food for its own survival, or set seed for its own reproduction.

Plant growth may be limited by competition from other plants of the same or different species, each drawing on the same reserves of soil and water, or shading one another from essential sunlight. Some plants secrete substances which inhibit the growth or establishment of other plants. A variety of organisms may prey upon plants, from the seed stage through the life cycle to the mature plant. It is obvious that the number of carnivores or meat-eating animals in any area is limited by the availability of the prey upon which they feed. Also there must be enough prey animals to enable the prey species to survive and reproduce, the predator cannot eat all of prey, or both would become extinct. Most prey animals have developed behaviour patterns in relation to their habitat conditions that permit some of them to escape predators. Predators seek the most valnerable and available prey, and usually do not hunt down and capture the more elusive individuals. Often the individuals thus captures are either very young and very old or the most diseased or genetically least vigorous stock, therefore, natural predation tends to have overall beneficial effects on the population of a prey species.

The relationship of the abundance of predators and prey is sometimes illustrated in the form of a **biotic pyramid.** Green plants occupy the base of the pyramid and must always have a greater total volume (biomass) than the plant-eaters that feed upon them. The latter, the herbivores, form the second step be wider and represent a greater biomass than the third step, representing the carnivores that eat other carnivores they must be fewer in number and contain less biomass than their prey.

Each succeeding level in the biotic pyramid also represents a consistent loss of energy from green plants of herbivores to predators, since at each transfer of energy is necessarily lost. Far more calories are available at the lowest level of the pyramid than at any higher level.

The sequence of plants and animals feeding upon one another is called **'food chain'**. Food chains are interconnected, since more than one herbivore may feed on a plant and more than one kind of carnivore may eat a herbivore. These interconnected chains form a **'food web'**.

As elements pass from soil (or atmosphere) to plants, and are then eatern by herbivores and in turn by carnivores, they are often concentrated in varying degrees by a process known as **'biological magnification'**.

Thus, the element iodine may be present in the soil in small quantities and taken up by plants as it goes into solution and reaches plant roots. It has little direct function in plants, but is essential to plant eating mammals. They must obtain enough iodine from the plants they eat and concentrate it in their thyroid glands for there glands to function properly. Therefore, the level of iodine in an animal's thyroid is far greater, than in either the plants or the soil.

Although the number of herbivores is limited by the supply of plants, and the number carnivores is determined by the number of their prey, the reverse is also true in varying degrees. The abundance and distribution of plant can be limited by the presence of herbivores. If a plant is introduced into an area where there are no species that feed upon it, can spread rapidly and become transformed into a weed or pest. Similarily, the abundance and distribution of plant-eating insects and other animals is often controlled by a wide variety of diseases, insects or other predators that feed upon them. If the predators are destroyed, their plant eating prey can increase suddenly and explosively, since its reproductive rate in nature is adjusted to the need for survival under constant predation. Sudden increases in number of rodents or other plant-eating mammals have often been related to extermination of the predators that formerly held them in check.

Populations of many animals species are limited by the effects of interactions among individuals within a species. The species concerned are described as *territorial* and comprise a proportion of individuals which persistently or seasonally occupy a particular area to the exclusion of other individuals of the same species. Commonly, territorial animals will tolerate or encourage the presence of certain other members of their species a mate or mates, their juvenile offspring, and sometimes the members of a larger social group, a herd, troop, flock, or pack. However, they will drive off or otherwise exclude animals that do not belong to the tolerated category. Territorialism tends to limit the number of animals of any one species that occupy an area and to reserve for the territorial individual or group an adequate habitat and food supply, however, there are many kinds and degrees of territorial behaviour, and not all of them serve directly to limit population increase. Plants might also be considered to compete for 'territories' the well-established individual holds its ground against competitors. Their territorial defence mechanisms include the shading out of competitiors and the secretion of chemical which prevent rival from germinating or growing.

Numerous studies have now been made of the effect of overcrowding on a variety of animal species under condition where food supply is abundant, and all other essentials (except space) are present is adequate supply. All of these studies show adverse effect upon individuals in a population where numbers exceed a certain level. These adverse effects are caused by social interactions, and vary from mild behavioural disturbances to serious forms of beahvioural pathology, leading to increased mortality and a decline in birth rate.

HABITAT AND NICHE

A community, or *biocenose*, is an aggregate of organisms which form a distinct ecological unit. Such a unit may be defined in terms of flora, fauna, or both. Community units may be very small like the community of invertebrates and fungi in a decaying log. The extent of a community is limited only by the requirement of a more or less uniform species composition.

A different community occurs in each different habitat and environmental unit of larger size, and in fact the composition and character of the community is an excellent indicator of the type of environment that is present. Since plants and animals, bacteria and fungi, all occur together in the same habitat and have many interrelations, they can scarcely be considered independently of each other. Together they make up the **biotic community.**

Communities may be distinguished as major or minor. Major communities are those which, together with their habitats, form more or less complete and self sustaining units or ecosystems, except for the indispensable input of solar energy. Minor communities, often called **societies**, are secondary aggregations within a major community and are not, therefore, completely independent units as far as circulation of energy is concerned.

The biotic community along with its habitat is called an ecosystem. The term "ecosystem" has been loosely applied to units of various sizes and characteristics but had best he limited to distinctive combinations of air, soil, water conditions with vegetative, animal and microbic life that possess functional unity. In short one can say that biotic community is a grouping of different but interacting populations of different species which live harmoniously in a given locality, e.g. pond community, lawn community may further be split into animal community, plant community and microbe community. Plants provide food, shelter and oxygen to animals. The latter provide CO_2, plough the soil, help in pollination and dispersal. Microbes take part in decomposition of dead bodies and release of minerals.

SPECIES INTERACTION

They may be neutral, positive or negative. Various kinds of interactions are as follows :

(*i*) *Scavenging :* Feeding on dead bodies. Animals feeding on flesh of dead animals are called 'scavengers' e.g. Vulture, Jackal, Hyena (eat left over from lion/tiger's kill), Crow (actually omnivorous) Ant (actually omnivorous). Scavenging keeps the earth clean.

(*ii*) *Commensalism :* One is benefitted without the other being harmed e.g. *E. coli* in human intestine and epiphytes perched on other plants for space only.

(*iii*) *Mutalism :* It is a mutually beneficial relationship/interaction between individuals of two different species.

Mutualism and symbiosis are synonyms though symbiosis was formerly considered to be any interaction between two different organisms. e.g. (*i*) Association between fungus (protection, fixation and absorption of water) and alga (food manufacture) in lichen. (*ii*) *Rhizobium* (nitrogen fixation) and root (shelter, food) in nodulated legumes etc.

(*iv*) *Protocooperation :* It is non-obligatory beneficial relationship that develops when two different organisms get associated. Cattle Egret feeds on lice and ticks of cattle.

(*v*) *Amensalism :* Without deriving much benefits, one inhibits the other by secreting allochemics, e.g. *Pencillium* on *staphylococus* (Flemming, 1928) by *Penicillin*. *Juglans* (walnut) on other nearby plants by *Juglone*, *Tagetes* on soil nematodes. *Chlorella vulgaris* against diatom *Nitzschia frustrulum*.

(*vi*) *Competition :* It is rivalry for obtaining the same resource. Intraspecific competition reduces the size of population. Interspecific competition causes one to be eliminated (*Gause hypothesis/principle of competitive exclusion*) or undergo different adaptations (e.g. 14 species of Finches in Galapagos Islands or 20 species of Antelopes in Sergneti plains, roots of different depths).

(*vii*) *Mimicry :* Mimicry is the resembling to another organism, structure or surroundings (camoulflage).

(*a*) *Protective :* Concealing type provides protection from predators, e.g. Stick Insect, Leaf Insect, Dead leaf Butterfly. In warming type, the mimic resembles a ferocious/poisonous/distasteful organism, e.g. Vicerory Butterfly mimics Monarch Butterfly.

(*b*) *Aggressive :* In *concealing type*, a predator resembles the surroundings, e.g. *Praying Mantis*. In *alluring type*, the predator has resemblance with a favoured article, e.g. mouth of African Lizard resembles a flower. Flower of *Ophyrs* resemble female wasp (Colpa) and are pollinated by male wasp.

(*vii*) *Parasitism :* One organism called parasite obtains nourishment from another organism called host.

(*a*) Non pathogenic (e.g. *Entamoeba coli*) and pathogenic (e.g. *Entamoeba histolytica*).

(*b*) Temporary/Intermittent (e.g. female mosquito) and permanent (e.g. *Ascaris*).

(*c*) Ectoparasite (e.g. Aphids, Lice) and endoparasite (e.g. intracellular *Plasmodium*, tissue parasite *Trichinella*).

(*d*) Holoparasite (complete parasite, e.g. animal parasites) or hemiparasite (semiparasite e.g. *Lovanthus*).

(*e*) Stem parasite (e.g. Cuscuta, stem borer) root parasite (e.g. *Rafflesia*, rootnematodes).

(*f*) *Hyperparasite :* Parasite over parasite e.g. *Cicinnobolus cesatii* on powdery mildew.

At times the parasite spread in *epidemic* form and causes large scale misery.

(*ix*) *Predation :* One organism called predator captures, kills and eath another organisms called prey. Predators are carnivorous but some herbivores which destroy whole plants/seeds are also called predators. A predator may become prey for another.

(*x*) *Negative Human Interactions :* They include primitive shifting agriculture (jhoom), felling of trees, hunting, overgrazing, scarping and litter removal, introduction of weeds, forest clearing and human induced forest fires.

BIOTIC STABILITY

It is the absence of major fluctuations and the ability of a biotic community to undergo homeostasis or achieving equilibrium after a disturbance. It depends upon species diversity, presence of biological control, population density and carrying capacity of environment, biogeo-chemical cycling, seeding growth, degree of disturbance, climax/seral community, etc. The larger the number of species present in a biotic community, the more stable it is.

Maintenance of almost same number of different types of organisms within an ecosystem or biotic community is called 'balance of nature.'

COMMUNITY ECOLOGY

INHIBITION

Sometimes the changes in the habitat caused by one species, while favouring other species, inhibit the growth of the species that caused them. Alders, for example, do not grow as well in acidic soil as the spruce and hemlock that replace them.

As ecosystem mature, and more K-selected species replace γ-selected one, species richness and total biomass increase but net productivity decreases. Because earlier successional stages are more productive than later ones, agricultural systems are internationally maintained in early successional stage to keep net productivity high.

Primary succession takes long time of 1000 years or more while secondary succession takes 50-100 years for grass and 100-200 years for forest. *Ferns* are generally the first to grow after forest fire because of their underground rhizomes. Secondary succession is not completed if invaded by weeds e.g. *Sphagnum, Eichhornia, Lantana, Eupatorium.*

Pioneer Community : It is the first biotic community on a base area.

Seral Community : Transitional community appearing in an area during biotic succession.

Climax Community : Stable, self-perpetuating and final community appearing in an area and at the end of biotic succession which is in perfect harmony with climate of the area-hence *climate climax community.*

Dominant Species : It is the most numerous and generally the largest of the species present in a seral/climax community which exerts the maximum influence.

Sere : It is the sequence of developmental stages from pioneer to climax communities, e.g. Lithosere (on rock), psammosere (on sand), hydrosere (in water). *Xerarch/Hydrarch* : series of developmental stages in an area/water body. Biotic succession involves changes to long-lived plants, greater species diversity, niche specialisation, increase in biomass, higher soil humus, food webs, stable biotic community and mesic conditions.

So one can say that causes of succession are as follow :

(*i*) Baring of an area

(*ii*) Changes brought about by pioneer and seral communities not favourable to them but favourable to next ones.

LITHOSERE-XEROSERE (SUCCESSION ON BARE ROCKS)

(A) Lichen Stage : Bare rock is invaded first by *crustose* lichens (e.g. *Graphis, Rhizocarpon*). They corrode the rock at places causing *foliose lichens* (e.g. *Parmelia, Dermatocarpon*) to invade, eliminate crustose lichens and creating conditions for invasion by mosses. In tropics, blue green algae are pioneers instead of lichens.

(B) Moss Stage : Mosses capable of tolerating drough invade the human rich holes created by foliose lichens, e.g. *Tortula, Grimmia, Polytrichum.* They create more humus and shade to eliminate lichens.

(C) Annual Grass Stage : Annual grasses are slowly replaced by perennial grasses with runners and rhizomes, e.g. *Heteropogon, Cymbopogon.* Several small animals begin to reside. Herbivorous animals visit the site.

(D) Shrub Stage : Shrubs begin to grow in area occupied by perennial grasses. They increases soil and humus contents besides moisture, e.g. *Rubus, Rhus, Capparis, Zyzyphus.*

(E) Climax Community : Initially hardy, light demanding small trees invade the area. They make the habitat shadier and move moist. Ultimately, trees shrubs and herbs representing the climax community begin to grow in the area.

HYDROSPHERE

(A) Plankton Stage : Phytoplanktons (diatoms, flagellates, blue green algae and green algae) are the pioneers in a freshly formed water body. They are almost immediately followed by zooplanktons that feed on phytoplanktons. Plakton growth produces organic matter which gets mixed with bottom silt for growth of next stage.

(B) Submerged Stage : *Hydrilla, Potamogeton* and *Najas* form dense growth at bottom enriched with organic matter.

(C) Floating Stage : In the shallower regions appear plants with tuberous rhizomatous and creeping stems and leaves floating on the surface of water, e.g. *Nymphaea, Nelumbo.* at places, free floating plants also appear (e.g. *Azolla, Wolffia, Lemna*) to cover to the water surface. Humus rich bottom begins to rise making water shallower.

(D) Red Swamp Stage : In shallower water, amphibian plants (with emergent leaves begin to grow (e.g. *Sagittaria, Typha, Phragmites*). They add more silt and humus at the bottom so that shoves built up.

(E) Sedge/Marsh Meadow Stage : On newly built up shores, *Larese* (Sedge), Juncus, Cyperus, some grasses and herbs (Themeda,Caltha, Polygonum) grow rapidly and lower the water table.

(F) Woodland Stage : Rhizome bearing shrubs and small trees capable of tolerating excessive light and water logged conditions appear on the edges of sedge/marsh meadow, e.g. *Cormus, Cephalanthus, Populus, Alnus.*

(G) Climax Stage : New trees, shrubs and herbs appear which are in perfect harmony with the climate of the area.

CONCEPT OF BIOSPHERE

Biosphere/ecosphere is the living mantle or biologically inhabited part of earth (soil, water and air from depth of oceans to tops of mountains) alongwith its abiotic physico-chemical compound. Biosphere extends to some 22.5 km. Life is most abundant at the interfaces of sea, air and earth. Foundation/maintenance of life is based on (*i*) Flow of energy (*ii*) Circulation of nutrients or biogeochemical cycles.

Subdivisions of Biosphere : Biosphere consists three interacting subdivisions, viz., atmosphere, lithosphere and hydrosphere.

(i) Atmosphere

It is the transparent gaseous mantle surrounding the earth which extends to several kilometers and in differentiated into troposphere (10-18 km), stratosphere (18-50 km), mesophere (50-85 km), thermosphere (85-500 km) and exosphere (500 km to about 1600 km). Troposphere shows lowering of temperature with height (15°C to – 55°C), cloud formation and manifestation of weather conditions. Dust particles are restricted to its lower part. Stratophere contains an *ozonosphere* or ozone layer (for filtering ultraviolet rays) at a height of about 25 km. Ozone (O_3) is produced by action of ultraviolet and other high energy radiations on oxygen, resulting in splitting and interaction of oxygen molecules ($3O_2 \rightarrow 2O_3$). *Ionosphere* is a region of thermo-sphere which is protective and radioreflective.

(ii) Lithosphere

It is outer solid crust of earth. The exposed part or soil supports terrestrial life. It possesses minerals, moisture and organic matter.

(iii) Hydrosphere

Hydrosphere is liquid mantle of earth. It is differentiated into fresh water sea water. Both air and water are essential for supporting life.

CLOSED AND OPEN SYSTEM

Earth is an open system of energy. It is continuously receiving solar energy. A fraction of it is trapped by autotrophs. Rest is emitted back as heat waves. Earth is closed system for materials, neither receiving (except for occasional meteorites) nor giving out anyway. There is recycling of materials/matter between biotic and abiotic components of biosphere. Energy flows through the biosphere to consumers, consumers to consumers organisms to microbes, as also dissipating as heat.

ECOLOGICAL SUCCESSION

It is the successive development of different biotic communities at the same site till a climax community develops there.

Even when the climate of an area remains stable year after year, ecosystems have a tendency to change from simple to complex in a process known as *succession.* This process is familiar to anyone who has seen a vacant lot or cleared woods slowly become occupied by an increasing number of plants, or a pond become dry land as it is filled with vegetation encroaching from the sides.

(i) Primary Succession

Primary succession occurs on base, lifeless substrate, such as rocks, or in open water, where organisms gradually move into an area and change its nature. Primary succession occurs in lakes left behind after the retereat of glaciers, on volcanic islands that rise above the sea, and on land exposed by retreating glaciers. Primary succession that occurs on land in called *XERARCH* succession, to distinguish it from the *hydrarch* primary succession that occurs in open water. Primary succession on glacial moraines provides an example. On bare, mineral-poor soils, lichens grow first, forming small pockets of soil. Acidic secretions from the lichens help to break down the substrate and add to the accumulation of soil. Mossess then colonize there pockets of soil, eventually building to take hold. Over a hundred years, the alders build up the soil nitrogen levels until spruce are able to thrive, eventually crowding out the older and forming a dense spruce forest.

In a similar example involving *Hydrach succession*, an *oligotrophic* lake (poor in nutrients)—may gradually, by the accumulation of organic matter, become *eutrophic*—(rich in nutrients).

Primary succession in different habitats may over the long term arrive at the same kinds of vegetation—vegetation characteristic of the region as a whole. This relationship led American ecologist F.E. Clements, at about the turn of the century, to propose the concept of a final *climax vegetation* (and the related term 'climax community'). With an increasing realization that (1) the climate keeps changing, (2) The process of succession is often very slow, and (3) the nature of a region's vegetation is being determined to an increasing extent by human activities, ecologists do not consider the concept of 'climax vegetation' to be as useful as they once did.

(ii) Secondary Succession

If a wooded area is cleared and left alone, plants will slowly reclaim the area. Eventually, traces of the clearing will disappear and the area will again be woods. This kind of succession, which occurs in area where an existing community has been disturbed, is called *secondary succession*. Humans are often responsible for initiating secondary succession, but it may also take place when a fire has berned off an area, or in abandoned agricultural fields.

WHY SUCCESSION HAPPENS

"Communities evolve to have greater total biomass and species richness in a process called succession." In other words, succession happens because species alter the habitat and the resources available in it, often in ways that favour other species. There dynamic concepts are of critical importance in the process : tolerance, inhibition and facilitation.

(A) Tolerance

Early successioal stages are characterized by weedy-γ-selected species that do not complete well in established communities but are tolerant of the harsh, abiotic conditions in barren areas.

(B) Facilitation

The weedy early successional stages introduce local changes in the habitat that favour other, less weedy species. Thus, the mosses in the Glacier Bay succession fix nitrogen that allows alders to invade. The alders in turn lower soil pH as their fallen leaves decompose, and spruce and hemlock, which require acidic soil, are able to invade.

ECOLOGICAL FACTORS

Ecological Factors : Ecology is the study of plants in reciprocal relationship with their environment. The two aspects of ecology are :

(*i*) Autoecology : Ecology of individuals.

(*ii*) Synecology : It is the study of interaction between all the living organisms in a natural community.

ECOSYSTEM

It is a system of interacting organisms and non-living substances. Ecosystem may be large or small, complex or simple.

The common ecological factors are

(A) Physical Factors

(B) Chemical Factors.

(A) *Physical Factors :* They include temperature, light, wind, gravity, soil conditions, pressure and presence or absence of natural barriers. Most organisms have an optimum temperature for their living and minimum and maximum temperature beyond which they cannot survive.

Adaptations such as aestivation, hibernation and diapause help the organisms to overcome adverse temperatures. Light also plays a major role in life of plants and animals. The organisms active during the day are **diurnal** and those active in the night are **nocturnal**.

Wind, rather the velocity and direction of wind affects the usual course of animals.

(B) *Chemical Factors :* They include quality of soil and water, oxygen, carbon dioxide, obnoxious gases and the quality and quantity of usuable foods.

LIMITING FACTORS AND THEIR OPERATION

Limiting factors are often classified in two categories: (a) Density Dependent and (b) Density Independent.

The effect of the former on a population increases as the population increases in density. It is essentially a stabilizing influence on growth and causes a population to level off at carrying capacity. A density-independent factor, coversely, affects many or few individuals without reference to the population level.

Food supply is generally density dependent. The more there are to eat it, the less there is for each individual and the greater the effect of food scarcity. By contrast, a flood is density independent, since it may wipe out an entire population of a species, whether there are few or many.

BIOGEOGRAPHY

(A) FOREST TYPES IN INDIA

The word 'Forest is derived from Latin 'Foris' meaning *outside*, the reference being to village boundary of fence, and must have included all uncultivated and uninhabited land. Today a forest is any land managed for the diverse purposes of forestry whether covered with trees, shrubs, climbers etc. The Indian word 'Jungle' has been adapted in the English language to describe a collection of trees, shrubs etc. that are not grown in a regular manner, as contrasted with 'forest, which is any vegetation under systematic management. Legally, a forest is any land, including the vegetation growing on it, that has been so declared under a legal enactment. *Forestry has been defined as the theory and practice of scientific management of forests, including their creation when necessary for the continuous provision of produce and services.'*

Forests are one of the most striking features of the land surface. They vary greatly in composition and density, and stand in marked contrast to meadows and pastures. The seenic effect of forests changes with the season like the patterns in a Kaleidoscope. Certain forests are evergreen, like the Deodar forests of Kashmir, while others are deciduous, becoming leafless, either before the advent of winter when vegetative activity almost ceases, such at the oak forests of the Himalayas, or else just before the onset of intense dry summer, to reduce transpiration to the minimum, like the teak forests of the Central India. The falling leaves in some species becomes bright oranges or golden yellow. In others the young foilage is pink. Such autumnal and vernal tinges are a vivid contrasts to the general green or straw-coloured background and are extremely pleasing. Unlike animals, plants do not have the power of locomotion. They also cannot construct shelters or generate heat to withstand the adverse effects to the environment of which they are a captive. Therefore, to survive, they wear the evidence of this fact in the form of structural adaptations such as leaflessness in summer to minimize transpiration, thorns to ward off browsers, poisonous sap etc.

In the Indian subcontinent, the term forest does not merely mean an area covered with trees but it carries the impression of an entity that in sum total of ecological, edaphic and biological parameters. According to the cultural traits of the country, forest hold a very important place in the life and philosophy of the people apart from the material gains that it brings about continously ever since the birth of civilization.

Forests are a renewable source and contribute substantially to economic development. They have a major role in enhancing quality of environment. India has an area of 752.3 lakh hectare notified as forests, of this, 406.1 lakh hectare area is classified as **reserved** and 215.1 lakh hectare as **protected. Unclassified** Forest Area is spread over 131.1 lakh hectare. About 19.47 per cent of the total geographical area is under actual forest cover. However, independent forestry experts put the figure much lower. They say not more than 11 per cent of India's total area is under forest cover.

Forest Types

The vast expanse of the country spraed over regions from temperate to sub-tropical zones coupled with wide varieties of relief, temperature and rainfall, the country provides ideal natural condition for the growth of forests that would represent the range and variety of forests species that could rarely be found in any single country of the world.

A broad review of the natural growth of forests will reveal the astounding range of varieties that exists. Thus Tropical Wet Evergreen Forests occur in the Western Ghat, and hilly areas of Assam and Northeastern regions. These areas are those having the highest rainfall in the country (around 2500 mm/year). The rainfall regimes of 1900-2500 mm/annum holds Tropical Semi-evergreen varities. Tropical Moist Deciduous type finals their natural habitat in the regions having annual rainfall of 1250 mm to 1900 mm. The next below rainfall regime, 750-1250 mm holds the Tropical Dry Deciduous type of Forests. Areas having lesser rainfall have developed Tropical Thorn Forests ultimately leading to a practical absence of vegetation in the arid and desertic tracts. A very different variety of forests exist in the different zones of Great Himalya. The southern most ranges of the Western Himalaya holds the subtropical pine forests. Higher rainfall in the Eastern Himalaya brings about a belt of Wet Temperate Forests immediately about that. These are followed northwards or in other words in the higher ranges by Moist Temperate and Dry Temperate forest ultimately leading to the Alpine Forests in the highest ranges.

The two broad types that emerge from the above discriptions are those of tropical/sub-tropical and the temperate. Again, broadly speaking, the two groups on general terms could be grouped into broad-leaved or coniferous and narrow-leaved or coniferous. Majority of the species that grow in the broad leaved non-coniferous zone are deciduous, whereas the coniferous species are predominantly evergreen.

(B) AFFORESTATION

Forests occupy central position is nature. They restore ecological balance of all ecozystems, maintain biological diversity, act as catchments for soil and water conservation, prevent floods and safeguard future of tribal people. In order to meet such needs, we need to develop massive afforestation programmes of indigenous and exotic fast growing species for production and protection of forestry on suitable land including wasteland. A massive social forestry programme is needed to meet demands of local people for fuel, fodder, timber, etc. Then there is need for wood-based industry. Today, the two major goals for forestry are :

(*i*) Supply of goods and services to people and industry by a well thought out plan of production and long term ecological security through conservation of forest cover and its retoration.

(*ii*) Conservation of forest or Reserve forests i.e. National Parks, sanctuaries, sacred groves, biosphere reserves and all ecologically fragile areas are covered by Government of India. No commercial exploitation can be allowed in these areas.

India Forest Policy aims at 60% forest cover in hills and 20% in plains. For this sustained efforts are made for afforestation and reforestation. Tree plantation movement or Van Mahotsava is being carried out in India since 1950 whereby both government and private agencies perform tree plantation during July and February every year. Conservation of forests aim at management of forests in such a way as to maintain them at optimum form and derive optimum sustainable benefit for present as well as future generations.

Limited Production Forestry : In these forests, the annual increment may be harvested in a very careful and controlled manner so as to avoid soil and tree damage. These forests are present in hilly areas at the height of more than 100 meters.

Production Forests : These are forests of plains. Their scientific exploitation does not pose any threat to environment.

Intensive Plantation : This includes planting of all the available land from village fields, to community land and to road/rail sides and available space. Social and agro-forestry programmes are included in this category.

Production Plantations : This is entirely commercial forestry developed to meet the need of the forest based industry. Plantations are to be done on fallow land not being used for agriculture, mostly free grazing lands. Short rotation species are to be preferred over long duration sal and teak.

(C) DEFORESTATION

It is a threat to the economy, quality of life and future of the environment. Main causes of deforestation in India are explosion of human and livestock population, increased requirement of timber and fuel wood, expansion of cropland and enhanced grazing. Another cause of forest degradation is construction of roads along the mountains. Increased demand for fuel-wood, wooden crates, paper, board and newsprint have led to large scale tree felling. Ideally one third (33%) of land of a country must be covered by forest. In India forest cover is only 19.43%, out of which only 13% are thick forest. Rest is bushy land. Deforestation has caused intensified soil erosion, accentuated floods and draught and loss of precious wild life and has led to deterioration of economy and quality of life of two weaker sections of society.

India is losing about 1.5 million hectares of forest cover each year. Nearly one per cent of the land surface of India is turning barren every year due to deforestation. In the Himalayan range, the rainfall has declined 3 to 4 per cent due to deforestation.

CAUSES OF DEFORESTATION

(*a*) *Jhuming :* Prevalent in early stages, even now in some 30 million ha. Jhum of N.E. India is called podu in A.P., bewar or dahza in M.P., dahi (firing) in Orissa, gudia and chas. Technically it is known as shifting cultivation. In India about 5 lakh hectares of land is cleared every year through lopping, burning the remainders, mixing the ash with soil and sowing the cleared land with crop seeds. The land is used for 2-3 years without manuring. This results in nutrient depletion, reduced moisture retention and increased soil erosion. Weeds may grow in such areas e.g. *Eupatorium, Parthenium, Eichhornia.*

Even otherwise jhumed sites initially encourage the growth of animals.

(*b*) *Hydroelectric Projects :* Dams, reservoirs and hydroelectric projects submerge forest tract, killing all plants animals.

(*c*) *Forest Fires :* Huge forest fires engulfing areas of 40,000 km^3 have occurred in Indonesia in 1983 and 1997.

(*d*) *Human Establishment :*

(*i*) *Mountain and Forest Roads :* Construction of roads and railways in the hilly forested areas brings about a lot of deforestation, land slides and soil erosion. Large sections are dynamited. This weakens the already fragile mountain system. The fragments pore into valleys and streams. They weaken the slopes and increase soil erosion.

(*ii*) *Canals :* Sarda Sahayak Canal Irrigation Project was commissioned in eastern UP in 1974 to irrigate 16 lakh hectares of land. In 1987, Singh and Afroz found that seepage from canals has damaged 13,677 houses, harmed 2200 cattle, killed about a million mature Sal trees and put about 1,42,000 hectares of land out of cultivation.

(*iii*) *Overgrazing :* India with 2.4% geographical area has some 500 million livestock population. Grazing area is only 13 million hectares where one hectare of land supports only 6 livestock heads. The remaining livestock naturally graze in forests trampling seedlings and causing compaction of soil. The latter reduces water storing capacity and increases runoff.

(iv) *Requirement of Wood :* It is rising. Some 300 million m^3 for fuel and 40 million m^3 for industry, mostly timber and paper industry. Naturally several million hectares of forest land is stripped to meet this demand.

(D) SOCIAL FORESTRY

Started in 1976 by NCA. Raising quick growing multipurpose plants in common village lands for meeting requirement of fodder, firewood and small timer. Social forestry seeks the use of public and common land to produce firewood, fodder and small timber for the use of the rural community to relieve pressure on existing forests needed for soil and water conservation. The programme includes raising, planting and protecting trees with multiple uses (firewood, fodder, agrticultural implements, fruits etc.) for the rural commiunity.

The National Forest Policy 1988

Stressed peoples involvement as one of the essential components of forest management in the development and protection of forests. The **main features** of the 1988 Forest Policy are :

(*i*) Maintenance of environmental stability through preservation and restoration of ecological balance.
(*ii*) Conservation of natural heritage.
(*iii*) Check soil erosion and denudation of catchment areas of rivers, lakes and reservoirs.
(*iv*) Check on extension of desert areas.
(*v*) Substantial increase in forest density through afforestation.
(*vi*) Steps to meet requirements of fuelwood, fodder, minor forest produce and timber for rural and tribal populations.
(*vii*) Increase in productivity of forest to fulfil the natural needs.
(*viii*) Encouragement of efficient utilisation of forest produce and optimum substitution of fodder and fuel wood and
(*ix*) Steps to promote peoples participation in forest conservation.

(E) ENDANGERED PLANTS

The species which are in danger of extinction and whose survival is unlikely if the causal factors continue to be operating. Their number have been reduced to a critical level or whose habitats have been so drastically reduced that they are deemed to be in immediate danger of extinction.

The forest administration in India is more than 100 years old. Efforts to identify plant species as a part of wild life and to recognize the importance for providing special protection to endangered plant species have so far been negligible. While the rapid disappearance of some beautiful animals stimulated efforts to protect fauna. In 1968 is an International Conference (UNESCO 1968) problem of conservation of Flora and Fauna was appreciated and several recombinations were made urging the **International Biological Programme (IBP),** the international union for conservation of Nature and Natural Resources (IUCN) and various national and international organisation to initiate studies in to the problems involved, particularly the problem of protecting and preserving wild fauna and flora in their natural habitat/ecosystems establishing nature reserver. Later at the 10th General Meeting of the IUCN, the survival Service Commission reviewed the status of endangered species of plants and their habitats. The recent promulgations of the United States Endangered Species Act (1973), the UK Wild Creatures and Wild Plant Act (1975), development of international conventions on conservation (wetlands convention) and the setting up of Biological records centre of the Nature Conservancy, UK, and threatened plants, orchids, lycads, treewide awakening of the need for the conservations, preservation and protection of floras of the world.

According to the volume 5 of Red Data Book on angiosperms started by Survival Service Commission of the IUCN in the year 1970 (Melville, 1970), it is estimated that out of the total of three lakhs (0.3 million) species of plants in the world, over 20,000 were in the category of either **endangered or vulnerable and threatened with extinction by the year 2000 A.D.**

Example : (*i*) *Cypripedium cordigerum* D.Don. (orchidaceae) (Lady's Slippes Orchid), threatend due to trade. (*ii*) *Cypripedium elegans* (*Cypripedium himalacicium* (*iii*) *Cypripedium, Macranthon* (*iv*) *Dendrobium densiflrum.*

RED DATA BOOKS

IUCN is International Union for conservation of Nature and Natural Resources with head quarters at Morges, Switzerland. It maintains a *red data book* (two volumes) about threatened species. The book has enlisted 277 mammals and 321 birds. India has the maximum number of threatened species in this Red Data Book. The number of threatened plants is over 100 e.g. Pitcher plant, Indian Podophyllum, Snow Orchid. It has classified threatened species on the basis of distribution (past/present/continuous/ discontinuous) abundance and quality of habitat, decline in population, biotic potential and potential value. The book has pink pages for critically endangered species. As soon as a species recovers, it is deleted from the pink page and entered on a green page.

Endenism

Endemic species is a species which is found in a particular natural habitat beyond which it is unkonwn. India has a large number of endemic species.

(*i*) *Elettaria cardamomum*
(*ii*) *Ficus religiosa*
(*iii*) *Butea monosperma*

Endemics, which are confined to narrow, restricted areas or specialized ecological niches, also in some respects fall in the category of threatened plants. Some phytogeographers believe that endemic species or genera are the survivors of the one time widely distributed groups, which are now in the course of gradual extinction. Other maintain that they are newly evolved and recent forms still in the process of extending their geographical range of distribution. In such cases, due to their rarity they are to be considered as threatened plants, because any disturbance or imbalance in their narrowly confined ecosystems/habitats could mean extermination of the species.

Isolation, as in the case of island floras, and natural barriers such as mountain ranges are consiered main factors resulting in endemism.

India has a very rich element of endemics in its flora. According to Chatterjee (1940) Indian subcontinent has about 7,000 endemic species and 134 endemic genera. Of these, the Himalayas and the Khasi Hills account for about 3,000 and Deccan peninsula for about 2,000 endemic species. The figures speak eloquently of the great need for protecting the endemics. This can be done effectively by carefully analyzing the floristic composition of the various phytogeographical units of Indian flora and by selecting suitable natural forests is these units and preserving them us 'Biosphere Reserves'.

Sapira Himalagana, Uvaria lurida, Alcimandra cathcartii, Magnolia gustavii, M. Peliana, Pachylarnax Pleiocarpa, Nepenthes Khasiana, Dicentra royler, several species of *Primula* and *Rhododendron* and the Lady's slipper orchids. *Paphiopodilun insigne, P. hirsutissimum, P. faireenum, P. spicenianum, P. venusturm*, are some of the noteworthy endemics of the Himalayas and Khasi Hills. *Antiaris toxicarai, campanual cytinoids, Pedicularis perroter* and some species of the Podostemaceae are endemic to western ghats or the Nilgiri Hills South India.

(F) BIODIVERSITY

Biodiversity is the number of species of different organisms present is an area. Thus, biodiversity includes all plants, animals and micro-organisms of an area. Earth is endowed with an immensely rich variety of life forms which roughly consists of 30,000 green plants, 8,00,000 insects, 23,000 fishes, 2,000 birds, 6,500 reptiles, 4,100 mammals and few thousand microbes. Thus, *biodiversity* means variation and abundance of species and their habitats. According to the *World Resources Institute*, 'biodiversity' is variety of the world's organisms including their genetic diversity and the assemblage they form. It is the blanket term for natural biological wealth that underguards human life and well-being. India is recognized as a country uniqluy rich in biodiversity, because of its tropical location, varied physical features and climate. It consists of approximately 850 bacteria, 23,000 fungi, 25,000 algae, 1,600 lichens, 2,664 bryophyts, 1,022 pteridophytes, 64 gymnosperms, 15,000 angiospersm, 53,430 insects, 5050 molluscs, 2,546 fishes, 204 amphibians, 456 reptiles, 1,228 aves, 372 mammals.

CONSERVATION OF BIODIVERSITY

There is currently an enormous amount of general concern over the threat to biological diversity. Extinction of species may be natural or man made. However, the cause of concern is the rate at which species are becoming extinct today due to human interference. Some of the other causes for the loss of biodiversity are :

(*i*) degradation and destruction of habitats due to human needs.
(*ii*) Husting and over-exploitation mainly for commercial purposes.
(*iii*) Introduction of exotic species.
(*iv*) Pollution and poisoning stress on ecosystem.
(*v*) Global warming and green house effects.
(*vi*) Improper use of agro-chemicals and perticides etc.

The loss of biodiversity is not only an ethical tragedy, but also a great social, economic and cultural one. Without biological diversity use should perish. Hence, efforts are being made to save biodiversity. Conservation of biodiversity can be divided into two categories : *In-situ conservation* and *Ex-situ conservation.*

(a) *In-situ* conservation

This is the conservation of biodiversity through their maintenance within natural or even human-made ecosystems in which they occur. This type includes a system of protected areas of different categories, managed with different objectives to bring benefit to the society. National Parks, Sanctuaries, Nature Reserves, Natural Monuments, Cultural Landscape, Biosphere Reserves, etc. belong to this type of conservation.

(b) *Ex-situ* conservation

This is conservation outside their habitat by perpetuating sample populations in genetic resource centres, zoos, botanical gardens, culture collections, etc. or in the form of gene pools, and gamete storage for fish, germplasm, banks for seeds, pollen, semen, ova, cells, etc. Plants are more readily maintained than animals. In this type of conservation, seed banks, botanical gardens, pollen storage, tissue culture and genetic engineering have been playing important role.

(*i*) *Protected Area Network :* In-situ conservation of wildlife includes a comprehensive system of protected area. There are different categories of protected areas, which are managed with different objectives for bringing benefits to the society. These include (*a*) National Parks (*b*) Sanctuaries (c) Biosphere Reserves (*d*) Natural Reserves (*e*) Natural Monuments (*f*) Cultural Landscape.

(*ii*) *Sanctuary :* It is an area where killing or capturing of any species or bird or animal is prohibited except under the order of the competent authority and whose boundaries and character should be sacrosanct as far as possible. A sanctuary is the whole or portion of a reserved or protected forest as declared by the Government.

(*iii*) *National Park :* It is an area dedicated by statute for all time to conserve flora and fauna and historical objects of national significance and wild life, and where provision is made for the enjoyment of the same by public. A National Park is created by legislative action and can be abrogated or modified by the Legislature of the state concerned. There are 67 National Parks and 394 Sanctuaries with a total area of about 1,41,298 sq. km. representing roughly 4% of the country's geographical area.

(G) BIOSPHERE RESERVES

The idea of 'biosphere reserve' was initiated by UNESCO under the aegis of Man and Biosphere (MAB) Programme, to provide a global network of protected areas for conserving natural communities. It was a new concept which was elaborated by a workshop convene by UNESCO, in 1973, which highlighted the need to conserve diversity of living organisms essential for economic, scientific, educational and cultural needs of the present and future generations.

Following are the objectives of biosphere reserves :

(*i*) To conserve representative samples of ecosystem of the world as opposed to species or habitat conservation.

(*ii*) To promote and facilitate ecological and environmental research.

(*iii*) Provide opportunities for education and training to local people regarding biosphere and its conservation.

(*iv*) Promote appropriate sustainable management of the living resources.

(*v*) Promote international co-operation.

In brief, it combines below mentioned areas :

(*a*) Conservation

(*b*) Research

(*c*) Education

(*d*) Local Involvement.

They include a wide range of ecosystems, ranging from undisturbed communities to degraded areas. In a biosphere reserve, multiple land use is permitted by designating various zones, the *Core Zone* (where no human activity is permitted), the *Buffer Zone* (where limited human activity is allowed) and the *Manipulation Zone* (where a large number of human activities would go on).

The core area of biosphere reserve should be kept completely free from tourism or any other activity. The buffer zone can be used in a limited way for wildlife educational tourism and related (non-destructive), social, cultural and economic activities by the local population.

(H) CONVENTION ON BIOLOGICAL DIVERSITY (CBD)

The United Nations Convention on Biological Diversity in intended to ensure effective international action to curb thg destruction of biological species, habitats and ecosystems. It was opened for signature at the UN-conference on Environment and Development the Earth Summit—in Rio de Janeiro, Brazil on 5th June, 1992. The convention subsequently came into force on December 29, 1993.

CBD sets three goals as given below :

(*i*) The conservation of Biodiversity

(*ii*) Sustainable use of biological resources

(*iii*) Equitable sharing of benefits which would accrue from such use.

It recommends *in-situ conservation* as the fundamental mechanism and ex-situ method's as complementary mechanism. The convention encourages research on resources to be carried out in the country of origin. They should share benefits arising from the commercial use of genetic resources with the country providing the resources.

CLIMATE CHANGE

Back in the 1960s and 1970s, after some year of careful observations of CO_2 in atmosphere, it became evident that its concentration was increasing. In this context, earlier findings which indicated a possibility of climate change due to so called 'green house effect' of carbon dioxide and other radioactive gases assumed great significance. The increase of concentration of CO_2 and subsequently, observed increase of concentration of methane and other green house gases were attributed to a considerable extent to human activities, in particular, to emissions of green house gases into the atmosphere from the burning of fossil fuels. It was recognized that global climate can be modified by inadvertent humans action. We can study the global climate change under the following three sub-headings (*i*) Global Warming, Green House Effect, Ozone Depletion.

Global Warming

Global warming has often been described as one of the most serious environmental problems ever to confront humanity as this problem is closely linked to the process of development and economic growth itself.

While the pattern of future warming is very much open to debate, it is indisputable that the surface of the earth has warmed, on an average, 0.3 to 0.6°C since the late 19th century. The ten warmest years in the last 130 years, have all occurred in the 1980s, and 1990s. And within this ten years the three warmest years were in 1990s.

Global climate models show that due to a temperature rise, warmer ocean release more energy into the atmosphere, leading to more intense and violent storms. Illustrative of this is the 1991 cyclone of Bangladesh and more recent is Orissa cyclone of 1999.

The frequency and intensity of El Nino have been increasing. We have faced a strong El Nino is 1997-98, which, in turn, was responsible for forestfires in Indonesia and Sumatra. The seasonal rain which could behave doused the fire did not arrive due to El Nino. All this supports the theory that what is altering the Earth's climate is the accumulation in the atmosphere of green house gases generated by human activities.

Scientists continue to be worried by the phenomenon of global warming. Notwithstanding the highly exaggerated predictions by environmentalists, scientists are veering to the view that the world is indeed facing a grave threat from the effects of global warming scientists have recently discovered that the Quelccaya ice cap in the South American Andes—the hemisphere's largest glacier is melting.

There are other precurious indicators too : half the glacier ice on the European Alps has dwindled over the past 100 years. Antarctica is experiencing its hottest temperatures in over 4,000 years. In October 1998, an iceberg, 7,125 sq. km in area, separated from the Ronnieë ice shelf, the second largest ice cap in Antarctica. The Arctic ice, too is now one third thinner than it was in 1976. Meanwhile, the Inter-governmental Panel on Climate Change (PCC) in its scientific consensus has warned that global mean temperature will rise by 1 degree = 3.5 degree in the 21st century statistical evidence also speak for themselves. Thirteen of the 14 hottest years is history of the planet have occured since 1980 and six of the eight months of 1998 were the warmest since 1866, with July being the hottest single month ever recorded.

EL NINO

El Nino literaly means Child Christ in Spanish. It takes its name from the fact that it arrives usually during season of christmas. This weather phenomena which occurs in cycles, resulting in a reversal of wind flows. Instead of blowing from South America towards Asia across the Pacific, El Nino results in the reverse flow from Asia towards South America. So instead of bringing in rains to Asia, it takes away the moist air and dumps unwanted rains across the Pacific, causing floods. For Asia, it leaves large tracts like Indonesia without rains and creates drought in some South Pacific Islands or even Australia. It occurs because of the warming up (which is generally cold during winter) of the coastal waters of the eastern pacific in South America, off the cost Peru. This warming spread westward into the Central Pacific. The stronger the El Nino, the more intense the changes in the weather. Due to warm waters, a low pressure is created over southern pacific ocean (which usually has a high pressure) and to balance it a high pressure develops over indonesia (which usually has a low pressure over it). As a result, the reversal of wind flow occurs. The 1997 El Nino was worse for Asia, particularly, Indonesia. Papua New Guinea faced severe droughts. Forest fires in Indonesia, worsened by the drought and dry weather are supposed to be caused by El Nino.

GREEN HOUSE EFFECT

The green house effect is a fundamental property of the Earth's atmosphere. The atmospheric green house effect warms the Earth surface by reflecting back down to it a portion of the solar heat energy, the Earth surface sends skyward. The atmosphere is transparent to the Sun's visible light (short-wave), which is absorbed by the Earth's surface. The Earth then slowly expels this stored heat in the form of invisible infra-red radiation (long wave radiation). But, the atmosphere acts something like a one-way mirror, reflecting some but not all of this radiated heat energy. It comes back down to earth to warm its surface further.

The chief green house gases are water vapour, CO_2 methane, nitrous oxide and various complex human-made compounds. They are entirely responsible for reflecting downward heat that the Earth's surface would otherwise send into space. The gases that makes rest of the atmosphere, nitrogen (78%), oxygen (21%) and Argon (0.9%) are transparent to heat as well as to light and contribute nothing to the green house effect. Without this effect, the Earth's surface on an average would be 33 degrees celsius colder, yielding an ice-covered planet inhospitable to life as we know it. Having some green house gases in the air, thus, makes life possible. But if their concentrations exceed critical levels, conditions could become less favourable for human beings and other species.

Today, however, concentration of most of the greenhouse gases are rising due to the growth of a relatively new influence on the atmosphere-people, with their modern consumer life styles and their large numbers. Human activities have come to rival natural processes as a source of heat trapping gases without producing comparable sinks to aid in the gases removal from the atmospher. As a result of this imbalance, green house gases are accumulating in the atmosphere.

(A) The Green House Gases

Although there are dozons of green house gases, four of them are most important, which are closely linked to common human activities. These are as follows :

Green House Gases	Green House Effect
Carbon dioxide	55%
Methane	15%
CFCs	24%
Nitrous Oxide	6%

Carbon dioxide is responsible for more than half the human contribution to the green house effect, CO_2 concentrations have increased from 280 parts per million at the dawn of the industrial revolution to around 355 ppm today. Each year, human beings shift 6 billion metric tonnes of fossil carbon (coal, petroleum, natural gas) from the Earth to the air in the form of 22 billion tonnes of CO_2. The destruction of forests and the degradation of soils adds an estimated 5-9 billion tonnes of CO_2 to the atmosphere. About half of CO_2 released by human activities is quickly absorbed by the oceans and plants and half of the global emission remains, in the atmosphere indefintely, contributing to green house effect. Methane (CH_4) is released as a result of the combustion of carbon and microbial decays in the absence of oxygen. This occurs in the cultivation of wetland rice, the burning of plant material, land fills and the digestive systems of cattle and termites. Methane is also emitted from coal mines and the production and distribution networks of natural gas. Methane is 50 times more powerful in trapping heat than CO_2. Human activities have more than doubled its concentration from 0.7 ppm (parts per million) in pre-industrial times to more than 1.7 ppm today. Because it is removed from the atmosphere relatively rapidly by chemical reactions in the air, emissions, reductions of only about 15 to 20 per cent would be required to stabilize methane at its current high concentrations.

Nitrous oxide (N_2O) is produced by a variety of biological processes in soils and water. Although its concentration increase of 8 per cent since pre-industrial times (from 288 to 310 parts per billion) is because of human influence, soil cultivation, biomass burning and fossil fuel combustion—all play some role in nitrous oxide production. Bringing new land into cultivation may be largest source of the gas. Two recently identified major sources are the production of nylon and nitrogen fertilizers. It is estimated that a 70 to 80 per cent reduction in human emissions of N_2O would be needed in order to stabilize concentrations at their present high level.

(*a*) *Chloro Fluoro Carbons (CFCs) :* Industrial gases known as CFCs are powerful heat trappers. But, the net impact of CFCs on climate change may be natural because they also contribute to the depletion of upper atmospheric ozone layer. Production of CFCs is being gradually phased out under the Montreal Protocol (1987), but they are still abundant in the atmosphere. Some of the compounds being developed to replace them are also green house gases.

(*b*) *Ozone (O_3) :* It is a powerful green house gas in upper atmosphere. Ozone protects living beings from the sun's potentially harmful UV-β radiation. Near the Earth's surface, however ozone is a human made pollutant produced by the interaction of sunlight and industrial and vehical waste gases that damages living tissues of animals and some plants.

(*c*) *Water Vapour :* It is the most abundant green house gas. Its concentrations are regulated by overall atmospheric temperature and pressure, not human emissions. However, water vapour plays a major role in human-induced climate change through what is called a 'feed-back loop'. If increasing concentrations of CO_2 and other gases raise global temperatures that will draw more water vapour by evaporation and evapotranspiration into the atmosphere, complifying the warming.

(B) Impact of Green House Effect

It is estimated that due to the green house effect, the Earth's temperature will rise. On a world wide average, temperatures would rise by 1 to 3.5°C by the year 2100. If CO_2 concentration doubles, global sea level could rise from 8 to 29 centimeters by the year 2030 and by as much as one metre by the end of 21st century. A rise of one metre will permanently inundate thousands of square miles of low-lying coastal land.

Other effects would be :

- Polar ice caps will melt.
- Rising sea level will cause salination of land.
- Many animals and plant species will become extinct in the changed environment.
- Agricultural productivity will decrease because of changes in soil, water and microbial population.
- Human health may also be affected as rising temperatures expand the area vulnerable to tropical disease, malaria and dengue fever.
- By shifting precipitation pattern that determine placement of clean water supply and sanitation infrastructure, a warming climate could undermine these services.
- Farmers in wealthy countries, aided by lengthened growing seasons, are likely to fare better than those in most developing countries, because many tropical crops may not tolerate increased warmth. One per cent reduction in O_3 increases UV radiation on earth by 2%. This increase will induce skin cancer, particularly in white populations. In addition, the global incidence of severe eye diseases (e.g. Cataracts) can be expected to go up. It will also affect human immune systems. Risks involved for plants and micro-organisms are much more serious than direct effects on human health. Many crop plants are sensitive to ultraviolet radiation affect-ing their yields. UV induced reduction in the crop yields of crop plants, in turn, might have serious consequences with regards to global food supply and food security.

(C) Antarctic Ozone Hole

It was first discovered in 1982 by the *British Antarctic Survey*, an Institute of the *Natural Environmental Research Council.* By 1985, it was clear that the ozone layer is destroyed over antartic every year during spring season (sept-oct), heaving a hole in the startosphere. Through this hole, harmful UV-β ray can enter into the Earth's atmosphere.

Studies have shown that during winter, vortex of very cold air blow over the pole. So, neither sunlight nor warmer air from lower latitude enters in tis vortex. The concentration of chlorine monoxide (ClO) is usually very high in this vortex of cold air which is responsible for ozone destruction. But, it can not destroy ozone during this time, since ozone breakdown reactions require light, and antarctic winters are dark. With the onset of spring, sunlight returns and chlorine monoxide reacts with ozone breaking it down to oxygen. Under certain conditions, one molecule of ClO can destroy 10,000 to 100,000 O_3 molecules.

Ozone Depletion and Ozone Hole

The sun emits radiation over a broad range of wavelengths, to which humans eye respond in the region from approximately 400-700 nm. The range can be divided into three categories.

UV–A (ultra violet) 320-400 nm : Not absorbed by ozone.

UV–B (286-320 nm) : Partially absorbed by ozone.

UV–C (200-280 nm) : Completely absorbed by ozone.

Ozone produced is destroyed at a wide range of altitudes in the atmosphere. About 90% of the ozone is present in the stratosphere. The maximum concentration (about 0.5 ppm) occurs between the altitude of 20 to 35 km and the layer at this level is called *ozone layer.* The presence of ozone is an essential necessity for life on Earth. Stratosphere ozone layer absorbs dangerous UV β rays of the sun and thus protects the earth's surface from these high energy radiation.

Over the last few decades O_3 layer is thinning out because of man made pollutants which catalyse the dissociation of O_3 at a very fast rate. Major pollutants responsible for depletion of ozone are chloro-fluorocarbons (CFCs), nitrogen oxides, hydrocarbons and oxides of chlorine and bromine.

APPLIED ECOLOGY

POLLUTION AND ITS CONTROL

Environmental pollutions is a serious problem of the industrialised societies because people have converted the life. Supporting systems of the entire living world into their own resources and have vastly disturbed the natural ecological balance. Serious degradation and depletion have been caused through over use, misuse and mismanagement of resources to meet the humans needs and to satisfy the increasing demands.

The word "pollutionem" (means to make dirty), is the act of polluting the environment. *Environmental pollution* is defined as the unfavourable alteration of our surroundings, wholly as a by product of man's activities through direct or indirect efforts to changes in the physical, chemical and biological characteristics of land, air or water that harmfully effect human life or anydesirable living thing. Human population explosion, rapid industrialisation, deforestation, unplanned urbanisation, scientific and technological advancement etc. are the major causes of environment pollution.

(A) Pollutant : It is a substance, chemical or factor which has the potentiality to adversely affect natural characteristics of environment, natural resources and assets. Pollution may be a substance in wrong place, e.g. fertilizer causes water pollution.

(B) Primary Pollutant : Pollutant persisting in the environment in the form it is produced, e.g. carbon monoxide.

(C) Secondary Pollutant : Pollutant formed from a primary one through change or reaction. Nitrogen oxides and hydrocarbons react photochemically to produce peroxyacyl nitrate and ozone. The secondary pollutants may be more toxic than the primary ones. The phenomenon is called *synergism*.

(D) Qualitative Pollutant : It causes harm due to its nature. It is often produced due to human activity. e.g. insecticides.

(E) Quantitative Pollutant : It is a component which becomes pollutant only when its concentration reaches beyond a threshold value e.g. CO_2, CO.

(F) Degradable Pollutant : The pollutant degrades after some time, either automatically (e.g. heat) or through the agency of microorganisms (= biodegradable, e.g. sewage).

(G) Nondegradable Pollutant : The pollutant does not get degraded or broken down into harmless material, e.g. DDT, plastics.

(H) Atmospheric Pollution : It is the addition of particulate matter, gases and other ingredients into air which can produce an adverse effect on human beings, animals, vegetation, human assets and resources.

Major sources of atomospheric pollution are

(*i*) Combustion of fossil fuels in homes, factories, thermal plants, automobiles, aircrafts, railways etc.
(*ii*) Mining and processing
(*iii*) Chemical industries
(*iv*) Processing industries etc.

(a) Particular Matter

It consists of soot, flyash, dusts of various types, fur, hair, spores, pollen grains etc. Particulate matter is differentiated into settleable (larger than 10 μm) and suspended (less than 10 μm). SPM (suspended particulate matter is maximum in Calcutta (Tokyo is the most polluted city of the world). It is differentiated into aerosol (less than 1 μm), dust (more than 1 μm) and *mist* (liquid, more than 1 μm). Particles of 2 - 4 μm size are mostly deposited in the respiratory tract.

(*i*) *Soot :* (incomplete burning of carbohydrates), smoke, flyash (fine particulate matter passed out alongwith gases during burning of coal) and *dust* deteriorate the quality of articles, log stomata, cover leaf surface, produce allergic reactions, especially bronchial asthma.

(*ii*) Particulate matter from processing industries (e.g. cotton dust, iron mill dust, mine dust, flour mill dust, gem grinding) causes *pneumoconiosis, byssinosis, emphysaema, siderosis* and other pulmonary problems.

(*iii*) Dust and smoke produce smog.

(b) Carbon Monoxide

It is produced due to incomplete combustion and naturally by plants as well as animals. 70% emissions are from automobiles. Carbon monoxide combines with haemoglobin, produces carboxyhaemoglobin or COHb. At 50 ppm, CO converts 7.5% of haemoglobin into carboxy-haemoglobin with 8 hours. It impairs oxygen transport resulting in giddiness, headache, decreased vision, cardiovascular malfunction and asphyxia.

(c) Carbon Dioxide

It is a green house gas the concentration of which is constantly rising (0.033 from 0.029 and expected to be doubled by 2020). In excess it causes headache and nausea.

(d) H_2S

It is a product of putrefaction, treatment of sulphur containing over, refineries, chemical plants and bituminous fuels. It causes mottled *chlorosis* and defoliation in plants, decolourises paints, produces eye irritation, throat irritation and naurea.

(e) Hydrocarbons

They are produced naturally (e.g. marsh gas) as well as due to incomplete combustion. Hydrocarbons are carcinogenic, cause irritation of eyes and mucous membrane and bronchial constriction. There is increased mucus secretion and tearing of alveoli. They give rise to bronchial constriction. There is increased mucus secretion and tearing of alveoli. They give rise to secondary pollutants with nitrogen oxides. Methane (marsh gas) has the potential to destroy ozone.

(f) Sulphur Dioxide

It is produced during combustion of fossil fuels and smelting of sulphur containing ores. Sulphur dioxide produces *smog*. Maximum SO_2 pollution is found in calcutta. It causes membrane damage, destruction of chlorophyll (change to phaeophytin), necrosis and water soaked appearance. Lichens are most sensitive to SO_2 pollution. Mossess and garden pea are also destroyed. SO_2 corrodes metals, equipment, damages buildings, kmarble, paper and textiles. It produces eye irritation, damages respiratory tract, produces *asthama, bronchitis* and *emphysaema*. SO_2 alongwith nitrogen oxides produces acid rain that destroys vegetation and degrades various articles (like SO_2). Threat to Taj Mahal from Mathura refinery is due to pollutant gases comprising SO_2, H_2S and nitrogen oxides. They would convert $CaCO_3$ (marble) into calcium sulphate and calcium nitrate.

(g) Nitrogen Oxides

They are formed electro-photo-chemically in air, burning of fossils fuels and denitrifying bacteria. Maximum NO_2 pollution is recorded from Baroda. Nitrogen oxides causes *necrosis, defoliation*, dieback and death of plants. Like SO_2, they corrode metals and deteriorate paints as well as various articles. At less than 0.1 ppm, nitrogen oxides impair sensation of smell. The oxides produce eye irritation, lung oedema, dilation of arteries, injury to liver and kidneys. Carcinogenic, form Secondary pollutants.

(h) Fluorides

They are given out during refining of minerals (e.g. aluminium) as also from ground water. Fluorides cause *fluorosis*. In plants there is chlorosis and necrosis of leaf tips and leaf margins, followed by abscission. In animals, fluorides bring about abnormal calcification of bones and teeth (making them weak), frequent diarrhoea and swelling of knee bones. In humans, there is mottling of teeth, weak bones, boat-shaped posture, knocking knees, gastrointestinal and neuromuscular disorders.

(*i*) Chlorofluorocarbons/Chlorofluoromethane/Freon/Aerosols

They are chemicals used as refrigerants, propellants and solid plastic foams. The chemicals are release as aerosols by jets flying at high altitudes. Alongwith nitrogen oxides, chlorofluoro-carbons react with ozone of ozonosphere and depletes the same. Hole in the ozone shield over Antarctic region has widened from 129 to 133 dobson units in 1994 alone. This can increase the amount of ultraviolet radiations reaching the earth.

(j) Photochemical Oxidants

They are secondary pollutants (ozone, peroxyacyl nitrates, aldehydes and phenols) produced due to unsaturated hydrocarbons.

(*i*) *Ozone* : It destroys chlorenchyma, produces necrosis, hardens rubber, damages textiles, injures mucous membranes, dry throat, haemorrhages and eye irritation.

(*ii*) *Peroxy-Acyl Nitrates* : (PAN/PBN/PPN). Young and spongy parenchyma cells are destroyed resulting in silvering, glazing, bronzing and necrosis in leaves. In human beings they cause respiratory distress and eye irritation.

(*iii*) *Aldehydes* : Irritation in gastro-intestinal and respiratory tracts.

(*iv*) *Phenols* : Damage to Kidneys, liver, spleen and lungs.

(k) Other Air Pollutants

Mercury (burning of coal, smelting), methyl isocyanate (pesticide manufacture), phosgene (pesticide manufacture, dye industry), ammonia (fertilizer, dye and lacquer industries) and lead (automobile exhausts) are pollutants added to atmophere though they may not reside in them (e.g. lead in soil). *Bhopal gas tragedy* (Dec. 1984) was due to release of phosgene and methyl isocynate (MIC).

(l) Automobile Exhausts

Automobiles burn petroleum inefficiently causing 80% of air pollution and 75% of noise pollution in urban areas. They release hydrocarbons (13.7%), carbon monoxide (77.2%), nitrogen oxides (7.7%), sulphur oxides, ammonia, aldehydes and lead (90% of total lead poisoning). Lead is present in petroleum in the form of $Pb(CH_3)_4$ and $Pb(C_2H_5)_4$ as antiknock agent.

(m) Smog

Smog is opaque or dark fog having condensed water vapours, dust, smoke and gases (SO_2, H_2S, NO_2 etc.). It causes silvering/glazing and necrosis in plants, allergies and asthma/bronchitis in humans. Some famous smogs of the world are Los Angels smog (1946), London smog (1952), Tokyo (Rome, New York, Sydney, 1870). Smog is of two types :

(*i*) *Classical (London) smog* : It occurs at low temperature, contains sulphur gases (hydrogen sulphide, sulphur dioxide), smoke and dust particles.

(*ii*) *Photochemical (Los Angeles) smog* : It occurs at high temperature over cities and towns due to still air, emission of nitrogen oxides and carbohydrates from automobile exhausts and solar energy. Nitrogen dioxide splits into nitric oxide and nascent oxygen. Nascent oxygen combines with molecular oxygen to form ozone. Ozone reacts with carbohydrates to form aldehydes and ketones. Nitrogen oxide, oxygen and ketones combine to form peroxy-acyl-nitrates.

(n) Pollen/Spores

They cause allergic reactions or hay fever in certain persons.

CONTROL OF AIR POLLUTION

(A) Automibiles

(*i*) Two stroke engines fitted in two wheelers (waste fuel 20-30%) be changed to either four-stroke engines or fitted with catalytic converters specially designed for them. A low cost-catalytic converter has been developed at BHU.

(*ii*) Leaded petrol be replaced with unleaded one and diesel with low sulphur diesel.

(*iii*) Tune-ups (for high air-fuel ratio) and catalytic converters (for oxidising $CO \rightarrow CO_2$ and reducing $NO \rightarrow N_2$) be fitted in automobiles.

(*iv*) Periodic checkup of pollution control for all vehicles.

(B) Bagasse and Rice Husk

Bagasse should not be used as fuel. Rice Husk should be first converted into briquetts.

(C) Fly Ash

About 38% fly ash is produced by coal based thermal plants. It should be removed through wet method and used in building material.

(D) Industrial Pollution : (Control measures)

(*i*) *Tall Chimneys* : They disperse smoke more throughly.

(ii) *Gravity Setting Chambers :* Particles larger than 50 μm settle down.

(iii) *Wet Scrubbers :* A fine spray of water or alkaline fluid is used to remove soluble gases and particles.

(iv) *Bag Filters :* Porousbags of teflon or polyester filterout particulate matter.

(v) *Cyclone Collectors :* They cause settling down of particulate matter through centrifugation.

(vi) *Electrostatic Precipitators :* (ESPs). They are electrically charged plates or electrodes which remove most of the particles present in chimney exhausts.

(E) Vegetation

A broad strip of vegetation along road and around industrial areas reduces particulate pollution. Vegetation can also metabolise toxic gases like CO (e.g. *Ficus, Coleus, Daucos, Phaseolus*), and nitrogen oxides (e.g. *Vitis, Pyrus, Robinia, Rhamnus*).

ACID RAIN

Acid rain is the term coined by Robert Augus (1872). It is rainfall and other forms of precipitation with a pH of less than 5. The most acidic rain has occured over west Virginia, USA with a pH of 1.5. It is caused by large scale emission of acidic gases into atmosphere from thermal power plants, industries and automobiles. The commones ones are *sulphur dioxide, nitrogen oxides* and *hydrogen chloride*. Sulphur dioxide and nitrogen oxides are changed in the atmosphere into sulphuric acid and nitric acid by combining with oxygen and water.

Acid rain damages plants by direct effect on foliage and growing points-chlorosis, necrosis, defoliation, dieback. It causes leaching of essential minerals of soil. Toxic minerals left in the soil further kill the plants. 50% of natural forests have been destroyed by acid rain in Germany, Sweden, north east USA, Romania, Poland etc. Acid rain has also ruined fresh water reservoirs of most industrialised countries, e.g. 80% in Norway, 25% in Sweden, 20% in USA. Acidity dissolves toxic metals like Hg, Pb, Zn, Al. Both acidity and toxic metals kill all types of aquatic life except some algae and fungi. Acid rain corrodes metals, marble, painted surfaces, slate, stone, etc. The phenomenon is called *stone leprosy.*

OZONE DEPLETION

Ozone layer or shield is present in the stratosphere. It protects the earth from short-wave ultraviolet rays (below 300 nm) by changing the same into infra-red rays. A large hole has appeared in ozone shield over Antarctica (first detected by Farman, 1982), and a smaller one over North Pole. Size of the hole varies with the seasons. Thinning of ozone shield has also been reported elsewhere (e.g. 8% between 30°-50°N). Depletion of ozone layer allows harmful UV-radiations to reach earth. It is the major cause of *skin cancer, cataract, dimming of eye-sight*, decrease in immune system and increased susceptibility to herpes.

Thinning of ozone shield is being caused by a number of pollutants like chlorofluorocarbons (14% of total depletion), nitrogen oxides (3.5% depletion), sulphur dioxide, halon, carbon tetrachloride, being released by jets flying in the stratosphere and rockets being fired into space. Others are persistent in the troposphere and gradually pass into stratosphere. Maximum ozone depleting potential or ODP is of chlorofluorocarbon due to release of chlorine by it. A single chlorine atom converts 1 lakh molecules of ozone into oxygen. Consequently, chlorofluorocarbons *(CFCs)* are being replaced by hydrofluorocarbons *(HFCs)* and hydrochlorofluorocarbons *(HCl FCs).* Carbon tetrachloride, halogen and methyl chloroform also deplete ozone by a similar method. Nitric oxide (NO) and other gases released by jets directly react with ozone to form oxygen.

WATER POLLUTION

It is the degradation of quality of water due to addition of substances (inorganic, organic, biological, radiological) or factors (e.g. heat).

(A) Organic Wastes/Sewage

It is waste water having food residue, animal and human excreta, detergents, discharges from commercial and industrial establishments.

(*i*) Raw sewage contains a number of pathogens (dysentery, diarrhoea etc.) coliforms and enterococi.

(*ii*) It stimulates the activity of several decomposer organisms collectively called *'sewage fungus'*. The property of becoming decomposed through microbial activity is known as *'putrescibility'*. Degree of impurity of water due to organic matter is measured in terms of B.O.D. Biochemical oxygen demand or B.O.D. is the oxygen in milligrams required for five days in one litre of water at 20°C for the microorganisms to metabolise organic waste. Low pollution-below 1500 mg/l, medium pollution—1500-4000 mg/l and high organic pollution-above 4000 mg/l.

(*iii*) Water has a brown colouration and an unpleasant odour due to formation of secondary pollutants like CH_4, NH_3, H_2S.

(*iv*) Scum and sludge (H_2S+ metallic ions)

(*v*) There may be algal blooms and entrophication. The latter is due to phosphates present in detergent.

(*vi*) Animals may die due to depletion of oxygen by sewage fungus.

(*a*) *Primary Treatment :* This consists of shredding, churning, floatation, screening and sedimentation.

(*b*) *Secondary Treatment :* The organic matter is decomposed through sewage fungus by either **trickling filter method** (passing through thick bed of gravel) or **activated sludge method** (aeration/oxidation tanks). The cleared water is now chlorinated to kill pathogens. The water can be passed into fields as manured water or into water courses where it may cause eutrophication.

(*c*) *Tertiary Treatment :* Where water is to be recycled, the chlorinated waste water is mixed with alum, ferric chloride and lime for precipitation of salts. Zirconium is also a good precipitant. Another technique is *reverse osmosis*.

(B) Fertilizers

Part of fertilizers added to crop fields are passed down to water bodies during rains through surface run-off. Presence of extra nutrients brings about dense growth of plant and animal life. The phenomenon is called *'eutrophication'*. Eutrophication leads to organic loading, depletion of oxygen, death of animals and fouling of water.

(C) Pesticides

Pesticides spread over crops also pass into water bodies due to surface run-off. In excess they cause immediate and mass scale deaths of aquatic animals. Persistent-perticides (e.g. organochlorine or chlorinated hydrocarbons like DDT) pass into food chain and increase in amount per unit weight of organisms with the rise in trophic level due to their accumulation in fat. The phenomenon is called *biomagnification / bioconcentration/biological amplification*. e.g. 0.01-0.05 parts per billion in water, 10 parts per billion or 0.001 ppm in phytoplankton, 0.04 ppm in zooplankton, 0.4 ppm in clams, 3-8 ppm in fish and 18-75 ppm in water birds like Sea-Gulls. Higher amounts of pesticides cause cerebral haemorrhage, softening of brain, liver cirrhosis, hypertension, thinning of egg shell, malfunctioning of sex hormones. Population of Bald Eagle has declined due to it.

(D) Silt

Silt from soil erosion makes water muddy and unfit for plant growth. Silt may clog gills of fishes.

(E) Thermal Pollution

Hot effluents and hot water (e.g. thermal plants/ atomic reactors) bring about rise in water temperature. Warm water contains less oxygen, has lower rate of putrescibility resulting in increased organic loading, replacement of green algae by blue-green ones. Many animals fail to reproduce e.g. Trout, Salmon.

El Nino is warm ocean *Peru current* that recurrs after every 5-8 years. It kills marine animals and plankton over large tracts along Peru and Ecqudor coasts.

(F) Oil Pollution

Oil spills and refinery discharges cause oil pollution. It reduces oxygenation, inhibits plankton growth and kills animals.

(G) Industrial Effluents

(*a*) *Mercury :* It is changed to water soluble dimethyl mercury which undergoes biomagnification. Eating poisoned animals causes deformity known as *mina mata* disease which is characterized by diarrhoea, Lemolysis, impairment of various senses, meningitis and death.

(*b*) *Copper* : Hypertensions, uremia, occassional fever and coma.

(*c*) *Lead* : (also common from automobile exhausts) Anaemia, vomiting, convulsion, loss of appetite, damage to liver, kidneys and brain.

(*d*) *Zinc* : Vomiting, cramps, renal damage.

(*e*) *Cobalt* : Diarrohoea, hypotension, bone defects and paralysis.

(*f*) *Chromium* : Gastro-intestinal ulcers, nephritis, nervous system disorders.

(*g*) *Cadmium* : Anaemia, hypertension, testicular atrophy, damage to liver and kidneys, diarrhoea and skeletal deformities called *itai-itai* (ouch-ouch, first reported in 1947 in Toyoma city of Japan).

SOIL POLLUTION

It is alteration in soil caused by removal or addition of substances and factors which decreases its productivity, quality of plants and ground water. *Negative soil pollution* is reduction in soil productivity due to erosion and over use. *Positive soil pollution* is reduction is soil productivity due to addition of undesirable substances (e.g. perticides, fertilizers, industrial wastes, air pollutants washed down by rain, faulty sanition). *Landscape/third pollution* is converting fertilie land into barren one by dumping wastes (e.g. ash, sludge, garbage, rubbish, industrial wastes, broken cans, bottles etc.) over it.

(A) Pesticides

They include insecticides, fungicides algicides, rodenticides and weedicides. Pesticides are generally broad spectrum and function as biocides.

(*i*) Organochlorides/chlorinated hydrocarbons : The important ones are DDT (dichlorodiphenyl trichloroethane), BHC (Benzene hexachloride), aldrin, dieldrin and endrin. They are persistent, fat soluble and show biomagnification whence they prove harmful to higher trophic level organisms. Hence their use is being restricted.

(*ii*) Organopesticides : Degradable, but toxic to workers e.g. malathion, parathion, carbamates.

(*iii*) Inorganic pesticides : They contain arsenic and sulphur. Persistent. Hence, their use is highly restricted.

(*iv*) Weedicides : Often persistent and harmful.

(B) Fertilizers

Excessive use causes soil deterioration through decrease of natural microflora. Leading down causes pollution of underground water (third poison). Salts entering crop plants in excess may prove harmful. For example, nitrate rich leaves, fruits and water produce nitrite in alimentary canal that enters bloods, combines with haemoglobin forming *met-haemoglobin* and reducing oxygen transport. It may prove futal in infants. Organic farming involves used of biofertilisers, manures, pesticides of organic origin, biological control and resistant varitiets.

(C) Industrial Effluents/Wastes

They contain a number of toxic substances including cynides, chromates, acids, alkalis and metals like mercury, copper, zinc, lead, codmium etc.

(D) Mine Dust

It destroys vegetation and produces many deformities in animals and human beings.

(E) Soil Salination

It is increase in salt concentration of soil making the soil *halomorphic*. Salination is often accompanied by white incrustation over the surface. It makes the soil barren. Only halophytes can grow over it. Soil salination is caused by the following factors :

(*i*) Parent-rock.
(*ii*) Poor drainage and elevated water table.
(*iii*) Salt rich ground/canal water.
(*iv*) Excessive fertilizers.
(*v*) Salt blown from rocks/sea.
(*vi*) Plants that absorb ions.

In India, 6 million hectare soil is saline. They can be reclaimed by addition of gytosum/related chemicals, trenches and proper drainage, growing salt tolerant plants and blue green alage.

RECYCLING OF WASTES

Sludge from sewage treatment plants be burnt alongwith coal. Organic wastes be composted or employed in biogas plants. Paper, plastics and metals are now recycled. Agricultural wastes are used in manufacture of paper, hard board, annimal feed etc.

Land Degradation

Land becomes slowly unfit for plant growth due to following reasons :

(*i*) **Jumping/Shifting/Swidden Cultivation.** It is the practice of cutting down forest trees, burning of remains, raising crops on cleared area for a few years and then abandoning it. Thin degrades forests and disturbs soil stability. The practice is carried out even now by certain tribals in eastern states of India.

(*ii*) **Soil Erosion :** Removal of natural plant cover by deforestation, overgrazing, improper tilling and overcroping make a soil prove to erosion by wind and water. Soil erosion denudes additional 40,000 ha of land annually in India.

(*iii*) **Desertification :** It is the conversion of fertile land into barren sandy tract. Desertification is due to

(*a*) Overgrazing
(*b*) Drying of rivers/irrigation canals/dry weather
(*c*) Clean tilling, firre and felling of trees
(*d*) Nearness to sandy beach, sand storms and shifting sand dunes.

(*iv*) **Developmental activities** like mining, urban encroachment, human settlement, industrial estates, canals, roads, rail tracks, etc.

LAND AND WATER MANAGEMENT

India has

(*a*) Total land mass—305 million ha.
(*b*) Urban/Industrial area—18 million ha.
(*c*) Rock/Snow Bound—21 million ha.
(*d*) Forests/Pastures—83 million ha.
(*e*) Agricultural—143 million ha.
(*f*) Culturable Wasteland—17 million ha.
(*g*) Fallow—23 million ha. 87 million ha of land is erosion prone. Himalayas constitute major watershed (drainage water flow area) with high sedimentation due to absence of plant cover.

(A) Treatment of Catchment Area : Perennial grasses and trees be planted everywhere with regligible grazing.

(B) Canal Irrigation : This irrigation channels be brick-lined. Irrigation should not lead to water logging and salination.

(C) Ground Water : Abundant in India, but only 30% of the replenishable water is being drawn for agriculture. However, depletion has occurred is Punjab and Haryana.

WASTELAND DEVELOPMENT

Land not put to economic/ecologic use is wasteland. A lot of wasteland occurs even in the thickly populated country like India. It is of two types, culturable and nonculturable.

(A) Culturable Wasteland

It is barren/devastated land which can be reclaimed and put to agricultural use are, e.g. mining and industrial wasteland, degraded forests, saline soils, water-logged soils, stripland, ravinous and gullied land, marshyland, ihaming areas, sandy/arid tracts.

(B) Uncultivable Wasteland

It is barren land which cannot be put to agricultural use, e.g. rocky areas, steep slopes, snow capped mountains, glaciers.

RADIOACTIVE POLLUTION

It is degradation of environment due to release of radioactivity (emission of α-particles, β-particles and gamma rays) by changes in nuclides (atomic nucleus) of sunstable/radioactive elements causing short-range and long range harmful effects on living beings including humans. Radioactivity is measured is units called ROENTGENS or r.

(A) Background Radiation

It is radiation level found in naturally is biosphere due to cosmic rays reaching earth and radio-nuclides found in earth's crust. The naturally occurring radioactive elements are Dranium-238, Uranium-235, Thorium-232, Radium-224, Radon-222, Potassium-40 and Carbon-14. Half life is the time required for one half of radioactive atoms to disintegrate, e.g. 5000 years in C-14. Maximum background radiation is found in Keralal beach where 75% of thorium deposits of the world are found.

(B) Man Made Radiations

They are due to mining and refining of radioactive elements like Plutonium, Uranium and Thorium, nuclear power plants and fuels, preparation of radioactive isotopes, production and explosion of nuclear weapons.

Atomic Reactors

They employ controlled radioactive fission/fusion for liberation of energy. The effects of reactors include:

(*i*) The coolant water causes thermal pollution.

(*ii*) Small amount of radioactivity enters coolant water which undergoes biomagnification to some 75000 times in birds.

(*iii*) They release halogens and inert gases.

(*v*) A mishap can be dangerous as an atomic explosion, e.g. Chernobyl in Ukrain.

(*vi*) Radioactive waste is highly pollutant and its dumping requires several precautions.

Radio-Isotopes : They are used in research (e.g. metabolic pathways), induction of mutations in plants and microorganisms, radiotherapy etc. e.g. Co-60, P-32, C-14, I-25.

Harmful Effects : They were first recorded in 1909 in Uranium miners as skin burns and cancers. Many plants are killed even at low level of radioactivity. Young and recently divided cells are more easily damaged

Short Range Effects : Loss of nails and hair, subcutaneous bleeding, changed proportion of blood cells. Changed metabolic rates, damage to all organs, death in high dose.

Long Range Effects : Tumours, cancers, mutations, genetic deformities, short life span.

Nonionising Radiations : They are UV rays (100-300 nm) which have low penetration. They damage eye sight due to damage of corneal cells, injury to germinative layers, rupture of subcutaneous capillaries, blisters and reddening of skin (sunburn), mutations, skin and other concers due to inactivation of organic molecules and formation of pyramidine dimers in DNA. Damage to ozone layer will bring all these hazards. Thick cuticle, sporopollens, and carotenoids protect plants from UV radiations, especially at higher altitudes. Human beings can protect themselves by wearing sun-glasses. They have an enzyme system for repair of UV damage. Absence of this protective system produces a deficiency called *Xeroderma pigmentosum.*

NOISE POLLUTION

It is a physical form of pollution that affects the receiver directly. Noise pollution in due to release of unwanted sound generally with the value of 80 dB and above. Frequency of sound is measured in Hz (Hertz) while unit of sound in dB (deci Bel).

Range of human hearing is 20 Hz to 2000 Hz. Infrasonic vibrations (below 20 Hz) can be felt because some body parts resonate at this frequency. Ultrasonic vibrations (above 20,000 Hz) are used in imaging, cleaning, drilling cutting, welding and sealing. Moderate conservative produces 60 dB sound, loud conversation 70 dB, plying of trunk/bus 90 dB, jet aeroplane–150 dB, rocket 180 dB. Noise becomes uncomfortable above 100 dB. Sound is produced by loud speakers/public address system, transport vehicles, defence equipment, industries, domestic gudgets and outdoor equipment.

Effects of Noise : Noise brings about

(*i*) Damage to ear drum and impairment of hearing (a ten year exposure to 80 dB impairs hearing by 15 dB)

(*ii*) Interference in conversation and hearing.

(*iii*) Emotional disturbance, development of anxiety and stress (first effect).

(*iv*) Damage to eye sight, colour perception, night vision, etc.

(*v*) Hypertension, decreased heart output and gastric problems.

(*vi*) Startle reaction.

Control Measures

(*i*) Delimination of acoustic soning

(*ii*) Use of cotton pluges or ear muffs in occupational exposure

(*iii*) Developm. nt of quieter machines.

(*iv*) Restricted use of loud speakers.

(*v*) Acoustic furnishing and low voice radio/TV.

(*vi*) Regulation of noise on road.

(*vii*) Green muffler.

CONSERVATION BIOLOGY

Some of the man's activities like hunting of various animals, disrupts the food chains in which there animals normally take parts. The shortening of food chains due to man's activities leads to an imbalance in the functioning of an ecosystem and ultimately in the functioning of the whole biosphere. Modern argicultural activities use a large number of toxic chemicals like pesticides, weedicides and rodenticides, to protect the crop plants from pests and diseases. Some of these poisonous chemicals mix-up with soil and water and are absorbed by the plants from the soil along with water other minerals. In this way, the poisonous chemical substances enter the food chain right from the producer level. When man and other animals eat these plants or their products, the poisonous chemical substances are transformed to their bodies. During the process of food transfer through trophic levels, there harmful chemicals get concentrated at each successive level. The increase in concentration of harmful chemical substances like perticides in the body of living organisms at each trophic level of a food chain is called *biological magnification*. To consume ecosystem, such activities should be minimised.

ECOSYSTEMS AND THEIR CONSERVATION

Ecosystem or biocenosis is a segments of nature/biosphere consisting of a community of living beings and the abiotic/physical environment both interacting and exchanging materials between them. Ecosystem can be temporary (e.g. rain water pond) or permanent, natural or man-made (e.g. aquarium, agriculture), small or large.

Biotic Components : They include all living beings present in an ecosystem producers, consumers and decomposers. The component are connected through food, its contained energy and a web of interrelationships.

(A) Producers

They are autotrophs that manufacture organic compounds from inorganic raw materials with the help of solar energy. Producers are also called *transducers* as they convert solar radiations into chemical energy. Besides food, producers give out oxygen and take in carbon dioxide.

(B) Consumers

They are heterotrophs, mostly animals which feed on other organisms. Consumers are also called *phagotrophes* as they ingest food. *Herbivores/First Order Consumers*. They feed on producers. Also called key industry animals (Elton, 1927), e.g. Deer, Rabbit, Cattle, Goat/Sheep, Grasshopper, protozoans, molluscs, many crustaceans. *Primary Carnivores/second orders consumers*. Feed on primary carnivores, e.g. Owl, Peacock. *Top Carnivores*. Carnivores which are not preyed upon. e.g Lion.

(C) Decomposers

They are saprotrophs which decompose the organic remains by secreting extracellular digestive enzymes. Due to degradation of organic remains, decomposers are also called *reducers*. They are also known as mineralisers as they release minerals trapped in organic remains. *Detrivores* are decomposers, as well as scavengers. Scavangers are consumers of dead bodies, e.g. Vulture, Carrion Beetle. Parasites are consumers that feed on small part of a living being.

Abiotic Components : (*a*) Temperature (*b*) Light (*c*) Wind/Air current (*d*) Humidity/Precipitution (*e*) Water (*f*) Topography (*g*) Back ground.

TROPHIC LEVELS

They are steps or divisions of food chain characterised by specific method of obtaining food. Producers belong to T_1 or first trophic level, herbivores/primary consumers T_2, primary carnivores/secondary consumers T_3, secondary carnivores T_4 etc. Parasites do not have any fixed trophic level. Decomposers constitute the last or deteritus trophic level. *Guild* is the group of species belonging to the same trophic level and exploiting the same resource.

(A) Food Chain

It is the sequence of populations/organisms through which food and its contained energy pass in an ecosystem with members at one step becoming food of later step of the sequence. Common food chains are predator food chains.

Detritus food chain is the *shortest*. Parasitic food chain is the third type.

(*a*) *Aquatic Food Chain* :

Phytoplankton → Zooplankton → Small Crustaceans → Water Insects → Small Fish → Larger Fish → King Fishes.

(*b*) *Land Food Chain* :

- Grass → Grasshopper → Frog → Snake → Peacock → Falcon → Eagle.
- Herbs → Rabbit → Fox → Wolf → Tiger

(B) Food Web

It is a network of food chains which are interconnected at different trophic levels so as to form a number of feeding connections amongst members of a biotic community. e.g. Rabbits preyed upon by Wild dog, Fox, Wild cat and Jackal. These carnivores can also prey upon mice, shrews, and squarrels. Wolf preys upon Jackal, Fox, Wild cat and Sheep/goat. It is eaten by Tiger. Tiger preys upon Deer, Antelope and a number of other animals. In Sunderbans, Tiger does not have its natural preys. It feeds there on fish and crabs.

FLOW OF ENERGY

Ecosystem is continuously obtaining solar energy which is trapped by producers—1.15% in grasslands, 0.9% in Savannah, 0.81% in mixed forest, 5% in crops and 10-12% in sugarcane. The rest is dissipated as heat. A part of energy stored in food is released during respiration. Some of the released energy is used in carrying out body activities while the rest is dissipated. Herbivores feed on producers. Part of the food energy is wasted in digestion and assimilation. Some of the assimilated food is broken down to release energy for performing body activities.

Some of the energy is lost as heat. A very small portion becomes part of the body of herbivore. Herbivores are eaten by primary carnivores, the latter by secondary carnivores and so on. At every step, a lot of energy is wasted. Flow of energy in an ecosystem is unidirectional.

ECOLOGICAL PYRAMIDS/ELTONIAN PYRAMIDS (ELTON, 1927)

Ecological pyramid is the graphic representation of an ecological parameter (number, biomass, energy) sequence-wise in various trophic levels of a food chain. It can be upright, inverted or spindle-shaped.

(a) Pyramid of Numbers

It is an ecological/eltorian pyramid which employs the numbers of individuals per unit area at various trophic levels sequence-wise with producers at the base and various consumers at successively higher levels. It is generally *upright* as maximum number of individuals occur at the producer level, followed by smaller number of herbivores, fewer primary carnivores and still fewer higher levels of carnivores. However, a single large-sized tree can provide food to several herbivores (e.g. birds, squirrels) which support a few carnivores. Such a pyramid of number is *spindle shaped*. When the herbivores support a large number. of ecotoparasites, which are further parasitised by still larger number of hyperparasites, the pyramid of numbers is *inverted.*

(b) Pyramid of Biomass : Biomass

It is the amount of living matter present in the individual/population/community/trophic level/ ecosystem. Biomass is measured on both fresh and dry weight basis. It is ecological/electronian pyramid which represents the biomass in various trophic levels. It is more real than the numbers at various trophic levels. Only 10-20% biomass is transferred from one trophic level to the next – 10% law. 1000 kg (one tonne) vegetation shall form only 100 kg of herbivore, 10 kg of primary carnivore, 1 kg of secondary carnivore and only 0.1 kg of tertiary carnivore. Therefore, with increasing dependence on animal diet (nonvegetarian), the human population will require higher amount of farm produces—total nonvegetarian 10 times, 50% non vegetarian 5 times, vegetarian with milk 1.5 times. Pyramid of biomass is upright, exception equatic food chain involving short lived plankton (biomass at one time will be less than consumers at higher levels.

(c) Pyramid of Energy

It is ecological/eltorian pyramid that gives graphic representation of amount of energy trapped by different traphic levels per unit area. It is always upright because during transfer of energy from one trophic level to the next, a lot of wastage occurs in feeding, digestion, assimilation and respiration.

HOMOESTASIS/BIOLOGICAL EQUILIBRIUM

It is the maintenance of a functional dynamic balance or state of equilibrium amongst various components of an ecosystem. Homeostasis is maintained through a number of controls/cybernetics/limitations like :

(*i*) Carrying Capacity : It is the maximum number of individuals the environment can support. Near it, the rate of population growth begins to decline. Beyond it, the population decreases rapidly.

(*ii*) Recycling of Wastes : It controls the availability of raw materials and space.

(*iii*) Self regulation : Mortality decreases and natility increases in case of small population while reverse is true in case of larger population.

(*iv*) Feedback System : It is of two types, positive and negative. In *positive feedback* the increased availability of a resource increase number of utilisers. For example, predator population will increase with the increase in population of prey. In *negative feedback*, the increase in number of members of a higher trophic level will decrease the number of individuals at the lower level which in turn shall reduce their number as well.

Habitat : It is a specific place/locality delimited by a combination of factors and barriers where an individual/population/community resides, e.g. pond, desert, river, bark of tree, burrow, intestine.

Microhabitat : It is part of the habitat having a specific property, e.g. forest floor, tree canopy, tree trunk, edge of a pond.

Niche/Ecological Niche : It is specific/part of habitat occupied by individuals of a species which is circumscribed by its range of tolerance, range of movement, microclimate, type of food and its availability, shelter, type of predator, timing of activity. Tadpole and adult frog occupy different ecological niches as the former is herbivorous aquatic while the latter is carnivorous amphibian. Water Bug and water Boatman live in shallow edges of ponds but occupy different niches as the former is predator while the latter scavenger. Both owl and cat feed on shrews and mice. They occupy the same niche because of being *ecological equivalents* though their habitats are different.

LIFE FORMS

Raunkiarer (1934) has distinguished plants into five forms on the basis of size, shape, branching, crown, life span and perennation.

(*i*) *Therophytes :* Annual plants which perennate in the form of seeds.

(*ii*) *Cryptophytes :* Perennial plants with underground storage parts,

(*a*) *Geophytes :* Subterranean perennating structures (root, root tuber, bulb, stem tuber, rhizome, corm).

(*b*) *Helophytes :* (Marshy plants). Perennating structures are embedded in mud.

(*c*) *Hydrophytes :* Aquatic plants.

(*iii*) *Hemicryptophytes :* Peremating structures occur at ground level. Aerial shoots die on the onset of winter, e.g. rosette plants.

(*iv*) *Chemaephytes :* Small plants of cold areas where perennating buds or shoot apices lie at or above the ground level.

(*v*) *Phanerophytes :* Pernnial herbs, shrubs, and trees, epiphytes, succulenty lianas etc. where perennating buds occur at 10 cm or more heigh above ground level.

BIOMES/MAJOR ECOSYSTEMS

Biomes are major ecosystems delimited by particular climates or geographical areas, e.g. Marsh, Desert, Tundra, Pond, Sea.

Ecotone : It is transitional or overlapping zone between two biomes where plants/animals of both the biomes are found.

Major Biomes : They are of two types, terrestrial and aquatic. The terrestrial biomes include tundra, taiga, deciduous forest, tropical rain forest, chapparal tropical savannah, grassland and desert. Aquatic biomes include ocean lake, pond, marsh and stream.

(A) Tundra/Arctic Tundra

It lies north of 60° N in North America. Europe and Asia. Precipitation is 25 cm/yr, mostly as snow. Winter temperature is – 30° to – 40°C. Summer is for 45-75 days with highest temperature of 10°C. Ponds, pools, marshes, bogs occur during summer.

Lower part of soil is under permafrost. Tundra is *arctic desert* with *mosses* (e.g. *Sphagnum*) lichens (*Cladonia*), grasses, sidges, dwarf willow (*Salix*), dwarf birch (*Betula*) and a few shrubs. Amphibians and reptiles are absent. Arthoropods and worms appear during summer. Common animals are lemmings, Snow Grouse, Snow Owl, Arctic Fox, Polar Bear, Arctic Hare, Caribou, Reindeer. Polar Bear, *hibernates* during winter while Reindeer and caribou migrate to less cold areas.

(*a*) **Alpine/Alpine Tundra :** It is treeless area on high mountains (above 3500 m) which has snow for long months. It is well drained and sloppy. Plants include lichens, mosses, grasses, herbs, small shrubs (e.g. *Artemesia, Primula*) and dwarf trees (*Juniperus*). Animals are Snow Leopond , Snow Bear, Mountain Goat, and migratory birds.

(B) Taiga/North Coniferous Forest

Taiga occurs is temperate areas (mostly Northern Hamisphere, parts of New Zealand) with precipitation both as snow and rain (variable). Winters are chilly while summers are pleased. Marches have cotton grass and *Sphagnum*. Vegetation consists of evergreen conifers—Deodar (*cectrus*), Larch, Juniper, Spruce, Fir, Pine, Hemlock, Yew. They are adapted to severe cold winters. The needle like leaves lose very little in transpiration. Being green, they continue to manufacture food, Broad-Leaved Birch, Mple, Poplar and Aspen occur at places. Lichens, mosses, ferns and herbs are abundant. Ground has thick covering of fallen needles us the latter decay slowly. Fauna includes Wolf, Deer, Rabbit, Hare, Weasel, Elk, Beaver, Pumas, Squirrels, RAven, Muskrat, Porcupine, Lynx, Grouse and Jay. Migration from Tundra (Reindeer, Caribou) and from here to warmer places is quite common.

(C) Temperate Deciduous Forests

The areas have warm summer and moderately cool winter. Rainfall is 75-150 cm. Dominant trees are Oak, Elm, Birch, Maple Ash, Chestnut, Hickory, Beech, Poplar and Magnolia. Conifers occur at places. Shrubs, herbs, ferns, mosses, lichens, grasses vines and epiphytes are abundant. Most trees shed their leaves during autumn or fall making the soil brown. A mixed coniferous-broad leaved forest occurs in Indian hills between 1500-3500 m. Trees height can reach 30-40 m. Fauna consists of Deer, Fox, Beaves, Wild Cat, Racoon, Opossum, Squirrel, Rabbit, Hare, Snakes, Lizards, Salamanders, Thrushes, Owls, Sparrows, Song birds.

(D) Tropical Deciduous Forests

Climate is warm with alternate wet and dry periods. Rainfall is 100-200 cm. Vegetation includes broad leaved trees which shed their leaves during dry season, e.g. Butea, *Bonbax,Shorea, Dalbergia*. Famous Sal (*Shorea*), Teak (*Tectona*) and Samdal (*Santalum*) forests of India belong to their category. Animal population is similar to evergreen tropical forests.

(E) Tropical Evergreen/Rain Forests

The biome occurs over equatorial/subequatorial regions with abundant warmth and rainfall (200-1000 cm/yr) almost throughout the year. The forest are impenetrable (= jungle) with maximum *diversity*, 200 types of trees in one hectare, 70-80% of all insects and 80-85% of all birds. *Productivity* is also maximum 12,000 K cal/m^2/yr as compared to 2000 K cal/m^2/yr for taiga. The forests occurs in famous congo basin of Africa and Amazon basin in South America. In India they occur in Western Ghats, Assam and Andamans Vegetation shows *stratification* (layering), emergent tree layer (50 m or more), understorey tree layer, shrub layer and ground layer. Epiphytes, climbers, mosses, ferns and orchids are abundant. Trees include Cinnamon, Mahogony, Ebony, Rosewood, Rubber Tree, Nutmeg, Artacarpus, Fig etc. Palms, plantains and bamboos occur here and there. Fauna consists of Deer, Goat, Antelope, Tapir, Elephant, Leopard, Jaguar, Snakes, Lizards, monkeys, lemurs, bats, sloths, parakeets, Toucan, Birds of Paradise and several others.

Chapparal : It is a broad-leaved scrub-forest (sclerophyllous or thick leaved shrubs and small trees) found in Mediterranean and pacific coast of several countries with winter rain and dry summer. Bush fires are common. Several plants are fire resistant including *Sage, Arctostaphylos, Adenostemma* and *Coenothus*. Trees of Oak and *Euealyptus*, (in Australia) occur at places. Fauna consists of rabbits, chipmunks, deer, tiger, rats, snakes, lizards and birds.

(F) Tropical Savannah

It is a warm climate plain with coarse grasses, scattered shrubs and trees, seasoned rain (wet and dry periods) and frequent fire. Savannah is named after dominant tree like *Acacia, Phoenix, Euealyptus.* Hoofed herbivores are quite common. Animals include Antelope, Zebra, Giraffe, Goat, Gazelle, Rhino, Elephand, Fox, Wolf, Lion. Tiger, Kangaroo (in Australia).

(G) Grassland

Grases are dominant with nongraminaceous herbs, scattered bushes and occasional tree, e.g. prairies of USA/Canada, pampas of South America, Steppes of Eurasia, tussocks of New Zealand and Veldts of South Africa. There is hot summer, cold winter, seasonal 25-75 cm rainfall. Grasses can be short or long. Fauna consists of Deer, Elk, Bison, Wolf, Prairie Dog, Bear, Bighorn Sheep, Rabbit, Mice, Budges, Coyote, Burrowing owl.

(H) Desert

It occupics about 1/5 of land. It lacks rain (less than 25 cm) due to either being present in rain shadow (area beyond high mountains which cut of clouds, e.g. Tibet), lack of cloud intercrepting mountains (e.g. Thar) or leging away from cloud seeding regions, e.g.

Death Valley (Great Western Deserts) of USA, Shara (Africa), Gobi, Arabian and Thar of Asia. Rajasthan lies in the Thar desert. Deserts can be cold (e.g. Tibet, Gobi) and hot (e.g. Thar, Sahara). Ground is sandy or rocky. Vegetation is sparse consisting of Cacti, euphorbia (succulents) *Acacia, Phoenix, Tamarix, Echinops, Aerua* etc. Animals are Kangaroo Desert Rat, Hare, Fox Jackal, Cat, Rattle Snake, Coral Snake, lizards (Gila, Monster, Horned Lizard), spiders, scorpions, locusts, ants, wasps and a number of birds like Swifts, Swallows, Quails, Doves, etc. Camel is adapted to desert conditions as it can protect its eyes and nostrils from dust, has insulated spreading feet, and is capable of tolerating dehydration upto 40% with highly reduced urine output.

(I) Oceanic Biome

Oceans occupy 75% of earth's surface with salinity of 3.5% (0.5% in Red Sea and 1% Baltic Sea), temperature of 28°C on surface in equatorial region (colder below) and 0°C near poles (warmer below). Continental shelf is gradually sloping (0%) sea shore upto 160 km and depth of 8-200 m. It passes into continental slope (3°-6°) which leads to *ocean floor* at a depth of 6 km-10 km. There littoral zone in continental shelf and a neritic zone above the same. The open seal pelagic part is differentiated into *photic zone* (upto 200 m depth, light penetrates the zone), *aphotic zone* (200-2000 m depth, little light) and *abyssal zone* (dark zone), *epipelagic* (photic zone), *mesopelagic* (alphotic zone), *bathy belagic* (2000 m to near ocean floor) and *abyssopelagic* (ocean floor).

(J) Open Ocean

Productivity is 1000 K cal/m^2/yr. The surface has phytoplankton (diatoms, dinoflagellates, other unicellular and multicellular algae, some luminescent flagellates), 300 plankton (protozoans larvae, crustacens) and *neuston* (photosynthetic like *Sargassum*, phagotrophic like some crabs, gustropods, jelly dishes, *physallia*). The surface as well as lower part has necton/nekton or swimming animals like turtles, snakes, squids, fishes, marine birds, etc. producers are absent in deep water. The abyssal zone contains only carnivores/predators. Some of them have luminescent organs (e.g. Devil Fish, Hatchet Fish), baits (e.g. Angles Fish), large heads (Granadier Fish, Gulper Eel). The benthonic region has scavengers and decomposes.

(K) Coastal Region

Productivity is 2000-6000 K cal/m^2/yr.. The important producers of intesdial regions are *Dictyota*, Ulva, *Fucus*, *Polysiphoria*, *Enteromorpha*, *Cladophora*, *Zostena* (the only seed plant) besides phytoplankton. Consumers include Zooplankton, biralves, snails, crabs, barnades, sponges, bryozoans, *Nereis*, Star Fish, Sea Urchin, tunicates etc. In littoral zone there are strong waves. Attached algae include *Laminaria*, *Macrocystis*, *Neroecystis*, *Alaria*, *Gelidium*, & *Corallian*.

Lithothamnion, consumer of the area are sponges, corals, polychaetes, tunicates and sea anemones. Nekton of the neritic zone also visit the area. *Neritic zone* (constant water, pelagic) has plankton, neuston and necton. *Coral reef* is the area of maximum productivity and diversity.

(L) Estuary

Tidal mout of river/coastal bay where there is mixing of fresh and sea water. Highly productive due to turbulence. There are fluctuations in temperature and salinity. Species found are phytoplankton (blue-green algae, green algae, diatoms, dinoflagellates), zooplankton (protozoans, crustaceans, rotifers), necton (fishes and some crustaceans) and benthon (attached algae, snails, clams, prawns etc.)

(M) Pond/Lake Biome

Ponds and lakes are stationary fresh waters. Deep lakes and brackish lakes are oligotrohic with sparse biota due to little circulation of nutrients. Shallow lakes and ox-bow (from main stream of river) lakes are *eutrophic* with rich biota and quick circulation of nutrients. Ponds are generally shallower with depth less than 2 m. Producers includes phytoplankton (e.g. diatoms, desmids, *Chlorella*, *Chlamydomonas*, *Spirogyra*, *Oedogmium*, *Zygnema*, free floating macrophytes (e.g. Lemna, Pistia, Azolla, suspended macrophytes (e.g. Utricularia, Ceratophyllum, Hydrilla), submerged, anchored plants (e.g. Scirpus, Sagittaria, Phragmites).

Consumers comprise zooplankton (ciliates, flagellates, rotifers, small crustaceans like *cyclops* and *Daphnia*, larvae), necton (e.g. Water Boatman, Water Spider, Diving Beetle, amphilians, burtles, fishes) and benthon (e.g. snails, clams, mussels, crabs, prawns). A number of decomposers also occur on the bottom. Water birds include Duck, Heron, Crane and Kingfisher.

(N) Marsh Biome

It is turbid muddy biome with little planktons. Flora includes emergent hydrophytes (e.g. *Typha*, *Phragmites*), *Sphagnum* and *Eichhornia*. Fauna consists of snails, mosquito larvae, some insects and frogs.

(O) Lotic/River Biome

It has high speed and low temperature in upper reaches. Water becomes muddy during rains. Detritus form land constitutes important component of food. Produces grow along shallow banks with very slow moving water. They include attached algae, encrusting diatoms, aquatic mosses (e.g. *Fontinalis*) submerged seed plants, reeds, water grasses etc. Consumers are more abundant including flatworms nymphs, larvae, snails, fishes, otter, mink, muskrat, crocodile etc.

(P) Man-Made/Artificial Ecosystem

They include aquaria, dams, parks, gardens, orchards, plantations, human settlements and agriculture. Artificial or man-made ecosystems have little diversity (generally monocultures), little recycling of nutrients and no self regulatory mechanisms. Agriculture (crop raising, animal husbandry) has created an agroecosystem which differs from place to place depending upon climate, latitude, topographic and edaphic factors. *Agroecology* is the study of relationships between agricultural crops and there surrounding animate as well as inanimate environment. Biotic community is rich when crop is in the field-crop, weeds, pests, birds, polinators, nematodes, earth worms, insects, rodents, birds and decomposers. Since there is little circulation of nutrients, agroecosystem is artifically irrigated, provided wil biogenetic nutrients, protected from weeds, pests and pathogens. There is little accumulation of biomass. Manure is, therefore added. Technology is being increasingly used in creating new varieties, sowing and reaping.

Multiple Choice Questions

1. Coelom developed from mesoderm cells is called
(*a*) Entocoel (*b*) Pseudocoel
(*c*) Hydrocoel (*d*) Schizocoel
2. Radially symmetrical phylum are
(*a*) Platyhelminthes and Nematoda
(*b*) Cnidaria and Porifera
(*c*) Echinodermata and Arthropoda
(*d*) Cnidaria and Annelida
3. Spherical symmetry is present in
(*a*) *Volvox* (*b*) *Hydra*
(*c*) Round worm (*d*) Flat worm
4. Blind sac body plan is exhibited by
(*a*) Porifers (*b*) Coelenterates
(*c*) Annelids (*d*) Arthropods
5. The deuterostomic animal is
(*a*) Pearl oyster (*b*) Earthworm
(*c*) Star fish (*d*) Round worm
6. The animals float or swim in the surface water is
(*a*) Neuston (*b*) Seston
(*c*) Tripton (*d*) Benthic
7. Animals lives in burrows are called
(*a*) Cursorial (*b*) Fossorial
(*c*) Cave dwellers (*d*) Scansorial
8. Shoal is the aggregation of
(*a*) Deers (*b*) Horses
(*c*) Fishes (*d*) Whale
9. Cellular level of organization is present in
(*a*) *Protozoa* (*b*) *Hydra*
(*c*) *Taenia* (*d*) *Sycon*
10. Protostomous plan is exhibited by
(*a*) Hemichordates (*b*) Chordates
(*c*) Arthropods (*d*) Echinoderms
11. Branchial respiration takes place through
(*a*) Skin (*b*) Gills
(*c*) Lungs (*d*) Trachea
12. Annelids have
(*a*) Cell aggregate body plan
(*b*) Blind sac body plan
(*c*) Tube within a tube body plan
(*d*) Hollow sac plan
13. In arthropods, body cavity is called
(*a*) Coelom (*b*) Haemocoel
(*c*) Pseudocoel (*d*) Eucoel
14. Cephalization is present in
(*a*) Coelenterates (*b*) Porifers
(*c*) Flatworms (*d*) Protozoans
15. The appendages of locomotion in echinoderms is/are
(*a*) Foot (*b*) Fins
(*c*) Tubefeet (*d*) Parapodia
16. What is common between porifers and coelenterates
(*a*) Monoblastic and acoelomate
(*b*) Diploblastic and acoelomate
(*c*) Triploblastic and acoelomate
(*d*) Triploblastic and pseudocoelomate
17. *Neopilina galathea* exhibit the characters of
(*a*) Annelida and arthropoda
(*b*) Arthropoda and mollusca
(*c*) Mollusca and echinodermata
(*d*) Annelida and mollusca
18. The largest living vertebrate is
(*a*) Shark (*b*) Elephant
(*c*) Whale (*d*) Camel
19. Most vertebrate exhibit
(*a*) Bilateral symmetry
(*b*) Radial symmetry
(*c*) Biradial symmetry
(*d*) Spherical symmetry
20. The living jawless vertebrates belong to the class
(*a*) Ostracoederms (*b*) Placoderms
(*c*) Chondrichthyes (*d*) Cyclostomes
21. Pseudometamerism is the characteristic feature of
(*a*) Roundworm (*b*) Liver fluke
(*c*) Tape worm (*d*) Silverfish
22. Round worms are
(*a*) Acoelomate
(*b*) Pseudocoelomate
(*c*) Eucoelomate
(*d*) Haemocoelomate

23. Schizocoel theory was put forwarded by
(*a*) Lankester (*b*) Sedgwick
(*c*) Goelta (*d*) Hasselbalch

24. Mammals are
(*a*) Endothermal (*b*) Ectothermal
(*c*) Mesothermal (*d*) All of the above

25. Green glands are organs of excretion in
(*a*) Platyhelminthes (*b*) Crustaceans
(*c*) Molluscs (*d*) Annelids

26. Aminotelic animals are
(*a*) Insects (*b*) Bony fishes
(*c*) Echinoderms (*d*) Birds

27. Protandrous condition refers to
(*a*) Testes mature with ovaries
(*b*) Testes mature earlier than ovaries
(*c*) Testes mature later than ovaries
(*d*) Nonfunctional testes

28. Ladder type nervous system is present in
(*a*) Earth worm (*b*) Molluscs
(*c*) Coelenterates (*d*) Flatworms

29. Tissue grade organization is originated from
(*a*) Protozoa
(*b*) Porifera
(*c*) Cnidaria
(*d*) Platyhelminthes

30. The animals, which are active during evening hours
(*a*) Crepuscular (*b*) Vespertine
(*c*) Auroral (*d*) Nocturnal

31. Minute cytoplasmic connections between cells of epithelium is known as :
(*a*) informosomes (*b*) microsomes
(*c*) desmosomes (*d*) mesosomes

32. The descending limb and the ascending limb of Henle's loop of nephron in mammals is lined by :
(*a*) simple squamous epithelium
(*b*) stratified squamous epithelium
(*c*) simple columnar epithelium
(*d*) transitional epithelium

33. Exocrine glands containing glandular cells which shed themselves to secrete their products are known as :
(*a*) ductless glands
(*b*) apocrine glands
(*c*) mesocrine glands
(*d*) holocrine glands

34. Sensory epithelium is seen :
(*a*) on skin surface
(*b*) on the olfactory mucosa and taste buds of tongue
(*c*) on the ears
(*d*) All of these

35. Example for a holocrine gland is :
(*a*) salivary gland (*b*) sweat gland
(*c*) sebaceous gland (*d*) mammary gland

36. The mucosa is seen in :
(*a*) cavities of the respiratory passages
(*b*) cavities of the urogenital tract
(*c*) cavities of alimentary tract
(*d*) All of these

37. Mesenchymal epithelium is seen in :
(*a*) liver
(*b*) lungs
(*c*) subdural and subarachnoid spaces
(*d*) kidneys

38. The largest volume of adult tissues in the body is derived from (in vertebrates) :
(*a*) ectoderm
(*b*) endoderm
(*c*) mesoderm
(*d*) ectoderm and mesoderm

39. Mesothelium is the name given to :
(*a*) lumen of gut
(*b*) coelomic cavities
(*c*) lumen of blood vessels
(*d*) organs derived from mesoderm

40. An epithelium with more than one layer of cells is seen in :
(*a*) inner lining of stomach
(*b*) inner lining of intestine
(*c*) all parts of alimentary canal
(*d*) buccal cavity and oesophagus

41. The attachment between two epithelial cells is due to :
(*a*) connective tissue
(*b*) intercellular fluid
(*c*) intercellular cement
(*d*) intercellular fluid and air spaces

42. Epithelial cell differs from connective and supporting tissues :
(*a*) by the presence of more cellular substance

(b) by the presence of two or more nuclei in the cells
(c) by the presence of more inter-cellular substance
(d) by the presence of more cytoplasm

43. Inner lining of our trachea is formed by :
(a) simple squamous epithelium
(b) pseudostratified epithelium
(c) stratified epithelium
(d) simple glandular epithelium

44. Stratified squamous keratinised epithelium seen in :
(a) oesophagus (b) kidney
(c) liver (d) epidermis of skin

45. All glands whether exocrine or endocrine originate in mammals from :
(a) epithelial tissues
(b) some from epithelial tissues and others from connective tissues
(c) some from epithelial tissues and others from muscular tissues
(d) Some from epithelial tissues and others from nerve tissues

46. Monocotyledonous leaves have reticulate venation in :
(a) *Calophyllum* (b) *Smilax*
(c) Maize (d) *Cocos*

47. Which modification of root does not store food material?
(a) Tuberous (b) Stilt
(c) Conical (d) Napiform

48. Artabotrys is a hook-climber in which hooks are modified :
(a) inflorescence (b) petioles
(c) roots (d) stipules

49. The oil reserves of groundnut is stored in :
(a) embryo
(b) underground tubers
(c) endosperm
(d) cotyledons

50. Phyllotaxy is the arrangement of :
(a) leaves (b) veins
(c) branches (d) flower buds

51. Sundew, dionaea and pitcher plants are :
(a) saprophytes (b) carnivorous
(c) insectivorous (d) heterotrophs

52. The food is stored in which of the following?
(a) Fasciculated root (b) Tap-root
(c) Fibrous root (d) Respiratory root

53. Bipinnately compound leaves are found in :
(a) Mimosaceae (b) Papilionaceae
(c) Ranunculaceae (d) Poaceae

54. Main function of leaf is :
(a) exchange of gases
(b) trapping of gases
(c) synthesis of food
(d) process of transpiration

55. A rootless aquatic herb which forms leaf bladders to trap insect is :
(a) *Drosera* (b) *Sarracenia*
(c) *Dionaea* (d) *Utricularia*

56. Buds are found at the :
(a) tips of roots and branches
(b) base of leaves only
(c) base of leaves and tips of branches
(d) apex of axil of leaves

57. Tuberous tap-root is found in :
(a) *Raphanus sativus* (b) *Colocasia*
(c) *Solanum* (d) All of these

58. Which of the following monocots has reticulate venation?
(a) *Smilax* (b) *Ficus*
(c) *Allium* (d) *Yucca*

59. *Santalum album* is a :
(a) partial stem parasite
(b) total stem parasite
(c) total root parasite
(d) partial root parasite

60. Suckers are meant for vegetative propagation in :
(a) Hydrilla (b) Chrysathemum
(c) Jussia (d) Pistia

61. Osmosis is a form of diffusion in which
(a) the solute moves freely from a region of higher concentration to lower concentration through semi-permeable membrane
(b) the solvent move through a semi-permeable membrane from region, where a solute is in higher concentration to region of lower concentration

(c) the solvent moves through a semi-permeable membrane from a region where is a solute is in lower concentration to a region of higher concentration
(d) None of these

62. Which of the following is a function of plasma membrane?
(a) structural barrier and cell communication
(b) metabolic activities and cell adhesion
(c) mass flow regulation, active transport, diffusion, endocytosis and exocytosis
(d) All of thse

63. Select the *false* statement
(a) facilitated diffusion is faster than simple diffusion
(b) facilitated diffusion exhibits saturation kinetics
(c) facilitated diffusion is not very selective
(d) facilitated diffusion can be inhibited by agents known to denature proteins

64. 'Permease' a carrier protein, present in the plasma membrane is involved in the
(a) passive transport of molecules
(b) active transport of molecules
(c) Both (a) and (b)
(d) None of these

65. In simple diffusion process, molecules cross the plasma membrane
(a) against concentration gradient
(b) along concentration gradient
(c) do not depends on concentration
(d) with the help of energy

66. Purple cabbage leaves do not loose their colour in cold water but do so in the boiling water because
(a) boiling water can enter the cell cavity
(b) plasmalemma get killed in boiling water
(c) the pigment is not soluble in cold water
(d) cell wall is killed in boiling water

67. Transport of molecules through channel protein present in the plasma membrane is
(a) always passive
(b) always active
(c) may be passive or active
(d) None of these

68. Normally the process of osmosis, the net flow of water molecules into or out of the cell depends upon differences in the
(a) concentration of water molecule inside and outside the cell
(b) rate of molecular motion on either side of the cell membrane
(c) concentration of solute molecule inside and outside the cell
(d) None of these

69. If a subcellular fraction from liver tissue exhibits a high level of acid phosphatase activity, it most likely contains
(a) nuclei
(b) lysosomes
(c) endoplasmic reticulum
(d) coated vesicles

70. Free fatty acids enter cell by
(a) passive diffusion
(b) active diffusion
(c) cannot enters into the cell
(d) None of these

71. Which of the following is *not* related to facilitated diffusion?
(a) solutes are moved by a change in shape in the carrier protein
(b) the process is passive
(c) the process require energy input
(d) Both (a) and (c)

72. Ca^{2+} ATPase, present on sarcoplasmic reticulum, increases Ca^{2+} concentration in
(a) sarcoplasmic reticulum as compared to cytosol actively
(b) cytosol as compared to sarcoplasmic reticulum
(c) sacroplasmic reticulum as compared to cytosol passively
(d) None of these

73. Movement of substances across cell membrane is controlled by the
(a) size of permeating particles
(b) permeability of membrane
(c) membrane proteins
(d) All of these

74. Which of the following events require energy?
(a) pinocytosis (b) $Na^+ - K^+$ pump
(c) phagocytosis (d) All of these

75. A poikilothermic organism living in the Arctic would have, compared to that organism living in the temperate climate zone, a plasma membrane richer in
(*a*) cholesterol
(*b*) long chain fatty acids
(*c*) protein
(*d*) unsaturated fatty acids

76. Diffusion across the plasma membrane is more rapid if a substance is
(*a*) a protein
(*b*) hydrophilic
(*c*) high in its oil: water partition coefficient
(*d*) large and globular in shape

77. A difference between simple diffusion and facilitated transport is that facilitated transport
(*a*) is concentration dependent
(*b*) occurs across plasma membrane
(*c*) requires membrane proteins
(*d*) utilizes a substance moving with its concentration gradient

78. In plasma membrane, carbohydrate present on the
(*a*) both layer of lipid
(*b*) only on cytoplasmic side of lipid layer
(*c*) only on non-cytoplasmic side of lipid layer
(*d*) None of these

79. Most abundant lipid in plasma membrane is
(*a*) cholesterol (*b*) sterol
(*c*) glycolipid (*d*) phospholipids

80. In biological membrane, integral proteins and lipids interact mainly by
(*a*) covalent bond
(*b*) H-bond
(*c*) hydrophobic interactions
(*d*) van der Waal force

81. In muscle cells, Ca^{2+} pump is responsible for pumping Ca^{2+}
(*a*) from cytosol into the sarcoplasmic reticulum
(*b*) from sarcoplasmic reticulum into the cytosol
(*c*) from sarcoplasmic reticulum to the extra cellular matrix
(*d*) Both (*b*) and (*c*)

82. Liposome is
(*a*) closed, solvent filled vesicles have a single bilayer of fatty acid chain
(*b*) closed, solvent filled vesicles have a single layer of fatty acid chain
(*c*) a structure made up of protein
(*d*) Both (*b*) and (*c*)

83. Major force responsible for the formation of lipid bilayer
(*a*) van der Waal force
(*b*) covalent bond
(*c*) electrostatic interaction
(*d*) hydrophobic force

84. An artificial membrane composed only of phospholipids has significant permeability to
(*a*) water (*b*) Na^+
(*c*) sucrose (*d*) glucose

85. Which of the following will affect active transport?
(*a*) absence of O_2 (*b*) cyanide
(*c*) denaturing agents (*d*) All of these

86. Desmosomes differ from tight junction in that desmosomes
(*a*) allow molecules to pass in the intercellular space
(*b*) are non-communicating
(*c*) are present in plants
(*d*) lack proteins

87. Hemi desmosome differs from spot desmosome because hemi desmosome
(*a*) connect cell to cell
(*b*) connect extracellular matrix to extracellular matrix
(*c*) connect cell to extracellular matrix
(*d*) having tonofilament, made of intermediate filament

88. Tight junctions
(*a*) are essential for metabolic coupling
(*b*) don't occur in vertebrates
(*c*) have the closest approach of two plasma membranes of any junction
(*d*) surround connexons

89. The most important difference between gap junctions between animal cells and plasmodesmata in plants is that in plasmodesmata

(*a*) ionic coupling occurs
(*b*) metabolic cooperation occurs
(*c*) pore diameter is 1 mm
(*d*) two adjacent plasma membranes are fused

90. Which of the following is *correct* statement? In animal
(*a*) concentration of Na^+ is high inside the cell than outside
(*b*) concentration of calcium is high inside the cell than outside
(*c*) concentration of K^+ is high inside the cell than outside
(*d*) concentration of Mg^{2+} is high inside the cell than outside

91. During non-cyclic photophosphorylation, plants and cyanobacteria produce
(*a*) ATP (*b*) NADPH
(*c*) NADPH and ATP (*d*) NADH and ATP

92. The first carboxylation product of a C_3 plant is
(*a*) phosphoglyceric acid
(*b*) oxaloacetic acid
(*c*) malic acid
(*d*) phosphoglyceraldehyde

93. Consider the following compounds
1. phosphoenol pyruvate
2. malic acid
3. pyruvic acid
4. oxaloacetic acid

What is the correct sequence of these intermediate compounds as they form in C_4 dicarboxylic acid pathway following the PEP-carboxylation reaction?
(*a*) 1, 2, 3, 4 (*b*) 2, 4, 3, 1
(*c*) 4, 1, 2, 3 (*d*) 4, 2, 3, 1

94. Consider the following
1. cytochrome b_6 2. cytochrome f
3. plastocyanin 4. plastoquinone

What is the sequence of these in the photo-induced electron carriers between PSII to PSI in photosynthesis?
(*a*) 4, 1, 2, 3 (*b*) 3, 4, 1, 2
(*c*) 1, 2, 3, 4 (*d*) 2, 3, 4, 1

95. The total requirement of ATP and NADPH for each molecule of CO_2 fixed and reduced in photosynthesis in the Calvin cycle is
(*a*) 2 ATP and 2 NADPH
(*b*) 2 ATP and 3 NADPH
(*c*) 3 ATP and 2 NADPH
(*d*) 4 ATP and 3 NADPH

96. What is the step in photosynthesis that contributes the greatest number of protons to the generation of a concentration gradient across the thylakoid membrane?
(*a*) the Q cycle
(*b*) reduction of $NADP^+$ to NADPH
(*c*) oxidation of water to O_2
(*d*) none of the above contribute to the proton concentration gradient

97. What is the strongest reducing agent in photosynthetic electron-transfer reactions?
(*a*) Plastoquinone (*b*) P680*
(*c*) P700* (*d*) P700

98. In the presence of light, pH of the lumen of thylakoid
(*a*) increases (*b*) decreases
(*c*) remain same (*d*) None of these

99. If the thylakoid are treated with detergent to stabilize lipids and then the proteins gently isolated, the following complexes will be observed, *except*
(*a*) ATP synthase
(*b*) cytochrome oxidase
(*c*) light harvesting complex
(*d*) pheophytin

100. In the chemiosmotic hypothesis for energy generation in chloroplast
(*a*) electron transport carriers set up a proton gradient
(*b*) a pH gradient drives the hydrolysis of ATP to ADP
(*c*) ATP must be continually translocated into the chloroplast
(*d*) electron transport carriers, use energy of moving electron in uphill direction to form ATP

101. In chloroplast, photochemical reactions occurs in
(*a*) thylakoid membrane
(*b*) thylakoid lumen
(*c*) stroma
(*d*) inner chloroplast membrane

102. In chloroplast, PSI present on the
(*a*) apperased membrane of the thylakoid
(*b*) non-appearased membrane of the thylakoid
(*c*) lumen of the thylakoid
(*d*) inner membrane of chloroplast

103. Which of the following statement is *correct?* Rubisco
(*a*) catalyzes the fixation of CO_2
(*b*) can function as an oxygenase
(*c*) is the most abundant protein on earth
(*d*) All of the above

104. C_4 plants able to minimize photorespiration because C_4 plants
(*a*) do not carry out the Calvin cycle
(*b*) use a more efficient enzyme to initially fix CO_2
(*c*) exclude Calvin cycle
(*d*) None of these

105. Photorespiration
(*a*) occurs because oxygen rather than carbon dioxide links to the rubisco enzyme in the Calvin cycle
(*b*) occurs more in C_4 than in C_3 plants under identical conditions
(*c*) describes the up-take of carbon dioxide and the release of oxygen in chloroplasts
(*d*) All of the above

106. In non-cyclic light reactions of photosynthesis, electrons from chlorophyll molecules in photosystem I are used in the formation of NADPH. What is the source of such electrons?
(*a*) from light, which is converted directly into an electron
(*b*) from ferredoxin
(*c*) from mitochondria, which release the electrons at the end of the electron transport chain
(*d*) from photosystem II, which splits water molecules

107. Which of the following incorporate CO_2 into organic acids, and then release it for use in the Calvin cycle?
(*a*) C_3 plants
(*b*) C_4 plants only
(*c*) C_3 and CAM plants
(*d*) C_4 and CAM plants

108. Colours of light most useful in photosynthesis are
(*a*) green, yellow and orange
(*b*) red, violet and blue
(*c*) infrared, red and yellow
(*d*) red, white and blue

109. Which of the following is the correct sequence for the movement of electrons during the light-dependent reactions of plants?
(*a*) P_{680} P_{700} water $NADP^+$
(*b*) water P_{700} $NADP^+$ P_{680}
(*c*) P_{700} P_{680} $NADP^+$ water
(*d*) water P_{680} P_{700} $NADP^+$

110. The most original source of hydrogen that will ultimately be used to reduce or fix carbon dioxide in the Calvin cycle is
(*a*) glucose (*b*) ATP
(*c*) NADPH (*d*) H_2O

111. The synthesis of ATP in the chloroplast is associated with
(*a*) non-cyclic electron flow
(*b*) an accumulation of H^+ in the thylakoid lumen
(*c*) electron flow between photosystem II to photosystem I
(*d*) All of the above

112. Photoexcited P_{680} and P_{700}
(*a*) have the same chemical properties of the ground state molecules
(*b*) are strong oxidants-taking electrons from donor molecules
(*c*) are strong reductants-giving electrons to acceptor molecules
(*d*) transfer excited state energy to another molecule

113. All of the following are *false* for non-cyclic electron transport in photosynthetic light reactions *except*
(*a*) the components of electron transport are arranged asymmetrically across the thylakoid membrane
(*b*) electrons flow from low energy water to reduce high energy $NADP^+$ due to

absorption of photons of light (by PSII and PSI) (PS stands for photosystem)

(c) electron transport establishes a proton gradient across the thylakoid membrane

(d) electron transport between PSII and PSI produces ATP by substrate phosphorylation

114. The individual (or individuals) who demonstrated, using isolated chloroplasts, that splitting of water by light could reduce a dye solution as well as releasing oxygen is/are

(a) R. Hill (b) Ruben and Kamen

(c) F. F. Blackman (d) Melvin Calvin

115. If asked to pinpoint precisely the site of synthesis of 3-phosphoglyceraldehyde in plants, you would have to say that it takes place within the

(a) mesophyll (b) grana

(c) stroma (d) chloroplast

116. When photosynthesis rate is plotted as a function of temperature, the graph will be

(a) bell shape (b) sigmoid

(c) straight line (d) None of these

117. At low CO_2 concentration, photosynthesis is limited by

(a) the carboxylation capacity of rubisco

(b) ability of Calvin cycle enzyme to regenerate RuBP

(c) ATP + NADPH

(d) All of the above

118. According to British plant physiologist F.F. Blackman's law of limiting factor, at any given time, photosynthesis can be limited by

(a) light

(b) CO_2 concentration

(c) both light and CO_2 concentration

(d) either by light or by CO_2

119. Synthesis of sucrose during photosynthesis occurs at

(a) chloroplast (b) cytosol

(c) vacuoles (d) amyloplast

120. Total energy requirement for fixing one CO_2 by combined C_4 and C_3 cycle is

(a) 5 ATP + 4 NADPH

(b) 3 ATP + 4 NADPH

(c) 5 ATP + 2 NADPH

(d) 8 ATP + 2 NADPH

121. In muscle physiology, the latent period refers to

(a) the period of lost excitability that occurs when two stimuli are applied immediately one after the other

(b) the brief contraction of a motor unit

(c) the period of elevated oxygen use after exercise

(d) a brief delay that occurs between application of a stimulus and the beginning of contraction

122. In muscle contraction, what starts filament sliding

(a) an increase in Ca^{2+} concentration in the cytosol

(b) a decrease in Na^+ concentration in the cytosol

(c) the bending of the myosin head

(d) the release of energy from the breakdown of ATP

123. What would happen if ATP were suddenly unavailable after the sarcomere had begun to shorten?

(a) nothing. The contraction would proceed normally

(b) the myosin heads would be unable to detach from actin

(c) troponin would bind with the myosin heads

(d) actin and myosin filaments would separate completely and be unable to recombine

124. Which of the following are sources of ATP for musclecontraction?

1. creatine phosphate
2. glycolysis
3. anaerobic cellular respiration
4. aerobic cellular respiration
5. acetylcholine

(a) 1, 2 and 3 (b) 2, 3 and 4

(c) 2, 3 and 5 (d) 1, 2, 3 and 4

125. Match the following

Column: A	Column: B
1. A band	(a) point of contact between a motor neuron and a muscle fibre

2. I band	(b) invaginations of the sarcolemma from the surface toward the centre of the muscle fibre
3. Z disc	(c) myoblasts that persist in mature skeletal muscle
4. sarcomere	(d) plasma membrane of a muscle fibre
5. neuromuscular junction	(e) oxygen-binding protein found only in muscle fibres
6. myoglobin	(f) Ca^{2+}-storing tubular system similar to smooth endoplasmic reticulum
7. satellite cells	(g) the contracting unit of a skeletal muscle fibre
8. T tubules	(h) middle area in the sarcomere where thick and thin filaments are found
9. sarcoplasmic reticulum	(i) area in the sarcomere where thin filaments are present but thick filaments are not
10. sarcolemma	(j) separate the sarcomeres from each other

(a) (a)-5; (b)-8, (c)-7, (d)-10, (e)-6, (f)-9, (g)-4, (h)-1, (i)-2, (j)-3
(b) (a)-7; (b)-8, (c)-5, (d)-10, (e)-6, (f)-9, (g)-4, (h)-2, (i)-1, (j)-3
(c) (a)-10; (b)-8, (c)-7, (d)-5, (e)-6, (f)-9, (g)-1, (h)-4, (i)-2, (j)-3
(d) (a)-5; (b)-8, (c)-7, (d)-6, (e)-10, (f)-9, (g)-1, (h)-4, (i)-3, (j)-2

126. If the active transport of calcium ion across the sacroplasmic reticulum is blocked, if all else is normal, and if the motor neuron is stimulated 1 minute after the start of the blockage, then after stimulus delivery
(a) there will be no calcium ions leaving the sarcoplasmic reticulum
(b) the muscle fibre will contract and will stay contracted
(c) no new cross bridges will be formed
(d) All of the above

127. Calcium ions in skeletal muscle
(a) are stored in the transverse tubules
(b) bind to sites on troponin molecules
(c) only can bind to sites on actin molecules
(d) All of the above

128. When the length of a skeletal muscle decreases during an active contraction
(a) the A band remains the same size
(b) the H band becomes larger
(c) only can bind to sites on actin molecules
(d) All of the above

129. ATP is needed in which of the following processes in vertebrate skeletal muscle?
(a) cross bridge attachment and detachment
(b) movement of calcium ions into the sarcoplasmic reticulum
(c) movement of potassium ions into the muscle fibre
(d) All of the above

130. When a muscle increases in length
(a) the distance between the Z lines decreases
(b) the width of the H zone decreases
(c) the amount of the A band not in the I band increase
(d) None of the above

131. Which of the following statements are true for skeletal muscle?
(a) calcium ions bind to sites on the tropomyosin molecule
(b) the movement of the troponin molecule is the direct cause that allows the receptor site on the actin molecule to be available for binding
(c) the head of the actin molecule binds to the myosin molecule to form a cross bridge
(d) None of the above

132. Which of the following statements are true for skeletal muscle?
(a) actin molecules are located in the thick filaments
(b) acetylcholine receptors are located on the surface of the sarcoplasmic reticulum
(c) the heads of the myosin molecules attach onto the Z line
(d) None of the above

133. ATP is directly needed in which of the following processes in muscle?
(*a*) movement of potassium ions out of the muscle fibre
(*b*) movement of calcium ions out of the sarcoplasmic reticulum
(*c*) movement of tropomyosin molecules to expose binding sites on actin molecules
(*d*) None of the above

134. An action potential in an isolated healthy skeletal muscle fibre (with normal intracellular levels of ATP and no external forces on it) bathed in physiological saline will lead to an increase in the
(*a*) amount of calcium ion near the cross bridges
(*b*) amount of troponin that has calcium ion bound to it
(*c*) breakdown of ATP in the muscle
(*d*) All of the above

135. Which of the following are true for skeletal muscle cells?
(*a*) acetylcholine receptors are located on the external surface of then plasma membrane of the muscle cell
(*b*) actin filaments are attached to the Z line
(*c*) calcium ion conductance of internal membranes can be changed
(*d*) All of the above

136. Which are closely associated with thin filaments of skeletal muscles?
(*a*) troponin
(*b*) tropomyosin
(*c*) calcium ion binding sites
(*d*) All of the above

137. In the sarcomere of a skeletal muscle, there are
(*a*) actin molecules in the H zone
(*b*) myosin molecules in the I band
(*c*) both actin and myosin molecules in the region of the A band that is not in the H zone
(*d*) All of the above

138. An increase in the calcium conductance of all sarcoplasmic reticulum membranes of a skeletal muscle with no external forces on it leads to
(*a*) increased binding of calcium ions to tropomyosin
(*b*) a decrease in the amount of ATP molecules in the muscle
(*c*) an increase in the length of the H zone
(*d*) All of the above

139. When rigor mortis occurs in a muscle,
(*a*) there are adequate levels of ATP in the muscle
(*b*) cross-bridges can be easily broken
(*c*) sarcomere length remains constant
(*d*) All of the above

140. Which of the following is true in a skeletal muscle?
(*a*) movement of the cross bridge occurs only when the myosin head is detached from the actin molecule
(*b*) the binding of ATP of myosin causes detachment of the myosin head from the actin molecule
(*c*) the myosin head cross-bridge is activated (energized) by the conversion of ADP to ATP
(*d*) All of the above

141. The action potential of a neuron
(*a*) is initiated by efflux of Na^+
(*b*) is terminated by efflux of K^+
(*c*) declines in amplitude as it moves along the axon
(*d*) results in a transient reversal of the concentration gradient

142. The action potential of skeletal muscle
(*a*) has a prolonged plateau phase
(*b*) spreads inward to all parts of the muscle via the T tubules
(*c*) causes the immediate uptake of Ca^{2+} into the lateral sacs of the sarcoplasmic reticulum
(*d*) is longer than the action potential of cardiac muscle

143. The function of tropomyosin in skeletal muscle include
(*a*) sliding on action to produce shortening
(*b*) releasing Ca^{2+} after initiation of contraction
(*c*) binding to myosin during contraction
(*d*) acting as a relaxing protein at rest by covering up the sites where myosin binds to actin

144. The cross-bridges of the sarcomere in skeletal muscle are made up of
(*a*) actin (*b*) myosin
(*c*) troponin (*d*) tropomyosin

145. The contractile response in skeletal muscle
(*a*) starts after the action potential is over
(*b*) does not last as long as the action potential
(*c*) produces more tension when the muscle contracts isometrically than when the muscle
(*d*) produces more work when the muscle contracts isometrically than when the muscle contracts isotonically

146. Which of the following statements are *true?*
1. two or more neurotransmitters may be present in many neurons.
2. some amino acids, including glutamate and separate, are neurotransmitters.
3. the catecholamine neurotransmitter acetylcholine is synthesized from the amino acid tyrosine.
4. the simple gas nitric oxide functions as a neurotransmitter.
5. an excitatory neurotransmitter can never be inhibitory regardless of the neuron that produces it.

(*a*) 1, 2 and 4 (*b*) 2, 3 and 5
(*c*) 1, 3 and 5 (*d*) 1, 3 and 4

147. Which of the following statements are *true?*
1. the frequency of impulses and the number of activated sensory neurons encodes differences in stimuli intensity.
2. larger-diameter axons conduct nerve impulses faster than smaller-diameter ones.
3. continuous conduction is faster than salutatory conduction.
4. the diameter of an axon and the presence or absence of a myelin sheath are the most important factors that determine the speed of nerve impulse propagation.
5. action potentials are localized, whereas graded potentials are propagated.

(*a*) 1, 3 and 5 (*b*) 3 and 4
(*c*) 2, 4 and 5 (*d*) 1, 2 and 4

148. Neurotransmitters are removed from the synaptic cleft by
1. axonal transport
2. diffusion
3. neurosecretory cells
4. enzymatic breakdown
5. cellular uptake

(*a*) 1, 2, 3 and 4 (*b*) 2, 4 and 5
(*c*) 2, 3 and 4 (*d*) 1, 4 and 5

149. Match the following

Column: A	Column: B
1. graded potential	(*a*) a sequence of rapidly occurring events that decreases and eventually reverses the membrane potential and then restores it to the resting state; a nerve impulse
2. action potential	(*b*) a small deviation from the resting membrane potential that makes the membrane either more or less negative
3. excitatory postsynaptic potential	(*c*) period of time when a second action potential can be initiated with a very strong stimulus
4. inhibitory postsynaptic potential	(*d*) the minimum level of depolarization required for a nerve impulse to be generated
5. absolute refractory period	(*e*) the recovery of the resting membrane potential
6. repolarization	(*f*) a neurotransmitter-caused depolarization of the postsynaptic membrane
7. after hyper-polarizing phase	(*g*) aneurotransmitter-caused hyperpolarization of the postsynaptic membrane
8. threshold	(*h*) time during which a neuron cannot produce an action potential even with a very strong stimuli
9. relative refractory period	(*i*) polarization that is less negative than the resting level

10. depolarizing graded potential	(*j*) the hyperpolarization that occurs after the repolarizing phase of an action potential

(*a*) (*a*)-1; (*b*)-2, (*c*)-9, (*d*)-8, (*e*)-3, (*f*)-6, (*g*)-4, (*h*)-5, (*i*)-10, (*j*)-7
(*b*) (*a*)-2; (*b*)-1, (*c*)-9, (*d*)-8, (*e*)-6, (*f*)-3, (*g*)-4, (*h*)-5, (*i*)-10, (*j*)-7
(*c*) (*a*)-2; (*b*)-1, (*c*)-8, (*d*)-9, (*e*)-6, (*f*)-3, (*g*)-4, (*h*)-10, (*i*)-5, (*j*)-7
(*d*) (*a*)-2; (*b*)-1, (*c*)-9, (*d*)-8, (*e*)-6, (*f*)-4, (*g*)-3, (*h*)-10, (*i*)-5, (*j*)-7

150. Match the following

Column A	**Column B**
1. myelin sheath	(*a*) the part of the neuron that contains the nucleus
2. neurolemma	(*b*) rough endoplasmic reticulum in neurons
3. nodes of Ranvier	(*c*) store neurotransmitter
4. cell body	(*d*) the process that propagates nerve impulses toward another neuron, muscle fibre, or gland cell
5. Nissl bodies	(*e*) the receiving or input portions of a neuron
6. neurofibrils	(*f*) a multilayered lipid and protein covering for axons produced by neuroglia
7. dendrites	(*g*) the outer nucleated cytoplasmic layer of a Schwann cell
8. axon	(*h*) first portion of the axon
9. axon hillock	(*i*) site of communication between two neurons or between a neuron and an effector cell
10. initial segment	(*j*) form the cytoskeleton of a neuron
11. trigger zone	(*k*) gaps in the myelin sheath of an axon
12. nerve fibre	(*l*) general term for any neuronal process
13. synapse	(*m*) area where the axon joins the cell body
14. synaptic vesicles	(*n*) area where nerve impulses arise

(*a*) (*a*)-5, (*b*)-4, (*c*)-14, (*d*)-8, (*e*)-3, (*f*)-1, (*g*)-2, (*h*)-10, (*i*)-13, (*j*)-6, (*k*)-7, (*l*)-12, (*m*)-9, (*n*)-11
(*b*) (*a*)-4, (*b*)-14, (*c*)-5, (*d*)-8, (*e*)-7, (*f*)-1, (*g*)-11, (*h*)-10, (*i*)-13, (*j*)-6, (*k*)-3, (*l*)-12, (*m*)-9, (*n*)-2
(*c*) (*a*)-4, (*b*)-5, (*c*)-14, (*d*)-8, (*e*)-7, (*f*)-1, (*g*)-2, (*h*)-10, (*i*)-13, (*j*)-6, (*k*)-3, (*l*)-12, (*m*)-9, (*n*)-11
(*d*) (*a*)-14, (*b*)-5, (*c*)-4, (*d*)-8, (*e*)-7, (*f*)-2, (*g*)-1, (*h*)-10, (*i*)-13, (*j*)-6, (*k*)-11, (*l*)-12, (*m*)-9, (*n*)-3

151. Sporogenesis is
(*a*) Production of meiospores
(*b*) Formation of zygote and embryo
(*c*) Formation of spores
(*d*) Production of microspores

152. An anther has
(*a*) One microsporangium
(*b*) Two microsporangia
(*c*) Three microsporangia
(*d*) Four microsporangia

153. Pollen tube has
(*a*) Tip growth
(*b*) Three nuclear zones
(*c*) Cytoplasmic streaming
(*d*) Chemotatic growth

154. Meiosis is best seen in
(*a*) Microspores and anther wall
(*b*) Microsporocytes
(*c*) Cells of lateral meristem
(*d*) Cells of apical meristem

155. Point out the odd from the following
(*a*) Ovule (*b*) Antheridium
(*c*) Oogonium (*d*) Archegonium

156. Archesporium of ovule is
(*a*) Single celled lateral
(*b*) Single celled terminal
(*c*) Single celled central
(*d*) Single celled hypodermal

157. Microscopic structure that has polar nuclei is
(*a*) Male gamete (*b*) Embryo sac
(*c*) Pollen grain (*d*) Pollen tube

158. Meiosis occurs in
(*a*) Anther (*b*) Archesporium
(*c*) Pollen grain (*d*) Root tip

159. Karyogamy is
(*a*) Fusion of gamete protoplasts
(*b*) Fusion of gametic nuclei
(*c*) Delayed meiosis
(*d*) Delayed mitosis

160. Chalazogamy is found is
(*a*) Lily (*b*) *Casuarina*
(*c*) *Cucurbita* (*d*) All of these

161. Essential for fertilization is
(*a*) Fruit (*b*) Calyx
(*c*) Mature ovule (*d*) Corolla

162. Fertilization is synonymous to
(*a*) Syngamy (*b*) Homogamy
(*c*) Apogamy (*d*) Autogamy

163. Part of endosperm is liquid in
(*a*) *Datura* (*b*) *Passiflora*
(*c*) *Ricinus* (*d*) *Cocos*

164. Which of the following is/are not diploid ?
(*a*) Embryo (*b*) Endosperm
(*c*) Nucellus (*d*) All of these

165. Pollen grain gets germinated by
(*a*) Germ pore (*b*) Chalaza
(*c*) Integument (*d*) Micropyle

166. Which forms the embryo ?
(*a*) Fertilized synergid (*b*) Fertilized ovum
(*c*) Oosphere (*d*) Egg apparatus

167. Self pollination can be prevented by
(*a*) Herkogamy (*b*) Dichogamy
(*c*) Self sterility (*d*) All of these

168. Allogamy is best favoured by
(*a*) Homogamy (*b*) Dicliny
(*c*) Cleistogamy (*d*) None of these

169. In the microsporangial wall, tapetum is present in between
(*a*) Epidermis and middle layers
(*b*) Epidermis and endothecium
(*c*) Middle layers and sporogenous tissue
(*d*) Endothecium and middle layers

170. In an ovule, archesporium is
(*a*) Single celled and lie in the centre of ovule
(*b*) Single celled and hypodermal in origin
(*c*) Single celled and terminal in origin
(*d*) None of the above

171. *Zostera* and *Ceratophyllum* are submerged marine plants in which pollination is of
(*a*) Epihydrogamous type
(*b*) Hypohydrogamous type
(*c*) Entomophilous type
(*d*) None of these

172. Parthenogamy refers to
(*a*) Development of gametophyte from sporophyte directly.
(*b*) Development of embryo from haploid female gamete without fertilization.
(*c*) Development of sporophyte from gametophyte without the fusion of gametes.
(*d*) Union of two incompatible gametes.

173. Fleshy specialised buds produced in the axil of leaves which fall on the ground and produce new individuals, are called
(*a*) Offsets (*b*) Bulbils
(*c*) Tubers (*d*) Bulbs

174. Absence of double fertilization and endosperm formation is found in
(*a*) Orchidaceae
(*b*) Podostemonaceae
(*c*) Trapaceae
(*d*) All of the above

175. Stolon is a kind of vegetative propagation in strawberry which is a
(*a*) Subaerial stem
(*b*) Underground stem
(*c*) Leave
(*d*) Root

176. Recurrent agamospermy refers to
(*a*) Haploid parthenogenesis
(*b*) Diploid parthenogenesis
(*c*) Parthenogenesis
(*d*) None of the above

177. Air layering is a method of artificial vegetative propagation in plants which
(*a*) Do not produce adventitious roots easily.
(*b*) Branches fail to bent due to larger diameter.
(*c*) Stems are so mature that latent buds near the base do not sprout by other methods of layering.
(*d*) All of the above

178. Trap door mechanism is present in hypanthodium of *Ficus* in which pollination takes place through
(*a*) Birds (*b*) Insects
(*c*) Air (*d*) Bats

179. Dispersal mechanism of fruits and seeds in *Clematis* is by
(*a*) Parachute–like appendage
(*b*) Swinging of capsule in air
(*c*) Winged seeds
(*d*) Seeds with spongy air filled tissues

180. Embryo culture helps in
(*a*) Production of plant hormones auxins, cytokinin and florigen.
(*b*) Introduction of variations of high genetic quality.
(*c*) Preventing hybridisation.
(*d*) Producing plants resistant to pathogens and parasites.

181. A virus consists of
(*a*) Protein and nucleic acid
(*b*) Cell membrane and cytoplasm
(*c*) Nucleus and cytoplasm
(*d*) Cell membrane and ribosomes

182. Viruses are :
(*a*) Larger than bacteria
(*b*) Intracellular parasites
(*c*) Capable of autonomous replication
(*d*) Contains only DNA

183. Which of the following viruses has DNA as its genetic material ?
(*a*) Tobacco mosaic virus
(*b*) Influenza virus
(*c*) Polio virus
(*d*) Small pox virus

184. Which one of the following sentence is correct about viruses?
(*a*) They can integrate their genome into the host cell genome
(*b*) Their genes do not mutate
(*c*) Their genes are covered by histones
(*d*) They have small mitochondria

185. A bacteriophage has a lysozyme, which breaks the bacterial wall. When this gene of the bacteriophage is utilised?
(*a*) During lysogeny
(*b*) During lytic phase
(*c*) During both the conditions
(*d*) No such enzymes present

186. A virus can replicate its genome without killing the host cell. This is done when the viral genome is integrated into the host genome. As the latter replicates, the former (viral genome) is also replicated. This viral genes DNA is called
(*a*) Prophage (*b*) Virion
(*c*) Lytic virus (*d*) Retrovirus

187. A bacteriophage with lysogenic cycle integrates its genes with the genome, for which the bacteriophage genes must be
(*a*) RNA
(*b*) Single stranded DNA
(*c*) Double stranded DNA
(*d*) Double stranded RNA

188. The energy for injecting viral DNA into host cell comes from ATP. Where do these ATP molecules come from ?
(*a*) ATP molecules are is the tail piece during theformation of virus in the host
(*b*) ATP is produced by viruses themselves
(*c*) ATP is taken from the host at the time of penetration of DNA
(*d*) It comes from the head of the virus

189. All RNA viruses are
(*a*) Retroviruses
(*b*) HIV
(*c*) Oncogenic
(*d*) Provided with RNA within their coats

190. Viral genes are responside for causing tumour are called.
(*a*) Early genes (*b*) Oncogenes
(*c*) Late genes (*d*) Pseudogenes

191. Bacterial chromosome is
(*a*) Circular
(*b*) Devoid of histones
(*c*) Not enclosed in an envelope
(*d*) All the above

192. The transfer and integration of genetic materials from one bacterium to another through a vector (Phage) is called.
(*a*) Transduction (*b*) Transformation
(*c*) Conjugation (*d*) Fusion

193. The plasmid is
(*a*) Double stranded circular DNA
(*b*) Double standerd RNA
(*c*) Never integrated into the bacterial genome
(*d*) Never replicated

194. The plasmid that can integrate into the bacterial DNA are called
(*a*) Virion (*b*) Episome
(*c*) Nucleoids (*d*) Hyposomes

195. The end product of a metabolic pathway binds to a repressor to make the latter active enough to bind to the operator. The end product in such case is called
(*a*) Co-repressor (*b*) Aporepressor
(*c*) Inducer (*d*) Suppressor

196. A single messenger RNA is formed for all the structural genes of an operon. Such a RNA is called
(*a*) Regulatory RNA
(*b*) Polycistronic RNA
(*c*) Transfer RNA
(*d*) Uncommon RNA

197. The eukaryotic genes are regulated by–
(*a*) Enhancers (*b*) Exons
(*c*) Introns (*d*) Operators

198. The transcribed RNA of a split gene
(*a*) undergoes no processing
(*b*) is fully translated
(*c*) undergoes splicing
(*d*) is totally degraded

199. All genes produce–
(*a*) Translatable RNA
(*b*) Non-translatable RNA
(*c*) Enzymes
(*d*) RNA

200. What is recombinant DNA technology?
(*a*) It is a techniques for forming recombinant DNAand introducing them into living cells, where they replicate.
(*b*) It is the study of crossing over.
(*c*) It is the creation of DNA from RNA.
(*d*) None of these.

201. In recombinant DNA technology the plasmid vector DNA is cleaved by
(*a*) Exonuclease
(*b*) Ribonuclease
(*c*) Endonuclease
(*d*) Any nuclease

202. The bacterial resistance to antibiotics is a genetic qualification which is present in–
(*a*) Bacterial DNA
(*b*) Plasmid
(*c*) Virus
(*d*) Bacterial membrane

203. The restriction enzymes are–
(*a*) able to join DNA fragments
(*b*) proteolytic
(*c*) able to cut DNA at specific base sequence
(*d*) RNA catalysing enzyme.

204. The genetic material of influenza virus is a–
(*a*) Single - stranded RNA
(*b*) Double - stranded RNA
(*c*) Single - stranded DNA
(*d*) Double - stranded DNA

***Directions:** In the question 205-240, two statement are given, one is assertion (A) and other is reason (R). For the (A) and (R) statements, mark the correct answer as :*
(*a*) If both A and R are true and R is correct explanation of A.
(*b*) If both A and R are true and R is not correct explanation of A.
(*c*) If A is true but R is false.
(*d*) If both A and R are false.

205. Assertion : Workers prior to Mendel could not work out the principles of inheritance.
Reason : They considered the individual as a whole complex of characters.

206. Assertion : In practice, a large number of offspring must be counted to observe the expected results.
Reason : The gametes combine at random and in large number of offspring there are great chances that all possible types of male gemetes have fertilized all types of eggs.

207. Assertion : In the test cross, the F_1 plants are crossed with homozygous recessive plants
Reason : It is called so because it is used to test whether the individual showing recessive character in homozygous dominant or heterozygous.

208. **Assertion** : When two character taken into consideration for a cross such a cross is called dihybrid cross.

Reason : The number of gametes produced by a dihybrid is four.

209. **Assertion** : Gene loci on a chromosome can be mapped by measuring the frequencies of recombinants produce by crossing over.

Reason : By determining the frequency of recombinants we can get an idea of the map distance between genes.

210. **Assertion** : The larger is recombination frequency the less accurate is the map distance.

Reason : A cross over in one region affects the likelihood of cross overs in the adjacent region.

211. Which of the following statements about monoclonal antibodies is *incorrect?*

(*a*) they can be produced in large amount by growing many mice, each of which is immunized with the same antigen
(*b*) they are useful in quantifying specific proteins in human blood
(*c*) they can be used to purify scarce proteins by affinity chromatography
(*d*) they can be used to prepare catalytic antibodies

212. J chain is a glycopeptide chain associated with which of the following immunoglobulin?

(*a*) IgA (*b*) IgG
(*c*) IgM (*d*) IgE

213. Although T-cell and B-cell membranes contain some shared receptors, the receptor specific for B-cell membrane is

(*a*) pokeweed mitogen (PWM)
(*b*) phyto haemagglutinin (PHA)
(*c*) concanavalin A (con A)
(*d*) sheep red blood cells (SRBCs)

214. Most antibodies are synthesized by the

(*a*) central lymphoid organs
(*b*) peripheral lymphoid organs
(*c*) primary lymphoid organs
(*d*) macrophages

215. Pepsin digestion of immunoglobulin G yields

(*a*) $F(ab)_2$ fragment and low molecular weight fragments
(*b*) 2 Fab fragments and Fc fragment
(*c*) one heavy chain and one light chain
(*d*) only light chains

216. Immunosuppressive measures are most effective when administered

(*a*) just prior to antigen exposure
(*b*) one week before antigen exposure
(*c*) at the time of antigen exposure
(*d*) following antigen exposure

217. Aminopterine is used during the production of hybridoma cells because

(*a*) it blocks the *denovo* pathway
(*b*) it prevents the growth of B cells
(*c*) it prevents the growth of myeloma cells
(*d*) it blocks the synthesis of Ig by B cells

218. Which one of the following statements is *incorrect?*

(*a*) plasma cells are terminally differentiated cells
(*b*) IgA is the predominant class of immunoglobulin in sero mucous secretions
(*c*) the secretory component is associated with IgM
(*d*) the pentamers of IgM are formed by disulphide linkages

219. Antigenic peptides are presented to T cells by

(*a*) TCR / CD3 (*b*) CD28
(*c*) CTLA4 (*d*) MHC

220. The relative level of specific IgM antibodies can be of diagnostic significance because

(*a*) IgM is easier to detect than the other isotypes
(*b*) viral infection often results in very high IgM response
(*c*) IgM antibodies are more often protective against reinfections than are the other isotypes
(*d*) relative high levels of IgM often correlate with a first recent exposure to the inducing agent

221. Individuals exposed to smallpox virus are immune to same disease due to

(*a*) presence of larger quantities of antibodies
(*b*) presence of long lived memory cells
(*c*) healthy lifestyle
(*d*) generation of antigen specific macrophages

222. Which of the following cell/cells express MHCII on the surface?
(*a*) lymphocytes (*b*) macrophages
(*c*) dendritic cells (*d*) All of the above

223. Generation of antigenic peptide for MHC class-I occurs in
(*a*) endoplasmic reticulum
(*b*) cytosol
(*c*) golgi apparatus
(*d*) endosome

224. All humans starts producing antibodies only after they are
(*a*) infected with a pathogen
(*b*) immunised with an antigen
(*c*) exposed to an antigen
(*d*) None of the above

225. ....cells play a major role in defense against parasitic micro-organisms and constitute 1-3% of the white blood cell population.
(*a*) macrophages (*b*) neutrophils
(*c*) eosinophils (*d*) basophiles

226. Which of the following statements is *false* concerning the immune system?
(*a*) antigen presenting cells are found only in the primary immune organs
(*b*) B lymphocytes are capable of processing and presenting antigens to T lymphocytes
(*c*) T lymphocytes are capable of helping to activate B lymphocytes
(*d*) all nucleated cells have MHC class I antigens on their cell surface

227. Which of the following statement is *correct?*
(*a*) Tc cells recognize MHC II molecule on the surface of B cell and excretes cytokines
(*b*) Tc cells recognize antigen presented by MHC II molecule on the surface of B cell and attacks cancer cells
(*c*) Tc cells proliferate to from cytotoxic T cells and interact with MHC II along with CD4 present on their surface
(*d*) Tc cells recognize antigen presented by MHC I much on the surface of virally infected cells/cancer cells and leads to cell death/cytotoxicity

228. Tolerance refers to the finding that
(*a*) the T cell repertoire for recognition of foreign Ag is very diverse
(*b*) $CD4^+$ T cells do not respond to foreign Ag associated with MHC class I molecules and $CD8^+$ T cells do not responds to foreign Ag associated with MHC class II molecules
(*c*) in the absence of foreign antigen, mature T cells are non-responsive to the host's tissues and cells
(*d*) mature T cells responds to foreign MHC molecules at a high frequency

229. Which of the following chemical bonds is not involved in antigen binding by antibody?
(*a*) hydrogen bonds
(*b*) hydrophobic forces
(*c*) Covalent bonds
(*d*) van der Waal forces

230. A T-cell is most likely to be eliminated by the process of negative selection in the thymus if it expresses a TCR which can bind strongly to
(*a*) foreign MHC + self antigen
(*b*) self MHC + foreign antigen
(*c*) self MHC + self antigen
(*d*) foreign MHC + foreign antigen

231. Active immunity means
(*a*) resistance developed after disease
(*b*) resistance developed before disease
(*c*) increasing rate of heart beat
(*d*) increasing quantity of blood

232. Immunoglobulin in the serum of a newborn will be mostly
(*a*) IgM of maternal origin
(*b*) IgG of maternal origin
(*c*) IgG of endogenous origin
(*d*) IgM of endogenous origin

233. The major immunoglobulin family to which a particular immunoglobulin belongs can be determined by sequential analysis of the 100 amino acids beginning from the
(*a*) amino-terminal of the light chain
(*b*) carboxy-terminal of the light chain
(*c*) amino-terminal of the heavy chain
(*d*) carboxy-terminal of the heavy chain

234. Gell and Coombs classified hypersensitivity into 4 types. IgE mediated hypersensitivity belongs to
(*a*) Type I (*b*) Type II
(*c*) Type III (*d*) Type IV

235. Class switching takes place in
(*a*) Pro-B cell (*b*) Pre-B cell
(*c*) immature B cell (*d*) activated B cell

236. The following two organs are examples of secondary lymphoid organs
(*a*) spleen and thymus
(*b*) lymph nodes and thymus
(*c*) spleen and GALT
(*d*) bone marrow and MALT

237. CD3 molecular are present on the surface of both these types of cells
(*a*) B cell and Th cell
(*b*) Th cell and NK cell
(*c*) Tc cell and Th cell
(*d*) Tc cell and NK cell

238. Immunoglobulin G was fractionated by size exclusion chromatography and it was observed to have a molecular mass of 150 kDa. SDS-PAGE analysis under reducing conditions revealed two bands of size 50 kDa and 25 kDa. The oligomeric status of the protein consists of
(*a*) 3 polypeptide chains of molecular mass 50 kDa
(*b*) 6 polypeptide chains of molecular mass 25 kDa
(*c*) one polypeptide chain of 50 kDa and 4 polypeptides of mass 25 kDa
(*d*) two polypeptides of 50 kDa and two of 25 kDa

239. In immunoglobulin molecule, the complementarity determining region is present in
(*a*) V_H domain only
(*b*) V_L domain only
(*c*) V_H and V_L domains
(*d*) V_H and CH_1 domains

240. The antigen processing cell in higher organisms is
(*a*) T cell (*b*) macrophage
(*c*) megakaryocyte (*d*) eosinophil

241. Which of the following is not true about restriction endonuclease?
(*a*) restriction enzymes work in presence of Mg^{2+}
(*b*) type II restriction endonucleases do not require ATP for restriction activities
(*c*) it present in both eukaryotes and prokaryotes
(*d*) each restriction enzyme only recognizes the same palindromic sequences regardless of source of DNA

242. A mouse in which one particular gene has been replaced by its inactivated form generated *in vitro* is called
(*a*) transgenic mouse (*b*) knockout mouse
(*c*) nude mouse (*d*) mutant mouse

243. Identify the mismatch

(*a*) Alkaline phosphatase	1. remove phosphate group present at 5' end of DNA
(*b*) DNA polymerase I	2. nick translation
(*c*) SI endonuclease	3. cleaves only single strand DNA
(*d*) DNAse 1	4. cleaves only dsDNA

244. Genetically engineered male sterile crop plants may be produced by inserting
(*a*) BT toxin gene (*b*) barnase gene
(*c*) lectin gene (*d*) chitinase gene

245. Cybrids are produced
(*a*) by *in vitro* fusion of gametes
(*b*) by fusion of two cells and contain full nuclear genomes of the two parents
(*c*) by fusion of two cells and contain full nuclear genome of one and partial nuclear genome of the other parent
(*d*) by fusion of two cells and contain nuclear genomes of one parent and cytoplasmic genome of the other parent

246. For a plasmid to be a cloning vector, the minimum numbers of elements required are
(*a*) origin of replication, multiple cloning site, selection marker
(*b*) origin of replication, multiple cloning site, selection marker, promoter
(*c*) origin of replication, multiple cloning site, selection marker, translational start site
(*d*) origin of replication, multiple cloning site, promoter

247. Which of the following is incorrect about reporter gene
(*a*) gene whose phenotype can be assayed in a transformed organism
(*b*) β-galactosidase gene is an example of reporter gene
(*c*) test gene that is fused to the upstream region of the cloned gene
(*d*) none of these

248. Identify the incorrect statement for the model plant *Arabidopsis thaliana*
(*a*) its mutants can be easily produced and characterized
(*b*) its genome sequence is known
(*c*) all genes encompassing its genome have already been identified
(*d*) the molecular genetics of its flowering has been extensively studied

249. Polymerase chain reaction is considered as a revolutionary technology because all of the following, except
(*a*) it enables an unlimited production of a DNA fragment *in* vitro
(*b*) it is a highly sensitive technology
(*c*) its experimental protocol is simple
(*d*) it enables the direct production of a synthetic gene that did not exist before

250. Choose the mismatch

(*a*) phagemid	1. part of M 13 genome with plasmid DNA
(*b*) Pi-derived artificial	2. combine features of chromosome P1 vector and BACs
(*c*) shuttle vector	3. yeast episomal plasmids
(*d*) Ti plasmid	4. *Agrobacterium rhizogenes*

251. The term 'cDNA library' means
(*a*) collection of cDNA clones by an individual researcher
(*b*) compilation of cDNA sequences in the database
(*c*) pool of cDNAs generated from a specific tissue inserted into an appropriate vector that can be used as a source of the cDNA of interest
(*d*) it is manual for cDNA research

252. The genome sequencing of rice is important because
(*a*) the rice genome is very unique and contains genes not found in other plants
(*b*) the rice genome is very large compared to the DNA of other grains and so *more* genes will be identified
(*c*) it can identify genes associated with disease resistance, growth capacity, etc
(*d*) it has a rapid life cycle and has many identifiable mutations

253. Which of the following is *not* component of yeast artificial chromosome
(*a*) centromere
(*b*) telomere
(*c*) origin of replication
(*d*) cos site

254. Which of the following techniques would separate molecules based upon their sizes?
(*a*) gel exclusion chromatography
(*b*) antibody-affinity chromatography
(*c*) isoelectric focusing
(*d*) ion-exchange chromatography

255. Which of the following is used as a fusogen for plant protoplasts?
(*a*) sodium chloride
(*b*) sendai virus
(*c*) potassium chloride
(*d*) polyethylene glycol

256. Which of the following statement is *incorrect?*
(*a*) inactivation of a gene for determination of gene function of that gene is called gene knockout
(*b*) technique used to construct a clone by overlapping fragments of cloned DNA is called chromosome walking
(*c*) a clinical procedure in which a gene or other DNA sequence is used to treat a disease is called gene therapy
(*d*) none of these

257. Dideoxy DNA sequencing exclusively depends on one of the followings
(*a*) termination (*b*) ATP
(*c*) plasmid vector (*d*) vector primer

258. In order to isolate cDNA for a specified protein from a mice cDNA library prepared in lgt11 vector which of the following methods you will choose for screening?
(*a*) recombinational
(*b*) immunochemical
(c) polymerase chain reaction
(*d*) yeast two hybrid screen

259. Restriction enzyme digestion of a 4 kb PstI-digested DNA molecule with EcoRI yields two fragments of 1 kb and 3 kb each. Digestion of the same molecule with HindIII yields fragments of 1.5 kb and 2.5 kb. Finally, digestion with EcoRI and HindIII together yields fragments of 0.5 kb, 1 kb. and 2.5 kb. Based on this information, the 0.5 kb fragment is flanked by which of the following enzyme sites
(*a*) PstI-HindIII (*b*) EcoRI-HindIII
(*c*) EcoRI (*d*) EcoRI-PstI

260. Restriction endonucleases hydrolyzes polynucleotide from
(*a*) only the 5' end
(*b*) from either terminal
(*c*) at an internal phosphodiester bond
(*d*) a phosphodiester bond within a specific sequence

261. Most common reporter gene whose product can be directly visualized in transformed cells is
(*a*) NPTII (Neomycim phosphotransferase)
(*b*) CAT (chloramphenicol acetyl transferase)
(*c*) β-galactosidase
(*d*) GFP (green fluorescent protein)

262. Which of the following would be eliminated by *hot start* PCR?
(*a*) aerosol contamination from the barrel of pipetors
(*b*) addition of a nucleotide to the terminal end of PCR products
(*c*) infidelity of DNA copying by Taq DNA polymerase
(*d*) formation of primer-dimers

263. The first step in the PCR is
(*a*) denaturation (*b*) primer extension
(*c*) annealing (*d*) cooling

264. Bacteria protect themselves from viruses by fragmenting viral DNA upon entry with
(*a*) methylase (*b*) endonucleases
(*c*) ligases (*d*) exonucleases

265. A restriction enzyme *AluI* with an 4-bp recognition site produces restriction fragments that should
(*a*) 4096 bp (*b*) 256 bp
(*c*) 16 bp (*d*) 436 bp

266. Which of the following tools of recombinant DNA technology is *incorrectly* paired with its use?
(*a*) restriction enzyme-production of RFLPs
(*b*) DNA ligase-enzyme that cuts DNA, creating the sticky ends of restriction fragments
(*c*) DNA polymerase-used in a polymerase chain reaction to amplify sections of DNA
(*d*) reverse transcriptase-production of cDNA from mRNA

267. In recombinant DNA methods, the term vector refers to
(*a*) the enzyme that cuts DNA into restriction fragments
(*b*) the sticky end of a DNA fragment
(*c*) a plasmid used to transfer DNA into a living cell
(*d*) a DNA probe used to identify a particular gene

268. Identify the *incorrect* statement for cosmids
(*a*) cosmids are hybrid between a phage DNA and bacterial plasmid
(*b*) cosmids are basically a plasmid that carries a *cos* site
(*c*) cosmids can be used to clone DNA of 30-40kb
(*d*) cosmids produce plaques

269. The PCR is used to
(*a*) amplify a small amount of DNA
(*b*) cleave bacteria plasmids
(*c*) seal "sticky ends"
(*d*) identify target plasmids

270. pBR322 which is frequently used as a vector for cloning gene in *E.coli* is
(*a*) an original bacterial plasmid
(*b*) a modified bacterial plasmid
(*c*) a viral genome
(*d*) a transposon

271. In the following food chain, which one will transfer maximum energy to the next trophic level.
Grass → Grasshopper → Frog → Snake → Peacock
(*a*) Grass (*b*) Grasshopper
(*c*) Snake (*d*) Peacock

272. What scientific term is used for the circulation of the essential nutrient
(*a*) Biogeographic cycle
(*b*) Cycling of material
(*c*) Biological cycle
(*d*) Biogeochemical cycle

273. A pond as a
(*a*) Man made ecosystem
(*b*) Natural ecosystem
(*c*) Biome
(*d*) Macroecosystem

274. In a following food chain
Peacock → Snake → Frog → Grasshopper → Grass,
The peacock is
(*a*) Primary consumer
(*b*) Secondary cnsumer
(*c*) Primary decomposer
(*d*) Apex of food pyramid

275. Which ecosystem has maximum stratification
(*a*) Desert ecosystem (*b*) Grassland
(*c*) Coniferous (*d*) Tropical rain forest

276. The source of energy in the ecosystem is
(*a*) Sun (*b*) DNA
(*c*) Glucose (*d*) ATP

277. In aquatic ecosystem, the food chain starts from
(*a*) Phytoplankton (*b*) Zooplankton
(*c*) Small fish (*d*) Benthos

278. Snakes belongs to
(*a*) Net primary productivity
(*b*) Gross primary productivity
(*c*) Secondary productivity
(*d*) None of these

279. The % of sunlight trapped by producers is
(*a*) 1 – 5% (*b*) 5 – 10%
(*c*) 10 – 15% (*d*) 15 – 20%

280. The amount of energy utilized by the herbivores is
(*a*) 20% (*b*) 50%
(*c*) 10% (*d*) 0.1%

ANSWERS

1	2	3	4	5	6	7	8	9	10
(*d*)	(*b*)	(*a*)	(*c*)	(*a*)	(*a*)	(*b*)	(*c*)	(*d*)	(*c*)
11	**12**	**13**	**14**	**15**	**16**	**17**	**18**	**19**	**20**
(*b*)	(*c*)	(*b*)	(*c*)	(*c*)	(*b*)	(*d*)	(*c*)	(*a*)	(*d*)
21	**22**	**23**	**24**	**25**	**26**	**27**	**28**	**29**	**30**
(*c*)	(*b*)	(*c*)	(*a*)	(*b*)	(*c*)	(*b*)	(*d*)	(*c*)	(*b*)
31	**32**	**33**	**34**	**35**	**36**	**37**	**38**	**39**	**40**
(*c*)	(*a*)	(*d*)	(*b*)	(*c*)	(*d*)	(*c*)	(*c*)	(*b*)	(*d*)
41	**42**	**43**	**44**	**45**	**46**	**47**	**48**	**49**	**50**
(*c*)	(*a*)	(*b*)	(*d*)	(*a*)	(*b*)	(*b*)	(*a*)	(*d*)	(*a*)
51	**52**	**53**	**54**	**55**	**56**	**57**	**58**	**59**	**60**
(*c*)	(*a*)	(*a*)	(*b*)	(*d*)	(*c*)	(*a*)	(*c*)	(*d*)	(*c*)
61	**62**	**63**	**64**	**65**	**66**	**67**	**68**	**69**	**70**
(*c*)	(*d*)	(*c*)	(*a*)	(*b*)	(*b*)	(*a*)	(*a*)	(*b*)	(*a*)
71	**72**	**73**	**74**	**75**	**76**	**77**	**78**	**79**	**80**
(*c*)	(*a*)	(*d*)	(*d*)	(*d*)	(*c*)	(*c*)	(*c*)	(*d*)	(*c*)
81	**82**	**83**	**84**	**85**	**86**	**87**	**88**	**89**	**90**
(*a*)	(*a*)	(*d*)	(*a*)	(*d*)	(*a*)	(*c*)	(*c*)	(*d*)	(*c*)

91	**92**	**93**	**94**	**95**	**96**	**97**	**98**	**99**	**100**
(*c*)	(*a*)	(*d*)	(*a*)	(*c*)	(*a*)	(*c*)	(*b*)	(*b*)	(*a*)
101	**102**	**103**	**104**	**105**	**106**	**107**	**108**	**109**	**110**
(*a*)	(*b*)	(*d*)	(*b*)	(*a*)	(*d*)	(*d*)	(*d*)	(*d*)	(*d*)
111	**112**	**113**	**114**	**115**	**116**	**117**	**118**	**119**	**120**
(*d*)	(*c*)	(*c*)	(*a*)	(*c*)	(*a*)	(*a*)	(*d*)	(*b*)	(*c*)
121	**122**	**123**	**124**	**125**	**126**	**127**	**128**	**129**	**130**
(*d*)	(*a*)	(*b*)	(*d*)	(*a*)	(*b*)	(*b*)	(*a*)	(*d*)	(*d*)
131	**132**	**133**	**134**	**135**	**136**	**137**	**138**	**139**	**140**
(*d*)	(*d*)	(*d*)	(*d*)	(*d*)	(*d*)	(*d*)	(*b*)	(*c*)	(*b*)
141	**142**	**143**	**144**	**145**	**146**	**147**	**148**	**149**	**150**
(*b*)	(*b*)	(*d*)	(*b*)	(*c*)	(*a*)	(*d*)	(*b*)	(*b*)	(*c*)
151	**152**	**153**	**154**	**155**	**156**	**157**	**158**	**159**	**160**
(*c*)	(*d*)	(*a*)	(*b*)	(*b*)	(*d*)	(*b*)	(*a*)	(*b*)	(*b*)
161	**162**	**163**	**164**	**165**	**166**	**167**	**168**	**169**	**170**
(*c*)	(*a*)	(*d*)	(*b*)	(*a*)	(*b*)	(*d*)	(*b*)	(*c*)	(*a*)
171	**172**	**173**	**174**	**175**	**176**	**177**	**178**	**179**	**180**
(*b*)	(*d*)	(*b*)	(*d*)	(*a*)	(*b*)	(*d*)	(*b*)	(*a*)	(*b*)
181	**182**	**183**	**184**	**185**	**186**	**187**	**188**	**189**	**190**
(*a*)	(*b*)	(*d*)	(*a*)	(*b*)	(*a*)	(*c*)	(*a*)	(*d*)	(*b*)
191	**192**	**193**	**194**	**195**	**196**	**197**	**198**	**199**	**200**
(*d*)	(*a*)	(*a*)	(*b*)	(*a*)	(*b*)	(*a*)	(*c*)	(*d*)	(*a*)
201	**202**	**203**	**204**	**205**	**206**	**207**	**208**	**209**	**210**
(*c*)	(*b*)	(*c*)	(*a*)	(*a*)	(*a*)	(*c*)	(*b*)	(*a*)	(*a*)
211	**212**	**213**	**214**	**215**	**216**	**217**	**218**	**219**	**220**
(*a*)	(*a*)	(*d*)	(*b*)	(*a*)	(*c*)	(*a*)	(*c*)	(*d*)	(*d*)
221	**222**	**223**	**224**	**225**	**226**	**227**	**228**	**229**	**230**
(*b*)	(*d*)	(*b*)	(*d*)	(*c*)	(*a*)	(*d*)	(*c*)	(*c*)	(*c*)
231	**232**	**233**	**234**	**235**	**236**	**237**	**238**	**239**	**240**
(*a*)	(*b*)	(*d*)	(*a*)	(*d*)	(*c*)	(*c*)	(*d*)	(*c*)	(*b*)
241	**242**	**243**	**244**	**245**	**246**	**247**	**248**	**249**	**250**
(*c*)	(*b*)	(*d*)	(*a*)	(*d*)	(*a*)	(*d*)	(*c*)	(*d*)	(*d*)
251	**252**	**253**	**254**	**255**	**256**	**257**	**258**	**259**	**260**
(*c*)	(*c*)	(*d*)	(*a*)	(*d*)	(*d*)	(*a*)	(*d*)	(*b*)	(*d*)
261	**262**	**263**	**264**	**265**	**266**	**267**	**268**	**269**	**270**
(*c*)	(*c*)	(*a*)	(*b*)	(*b*)	(*b*)	(*c*)	(*d*)	(*a*)	(*b*)
271	**272**	**273**	**274**	**275**	**276**	**277**	**278**	**279**	**280**
(*a*)	(*d*)	(*b*)	(*d*)	(*d*)	(*a*)	(*d*)	(*c*)	(*a*)	(*c*)